I0129614

ELMER KEITH'S BIG GAME HUNTING

Painting of Cow and Bull Moose by Bob Kuhn

ELMER KEITH'S

BIG GAME HUNTING

Illustrated with drawings by
Bob Kuhn and the Author
and with many photographs

SILVER ROCK PUBLISHING

Published in 2016 by Silver Rock Publishing

All rights reserved.
Neither this work nor any portions thereof may be reproduced, stored in a
retrieval system, or transmitted in any capacity without written permission
from the publisher.

Original Copyright © 1948, by Elmer Keith

Elmer Keith's Big Game Hunting
ISBN: 978-1-62654-573-1 (paperback)
978-1-62654-574-8 (casebound)
978-1-62654-575-5 (spiralbound)

Cover image: Bull Elk, Blacktail Deer Plateau
by Neil Herbert,
Courtesy of Yellowstone National Park,
National Park Service

Cover design by Justine McFarland
Studio Justine

Dedicated

to the memory of my parents

FOREST EVERETT KEITH

and

LINNIE NEIL KEITH

Elmer Keith

HERE are two brief stories of Elmer Keith, the hunter, naturalist and outdoorsman, and an analysis of the writer.

Keith and a guide were scouting game ahead of a hunting party. They were not carrying rifles but both had a heavy pistol. In the middle of the afternoon they saw a grizzly bear below them, near the creek. Keith studied the situation briefly and then whispered to the guide, "I have always wanted to get a grizzly with a pistol." (I have no such ambition, myself.) "This looks like my chance. Give me your gun and climb a tree." He made a successful stalk and was about to open fire when a sound behind the animal drew his attention. A cub came tumbling out of the brush, and then another and still another. Keith reversed his stalk and returned to the guide. The grizzly family went on their way blissfully unaware of how near they had been to disaster. Keith's laconic comment: "I never wanted a bear bad enough to make orphans of three cubs."

*   *   *

Keith's writings are based on three aspects of his personality. The first is his remarkable gift for accurate, detailed observation. The second, his prodigious and exact memory. The third is his uncompromising honesty.

It is impossible for Keith to build up a story for a better effect or to tone one down to make it sound more plausible. He must tell it as he saw it, regardless of where or how it impacts. If a phrase seems provocative or a sentence challenging, it is not argumentative. It is his conception of the truth — defiant.

The reader who settles himself in an easy chair with one of Keith's books can let down the drawbridge of his mind and dismiss his mental sentries. Keith parades his thought openly. His sentences contain no *double-entendre*. His paragraphs offer ambush to no bravos of propaganda.

Keith is not a philosopher. Concrete facts interest him; abstractions do not. Psychologically he is inclined toward the decision-action type. He is never found sitting on an ideological fence.

When Keith writes there is some conflict between the technician and the artist. So far the disburser of facts has won most of the points but there are indications that the sensitive, imaginative Keith is gaining in strength. If so, it is all to the good. His occasional descriptive paragraphs of nature in action are the best of his work — etchings in prose. He should give us more canyons, mist-filled after a night of rain; more mountain peaks, copper-washed by the last rays of evening.

Keith is best known as an arms expert, a term he dislikes. At least twenty-five years have elapsed since his first gun article was published. There have been many since. Like General Hatcher (handguns), Colonel Whelen (rifles) and Major Askins (shotguns), Keith writes from personal experience and observation. He keeps his fingers on the pulse of world thought through an extensive correspondence that is nearly world wide. Hunters in Alaska and Canada, European sportsmen, a scientist in Africa, all write him long letters. He is careful about his statements of fact. They can be accepted at face value. His conclusions are open to question as is all personal opinion. But be warned. He has a penchant for getting ahead of current thought. Time frequently corroborates him.

Keith's knowledge of wildlife is categorical and intimate. It flickers in and out of his hunting stories but he has never quite given it a free rein. He could, if he were so minded, write a cradle-to-grave biography of any game animal, game bird, fur bearer or predator in the Rocky Mountains. He knows what they eat, how they live, the type of country they like, their romances, their natural enemies, and their geographical dispersion. He does not make "guesstimates." His comments, however casual, are authoritative.

* * *

Keith and I were hunting. We could have found deer but we were looking for something else. It was a rugged day. Half-melted snow and wet brush on the north hillsides — slippery rocks — mazes of crisscrossed down timber — tough going all the way.

Just after sundown we came out on a hill a quarter of a mile above camp and sat down to rest. There was a sound in the brush.

Two grand mule deer bucks, their noses up and their antlers thrown back, sneaked craftily along the edge of the timber forty yards below us. When they had passed out of sight I looked at him. His rifle lay across his knees forgotten. His pipe hung loosely from his mouth. The big hat was pushed carelessly up on the side of his head; his face was a picture of absorbed interest. He caught my glance. A twinkle came into his gray eyes.

"Beauties, weren't they?" he said softly.

To know Elmer Keith, an authentic brother of the backlands needs no more introduction.

DON MARTIN

September 1948

Contents

Illustrations

[xv]

[xvii]

ELMER KEITH'S BIG GAME HUNTING

I

How to Look for Game

REGARDLESS of how much is written on the subject, the amateur big game hunter will have to learn by actual experience in the field. When he first takes the field, in spite of expectations he will very rarely see game in the open in true picture-book style. Except in early morning and late evening, game is seldom out in the open unless traveling, and even then, if much hunted, it will remain in the edge of any cover available. Goats, sheep and antelope are the exceptions, and the latter especially stay out in the open and depend on their eyesight to keep them out of danger. While sheep and goats do the same, to some extent, they will also bed where they can be well hidden, if they have been hunted, while the antelope, in such a case, prefers plenty of open terrain on all sides.

One must learn what to look for and then where to look as well. In early morning, the game is apt to be feeding and one can well look for movement, while later in the day it will be bedded and one must then look over all likely bed grounds. Again in the late evening game will feed and one can watch for movement on all likely feed. Knowing what the animal is feeding on is of utmost importance and will save a great deal of hunting and searching; it is really the key to locating game.

In all mountain hunting of open terrain, look for the telltale white spots on the rumps of sheep, or mule deer, or the yellow patch on elks' rumps. It is always best to get out at daylight and if possible have the sun rise behind you, then you can search the hills and valleys beyond you, with the aid of the sun. It will invariably flash on those white spots, also the white necks of Fannin rams, and even a coyote will be picked up by the early sun rays and made to stand out in contrast with his surroundings. The yellow-gray color of his coat will show much more clearly with the early sun on it than at any other time of day. Antelope will flash in the sun, their various white patches catching and reflecting the early sunlight, and are then easily picked up. Watch the sky lines of all ridges adjacent to feed grounds, as you may see game silhouetted there. As the sun mounts higher and the light penetrates down into the deep canyons and valleys it is time to search them out. Deer, elk or moose will often be located by seeing the sun flash on their horns, and they will often be feeding in high brush, where only the horns are visible. You must learn to look for anything that seems out of place and not a part of the scenery. All dark objects should be closely examined if hunting moose or bear, and if hunting elk look for light buckskin-colored patches in the brush. Many thousands of black charred stumps I have looked over before finally seeing some of them move.

Mountain goats are nearly always mistaken for scattered small snowdrifts at long range. Examine with the glasses or telescope any suspicious white spots in the distant cliffs, if you are hunting either goats or sheep. When sheep are feeding, those white rumps will show for miles when the sun hits them, and the same is true of antelope and mule deer. You will always see more game while sitting down and quietly watching the terrain, if you get out early in the morning when you should, than by busting brush. The axiom should be to get out first and in a good vantage point and let the game make the first move, or come to you. Many times you will see a line of white rocks in the distance. Always investigate them with the glasses, particularly if they are in line or at the same elevation or in a small group.

Don't overlook the immediate foreground, as game may be feeding directly below you and often at short range. The old woodsman sweeps all the surrounding terrain regularly with his eyes and while there may have been nothing there a few minutes past, the game may suddenly feed out of the brush and stand in plain sight and often in good range as well. When hunting any of the mountain game, watch carefully any distant objects that do not appear to be a part of the scenery, and if they resemble ants in the distance, put the glasses on them. With good snow on the ground, game will be seen quickest and easiest, but on dry grassy slopes that more nearly match the fall coats of the game it will be much harder to see. It is surprising how well the coat of a bull elk will blend with the gorgeous colored leaves of mountain maple or aspen after a frost, and elk love to feed in these thickets. Later in the morning as the sun warms the slopes, game will often be seen working back toward the bed ground. The first two or three hours after daylight are worth more to the hunter than the rest of the day. If you do wound an animal you have all day to trail it up, while in late evening hunting you must make a clean one-shot kill, or find a dead and soured animal the next day.

While sitting quietly out of sight you have twice the chance of seeing early feeding game that you have when traveling, for the simple reason that you must spend half of your time looking where you are planting your feet when traveling. Animals seldom see or identify a still object but will instantly spot a moving object and then will not take their eyes off it until they decide whether it is dangerous or not. Many times I have had elk and deer and a couple of moose as well walk up in very close range of me before they saw me, because I sat motionless. Deer at such times are really comical.

Although you may be out for game, the killing of game should be only incidental, and you should be able calmly to enjoy the beautiful scenery, the ever-changing lights on the hills and forests and the game itself. It's much more fun to watch game about its daily business of obtaining a living than actually to kill it. When a worth-while specimen shows, or you are in need of meat, that is something else and immediate, but when you have the time and do not need the meat, then you should quietly wait for a real fine specimen before shooting. If the hunter goes about this business in such a manner he will usually see far more game in a day than the lad who travels all day and likewise busts brush in his hurry to get somewhere. To my notion there is no finer church than nature and man is closer to his God when calmly enjoying the grandeurs of beautiful mountain scenery than in any man-made house of worship. Many times I have climbed to some vantage point where I could inspect a good bit of feed and bed ground of the game I was after, then while quietly meditating on a misspent life I have actually seen much more game than others of the same party who covered ten times as much territory the same day.

After the sun gets high, the game will start for its bed ground. Then you will find the goats bedded on some narrow ledge while the sheep may select some high alpine basin among a jumble of rocks for their bed ground, or each animal may paw out a hole in the slide rock or grass down some 100 to 200 yards from the crest of the ridge for its bed. When hunting such game in the middle of the day, be careful to keep off the ridge tops unless screened by brush and never go over a ridge in a hurry. Always stop and get your wind, then very slowly approach and look over the top, advancing a little way at a time as you carefully scan every inch of ground below you. I have sometimes seen only one horn and eye of a wise old ram showing over a boulder. At other times only the white rump patch projected beyond a boulder.

Elk and mule bucks may be depended on to seek their beds on the shoulders of the ridge where little flat places afford good beds, and usually among some down timber, or at the roots of tree boles. Quite often mule deer will bed right out on an open side hill in some small clump of low red brush, while elk usually seek the north slopes and heavy cover. Moose will usually take to a stand of jack pines or willows or other brush for their noonday bed ground. Look closely for all dark objects and also for the flash of a horn. In all timber hunting of deer and elk, you will often see the horns but not the animal, as the horns project so much higher than the body. If you do see a set of horns at close range, it may often be placed where there are a lot of dry limbs for a background. All game is thoroughly adept at picking such a bed, often beside a big fallen log with many projecting dead limbs. Move very slowly when hunting the timber, stopping and spending twice as much time looking around as you do in traveling. Place each foot carefully and clear of all dead limbs, twigs or dry sunflowers. It's well to be above the game as sound travels uphill better than down; then, too, if the game is feeding it always makes some noise and you may hear it and then locate it exactly.

In the timber, watch for a horn, a flick of an ear or the wiggle of a tail, as well as outlines of head, or neck, or body. Watch also under the boughs of low-hanging firs for legs and their movement. Often the legs of game will be in view when the body is well screened by low-hanging boughs in such fir timber. Take nothing for granted and make certain of each object before moving on. Usually the experienced woodsman first sees something that just does not look right to him. He may not be able to put it into words or clearly define why the object is suspicious, but the longer he has hunted, the quicker he will spot any suspicious object and also the game. The novice, on the other hand, will often walk right onto game before he sees it and it will suddenly jump and run before he ever does see it, though it has been standing in plain view all the time. This is because he does not thoroughly cover the terrain with his eyes, searching out each minute detail before moving on. Don't look for game in the timber as a whole, look for the head, an ear, the tail or a leg or the nose. If you follow this procedure you will soon learn to see partly hidden game, and game in the timber is nearly always partly hidden, at least by limbs, boughs or logs. Many times you will see the head of an elk, moose or deer calmly regarding you over some big fallen log. At other times the tip of the nose and eyes may be seen looking at you below some heavy low-hanging limbs, or the rump may project around a tree bole. It's the little things that count in game observation, such as picking up any telltale tracks as you go along, seeing where a buck or bull has cleaned his horns or fed, his feed grounds and direction of travel to the bed ground. The old hillbilly has spent a lifetime at it so don't think you can emulate him on your first trip, but with practice and constant use of the eyes you will learn. The experienced woodsman sees more out of the corner of his eyes without moving his head than the average city hunter will with both eyes looking directly at the game. Many timber animals move quietly and slowly even when feeding, and if you are quiet you will suddenly see them in plain view and how they came there will be a mystery. Such occurrences will often surprise even the most experienced hunter. On the other hand, if you are hurrying along your first glimpse will be of a fast disappearing animal.

Pay particular attention to camp robbers, bluejays, pine squirrels, magpies and also ravens. They will locate much game that is invisible to you from your position. As a rule the color of the game blends in with the color of the terrain, and you will be surprised that such flashy-colored animals as Fannin rams in the north seem to blend perfectly with the country they inhabit — this for the reason that much of their range is blue slate rock, interspersed with white boulders. An old blue Stone ram on such a slide, or cliff, is almost invisible except to trained eyes. Elk blend well with frost-colored aspen, mountain maple and other brush, but show up all too plainly in green timber, while whitetails and mule deer both blend well with their usual surroundings. The mule deer's white rump often gives him away, while the whitetail is nearly invisible to the average human eye when not alarmed.

Watch for all movements of limbs or small trees as game browses, or for the swaying top of a small tree on which a buck or bull is cleaning his horns. Usually it is the little things that give them away and bring at least a portion of the animal into view. Do not expect to see game in the usual artist's stance for such a scene is rarely encountered in the timber. Study your game until you can recognize any portion of it that becomes visible. Above all, do not let your imagination run wild and shoot at some fellow hunter for a game animal. Game should never be shot at until you can see enough of the beast to enable you to pick out a vital area.

When hunting caribou, you will often see the horns projecting out of the grass or brush, or over the top of some ridge, before you actually see the animal itself, so familiarize yourself with what the horns look like well in advance of the hunt. While I have seen deer and elk both pull their horns down flat with their bodies as near as they could, in order to remain hidden when I had caught them in their beds, caribou do not do this, but even when they see you the horns remain erect, the same as antelope's. Moose will also carefully and slowly lower their heads in order to get as much out of sight as possible when caught in their bed. It is interesting to watch an animal in its bed that has seen you, but does not know that you have also seen it; how slowly it will go about making any move — even pulling its head down and laying it on the ground will take minutes for the complete movement, it will move so slowly. Game well knows that any quick movement will attract your attention. I have walked right on by many bedded animals, the while I carefully sized up their heads out of the corner of my eye, but never turned to face them. Then if they were good enough I walked slowly along until past them, brought the rifle slowly up almost to my shoulder, and then turned very slowly for the shot. At times in open country I have simply walked or ridden on past the game, apparently oblivious to its presence, until I found an excellent place to shoot from that would clear all brush and limbs, then have taken the shot from prone or sitting position, often at considerable range. The instant you turn or look squarely at game at close range, it will realize that you see it. Until it knows you see it, it may try to remain still and concealed, but once the animal realizes the jig is up it will be on its way.

The hardest job for the eyes is to pick out game in dense forest, where the sun seldom penetrates. Such work is very hard and trying and I have often had very tired eyes after a couple of weeks of elk hunting in the rainy, dense cedar-timbered Lochsa country. All is twilight in such dense heavy forest, even in midday, and everything is seen dimly. Likewise where some stray patches of sun do filter through on the rare clear day, they only make visibility the more difficult with their light and dark effects.

Game eyes are trained, you are not born with them. While it's only natural that the man raised in the hills, who has been hunting livestock and game from earliest childhood and also practicing the trailing of game, should be the more adept, still the novice can learn in time and can soon improve his game eyes with a little intelligent study and use.

II

Judging Trophies before Shooting

WHILE, in all probability, some 90 per cent of the hunters afield each fall in North America are out for meat, the other 10 per cent are out for worth-while trophies alone. Of the 90 per cent, there is every possibility that fully half of them would also like a decent trophy for mounting along with their meat supply. Though a great many hunters are forced through scarcity of the game to take anything that is legal and on the first opportunity, others will be hunting beautiful wild country, where game is plentiful, and where a selection of the heads taken is not only possible, but pays off in finer trophies. For this reason we believe the hunter should have a good basic knowledge of just what a respectable trophy of each species should look like in the field. In over twenty years of big game guiding we have many times asked our sportsman to wait for something better, only to have him kill the beast, then want to leave it to rot as the trophy was smaller than he wanted. Needless to say, under my guidance, he took the trophy whether he liked it or not, as I do not believe in ever killing an animal unless there is a use for it, or it is needed.

Estimating a trophy in the field, often at long range, is not an easy task, but there are some fundamental rules you can observe that will help. Even then, the best of us will occasionally get fooled. Even after years of hunting, you may think a certain head is a fine specimen when it is not and you must see some really good heads before you are competent to judge them on foot. Different conditions of light and background must also be considered, as they have a material effect on the appearance of a trophy. Usually game on bright sunlit snow, or silhouetted on the sky line, will appear larger than it really is. Likewise the range of the animal from the hunter must be carefully considered before a decision is reached. If you are in fine virgin country where really good trophies exist, and have the time, then it is best to look around a bit before shooting, but if that record head should appear on the first day of the hunt, you want to be able to recognize it as such, and take it while the opportunity offers.

Different species present far different problems, so we will take up each in turn, submitting what we have learned on the subject over the years for whatever it may be worth. The experienced old hunter needs no coaching, but the beginner surely does.

Deer will be hunted, probably, by more sportsmen than any other big game, so let us take up a few of their peculiarities of headgear. First the big mule deer, ranging from Canada south along the Rocky Mountain chain, clear down into Sonora, Mexico, and Tiburon Island in the Gulf of California, is the largest and finest of the deer species. Their horn growth varies greatly in size and weight of antlers, just as the animals vary greatly in size of body. As with all animals that shed their horns each year, the finest heads will usually be found on old mature bucks still in the prime of life. After they become too old the horn growth diminishes and often there will be a well-formed, five-point antler on one side and only a single long horn on the other. Likewise very old deer often grow short stumpy horns, sometimes with plenty of points and at other times the typical five-point head. In the West we speak of all deer heads by the number of points on one side alone, if they are the same, while in the East the total number of points is more apt to be named.

The typical mule deer head has four long points and a brow point to each side and more mature bucks will be found with this typical head than any other type. It may vary a great deal as to weight, as well as length of antlers, and particularly as to length of the brow points. Many old bucks will have none at all. In judging mule deer heads one must always give some consideration to the size of the animal's body. Really big mule deer in sections where plenty of feed is available the year around, as here on the Salmon River, grow to enormous size, and the rare buck will be found that will weigh a full 400 pounds, with all innards removed. Such huge old bucks if still in their prime usually carry fine heads, but if too old the head may be only a normal five-pointer, with very average weight and spread. Such was the head of the largest mule deer I ever obtained, an animal that weighed 400 pounds with all insides removed. One should look for weight and length of horns rather than symmetry, to my notion, and the more points the better. After studying deer long enough one learns to judge the extreme length of the horns in proportion to the length of the neck and height of the body. Spread is also important for a fine head and this can be best judged by the ears of the animal. If the head is turned facing the hunter and the horns run out parallel to about the tips of the ears and then turn upward, that head will usually go around 25 to 26 inches in spread. Rarely you will see an old resident whose great horns grow out past his ears, sometimes the full length of the ear on each side, and when you see such a head you need look no further, for you can bet it has both weight and length. Such heads are rare, even in fine deer country, and the writer has seen only three such in a lifetime of hunting.

Usually if you can see a snarl of points indicating a head with lots of points, it will be a good head and will generally carry considerable weight and some palmation of the antler as well. To our way of thinking such heads are always to be preferred to the typical slim, trim and usual five-point type. Many of the record mule deer heads now recorded are, to our notion, far inferior to many others whose main beam is not long enough to get them into the records at all, and for this reason we prefer the measurement system of James L. Clark to the older museum method which takes extreme length of main beam as the criterion. Generally speaking, if a mule buck will turn facing you, your best estimate of the head will be by the amount it projects on each side of the ear tips. Some heads, however, are of the narrow high type and a really high head is instantly picked out if the horns are clearly visible. These often run to more length than the usual head with horns turning upward at or near the ends of the ears. When you do see a head that appears massive and heavy and either of extreme height or else having the wide basket type of antlers that spread out well past the ends of the ears on each side, the further the better, then you may be sure you have located a good shootable mule deer head and one you can always be proud of.

My best mule deer head is not a large one, but all told has twenty-four points. My partner and I were trailing a band of elk, looking for our winter's meat supply, when I noticed an old doe walk out on a shoulder of a ridge just across a small spring from us and at about 60 yards. She turned her head and looked back, as my partner wished to continue after the elk. I asked him to wait a minute as there must be another deer behind her. Soon a handsome buck strolled out behind her and gazed in our direction. The tips of his horns came almost together at the top, yet it was not a high head and not large. I counted seven points on the off side before he turned his head, then could see nothing but a snarl of points projecting up on the right side, so without further ado I cocked the old .405 Winchester, placed the gold blade front sight through the center of the peep and square on his chest and pressed the trigger. My partner had started on, saying the head was no good and it was a hell of a place to ever get the meat out. At my shot the old boy dropped and slid down the mountain into some chaparral. The snow was up to our knees and he was then hidden from sight. My partner gave me the devil for shooting a worthless head, expressing surprise that I hadn't seen that the points came right together on top. However, examination proved I had been right.

In general there are two types of mule deer, in about every section I have hunted. The short-coupled, short-legged type, with short nose and a really pretty shaped head, and the big, rangy, long-legged and long-Roman-nosed type. The latter nearly always produces the few really fine record heads, while the smaller type is more apt to run to either a goodly number of points and short beams or else to a narrow high type of head. The really big old long-bodied, rangy type will invariably carry the widespread, heavier type of antlers. They are supposed to be all of the same specie but nevertheless there is a marked difference in their build, weight and general body conformation, the smaller deer being much the most shapely and having the prettiest shaped nose and face.

Though these big, rangy, long-bodied mule bucks may often carry only small mediocre heads, they are the type to look for when hunting a really big head, though the shorter, stockier bucks may often carry the more symmetrical head. Frog points that project out to the side of the main beams are always an indication of a good heavy head and enhance the beauty of any deer head. Sections of the West that have long had a buck law very seldom produce good heads. I remember seeing many really fine outstanding heads killed in Montana when I was a small boy, but now after many years of the buck law a really fine head is much more rarely taken. In Oregon the same applies and we have counted a hundred does without seeing a buck with other than a very small head. As the bucks degenerate from the buck law they tend to grow long two-point antlers without brow points, more like the typical Pacific Coast black-tailed deer. Here in this section of Idaho where the deer can drift down to low altitudes and winter in the sagebrush, there are many record heads killed each fall but very few are ever recorded, because they are usually killed by a meat hunter who cares nothing for the trophy. Only last fall a mile from this ranch we saw an exceptionally big heavy mule deer head with many long heavy points and frog points on each side taken by a young hunter who had simply chopped off the skull plate to hang on the garage at home. He was after meat and would never think of paying for the mounting of such a fine head.

Usually the really fine big bucks are solitary animals during October and only seen with the does during the rut in November or during the winter.

Bucks may be distinguished from does even at very long range when the horns cannot be seen, by the angle of the ears. The old bucks have carried their ears out horizontally so long in order to clear their horns that they continue so to carry them even in the late winter or spring after the antlers are shed. A doe invariably carries her ears more nearly vertical.

This section of Idaho and some parts of Colorado seem to produce the finest mule deer heads we have seen, with the palm going to the Colorado heads. No doubt there must be more lime in the water in the sections of the country producing the largest and finest heads, but abundant winter feed is also a prime requisite, permitting the bucks to recuperate from the rut and come through the winter in good shape. Over the years we have noticed that heads are usually small on the average after an exceptionally long hard winter and also that they run large, with many really fine heavy heads, lots of points and some of record proportions, after a mild or short winter. To our mind this proves that the better the condition of the buck physically in the spring, at the start of the horn growth, the larger the head he may ultimately produce in that coming short season.

Where the buck law has been in effect for a number of years, the bucks are usually killed off far too close, with the result that there will be a great many dry does and the bucks then deteriorate themselves, until there are not enough bucks to fight for each bunch of does. We believe this law a mistake and that whenever the deer are too scarce to permit shooting of does, then they are also far too scarce to permit of buck hunting alone. When Nature is left alone, only the largest, finest and strongest bucks propagate the species and the resulting fawn crop is usually fine strong animals. When man tries to impose his superior knowledge into Nature's business he usually makes a mess of things, just as has occurred with the deer in Pennsylvania, Montana and eastern Oregon to our knowledge.

When a mule buck turns his head broadside to the hunter, one can usually get a good idea of the top formation and the spread from the rear main beam forward to the tip of the main prong. The wider these front and rear points are spread on a broadside view the better the head and the more apt it is to carry many points. A slim appearing set of antlers is usually just that. A heavy set appears heavy at any reasonable range. Pick the heaviest antlers always, and you can also judge the spread of each side, from point of main beam forward to point of main branch, by using the length of the head from butt of ear to tip of nose as a measuring stick, always remembering that those short-legged pretty mule deer will have shorter heads than the big Roman-nosed mule bucks.

Hunters will simply have to examine enough heads, or live animals, to form a mental picture of how heavy and large a good head really appears before they will be able to judge them accurately on foot.

Whitetails

With whitetail bucks, one seldom has an opportunity either of correctly judging their horn formation or of selecting heads, as they are seldom banded up like mule deer in late season. In some sections of the country we have hunted whitetails were very thick, as at the head of Swan River in Montana, and then at times we would see several bucks in the little wet meadows of an evening and have a chance to pick the best head. Whitetail heads are differently shaped than mule deer heads and the main beam curves out and upward from the skull, then forward over the nose. Weight of antlers and length of the points from the main beam, as well as the spread of horns, should be the main points to consider in estimating a whitetail head. Always pick the heaviest head with the longest main beam and longest tines, and the more points the better.

Pacific Coast blacktails seldom run to good heads and to my notion do not make much of a trophy as compared with either whitetail or mule deer. Usually they carry only two to four good points to the side and very much resemble some Oregon mule deer we have seen where the buck law had been in force for many years, except that they were of course smaller. They seldom carry brow tines, or if they do these are short, and we have yet to see a really fine head from these species though no doubt some may occur. We would say pick the longest and heaviest head if a choice is possible. Like the whitetail, the blacktail is usually found in dense timber and seldom does one have a chance to size up the head before shooting. They are very small deer on the whole and a husky man can pack out a good buck on his back while he would have to be a giant to carry either a big mule buck or a big whitetail.

The Alaskan Sitka deer is usually even larger than the Pacific Coast blacktail and has similar-shaped horns, but more often larger and better heads, with more points. To our way of thinking, neither the Sitka deer nor the true blacktail in any way compares with a fine whitetail or a mule deer head as a real trophy. Sitka deer usually carry good brow points and are larger than Pacific blacktail heads.

The small, almost dwarflike gazelle deer, also called fantail, was never common and is probably now extinct. I have seen them near Seven-Up-

Pete's out of Helena, Montana, as a boy, also on the North Fork of the Blackfoot in Montana in 1917 and 1918.

These tiny deer carry beautiful little whitetail heads and are a sub species of the whitetail. An old buck of this species would weigh between 65 and 80 pounds when fully matured and fat. I remember seeing a half dozen of their skulls with excellent horns nailed on a barn on the Big Flat out of Ovando, Montana, in 1918. If a man would place the inside of his wrists together and then spread his fingers upward and outward, he would have about the size of a true fantail head — that is, provided his hands were not too large. In conformation they seemed exactly like the larger regular whitetail. One day while dragging a pack string up the North Fork of the Blackfoot we met one of these little dandies in the trail, in an open park. He was from all indications a typical whitetail but so small as to more nearly resemble an overgrown jack rabbit. He snorted and flashed his long whitetail and then disappeared in the brush at about 50 yards. A true fantail head today would be a very rare and beautiful trophy, and I now wish I had taken time to kill one really good specimen when I had the chance. However, at that time I was after venison, and who wanted to waste his license on so small an animal when a big 300-pound or larger mule deer was more easily obtained.

The southwestern Coues deer is often called the fantail, but all specimens I have seen were very much larger than those I saw in Montana when a boy.

Antelope

In the antelope we have an animal that nearly always permits a fair estimate of the head before shooting, unless jumped at close range. Really fine heads are not common and one usually has to look over a lot of bucks and study them at long range before making the stalk, after a good one is selected. There are some rules of thumb which will, however, help in selecting a good one.

First note whether the horns go straight up at the tips or whether they curl back in hooks or inward. Usually the straight-tipped heads will measure two or more inches shorter than those with good hooks. They are to be avoided. In selecting a good antelope head, I first size up the length of the horns, by noting how high the prong or paddle is above the eye; it should be as high above the eye as the tip of nose is from the base of the horn for a record head. Next the tip should carry on upward nearly as much farther above the prong as the prong is above the base of horn. Then, if the buck carries heavy horns and the prongs appear wide and the tips have a good curl to them, you can be sure you have located a worth-while antelope head. You must remember, however, that you may look over some five hundred bucks before you see one that will answer these descriptions. A really good head appears heavy and the horns look big and distinct even at long range.

Antelope heads vary a great deal in spread and there are some freaks. I remember one head that would have gone well up in the records. After a long stalk we found he carried one horn that turned out to the right, at right angles to his other horn, and we turned him down on this account, but he would have been a record for the species for spread and also he carried very long heavy horns. That same day I talked with another hunter who had also stalked to rifle range and then turned down this same buck for the same reason. At that time we were both looking for record heads but wanted symmetrical, fairly even ones. Antelope buck vary a great deal in size and one must take this into consideration in judging the horns. A fine old buck appears fat and heavy and the best one I have killed stood a good 6 inches higher at the withers than several other bucks in the same band that later measured 16 inches in length or over. However, he was an exceptional animal and his horns both went 17½ inches in length, with a spread of 17½ inches as well, and he proved about one fourth to one third heavier than any antelope buck I have seen before or since. His head still retains seventh place in the records.

One has little to judge an antelope head by, except the length of the horns from the prong down to their base, as compared with the length from base of horns to end of nose, and also the top length as compared to the prong to basal measurement. A good spotting scope of 20 power is almost a necessity, though at times heavy mirage may make it useless in the middle of the day. Quite often, the finest bucks will be found to be old solitary animals except during the rut. Many different types will be found, the very widespread type being the most difficult to judge accurately. I turned down one my last antelope hunt that I am sure was larger than the buck I finally secured. This particular buck ran past us broadside, at about 150 yards, and while his horns looked very heavy with exceptional prongs, they seemed very short, and it was not until after he went over that ridge and later came out on the sky line a half mile away that I was able to really size him up. The fact that his near horn tipped toward us at such an acute angle made it look short when in reality it was long, and I believe would have gone at least 17 inches. We had ridden onto this bunch of bucks and this old boy was much the largest of them all, but owing to their speed and the fact that they ran broadside, we did not know we had an exceptional head in nice range until after it was far out of range.

Many antelope heads will carry horns with white tips, and at a distance these white tips may be invisible; however, they help a lot when the steel tape is finally drawn along their contour for final measurement. Don't count on them though, and as a rule, if you cannot see enough length of horn to justify your taking the buck, better pass him up and wait for a larger animal if you are in good antelope country. Some of the finest heads are rough and have bumps on the horns and at times they will also carry additional prongs; and some have been killed with a smaller third horn.

Mountain Sheep

In the wild sheep we have another animal that allows a close estimate of the horns to be made under suitable stalking conditions.

Sheep vary greatly in size of animal and the larger the ram as a general rule the larger will be the basic measurement of his horns. In all sheep countries I have hunted, however, there have at times appeared some small undersized rams and usually they ran in bunches. At long range it is impossible to distinguish them from larger rams, unless they are banded together. Occasionally one of these small rams may carry an exceptional head as the world's record *stonei* did, but usually they will be much shorter and with smaller basic measurement. To form an accurate opinion of any species of sheep, one should measure and size up all the different specimens he can find of mounted heads from any particular locality and then he can better estimate one animal at long range. A big heavy ram, if he carries a fine head, usually has heavy appearing horns even at a distance. The points are also usually well broomed, on old bighorn or *Ovis canadensis*. If you can get a good side view of the head, try and pick one whose horns appear heavy and whose points come up to a level with the bridge of the nose, and if even higher, so much the better. A head with unworn points that come up to a level with the eyes from a side view will usually measure only about 35 inches in length, and the base is also apt to be smaller than desired.

Length of horns can be judged from a frontal view as well as from the side, but some may have a very close tight curl and appear as records when they will only measure 35 to 36 inches. We have seen Stone rams with such a tight curl that they appeared to be over 40 inches, with points coming high above the nose, yet they measured only 36 inches, and had small bases. Many friends who have hunted sheep in different sections report the same thing and the presence at times of small rams that appeared to have very fine large heads, but the whole sheep was small and the head correspondingly undersized. To the amateur, any sheep head is apt to look big, but the old experienced sheep hunter, or guide, will be able to size them up in most cases, and accurately as well.

While really fine heads are apt to be on old solitary rams, one does often find them among a band of rams. When a band is located, set up the spotting scope and study them carefully if you have time. Pick the largest, darkest colored ram in the band, if his horns appear large in proportion. A really fine ram will usually appear to be "all horns." Next, see if the tips of his horns are well broomed, and if a broadside is presented, then estimate the width of the horn tips as compared with tip of nose and chin. This will give you something concrete by which to judge. Always pick the heaviest head with the widest tips if they come up to a level with or above the bridge of the nose. On the other hand you may find that rare bighorn whose horns are not broomed and sweep upward and back well beyond the base of horns, and it then is a real trophy. From a frontal view, you must judge the diameter of horn tips as best you can and their height in relation to base of horns. Then select the ram whose horns come up to a level of the nose and also turn upward. You can also judge the spread, or extreme width, as compared with others in the band. An old sheep hunter will usually pick the best in short order, but the tyro will have to study them a bit, if time permits.

When one comes out on a shoulder of the mountain and jumps rams at close range, he must pass them up or else select the largest appearing ram in a fraction of a second and shoot before they are out of sight around the shoulder of the mountain. No real sheep hunter likes such an opportunity, but much prefers a longer standing shot that will permit his sizing up the bunch and picking the finest head.

With typical bighorn, usually the largest, darkest ram will carry the finest head, and the badly broomed horns, if they are of equal appearing length to the younger ones with perfect points, should always be selected, as they will not only carry larger bases, but usually greater length as well. The only exception to this rule that I know of is that rare specimen who may not have broomed off two or three years of his horn growth and whose horns will instantly appear for what they are, exceptionally long. From a frontal view they will be seen to curve outward above the nose and from a rear view one can also see them turn upward and outward. These always make beautiful heads and should be secured when the chance offers.

Because one horn of a ram appears fine, do not take it for granted that both are the same. Usually, one will be broomed more than the other and Westley Brown and I, while sizing up a bunch of Stone rams on the Musqua River, saw one particular beast that carried an excellent right horn while the left looked as if it had been sawed square off about six inches from his head, or where the inner bone core would terminate. How this ram ever broke that horn off is beyond me. Possibly it was hit by a rifle bullet and damaged and later broken in his annual battles. Don Hopkins, hunting on the Cassiar, also reported finding a similar head with one good horn and one that appeared through the glasses to have been sawed square off about six inches from the head.

Many heads will not be uniform; we have two hanging in this room as I write, with one horn setting at an entirely different angle on the skull than the other. This may also be caused by skull deformation during their annual battles, especially while the ram is young. They hit a terrific blow when they come together and it is a wonder the skulls are not fractured, or deformed, more often. Try if possible to see both horns, though at times this will be impossible. Among bighorn, as among all other species I have hunted, one will often see a type with very heavy bases that have a widely divergent curl and make a large open curl as well. This type usually brooms more than more compact curls and seldom reaches any great length. We have one such head of a *stonei* that carries a 15¼-inch base, very heavy for that species, but only a 35-inch curl. They dig roots a lot with their horn tips and thus wear them off, and we watched one fine old Fannin ram throw dust up on his back with his right horn and later killed him, to find this right horn was a wider curl than the left and swung lower on his head.

Real fine old rams are almost always "buck-kneed," and this feature can be seen as far as you can see their legs clearly through the glasses. If the front knees bend forward when turned broadside, then you can be reasonably sure he is an old ram.

In some sections of Montana and Canada, bighorn rams tend to run to a tight curl of horn, while some bands I have seen down the Salmon River of Idaho had a wide spread of horn more like some Mexican rams, and also some of the northern Stone and Dall species. Dr. Wilson L. DuComb, of Carlyle, Illinois, while hunting under my guidance on one Salmon River boat trip, obtained what is today the widest spread of bighorn listed in the present book of records of the species. This particular ram had 38½-inch curls and 26½-inch spread and carried very light horns. They were well broomed at the tips, with an exceptionally wide curl, but the bases measured only 13⅝ inches as I remember. From a frontal view, a wide-spread head is harder to judge for length than a narrower spread of horns. If the tips of the horns come up on a level with eyes and ears you may be sure it is a good head. While the bridge of nose and eye makes an excellent measuring stick from a side view, the ears in relation to the horn tips are the best aids in sizing up a head from a frontal view.

Mexican rams will be found with about all types of head, but usually they tend to a wider spread than *Ovis canadensis*. The *stonei* is merely a color gradation from the true white northern Dall sheep and gradually grades into the pure white sheep. Just the same we have observed the same general types of head on Stone rams as found on bighorns. The farther north one hunts the more apt he is to find the slim, tapering, wide divergent horns, on Stone and Fannin rams. Also the Fannin is more apt to carry wide-spreading, light base horns than the true *stonei*. Among the Stone rams we have seen everything from heavy bases with wide short curls to very close curls, both with heavy and light bases. No doubt some of those Stone rams run to over a 16-inch base measurement. Both Stone sheep that are nearly black and Fannin sheep with white necks and gray bodies will be found in the same band, at least on the Musqua River. Farther north they grade more to Fannin, and finally into pintos and then white sheep with dark patches of hair on their bodies.

Personally we prefer the widespread heads when they also carry good weight and length, and nothing is more beautiful in the trophy line than a large perfect sheep head of whatever species.

Good binoculars such as the 7 x 35 and 9 x 35 B & L or 8 x 30 are almost a necessity in hunting sheep, though experienced eyes can get along without binoculars if they have a good spotting scope to look over suspicious objects and to use in selecting heads. My choice is a 9 x 35 B & L binocular and a 20-X or 20 power Argus spotting scope, and these glasses have served mighty well.

Even an old experienced guide may be fooled on a sheep head at times, either in poor light, or with a poorly contrasting background, or when he runs onto a bunch of undersized rams that, though old, are simply the smaller type of that species. Their tracks will give them away, but one often find rams without first seeing their tracks.

I have never had the opportunity of hunting the pure white Dall sheep, but would expect the estimation of their heads at long range to present practically the same problems as the Fannin rams, since they usually carry the same type of horns. With the Fannin rams and also with those white Dall rams, a really good heavy base head with long curl will appear heavy, and if the horns appear slim and short, they probably are. Northern sheep in their short fall coat will appear differently than when fully haired out for their long winters, and this must also be taken into consideration in judging the size of the horn bases. I have heard an old and very experienced sheep hunter say the only way to size up a sheep head was to kill it and put the steel tape on it, but with this I cannot agree, for I have found that by careful estimation one can usually come close to sizing up the head before the taking, when time permits.

Caribou

Judging a caribou head is something that often has to be accomplished in record time. In Alaska during the migration, one may have plenty of heads to pick from and they may stay in sight for longer periods, but farther south in Canada where the great Osborn is found, they will seldom be seen in large numbers and are usually on the move, or else out of range.

The Osborn is much the largest, but the Barren Ground Alaska caribou will often have just as long and heavy antlers. Eastern and woodland caribou seldom carry as long antlers but they do often run to great palmation and number of points.

With all caribou it is well first to look for weight and length of main beam, next look at the shovels and see if there are one or two shovels or brow antlers. Double shovels are rare, but make the most beautiful of all caribou heads. We much prefer double shovels and a great number of points and weight to a long sprangly head with few points and only one shovel. If the length and weight of antler are good enough, and the beast carries at least one good palmated shovel, look next at the top formation. If it is wide and has a goodly number of points, then you have a good head located. Those double shovel beauties with 35 to 40 points are very, very rare and you should never count on seeing one. As a general rule the older the bull the farther back on his shoulder and side will run the white strip from the neck, and the younger the animal, the less conspicuous this white strip will be. On young bulls it will terminate at the base of the neck. Further, the older bulls will be lighter in general body coloring. This fact helps one to judge an animal at great distance where the horns cannot be seen. Height of the main beams above the body, in comparison with the height of the body, is a good measure for length of beam. Some heads run up and palmate, while others, particularly with the woodland and Barren Ground types, tend to curve forward with the main beam, and the more curve, the harder it is to estimate total length. A really good head will show up instantly as such and the animal will appear to be almost overloaded with antlers. I have looked over a lot of caribou bulls and seen to date just one outstanding head, and though I could easily have killed him at 400 yards as he stood looking at us, our sportsman wanted to get close for a better look and a closer shot and he never saw that bull again.

Among Osborn caribou, and I presume with other species as well, the heads vary greatly in conformation and there are many different types. Some will be short and heavily palmated, while others will run to extreme lengths, often with few points. One head killed by George Bates on my first trip to British Columbia in 1927 resembled an elk head in shape and points. The main beams ran back over the withers, with points projecting upward, just like an elk head. Another I killed for meat in 1937 between the Prophet and Siccanni Rivers carried 22 points, widely palmated, but it was such a tiny little head it would not have been much longer than the horns on a large mule buck. Real old bulls, like real old elk and mule deer, often have but a single long horn on one side with few or no points at all, and this clearly shows they are past the age when they will produce normal healthy antlers.

Wide spread always enhances the beauty of a caribou head; if it also has other good features and a really good double-shovel head with 30 or more points and good length and weight, it is a trophy for a king. If the beast is turned broadside, look for the length of the shovels in proportion to length of the nose and you have an excellent measuring stick. Next look at the bays to see if there are a good many points and good length; then the top formation and length, and you can arrive at a fair estimate of the head. At times you will find the caribou bedded or feeding around some little alpine lake or shoulder of the mountain and have ample opportunity to size up any bulls in the band. When traveling always look for the good bull to bring up the rear, as he herds his harem along. Thus if you are in timber or the caribou are coming over a ridge, it is usually best to wait and see what brings up the rear, if the band can all be kept in sight and range at the same time, as the old boy with white neck and white shoulders will probably be prodding along some recalcitrant cow. Once you have de-cided to take a caribou, it is well to put him down then and there, for they may suddenly jump up, apparently from a sound sleep, and tear off across the country as if the devil was after them and for no apparent reason whatever. Unless you are going to see the northern migration, do not count heavily on exceptional caribou trophies, as they are rare for the number of animals sighted and you may look over a lot of bulls before finding one with even a presentable head.

A fine one is a magnificent thing, to my notion even more rare than a good ram head, and if you do get a caribou with double shovels, good palmation, and 35 or 40 points you are well repaid for that trip and possibly others as well, as they are far from common. A poor caribou head, like a small moose head, is not much to look at, and unless meat is needed it is better to pass up the poor ones and wait for the chance of old King Caribou appearing in range. When you do locate a good one, go after it then and there, for if you wait until the morrow that particular bull may be twenty miles away. With sheep and goat, when undisturbed, you may reasonably expect to find them in the same vicinity the next day except during the rut, but not so with caribou, which are great travelers. Both sheep and caribou, as well as antelope and mule bucks, must often be examined and passed on, as well as killed, at long range. In the North long-range shooting is the rule rather than the exception on the caribou range, and the same applies to much of the northern sheep ranges as well.

Moose

Moose heads are not as hard to estimate as many other species, if the bull is in the open and good light is available, but when located in dense timber the hunter must often make a snap judgment, if he would have a shot at the moose, and then accurate estimation is much more difficult. Wyoming, Idaho and Montana moose, open under special license in these states, are smaller in horn growth than Canadian moose as a general rule, and the huge Alaskan moose of the Kenai Peninsula are by far the finest moose in the world. In Norway they have moose exactly like ours but call them elk, and their heads run much smaller than those of our moose.

In judging a moose head, remember that spread counts more than other measurements, and one should if possible obtain a frontal or rear view for a good estimate of the spread of horns. A moose is an ungainly brute, magnificent as to size, but appearing more like a Missouri mule than any animal we know of, and when a moose takes off and runs away, he presents just about the same degree of beauty as the south end of a mountain goat going north. Both animals appear ugly and clumsy, when in reality they are far from clumsy. Measure and estimate all the mounted heads you can before going hunting and try to form a mental picture of just how wide a really good head appears. Next, when you sight a moose, estimate the spread from base of horn to extreme side points of one antler at a time, then consider the other antler and just how much spread each antler has from base of skull; then by figuring the width between horn bases and adding the two sides, you will have a fairly accurate estimate.

Moose vary greatly in body size and thickness at the shoulders and this must be considered. The thickness of the body at the shoulders in proportion to the spread is your best measuring stick for spread, but body size must also be taken into consideration. A really good head appears huge and majestic and the palms sweep well out from the body on each side. Even a 60-inch head appears enormous in proportion to the width of the body, so the hunter must actually measure some good heads in order to form an accurate opinion. As with all other game, a really good guide who knows his stuff will tell you within a very few inches just what a certain moose head will go.

Once spread has been judged, look next at the palms, for width and also length and number of points, if the range is close enough to see them clearly. Wide long palms with an ample number of points are always to be preferred. However, the width and the length of the palm and the general weight of the antlers should be considered ahead of the number of points. Next examine the brow tines. Many fine heads have separate small brow palms, and this palmation of the brow points adds much to the general appearance and beauty of the head. Some even have two sets of brow palms or points on each side. Long, heavy and wide brow points or palmations of brow points are always to be preferred. The brow formation can only be judged accurately when the bull faces the hunter and both sides can be seen for general uniformity, but a fair estimation can also be obtained from a side view and at least one side of the brows can usually be studied for length and weight from this position. Likewise, the general length of the palm of the main beam can best be judged from a side view. Note how far back over the animal's back it extends, if it ends short of base of neck or extends back over the front of the withers. In the timber, or with a dull brushy background, it is often very difficult to form an accurate opinion of the number of points or the exact length of a set of moose horns. Usually they appear much larger than they really are, and we have seen a good many killed by hunters who thought they had a 55-inch head only to find when the steel tape was passed across the extreme spread that the head only went 45 inches. A 60-inch moose is a mighty good one for Canada and that means a 5-foot spread. You simply must be able to visualize just what a 5-foot spread looks like over a big moose's shoulders, and that takes practice. This is the reason good guides are paid good money, and they are worth it to any trophy hunter. Their long experience enables them almost instantly to judge a head for spread within a few inches, if they get one good look at it. On the Kenai Peninsula of Alaska, heads of 65 inches or better can be secured if one has about two to three weeks to look them over, and if anyone wants a real moose head, that is the best place to look for him. Some magnificent heads have been obtained in Canada, but larger moose, in far greater quantity, are available from which to make the final selection on the Kenai.

Some mighty good guides use the spread of the ears when a bull is turned facing the hunter as a measuring stick by which to estimate the spread of each antler and then the total spread of the head. At times it is very difficult to see both ears at the same time, on a really fine head, owing to the brow points or palms. Some hunters prefer a really pretty and uniform head to an extremely large one, but for our money, those wide, long and heavy heads, with many massive points and really wide and long palms, take the cake. Really good heads always appear very heavy and massive in proportion to the animal, but it must be remembered that a moose at close range is always an impressive sight, as he towers above you at times, and the hunter is inclined to snap judgment, when if he would just wait a few seconds and carefully consider the head from all angles presented, he might find it only mediocre in size. Heads from about 50- to 60-inch spread are very hard to estimate correctly; they are large enough to appear really big yet do not present the sweeping majestic hugeness of a really big head of over 60 inches. You will look over a lot of moose in all probability, even on the Kenai, before you find one that truly stands out as being exceptional in size, but once a really fine one is sighted there can be no doubt of his size.

Another good point to consider in estimating length of palms is the length of the individual palm from base to tip as compared with the length of the head from nose to ears, remembering always the variation in actual size of the animals as well. A big average bull of Canada will stand from six to six and a half feet at the shoulder and some a trifle larger. A really good Alaskan bull stands higher at the withers, probably from seven to seven and three fourths feet. When such a beast is encountered at close range the hunter has much the same feeling as when a big Alaskan brownie rears up on his hind legs and towers over him; he is very apt to consider him big enough to be a real trophy, even though his horns are not of record proportion. With all horned trophies, but moose especially, it is well to beware of snap judgment of a bull that appears silhouetted on the sky line, as his horns then appear larger than they will measure, and even though he looks good, better to clip six inches off your estimate before making a final decision, if time permits.

Mountain Goat

In the mountain goat we have one of the hardest of all big game heads to estimate before killing. Except during the rut, the really good old billies will practically always be found alone as they are usually solitary old gentlemen. Look for an old yellowish cast animal rather than a pure white one, for the really good old billies always have a yellowish cast. Estimation of horn length must almost always be made at a distance and a good spotting scope is a necessity.

A side view is necessary at all times. The only good measuring stick I have found for a goat is the length of the horns in proportion to the length of the head from base of horn to tip of nose. Even then the animals vary so much in size and also in length of skull that it is very, very hard to tell within an inch or two the total length of the horns.

As an illustration, a friend of mine whom I coached a lot was guiding a party down the Salmon River and they located an old yellowish billy. The glasses showed one horn broken off badly and the face of this goat appeared much longer than the one remaining good horn. Bob decided he was not worth going after, so Bill Carlson, the horse wrangler, asked if he could take him. Granted permission, he looked up that old goat and proceeded to fill him with .30–30s, finally getting him down. Examination showed he had been badly shot up years before and one hind leg was simply a wreck. It was drawn up until the foot would not reach the ground and the old boy had been using the hock joint to help him get around. The head and face were unusually long, making him appear horse-faced, and this had led Bob to believe the one good horn was short, but the steel tape showed the remaining horn to be 11¼ inches in length with large base. The goat had the longest, homeliest head and nose I have ever seen on a goat, yet proved a record head.

Usually a big billy will measure about 10½ to 11 inches from horn base to tip of nose, so one can use this measurement as a yardstick in estimating the length of the horns. If the goat is seen from the front or rear no accurate estimate can be made. From the front view the horns curve back out of sight and from a rear view the long hair on top of the withers hides all but the tips. The only way a fair estimate can be made, in my humble experience, is to compare length of horns with length of nose from base of horn to tip of nose, remembering that the needle-sharp points are hard to discern except in good light, and that the short facial hair covers the extreme base of horns, while that big stinking blue gland, behind each horn, also hides the base of horns at the back of each. With goats it's about as well to pick the largest, dirtiest old yellow billy goat you can find, then check this side measurement if you can get such a view before shooting. They vary a lot in size, so at best your estimate is none too accurate.

On the other hand if a representative specimen is desired, you must remember that the nannies often have just as long horns as the billies, but much smaller basal circumference. In fact the world's record was and may still be a nanny. Nannies always appear much whiter than the good old billies and will usually be found in bunches with the young stock. Owing to their whiteness, all goats appear large at first sight, but the experienced hunter can instantly pick out the good old billies when they do happen to be near the nannies and kids. Any billy whose horns appear as long as his nose from base of horns is a mighty good one.

Elk

We consider elk about the easiest of all the deer tribe to estimate. Possibly this may be due to the fact we have hunted elk so many years, both on our own and also in guiding other hunters. During this time thirty-one head of elk have fallen to my own rifle, not counting many "crips" followed up and finished for others. Elk heads are usually very uniform as to number of points on each side, and a long or heavy head is instantly seen as such if the light is good, or the animal is silhouetted against a suitable background. As with most other horned game, a great many average or mediocre heads will be seen for every one that will go in the record class. If you are looking for a record head you need give but a passing glance to the average bull to determine he is just another six-pointer or less. Really big heads stand out as such the minute you get your eyes on them, as they present no such problems as moose, deer, sheep or caribou.

One should look always for heavy massive beams, long brow points, and at the length of the sword points and how they project upwards from the main beam, then at the tip formation. Usually a good look at the tip formation is enough to pass on the quality of the head alone, but some heads that run very long may have a poor tip conformation and be really worth while. As a general rule, if a head makes only a small fork at the extreme tip, then you can put it down in your little red book as either a small young head or a short one. There are, however, exceptions to this general rule and some of the longest heads have poor and small tines at the extreme tip, so it is well to beware of this type. Usually the really good heads will have a very wide divergence of the last two points. When such is the case, the length of the main beam will be instantly apparent. In judging elk heads, I first look for a huge old bull. If it is during the rut, his bugle will be much coarser and deeper pitched as a rule than that of younger bulls. I have heard some who were so old and hoarse they could not really bugle and their call was more of a long-drawn grunt than the true bugle of an elk. Select the largest animal, then if he is also light colored you may be sure he is an old bull. However, he may also be too old to carry a good head and often such old-timers will have heavy, but short, stumpy antlers, or they may have just one long main beam on one side, with no projecting points at all. Younger large bulls will appear darker at a distance and with much darker neck and mane, and often these bulls, if large and in their prime, will carry the finest, most symmetrical heads.

After locating a promising bull, by either calling or stalking, look first at the size of the beams, next at their length in proportion to length of neck, if broadside. A good one should have horns coming back to or over the withers, depending on whether the head is outstretched or carried in the usual fashion. If the main beam appears long, then look at the distance between the third point up from the head on each side and the base of the sword point, then at the length and weight of the high sword point. Next look at the length from base of the sword point out to the last fork, if the usual six-pointer. If the last point makes a widely divergent fork from the tip of the main beam and has good length and weight, you may be sure you have located a fine head. Spread is secondary but also easily seen when the animal either faces you, or is going, or turned directly away from you, or when he swings his head.

To my notion, taking the main beam as a criterion of the size of an elk head is all wrong. I prefer James L. Clark's system of measurement which also includes weight and length of the various points. A fine bull elk at the start of the rut and when he is in his prime is the prettiest specimen of all the deer tribe, and the most magnificent. He is handsome from every angle and does not present the awkward ungainly appearance of a moose. Also his gait when he is jumped is agile and beautiful, and with his long sweeping antlers thrown back along the sides of his shoulders, his mane flowing, he is truly a sight any sportsman will long remember.

Though such may occur at times, in a lifetime of elk hunting, I have yet to see a really big head on a small elk. When you do sight a big, heavy and long head, it will nearly always be on a big animal and will instantly show up for the outstanding trophy it is. Such a bull, even though of great size, will appear to have enormous horns. If you have to study the head to see if it is big enough, you can be almost sure it is only of average dimensions. The tyro may, however, think any mature six- or seven-point bull a record, but after he has hunted elk a few seasons and really studied all the heads he sees, he will soon know them for what they are. In former years many fine heads were taken around Yellowstone Park, but in recent years fine heads are not so thick, as those elk have a hard time wintering and ranches prevent their reaching low-elevation winter range; hence they come through the winter in bad shape at times and for this reason do not make their normal growth. The finest heads and the heaviest we have ever seen occurred in the South Fork of the Flathead in Montana and on the Salmon River in Idaho, where the elk drift down to very low elevations in the sagebrush and bunch grass to winter, and for this reason come through the winters in better shape and put on a correspondingly greater growth the coming grass season.

Length of brow points can well be seen in proportion to length of the nose, when the beast is facing the hunter. The diameter of burrs and horn beams can clearly be seen in proportion to the width of the ears. With elk, a uniform, even head is usually much prettier than an uneven head, and the more points, the more apt that head is to be uneven. Freaks occur more often than most hunters would think and I have seen a goodly number. Occasionally an old bull may develop far above the usual number of points, with considerable palmation at the fork of the sword point. When such a head carries good length of main beam it is truly a prize, even though it will usually be uneven, in both number of points and angle to the main beam. We have obtained two perfect large heads that will go in the records — one of them a six-pointer of very heavy beams and long enough to go in the lower part of the records, and the other almost perfect in every detail with the great length of 62½ inches for one beam and 60¾ inches for the other. We have still another fine elk head with seven and eight points and 53½-inch spread that is very massive and heavy, but has short stubby horns with a length of only 49 inches, a very old bull.

However my best head carries the longest points I have ever seen on any elk head. The right horn is the best and from the back of the beam to the tip of the sword point measures just 24 inches; from tip to tip of the last prong, and the tip of the main beam, it is just 29⅜ inches — the widest fork at the end of the horns I have yet seen on an elk.

Elk, under good conditions, often live to very old age. One bull tagged in the ear and liberated near Missoula, Montana, in 1909 was killed the fall of 1944, which would put the old boy at thirty-five years old when killed. His horns showed age unmistakably as the points no longer carried their usual clean sweep, but the head was very large and with a tremendous spread.

Bear

Except in Alaska, black bear are seldom seen in numbers, or often enough to permit much choice. Though in good bear country, one can turn down any small bear and wait for the possible chance of a larger animal, either black or brown. Sows with baby cubs should never be taken as the little fellows need their mother that first summer and also hibernate with her the next winter, and if left to their own devices they often hole up on the south slopes and then thaw out in January, after which they may well starve before spring opens. Likewise they are too small to make rugs or trophies and the mother with baby cubs we believe in leaving alone.

Grizzly

Usually a sportsman is lucky enough to get a good grizzly in most sections of the northern Rockies on a fall hunt and will not be very choosy about him so long as he is a grizzly. In some sections of Canada and Alaska, where a spring hunt is undertaken, you will find enough grizzly to permit a choice up to a certain extent. When this is the case and several animals are seen at once, or over a period of a few days, then one should endeavor to pick the finest pelt of the lot, or the largest, so long as it is not rubbed. Again, we firmly believe in leaving in peace sows with baby cubs, though a sow with yearlings can well be taken, if the pelt is good. Two-year-olds usually have fine pelts, but are small and should never be taken if larger bear are available. It requires a period of some ten to fifteen or more years to grow a big bear and the youngsters should be allowed to grow up. Usually, any well-furred specimen of average size, or over, is a fine trophy. Care should be exercised, especially on spring hunts, to avoid killing a rubbed bear. Grizzlies, as well as browns and blacks, after they have been out of their dens for some time, may rub their rumps on a pitch tree, or stump, rubbing away all the guard fur. Grizzlies also like to play on snowslides, sliding down them for all the world like a bunch of children, especially the younger animals. A few days of this sport will spoil the finest pelt if there be much crusted snow.

If a pelt appears to have dark patches on it at a distance, or if the smooth even contour of the back is broken, one should if possible get closer and make a careful study of that bear before shooting. It may be that his pelt is wet from crossing a stream or lying in the snowdrifts or a wallow, while on the other hand it may be a badly rubbed place that would hopelessly spoil the pelt for a rug. Such rubbed pelts should never be taken; better by far to wait until he has grown another coat or else forgo the bear that trip, as a worthless pelt is never a trophy.

At times, through circumstances beyond his control, a hunter may be forced to kill a grizzly when he well knows its pelt is rubbed, but such instances do not happen very often. Grizzly pelts vary from jet black, without a single silver-tipped hair, to a pale blond color. I coached George Bates while he killed a black sow grizzly in British Columbia in 1927 that had no single white or silver-tipped hair on her entire body, yet her two yearlings were light-colored grizzly, as was a three- or four-year-old that was traveling with her. Again in 1939 we spotted and watched H. N. Busick kill a nine-foot Alaskan grizzly that also was coal black. He was an old male and a fair-sized bear but showed no trace of the usual silver-tipped coat. Of all the many color variations of the grizzly, we prefer the dark brown or almost black undercoat and legs with cream or silver-tipped coat over back and neck and shoulders. These pelts are outstanding in their beauty as the dark under fur sets off the silver tipping. A real good silvertip is one of our very finest trophies if not the absolute top.

Alaskan Brown Grizzlies

When hunting the big bear along the coast line of Alaska, the island of Kodiak or out on the Peninsula, one must be very, very careful, if he would obtain a perfect pelt. In southeastern Alaska, pelts average shorter in length of fur but are usually very even if taken soon enough after emergence from the winter den, or late enough in the fall to have enabled them to put on their winter coat. Farther north and to westward, it's a far different story, and most of the unattached bear up there come out of their holes badly rubbed. This fact is not generally known on the Outside and of course for obvious reasons is never mentioned in the ads from Alaska. In the spring of 1937 I personally saw 88 bear all on the Peninsula on the north side of the lower end of Cook Inlet. Of those 88 bear, 10 were blacks, the rest grizzlies or brownies. Of the 78 big bear, 30 head were sows and baby cubs, and for some reason every one of those sows, with young babies not much larger than a big house cat, was, as near as I could tell through the glasses and a 20 X Mossberg scope, a perfect specimen. The other 48 bear were males and sows with yearlings or two-year-olds, and of these 48 I honestly believe about 6 or 8 of them were perfectly furred; the rest were rubbed in various stages and we did not kill a single unrubbed specimen. Some of them we saw first break the crust of the snow and then dig out of their winter den, for the first time. One old chap we watched dig out looked for all the world like an African lion. His face and head were rubbed slick, but he carried a ruff of five- or six-inch fur and hair in a ring around his neck, the balance of his body being all rubbed down to the short under fur.

The fact that we saw so many badly rubbed specimens, when we were there before any bear trails showed on the snow and watched many actually dig out, proved that those bear rub in their dens and emerge in that sad state. The only way I can account for the fact that all the old sows we saw with tiny baby cubs were perfect is that they are afraid of injuring the babies and hence do not rub in the den as the others do.

If you just want to kill a record Alaskan brownie, pick the largest bear you can, and you are almost sure to find him rubbed in places or else so badly as to ruin his pelt and leave only the head for mounting. On the other hand if you want a fine specimen, then look over as many as possible and select a perfect one, and in all probability it will be a two- or three-year-old or that rare and exceptional big one with perfect coat.

Those bear wade around and swim the tidal arms that are filled with glacial silt and their pelts become impregnated with devil's-club needles during their summer of living on berries and salmon. So it is no wonder, what with their hides full of the festering needles and salty glacial silt rubbed in that they itch and proceed to rub all winter in their dens. I believe one would have a better chance of securing a perfect pelt in a late fall hunt, though hunting them then would be much more difficult and fewer would be seen. Then, too, the pelts would be shorter. A perfect and large brownie is a real trophy, but one that is not only very expensive but also hard to come by. I understand that the bear farther out to westward on the Peninsula are much better on the average and the Sikes expedition obtained many fine specimens. Many pelts we examined from Kodiak showed the usual rubbing, even when killed early. After the volcanic eruptions in that section following the turn of the century, much of the country was buried under ash, and that ash still permeates much of the tidal mud flats and glacial silt, so those bear have a real problem when their long shaggy pelts have a coating of such mud and devil's-club briers.

Bear pelts always grow all winter and the longest, glossiest pelts of all are obtained on a bear that has just emerged from his den. With mountain grizzly as well as blacks and browns and the black variation or glacier bear, the pelts are usually good and really at the finest when they first emerge in the spring. In the fall the pelt will be even and uniform but shorter, and at this time of year the younger bear will always sport the longest, heaviest coats.

The principal method of determining the size of bear trophies is to take the measurement of the skull, across the zygomatic arches, and the height as well as the length without the lower jaw. About all really big old grizzlies have a lower jaw that protrudes beyond the upper front teeth. The entire skull used to be taken for length, but lately only the upper skull is measured for length, though there must be a great many of the top record bear in the present records that were measured with complete skull.

The skull alone is not enough as some small bear carry huge ungainly heads, while some very large bear have small skulls in comparison, but it is still about the most accurate measurement for classification. The skin should also be measured as well as the body before skinning. Measure from tip of nose to root of tail and tip of tail, in a line down the back, and also circumference of neck in front of shoulders and just back of skull, as well as just behind the shoulders, and you have a very good check on the carcass measurements. Next, if the skin is spread out on the boat deck and a couple of husky men pull on nose and tail, then lay it down and do the same across the front paws, then drop them, being careful to stretch the skin to as nearly natural shape as possible, then take the measurements of the skin as it lies out smooth and flat, you have an accurate measurement. Of course if the vent is left a foot high on the backside of the pelt and a couple of husky guides stretch and sew it in a frame before measurements are taken, you can get some ungodly big bear, but it is not the true measurement and should never be measured in this way.

[33]

Cats

With both cougar and the jaguar of the Southwest, there will be little or no opportunity ever to select specimens, and the hunter will be lucky to obtain most any kind of a specimen. Usually only with the aid of dogs is it possible to get either animal, though occasionally one may be trapped. My advice is kill the cat, then measure his skull and pelt and body and see what you have for size.

In measuring the skulls of animals it is best to set them on a perfectly flat level surface and then use two steel squares to slide up against the skull, one at each end, and also the same for the zygomatic arch measurement, then carefully measure the space between the steel squares. This way you are not guessing, but skulls, like horns, are all prone to do considerable shrinking and measurements taken after killing will not agree with measurements taken a month or so later after the bone becomes dry and hard.

Arctic Game

Never having had the opportunity to hunt the great game of the arctic, I am not competent to pass on them, but arctic game, including musk oxen, polar bear and walrus, all present different problems than our more southern game. With bear, any sizable specimen is good in season, though the fur may be very short in summer, but a fall or early summer bear should carry maximum coat, especially the late spring and early summer bear. Summer is about the only time such game can be hunted unless one winters with the Eskimos. Musk oxen bulls and walrus bulls do present their problems in judging size and spread and weight of horns and length and base of tusks, but I am not competent to advise on these animals. With polar bear, usually the big old males have a yellowish cast, especially late in the summer, probably from seal oil, and the whiter specimens will usually be either younger bear or females. They sometimes grow just about as large as the Alaskan brownie, though these really fine specimens are now very scarce and few of the really big skins come out each summer. As with other bear, many years are required for them to reach such stature.

III

Still-Hunting

WHILE much Eastern hunting is still-hunting, the East does not have any corner on this type of hunting and many animals of the West must also be still-hunted for best results. Still-hunting is primarily timber or brush hunting, where the game feeds or beds in the timber or both. It is necessarily close range hunting, where you must see the game first. Usually, many years of experience are necessary to become a really good successful still-hunter. We learn by our mistakes, and with a relatively short part of the year available, usually not over two months of big game season, it is imperative that we devote all our faculties to the problem, if we would become really skilled in this phase of big game hunting.

Many things must be considered in still-hunting. We must consider the weather; condition of the forest, whether dry or wet; the type of browse or food the game is then feeding on, its hours devoted to feeding and the hours usually spent bedded. Direction of the prevailing wind or air movement must be carefully considered. Terrain must also receive due consideration, the places most likely for an animal to feed, or to bed for the heat of the day. Direction of the sun, if it is shining, must be noted. It is always best to hunt with the sun at your back, if at all possible. The rut must also be taken into account, and its effect on the hunting. Different species of game must be hunted differently, and in general to be a successful and accomplished still-hunter requires a great deal of woods knowledge. One must also know intimately the game he is after, if he would have a fair measure of success.

The moon is another important factor. In clear weather, when the game is much hunted, it will feed all night during the light of the moon and bed in some snug brush haven during the day. Likewise, in cloudy weather the game will be forced to feed later in the morning and earlier in the evening. With about all herbivorous timber game, the best time to hunt is the first two hours in the morning, after daylight, and the last two hours before darkness in the evening. If the weather is cloudy or rainy, game may feed more or less all day and bed at night. The approach of a hard snowstorm is always anticipated by the game, which will feed to capacity before a bad storm and then lie quietly bedded throughout the storm. In the mountains, it will often move down to lower levels well in advance of a bad storm. How animals know of the approaching bad weather is beyond the ken of man, but know it they do. Hunting is always hard in a bad wind, since the game seems more nervous and on the alert, probably because the wind makes so much noise in the forest that it drowns out all normal sounds of approaching danger which the game can usually hear and recognize well in advance of any hunter. For this reason, windy days are never the best for still-hunting, though at times the wind may help cover your approach and enable you to get onto your game, if you know the country and how best to approach the bed ground.

Bear are largely nocturnal and late evening is the best time to surprise them at feeding, while the early morning is next best. With hoofed game, the reverse is true and the morning hours are the best.

Practically all timber big game has exceptional hearing and sense of smell, both being many times sharper than the same senses in the average human being. Game also has the habit of feeding upwind, so it will be warned well in advance of any approaching enemy. When startled, if the beasts do not locate the hunter, they are very apt to go back over their tracks as they have just fed over that section and know the enemy is not there, while the country in advance is an unknown quantity. Big game does reason, in spite of the fact that many folks think it acts only on instinct. One has only to trail a wise old elk or deer for a day or so to see clearly that these animals not only possess considerable gray matter, but also use it.

The hunter should, wherever possible, wear soft woolen clothing, or if the weather is too warm for wool, then soft cotton, something that will not scratch or scrape against the boughs, limbs and brush. If virgin country and there are no city hunters about, then it should be neutral colored as well, but if the country is hunted much, it should be red for protection against some excitable fool who may shoot at anything that moves. Footgear for still-hunting must be carefully chosen. For level dry country, moccasins are very good, but in steep mountainous country they are too slick and about worthless. For wet boggy country or damp forest, Bean's leather-top rubbers are excellent, but in steep country the hunter badly

needs good heels to hold him when going downhill and for such hunting we prefer good White loggers with heels of about 1¼ inch height.
The soles should be soft rubber or composition and never slick. When
hunting in snow the leather-top rubber is almost a necessity. In some
sections containing much down timber, one is best off with a pair of
well-calked loggers that enable him to walk logs at every opportunity.
He can then get up above the ground and can see more, as well as being
able to walk logs without continually falling off when the bark peels.

Look your country over carefully, pick out the thickets, wet swamps
and usual feed grounds, then also pick out the low ridges and flat shoulders on the ridges where game is most apt to bed for the day. Also size
up the low passes through which moving game is most apt to travel in
moving from one feed ground to another. An experienced still-hunter can
very soon size up even new country and decide where to look for the
game during the feeding hours, as well as where he can reasonably expect
to find them bedded during the middle of the day.

Hunt always with the wind in your face, as a deer or an elk or a bear
can easily scent you a full half mile away, even on a very slight air current, many times further than you can ever hope to see them, and you
will see more game right from camp than you will when hunting downwind. Likewise, hunting is almost impossible when the ground is covered
with hard crusted snow, or if after a hard rain you get a freeze and the
ground is crusted badly on the surface. It's virtually impossible to sneak
up on game when such conditions prevail. At such times it is better to
locate a pass and keep out of sight, to windward of where the game may
cross, and watch during early morning and late evening hours.

In all still-hunting one must learn to travel noiselessly, always moving
very slowly and preferably with short steps and the weight on the ball
of the foot. The old army heel and toe is O.K. for marching an army down
the road, but is totally out of place when still-hunting. The weight should
be well forward on the foot and each step should be slow and careful,
feeling for possible limbs that may break and give you away. Remember,
nothing is ever gained in still-hunting by trying to cover a lot of country.
You may see game but it will usually be just a flash and no shot offered.
The skilled still-hunter slips along like a shadow, moving slowly, the
while he scans every foot of timber and brush, making absolutely certain
nothing is in sight before taking his next step. He keeps the wind or air
movement in his face. This can be done when the wind is very slight,
by dropping some soft rotten wood dust, or grass, or dust from the fingers,

or by wetting a finger and holding it up and noting which side gets cold first. We also believe in smoking. If you are a smoker, then enjoy your pipe or cigarette, and note which way the wind drifts the smoke.

Smoke will tell you the drift of the wind better than anything else. Remember also that any game animal can easily detect the man smell, many times farther than you can see in the timber, and a human being smells worse to any big game animal than smoke, or any other possible scent. Tobacco smoke will carry a long way but human scent will travel just as far, if not farther, and is more apt to stampede the game. Avoid all quick movements in the timber, travel slowly and move slowly. It's not the amount of territory you hunt, but how well and carefully you cover what you do get over. More game will be sighted and killed if a small section is hunted than if you barge across twenty miles of terrain in a day.

My own method of still-hunting may be of interest. I travel always up-wind, or quartering toward the prevailing wind, move a short distance and look everything over carefully, then move again a short distance. Whenever a log, stump or rock offers a suitable seat, I sit and smoke and watch and listen, usually from some vantage point, if possible, where a swale or basin, or open park, or other game feeding ground, may be constantly surveyed. If nothing shows after a time, I slip quietly along for a little way and repeat the performance. Of course it's little use to still-hunt so carefully unless the tracks indicate the presence of game. The time to travel is when no game sign is in evidence, but when you do locate fresh sign and it indicates feeding animals, then go slow and sit around and watch as much as possible. You can easily tell if the game is feeding or traveling, and if traveling, yet circling a bit, then you know it is looking for a suitable bed for the day, when every possible precaution should be taken. Once game is bedded, it has every advantage. It can hear you a long ways and if you do not keep the wind right it will get your scent and depart. Remember, game practically always circles around to windward of its trail before bedding, where the first enemy following that trail will give the game his scent, long before he gets in sight, or even hearing.

If you locate tracks of a traveling or slowly feeding band of game, never stay on the tracks, but always circle well to windward of them and then cut in occasionally, just often enough to keep the direction of the traveling game. All game habitually watches its back track and beds where it can get the scent of anything moving on that back track, so stay off the trail. Your circles should also be wide enough so that when you do catch up or get ahead of the game, you will work in from the side, where the animals will not be as apt to see you, and if you have the wind right they cannot smell you. When much hunted, a wary old moose, bull elk or whitetail will always do considerable circling before bedding, until he finds the best suited spot, usually where one jump will put him in cover from any direction. He will usually bed in some thick clump of second growth or behind a fallen log or at the root of a big tree, where his color blends into the landscape. Only by traveling very slowly and stopping often for a considerable time can the hunter hope to see the game first and get a decent shot. One good careful shot at standing game is always worth a battle after the game jumps. If you are on your toes and see the game first, you then have time to see how it is turned and what part of the game is presented. You can slowly raise your rifle and kill it. But when once it jumps, then you have only fleeting glimpses, usually between tree boles, and your fast snap shooting will be lucky to land on a vital spot.

If you see the game and it is watching you, raise your rifle very, very slowly, taking several seconds to get it to your shoulder. Then when the sights bear right, don't hesitate, but shoot the first time the sights lie right on the game. Many times we have surprised old buck mule deer and whitetails as well as elk and moose in the timber, at close range. Sometimes they saw us, at others they did not, and it is best always to pretend you do not see the game if it is watching you. Many times the animals were not just what we wanted, so we slipped quietly on our way, the while we watched them from the corner of our eyes, never looking directly towards them, as game instantly senses the minute you locate it. Some of those animals would begin to rise slowly out of their beds, taking over a minute perhaps to get to their feet, their movements so slow as to be almost imperceptible. The hunter can learn much from them. Often they would wait in standing position until they thought we had gone far enough not to notice their movements, then they would slink quietly away without breaking a limb or making a sound, until they were safe behind trees or brush. *Then* they would break into a run. Many times, when we wanted the animals and their heads were large enough to suit, we would walk slowly past as though we did not see them at all, then stop and slowly raise the rifle and turn just as slowly, and the instant the sights rested on the beasts we would let them have it. On the other hand, if we had stopped short the instant we saw them and jerked the gun up, they would have been out of their beds and running hard in a fraction of a second, presenting only a fast-running and difficult shot, whereas by our method we obtained perfect standing shots and instantly killed game.

When game is located and one wishes to get closer to it, then approach must be made when its head is down feeding, stopping the instant the animal raises its head. Game can see very well, but timber game cannot see as well as sheep and antelope. Bear are shortsighted, but even they can see a man a surprising distance if he is moving. When one stands still, the game may see you, but not recognize you for an enemy, but make the slightest movement and you are instantly spotted. This is just another reason why it is always best to hunt timber game during the feeding hours. Game makes more or less noise feeding and when the head is down or reaching high for browse, it is not as apt to detect you as when bedded and chewing its cud, when it has nothing to do but watch. We have often surprised such bedded game and proceeded to sit down quietly and observe it for a half hour or more, when the game was totally unaware of our presence. Every little while the animal would cautiously survey the surrounding terrain or tilt and twist its nose, in search of any enemy scent.

Many big game animals can do a surprisingly good job of slipping away in the timber without a sound. We have watched elk which had seen us and were showing only an eye and ear around a tree bole. Very slowly they pulled their head back out of sight, taking several seconds to complete the job, then slipped quietly away, without our ever seeing another hair of them, or hearing a single sound. An old and wise buck whitetail is notorious for this procedure.

When hunting low rolling country, it is well to work along just under the tops of ridges, where one is up high enough to look down into the basins where game usually feeds and see as much terrain as possible. In all timber hunting, more game will be seen and located when one is sitting quietly out of sight and watching such basins than when one is traveling along, even slowly and carefully. If possible do your traveling in early morning and with the sun at your back, as it is then much harder for the game to make you out. In late evening the sun is also best at your back. During the bedding hours of the day, it's just as well to work the low ridges, very slowly, keeping to windward of the most likely bed grounds. A stalk should always be made upwind and with the sun behind you as well, if possible.

In all big game hunting, there is no substitute for really knowing the habits of your game and also the particular section you are hunting. Experience learned in any one country will always help you in new country, but a guide who really knows that particular section and the feeding and bed grounds of the game will be of inestimable value, regardless of how long you may have hunted. One man can hunt alone to better advantage than with a companion, unless he and the companion have hunted together for a time and each well understands the other's movements. But never should more than two men hunt together. Three is always a crowd and will make too much noise.

When in country new to the hunter, it is always best to scout out the country quietly the first few days before attempting serious hunting. Get the lay of the land, learn the game crossings, their feed and bed grounds and the prevailing winds. Remember that in steep country, during the heat of the day, there will always be an updraft on south hillsides, and if you travel at that time of day and game is apt to bed on the ridges, it is best to circle along just over on the north slope, where your scent will not be wafted up to all the game in the country. Sound travels up better than down also. It is always best to work the higher ground where if you do jump game it will not be out of sight in two jumps.

When hard hunted, most all timber game prefers to bed where it can be out of sight in any direction in one or two jumps; then it is imperative that you do your hunting during feeding hours if possible. You might as well rest in camp during the heat of the day, but be out with the game as soon as you can see your rifle sights in the morning and again in the evening as long as shooting light lasts.

In the early fall in much of the West, both deer and elk like to eat mushrooms, and soon after the first heavy fall rains come they will be found on the north slopes in the dense timber, eating mushrooms in early mornings and evenings, and usually bedded along the north side of the ridges near the top in the heat of the day.

Whitetail in particular like old slashings and the tender reproduction growth affords ideal feed grounds, often right close to civilization. Elk and mule deer like more secluded country, particularly the elk. When conditions are bad for still-hunting, it is better to watch some old slashing, or second growth, or open meadow, from the security of timber or brush, than to go around breaking brush in a changing wind. Nothing can be more exasperating than a constantly changing wind and hunting under such conditions seldom pays dividends. In all still-hunting one should move slowly and look where he is placing each foot to avoid any noise, and the more time he spends quietly watching from cover the more apt he is to bag his game. The rifle should always be carried where it can be instantly brought into play, but unless the game is jumped and running, no quick movement should ever be made. Remember, you equal the game's senses only in the matter of eyesight, in all other faculties the game has you bested before you start.

Whenever you approach the top of a ridge, or a clearing or a point overlooking a basin, always try and stop behind the screen of a tree or log, and if you must sit down out in the open, then do so with a tree bole at your back, as you are not then outlined against lighter background or sky line. Game instantly spots any movement, but you can stand still in close proximity to game without its ever seeing you, if you have suitable cover or background and remain absolutely motionless. With about all hoofed timber game, elk, moose and deer, you will usually see the females first, while the old bull or buck will remain hidden, often behind the bunch, so it is imperative that you locate him before any of the band sees and identifies you for an enemy. The old boy with the horns will nearly always be along behind, or off to the side of the band and in good cover. He depends a great deal on the keen eyes and nose of the does or cows to warn him of approaching danger. Mule deer do not carry huge ears for nothing and they can detect clearly sounds that would be absolutely inaudible to the human ear.

Many times you will jump game, either elk, deer or moose, and they will make a couple of jumps and stop. This means they have heard you, but do not have you located. Always remain absolutely motionless at such times, at least until you have located the animal you want. Even then, if you would secure the trophy, you must move that rifle so slowly as to take several seconds, stopping the movement any time an animal looks your way, until you finally get it to the shoulder.

Moose and elk make considerable noise when they run and I have known many old hunters who ran right after elk when they jumped them in timber, stopping the instant the elk stopped and remaining absolutely quiet as long as the animals did the same. At times you can thus catch up with the last of the band and in it will usually be found the big bull you are after, if hunting trophies. It is only an expedient, however, and not always successful, and to be used only as a last resort. If the elk or moose or deer have winded you, it will avail nothing, as they will then travel a considerable distance. At times, however, they may have merely heard your approach and will run a few yards and stop, trying to get a look at what has disturbed them; then you may be lucky enough to get a shot, but if you make one jump after the game stops it will locate you and be gone for good. This was a favorite method of many old-timers when they hunted elk that were not used to man and which would run a short distance and stop for a look, but if they have been hunted much, you will hear only the continued crashing of the animals until they are gone out of hearing. I have fooled along behind a band of elk all day in dense cedar timber. The huge tree boles rose to tremendous height and blotted out the sun, then the fallen logs and second growth made visibility only a few yards. I could plainly hear the animals feeding slowly along, but sometimes I never did get sight of a single member of the band. At other times I have proceeded silently along, always to windward of the trail and circling in to check the tracks occasionally, until I reached more open timber or broken ridges and then was able to get good sight of the band and pick the animals wanted.

Snow hunting is the easiest when conditions are right, such as steady wind in one direction and no crust on the snow, or no wet snow that packs and pops under your feet. At such ideal times you can pick up tracks and circle always to windward and well away from the trail until you cut in ahead of the game and simply stand or sit still until it comes in view. If you can clearly get the animals' direction and get ahead of them, with the wind in your favor, then you can pick out good cover and sit still and have every advantage, but stay directly on their trail and they will be sure to circle enough to throw your scent to them and then they will be off for parts unknown.

The man living in the game country can pick his ideal hunting conditions, but the sportsman out for a limited time only has to take advantage of what time he can spare and must hunt whether conditions are good or bad. At times, however, even under the worst possible conditions, he will get a break and capitalize on being in the field and being ready. We have seen such things occur many times.

Two men used to hunting together over a period of years can do very well still-hunting, or working out the tracks of a band of game. One should always do the tracking, taking the lead and circling. In this way, he can cut in to the tracks just often enough to know their direction, and then cut back out in another big circle to windward. The second man can follow his footsteps with little thought to the placing of his feet or the trail, and devote his entire faculties to looking for the game. The man with the keenest game eyes should always follow behind the companion and search every inch of the surrounding terrain at all times. In this way, I have often had good luck in timber hunting. In partly open timber, the second man can also swing out a little apart from his companion and thus have more territory fully covered, and in case of jumping the game, it may and very often does circle to get your wind, when one or the other of the two may well get a good shot.

Except during the rut, the bulls and bucks will usually be the more wary and will on approaching a clearing or open space in the timber usually stop behind a screen of brush or boughs for a careful look-see, while the cows and calves will often barge right out into the open and go to feeding. This is true of whitetail, mule deer and elk as well, and the big bull or buck will usually be found tailing the herd, if possible under cover. As a general rule, before the rut, old buck mule deer and bull elk will be found alone or in pairs. Fat, lazy old gentlemen, interested only in their food and keeping out of harm's way. Moose usually will be found about the same and seldom with the cows until the approach of the rut.

You should simply sit down and look over the country, figuring out where the best feed is located and the most likely bed ground, remembering you are hunting solitary old gentlemen who well know how to take care of themselves. All is not bone between their horns.

When the country is particularly brushy and hard to get through without extreme noise, or when it is extremely dry, one can at times slowly work his way along old wood roads, or pack trails. At other times, back in virgin country, you will nearly always find game trails leading from one batch of cover to the next and to the favorite bed and feeding grounds, usually through low saddles in the hills. You can always slip along such trails more quietly than if you simply take off through the brush, and we always try to locate and travel such trails. Then too, a little noise on such a game trail is not as apt to frighten the animals as if it were coming from some other direction, as they expect other game to traverse those same trails.

Elk and moose, in particular, have well-used trails in any country they inhabit, and these usually circle through the high basins and pass through the low saddles in the range from one basin to another. These game trails are always the best way to get through difficult country. When two men desire to work out a gulch or along a small stream, it is well for one to take each side of the gulch and always upwind. When such procedure is followed, one man may see game across the gulch or canyon that is hidden from his partner and vice versa. Likewise one man may jump game and have no chance of seeing it, when it will be in plain sight of his partner across the gulch. At other times game jumped by one man, particularly deer of all species, will circle across the canyon in an endeavor to get the wind of the hunter that jumped it and thus run directly into the second hunter.

Once an old bull or buck has seen or winded you, there is no earthly use in keeping after him as you will not see him again, barring pure accident, at least that day. We have watched an old bull elk gather up his band of some fifteen cows during the rut, when our pack string came into the basin fully a half mile away. They got our wind and that old bull picked up every member of his harem and prodded them along the main divide for a full ten miles before he allowed them to turn off into another heavily timbered basin, as the tracks clearly showed the next day.

At times caribou must be still-hunted in the timber, but usually they are found in the high, open, alpine meadows, when they do stick to the timber they are much harder to hunt. During early seasons, mountain and woodland caribou will often be found in dense timber and must be still-hunted just as moose, deer or elk; they have an excellent sense of smell as well as excellent eyesight, but their ears are not the equal of deer and elk. The size of an animal's ears is well worth noting. Ears denote plenty to the old still-hunter. Moose have the largest and longest noses of all American game, but I do not believe their sense of smell is any better than, if as good as, that of an elk. I have many times watched an old bull elk stop and sniff my tracks, for all the world like a hound dog, then whirl and run. But once I had a moose pass within three feet and not scent us.

If approached upwind, moose, back in the virgin country, are not very wild and will often stand for some time while you look them over, and many times I have run onto them while hunting horses early in the morning, but let them get a mere whiff of the dreaded man scent and they are on their way.

The early mornings and late evenings are always best for moose hunting, especially along streams or shallow lakes where most of their feeding is done. During the middle of the day they will usually bed in some dense thicket on a low ridge adjacent to such lakes or wet meadows and they must then be approached upwind and with the utmost care. A moose, for all his size and bulk, can do a first-class job of hiding and also slipping away in the timber. During the first two weeks at the beginning of the rut moose may be called very easily by an experienced moose hunter, under the right conditions, but that is not still-hunting in the full sense of the word.

During the rut of hoofed game, if hunting upwind, or quietly sitting near a crossing, one will have many opportunities to bag a nice animal. They do not seem nearly as wary as a few weeks earlier and being on the go themselves offer many more opportunities for the hunter. They are also much bolder during the mating season, and will seldom leave a band of does or cows, though they may well sneak off into the timber to one side or the rear of the band. Lone bucks or bulls travel almost night and day until they find cows or whip some smaller bull, or buck, away from his band. We have heard old bull elk bugling all night long during the start of the rut and have also seen mule bucks traveling by the moonlight many times. This is by far the easiest time of the year to secure good heads.

The actual time of the rut varies from year to year, but as a rule occurs from the first to the fifteenth or twentieth of October for moose and from the first of September to the twentieth for elk, while deer are usually later. As a general rule the deer rut does not start until after some hard freezes or very hard early frosts. Here in Idaho and Montana it usually starts about the first of November, but some seasons may start a week earlier and some seasons may be a week later in November. Snow does not affect the fall range of elk, unless very heavy. Moose also get along very well in quite deep snow, but in mountain timber hunting the mule deer will nearly always be found during the rut at about the snow line. They may bed up in the lower edge of the snow but will feed down out of it during the morning or evening or during moonlight nights. The really good bucks will nearly always be a little higher than the does on the same range, until the rut is in full swing, and before the rut look for the big bucks up on the high ridges when hunting mule deer. Toward the close of the rut the best old bucks will usually work off to themselves, unless hunted hard or a cougar is working on them. When the big cat is working on a band of mule deer, they will usually band up and feed and often bed as well out in the open where they can spot him from any angle of approach.

In all timber still-hunting of steep or mountainous country, try to keep above where you believe the game is either feeding or bedded, as game for some unknown reason looks for danger from below rather than from above. Also if you jump an animal below you, it will invariably circle around the slope offering a good running target, while if you are below the game, it usually fades out of sight in one or two jumps unless in sparsely wooded country. Air currents usually range upward as well, which is another good reason for you to try and keep above the game. Sounds also carry upward.

In all still-hunting pay attention to the slightest movement or noise. It may only be the falling of a bunch of snow from a limb, yet a feeding animal may have caused it. Also listen for the scolding of the jays or of a red squirrel. They often fuss and scold at game, and magpies in the West very often follow deer and will soon find a wounded or bleeding animal. In dense-timbered elk country, the big black ravens have a habit of circling while they utter their hoarse croaks over a band of elk. Possibly it is because they always get a feed of fat offal when a hunter makes a kill, but the fact remains that you can often locate a band of elk at considerable distance by the circling ravens.

One should also use his own nose at all times. If you are above the game you can usually smell a deer or bear for quite a distance, and an old bull elk or moose in the rut can be scented by a human for a quarter mile at times. Many times while working along a ridge I have had the strong rank smell of an elk brought to me by the breeze. They smell much like a barnyard and when one has been out in the clean fresh air of the mountains for some time, and particularly if he has enough of a head cold to at least moisten his nostrils, then the rank smell of an elk will often carry nearly a quarter mile. I have worked down on the scent alone several times and thus secured my elk.

One hard day spent in still-hunting elk in very dense cedar timber and on very steep mountain slopes in the Lochsa will long stand out in my memory. Four of us had camped below Powell Ranger station and hunted hard for six days with no success. One day while working back through a dense cedar forest I climbed up on a log and instantly saw a yellow patch about 60 yards away, but for the life of me could not make it out, whether an elk or a patch of bark-peeled log. It had been raining steadily, night and day, all the time we had been in the country that fall and was still raining like all possessed. I slipped the safety on the old .400 Whelen, covered that yellow patch and waited for some sign of life, or for it to take shape, until my arms ached and I had to lower the rifle. Then, just as I had about decided it was a bit of peeled log in the dim forest light, it moved and I had a glimpse of an elk's neck and head crossing another open space between tree boles and the dense cedar scrub. No chance for a shot. Another day two of my friends and I worked along the top of a steep ridge, the south slope of which was studded by more sparse but huge cedars. We jumped a five-point bull below us and as my companions were well down below me, they were much closer to the bull than I, so I waited for them to kill him. Both dropped to sitting positions, and both fired with their old Model '95 Winchester .35-caliber rifles. I could hear the bull running, even after he went out of sight in second growth, so foolishly I asked if they had hit him. Both assured me they had, but when I continued to hear him crash through the timber, I ran to the next ridge and arrived just in time to see him go over the top with his tongue hanging out, at about 150 yards. He was gone before I could even raise the rifle, and examination of the trail for a couple of miles proved he was not hit.

After six days of this in a soaking rain every day, we were getting desperate. The only wood that would burn at all was pitch stumps which we dug out; then had to poke a pole through our stovepipe once a day to clear it of soot. On the seventh day the others elected to stay in camp and rest up and build a big mulligan, while I decided to try and kill for all of us, so we could get the job over with and go home. That morn, I left camp at daylight and legged it down the forest trail for seven and a half miles, then turned up on a low bench that probably covered some thirty acres and all very heavy cedar forest. A good many fresh elk tracks crossing the trail led me to believe I would find them on that bench eating mushrooms and ferns.

After getting back well away from the trail, I loaded and lighted my pipe, to get the very slight air movement, and found I would have to hunt back toward Badger Creek, as the wind was drifting down the Lochsa canyon. I had not gone over 50 yards when the smell of elk warned me that either elk or fresh beds were not far upwind. Stopping by a giant cedar, I surveyed every inch of the forest ahead of me and soon spotted something that did not look right. By moving very slowly to the right I could make out the neck and mane of a big cow elk, also see her ribs just back of the shoulder. A tree bole about a foot in diameter covered the shoulder. That was enough, so slipping the safety I very slowly and carefully raised the .400 Whelen, until the gold bead centered in the Howe-Whelen peep sight and over the middle of the lung cavity just behind the shoulder. Then I pressed the trigger, and had a momentary glimpse of elk running in almost every direction in front of me. Visibility was not over 60 yards and they were soon out of sight, even before I could work the bolt. Then I sat down on an old log and enjoyed my pipe. After knocking out the ash, I slipped over to where the cow had stood, finding a spray of blood on the other side, some pieces of lungs, and where the heavy 350-grain W.T.C. Company bullet had hit a small sapling and bounced away, evidently about spent after passing through the elk. Then I trailed her up and found her in about 80 yards. She had attempted to jump over a huge tangle of fallen logs some ten feet off the ground and had died in the air. There she was in the very top of that tangled log jam on her back, with all four feet sticking up in the air.

Without an ax, I had an awful time dressing that elk, but finally managed to open her full length after removing a forefoot to use as a club in pounding my heavy sheath knife through pelvis and breastbone. Then I turned her on her side enough to prevent the rain from beating into the abdominal cavity and brushed her with scrub cedar.

I could hear some more cows in the band barking at me as I finished the job. Then taking their trail, smoking and watching the drift of the smoke in the rain, and with my pipe inverted so the rain would not put out my light, I stayed clear of the tracks, only cutting in to them occasionally to get their direction, then circling again downwind from the trail. That band of elk led me back to the divide, then back down to the Lochsa and part way back up on the first high ridges, before I finally obtained another chance at them.

Had just noted that they had stopped traveling and were feeding, as it was fast getting dusk, when they worked around onto the steep slope of badger creek. There seemed to be about a dozen head in the band all told, and I saw tracks of a couple of bulls with the band, probably young animals. I climbed higher along the rim, so I could cut across the narrow gulches above the elk. Coming out on the brink of a gulch head some 60 yards across, I saw an elk jump, and as the cow's rump flashed over a fallen log across the gulch I hung a 350-grain .400 Whelen slug on it and heard her roll down the mountain. Instantly I threw the bolt and as soon as the bolt closed, another big fat yellow rump flashed over that fallen log and again I hit it solidly. This I saw by his horns was a bull, and heard him roll far down the mountain. As soon as I could recover from the recoil, I threw the bolt again, only to see another big yellow rump go sailing over that log. Again I planted a slug in it and again heard an animal roll.

Thinking I had our four elk down, I started looking for possible cripples as it was fast getting dark. I soon located a big cow and at sight of me she started grinding her teeth and pawing herself toward me and with the mane on the back of her neck all standing on end. She was a mad cow and wanting to end her suffering instantly I shot her through the brain, blowing out the back of her head. Next I found the bull wrapped around a big tree bole, but search as I would could find no trace of another wounded animal. The bull was dead as a mackerel. I found where all three elk had rolled down the mountain on the other side of that fallen log and found two of them, but the third had gotten up and as near as I could tell in the maze of tracks and fast approaching darkness had gone back up and across that log again. Going to the big barren cow I ran my hand along the ribs on one side, found a lump and cut out a 350-grain slug, then turning her over I felt along the ribs on the other side and soon located another lump, which proved to be another 350-grain slug. Then I knew that cow had made two trips over that log and received the two hits, and I had but two elk down instead of three at that place. It was dark as ink by the time I had the cow dressed, but I worked on down the mountain and finally found the bull and dressed him by feel alone, in the rain and darkness. However I did a good job on him at that.

It was two o'clock in the morning before I finally reached camp and saw that welcome glow of the gas lantern. One of the boys had killed another bull that day and thus completed our quota. We split up next day and went back and skinned out and quartered all four elk and hung the quarters from 80-penny spikes driven in trees. Then we were ready for the pack string. Had there been any old bulls in that band I would probably have had but the one first shot, but the younger bulls followed the cows. That hunt was many years ago, but stands out in my memory as one of the toughest days elk hunting I have put in. After the first shot in the morning, those elk were never jumped again, nor did they at any time wind me, until I came onto the band in the evening.

In still-hunting, beasts often sense the fact that you are after them, even though they neither sight nor smell you. It may be some sixth sense that warns them of your approach, or it may be their keen ears give them warning. Many times when trailing old wise mule bucks or whitetails as well as elk, I have found where they had doubled back on their trail, then jumped high and wide over some big windfall in an effort to confuse anyone tracking them. Wounded game invariably does this stunt, but often wise old bucks I had neither seen nor heard and had been very careful never to give my wind knew somehow I was circling after them. To have stayed on their trail would have given them my scent in no time, as they had many times circled to windward in an effort to get the scent of whatever followed them. Once wise old buck mule deer or old bull elk are jumped, you have relatively little hope of ever getting another chance at them, if they either see or wind you, but a Pacific Coast blacktail or whitetail will lie very close and will play hide-and-seek with you in dense timber all day long and never be more than 200 to 400 yards in advance of you.

A cougar will do the same thing, and I have spent over two months, all told, trailing cougar on foot, without dogs, in an effort to beat them at their own game, but never with any success whatever. For my money the cougar is the greatest still-hunter on earth.

Many days I have spent trailing a cougar around in a few acres of dense timber on the north slopes without ever even getting a glimpse of his tawny hide. Often he would circle right back on my tracks, and many times I have had a hunch the cat was closer on my back trail than I was on his, and when I turned and backtracked a short distance would find where I had jumped him again and he had in turn been trailing me. It's almost uncanny the way they can slip away with never a sound. Their hearing must be so much more acute than that of a man as to leave him no hopes of ever still-hunting them successfully. Many friends of mine here have seen and killed cougar while hunting deer or along old roads or pack trails, but I have never been so fortunate. Have had them trail me many times but always keeping just out of sight. The only successful still hunts I know of on cougar have been when the hunter sensed he was being followed and after crossing some open timber, or an open park, he circled back and watched from good cover. Several times this system has worked when the wind was favorable. I also know of other hunters working in pairs, and after jumping a cougar one would get to windward of the trail and sit down out of sight, while the other hunter continued to trail the big cat. Several times this has worked and when the cougar started following the hunter he soon circled back past his waiting companion, who wrote finis to his days of deer killing. Though I have one cougar to my credit going third place in the records, I trapped that cat after he had eaten the whole after end of a big mule buck I wanted for my own meat.

Bear, like elk, moose and deer, have exceptionally good ears and can hear your approach long before you come in sight as a rule. At times in the fall bear can be successfully still-hunted in the West when they are working the high alpine basins digging out the pine squirrels' cache of pine nuts. At such times they cover practically every high piñon pine basin and surely deal the squirrels a lot of grief. If you circle such basins in the very edge of the timber, and spend a lot of time sitting quietly on a log or rock and listening, you can often locate a bear by hearing him dig or tear out old stumps or logs. Usually, also, you can locate him by the scolding of the squirrels. Then it's merely a case of quietly slipping down on him with the wind in your face, moving very slowly and stopping very often, so that if he does hear you the sound of your approach will not be continuous and alarm him. Grizzly as well as blacks and browns can sometimes be obtained in the fall by this method. In the spring bear hunting is much easier, but it then becomes a stalking proposition rather than true still-hunting.

In the East, in Maine and other states, bear will often be found in the fall eating acorns along the hardwood ridges, and the same country is also excellent feeding and bed ground for whitetail bucks. Many are taken in such country each fall by careful still-hunting. Further south, in the West, in Utah and parts of Arizona and New Mexico, both mule deer and black bear feed a considerable part of the time each fall on acorns. It's often a dense timbered country and more game will be seen across the steep narrow canyons than will actually be seen on the ridge you are hunting. No animal has a better nose than a bear or wolf or coyote.

Regardless of where you are still-hunting, the old fundamentals of watching the wind, moving very slowly and carefully, stopping often to watch and listen and if possible sit down on log or rock and watch, will pay dividends. It's better to hunt one mile carefully than ten miles haphazardly and hastily.

The coastal bear hunting in southeastern Alaska, where the salmon streams are so densely forested, is practically all still-hunting, with the emphasis on quietly watching some likely bit of salmon stream or slide with the wind always in your favor. As in all big game hunting, there is little use in spending much time until the tracks indicate the presence of game. Even back in virgin game country, you will find miles of terrain that seem from all indications of both feed and cover to be ideal for the game sought, yet you will find no game sign whatever, or very little. Move over into another valley and it may be teeming with game of several species. This has held true in all sections I have hunted — why, I do not pretend to know. You will find game pockets and other valleys that seem just as good or better from every possible viewpoint, yet the game will not be there and often there are no signs whatever. Big game travels a lot at times and in some sections. Bears have quite a range at times but usually make a circle. Likewise mule deer often have a ten or fifteen mile circle they will make in the fall during the rut, and though they may be thick on a certain mountain one day, the next you may find only tracks, showing that they have moved on to another section of their range. Usually their travels will in the course of a week or ten days bring them back to the same section again. Elk also have quite a range and drift along for no apparent reason. Whitetail and West Coast blacktail, however, seem to stick in one locality much more than other game. Caribou are great wanderers, here today, twenty miles away tomorrow. Even moose move around a good bit, much more than whitetail or West Coast blacktail, but not as much as many other animals.

Any game may quit a certain section if hard hunted or if they wind a hunter on several successive days, then they will usually move. Elk in particular will often move a considerable distance, while deer will usually move over into another valley or portion of their range. All these things must be taken into consideration in still-hunting, and as before stated, the man who best knows the habits and range of the game hunted will usually have the best chance of filling his license.

I V

Timber and All-Around Rifles

IN selecting a proper big game rifle, one must consider, first, the game to be taken, second the type of terrain hunted and lastly the ability of the hunter, as to skill in both hunting and stalking, and also his ability to place his shots under every conceivable condition. Weight of rifle one can carry must also be considered as well as the amount of actual knock-down shock effect necessary for each species hunted.

Recoil of the rifle is secondary, and will seldom, if ever, be noticed in actual game shooting. Stocks and sighting equipment are a prime desideratum. The requirements for close range woods hunting are entirely different from those necessary for long range, open or mountain stalking. Woods hunting will be largely offhand work, which places a definite limitation on the accuracy requirements, and speed of fire may at times be more important for such work than the last fraction of a minute in accuracy standards.

Long range stalking in mountains or plains, on the other hand, necessitates the use of the most accurate long range rifles and cartridges available and also points to the hunting scope sight for finest results. With these points in mind, let us first consider rifles and loads for timber shooting and usual close range work on all American species, then take up long range rifles for the open country, plains or mountain hunting. To simplify matters, we can also classify the loads best suited to the different types of hunting along with the rifles. This is also a good time to set a definite limit on calibers. We believe firmly in clean one-shot kills wherever possible and for this reason would eliminate anything from the list below 6.5 mm. or .256 caliber. The 6.5 mm. Mannlicher Schoenauer and the .256 Newton are the two smallest loads we would classify as big game cartridges. They are suitable for our smaller game and for use against larger game only when long heavy bullets are used and by an expert rifleman. For our larger species, namely elk, moose and grizzly bear, the sky is the limit and no one will find any rifle load that he can shoot accurately from the shoulder too large at times and under some conditions.

Many folks may question these statements, and this writer makes no pretense at knowing it all, or being an authority on anything. These statements are, however, based on over thirty years' actual big game hunting experience on this continent, during which time I have personally killed 127 head of big game, not counting many cripples followed up and finished for others. I have also seen something over 600 head killed during this time and this includes most species of American game. In addition, I have killed a great many crippled horses and cattle, so I give my opinions for whatever they may be worth.

In all big game hunting, you should strive to do a clean one-shot job. You owe it to your own conscience, as well as the fine game animals you are privileged to hunt. If possible, do all your hunting before you shoot. Filling your license with one clean shot conserves the game supply; crippling and losing two or three animals for every one bagged with a small bore does not. This business of trying to kill big game with the smallest possible rifle, even including .22 calibers, is the opposite of game conservation. Your appearance in the hills with such popguns will not endear you to the old-timers, for they well know you already have two strikes against you and that you will leave cripples in the hills for the coyotes.

Sometimes I think it is just too bad that we do not have a few African lions or more grizzlies around, to balance the score against some of our small bore addicts. Either animal would very soon teach them the error of their ways. Killing big game with small inadequate calibers is just like skinning a big buffalo bull with a tiny penknife; it can be done, when no better tool is available, but surely reflects no credit on the mentality of the user.

For timber shooting, where the ranges are short, always select the longest, heaviest bullet your rifle will handle. This for the reason that you very often must shoot through heavy brush and limbs, and need a long, heavy, low or moderate velocity slug which will penetrate through the beast when turned broadside to insure a blood trail. Ultra high velocity-loads will expand their bullets on the slightest obstruction. A leaf, a blade of grass or even a sunbeam is enough to explode some of those high velocity small bore bullets, such as the .220 Swift and the .250 Magnum. They are open country vermin rifles and have no place in the timber on big game.

The faster you drive any given expanding rifle projectile, the faster it expands on impact. Timber shooting is usually close range, often well under 100 yards, and long range sniping rifles invariably explode their bullets at such short range with little penetration. Further, if any twigs or limbs are struck before they reach the game, it is then usually sprinkled with bits of jacket and lead core and, if it is hit squarely, often the wound will be a surface blowout owing to the extreme velocity at short range. Further, do not try to use thin jacket bullets intended for low velocities when speeded up several hundred feet faster for timber shooting, or you may get surface wounds, just as Gene Wilkinson did last fall on elk with the 250-grain .35 W.C.F. bullet speeded up to about 2700 feet from the .35 Whelen.

What you want for all timber shooting is a heavy slug, preferably of large caliber, with plenty of lead exposed and driven at low or moderate velocities. It will then wade through an awful lot of brush and even penetrate small saplings at times and still hit the game. Being of low velocity, it will not explode on impact and blow out a bad surface wound. You must have expansion, but you also need plenty of penetration, sufficient to insure the bullet's going through the beast when hit broadside at all times, if it is a proper load for the game hunted. Otherwise it would have no chance of ever getting forward into the boiler room from a rear raking hit. The novice gets a lot of such shots.

Timber rifles should balance well, and short rifles are very handy in dense cover. They should of course have more weight than your favorite upland shotgun, especially forward of the balance to make them swing slower, but they should balance and come up and on the mark quickly. Proper stock fit is also very important for fast timber shooting. Usually a little more drop is needed for such fast offhand work than for prone work, but the longer one hunts and the more he shoots, the straighter will be the stock that fits him. A drop of 1¾" x 2¾" is very good for offhand work but a bit on the excessive side, for most match-trained riflemen or military riflemen and most experienced shooters will get along nicely with a drop of 1⅝" x 2¼". Some hunters will have higher cheekbones and can use less drop, and some will have low cheekbones and need more, and the long-necked individual may also need more drop. Select a stock that fits and when the rifle is brought to the shoulder, the sights bear right where you are looking with no movement, except possibly dropping the head forward on the stock. Excessive drop means heavier recoil, especially facial recoil, as the rifle has more upchuck with a crooked stock. With a straighter stock it drives straight back and the thrust is more on the shoulder where it belongs. Facial recoil by the comb of the stock hurts and is the only type of recoil that should bother any seasoned hunter. It can be entirely eliminated with a properly shaped Monte Carlo comb stock.

Rifle stocks should all be fitted with large shotgun type butt plates to spread the recoil properly over a large surface of the shoulder and also to assure a firm grip on the shoulder. They should be either checkered or engraved steel that is rough and will cling to the clothes. Rifles of heavier recoil should be fitted with a good big soft rubber recoil pad.

Forestocks should be large enough to afford a good firm grip, but the beavertail fore end in any form has no place on the hunting rifle. A fine compromise is the fore end on the Winchester Model 70 rifle. It should be long enough so the left hand can be well extended in offhand shooting, to insure a good steady swing in following running game, and also to combat a side wind at times as well. All hunting rifles are better off with a good pistol grip and cheek piece. The comb should be medium heavy and thick enough to be comfortable in any position and my vote goes to the Monte Carlo type, higher near the bump or butt plate than the point of comb, so it will simply slip out from under the cheekbone in recoil. Down pitch should be one to not over two inches for most rifles for prone and sitting positions and even this small amount of down pitch works well for offhand shooting with bolt actions. However, with lever action rifles, one should have a little more down pitch to the stock, so the heel of the stock is a trifle longer and holds the butt securely to the shoulder during rapid fire work. A down pitch of two to three inches is about right on most lever action rifles.

Next let us look into the actions suitable for our timber rifle. Anything from the old single shot to the autoloader is useful in the timber, depending on your skill as a still hunter. In a fine double-barreled hammerless ejector rifle, we have to my notion one of the nicest, if not the nicest, of all timber rifles. It balances about like your favorite shotgun yet has more weight for steadiness, low easily defined open sights that swing easily onto the mark and the fastest of all safeties. Further, the double rifle is closed tighter against rain, snow, sleet or falling pine and fir needles than any type of repeating rifle. You have two shots, instantly available without working any pump action, lever action or bolt, or the rattling jar of an autoloader. Many times, if the first shot misses, the game will stop absolutely still, trying to locate you, and with the double rifle you can then get in a killing shot. If you have to work a lever or bolt, the game will hear that rattle, spot you and be on its way. Also you can kill two animals from a band easier and quicker with the double rifle, when they have not located you, than with the noisier repeating rifles. There is no other rifle quite so utterly reliable as a fine double, because you have two separate locks and they are not both going haywire at one and the same time.

By carrying two or three extra hulls between the fingers of the left hand you also have an instant reload. All double rifles should have automatic ejectors, but nonautomatic safeties. I have seen bolt actions fill up inside the bolt shell from rain, so that when fired they squirted water back in the eye and temporarily blinded the shooter. I have also seen about all types of lever and bolt guns freeze up, automatics as well when any surplus grease was left in the action. When the mercury buries itself down to about twenty to thirty degrees below, then any rifle action with excess oil or any oil at all in most cases will freeze up. Not so the fine properly cared for double rifle. It will work, come hell and high water, day in and day out, better than most of the repeaters. It is closed more completely against snow, rain or dust than any other type of rifle action. On the debit side of the ledger is its high cost, and it is high time American manufacturers brought out a good accurate double-barrel hammerless ejector at a price within the range of our fine, custom, scope sighted bolt actions. There is no nicer timber rifle if you can afford one in suitable caliber. Usually, a couple of shots are about all you have time for, or will get in the timber, and the double rifle places them at instant disposal.

Next we have the autoloader, best exemplified by the well-liked Remington Model 81 in .35 caliber and also the Belgian-made Browning rifle which is an almost exact duplicate. It is sometimes made in 9 mm. Mauser. We also have the Winchester autoloading .401 caliber. For the man who likes the rapid machine-gun-like rapidity of fire, these rifles will suit him. Personally, I never did like automatics for game rifles. For one thing, in trained hands they are very deadly, but in untrained hands are dangerous, and lead to a lot of wounded game through rapid shooting and poorly placed shots. Many folks prefer them, however. Of all of them I have seen in use, my choice would be the Remington .35 or the Browning 9 mm. for heavier game. Properly cared for they are very reliable rifles and quite accurate as well.

In a trombone or pump action, only the Remington Model 141 is made at present. In the .35 caliber Remington we have a splendid pump action rifle for timber shooting. Well stocked and with low, quickly caught sights, it handles very fast; in fact it is next to the double or autoloader for rapid fire work and if anything a trifle faster than the lever action. Formerly we also had the fine old Colt black powder Lightning Model, the first trombone action in calibers .40–60 and .45–85, both good rifles. These are now seldom seen in good condition. The trombone action is not suitable for any but Flat or Blunt Point bullets and does not have as powerful an extraction system as the lever or bolt actions, but works mighty well when fed only good clean factory loads. For the man or woman wanting a light, short and fast rifle, it is a mighty good one to consider, and is very fast for rapid running shooting. The forearm usually rattles on most trombone actions.

Next we have the time-tried lever actions. Primarily timber rifles, owing to the fact that their locking lugs or bolts are placed at the rear end of the breech bolt, they in time often develop some head space and for this reason are not in the class of the bolt action for fine accuracy. They are very fast and usually very reliable as well. We have the Savage '99, the Marlin 36 and older models, the Winchester '94 and its later versions, the Winchester Model '86 and its later Model 71, and the time-tried Model '95 Winchester. A good lever action is amply accurate for usual timber shooting and can be had in about any desired weight or caliber.

Lever actions can be had in carbine length or rifle length to suit any-one's taste. For close range timber shooting, either will do nicely. The lower velocity of the carbine will give slightly less expansion but more penetration over the performance of the rifle. The two-piece stock of the lever, pump and autoloader is not conducive to fine accuracy, as is the stiff one-piece stock of the bolt action. For this reason again, they should never be selected as long range rifles.

In lever actions, only the Model '99 Savage and the Model '95 Winchester handle sharp pointed bullets well and it's poor policy to try to use such bullets in any tubular magazine, as recoil of one load has been known to drive a bullet point forward into a primer and set it off, thereby wrecking the rifle magazine. The new Silver-tip Flat Point bullets are simply made to order for all lever actions.

Trigger pulls should be clean and snappy, like breaking glass, and should be from three to four pounds, not more. We never did like the take-up military pull as well as a clean single pull trigger. You want something that will fire almost at will, when the sights swing onto your game. Set triggers are a great advantage for any still standing shots, either off-hand or from sitting or prone position. However they are a handicap for any running shooting or for work on dangerous game. Timber rifles should have safeties that are instantly moved as the rifle is raised. All the visible hammer lever actions are fine from this standpoint. The Savage safety is slow and awkward and most trigger guard safeties are slow, for me at least. The shotgun safety on top of the small of the stock is the fastest for me of all. Next comes the visible hammer that has to be cocked and the Remington and Enfield safeties. The Tilden and Pachmayr safeties for the Model 70 are also very good, but the standard Model 70 safety is a slow awkward creation. The wing safety of all Mauser and Springfield actions is also slow and the Model 54 Winchester falls into the same category, as well as the time-tried old Krag.

In the timber, if you jump a beast you want, you may well have only a split second to move that safety, swing the rifle up to your shoulder and align the sights on or ahead of the beast as it crosses an opening in the timber, and you must have something you can bring into action instantly. Most all of our sporting rifles are amply accurate for short range timber shooting, so it's largely a matter of personal preference as to make and model, based on what loads the different actions will handle.

Sights should be easily and quickly defined in almost any shooting light. Bead or blade front sights are best, preferably gold or copper faced. If no snow is present the ivory bead is excellent, but if hunting on snow, the colored gold or copper is much to be preferred. They should be of a size to suit your individual eyes and the type of shooting afforded. The open rear sight when correctly made is probably the fastest of all iron sights, or any sight for that matter, at extremely close range on moving game, say twenty-five yards or less. It is never as accurate as an aperture sight, but is the fastest of all for real close range and with good keen eyes will do good work out to long range. The older one's eyes become, the more time will be required to focus the rear sight and target and front sight and the longer the eye will need for this accommodation, hence aperture sights are better for older eyes except at real close range. The best of all open sights are the very wide shallow English V with platinum or gold center line and bead or blade front also faced with gold.

Next best rear sight is a perfectly flat-topped bar with a shallow notch or U or else plain with a platinum center line. Forget all old high horned, so-called buckhorn open rear sights, as they have long been obsolete and were the worst possible type of open rear sight, because they covered up nearly all of the game when lined up. They are just as obsolete for sights as the Texas longhorn is for beef cattle.

In aperture or so-called peep sights, we prefer the receiver type or else the bolt sleeve type, never the tang peep. The latter can blind people by driving back into the eyeball when used with too short a stock or when shooting uphill. It gives too much sight radius and one is far better off with the safer receiver type, even though sight radius is not as great. The tang peep is fine on small game rifles and good for no other purpose, except target rifles. Tall verniers are safe but cumbersome.

Rear apertures should be large and easily seen through. Remove all cup discs and turn down apertures and hide them, as they are totally out of place on any timber rifle. You want something you can see through and instantly at that. If you can see the game and forty acres of surrounding woods at the same time, so much the better. Your job is simply to look through that rear aperture, pick up the front bead and place it where you want to hit on the game and squeeze. Timber shooting seldom affords time for any monkey business, or any delay in getting the shot off. The excellent Lyman, Redfield, Marbles Pacific and other good receiver type of peep sights, such as the King Little Giant, are all fine for the purpose. The rear aperture should be at least one tenth inch in diameter. There is no better rear aperture for rifles of heavy recoil than the Enfield Service rear sight. Aperture is correctly placed and is just about the best possible size for quick, accurate shooting. When a long shot is afforded the eye naturally finds the center of it anyway.

Next comes the hunting scope. For all shooting, except at very close range, it is better and more accurate than any type of iron sight. On dangerous game at close quarters, I, for one, do not want to peer through any peep or scope sight and see only a field completely filled with hair, as it is then more difficult properly to place your shots on the beast. But out at any range beyond twenty-five or thirty yards, and for all non-dangerous game, the good wide field hunting scope will give you the quickest, most effortless aim of any sight. It will also enable the oldster to shoot accurately long after his iron sights have grown a heavy crop of whiskers.

Select the widest possible field and best illumination, and for this we would heartily recommend the Weaver K 2.5 and the Lyman Alaskan 2½ as being about the finest scopes ever produced for timber shooting. Noske also made some very good so-called 2½ powers that were really only about 1½ power but were mighty good timber hunting scopes. For real fast running shooting, at close range, the 1 X Weaver shotgun scope is also excellent and offers the widest field of all. Mount the scope as low as possible, and in a good dependable mount, such as the Stith, Weaver top mount, Turner, G & H, Neidner, Hart, Pachmayr or other reliable mount. The greater space between scope clamp arms, the greater the strength. Probably the two strongest mounts are the Oneil-Hopkins fixed mount and the Stith, either fixed or detachable. Both offer considerable protection to the scope. In all timber hunting you will at times run into conditions where the scope must be carried covered or else removed on account of hard rain or wet snow. A circle cut from around an inner tube and stretched from one lens to the other will keep the lenses dry in inclement weather.

With detachable mounts you can remove the scope and use your iron sights in rainy or bad wet weather. With the Pachmayr, you can simply swing it up out of the way and use the iron sights. If the scope is in a fixed mount, like the Stith or Oneil-Hopkins, then it's best to carry a section of inner tube stretched from front to rear lens in bad weather and flip it off when the shot offers. You can shoot with considerable moisture beads on the front or objective lens but little is needed to hopelessly blur the rear or ocular lens.

Mount the scope low down central over the bore wherever possible. With these long eye relief scopes, one can usually mount the scope ahead of the bolt lift, on about all bolt actions, so safety and bolt alteration is unnecessary, unless you shoot with head well back on the stock, in which case you may need the ocular lens farther to the rear. Never tolerate a high-mounted scope. It is worthless and unless you can comfortably bed your mug down good and snug on top of the stock comb, then you cannot do as good shooting with a scope as with iron sights.

With top ejection lever actions and the Remington autoloader you must offset the scope somewhat, but it can still be mounted fairly low. M. L. & M. J. Stith do about the finest job possible on these rifles and Pachmayr also has a splendid mount for them. When they are offset slightly to the left of center to clear ejection, one should fit a Rowley cheek pad to bring the comb of the stock over in line and in sighting the rifle make no attempt to bring the line of sight and bullet strike exactly together, but let the bullet print just as much to the right of point of aim as the axis of the bore bears to the right of the axis of the scope. Then it will not cross fire at longer ranges. With the '95 Model Winchester, the scope can often be mounted to the right of center, leaving iron sights also available, and you simply press the cheek harder against the comb of the stock to bring your eye in line with the scope sight. Savage and Marlin rifles are well suited to perfect low scope installation, as are about all double and single shot rifles. The Mannlicher Schoenauer is best fitted with a Lyman swinging arm receiver sight or a cocking piece sight. Beware of most cocking piece sights as they are often positioned too close to the eye, like the Lyman 103 on the Krag or Springfield, and unless you have a long stock will cut your eyebrow or eyeball. I once had one on a .400 Whelen but when I busted a buck up a steep mountain, it cut a beautiful buttonhole in my eyebrow. So much for sights and sighting equipment. The timber rifle should be zeroed for the range you are most likely to use it on, and if your shooting is all very close range, under 60 yards, it is often best to zero it for that range, but if longer ranges occur, then sight for a longer point-blank. A lot hinges on the velocity and trajectory of your rifle. In much timber shooting you may want to shoot just under a big limb or just over a fallen log, and you must know where the gun prints to an inch, at any range, to do so.

I carried my .400 Whelen for years sighted for 150 yards, and it gave about 2300 feet velocity with the 350-grain W.T.C. Company bullet. I used it for all timber hunting during that time. My .45-70 Winchester featherweight 22-inch nickel steel barrel rifle is sighted for just 100 yards with 405-grain Soft Point and a .38-55 Winchester was sighted for 100 yards for timber shooting. If ranges are longer or you are using a flatter trajectory rifle like the .06 or .270, then sight for 200 yards point-blank. I carried the .35 and .405 Winchesters zeroed for 150 yards for years.

Timber rifles should have sling straps for carrying the rifle only, as you will seldom use the sling in the timber and it will catch on brush and limbs and be in the way. Further, when you raise the rifle for a quick shot, especially if you jerk it up for a quick shot at running game, then a heavy sling will swing from side to side and make aim slow and difficult. The sling should be detachable so you can remove it for usual close range timber shooting, and if the timber is more open, where longer shots will occur, you can carry it on the gun and use it for sitting and prone shots, which will occur rarely in the timber. The sling is absolutely of no possible use in offhand game shooting, but is worth its weight in gold for sitting or prone shots.

Next, let us look at the calibers suitable for most all timber shooting. Being close range shooting, we do not need high velocity, nor is it desirable. For deer, black bear and similar-sized game the .30-30-170, .32 Special and .303 Savage, as well as the .38-55-255 Soft Point loads, are all adequate if planted right and at close to reasonable ranges. More powerful rifles are better and we would recommend more powerful cartridges whenever a new rifle is to be purchased. However, if you have such rifles in good condition, and will use them right, they will serve the purpose. At over 150 yards they lose considerable energy and have not the knockdown shock for ranges much beyond that. Of the four cartridges, we have seen best average results over the years from the .303 Savage 190 grain and the .38-55-255. These two loads penetrate much better for all raking shots than either the .30-30 or .32 Special and have over the years proved the more reliable under average conditions. They are all either single shot or lever action cartridges.

In the 6.5 mm. with 160-grain Soft Point, we have the smallest cartridge that I consider really effective for such game. Its penetration is excellent, in fact sufficient for our largest game if placed right. Under average conditions it has shown more cleaner one-shot kills on deer and black bear for us than either the .30–30 or .32 Special. This is due primarily to its great sectional density and excellent penetration. For the person who absolutely must have an extremely light rifle and a cartridge of little recoil, the 6.5 mm. Mannlicher Schoenauer will take any game on this continent, but it must be placed exactly right so it will reach the vitals. Even then do not expect instant kills unless brain or spine is hit, as it will produce fatal wounds, but does not have the knockdown shock of larger calibers.

The 7 mm. Mauser with 175-grain bullet is an even better timber load and will do all the 6.5 mm. will and more. It is usually more accurate, longer ranged and has considerable more shock effect on the game. Boys, small women, and men who cannot handle heavier rifles with more powerful cartridges through physical handicaps, will do well to select the 7 mm. Mauser cartridge and use it in 175-grain Soft Point. It will penetrate just as well as the 6.5 mm. and many much larger cartridges and is exceptionally accurate. Either the 6.5 mm. with 160 grain or the 7 mm. with 175 grain can be depended on to penetrate to the vitals of even large grizzly, Alaskan brownies or moose and elk, if it is planted with extreme care. For the person who must use a lightweight rifle of very light recoil and who wishes to hunt our heavier game as well as deer and black bear, these two loads will do the work, if properly placed; but unless placed exactly they will only wound the poor beast. Users of such rifles on our larger game should make every effort to become expert riflemen and should then shoot only when they can be sure of exactly placing their shots. The old-timer with years of game experience, who is also an expert rifleman and who can no longer handle heavier rifles due to failing health, can still kill the game with these two small bores, by shooting only when he can exactly place his shot.

For the average hunter, better cartridges for average deer and black bear shooting in the timber are the .33 W.C.F. and the .35 Remington. Both are quite accurate loads and I have seen both stay in a six-inch bull at turkey shoots at 200 yards during a day's shooting, so they are amply accurate for all timber shooting. Both should be used with the 200-grain Soft Point loads, or the Silver-tip version which is also a Soft Point in reality. For average timber shooting of these two species it is doubtful if better loads can be found for their size. The .33 W.C.F. is available in the excellent lightweight Model '86 Winchester and the .35 Remington in the autoloading and pump action Remington rifles. I have also seen it used in the old Stevens side ejection lever action and in remodeled '99

Savage rifles. There is little difference in actual killing effect of the two loads although the .33 Winchester has a slight edge in sectional density and is slightly the better for ranges over 150 yards. A lot of game would have to be killed with both loads, however, to show up this small difference, though it is more pronounced than in the .30–30 and .32 Special. We have seen both loads used a great deal on elk and while they never did suit us for such work, or prove ideal from any standpoint, they have killed fairly well at close range when planted in the lungs, and with certainty when the heart was hit. For all close range timber shooting of deer and black bear, the .33 Winchester and .35 Remington are two cartridges I can heartily recommend.

In the .300 Savage we have one of the nicest lever action .30 caliber deer and black bear cartridges. With its light recoil and made for a light rifle, it is a splendid cartridge for the boy or lady who must have a light rifle. With the 180-grain Soft Point bullet, it is capable of penetrating considerable brush, but owing to its higher velocity is not quite as good a brush cutter as the .33 W.C.F. and .35 Remington, nor does it pack the actual knockdown wallop of those two fine loads. It is, however, a more versatile load, in that it can also reach out to longer range. Likewise its higher velocity usually kills deer mighty well with lung shots. The 180-grain bullet should always be used in dense heavy timber for close range, but where the timber is more open and that occasional 200-yard shot is offered, the 150-grain load is then better. Effective range is extended out to about 250 yards with the .300 Savage. Trajectory is much flatter than either the .33 Win. or the .35 Rem. and for this reason hitting is easier over 150 yards. Beyond 200 yards velocity has fallen off considerably, until at about 250 yards you are about done, as to both accuracy and remaining energy. At longer ranges it often drills through an animal with little or no expansion.

The rifle is short stocked, balances well, yet is light in weight. We particularly recommend the Model '99 R or RS and with a receiver peep sight or a good hunting scope like the Lyman Alaskan or Weaver K 2.5 in Stith Install-It-Yourself or other good mount. We have seen a lot of game killed with this load. It was first brought out to practically duplicate the old 2700 feet 150-grain ballistics of the old .30–06 Service load, which it cannot quite equal and with modern powders cannot come within 300 feet of duplicating, but it is a fine little load for deer and black bear and superior to any of the .30–30 clan. It is definitely inferior to the .30–40 but is used in a lighter rifle.

Next we have the old .30–40–220 Krag and Winchester load and its British cousin the .303 British 215 grain. Both are about identical in actual results on game, so we will discuss the .30–40. This is one of the best balanced, most reliable of all big game loads for its size, for close to reasonable range timber shooting. Like the 6.5 mm. and the 7 mm., the .30–40 with its long 220-grain Soft Point with plenty of lead exposure is a mighty good load for punching through brush and small limbs and twigs, and again like the 6.5 and the 7 mm. with heavy bullets it will penetrate to the vitals of our largest fauna when placed right. We consider it too small for elk, moose and big bear under average present-day hunting conditions, but in the hands of one who will shoot only when he can place his shot it will take anything on this or any other continent with proper loads. With full patch 220-grain bullets it's a fine elephant load, for brain or heart shots by an experienced ivory hunter, under favorable conditions.

Aside from the old Blake rifle, now seldom seen outside a few collections, we have the Krag, the Winchester Model '95 and the Winchester single shot. All are mighty good reliable rifles. We really need a fine double-barrel hammerless ejector for this load for timber deer and bear shooting. The '95 Winchester and the single shot are the strongest actions now made for this load, but Mauser and other actions can easily be altered to handle it by fitting tapered plates in each end of the magazine well to stagger the cartridges, so the rim of the upper load lies forward of the rim of the load below it, in the magazine. The old Krag is one of the slickest bolt actions ever produced, if not the slickest, and while it is limited as to permissible pressures, still it's amply strong for all 220-grain factory loads we have seen. It has one of the smoothest of all bolt throws, slick as grease, and a magazine that can be opened and more hulls poured in while keeping the bolt closed and cocked on a loaded round, as when watching down and wounded game. This is a mighty good feature, common only to the Winchester Models '94, 65, '86, 71 and the Marlin lever actions.

If you have a good accurate Krag rifle or carbine, then you have as good a bolt action rifle for deer and bear in the brush as any if you use the proper ammunition. The 220-grain load will practically always drive through shoulders or lungs of any deer or black bear, at least to the skin on the off side. It expands perfectly when plenty of lead is exposed, yet does not fragment or blow up as do about all high velocity loads at close range. It produces very reliable and uniform wound channels in any beast and is a thoroughly reliable cartridge from any standpoint. Under my observation, at least, it has produced far more uniform and reliable results on all American game than has the .30–06 with any bullet of lighter weight than 220 grain. A few of the old Remington-Lee .30–40 rifles are still giving good service in this neck of the woods.

With 150-grain bullets in rifles throated for this shorter slug it will beat the .300 Savage cartridge slightly and will do nicely out to 250 yards and sometimes to 300 on deer and black bear with a thin jacket bullet. With this load a full 2700 feet velocity can be had, while it will also handle the 180 grain to 2500 feet. These lighter bullet loads place the .30–40 in the list of stalking rifles for our lighter game to about 300 yards.

The Winchester .401 caliber Self Loader with 200-grain Soft Point is also an excellent close range deer and black bear load.

Next we have the .30–06. For timber shooting of deer and small bear, it is a swell load with 220-grain Soft Point with plenty of lead exposed like the old Winchester, Remington and Peters Soft Points in that weight and will give a very good account of itself on such game. It has a bit more shock on such game with the 220-grain bullet than the .30–40 and also is flatter in its trajectory and can well be sighted for 200 yards with 220-grain bullets.

However, over the years I have seen more big game lost wounded with the .30–06 than with any other single cartridge, and for this reason consider it the most overrated cartridge on our entire list. In all fairness one must say that practically all the failures on our lighter big game have occurred with the lighter-weight bullets of 180 to 110 grains in weight. When the long heavy 220-grain bullet was used with proper amount of lead exposure at the tip, it has always given a good account of itself on the lighter game. When turned on the larger game, such as elk, moose and big bear, it has performed well with 220 grain for its small size, but it must be remembered it is still a small bore cartridge and is not adequate for our larger game with any bullet made unless that bullet be planted exactly right. Even then, unless brain or spine is struck, it will not drop the big beasts with certainty. I used it for years, but after it let me down a few times on elk and other game for sportsmen I was guiding, I decided it was not the cartridge for game larger than deer and black bear, or at most caribou. For timber shooting of the smaller species, it is a good reliable killer with 220-grain slugs up to 300 yards range, and when it must be used on our larger game, then the 220 grain should always be used. The Western tip of lead Soft Point Boattail is a wonderful bullet for the .30–06 when it must be used on the larger game, but like the 6.5 mm. and the 7 mm. and Krag .30–40–220 it must be planted just right or game of the larger species will be lost.

I have never yet seen the man who could, under average shooting conditions, always place his bullet just right. The game will move, just as you shoot, or it will not show any vital point in the timber between tree boles and the hunter will have to shoot it behind the belt, or take a chance, unless he passes up a great many chances. The old experienced hunter will pass up such shots, but the average inexperienced sportsman will not and will shoot at the game regardless of how it's turned, or whether it be in full run. Many of our authorities will class the .30–06 as an all-around rifle and as being adequate for our great Alaskan brown bear, when they have never themselves either killed or seen one of the great bear killed. This, combined with the fact that so many of our arms writers have been military men, has tended to create a false impression about the .30–06 and to give it a reputation which has never stood up under actual game-killing experience. It is one thing to kill African antelope out on open plains, or our lighter game such as caribou, sheep and goats, in similar country, where several hits can be registered when needed. It's quite a different proposition to kill our heavier game in dense timber and brush, where one must take most any kind of shot or forgo the shot altogether. Many times a hunter will have but the one chance offered and the .30–06 is just too small to anchor such game, unless hit exactly right. I could fill a whole volume with factual accounts of .30–06 failures on our larger species, as well as our lighter species when trick bullets did not expand properly, but what is the use. Sometimes I think the old adage, "The public likes to be fooled," is true.

The cartridge with any bullet short of a Full Patch, or Hard Point, or the 225-grain Peters belted slug, which does not give enough expansion, will not shoot through the shoulders of our larger game, and any cartridge that will not drive its Soft Point expanding bullets through the shoulders of an animal broadside on has no possible chance of ever getting forward into the boiler room from a rear end raking shot. To be adequate for any game, a cartridge must always drive through the chest cavity when broadside shots are offered, and on a rear end shot must have penetration enough to go forward through hips, paunch and intestines into the lungs, and if it won't do just that, then to my notion it is not adequate for the game hunted. To prove my point I will cite throughout this volume plenty of instances where the .30–06 has failed, but this is a rifle chapter and will be devoted only to that subject.

Under my observation, the .30–06 has delivered its best average killing results with 220-grain bullets in timber shooting. I have seen a good many black bear killed with this load. When broadside shots were obtained, the bullet nearly always penetrated through and broke both shoulders but lodged under the skin on the off side. The 225-grain Peters belted bullets would go clear through black bear and even small grizzlies on broadside shots but did not expand enough to put them down, unless spine or both shoulders were broken. Even when the tip of lead Western 220-grain Boattail was used, the expanded slug always stopped under the skin on the off side, when broadside shoulder shots were obtained. With the 220-grain bullet of proper Soft Point exposure, it will give fine average results in the timber on our lighter game, but is not and can never be an adequate rifle for our larger game under timber hunting conditions. Paper energy figures don't mean a thing to me any more: there are too many other factors that enter into actual killing power. Some loads with far less muzzle energy are always better killers, since such things as expansion, entrance and exit holes must also be considered. In my experience there is no substitute for caliber and bullet weight when the larger species are on the agenda.

When the 220-grain .06 load is used on our larger species for rear raking shots, you will usually see the animal jump and kick at its belly and depart, unless it is a bear. It will usually swing its head and snap at the bullet entrance, then run, or turn and look for you. If the spine is hit, the beast is anchored, but if not, it may travel many miles.

The .30–06 case extends the killing range slightly over the .30–40 when both rifles are used with 220-grain bullets, but not as much as some might think. The added velocity will give the same shock effect out to slightly less than 100 yards greater range, not more than that. The faster we drive any given bullet, the faster it expands and the less it will penetrate. For this reason, penetration is usually greater at close range from the .30–40 than from the .30–06 when the same bullet is used in both rifles. At long range, where velocity has dropped greatly, the bullet may expand very little from either rifle and penetration is then adequate for most anything, but expansion is not. A .30 caliber hole through an animal's lungs will not stop him in time to be recovered in the timber, unless one is an expert tracker. Many animals will recover from such wounds. I once lost two mule deer shot through the lungs at about 200 to 250 yards with the .30–06 and 172-grain W.T.C. Company early issue thick jacket bullets, that did not expand. We trailed those deer three days, until they both joined a band and started feeding when bleeding had practically stopped. Elmer Hagel killed one of them about seven or eight years later, fat as a seal, but with a rib cut on each side from my slug. A large caliber bullet that does not expand at all, like the various .45 calibers, will kill with lung shots in time, but a .30 caliber often will not. One winter I lost just fifteen coyotes, shot through the lungs with 1925 National Match Boattails from the .30–06. Many of them were trailed for miles.

In the 8 mm. Mauser we have a fine timber cartridge, at its best for such shooting with the long exposed 236-grain Soft Point bullet. This is a very reliable load, producing reliable and deep wound channels on most all species. We consider it, like the .30–06, light for our larger species, elk, moose and big bear, but have seen much better average results on such game with the 236-grain load than from any .30–06 factory load made. Normally it is underloaded in this country, as the cartridge also fits the old Haenel Mannlicher carbine with its single locking lug. However when good Mauser actions are used one can hand-load the 236-grain Soft Point to a full 2450 feet velocity with 49 grains of Dupont 4064 powder. The loads should be worked up carefully, however, as German groove diameters have the bad habit of varying a bit and also some of the later German service rifles may have shorter throats that would greatly increase pressures.

This load seldom produces instant kills with lung shots on either deer or black bear, and in fact we have seen both animals go a long ways after being so hit, but they did leave a blood trail. On raking shots, however, it proved excellent, or wherever heavy bones such as shoulders were struck. It will not kill a deer with a lung shot as quickly as when the light 154- or 170-grain bullet is used at higher velocity, but is much more reliable in the timber, with the long heavy slug. I have seen a good number of elk killed with this load and expansion was better on them than lighter game, with factory loads, but was usually ample for anything when the above hand load was used. With that 236-grain hand load, I would prefer a good 8 mm. Mauser to any .30–06 for timber hunting if game larger than black bear or caribou was to be killed. Some folks may not like to see an American make such a statement, but I believe in giving the devil his due and can only write what actual experience has taught me. In the way of heavy calibers for our larger game or for the great game of Africa and India, we are far behind in sporting armament and have much to learn from the British especially.

The German 8 x 60 Magnum is a much more powerful cartridge than the German 8 mm. service cartridge with any weight bullet. Now no longer made in Germany, it is problematical if it will ever be made again, unless English or Norwegian firms take up its manufacture. My friend Frantz Rosenberg of Norway, speaks very highly of the effectiveness of this cartridge on their Norwegian moose which they call elk.

Another fine cartridge not generally known in this country is the British .318 Westley Richards. With the 180-grain bullet at 2700 feet it just about duplicates our own .30–06–180 ballistics as a stalking rifle, but with the 250-grain bullet at 2400 feet it is a very fine, well-balanced and reliable timber load and much used in Africa by old experienced hunters as a light rifle for all species with proper bullets. Its penetration is excellent with the 250-grain bullet and it will drive to the vitals of all American game owing to its tremendous sectional density. Many African hunters use it with solids or full patch as we call them for the great game of that continent. We would much prefer the 250-grain .318 Westley Richards load for timber use on game larger than our caribou to any and all .30–06 loads, owing to its longer heavier bullet.

Above the 8 mm. and the .318 Westley Richards, we run into the first cartridges that can truly be classed as all-around rifles for all-American game. An all-around rifle must use a cartridge perfectly adequate for taking our largest game under average hunting conditions, not just picked shots. It should also be capable of either killing or putting the beast down, or stopping him in a short distance with a single reasonably placed body hit. It simply must have sufficient penetration to reach the chest cavity with rear raking shots. In my humble opinion, about the smallest load that can qualify is the .35 Winchester with 250-grain bullet at 2200 feet. Long ago I decided that for my own use the minimum should be .33 caliber and minimum bullet weight of 250 grains for an all-around rifle. If the shooting was at close range, then the 250 grain at 2200 feet would do or a heavier bullet at lower velocity. If at long range, then more velocity was needed. An all-around rifle should also be capable of taking game at either short or long range, which puts the bolt action in the top bracket for such a rifle.

For general all-around timber shooting, the .35 Winchester is excellent, also the .405 Winchester. Both are more powerful than necessary for deer or small black bear, but will do the job with certainty and are adequate for moose, big bear and elk at close to reasonable ranges.

The old Model '86 Winchester .45–70 Featherweight with 22-inch nickel steel barrel is also an excellent all-around short ranged timber rifle, with the 405-grain Soft Point smokeless load. Another equally good one is the model '86 Winchester in .50–100–450, especially for the larger species. My friend Jack Wagar has long used this cartridge on elk and similar game and has secured more clean one-shot kills with it than with any other load. Owing to rapid loss in velocity due to a blunt Flat Point bullet and low initial velocity, neither is a good long range load, because the trajectory is far too high for certain hits at unknown ranges.

Both are, however, very reliable loads for close range timber work, and absolutely deadly on any American game if at all well placed. They will stop all our smaller game with most any body hit. They both penetrate very well and can be depended on always to open large wound channels and leave a good blood trail. In dense timber I would far rather use a good model '86 Featherweight .45–70 with 405-grain Soft Point loads than the finest .300 Magnum or .270 Winchester ever produced.

Getting back to that all-around rifle. The best cartridge and rifle made in Britain for such purposes is undoubtedly the .333 Jeffery with 250-grain spitzer for long range and 300-grain Soft Point for closer range or the 300-grain solid for brain shots on African game. In this country, I think the best is the 333 O.K.H. designed by C. M. Oneil, D. S. Hopkins and myself. It throws a 250-grain spitzer at 2635 feet from a 24-inch barrel and a full 2400 feet with 300 grain, either Soft Point or solid. It is the same as the British .333 Jeffery load except that it drives its bullets faster and from the revamped .30–06 case. It is probably the nearest approach we will ever see to a perfect all-around rifle.

This fall George Smith borrowed my old .333 O.K.H. Enfield and a quantity of 250-grain Soft Point loads at 2635 feet. He and his party accounted for three elk, two cows and a bull and two brown bear with five shots from this rifle. All were clean one-shot kills. All three elk were shot through the lungs, two close behind the shoulder broadside, and quartering forward on the bull with the bullet placed behind the shoulder. One small brown bear was shot standing on hind feet between the shoulders from behind, the 250-grain slug tearing a large exit hole through the front of chest, while the big bear was hit under the chin facing the hunter quartering and the slug came out behind the left shoulder. All five animals showed very large wound channels and all were perfectly bled out when dressed. All shots were at close range, around 60 yards in the timber. Such results are in startling contrast to some of the results I have recounted from the .30–06 with 180-grain bullets.

Other excellent cartridges for all-around use are the .35 Whelen and .350 G & H Magnum, both now handicapped by lack of a good commercially made bullet. Like the .333 O.K.H. they are also hand or custom loads. The .333 O.K.H. has much greater sectional density than either and does not shed velocity so fast per hundred yards of range, hence soon outranges either load. The .400 Whelen is a fine cartridge for our heavier game at close to reasonable ranges, but since W.T.C. Company dropped manufacture of their fine 350-grain bullet we have nothing available heavier than the thin jacket, 300-grain .405 Winchester bullet, which is far from ideal for this cartridge.

In a factory made load and rifle, the Model 70 Winchester, caliber .375 H & H Magnum is the best all-around rifle now made in this country. It is of course unnecessarily powerful for deer and small black bear and similar game, but is a wonderful cartridge for use on elk, moose and big bear or the heavy arctic game. Further, you can shoot a deer for meat with the 300-grain .375 with less mutilation and damaged meat than with either a .270 or .300 Magnum, if shots are placed at all right. With the 300-grain slug it is a very good cartridge for any game on this continent at close to reasonable ranges, or in timber and brush, and with the 270-grain bullet it just about duplicates Springfield 180-grain .30–06 trajectories for longer range shooting. It will produce more clean one-shot kills than any other modern American cartridge. Only the old Sharps Creedmoor and Buffalo rifles in calibers .40–90–370, .45–120–550 and .50–170–650 to 700 beat it for killing power. Those old Sharps were the most deadly rifles ever produced on this continent for sporting purposes.

The old Model '95 Winchester in .35 caliber has long been a favorite timber rifle with me. Clumsy, awkward to load and with a protruding magazine box that looks like a poisoned pup that had lain too long in the sun, it nevertheless is one fine, reliable and strong old rifle. The .405 is an even better cartridge in the same model for our larger game at close range but does not carry up quite as well as the .35 at longer ranges from 150 to 250 yards. Both are very reliable loads.

The Model 71, the modern '86 Winchester in caliber .348 is also a fine timber rifle, with the latest and most modern of all lever actions. Its 250-grain Silver-tip load is the best for all shooting to my notion. The 150 grain proved a frost for us on goats, while the 200 grain worked well on the lighter game, but the 250-grain Silver-tip at 2310 feet tops all loads in this caliber for timber shooting. It has a trifle over 100 feet more velocity and slightly greater sectional density than the time-tried .35 Winchester, so well supersedes that load. Also the rifle is a well stocked, perfectly balanced, modern arm in every way. Like the old '86 Winchester the Model 71 permits recharging the magazine while the arm is loaded and cocked, a great advantage at times, especially with wounded game. I have asked Winchester repeatedly to bring out this rifle for more powerful loads based on the same .348 case but with larger caliber. One to be a .375 caliber with 300-grain Flat Point Silver-tip bullet at 2200 feet and the other a 350-grain .40 caliber at 2000 to 2200 feet. Either load I believe is possible from this rifle and case and they would make the perfect short range, lever action combination for all our larger game under difficult conditions, as well as being a very useful rifle for much African and Indian shooting if loaded with both Silver-tip and Full Patch bullets. I have long been a firm believer in one load for one gun for timber shooting.

Another excellent timber cartridge for all species, that gives about the same average results on game as the .35 Winchester and the .348, but with even greater sectional density and bullet weight, is the 9 mm. Mauser and Mannlicher. When loaded with the 280-grain Soft Point we have every confidence in it. It is amply accurate and always leaves excellent deep wound channels in most any beast. The lighter bullet loads in these calibers are not so effective on our larger species, but the 280 grain is a very reliable killer. The Mannlicher Schoenauer makes a very light fast timber rifle for the shorter cartridge and the Mauser can be had in a heavier weight with less recoil. It is also a faster bolt action, as the Mannlicher bolt is poorly shaped and positioned for rapid fire work. Though not as powerful as the .405 Winchester the 9 mm. usually gives much deeper penetration.

The 9.3 x 74 German cartridge is also an excellent one for single shot and double rifles, but ammunition must be imported or custom loaded. Other heavy caliber German cartridges for the bolt action fall into the same category, and like the excellent .30 and .35 Newton will probably never again be made.

We have already covered the .333 O.K.H., .333 Jeffery, .35 and .405 Whelen and the .375 Magnum. The .400 Whelen with 350-grain bullet seemed to me an even better killer under 100 yards than the 300-grain .375 Magnum load, but over 100 yards the .375 is the better load.

Two more excellent British loads for our larger species under difficult conditions are the .400 Jeffery rimmed for single shot and double rifles and the .404 Jeffery Mauser. These are about as large calibers as are ever needed, even for the most difficult conditions on large Alaskan brownies, at close range in dense alders, and are excellent tools for the job. We have never used the .404 on game but have used the .400 Jeffery a good bit and like it very much. It will drive its 400-grain Soft Point through the shoulders of elk and moose and through big brown or grizzly bear to the hide on the offside, and is a wonderful close range stopper on any game on this continent. For crawling along an Alaskan bear trail where you may meet a big bear at a distance of feet instead of yards, we much prefer a good double hammerless ejector rifle for the .400 Jeffery cartridge to anything smaller, or anything in a bolt action. For such work the double rifle and the heavy caliber Winchesters always appealed to us more than the bolt action, because of rapidity of aimed fire when needed. With the big double the two heavy slugs are adequate for any bear if you plant them right, and with the big Winchesters in .45–70–405 Smokeless, .50–100–450 or the .405 you have at least five shots at your disposal, as fast as you want them, for you can operate the lever during recoil of the rifle. If Winchester will only bring out a larger caliber as I have suggested in the present 71 Model, we will have the finest of all lever actions for such work.

This about sums up the best rifles and loads for timber shooting as well as all-around shooting. While many may think I am advocating much more powerful rifles than are needed, these recommendations are based on over thirty years' hunting. During over twenty years of guiding I have seen altogether too many fine animals escape wounded, and much prefer to see a heavy rifle used which will in many cases eliminate a lot of trailing and leave more game alive in the hills for the number actually brought to bag. The use of an adequate rifle on our big game is just as important from a conservation standpoint as the use of a good dog in pheasant and duck shooting. Each fall more big game is wounded and lost here than is brought to bag.

One thing can be added to this chapter, and that is the fact that heavy bullets of moderate velocity seem to kill better on an average of all shots from different angles than does any type of high velocity bullet. While it is perfectly true that high velocity light bullets that simply explode on impact are very deadly when placed in the chest cavity of our smaller big game, the reverse is usually true when larger animals are so hit. The faster we drive any expanding bullet the sooner it stops or disintegrates; thus penetration is often lacking from all high velocity missiles on our larger game. There seems to be a time element that enters into killing power, but it is something that is quite hard if not impossible to explain, yet we have noted it many times. The heavy slug at 2000 to 2400 feet with great sectional density has a wallop and a smash to it that seems lacking in the high velocity light bullet types. Game hit with the heavy bullet either goes down or becomes too sick to travel, while when hit with the light high velocity bullet it is killed outright if hit in heart or spine, though it seems to recover from the shock of such light bullets, when they do not penetrate to the vitals, much quicker than when hit with the heavy bullet. Even the electric chair requires a sustained circuit to kill a man and there seems also to be a time element in the killing of game. The lower velocity heavy bullet is by all odds the most reliable when you can get close enough to place it effectively. Large calibers also have a slap to them that is not imparted by the sharp point high velocity spitzers. We need those streamlined missiles for just one purpose, namely to retain their energy and velocity out to long range and to give flat trajectory, but when game can be approached to within decent ranges the old long round nose or flat point heavy bullet is always the more reliable in its action.

This last fall I used my Watson double ejector for the .400 Jeffery cartridge for my elk. A spike bull was located through a tiny crack in very dense lodgepole pine. Though I had but an inch space to shoot through and the bull stood a good 150 yards away, with his rump toward me, the cartridge and rifle did the trick nicely. A heavy lodgepole pine some twelve inches in diameter covered the center of his rump and the back of the head. Only the right hind leg and the left front leg and a fringe of the left hind leg and the tip of the nose were visible. The bull had heard us and was standing still listening, trying to locate us. By resting my left shoulder against a tree bole and shooting from a sitting position, I held on the left flank just far enough to the left to clear the left ham of the animal. He was quartering away from me but at such an angle as to be facing almost directly away. I thought I was shooting a big cow elk. At the shot, he humped up and turned into a run over the ridge and down the steep slope. After giving him some time, as I knew the 400-grain Soft Point should have raked full length of the left lung, we trailed him up. Soon he was losing blood from the mouth, proving the lung shot, and after a quarter mile of trailing through deep snow, we found him, down but still not quite dead. That 400-grain Soft Point had struck the left flank, penetrating through paunch, diaphragm and left lung, and had severed three ribs close to the spine, then emerged in the front of the chest at the base of the neck. A high velocity bullet would simply have blown up in the paunch and we might never have obtained that fine piece of meat.

Large caliber bullets kill well when placed right, even though they do not expand, while all small bore high velocity missiles depend entirely on expansion for killing power. The slap of a heavy bullet can well be compared to the blow of a sledge hammer, while the small bore lightweight bullet is more the thrust of a rapier. We have no high velocity rifle large enough in bore and bullet weight to impart the same shock effect to our larger species that present small bore high velocity cartridges impart to small game of the deer and sheep class. The larger animals like elk, moose and big bear are just too large and we would need something like the .50 caliber machine gun load to equal the shock effect on them that the .300 Magnum 180-grain load imparts to the smaller big game.

V

Bear

Grizzly Bear

NORTH America may truly be called the home of the bear, as this continent supports more bear than any in the world. Formerly, the grizzly ranged in great numbers from Mexico to Alaska along the Rockies and Pacific coastal ranges, but now is probably gone except from British Columbia north along the coast, and only scattered grizzlies occur the length of the Rocky Mountain chain. No great number of grizzlies exist anywhere south of the Yellowstone Park.

The park still contains a nice complement of grizzlies, and Montana, Idaho and Wyoming, where they join the park, have a few, including the overflow from the park. Northward, however, we have grizzlies in increasing numbers, beginning at about the head of the Blackfoot River, the head of the Dearborn and the South Fork of the Flathead. From the section where these three rivers head on north, grizzlies occur in ever-increasing numbers. The divide between the South Fork of the Flathead and the Sun River is still fairly good grizzly country. To the west the Swan River and the Mission range contain grizzlies. Here on the head of the North Fork of the Salmon we still have an occasional grizzly and I saw a fresh track on the Divide last fall. The Bitterroots today have only a few of the grizzlies left that formerly ranged these mountains when Theodore Roosevelt hunted along this Divide in the eighties. We still have an odd grizzly in the Middle Fork country of the Salmon River and I saw four one evening, in a high alpine park this side of the Middle Fork. A stray grizzly shows up occasionally on down the main Salmon from Horse Creek to Sheep Creek. North of the main Salmon River in Idaho, we have the Selway and Lochsa branches of the Clearwater River and these all contain some few grizzlies; probably more are still around the heads of the streams on the Divide between the Selway and the Lochsa than elsewhere on the Bitterroot range today.

A very small desert specimen is said to still exist in the Craters of the Moon, south of Arco, Idaho. I have flown over the Craters a couple of times and crossed through their upper edge many times, but never have been out in them on foot, so do not know whether any of this small sub-species of grizzly still exists or not. My friends the late Julius Maelzer and Fred Carl of Salmon have both told me of seeing skins brought out of the Craters by sheepmen, and they were of a small, big-headed grizzly, probably dwarfed by centuries of existence in that desert section of lava flows. Maelzer had hunted them there and seen plenty of tracks, leaving no doubt they were grizzly, but failed to get a shot at any of them.

A very few may still exist in Colorado, New Mexico and in the Mogollons in Arizona, but they are now very scarce and should have permanent protection in those states. Glacier Park in northern Montana has a nice bunch of grizzlies left and they extend ever northward along the Continental Divide into the edge of the arctic. Some grizzlies also inhabit the flat lowlands to the east of the Divide in the north and even out on the Barren Grounds of the arctic.

When my old ancestor, Captain William Clark of the Lewis and Clark Expedition, came up the Missouri River in 1804, they had considerable trouble with grizzlies, especially about where Fort Benton and Great Falls, Montana, now stand. Civilization has pushed him back and made a strictly mountain animal of the grizzly in the United States, but farther north he still inhabits the lowlands east of the Divide. I saw many fresh grizzly tracks on the Siccanni, Prophet, and Musqua Rivers, a couple of days' pack east of the mountains and along where the Alcan Highway now runs north from Fort St. John, British Columbia. What that highway has done to the species in that section I do not know, but it cannot help their existence in any section.

The great brown bear of Alaska are also grizzlies, differing in size due to the great abundance of sea food they have available, and are larger than the mountain grizzly for this reason. Formerly the great California grizzly also attained great size, as he too fed on salmon a good part of each summer, but the California grizzly is now probably extinct. If any section of that once great grizzly range is still wild enough, especially in the parks, then some bear should be removed from Alaska and again planted in their old range in California.

Black bear do well living near civilization, but not so the grizzly. He is an animal with considerable ranging qualities, and likes the remote sections as far from civilization as he can get. While the Yellowstone and Glacier Park grizzlies have been fed so long they have become used to

[77]

seeing people, the wild grizzly is a different animal entirely, in this respect. Formerly there were a good many grizzlies along the park on the West Gallatin, and the fall of 1917 I trailed seventeen different grizzlies on that watershed and all went into the park, where I could not follow. They were digging out and eating the winter cache of piñon nuts of the pine squirrels and their huge droppings were a solid mass of pine nut shells. They were out quite late that year, well into November, and traveled ever higher into the park. I trailed every fresh track I could locate in the snow, but never got to see any of them.

Today, in the United States, the grizzly inhabits only the high rugged mountain ranges and, with the exception of the parks, as far from civilization as he can get. The more remote places without any pack trails are today his main range.

Grizzlies vary in coloration from a very light creamy yellow to jet black without a single white hair. No section of the continent seems to have any corner on a certain color phase. The grizzlies of the Bitterroots here in Idaho and Montana seem to run more uniform in color than those farther north, being usually a very dark undercover of brown to almost black on feet and legs, with more or less silver tipping over neck and shoulders and extending back to the hips and at times to root of tail. In the Brazeau district in Canada, many jet-black specimens occur, and this same color occurs north of Jasper Park on Fish Creek. We have seen one old sow there that was jet black but had two yearlings that were almost yellow and a silver-tipped four-year-old with her when killed. On Admiralty, Chichagof and Baranof Islands in southeast Alaska about all color variations occur, with a great many jet-black specimens. Up the Unuck River out of Ketchikan are found many of the jet-black grizzlies. The former world's record for grizzly before I killed that old sorehead at Snug Harbor was a jet-black bear named Old Groaner, killed by Bruce Johnstone of Ketchikan. He had been much shot up and one eye and zygomatic arch completely shot away, and bullets were imbedded in his frame in various places. Farther north, I saw bear that were almost silvery in color all over, like a silver badger. You will see all color variations in different localities. Often you will see these extremes of color variation from jet black to silver or blond in one section of the country.

The grizzly never inhabited the eastern part of this continent, being content with the Rocky Mountain and Coast Ranges and the northern barren ground for some distance east of the Rockies. Skull conformations differ greatly between the mountain and coastal bears, the largest skulls and bear being on the Alaskan Peninsula and on Kodiak Island. The peninsula bears (*Ursus gyas*) have long narrow skulls, while the Kodiak species (*Ursus middendorffi*) have much higher, wider, broader and more massive skulls. Some folks think the largest bears are all on Kodiak but I for one believe just as large bear live on the Alaskan Peninsula. In weight, a very big mountain grizzly would probably seldom go over 1000 to 1200 pounds today, but the huge coastal grizzlies of the peninsula and Kodiak Island may run to 1600 or even 1800 pounds in rare instances when hog fat, before holing up in the fall. The C. E. Sykes expedition obtained one enormous bear on the peninsula, but with most of the real big ones there are almost never facilities at hand for weighing them. When it comes to the size of bears, several very experienced hunters who have hunted the arctic claim that it is very rarely they find a polar bear that is as large as the big Kodiak and Alaskan Peninsula bears—and of course very much differently shaped. D. S. Hopkins killed the world's record.

Pelts of mountain grizzlies will average best late in the fall just before they hole up, usually in November in this country and earlier farther north, whenever winter sets in. In the spring when they first come out the pelts will be even longer, glossier and heavier as a rule, but some will be found that have badly matted during hibernation, also some that have had water and ice freeze on the guard hair and pull it out, or have rubbed some in the den. Later, when they come out, they will rub as soon as the sun gets warm. Further, they like to rub on some old pitch-covered bear tree.

In any mountain grizzly country, you will see many trees where the bear have reared up and bitten out chunks of bark and wood as high as they could reach. Whether they do this as a sort of signpost of their domain, to tell other bears of their presence, or just for the hell of it, I have never been able to tell, but bite trees as high as they can they do all over their range. The grizzly cannot climb trees, except as a little cub, on account of its long, straight or slightly curved claws. The longest claws will always be found on spring-killed specimens that have just come out, as the claws continue to grow throughout their lives. In the fall the claws are often worn off fairly short from much digging, but by spring will be grown out beautifully. The longest claws I have heard of were on a brownie killed in the spring and went six inches for the longest on each front foot. The hind claws are very short, not used for either digging or fighting.

The strength of a grizzly is prodigious. They can kill any beast on this continent with one blow of their paw, even the bison or moose. They can kill a full-grown five-year-old steer and pick him up and carry him over an eight-foot corral and pack him away. We have seen where they had carried off full-grown bull elk, and only horns and feet dragged as near as we could determine from the trail. Where the White River flows into the South Fork of the Flathead, a trapper in 1920 told me to take a look at the remains of his Newhouse No. 15 bear trap. There to the right of the trail as I was coming up the South Fork stood a big yellow pine and I rode over to it. As high on the tree as I could reach while sitting in my saddle were pieces of trap embedded in the tree, and the balance of the broken trap and toggle lay at the base of the tree. He had caught a grizzly, but the old bear had simply raised up on his hind feet and smashed the trap against the tree. It takes enormous strength to break such a trap to pieces.

Mountain grizzlies, when they first come out of the den in the spring, will eat a bate of skunk cabbage or other herbage to doctor up their old tummy; then as soon as their tender feet toughen somewhat, they will work the bottoms of the snowslides and eat any big game they can find killed by the slides. They can often scent a game animal under an unbelievable amount of snow and proceed to dig down to him. Probably no animal has a better nose than the grizzly, not even the wolf and coyote. While they are working these slides for dead big game animals, they often run onto big game that is thin and poor from the winter and are able to stalk it and carry it down with a rush, before it is aware of their presence. This meat, when they can get it, is also varied with a diet of grass and roots. Mountain grizzlies in particular will dig up acres of the Divide each spring eating various roots, much as a hog roots them out. We have seen the whole Divide north from the head of the Dearborn River in Montana literally plowed up where grizzlies had dug out roots in the spring.

Their spring and summer diet is further varied with small rodents, ants, bugs, and such until summer brings on the berry season, when they spend a great deal of time eating various berries. Huckleberries and serviceberries are prime favorites with them, but they will eat almost any berry fruit they can find. They consider honey a delicacy and will tear up an old log that has a bees' nest in it, to get the small amount of comb and honey it contains. They are also very fond of ants. While the big bear eat elk, moose, caribou and other big game when they can catch it, as well as cleaning out the dead animals from under the tangle of logs and snow at the foot of the slides each spring, their summer diet is largely berries, rodents and bugs of various kinds, combined with grass and roots. If salmon run the streams adjacent to their range, the grizzlies will spend much time there and practically live off the salmon as long as the run continues. They will also eat the old dead salmon later in the season as well as what berries they can find.

After fall freeze-up the mountain grizzly usually works up near the top of the Divide in this country and systematically combs all the high timbered basins for caches made by the pine squirrels. He will dig out and eat every squirrel cache of piñon nuts he can locate, and often almost every big tree will have such caches among its roots. When the bear finally hole up these are largely dug up and eaten so that the squirrel who collected them often has to go hungry.

While a grizzly will kill a man in anger, I have never known of one eating its victim. Many years ago, after an enormous number of the Canadian Indians on the east side of the Divide had died from smallpox and their few relatives had simply abandoned their lodges and dead, the grizzlies of that section, south from Jasper Park to Montana, learned to eat human flesh and cleaned up many of the dead Indians. For thirty years thereafter, mean grizzlies occurred in that section, who had formerly eaten human flesh and would attack a man unprovoked. We obtained this information from old hunters while living in Montana. They had not only seen the dead Indians and where the bear had eaten them, but had also been attacked several times by those bear. Probably some of those real old grizzlies are still living today in that section along the Divide north of Glacier Park.

A trapper at Fort St. John also told me of a man being camped alone some 300 miles north of that little hamlet, when a grizzly came into camp and was simply rolling him over out of his blankets with his nose when he awakened, crawled away from the bear to his rifle, where it leaned against a tree, and shot the bear. I do know the guides up there that I was out with prefer to sleep with their feet toward the front or opening of the lean-to tent and with a loaded rifle or sixgun in easy reach at all times.

Though I saw many blacks on Salmon River boat trips, the only grizzly I saw on any of them was one I got Mrs. G. G. Nesbitt a shot at below Horse Creek, and he had probably strayed in from the Selway or from the Middle Fork section. However, Captain Guleke showed me many sections of the river where he had often seen grizzly rise up and look at him as he flashed by in his big scow in earlier years. With the exception of those grizzlies who ate dead Indians, I have never known of grizzly bear eating human flesh, though I have talked to many men who have been mauled by grizzlies at different times. Some of them were a sight and crippled for life. Captain Guleke buried a drowned man and bear later dug up and ate his body.

The rut occurs in late May or early June in Alaska, and I have seen huge old boars chasing the females up there on the north side of Cook Inlet over cliffs that looked passable only to a mountain goat. A grizzly is, however, a great climber and can go about anywhere in the cliffs, when he decides to do so.

The young, often only one but usually two cubs, and rarely three or four, are born in the den, usually in January, and are then about the size of a squirrel. They nurse their mothers the rest of the winter in the den and usually emerge in spring about the size of house cats. We saw one huge old brownie at Iniskin Bay in Alaska with two tiny cubs no larger than cats. The cubs den with the sow the next fall, and may do so again the succeeding fall unless she is to bring cubs again; when this is the case she will spank the yearlings on their way and make them hunt another den site. Usually they breed only every other year, and often only every third year, so the big bear do not increase fast like many of our hoofed animals. Many times we have seen sows with yearlings and quite often with two-year-olds and no young cubs. This tells the tale.

Usually the finest grizzly pelts come from Alaska or far northern Canadian provinces. We have seen pelts of grizzly killed in interior Alaska late in the fall, with silky fur fully six inches long and so soft that you could hold up the pelt by either head or tail and the fur would immediately drop down and point to the ground. Such pelts, when well marked by silver-tipped or cream-colored guard hair over the shoulders, are the finest obtainable of the mountain grizzly. Some few of the big brownies on Kodiak and the Alaskan Peninsula also have long six-inch fur, but usually the guard hairs are much coarser than on those beautiful specimens from interior Alaska and the upper reaches of the Yukon and adjacent sections of the Continental Divide.

I killed a grizzly with such a pelt in '37 on the Divide between the Halfway and Siccanni Rivers, except that it was shorter, being killed earlier in the fall. At that it is a much longer and heavier grizzly pelt than a much later skin killed in this section, as snow and winter come early that far north. This bear, a male whose skull will just go in the bottom of the records, was very dark on the legs and under fur, but with cream-colored tips to all the guard hair over the neck and shoulders and extending well down the back. The face was very light-colored tan and the front of the ears jet black, making a strikingly colored grizzly. His fur is almost as soft as a fox.

Grizzlies have a comparatively large range, and may travel along the

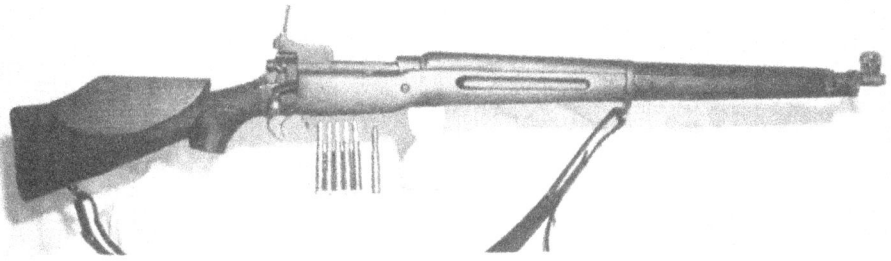

Author's .333 O.K.H. Enfield with Paldani rear sight, rifle and stock alterations
by C. M. Oneil

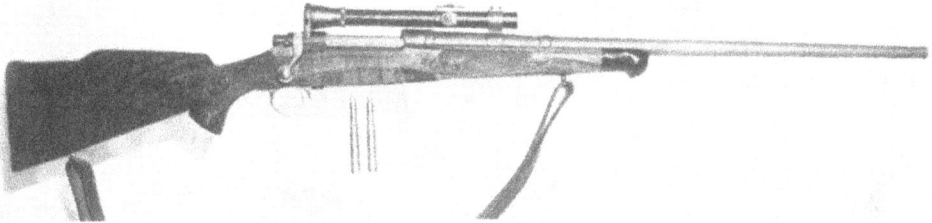

Author's .334 O.K.H. by Oneil, stocked by Frost to author's specifications. Lyman
Alaskan scope in Oneil-Hopkins mounts

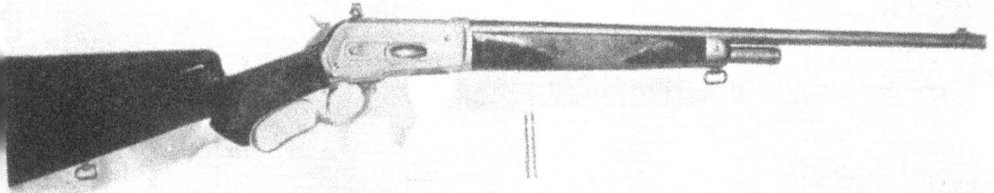

Author's pet .45–70 lightweight Model '86 Winchester with single set trigger. This
rifle, originally presented to Walter Shoup by President Cleveland, was later acquired by F. L. Gibson, who fitted it with a new 22-inch nickel-steel barrel and
Gibson stock

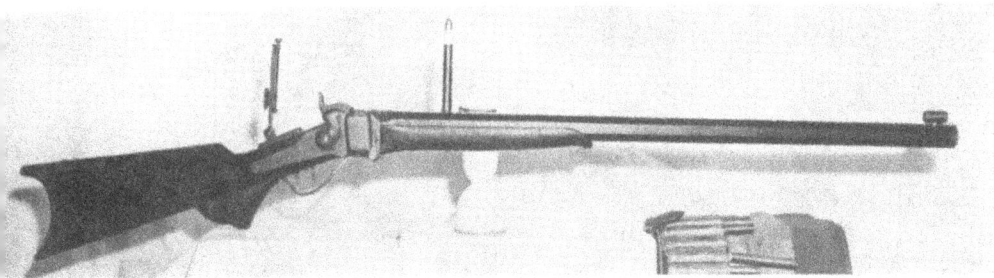

Photos courtesy Keith Barrette

Author's 16-pound .45–120–550 Sharps buffalo rifle used in the Dakotas during the
buffalo hide-hunting days

Grizzly

Bert Miller and his Alaskan grizzly

Record Alaskan grizzly killed by author with three shots from .35 Whelen rifle at 12 feet

Westley Brown with grizzly killed by author with .375 Magnum

Black bear

Divide between some watersheds for 50 to 100 miles, but they will always complete their circle and come back. Each season their wanderings in search of different food at different elevations will take them over a great many miles, but they will very often come back and hole up in the same den used the preceding winter. If the snow has not melted and run under them during hibernation, thus pulling or matting the guard hairs, they will have the very finest and glossiest pelts when they first come out of the den, but as the sun warms them later they soon rub. They particularly like to back up to some old pitch stump or tree which they have previously bitten into and whose sap has exuded and plaster their pelts with pitch. This soon pulls out the guard fur and spring grizzlies must be looked over very carefully if they have been out for any time, or you may shoot one with a worthless skin.

Grizzlies are easily distinguished from black bear as far as you can see their contour. The back is much straighter and the hips do not drop away so fast as the black bear's. There is a decided hump on top of the shoulders and usually the longest fur on the entire skin, as well as the heaviest, is on this high shoulder hump. The side view of the head looks more like the profile of a Newfoundland dog, with considerable arch to the skull at the eyes, while the black skull and head, from a side view, are just a gradual curve from snout to the back of the head, with no high rise at the eyes. Tracks are also easily distinguished at a glance, the grizzlies' heels being more pointed than the blacks' and the front claws always striking well ahead of the ends of the front toes. In addition they are usually much larger than the tracks of black bear.

Mountain grizzlies, that spend their lives in the high country and do not live on salmon on the Pacific Coast streams, are usually good eating. I have cut the loins out of several and they made most excellent mountain pork chops which were quickly eaten up when taken to camp. A young grizzly is also very good roasted and very similar to pork. It depends a lot on what they have been feeding on when killed, when living on berries, small mammals, and grubs, at high elevations, they are usually very good meat, unless too old and tough. A grizzly normally lives a long time and old ones are naturally tough, but a yearling or two-year-old is fine meat. Likewise the fat from a grizzly of the mountain species makes about the finest pastry lard you will ever find. It is held in high esteem by cooks and many ranchers' wives in the high country. Lard rendered from grizzly fat in the late fall makes up into clear white lard not so easily distinguished from hog lard, but the fat rendered from a spring-killed bear is merely an oil and good only for greasing shoes and such. I do not care for the meat of a spring-killed bear; it is usually tough and gets bigger the longer you chew it.

Bear meat is like that of other game animals, best in the late fall, when they are in prime condition and fat. No game animal, and no livestock either for that matter, is good meat when in poor condition. Grizzlies often come out of the den in the spring with considerable fat left on their frames, but it quickly leaves them after they are out. The fact that their body has consumed the best part of the fat during the winter hibernation probably accounts for the fact that they are usually tough and poor eating in the spring.

Though grizzlies probably travel more in the spring during the rut, from about the fifteenth or twentieth of May on through June, than at any other time, and may be found then in almost any place, as the females often lead the males a merry chase, they also travel a great deal just before holing up for the winter. In the late fall they may travel miles of their range searching for the exact spot that is to their liking for a den. Just before denning for the winter, they seem to stop eating altogether, and finally just before hibernation usually eat a quantity of fir or spruce needles. This is probably to keep their stomachs from completely collapsing, and on several occasions I have found a wad of such fir needles in the stomachs of spring bear when they first came out.

During the mating season, the old males fight a lot and Jim Allen, a guide at Petersburg, told us of once watching such a battle to the finish. Many of these old males get badly chewed up at that time of the year and are cranky. The term "sore-headed bear" is very appropriate, and the hunter is much more apt to get an unprovoked charge at this time of the year than later in the season. The bear may have neck, chest and shoulders covered with pus-filled fang and claw wounds, and to add insult to injury his lady friend may have jilted him in favor of his adversary. Under such conditions most men would fight if they possessed any guts at all, so it is no wonder the old males are then very cranky. Females with young cubs, or even yearlings, are always cranky and will fight at the drop of the hat if you get between them and their cubs, or scare a cub and it squalls for its mom. Bear are, however, individuals, and very intelligent individuals at that, and what one bear does is no criterion as to what the next one will do. Westley Brown and a couple of companions once caught a fair-sized grizzly cub and put it in one of their packsacks. It howled bloody murder and its mother ran back and forth on the opposite bank of the river, the while she huffed and growled but never did come across and charge them, though they fully expected to have to kill her. This shows there are exceptions to all rules. Bear are very intelligent, but differ in temperament just as much as do human beings.

The advice of our most experienced old bear hunters, like Earl Olmstead, Andy Simons, Jay Williams, Ned Frost and many others I could name, is, wherever possible, to get up above a bear before you start hostilities. Wounded bear usually react to the impact of a rifle slug quicker than most any other animal except cats. They will drop and roll down the mountain, as a rule, from most any body hit and often from only a leg hit. Though they may drop as though killed and often lie for a time when they quit rolling, they may not be badly off at all and will suddenly jump up and charge or depart.

So always get above a grizzly before you shoot if possible to do so, for you can depend on him to roll downhill when hit and he will often decide to go downhill anyway in making his getaway, as he can travel faster down than up or around the side of the slope. Bear have good ears, I believe equal to moose, goats, caribou and sheep, but probably not quite the equal of elk and deer, and while they appear at times to be nearsighted, we have also had them spot us when we were clean out of effective range — 500 to 600 yards in fact. If you are still and not moving or standing up, they are not so apt to see you, but if you are moving, then for my money a bear's eyesight is plenty good at times.

In all spring bear hunting, it is far better to establish a good lookout where you can comb the slides with your glasses and also search the snow fields and slides for tracks. If you do this day after day, you will see all the bear in that section and you will not track up the country in so doing. In this way you will be able to see the best bear and can then stalk them to effective range. Busting brush will get you absolutely nowhere in bear hunting. Remember the old males will den highest and will be the last to come out in the spring, so you should not be in too big a hurry to take the first bear you see, if in good bear country. The sunny south slopes of the mountain, where the avalanches have roared down during the winter and swept the snow clear, will be the first to turn green in the spring in mountain country and the same is often true in Alaska. There is where the bear will come first for their pottage, and that is the best place to stalk and kill them.

Never camp too close to your prospective bear country, as the smoke and scent from your camp will suck up the canyons for miles and one whiff of it will warn any grizzlies in the country. It's best to camp over some ridge or on some other creek from the one you expect to hunt, and a few miles' walk each morning is better than chancing giving them the scent of your camp. Usually the best place for a lookout is across some wide canyon or on some point overlooking a big basin, where you can cover a lot of likely bear country with the glasses. You will see and get more grizzly by this method than any other, in the spring.

If any dead game animals were caught by the snowslides of the winter, so much the better, as the grizzlies will find them when they start working the slides. Then you have a good bait that they will return to until it is cleaned up. If you can find a bear kill that is not eaten, it is a sure bet for the big bear.

Regardless of how good a rifle shot you may be, never chance a long range shot at a big bear if it is possible to get closer and into more effective range. Out at long range a rifle has plenty of penetration but little shock effect left, so get close enough to give your bullet its maximum knockdown shock effect on bruin and you will have far fewer cripples. If you do wound a big bear and he goes into a small patch of timber, or alders, it's best to try and find some vantage point from which you can watch the surrounding terrain and try and kill him when he comes out, and if he doesn't come out, give him plenty of time to stiffen up before you go in after him. A wounded grizzly is one of the most dangerous beasts on this earth, if not the most dangerous, for once he decides to square accounts, nothing but death will stop him. Leslie Simson the old African hunter once told my partner, Arthur Kinnan, that he considered a grizzly or brownie in the alders or timber just as dangerous as any beast he had ever been up against in his lifetime of collecting all over the North, as well as in Africa. Simson has probably killed more African game than any other American so should know whereof he speaks.

Today our grizzlies have been forced back into the mountains over all their southern range, owing to the inroads of civilization, and for this reason remain denned up longer and have less growing time each summer; hence they are today over the southern part of their range smaller animals on the average than they were fifty to seventy-five years ago. The mountain grizzly, inhabiting only the roughest and highest, as well as longest winter sections of our Rocky Mountains, never did attain the huge size of grizzlies that formerly ranged well out on the plains and had an abundance of game as well as berries and roots to live on. The grizzlies of the Bitterroot Mountains here used to have the name of being the smallest and meanest of all grizzlies. As a rule a mountain grizzly is much more apt to fight than are the huge coastal grizzlies and brownies of Alaska. He is grand game, second to none on this continent, and to my notion is an even finer trophy than a good ram — certainly harder to obtain and offering much more sport and thrills in the taking. The real big ones are always bear of very old age, twenty to forty or more years old. Many have lived to be fifty years of age, and when you consider that at least ten or fifteen years are required for a bear to attain his full stature, and he then fills out and gains weight for many more years, it's no wonder that a lot of time is required to produce a really big grizzly.

Two old grizzlies used to range the headwaters of the South Fork of the Flathead and I heard of them often for twenty years. One was called Gordon Bill and the other White River Jim, as they frequented those two streams. Many hunters of my acquaintance who wanted a grizzly turned back when they saw the tracks of those old boys and decided they had lost no bear at all. Lately I heard that someone had killed Gordon Bill but I never have heard of their getting old Jim. Both were very big grizzlies. I have seen their tracks when old several times, and a friend and I trailed old Jim along the divide for three days on one light lunch, but never did catch up with him in a light snow. We slept out under a tree each night and hoped to have a meal off that great bear if we caught up with him, but the last I saw of his tracks they were pointed for the head of Sun River and still going. They were enormous tracks for a mountain grizzly.

The spring is by far the best time to get a grizzly and you should be out at daylight and where you can cover all the slides possible, then watch them until about ten o'clock in the morning, after which you might as well take a snooze, until about three in the afternoon. The bear will work out of the deep snow in the timber and feed from early morning until about nine or ten o'clock, then they will usually go back in the timber or brush and bed up until towards evening. If you are in good grizzly country you will find them in this way, but in the fall, bear hunting in the mountains is very uncertain, more a matter of chance than in the spring, unless you have some old horses shot for bait a week or so in advance or have made elk or moose kills and watch the offal for a chance bear. As soon as the offal reaches a high state, a grizzly can smell it and will come for miles. A bait is by far the best method of getting a grizzly in the fall. Even then, if much hunted, the sows and cubs will usually feed on the bait in daylight, while a wise old male will usually wait until after dark to approach it. In remote sections of Canada and Alaska, where they have not been hunted to any extent, the old males will often come out and feed just before dark.

Sows with cubs will be the most active and will be seen more often than the big males, because they have a family to support and must be on the go a great deal more than the solitary old males. Today you will be very fortunate in killing a grizzly along the Rocky Mountain chain that will weigh from 800 to 1000 pounds, but formerly grizzlies were killed that weighed 1600 pounds or more and some are said to have reached 1800 pounds in the old days when buffalo and all game were plentiful. The record bear I killed at Snug Harbor was poor and we estimated him at 1200 pounds, and I for one am certain in my own mind we did not overestimate him, as it required all four of us to roll him over, using his legs as levers. He would have easily carried 400 pounds of fat or more when hog fat, in late fall. Grizzlies have been killed in late fall that had a layer of back fat from six to eight inches thick. Even caribou often have a layer of fat four inches thick on the back. Anyone can readily see how much heavier a fat animal will be than a poor one.

In the spring as the snow melts back, the bear usually work along the lower edge of the snow line. They are still heavily furred and like to bed in the snow during the heat of the day, and for this reason will usually be found following the snow line back and up. Watching slides and meadows from some vantage point is the easiest way to hunt them and watching a bait in early morning and late evening the next easiest, and the hardest way of all is to pick up a fresh track and trail up the bear. In the timber, where he will usually be found, the big bear has every advantage in both hearing and smell. He is even harder to still-hunt than either deer or elk, and they are both hard enough. One will simply have to watch the slightest wind at all times and also where he is putting his feet, for the cracking of a small dead limb is usually enough to warn the bear and send him on his way. If you do run onto him in the timber it will be at close range, and after your first shot, if it is not an instant kill, anything can happen. Jim Simpson, an old Wyoming guide, once told me of trailing up a good grizzly on a light fall of snow. Jim had only a .250 Savage Model '99 rifle for the job and he finally found the old bear asleep in a windfall and approached very close, then carefully shot him between the eyes. He got away with it all right, but if that tiny slug had missed the brain, the chances are more than even that the bear would have killed Jim.

I have noticed that all experienced guides of the North hold the bear in wholesome respect and always take every precaution before shooting. Certainly there can be no greater thrill in big game hunting on this continent than trailing a big grizzly through dense alders, or timber, where you never know when you may walk right onto him and have to kill him before he can reach you. Such timber hunting is also most apt to produce a charge by a wounded bear. If hit at long range, or even moderate range, the bear has an even chance of getting away, but if surprised at close quarters and wounded, he will usually charge on sight. When he does do so it is an awesome sight and you may well know he must be killed to stop him. I saw one sow grizzly charge out at the hunter from some brush twice and each time he knocked her down, but the third time she came in earnest and we could plainly see the bottom flats of her hind feet as she reached right out past her ears with them at each jump. He had first knocked her down and she went back in the brush, after which her two yearlings came out walking on their hind feet. He killed each with a single chest shot, using Western Open Point 180-grain .30-06. Then the old sow came out again and was again knocked down, after which she went back into the brush, growled and whined for a time, then with a bawl of rage came for us. That hunter is dead now, but I'll bet he remembered that grizzly charge to his dying day. The last cartridge in his rifle put her down for keeps. Those 180-grain Open Point bullets expanded well but did not have enough penetration to break the shoulders down on the first shot, and later shots into the chest seemed to have no more effect than if we had thrown rocks. However on skinning out and opening that small grizzly, the heart and lungs were found to be demolished, and how she lived so long is another one for the book.

One day George Bates and I were working the rim of a high basin on a branch of Fish Creek in British Columbia for caribou and that odd grizzly. Coming out on a rim we looked down into a huge amphitheater. Heavy fog rolled into the basin and covered it entirely below us. Occasionally a wind would suck up the basin and blow the fog away so we could see patches of the terrain below. Finally, in a rift in the fog, I saw a huge old grizzly waddle along down one side of the gulch and then go into it, searching and digging for roots or small rodents. As the wind was directly behind us, I jumped up and ran back over the ridge and Bates followed me, asking what all the hurry was about. I told him of seeing the big grizzly about the center of the basin and that we would have to make a long two-mile circle and come down from the other side, in order to have any chance of keeping the wind in our favor. Bates remonstrated, saying I had probably seen only a porcupine and insisted on going directly down that long shale slide to the bear. I told him we would never get him if we did, but he was sure I had mistaken a porcupine for a grizzly, and as this was his first big game hunt in the fall of 1927 I finally became disgusted and told him all right, "It will save me a hell of a big skinning and packing job anyway." So down that slide we went, as carefully as possible. The fog had closed until we could not see ten yards and when we reached the edge of the gulch, where I had last seen the great bear, I sat down to listen. Bates stayed on his feet and started walking along the rim of the narrow gulch to see what he could see. Soon we heard a snort and then rocks rolling, as that bear tore up the other side, completely hidden by fog. Startled, Bates asked, "What was that?" and I answered, "A porcupine I guess."

Later on that same trip we had crossed Fish Creek and were working our way back toward a low divide over the Rockies to the north of Mount Ida. We had camped for the night, in a wide beautiful valley. Next morning as I was just ready to start packing up the cook outfit and was polishing off one last Dutch oven biscuit, wrapped around a choice fat slice of mountain sheep loin, I happened to glance across the valley. A lifetime in the hills has trained my eyes until they are always searching for game, regardless of what I am doing, and that one glance revealed four grizzlies working down a rock slide between thin ribbons of fir shin-tangle. Harry Snyder was standing near by, so I said, "Harry, put your glasses on those four animals and see if they are not porcupines." Harry was an old experienced big game hunter and knew his stuff. I had told him about losing the other grizzly. One look through his glasses and he pronouned them grizzly, a sow and two yearlings and a three- or four-year-old. Instantly he yelled at Jim Ross, the head guide, and the camp was in turmoil as the three Calleau boys, Cree Indians, named Sam, Pete and Joe, all ran for the horses. We soon saddled up and forgot about moving camp for that day.

Jim Ross detailed Pete to back up and guide the Skipper, our nickname for Carrol Paul, and I was to guide Bates again, while Jim guided Harry Snyder. We rode across the valley well downwind from the feeding grizzlies and tied our horses. Then, splitting into three groups of two each, we started spreading out and working back into the wind, toward the last position we had seen the feeding bear. Pete and the Skipper climbed highest, while Bates and I took the center of the line and Jim and Harry the lower end. The shin-tangle tapered out to only a foot high above us some 400 yards on the mountain, but where we were cutting across those narrow snow-slides and patches of shin-tangle the fir trees were from breast high to six feet or more. We had gone about a quarter mile when I came through another strip of shin-tangle and stopped to look over the next slide, before showing myself. Bates followed close on my heels. Just as I had covered the whole slide, both above and below me, seeing nothing of either Pete and the Skipper above or of Jim and Harry below, the old sow walked out of the brush about 100 to 125 yards above me. She promptly turned her rump to us and started digging. She was a jet-black grizzly of about 500 or 600 pounds weight at most, a rather small sow. I whispered for Bates to take her and to sit down so he could hold steady in the hard wind. Told him to bust her right over the base of the tail and be sure and center her rump, as she was up the steep slope above us and I well knew the other three were somewhere in that strip of shin-tangle she had just vacated. Bates would not sit down but insisted on kneeling, and in that position I could clearly see the wind move his rifle muzzle. He was using a Webley & Scott .300 Magnum and Western 180-grain Open Point ammo, when I had advised 220-grain for the job.

At the shot, the bear dropped and rolled end over end down toward us for 30 to 50 yards, then she regained her feet and reared up on her hind legs. I could see instantly that Bates had muffed the shot and hit the right hip, breaking it, and the slug had emerged on the belly, letting out a hatful of intestines. I have never seen a madder bear. She bawled for all she was worth, the while she looked all around for us, but we were well hidden in the shin-tangle. I told Bates to bust her again, between the forelegs. At the same time the two cubs or yearlings, I think they were, ran out into the slide, followed by the four-year-old. Instantly Harry Snyder put a 172-grain W.T.C. Company hand load of mine through the four-year-old's lungs, close in behind the shoulder. The bear snapped at the bullet entrance and went back into the brush. Bates shot again and again the sow went down and rolled closer to us, then regained her feet and again stood up on that one good hind leg while she bawled, then reached down and bit off six-foot sections of her intestines and flung them aside with a shake of her shaggy head. I now heard the Skipper shoot twice where the four-year-old had run through the brush and the two yearlings came down the slope on an angle toward us. I told Bates to bust the sow again and sit down and place it right, then rolling the safety over on my Hoffman .300 Magnum I held well ahead of the lead yearling and fired into the slide rock in an effort to turn them back out into the open where Harry could get in a shot. My shot threw up a cloud of white rock dust, but those two yearlings ran right through it and into the strip of shin-tangle, within 20 yards of us. At the same time Bates shot again and again the sow went down and rolled. She was now getting very close and was terrible in her rage, but did not seem to be able to locate us as she evidently heard the Skipper's shots above us and back on the other side of the shin-tangle. Again she bit off a long section of her intestines and flung it aside. I knew she was bawling as her mouth was wide open and now flecked with blood from Bates's last lung shots, but neither Bates nor I could hear her make a sound, though both Pete and the Skipper above us and Jim and Harry below could hear her plainly and the boys in camp three miles away as well. Some freak of the wind prevented our hearing her bawling.

I asked Bates to bust her again, but he said he did not want any more holes in her hide. By this time I was thoroughly disgusted with him, as I well knew that sow would charge and be on us in a flash if she ever looked down the steep slope. Just behind me an opening ran up the mountain in the shin-tangle for 20 yards and I determined that if the sow did charge, I would duck back up the hill in that open strip and let her take Bates for a merry chase. He was a big six-foot athlete and could run like a scared jack rabbit, so I had hopes of seeing a damn good race before I busted the sow in the top of the rump to stop her. However, Jim Ross, one of the wisest old heads in the guiding business in that section of British Columbia around Hudson's Hope, spoiled my chances of seeing Bates run, by yelling to him, "Shoot that sow again or I am going to." Bates shot again and got her down to stay. Then Jim and Harry came up the mountain and Jim ordered Bates to bust her again through the shoulders, which he did. That shot finished the sow, but we stayed back and heaved rocks at her until certain. Then the Skipper and Pete came out in the slide about where the four-year-old had disappeared. The Skipper had accidentally fired his gun in the air the first shot as the four-year-old came out on them, as he always wore gloves and could not feel how much pressure he had on the trigger of his G & H Springfield. Then the four-year-old had reared up and looked at him at close range but he had missed as he was plainly disconcerted, hearing the savage bawling of the wounded sow just through that thin strip of firs and right behind his back. The yearlings had also almost run over him and Pete.

Taking stock of the situation, Harry Snyder sent Pete to trail up the wounded four-year-old and finish him off. I offered to do the job, but at that time I believe Snyder had more faith in the Indians' tracking ability than mine. Evidently Pete had lost no wounded grizzlies, as he never caught up with it and soon lost the trail, he said, though it was bleeding freely. After skinning Bates's sow I went on after caribou that day. No doubt Harry's grizzly died, as he was plugged square through the lungs and the same load had simply demolished the lungs of a bighorn a short time before. I doubt if that bear went a mile. Bates had his "porcupine," but I still do not know how fast the laddie could have run. The sow was well furred, but jet black, with not a single gray or silver-tipped hair. The yearlings were very light-colored grizzlies, real blondies, while the four-year-old was a normal colored silver-tipped bear.

Hunting grizzlies with a small bore rifle is to my way of thinking simply asking for trouble, with every possibility of wounded bear escaping, or in rare instances charging home. Most grizzlies are content to mind their own business, and unless wounded will usually do just that, but once their anger is aroused you have an adversary worthy of the best that is in you and one that will come with determination. When a bear is wounded out in the open, there is no excuse for allowing him ever to get to close quarters, but when a wounded bear is trailed into dense cover, he then has the advantage and anything can happen quick. If a charge occurs around the side of a steep mountain, remember you can roll a fast-moving bear down the hill with a shoulder shot with more certainty than you can reach the relatively small brain pan in the back of the skull. Always break the lower shoulder. Large caliber, low or moderate velocity heavy bullets are the best for such work. Today the old grizzly is about done in the U.S. with the exception of a few very remote areas and the two National Parks, but he is still plentiful in the North and I hope he so remains, as the grizzly is the grandest game animal on this continent.

He asks nothing from any man or any of his kind except to be let alone and given room to live in. Man is about his only enemy, though wolves may at rare intervals tackle an orphaned cub. When livestock was run on his natural domain in the States, the great bear very naturally killed and ate some of them and was in turn wiped out by livestock interests.

The same thing is happening today right here, in regard to the little black bear. The Forest Service usually shows every possible preference for sheepmen, and while the North Fork of the Salmon is far more of a natural game country than a stock country, the Forest Service allots range here to three bands of sheep each summer and the sheepmen are privileged to kill any and all bear that their herders claim are bothering the sheep. The net result of this is that these three camps and bands of sheep destroy from a dozen to twenty-four bear each year.

As a sporting animal in the United States, the grizzly is gone, and the few remaining specimens should be protected wherever possible the year round. My sympathy is all with the great bear.

Domestic sheep drive about all the elk out of this section each spring over into the Big Hole of Montana where they summer in peace with the cattle there, but the much colder winters of that section drive them back in the fall, after the sheep have reduced their range and winter forage.

When *Outdoor Life* magazine, under the editorship of Harry McGuire, instigated the grazing hearing in the U.S. Senate, I filed a seven-page brief on conditions relative to the game of this section and the domestic sheep. It was published in the *Congressional Record* for that year, about twelve years ago I believe. Conditions have not changed since that time. While three bands of domestic sheep benefit three sheepowners, this section of

Idaho would benefit untold numbers of sportsmen if those sheep were removed forever from this range. The wool growers are well organized while the sportsmen are not, but steps will have to be taken along the line of the present waterfowl study, to maintain big game in this section of the National Forest. The Forest Service itself is too well controlled by the powerful wool-growing lobby in Washington to do anything.

Black Bear

Black bear are clowns, the most comical animals in all the world. They are in the main timber animals and must be hunted in the timber. They are largely nocturnal as well, especially if much hunted. They will increase and live right near civilization if given any protection at all. While an old bear will occasionally kill sheep, bear are far better citizens in any section of our National Forests than the domestic sheep they destroy. After sheep have been run for years on a certain range, the bear naturally find and eat sheep that have died of old age and poison, such as hemlock and larkspur, then in time they may turn sheep killers themselves. Big game and domestic sheep simply cannot be maintained on the same range, so the Wool Growers Association has taken over this section of Idaho game country for their own, and though it costs the Forest Service, each year, more to maintain domestic sheep in our National Forests, to the detriment and extermination of such game animals as the black bear, than all moneys derived from grazing permits, the sheep are still permitted to use the range and the sheepherders to kill every bear they see at any and all times. Such is the status of the black bear in our National Forests wherever domestic sheep are normally run during the summer.

The little black bear has the widest range of all bear, extending from Florida to Maine and on north well into Canada on the east coast and from old Mexico, to well north of the Alaskan Peninsula. Black bear very rarely kill any livestock other than domestic sheep. Their diet is largely small rodents, grubs, ants, berries and roots. Rarely they will catch the young of our big game such as elk and deer if the mother is not around at the time, and eat them, but their diet is largely as above stated.

The rut usually occurs in May or early June and the cubs are born in the dens during the winter, usually in January or February. Sometimes only one cub is born, but two are quite common and three are not rare, and they may on rare occasions have four as does the grizzly. At birth the cubs are little if any larger than pine squirrels, but they grow very fast.

The cinnamon or small brown bear is merely a color phase of the black bear and we have many times seen an old brown cinnamon sow with black cubs and vice versa, and some families may have both black and brown cubs in the same litter. Man is their chief enemy, and in this section of the West sheepmen account for 90 per cent of black bear kills each year, while the sportsmen take the other 10 per cent. They usually den in November or early December on rare warm seasons and come out of the den in late February, March or April, depending on how high they happen to den and on the seasons. Before denning up, they usually eat a quantity of fir needles and go for some time without food when hunting a suitable den, or place to dig one. Usually they dig out under a fallen log or the roots of a big tree and let the snow cover their den. They pack large quantities of bear grass or other grass into the den and make themselves a very nice warm bed, much as a domestic hog will do. Cubs remain with their mother the first year after birth and often the second winter as well, unless she is again to bring cubs, which is rather rare. In this case she will force the yearlings to den alone. These young bear that are thus kicked out of the family circle early in life often den on the south slopes, where they may thaw out much earlier than usual, and we have seen them rambling around trying to make a living in early February at times. If they live and grow older, they will learn to den in a proper place where they can sleep until spring. Like the grizzly, they have excellent ears and a nose second to none; their eyesight, while not equal to that of many other big game animals, is surprisingly good and they will see you a considerable distance if you move. Like the grizzly's their eyes are set fairly close together and in the front of their face, so that they do not see to their rear or much to the side and can be easily approached if the wind is right and you make no sound and keep absolutely still when the head is turned broadside, and move forward only when the head is turned away from you.

Black bear are great travelers and while their range is not usually as extensive as the grizzly's, nevertheless they travel a lot. In the East the coat is always jet black, while in the West it has many variations of cinnamon and blue gray. The glacier bear of Alaska is another offshoot of the common black bear, and is a peculiar blue color. The white Kermodie bear inhabiting an island on the coast of British Columbia is also said to be an offshoot of the black bear. I have never seen a skin of this animal and my own experience is entirely with the blacks along the Rocky Mountain chain from Mexico to Alaska.

The black bear has no hump on the top of his withers as do all species of grizzly. The middle of the back is the highest part of the body except the head, and from the middle of the back the rump slopes away sharply to the hind legs. The skull and head are also much different in shape from the grizzly's, the top of the skull being more convex in contour. The claws are short and sharply curved and these bear of all color variations, as far as I know, can and do climb trees. They do not turn over acres of mountain grassland for roots as do grizzlies, but spend far more time in search of ants and grubs and bees' nests as well as all kinds of small mammals, frogs, snakes, and in fact about anything that is edible in the forest.

In the southern extremity of their range, black bear do not hibernate to the extent that they do farther north and may be out all winter in some sections of Florida and Mexico. Wherever long hard winters are the rule, the black bear hibernates like the grizzly. They go into the den in the fall hog fat and come out usually with considerable fat still left on them, but soon lose this when they start eating grass and roots.

In the late fall when hog fat, black bear are excellent eating if not too old, and no finer roast is possible than a ham or saddle of a yearling or two-year-old black bear in prime condition that has not lately been eating carrion. It is, however, even greasier meat than a beaver and all surplus fat should be trimmed off and rendered for lard. It makes wonderful pastry lard, clean, hard and white when rendered from late fall-killed bear. In the spring, I for one do not care for their meat at all, as it is then tough and strong and totally unlike that of a fat fall-killed bear.

Black bear are the most playful of all animals, though solitary, except for sows with cubs or during the rut in the spring. The average black bear is a hobo, eating here today and what he can find some other place tomorrow, and seemingly not caring when or what his next meal will be. In the early spring they work the slides much as do the grizzly and eat any dead big game animals they can find killed by snowslides, or winterkilled. For this reason they are more apt to be carrion eaters in the spring than later in the summer or fall.

Pelts are usually very good in late fall, just before the bear den up, but even longer and glossier in spring when they first come out. However they soon rub and shed and a spring pelt must be obtained just when they first show up, if it is to equal the late fall pelt. If killed when the bear first emerges from his hole it will be the finest pelt obtainable.

Wherever fish can be caught the bear will live on them, as along the salmon streams of Alaska, and Jim Allen directed our course to a couple of islands in southeast Alaska that were inhabited only by deer and black bear. The salmon streams were choked with a fall run of humpies and the black bear were living high. I saw more black bear there in a few days than I have seen in years on the mainland farther south. They were fishing constantly and would pin a salmon down just as do the grizzly, then reach down and grab it with their teeth. Though bear may at times flip salmon out on the bank to their cubs as most artists portray them, I have never seen one do this. Those I have seen have always caught the fish with their paws, then reached down and grabbed it with their teeth, then dragged it ashore for a meal.

In this section, their earliest spring diet is usually skunk cabbage and other bulbous plants that they dig out, supplemented by early grass. Later, they will turn more attention to bugs and ants and the occasional rodent they may be able to dig out. Of course they scout the country for any winterkills, or snowslide kills of big game, and eat these up. They feed in the open on slides more in the early spring than at any other time of the year and for this reason are more easily obtained then than at any other time. Later in the season they will stay more in the timber at all times and feed in the late evening and night, to a great extent. They are very fond of mushrooms and eat them whenever encountered. In the fall after hard early rains they will often be found in the dense timber, on the north slopes, living on mushrooms almost entirely after the berry season is over. We prefer to hunt them only in the fall when they carry a lot of excellent lard, a good pelt and good meat as well, if the bear is young. For obvious reasons we do not intend telling anything of trapping methods for any of our bear. They are now getting too scarce in the U.S. at least to be trapped for the skins alone.

Black bear dearly love honey and will spend hours tearing up an old log or trying to break into a bee tree to get what honey is available. A bear also digs out every yellow-jacket nest he can find in spite of the stings of the angry bees, for the fat larvae as well as any comb or honey. Later in the summer, when wild currants first ripen, he will feed on them, and still later on the serviceberries, then when the huckleberries ripen the black bear will simply live on them for weeks at a time. He will strip off leaves, berries and cram all into his little open mouth. Bear consume gallons of them each day and their dung will be a mass of such fruit. They also vary this diet with fat picket pins and woodchucks when they can find them and will dig for hours to obtain them. However they almost never make the huge excavations that a grizzly will for such a small morsel.

Black bear usually range in the same sections as our deer — whitetails in the East and mule deer in the West and Pacific Coast blacktail on the extreme West Coast. Just as the grizzly will be found up high in the range of the sheep, goat and caribou, so the little black bear will be found lower on the range of the deer and elk as a rule.

Many times I have run onto black bear sows with young cubs in the berry season and sometimes in the fall when hunting deer and elk. I never shoot a sow with cubs so have always watched them, and they are usually good for a half hour of entertainment, if not traveling. Their actions are absolutely unpredictable. The cubs will wrestle and play and often stand up and box as though they supposed they were men, at other times they will chase each other up trees and even jump on their mother's back in their play. The cubs seem to be eternally interested in either food or play. At times they will mimic their mother's actions; if she turns over a rock, they will find one and do likewise. If she starts to dig they will dig. They are clowns and good for a laugh at any time. In hot weather they like to wallow in some cool muddy spring and will spend hours playing in it with their mother.

I once watched an old black sow convoy her cub across a deep and wide stream. She pushed him in with a paw. He could swim, but did not like it at all, and when the old bear dived in he promptly grabbed her tail in his little teeth and hung on while she towed him across and up the other bank of the river. At other times, I have seen sows teaching the cubs to fish and to dig out grubs. It was most interesting.

Black bear do not average very large, probably 300 pounds on the average, for mature specimens. They mature much quicker, or so it always seemed to me, than grizzlies. A real large one may go as high as 600 pounds, but personally I have never seen a black or cinnamon of over 400 pounds in weight. The nose is usually tan colored and quite often there is a white spot in the center of the breast. The teats of the sows are located high, almost between the front legs, and it is most amusing to watch an old sow sit down while the cubs stand up and plant their forefeet on mother's breast and nurse. When scared, the cubs usually let out a bawl and head for the last known direction of mother. When the old sow has young cubs she is very savage toward any old males that come around and they usually give her a wide berth. She will fight to the death for her cubs against most any animal but will usually run from man.

Usually black bear are harmless, but not always, and many Alaskan guides have told me of having black bear come for them and also chase them into their cabins. I have seen several show fight when badly wounded, but most of them continue to try to get away. Bob Hagel had a wounded black come for him even with a broken back, and that black pulled himself forward with his front paws, the while he bawled his rage. Captain Guleke also had a big one charge him when wounded, and this bear took hit after hit and was reaching for Guleke's cap when his last-shot powder burned its face. The only unprovoked black bear charge I have ever seen occurred between the Prophet and Musqua Rivers in British Columbia. Westley Brown and Edgar Dopp were afoot, cutting through dense growths of arctic willow and scrub spruce, while four more of us followed with their saddle horses and the pack string. A big-headed old black boar, that would not have weighed over 250 to 300 pounds, jumped up out of his bed when Westley disturbed him with his chopping and chased Westley back toward the pack string. Westley yelled, "Look out for the bear" as he ran back, in an effort to reach his saddle and his .30–30 carbine. He still carried his four-pound chopping ax. When he saw the bear was going to catch him before he could make the horse, he stopped and swung the ax up high for a blow at the bear's skull. Just then, Ed Dopp pulled his glove off with his teeth and jerking out an old .455 S & W Triple Lock, he took it in both hands and centered the bear's brain with a heavy slug. That black turned head over heels toward Westley and stopped with his head on the stump of a small tree Westley had previously cut down. Wes promptly sunk the chopping ax in the back of his head clear up to the handle, but the bear was already dead as a mackerel from Edgar's heavy sixgun slug in his brain. The wind was directly behind us and that bear came upwind of six men and twenty-three head of horses. I was back in the middle of the string and though I stood up in my saddle could not do anything, because of two men and plenty of horses ahead of me. However I saw enough to know that bear was plenty mad. His upper lip was extended toward Westley and his teeth were showing and ears laid back flat with his skull.

Incidentally, mad bears all have the same expression on their faces, whether grizzly or blacks. The upper and lower lips are extended forward to the limit and the teeth show, while the ears are laid back flat alongside the skull. They never have the cat snarl that most artists portray in their pictures, with the upper lips drawn back and upward. A mad bear looks almost identically like a mad boar hog. After death, the old grizzly I killed at Snug Harbor had his lips still extended. To give the tyro an idea of the length of the snout, I placed the tips of the fingers on my right hand back against the front teeth of that bear and then the upper lip extended clear across the length of my extended hand to my wrist, fully six inches from the tip of that upper lip to the front teeth.

Though more hunters try for black bear each fall and spring than all other species of bear combined, they are usually killed by accident more than when actually hunting them. By this I mean that getting a shot at a black is more apt to occur when hunting other game and is just a chance shot, rather than due to the efforts or knowledge of the hunter. The sense of smell and hearing of the bear is so much greater than that of human beings that a hunter will seldom get a shot in timber still-hunting. When watching a bait, or a salmon stream in Alaska, or some garbage dump, it is another matter. But just to go out in the timber and still-hunt for black bear without snow is usually about the hardest possible still-hunting I know of, and one that is seldom productive of results.

Hunt always upwind, and if a good breeze is blowing that will muffle your footsteps so much the better. The late evening is always much the best time to hunt bear in the fall. If you make a deer, elk, or moose kill, then you will have a far better chance of getting a bear by watching the offal each evening from some vantage point than you will in actually still-hunting. In the East, bear are very fond of acorns and nuts and will frequent ridges where they can be obtained. They are also likely to frequent any old deserted orchards and berry patches, as they are very fond of any fruit. Even here in Idaho they very often come down and work our orchards of a night, or late in the evening. In Utah and the more southern ranges they feed a great deal on acorns in the fall. They also like to lie up along some steep rocky watercourse that is well covered with brush or berry bushes, and in hunting them in the West you can often jump them by working down a watercourse and keeping to the windward side of these small creeks and watching as you go. Even so, more bear will be seen and killed while hunting other game than when actually bear hunting.

In the late fall, they will often be found to frequent extensive patches of wild roses, where they eat the small red seed pods. They also frequent alder and willow thickets, where they eat the swollen larvae of the gallfly, which is encased in a red swelling of the leaves and often is nearly as large as a marble. At such times, when such thickets of willow and alder or wild roses can be located, it is well to get across the canyon and high enough so that you can have a good view and wait for the bear in late evening. The same is true of berry patches. Often the frozen huckleberries and serviceberries still remain on the bushes and you can then have a very good chance if you find where the bear are feeding and lie up and wait for him. Be sure always to locate your lookout where the wind cannot carry to him, or you will never see the bear. In all bear hunting and for that matter all big game hunting, one must know exactly what the game is feeding on at the time, to have much chance of success. Once you locate what the bear are feeding on and find a good patch of such food, then you have the battle half won. Always pay strict attention to any scolding of the pine squirrels, camp robbers, or blue jays and magpies, as all these birds, as well as the squirrels, will fuss at and scold a bear as long as they can see him. The squirrels hate him anyway, on account of his digging out their pine nut caches, and the magpies and jays and camp robbers will always scold him as long as he is in sight. Ravens as well will often circle over a feeding bear, just to see what he is eating and if by any chance it may be carrion and they can obtain a feed when he leaves.

In some sections of the country, wild thorn apple occurs and bears feed on these a great deal in season. By fall the black bear is usually rolling fat and after a few hard frosts his coat takes on a glossy appearance. He is busiest at this time of the year as he makes final preparations for his hibernation and is constantly on the go, always in search of food and ever more food, as his appetite is then insatiable. In most sections of the West is found a small red berry growing on very low vines and in a solid mat at high elevations. The vines have a green waxy appearance and slick leaves, the berries are small and mealy and the grouse, both blue and ruffed, feed on them a great deal. In Montana when I was a kid they were called grouse berries, but others have called them bear berries. At any rate, black bear eat them in quantities in late fall. They also feed on the scarlet-colored berries of the mountain ash before denning, probably to give their intestinal tract a thorough cleansing before taking on a couple of handfuls of fir needles to keep the old tummy from completely collapsing during their hibernation.

One spring, Bob Hagel was hunting up Sheep Creek a few miles above my ranch. He located a nice bear digging out a gopher across a canyon from him on an open sidehill. The bear had his head in the hole and was digging for all he was worth, probably being able to smell the gopher, when Bob took a long-range shot across the canyon at him. The .30–40 slug went low and the bear in his haste to get away started throwing the dirt with his hind feet. He made several passes with his hind feet, up and down the slope, while his head was still imbedded in the hole, before he ever got his head out and took off, over the ridge. Bob laughed at his antics so much he was unable to shoot again.

Ed Lovedahl and I were working up the tidal arm that swings to the right just above the mouth of Snug Harbor on the north or rather west side of Cook Inlet, looking for brown bear sign, when we saw a nice black. Wanting to try out my .35 Whelen, which I had sighted at 4100 feet here in Idaho before going to Alaska, I held on the bear's chest just back of the shoulder at 200 yards from a comfortable prone position and shot. The rifle sighted at 4100 feet, shot at least 18 inches low there in Alaska, and the 275-grain slug went under his chest and threw up a big splash of water on the other side. Seeing the slug had gone so low with a perfect hold I next held level with the tops of that black's ears, as he turned and ran straight away from me. This 275-grain slug caught him in the seat of the pants and came out well forward, near the brisket, but did not expand at all. The bear dropped, but was up and into the alders while I was throwing the bolt of my rifle for another shot. Ed and I spent a half hour searching that bit of alders before we found him, too sick to continue, and Ed gave him a 220-grain .30–06 Western Soft Point Boattail in the shoulders broadside. It broke both shoulders but lodged under the skin on the off side. My 275-grain W.T.C. Company bullet, with too heavy a jacket at the tip and too small a hole in same, had not expanded at all. Needless to say I resighted my rifle. Others have found the same trouble and rifles sighted at sea level will invariably shoot way high up at high altitudes and those sighted at high altitudes will shoot low at sea level. Don Martin sighted in his rifles here before going to Alaska to serve as deputy U.S. Marshal for seven years, and when he reached Alaska found all his rifles shot way low there at sea level. It's something well worth remembering.

One day Al Ellinger stalked a nice black, but just as he was getting in good range the black must have seen or heard him and lit out in a hard run for the alders. Al was using his .375 Magnum double rifle by Webley & Scott, with 300-grain bullets, and rolled this bear over in great style. He was running so fast he simply turned somersaults and laid there, then, when Al had taken down his rifle from his shoulder, thinking the bear was done, he was up and into the alders in a flash and we never did find him.

I shot another one up the river with the .35 Whelen and lost him. We had just anchored the boat and rolled out our beds and camp for a shore camp when a nice black scamp came out on a big rock about 100 yards above us and poked his head over, watching us. His chest was fully exposed and I had only to roll over from where I lay against my bedroll and turn the safety on my .35 Whelen by G & H and had a dead rest. I placed the top of the front sight square in the bottom of the white spot in his chest. He was turned slightly quartering toward us and though I struck his chest square, the bullet no doubt ranged through him to the right of the spine. Anyway, at the shot he simply curled up around the bullet entrance as he bit at it, then took off in a hard run through the alders. In spite of our best efforts we lost his trail over that huge jumble of slide boulders in the rain. This shows the fallacy of using too stiff and heavy bullet jackets for black bear. Though his shoulders will usually stop a 220-grain .30-06 slug from a broadside shot, you want a bullet with a large hollow point or else plenty of lead exposed, that will surely expand on impact, for though the black bear is not nearly so hard to kill as a grizzly, he can carry off wounds that would usually put almost any hoofed animal down except goat and elk.

I believe in using fairly heavy rifles, with ample power, even for black bear, and the .300 Savage, .30–40 Krag and Winchester, the .33 W.C.F. and .35 Remington are all excellent timber rifles for black bear. When the bear is hunted in more open terrain, such as the tide flats of Alaska or the more sparsely wooded sections of the Southwest, where long shots will often occur across canyons, then such rifles as the .270 Winchester, .30–06 with 150 or 180 grain and the .300 Magnum are excellent. For most black bear hunting in the timber one should use either a big wide field hunting scope, with plenty of illumination, or a fair-sized gold or ivory bead, as most shots will be had very late in the evening, usually long after sundown. I particularly like the .35 Winchester load for black bear in the timber, a bit strenuous on the pelts perhaps, but a sure bear producer. The .256 Newton, 6.5 mm. and the 7 mm. are also excellent for black bear, but be sure and use bullets that will expand reliably on them. Al and Mrs. Ellinger have had great luck with the .300 Savage, while Frank Mosteller has used the 7 mm. with a Hi-Speed W.T.C. Company bullet hand load, with perfect success. I have killed them with about everything from a .44 Special heavy sixgun load to the .35 Whelen. With black bear, as in all bear shooting, strive to break down their skeletal structure on the first shot, particularly the spine or shoulders, and you have them.

In some sections of the deep South and also in some brushy sections of the Southwest, bear will rarely be obtained except by the use of dogs and traps, and when such is the case their use is justifiable, and many exciting chases may be had with a good pack of dogs. In other sections, I believe in hunting the little bear without dogs. Though a comical clown, he is very intelligent and well worth the highest skill of any still-hunter.

V I

Moose

MOOSE, like caribou, occur clear around the globe. In Norway my good friend Frantz Rosenberg calls them elk, which is of course the correct name even though they are identical with our moose, except that they have smaller heads. Our scientists recognize just three species of moose in America. The most common is of course *Alces americana americana*. This moose inhabits the whole of Canada, mainly east of the Rockies, and from the northern part of the United States to about Hudson Bay in the east and beyond the Arctic Circle in the west as far north as willows and browse occur in sufficient quantities for food. In the U.S., this species occurs from Maine, Minnesota, North Dakota, into Montana and British Columbia. They are much more plentiful east of the Continental Divide, but a goodly number occur near Ketchikan, Alaska, near the coast.

A smaller species, known as *Alces shirasi*, occurs in and around the Yellowstone Park. It is a paler brown, with lighter colored ears, and the heads also run smaller than in the Canadian moose. We have a considerable number of moose on the Lochsa here in Idaho, also some on the North Fork of the Salmon and down the main Salmon and Selway Rivers. Just which group they belong to I do not know, but would suspect them of belonging to the main Canadian species of *Alces americana americana,* though they might belong to the *shirasi* group. We also have a goodly number of moose in Montana and near Ashton, Idaho. The latter of course belong to *shirasi*.

On the Kenai Peninsula in Alaska occurs the world's finest moose, known as *Alces gigas*. This is also the largest known species, with extreme weights for fat bulls running to 1800 pounds and extreme height at top of withers running as much as 92 inches. It is also longer bodied than the Canadian moose or the typical Wyoming moose and extremely large specimens will run a total length of 120 to 122 inches. The Canadian moose, in comparison, will run to 1400 or 1500 pounds extreme weight, a total height in extreme cases of as much as 78 inches and a total length for largest specimens of 108 inches. Our moose here in Idaho, in the Lochsa region, I believe will run just as large, but those in eastern Idaho, around the park, are smaller, as are the moose on the North Fork of the Salmon.

Moose are a browsing animal and fond of just about all aquatic plants, such as water and pond lilies and water moss and willows. They will, however, eat most anything when forced to do so by a hard winter and we have even seen them eat small conifers while yarded up here when the willow and quaking aspens were cleaned out. While the moose has slim, trim legs and feet, the latter shaped almost identically like those of a large deer, the rest of the animal bears little resemblance to deer, though it is the largest of all the deer tribe. Moose are homely brutes, and except for the horns of the bulls resemble a Missouri mule that went wrong early in life. Moose have an awkward, lumbering gait when they start off at a trot, not unlike that of a mule or mountain goat, but their long stride carries them very fast. When they break into full run, they still appear awkward and ungraceful. A huge bull with a big wide head is truly a majestic sight, but by no stretch of the imagination can he be classed as a beautiful animal. The long legs, long neck, and particularly the long skull and nose, are particularly adapted to his way of life and usual methods of feeding under water.

In color they run from dark brown to black over most of the body, with the hind legs up above the hock joint often being a dirty white or blue gray. Some white also appears on the back of the forelegs at the knee. Dew claws are sharp and well developed and show in the tracks in the mud. In general, the tracks resemble a gigantic deer track and the hoofs are just as long and pointed in proportion.

Moose are grand game, particularly to the Indians and trappers of the North, as they furnish a great deal of the winter meat supply for many Indians, as well as whites, living away from the caribou ranges. The meat is coarse and dark, but very good eating when fat and it has hung long enough to age.

The rut usually occurs in late September, extending on into the middle of October. The calves are usually born in late May or early June. Young heifers usually have just one calf and thereafter usually two. Three have been seen at times with a single cow, but this is rare. Having no horns, the cow moose is the ugliest of the two sexes and resembles a mule even more than the bull. Moose are great travelers and may range over great distances if food becomes short and scarce. On the other hand, they may remain in one locality most of their lives if both summer and winter food is plentiful. During the summer and early fall months, they will be found mostly adjacent to lakes, ponds and streams, where they can get the aquatic plant life they so dearly love, but in winter their food is all browse and when snow gets deep they will usually yard up in small bands and break out trails to all available browse.

Moose are excellent swimmers and will not hesitate to swim the largest lakes and rivers. At times they have been found far from shore in our larger lakes. During the rut, the bulls do considerable traveling until they find a mate, and at this time of the year they are often very cranky. At times they will put a man up a tree. I have talked to many Alaskans who have been treed by moose during the rut. In fighting they use both horns and forefeet but usually the horns, while the cow uses her front feet chiefly. A mad bull moose is truly an impressive sight, with the hair along the top of his neck and back erected and his little brown eyes glowing. He looks like nothing else on this earth. I have seen them thus in the rut, when they were called out and expected a rival rather than man, but all I have seen always ran when once they got the man scent.

The largest Canadian moose I ever saw was on the head of the Wapiti River in British Columbia. I had made a long circle some 12 to 15 miles from camp in search of grizzly and ran onto this huge bull in a little wet meadow, surrounded by fir and spruce. He started toward me, grunting at the first sight of me, and when I answered with a hoarse grunt he came at a fast swinging trot, with hair erected on top of his neck. His head was the largest I have seen of that species and I honestly believe would have gone 60 inches. Though I had a license for a couple of moose at the time, I had no intention of killing him, as it would have required the combined efforts of a couple of good men for three days to lug that huge skull and cape out of that section and I did not have the time. He came on toward me until very close, as I turned the safety over on my rifle and circled frantically into the wind. I did not want to kill him, though I would very much have liked to have his head, had it been where I could have reached the kill with a pack horse. As soon as the wind blew from me to him, he stopped, took one good sniff, and immediately the hair on his neck and back dropped down and he whirled and ran. He had exceptionally long and wide palms, with an enormous brow formation, palmated as well, and many long points extending out from each side of the palms.

Moose can be called in the West as well as the East, and I have watched the Indians call them. I have never heard of the Kenai moose being called,

Courtesy A. E. Ellinger

A. E. Ellinger with three fine Maine black bears

Courtesy A. E. Ellinger

Black bear killed in Maine, 1939, by
Mrs. A. E. Ellinger

Courtesy Bob Becker

Michigan black bear

Courtesy J. O. Cole

Bull moose in Alberta

Courtesy Kenneth Call, Alaska

Fine set of Alaskan moose antlers

Courtesy J. O. Cole

Cow moose picture taken by J. H. Shirk

but I will be willing to bet they would answer. They are very thick in the moose pastures of the Kenai Peninsula and there it is mostly a matter of looking over a great many moose, in order to pick the finest head available. If time permits, a really outstanding head can be had from 60 inches up in spread. The grunt of an old bull, at close quarters in the brush, is apt to raise your hair the first time you hear it, if the call is unexpected.

One fall we were hunting elk in the Lochsa and Frank Behrman, one of our party, while going through some very thick brush and spruce on Brushy Creek, suddenly heard a big bull grunt at close range. Frank said he jumped ten feet and his hair all stood on end, as he thought such a noise could only have come from a grizzly. We found the bull's tracks the next day and he had been less than 20 yards from Frank when he challenged him. Many times we have teased them in the rut, just to have a good look at them.

When it comes to sense of smell and hearing, the moose is very well equipped. Before the rut, he can usually hear you in the timber long before you get in sight of him, unless you are an extraordinary still-hunter. In the East, moose hunting is largely still-hunting, either on foot in the timber, or by canoe or boat on the lakes and rivers. In the mountains of the West and North, you may hunt him either by still-hunting or stalking, the latter method usually being much the best.

More moose are probably taken each year in the East by calling along streams and lakes than by still-hunting. During the rut, the call of the cow moose will nearly always bring an answer from any bulls present. It is a peculiar sound and while I have learned from the Indians and the animals themselves to make a fair imitation of this long-drawn call of the cow, I find words, or letters, totally inadequate to describe it. The bull's call is much harsher and deeper and ends in a hoarse grunt. At times he may answer only by a hoarse grunt, as he comes to investigate. Experienced guides are a necessity, if you would have a good hunt in eastern Canada. While the moose in these sections spend much of the summer in the low-lying swamp lands, they spend considerable time in the fall on the higher adjacent hardwood ridges. They also frequent the ridges to get away from flies in the summer. Most of their beds will also he found back along these low ridges and away from the lakes and swamps where they feed. Late evening is usually the best time to call, particularly when the air is still. If you trail the moose, remember he will invariably bed where he can get the scent from his backtrack. By circling before bedding, moose nearly always bring their back trail upwind of their bed. They are very fond of maple thickets, and even in the West will use the scrub or mountain maple for food, whenever it can be obtained. In still-hunting, a moose will invariably hear you before you get in sight, when he will usually get up out of his bed and circle or move his position. During the rut, a deep grunt from you will often bring an answer and disclose his position; but getting close enough actually to see him is something else. He cannot see so well, but those ears and that ungodly long nose will tell him all he wants to know about you in most cases. It is well to stay clear of the trail as much as possible, circle always to windward and cut the trail just enough to keep its direction. Move with infinite caution and patience and stop often to look and listen, if you are in the section where he is likely to bed. You simply cannot be too careful and I honestly believe a moose that has been much hunted is fully as hard to still-hunt as a wise old whitetail buck. Where they have not been hunted at all, I have seen them act dumb and allow you to approach to close range, then stand and look at you for a considerable time before trotting off. We found several on our last trip into British Columbia that did not seem the least alarmed at sight of the whole pack string.

But if a moose is much hunted, you can depend on him to be a tough customer to outwit in the thickets along the ridges, where he will usually shack up for the day. If you have snow that is neither crusted nor wet and poppy, you have an excellent chance, but moose that are hunted will usually bed in a place where it is very hard for you to sight them, without first warning them by your advance. I honestly believe they can hear you farther than any other animal, with the possible exception of mule deer and elk. When you do see them in the timber, it is often very hard to determine how the beast is turned and whether you are looking at the head or tail end. The tail is short and inconspicuous and the color of the legs, when they can be seen, is usually the best indication as to how the beast is turned. If you can see that telltale dirty white, or tan, of the hock joints and above them, then you know a rear view is presented. Usually, however, there will be intervening tree boles and limbs and one will have to stand absolutely motionless for minutes waiting for the moose to make the first move and disclose his position.

Though as a rule moose will not go as far as elk when any body hit is received, they may get a long distance from where you want them before stopping to bed, and it is always best to shoot only when you can place your shot properly. I have never seen a wounded moose offer to fight, but others have told me of having them turn when wounded, and several human and moose skeletons have been found together in various parts of the country, showing beyond doubt that they do fight at times.

One such pair of skeletons was found in Montana with an old rusted .45–70 rifle and a long sheath knife. We believe in using only heavy caliber rifles for moose, nothing smaller than the .348 Winchester and .35 Winchester for timber moose hunting. It's better to put them down where you want them than to have them go off and probably die in some lake or stream, or in some dense thicket, where they are very hard to pack out.

After the rut starts, moose, especially bulls, are great ramblers, and even though you have snow, a moose may lead you a long trail, unless he finds a cow and stops. Calling is usually much more successful than still-hunting, but you must have an expert at it, for best results. It takes time to learn to call moose properly, just as it does elk or other game, and you must have dead calm, clear weather, for best results. Though far less sporting than still-hunting, it is more productive of results. Calling is successful only for the first two to possibly three weeks of the rut. I have called bulls in the Lochsa in October several times, just out of curiosity, and while they did not come as did those in Canada, they would answer and thus enable me to work around to windward, to where I could see them. Possibly my call was not just right, or possibly they do less calling here. At any rate they would answer, both the call of a cow and the hoarse grunt of a bull. They have not been hunted, though each fall elk are killed all around them and occasionally some trigger-happy dude kills a moose for an elk and usually lets it lie, just as two were killed about six miles from this little ranch last fall.

If caught out in some lake a moose will usually swim ashore and, if scared, disappear in the timber, but if not badly frightened he will stop for a further look at you before beating a retreat. If shot in the water, he often lunges toward the nearest shore line, and if his direction leads him past your boat you may think he is charging, when in reality he is not. If shot through the heart he will nearly always run in the direction he was pointed just as other game does. I believe the sportsmen should kill one or two good heads and otherwise leave moose alone unless in need of meat. If you want the finest obtainable, it is best to wait and go to Seward, Alaska, get a good guide and spend a couple of weeks on the Kenai, where you can obtain a really outstanding head. I hope to do that myself someday. While I could have killed many moose over the years, I have passed them up, unless guiding sportsmen or helping in that capacity on trips. Altogether too many young bull moose are killed when their heads are not suitable for trophies at all, and many men kill them just to be able to say they have killed a moose. I cannot understand such logic, nor can I see any reason for killing a moose except for food or an outstanding head.

George Bates, Sam Calleau and I made a short spike trip from the main camp in '27 for moose and we saw an awful lot of bulls on that trip, but nothing that I figured would go over 45 inches in spread, and as George had already killed one of that size, he did not want another small head, so we passed them all up. We did get uncomfortably close to one moose on that trip. I had seen a bull's horns in the distance, that looked good, so we went down across a little creek and wet meadow and up another ridge, intending to go on over it into the basin, where we had seen the horns flash, and look him over. When nearing the top of the ridge, I saw a set of horns coming our way and not over 10 yards away. We had just time to slip over a huge log that lay on the lower side of the trail and lie down close in under it, out of sight, before the bull heaved his bulk over the ridge and came right down the trail we had been on. There was a slight breeze blowing down the hill from the trail over us, but how he could come so close and not smell us is still something I cannot understand, for he passed right down the trail with one palm projecting out in plain sight over us, as we lay behind the log, not daring even to breathe until he was past. He went out in the wet meadow and started feeding and, as his head was small, I took Bates's movie camera and stalked him each time his head went under water. In this way I managed to get very close, too close in fact. When he raised his head, I focused him in the finder and started the movie. He swung his ugly head and looked at me, then took off in a shower of spray and water, but I had his picture well recorded and Bates later wrote that the movies turned out fine.

In hunting moose in the West, one can usually do best by getting up on some good observation point and watching over as much country as possible with the glasses, until the flash of a horn is seen or an animal is located, then going down to stalk and investigate it for a possible trophy. Moose feed in early morn, but seem to feed even more in late evening. If you are in good moose country during the rut you have an even better chance, by watching a lot of terrain, as the bulls are on the go until they find a mate, and you may see several in a day. Often you can see an animal plainly from some lookout point, but when you go after him he is very hard to locate, or he may move while you are making your stalk. You should always locate his position with relation to trees, rocks or lakes and also note the time of the day, if he is feeding, or about to bed, or is traveling in search of cows. Quite often the moose that is clearly visible from some high point of land will be almost invisible down in the timber and on the flat land, and you will then have to resort to still-hunting to get in sight and range. A moose is a tall animal and while you can see the tops of his horns above brush and scrub timber, they may be invisible when you get down on his level. When such is the case, it is best to still-hunt, just as carefully as you possibly can, making absolutely sure of the wind at all times. When you do see him, you may be too close and jump him, without getting time for a careful check on his horns, having then either to pass him up, or make snap judgment and do snap shooting as well.

If he is feeding you have every advantage, and have only to keep the wind from him to you and advance only when his head is down and with no noise. In this way you can soon slip up in range. When the ground is covered with water or is muddy, it's much harder to get by without making a noise. If you have to wade, do not lift your feet up out of water at each step, but slide them forward slowly and you can move with less chance of splashing water and alarming your quarry. When you do see him he may be bedded, or turned so you cannot see the horns if in the brush; then it is best to wait and watch and let him make the first move. You have a better chance by watching as soon as you get in good effective range rather than trying to get too close, as stray changes in the wind may give you away at close range when they would not if you were farther away. When taking photos, of course, you want to get as close as humanly possible, but you are then not interested as a rule in killing the beast, or in the exact size of his horns. In remote sections you may run onto moose that appear dumb, simply because they are not familiar with man. On one trip we had one walk up to close range of the pack string and stand there watching us for several minutes after we stopped. In fact we tightened the cinch on a pack, readjusted another pack, climbed back on our horses and moved on and he was still standing there gazing at us, within 30 yards. The wind was from him to us, but he made no effort whatever to circle and get our scent. This was one of the most peculiar-acting moose it has been my pleasure to meet.

On the last trip to B.C., when climbing up out of the head of a creek flowing into the Musqua River, a fair bull jumped up and stood and gazed at us within 50 yards. Dick Brown wanted him and jumped off his horse and ran to me. He had just turned the safety on my .375 Magnum to shoot when the bull disappeared in the timber. Had Dick shot with his own rifle, as soon as he stepped off the horse, he could have gotten him nicely, but I for one was well satisfied he got away, as we did not need the meat and the head was nothing out of the ordinary.

Two bulls will often run together during the summer, but they soon separate when the rut starts and after that you will seldom see two bulls together unless fighting until after the rut is well over — except in Alaska, where a herd of bulls may be seen in a small area.

Abundance of food and a mild climate no doubt account for the huge size of the Alaskan moose in the Kenai and Rainy Pass sections. The climate there on the Kenai Peninsula is mild as compared to interior Alaska and favored by the warm Japanese current that also hits Kodiak Island. Much of the Kenai has been burned off and this has in turn grown up with aspens and willows and other small second growth, ideal for moose. Stalking is also easy on the Kenai, as compared with moose hunting in the interior, where you run into heavier stands of timber. You can often locate moose in the timber from a lookout, but when you leave the lookout they are then hard to locate again and harder still to size up and estimate, when you do see them. For these reasons, and also the size of the game as well, probably no other place exists that is so favorable to securing a really good moose head as the Kenai Peninsula.

If you go there and are on the ground by the first of October and figure on spending two or three weeks looking over moose, and get a really good guide, such as Earl Olmstead, Andy Simons, Tom O'Dale, Jack Lean, Ward Gay or any number of other good men in that section, then use your own judgment as well as the guide's advice, you should get a head without difficulty that will go from 60 to 70 inches and sometimes even larger. It's a great moose country, the best on earth. A really fine moose head is an outstanding trophy, but a small head always looked more to me like a mule with a set of antlers added. You can reach the very best moose hunting on the Kenai by plane in a very short time from either Anchorage or Seward and have outstanding hunting. On the Kenai, right up until the rut is in full swing, you will find bull moose in bands, as they are very plentiful. You will see so darn many moose it is hard to judge them accurately, and that is where your guide will be of inestimable value in helping you select a really fine one. The best heads will be on bulls in the prime of life, or a trifle older, and real old heads will be short and scrubby as a rule, the same as with about all our other game of the deer tribe.

Moose must clean their antlers of velvet in August, like elk, as all I have seen during September, October and November, were clean and hard. They put on the heaviest of all horn growths in one season of any living animal today. When you do get a good moose, always remove the cape well back on the shoulders, as you need plenty of the shoulder and brisket showing on the finished mount to make it really balance up with a big wide set of antlers. A heavy, well-shaped sheath knife is needed, as the skin is both tough and very heavy, and a couple of pack boards are best to transport skull and antlers and cape back to camp. You will need a good back-packer to handle the head, as it will usually go around 100 pounds or more green, even though you have shaved down the meat and removed the brains. The cape alone will make one man a mighty good load.

I believe cow moose bring calves every year, or at least to a much greater extent than elk, as you often find cow elk with yearling calves. In the North, probably few cows succeed in bringing both calves through the summer, due to the wolves. Wolves and man are the moose's worst enemies. A cougar may occasionally kill a calf in the southern part of their range and a grizzly will occasionally stalk and kill a moose, but by far the greatest loss from animals is due to the big arctic wolves. In 1937, we found many wolf kills of moose for 200 miles north from Fort St. John along the section where the Alcan Highway now runs. We also saw a lone wolf chasing a cow and calf moose out on the tundra and muskeg while we were climbing around a low hill with the pack string between the Prophet and Musqua Rivers. I have little doubt that the wolf finally ate that calf. He was completely out of rifle range or we would have taken a hand, if only to scare him off. Wolves kill a great many more moose in winter, when they pack up, and woe to the moose they cut out from a yard. Sooner or later, one wolf will hamstring him, then the others will soon finish the job. From the number of summer kills we saw that season, I wonder how many are killed in winter by wolves. Certainly a great many more moose are pulled down in the winter by wolves in that section than are ever killed by man.

One peculiar trait of the moose is that they will reach far under water for their favorite food. I have seen them standing out in lakes so deep that only the top of back and head showed; they would get a good breath and submerge their head completely for about a minute while they cropped off water plants far below the surface. Several guides have told me of surprising them in lakes and of having them dive under, then come up and show only their heads with horns laid on their backs and just the eyes and nostrils and horns showing, and hold that position for several minutes in an effort to evade detection.

The only time I have ever seen two bulls killed right together was in 1927. Harry Snyder, Bates and Carrol Paul were in the lead of the pack string, while the Indians and Jim Ross worked along in the middle of the thirty-two head of horses. Prentiss N. Gray, one of the finest men and sportsmen I have ever been out with, walked along with me in the rear of that long pack string. We had both given up our saddle horses and packed them to lighten the loads of the others and had spent the day following the string, unpacking and tailing bogged pack horses out of the muck and repacking them. We were both plastered with black swamp mud from head to foot. Sam and Pete Calleau had come back and relieved us, so that we started to scout on ahead of the slow-moving string. Just then the lead ran into two big bull moose, right in the trail. We were nearing the Wapiti River at the time. Bates and Paul fell off their horses, each selected his animal and proceeded to plant three slugs in his chest as the two bulls faced us at close range. During the excitement, Gray unslung his old Springfield and gave each bull one 180-grain Western open point in the chest, then turning the safety he winked at me and slipped the sling back on his shoulder. I do not think anyone saw his action, or knew he shot, as his shots blended with the others. The two bulls then wheeled and ran about fifty yards and both fell dead together. They had stood and taken four slugs in the chest each and had broken and run off together, and they had fallen dead side by side. Any one of the four slugs in either bull would have killed him if given a little time. Paul used a 20-inch Mannlicher type .30–06 Springfield and either 180- or 220-grain bullets and Bates used his Webley & Scott .300 Magnum and Western 180 grain. That evening as we made camp near a small lake, a very tiny little diving duck alighted about 100 yards from camp. Prent Gray picked up his old Springfield and, taking careful aim from a sitting position, blew the little mud duck to atoms. When questioned about shooting, he said he just wanted to see if his rifle was sighted, while he again gave me a knowing wink. Not knowing if either Bates or Paul had hit his moose right, Gray simply made sure those two bulls did not go far as he was in a hurry to reach sheep country. Prent Gray was later killed in a gas boat explosion down in Florida, and Paul has no doubt crossed the Divide to better hunting country, ere this is written.

Sometimes during the rut moose can be called by simply rubbing a heavy limb up and down a tree trunk, the same as we do when bugling out a bull elk in the fall. The bull naturally thinks it is another bull cleaning his antlers and will come to investigate. If he has been hunted, he is usually too wary for this sort of thing, but in remote sections where he has little fear of man, he may do anything. Though many hunters credit moose with having better sense of both hearing and smell than deer and elk, I have never found this to be so. In my experience an elk or mule buck will usually take alarm far sooner than a moose. Moose pay very little attention to rifle shots, as a rule, unless they have been hard hunted, or shot at. I have seen them remain in one small patch of timber while elk were killed near by, and they were still there when the elk had been dressed out and quartered. Of course these moose had long enjoyed a closed season and had no cause to be alarmed, but the fact remains that they do not seem to associate the sound of rifle fire with man, as do other game animals.

During the rut, bull moose will often grunt when they hear you breaking brush, as you force your way through thickets; further, if you sit still and listen when in a thickly inhabited moose country, you will hear them grunting continuously at times, not only in daytime, but in the dead of night as well. A moose that has been hard hunted is a totally different animal in his actions than one in a remote section, where man has seldom penetrated and he has not been molested. On the whole I would class moose hunting, at least in the West, along the Rockies and in Alaska, as much the easiest hunting of all our deer tribe. In my experience at least moose have been much easier to come onto than elk, deer or caribou.

In eastern Canada, moose are often called from a canoe on moonlight nights. A birch-bark horn is used to amplify the call. For calling a moose that is suspected of lying up close by, the call is held near the water and used more softly than when the call is desired to carry a mile or two away. If there is any wind movement, calling is seldom productive of results, as the animal cannot hear it against the wind and if he is downwind he will circle and pick up your scent. Further, such moose shooting offers little or no chance of sizing up a head. It is a good method of securing meat and is also apt to lose wounded animals, due to badly placed shots in the night. I believe such practices should be abandoned in favor of calling just at daylight and again in the evening.

Many moose will answer your call that will not come anyway, and if the calling is done in early morning, you can then proceed to still-hunt a moose if he answers but will not come. In the gathering dusk such would be a poor procedure, as you would hardly have enough light left for a stalk, and if you only wounded the animal, darkness would settle before you could trail up and finish him. So for practical purposes and the securing of a good representative head of the Canadian moose, we would suggest calling in the early morning and later evening and still-hunting in the early morning or during the day. At least you can then see your sights and have a fair idea of the size of the head you are taking.

Hunting moose in the dense flat lands of eastern Canada is a much harder task than hunting them in the mountains of the West, where you can get up on some point, or mountain, and comb a lot of country with the glasses, until you locate a moose. They will inhabit the timbered basins and streams and lakes bordered with willows, well up in the mountains, and you can spy them out much easier than you can locate them by ordinary still-hunting in the timber. You can also size up the heads and determine if they are worth going after or not.

Moose will sometimes stampede when hit by a rifle bullet, and at other times they will simply stand around and hump up, or walk slowly away. They seem to be able to take it, much like an elk, but as a general rule a wounded moose will stop and wait for you, when a wounded elk will continue to put miles between you as long as life lasts. It is imperative that you get your slug into the chest cavity on any moose, if possible. Further, use a good, powerful, heavy-caliber rifle. From what moose I have seen killed and wounded, I would say that you are not going to spoil either meat or trophy with any rifle, regardless of how big it is. Even an elephant rifle is not too large if you can handle it quickly and accurately. Such calibers as the .348, .35 and .405 W.C.F., .45–70–405 Smokeless and the .375 Magnum are ideal, as well as the .35 and .400 Whelen and the .333 and .334 O.K.H. These cartridges with heavy bullets will stop your moose a lot quicker than anything smaller if he does jump and run at the shot. High velocity small bores are out with me, unless they can be used in fairly open country. In the timber, you will usually have to plow through some brush and this will explode any high velocity bullet before it even gets to the moose. Thirty-caliber rifles will kill him nicely with heart shots, but are very unreliable for any raking shots, and unless the spine, or rump, is broken, they won't stop him and won't go through the paunch. Some experienced moose hunters prefer Hard Point Round Nose bullets in .30–06 and .303 British calibers for moose, for all rear end raking shots, something that will if possible go the length of him, but such bullets are almost useless on broadside shots unless heart or spine is struck.

Buck Harris of Ketchikan, Alaska, tried out a .257 Roberts on moose and fired about seven shots, as I remember, at the neck broadside at fairly close range, attempting to break the neck. Even the heavier Roberts bullets would not break the spine. The shots were planted from the skull back to about the front of the shoulder in line with the spine. They finally got the moose down and finished with head shots, but that one experience was enough to prove the .257 Roberts totally inadequate on moose, even when well placed. The bullets ground up on contact with the spine and would not break it. One .375 Magnum or even a .30–06–220 in the same place would have produced results.

In conclusion, I would say, kill your moose if you need meat, but if you don't need meat and want only a good head, then wait until you find such a head and pass up the smaller younger bulls, whose head would not satisfy you after you had killed them.

V I I

Alaskan Coastal Bear Hunting

HUNTING bear along the Alaskan coast line presents many problems. For one thing, it is usually boat hunting, either along some river or tidal arm. In either spring or fall, Alaska is usually a very wet inhospitable land. Average rainfall in southeastern Alaska is around 155 inches per annum, and though it rains less to the north and out on the Peninsula, it blows more and is much colder. Tides are also higher in Cook Inlet and along the Peninsula. Experienced guides or sourdoughs are an absolute necessity for the Cheechako if the hunter would keep out of trouble on his first trip. Also, Alaskan law necessitates the hiring of a registered guide for either hunting or bear photography. Many of those guides are mighty competent men, who well know their business and are worth their pay, while others are not worth the food you will feed them. Their pay before the war was fifteen bucks per day from start to end of trip, whether hunting, or smoking in the cabin of the boat. Some are wise old heads and mighty competent, some are competent only at the table and at collecting their pay. Some in the service are too old, and when you find one who will argue that a 1000-pound brown bear seen through a 20 X spotting scope is a whistler or woodchuck, then you well know he is too old for the job in hand and does not want to make the climb.

Alaska is the greatest bear country in the world. A combination of remote areas accessible only by boat or plane, combined with a great variety of berry foods and the greatest runs of salmon in the world, make Alaska a veritable paradise for the bear, both big and small. Alaska has the bear all right, make no mistake on that score, but a lot of malarkey has been spread about them and you seldom if ever see any mention of the fact that most of them along Cook Inlet and the Peninsula as well as on Kodiak Island are badly rubbed when they first break through the snow and come out in the spring. The big bear usually come out of their dens around the latter part of April. Some seasons they may beat this time in some localities, particularly down in southeastern Alaska, and some seasons they may not be out in numbers until early in May. The sows and cubs and young bear usually hole up at the lower elevations and come out first, while the big males usually den at higher elevations on the north slopes and come out last. On a month- to two-month trip, in either the southeast or north on the Peninsula, you will see plenty of bear if under a good guide, but how many shootable specimens you will see is something else entirely.

The spring of '37, while hunting along the north shore of Cook Inlet on the Peninsula, in Iniskin, Chinitna and Snug Harbor, I saw just 88 bear that I felt sure were all different animals, and also saw several of these repeatedly. Of the 88 bear, 10 were blacks and the other 78 were grizzly or brownies. Of the 78 big bear 30 head were sows with baby cubs and every last one of these sows had a perfect pelt, as near as I was able to determine with a 20 X spotting scope. Of the other 48 big bear, I do not believe over six or eight at the most carried a worth-while, shootable pelt. This shows what you are up against, and once you see a bear and the guide tells you to shoot, he is then your bear, whether good or bad as to pelage. Just after the turn of the century that country was all covered with a fine volcanic ash, and the ground and tidal arms are still impregnated with it. Those big bear swim the tidal arms a great deal, also pick up countless devil's-club thorns each summer, so with their pelts full of thorns and salty glacial silt impregnated with volcanic ash, it is no wonder they rub a great deal in their dens. Many of them looked like maned African lions when they first came out, with a big collar or ruff of six-inch fur around their necks and the rest of their body practically bare. I watched one specimen break the snow crust over his den and then emerge for the first time, and the above description fitted him exactly as to pelage.

In southeastern Alaska you have a much warmer climate, the mercury seldom dropping much below zero in the winter, and the fur will be much shorter on the big bear but also more uniform, and without that volcanic ash there is less tendency to rub in the dens. The season, however, used to open the first of August, which was much too early for bear of that section as the pelts of all big ones are then very short, merely thin sparse hair all along the top of the back. A yearling or two-year-old will be well but shortly furred all over, but the big fellows, either sows or males, will have little hair and no fur in the center of the back. The season should not be opened in that area before the fifteenth of September. Spring bear in southeastern Alaska will, unless rubbed, have an even coat of fur, but shorter than those to the northward. Thus the spring is the time to hunt them. Fall skins will be good and without any rubbing if killed late in the season just before the bear den up, but by that time the salmon runs are over and most of the berries are gone as well, making hunting them very uncertain. Farther inland on the Stikine and other rivers such as the Unuck, the big bear will be found at times late in the fall, right up to freeze-up, and are then in excellent condition.

In the late fall you can well expect bad weather, by the time the bear are well furred, so for this reason too the spring will offer the best hunting. On Kodiak Island and the Alaskan Peninsula, I believe more good pelts will be found in the very late fall, just before winter sets in, than in the spring, but hunting will usually be tough at that time of the year. Hard storms will also be prevalent, which in turn means a lot of trouble finding a safe anchorage for the boat, as well as very uncertain and high tides and winds that blow at terrific velocity and from every conceivable direction, including straight down. The Alaskan williwaws, as they are called, are really something and must be endured to be fully appreciated. If caught out in the Inlet or in some unprotected bay, you will have to ride out some mighty high and rough seas, and even in a snug anchorage you will have much trouble from the hook's dragging or pulling out of the mud.

Conditions have no doubt changed a great deal in Alaska since we hunted up there last, but the weather will remain the same. Many reports have been received from men who have been on the scene of the Army Air Corps machine-gunning the big bear on numerous occasions, as well as moose and other game, and the country adjacent to about all the big army camps has been subjected to plenty of hunting. Only recently we had a letter from Fairbanks telling of some of this misuse of the game supply near army camps. It takes ten to twenty years to grow a big bear and if they are killed needlessly from the air, that section may long be depleted of good specimens. Much of the bear country is covered only with alders, which, when leafless, offer no cover whatever from the air. The army has no cause to be proud of some of the things that have happened up there during and since the close of the war.

There are two usual methods of hunting the big bear. One is to be dropped with shore camp and sea dory and kicker on some good bay by a mail boat or fishing boat. The other is to hunt from and camp on a small boat especially rigged for the purpose. To our mind this is much the best and most comfortable method, and we have tried them both. If you are put off in a shore camp, your range is limited and heavy weather may hold you in camp, or close to it, for days or a week at times, when the bay may be altogether too rough for your open boat. Further, shore camps are invariably cold and wet. Up on the Peninsula the ice is never much more than a foot underground, and you will need a cot, or plenty of spruce bough insulation. Bedding soon draws moisture, as well as clothes and guns, unless a good fire can be had in a warm tent. Even then it creeps out at night and soaks your belongings.

Another thing — the less tracks you leave in the bear country the better. Probably no animal has a keener sense of smell than a grizzly, and we have seen them pick up our tracks that were three days old and immediately depart the place. As the wind shifts, a shore camp is very apt to disturb all bear within a mile of it, and often much farther.

You will wear slickers, rain hat and hip boots daily and if there is any harder work than dragging them up out of that slimy glacial silt at each step, then I have not seen it to date. In Southeast Alaska you have much better footing as a rule, but out on the Peninsula you can expect to find the hardest possible going. Those tidal flats are one huge glacial silt morass, deeply eroded by the tides, and you often sink in nearly to the top of your boots, then while you extricate one foot the other sinks deeper. When you do hit the hard ground of the hills they are covered either to a foot or eighteen inches in depth with dead springy grass or a solid mat of dense alders and devil's-club. The alders first grow out down the slope, then turn up, and you can negotiate them only by using the bear trails or working along some snow slide. The devil's-club carries a myriad of tiny thorns on its leaves which are almost impossible to find in your skin until they fester, and fester they will in short order. Don't get choke-bored pants or choke-bored hip boots with their tight ankles and knees. The tight-kneed pants will become impossible when you have some steep climbing and they become soaked with water or perspiration, and those tight-ankle hip boots, while they stay on wonderfully in going through glacial mud, are a curse to remove when you do get back to camp or the boat. You will perspire a lot and your socks will become soaked, making those tight-ankle boots almost impossible to remove, and you will spend much time cursing them while a husky guide drags you around on the seat of your pants, as he endeavors to plant one foot in your crotch or tummy the better to remove said boots. Get good roomy boots, but if possible with straps that will tighten them on your foot while negotiating those tide flats.

Actual hunting is best done by keeping a lookout on the boat, where it is anchored in the bay, and one man there can usually spot any fresh trails or bear high on the slides. You can also take the sea dory and kicker and run up those tidal arms and rivers and scout both sides as you do so.

However, the kicker will disturb the bear and it is often better to float in on a rising tide and come back down on the next one. Tides average about 34 feet at anchorage, so you must always park your boat with the painter and anchor run up to high ground that you can reach at high tide. Many times we have been caught by the tide, even when working with experienced sourdoughs. A strong wind would blow in a higher than normal tide, and when we wanted to get back to the boat we would often find some deep tidal arms filled to the brim between us and the boat and no chance of getting to it until the tide ran out. At other times, rather than wait in the rain, we have climbed steep jungle-covered mountains to reach the boat. At still others we have taken the dory too far back in some tidal arm, then when the tide ran out and we wanted to get back to boat or camp, we would find it marooned in the mud and have nothing to do but wait until the return tide floated our dory.

Southeastern Alaska is much easier hunted than the northern parts, in many ways. For one thing it does not have as bad weather as a rule, and also there is less glacial silt and the tides are lower. Much of this southeastern section is a veritable jungle, with huge timber almost tropical in appearance, and you will do most of your hunting there along the salmon streams, occasionally climbing a mountain when a big bear is located high on some snowslide, if on a spring trip. As you will park the boat and work up the streams mostly, it is best wherever possible to wade in the streams rather than track up the bank if any big bear are present. They will often pick up your tracks and depart if you leave a lot of scent along the banks of the streams. In the fall it's mostly a matter of finding big bear tracks and waiting from some vantage point to windward of his favorite fishing riffle for him to come out, usually in late evening. The really big boys den higher, and also come out later in the spring and then feed more by night than in daytime. Nowhere on earth are there so many bear, but the real big trophy animals are not thick anywhere we have been. There will be a big old fellow in one bay and maybe ten or more miles away another one. The old guides have most of them located and know where they range. In a fall hunt, if you scout a stream carefully and find no big tracks, you might as well get back to the boat, pull the hook and go some other place, for if the big ones are there they will leave tracks, from 14 inches up in length of the hind foot.

You will find about all color phases of the big bear. They are all grizzly, but many different subspecies occur. In southeast Alaska on some of the islands and up the Unuck River you will find jet-black grizzly and also true brownie types, and even on the Peninsula I saw one huge old boar that was jet black, while we also saw many light-colored blondies. Some were solid brown and others silver-tipped. In fact you will find every color phase of the grizzly in Alaska.

It's a healthful country, and once you get clear of civilization you will rarely ever have even a cold, regardless of how wet you get and how much exposure you go through. You will eat and work like a horse and have the time of your life. You will also find you require very little sleep up there in the spring; three or four hours per day seems to keep one going nicely, though in the fall you will require much more. It must be the effect of the sunlight — that is, when the sun shines, which is not so often as some might think, old sourdoughs sleep very little, but when winter comes they almost hibernate like the bear, unless out on trap lines.

When scouting a country for big bear, look for wide trails. If the center of the trail is also worn out, you know there are sows and cubs around, but if the trail takes the form of two parallel trails, two feet or more apart, and with the center grown up with grass, then you know you are in the home range of the big boys, as they are wide-tread bear. In a fall hunt when no big tracks are around the salmon streams, you might as well move camp to another section, but in early spring the streams and slides may be well tracked up by small bear before the big boys thaw out of hibernation on some steep north slope. The guide will know if any big bear are in that section, so it is imperative to hire a guide who knows his country, and then abide by his decisions.

Little love is lost between the fishermen and the big bear. They tear up many salmon nets and smash up some dories as well, and most fishermen never lose an opportunity to shoot at a bear from the safety of a boat. The natives are particularly bad at this and will plunk an old brownie in the belly with a .30-30 in hopes he will go off and die, when they can do so from the safety of a boat. This makes the bear very wary; it also makes many soreheaded, wounded bear that will fight when surprised at close range. Many old guides have told me they seldom took a really big bear from twenty to thirty or more years old without finding bullets incised in scar tissue someplace on his frame. The bear as a rule have a wholesome respect for man, but many of those old wounded bear will fight, and a sow with baby cubs or even yearlings can be depended on to fight. There are usually a few fatal bear encounters each year up there and also a few that are unprovoked bear charges. Much of this is kept out of the papers and especially the sporting magazines, but is a fact nevertheless. Treat those big bear with the respect due them and you will get along much better. They are grand game, the largest carnivora on the face

Alaskan brown bear

Courtesy Arthur H. Kinnan

Alaskan brown bear killed with .348 Winchester

Courtesy Helen R. Peterson

Helen R. Peterson and her guide with an Alaskan brown bear she killed with a
Hoffman .375 Magnum in 1938

of the earth, and they should be given adequate protection to assure an adequate supply for all time.

Never go anywhere in bear country without your rifle. It should be part of your everyday apparel. You would not think of walking down town without your pants, but you may be much worse embarrassed if you ever meet a big bear on the prod without a rifle. Many men have been mauled because they neglected to take their rifle along. If you have a shore camp, always take that rifle along, even though you are going only 100 yards to a brush toilet or for a pail of water.

In Snug Harbor, we often rowed ashore and up a small tidal arm to where a creek came in for a supply of clear fresh water; then, before that trip was over, a big old boar grizzly picked up the tracks of the guide at that same creek and trailed us back inland a half mile and made an unprovoked charge. My yelling only speeded him up and I had to kill him at twelve feet, even though his pelt was worthless. You never know when you may run onto some old sorehead like that, or get between a sow and her cubs. In either case you are simply out of luck without your rifle. Usually a bear can be talked out of a charge if you maintain a firm fearless attitude and talk to him or her, but you need something besides intestinal fortitude to back your assertions if cussing fails to change bruin's mind. An old bear that has been wounded, or one that has been recently chewed up in a fight with another bear, is apt to come for you when surprised at close range. He may be just as badly scared as you are, but if he gets in one little pat with one of those huge paws, you are done for. Also when in a shore camp, sleep always with your rifle loaded and either under the tarp in your bed or in easy reach. You may live in bear country a lifetime and have no trouble with them, or you may run into an unprovoked charge on your first trip to Alaska as I did.

Much of the bear shooting will be close-range work. In southeastern Alaska you will have 90 per cent of the shots at fairly close to very close range, owing to the nature of the country. It's heavily and densely wooded and also covered with devil's-club and other brush growths. Even though you may spot a big bear at long range and make a stalk, unless he is high on some mountain you will usually be in very close range when you do get to see him again. Sometimes you may get long shots along the salmon streams or on snowslides in early spring hunting, but when hunting the stream during the salmon run, and also when stalking bear that have been previously located on some mountainside, you will usually find yourself at close quarters for the shot.

No animal has a better nose than a bear and few have better ears, so all I have written on timber hunting will be applicable when hunting the big bear in Alaska. You may locate a bear fishing along some salmon stream, or bedded in some snowslide, and start your stalk, which will often take you out of sight of the bear for minutes at a time or longer. Then you may arrive at where the bear was, only to find him long since gone. At other times, the bear may decide to move while you are making your stalk and is just as apt to come your way as go in the opposite direction; you may be down on hands and knees, crawling along a bear trail through dense alders and devil's-club, and meet the old boy face to face at ten feet or less. Or in making your stalk on one bear you may almost step on another one. Usually they will hear you and leave, but at times waterfalls or the river may make too much noise and you may meet one at very close quarters. You may start to climb over a fallen log only to find a bear bedded on the other side. When surprised at such close range, they are very apt to fight first and think of running too late to do you any good.

For this reason you should always be on your toes when in grizzly or brownie country. Remember you are hunting an animal with plenty of intelligence, and carry your rifle fully loaded and in a position for instant use. I would not advise a rifle of less than .33 caliber nor a bullet weight of less than 250 grain for this work, and even heavier cartridges are much to be preferred. In fact for such close range work in the alders you can't find any shoulder rifle that is too heavy for those big bear if you can handle it fast and shoot it accurately. A small caliber may kill one by repeated hits, but if you have to kill one at very close range — feet, not yards — then you may not have time for more than one shot and some men have not even had time for one shot.

The country is all in favor of the bear. He can go through ten-foot alders as easily as a pig through a hazel brush thicket, yet you can only get through them by following the bear trails. Bear are very deceiving. They appear slow and clumsy, yet in reality are quick as any cat, once aroused. They can catch the fastest horse that ever lived in the first hundred yards from a standing start; further, when necessary they can negotiate that steep, heavily alder-covered country faster than any other living animal I know of. Your guide will usually keep you out of trouble, but the more you know yourself, the easier will be his task, so long as you take his advice at full value.

Much of the country will be covered either with knee-deep dead grass or decomposed leaves, brush and such, making a soft carpet into which you sink at each step, when you get away from the rocky stream beds or muddy tidal flats. You will make little or no noise in covering such terrain, so you may well surprise a bear at very close range.

We do not believe in carrying any rifle with the safety off, but do believe in having a safety that is easily and instantly removed. Nothing beats a double barrel hammerless ejector rifle with its top safety for such close range work when of suitable caliber, such as .375 Magnum, .405 Winchester or even the .400 Jeffery. Next we prefer a lever action for fast work at close range, such as the Model '86 Featherweight Winchester in .45–70 with 405-grain Smokeless Soft Point load. That big punkin will cut a full-size entrance hole with its flat soft point and will penetrate to the center or beyond with very big bear at its relatively low velocity. It is a killer and can be fired much faster than any bolt action rifle. Also, you can reload the magazine while keeping a loaded round in the chamber and the arm cocked. Its big visible hammer is very fast, practically equal to the shotgun safety on the top of the double rifle grip. The .405 Model '95 Winchester has long been a prime favorite with experienced guides in Alaska for such work. It can be cocked and brought into action almost as fast as the lighter weight '86 Model and fired just as fast, but is a much slower gun to reload. Of the two loads at close range, I personally prefer the deeper penetration with Soft Point and the larger caliber of the .45–70. The .45–90 Model '86 when reloaded with the 405-grain bullet is also very good, but we prefer the quicker 20-inch twist of the .45–70 to the slower 32-inch twist of the .45–90. One of the Johnstone boys of Ketchikan still uses and prefers his old .50–100–450 Winchester Model '86 to all modern rifles for the big bear in the brush at close range. It's a very good rifle and load but we prefer the short, handy and fast .45–70 Featherweight for our own use. In the bolt actions, in a commercial caliber, the .375 Magnum with 300-grain bullet is by all odds the best tool available at present, and in the custom loads we prefer the .333 O.K.H. with 300-grain bullet in bolt actions.

The double and lever action rifles are best in the timber at close range and the bolt action rifles with peep or scope sights are of course best for more distant shots and are more accurate. They are more suitable for all long range work or shooting in dim lights if fitted with a good scope. The ideal combination is for the hunter and guide to carry a rifle of each type. The hunter can carry the short, fast lever action or double rifle and the guide can carry the longer ranged bolt action and they can swap arms as the shot is offered. Many old guides, however, won't be without their own favorite bear stopper and for obvious reasons. Jay Williams, a very experienced Alaskan guide, who has probably killed as much or more game of about all species as any guide or sourdough in all Alaska, prefers a Model 70 Winchester in .375 Magnum caliber when guiding.

The sportsman gets the standing shot and if the big bear does not go down at the shot, or starts for cover, it's then up to the guide to help him stop said bear. If you wound one and he gets away in the brush, you are in for trouble, and unless you have some good dogs available, trailing a wounded grizzly up in such country is dangerous business. I have done it, but cannot say that I enjoyed the experience. Unless hit very badly, and nearly dead, bear very often circle and lie up where they can watch or scent their back trail, then be in a position to jump you, when you follow them. Wounded bear will often dig out a hole under tree roots in soft earth, or some bank, where they can cool their wounds in the soft wet earth, and you may almost step on them before you see them. Given any chance, the bear will nine times out of ten attempt to get away, but you must also be prepared for that odd bear that will show fight.

Safeties on bolt actions should be instantly available and we do not like the Model 70 safety at all. However, both Tilden and Pachmayr furnish excellent safeties for the Model 70 in any caliber. The Remington and Enfield safeties are excellent in every way on bolt actions. The British .333 Jeffery Mauser with 300-grain Soft Point is also a most excellent outfit for the big bear in a bolt action.

The hide and skull of a big bear make a hell of a load for any man, from 200 to 225 pounds, depending on how close you skin it, and even smaller bearskins will, with head and feet attached, often run around 150 pounds. A good pack board is the only way to lug them out. If time permits, the bear should be skinned as soon as killed, as they skin easier then than after *rigor mortis* has set in. Also, if time permits, the head can be skinned out and one man can lug out the heavy skull while the other takes the skin. If darkness sets in and you have to postpone skinning until the next day, it is best to open the belly down the center to prevent gas from forming, and also straighten out the legs so they will be in shape to use as levers next day, in turning the big brute over. Big ones require the strength of two to four men to roll them over, when on rough terrain.

Never go up to a bear until you are certain he is defunct. His little pig eyes are so small it is hard to tell by them when he is dead, unless you are closer to him than you should be. Give him plenty of time to die and it's best to thump his nose with a rock or probe an eye with a long pole, while your partner keeps a ready rifle on him, before taking any liberties with his carcass. We have seen them come alive when they were supposed to be dead, and one such experience is usually enough for anyone. In all bear shooting, stalk to a range commensurate with your own skill as a rifleman, and make every effort to make your first shot all that is needed.

Before holing up for the winter, the bear usually eat a quantity of fir or spruce or other conifer needles. These become wadded into a tight ball during hibernation. In the spring when they first come out, their feet are very tender and they are almost blind when exposed to bright sunlight. We have watched them emerge from their holes for the first time, and they usually make only a short circle and pass their rectal plug, a hard substance that completely closes the rear end of the colon during hibernation. Then they go back in. Next day they may take another short stroll and also bed in the sun for a time. As soon as their tender feet become tougher, they extend their travels and feed mostly on grass and small plants. Later they will eat salmon, from the first runs on through the summer, and finish off on berries and more old dead salmon along the streams before again holing up.

As I have said, some will hole up in a poor place and snowslides, melting snow, or other causes will drive them out, so that bear tracks may at times be seen all months of the year. It is not uncommon for trappers to see an occasional bear trail even in the dead of winter. Their eyes are not overly keen and they are not apt to see you at any great distance unless you are moving, when they can spot you for a long way. Their nose, however, is unexcelled and their ears almost as good. Mrs. Ellinger, Doc Reising, the guide and I were watching a pair of three-year-old brownies play on a snowslide across a deep canyon from us, at the forks of the Iniskin River on the north side of Cook Inlet. The wind was blowing upstream, but suddenly shifted and blew from us up that left fork.

We knew they would soon get our scent and sure enough, they suddenly stopped their play and one rose up on his hind feet and turned his nose first one way and then the other. Soon he got it and turned away in a hard run over the ridge and out of sight. The other bear did not rise up to his hind feet but took off in the opposite direction into another gulch. Those bear were fully three fourths of a mile away. Another time Ed Lovedahl and I were crossing Iniskin Bay in the sea dory with the kicker. A huge old brownie rose up on his hind legs on the beach and a mile or two away. We could see him plainly through the glasses and he was twisting his head first one way and then the other and listening to our little motor. Ed said, "Watch him when we cross the wind." We did, and when we progressed far enough across the bay for the wind to carry our scent to him, he immediately dropped to all fours and took off in a hard run through the deep snow. The last we saw of him he was three miles away, going over a high ridge and still running.

While watching for bear with Tom O'Dale, the guide, one evening, I spotted the largest specimen I have ever seen. He was bedded high on the mountain across the Iniskin River from us. I pointed him out to Tom and after a long and careful examination he pronounced him the finest and largest brownie he had ever seen. He was bedded in the snow on the top of a ridge, just down below the summit, and comparison with a huge old wind-twisted tree gave us a very good indication of his great length. Next day Ellinger and Doc Reising, his guide, with Ed Lovedahl to help with the skinning and packing, went after him. I was busy cleaning bear skulls on the boat and had a ringside seat at the stalk. However, long before they reached the top where the big boy was again bedded, they jumped a smaller bear that they thought was their quarry and missed him. The big fellow jumped out of his bed instantly and the last I saw of him he was still running hard, back along that ridge top. Usually one will have to take a light camp and back pack and go back and up, high for the really fine old boars, as they are very wise and have lived long enough to know the danger of the tide flats and seldom work down to the salmon streams until the alders leaf out and afford cover. There can be no question but that those old bears often live to be thirty to possibly fifty years old, and with such a lifespan it's no wonder they become very wise.

While hunting Iniskin Bay region, we spotted a big bear and watched him travel across a snow-covered slide and into a patch of heavy alders. Mrs. Ellinger, the guide and I started a long stalk upward. The snow increased in depth as we climbed and finally was over two feet. This, combined with large and loose slide rock underneath, made very treacherous footing. Finally we reached an alder-covered ledge just below the old bear's bed in snow hip deep. Then the guide foolishly started talking aloud. Both Mrs. Ellinger and I signaled him to be quiet but the damage was done. In a few more minutes we could have been above him and had a good look at the old chap in his bed. He snorted and ran out across the slide above us. I saw instantly that he was no good for a rug, as he was completely rubbed. Mrs. Ellinger was in no position to shoot and he was out of her sight in a couple of seconds. I ran to the top of the ridge, or rather floundered there through the deep snow, and watched him cross the next big slide and stop on the farther side. I could easily have killed him with my scope-sighted .35 Whelen but he was worthless. Plainly he was a very old bear — he often stumbled in the deep snow and twice he fell flat on his nose. He had not been out more than a day or two and no doubt his feet were very tender. I laid the cross hairs on his shoulder and wished him luck as he was worthless as a trophy. His pelt did not have enough hair on it to make a hat, and his muzzle was turning gray with age. He soon hobbled on over the next ridge out of sight.

While we made this stalk Al Ellinger and Doc Reising climbed the opposite slope across the Iniskin River from us and stalked a bear bedded in the alders. They worked down on him from above and Al killed him with three center shoulder shots from his .375 Magnum double rifle, using the 300-grain slugs. They slowly worked their way down to the river and our boat in the evening, Doc heavily loaded with the heavy skin, which he carried over one shoulder with the hind legs dragging in the snow behind him.

One day we watched nine bear playing on one snowslide. They were old sows, their yearlings and three-year-olds all traveling together. They would climb to the top of the slide, sit down like a bunch of kids and slide to the bottom in a cloud of snow spray. There was nothing in the bunch we wanted, but finally a huge old black male in excellent fur came out above them on the top of the slide. Almost instantly they got his scent as the wind was blowing down the mountain at the time. The entire bunch jumped up and into the alders and went up the mountain to one side of the slide. Al and Doc started off immediately after the big male, though I had begged Al to use my scope-sighted .35 Whelen and hold up over the big bear and shoot from our position on the tide flat. He was afraid he would not connect with a strange rifle, so decided to climb the mountain and try and get a shot at closer range. The last I saw of the big fellow he was still chasing those sows, cubs and three-year-olds over the top of the mountain. He was one of the few really fine ones we saw on the trip, but Al and Doc never got in sight of him after leaving the flat in those dense alders. While watching them and the bear, I spotted another even larger bear to one side of them. They passed within 100 yards of him unaware of his presence, nor could I locate them in any opening long enough to catch their eye and signal them of his presence. When they did get back down off that steep alder-covered slope, I had neglected to move the dory back down the tidal arm as the tide receded, being intent on keeping that big bear in sight for them. The tide ran out, leaving the dory stuck fast in the mud, and we had to wait until two in the morning for the next tide to float us, while the rain poured down. Such is bear hunting on the north side of Cook Inlet. We made many unsuccessful stalks on that trip, and at other times our approach was successful, only to find badly rubbed bear at the end of it. We were there and on the job before any bear came out that spring of '37, but only too few bear were shootable specimens when they did dig out of winter quarters.

Another day I located three bear on a snowslide and Doc Reising and Ed Lovedahl and I made the stalk. Before we reached the slide, we came around a stand of heavy alders and there were our three bear within 20 yards. They proved to be an old badly rubbed sow and two yearlings. She immediately spanked the yearlings up the steep slope, then whirled around and hissed and blew at us while she chopped her teeth together. I was in the lead, so started talking to her and backing up as I did not want to have to shoot her. When I backed up she moved forward, so I had to stand my ground and tell her what I thought of her and all her ancestors. This held her to her position but she continued to blow and show her teeth and chop them together like a mad hog. Clearly she was ready for anything. Ed and Doc spread out on each side of me and continued backing up. I would stand my ground and cuss her in a low steady voice, then back up a few steps. Finally I talked her out of it and we backed up until we were even with the alders, when she turned and followed her yearlings up the slope. She was a grand old brownie but rubbed from stem to stern.

The claws of large specimens of grizzly and brownie will run from four to six inches in length on the front feet. The skulls of the typical brownie differ from those of the typical grizzly, especially in the contour from the nostrils back over the crown of the skull. The brownie skull usually rises in a steep shoulder at the eye sockets and the forehead has a pronounced rise at this point, while typical grizzly skulls make a gradual curve from the nostrils back over the eye sockets and top of the head to the rear end of the skull. Many other minor variations occur and there are a great many subspecies since both grizzly and brownie interbreed until they are truly a mixture, both on the upper part of the Peninsula and on the coastal islands. Out on Kodiak and the western part of the Peninsula the true brownie type occurs. Skulls from $16\frac{1}{2}$ to possibly $16\frac{3}{4}$ inches in length mark the limit on the true grizzly while the brownie runs to over 18 inches in total length of skull. Very large bears will be found with small skulls and very small bears with huge record skulls.

You will see tall rangy bears, long-bodied and long-legged, that will stand five feet at the withers, and you will find short-legged chunky bears, with shorter bodies that may weigh even more than the longer-legged, rangy type. When a really big one rises up on his hind legs to his full height, he is truly an impressive sight, and if this occurs at just twelve feet and he is a mad, bawling, wounded bear at that, as was the case with mine, then you will never forget it. I really believe a big bear stands ten feet high when he rises up to his full height. I do know I was slightly above the one I killed when he was up on his hind feet and had to raise my rifle above the horizontal to shoot him through the heart. So it's a safe bet that they will range from nine to ten feet tall or possibly more when standing erect.

Many times when you run onto bear in the alders at close range they will stand up and look you over, the while they twist their nose and endeavor to get your scent. One not familiar with the big bear has little or no conception of their enormous strength. One day Al Ellinger, the guide and I had run the sea dory up on a high tide in Snug Harbor, up the river that flows down from the glacier on Mount Illiamna. We had located what appeared to be a good brownie high above us in a little park in the alders and Al and the guide went after him, while I maintained watch on the dory in the fast changing tide. Soon another bear came out in the park. He was plainly a boar and anxious to court the sow, who was feeding there. She would have nothing to do with him but I never saw a bear go through more comical antics trying to win her attention. Each time he approached too close she would give him a cuff and put him back in his place again. Then he would climb up to the top of that steep grassy park and sit down and watch her for all the world like a small boy.

Finally the sow left and the male started to graze. Bear bite the grass and crop it with a lift of the head just about like an old cow, and in fact at a distance they appear much like a grazing cow. Al and the guide finally made that awful climb, nearly straight up and through dense alders, until they were above the bear. He heard or saw them, however, and rose to his full height. Al took a quick snap shot at him through the alders but missed with his .375 Double. That bear then traversed that mountainside in far less time than it takes to type down a description of it, or so it seemed to me at the time. At the shot he simply dropped to all fours and took a flying leap twenty feet or more down the mountain into those ten-foot alders. Then, seemingly, he floated in the air, only to come down again in the tops of the alders, when he would kick with all four feet and again sail down the mountain. He was never completely out of sight, and the alders were a good ten feet high. Of course he was going down a very steep mountain and the alders smashed forward under his weight, but the fact remains he went down that mountain through such alders fully as fast as any race horse could travel on level ground. No other animal on earth could negotiate such terrain at such speed. He came down a half mile, then swung around to the left, crossing the tracks of Al and the guide, and was soon out of my sight around a shoulder of the mountain. I had a ringside seat and was watching through a Mossberg 20-power spotting scope while lying in the boat.

Next I located another big bear to the north, about a mile away, while waiting for Al and the guide to return. I had the boat anchored on a steep bank where the tide could drop and be hanged and the river still floated me. This bear was after some small animal under a huge boulder. He would first dig on one side, then rush around to the other side and dig there. The earth flew in great clods. Finally he tired of running from one side to the other of that big boulder imbedded in the steep slope, so he reared up and grappled it with both forepaws. He tugged and heaved for some time, finally jumping nimbly to one side as that huge rock, weighing tons, went crashing down the slope. Instantly some small animal darted up the slope above where the rock had been, but he was not quick enough. One huge paw flashed out and pinned him to the ground, then the big bear reached down with his nose and nibbled the animal out from under his paw. It may have been a big picket pin or a small whistler, as they call the rock chucks in that country. I saw both up there, so never knew which it was. At any rate this shows the prodigious strength of a grizzly and his speed when speed is necessary. That rock was much larger than the bear and would have weighed many times as much. It's almost unbelievable, the amount of rock and dirt they will move to get a choice morsel of food.

Al and Mary Ellinger each killed a couple of brownies and Frank Mosteller killed one on the trip, and each of us got a good black, but I killed only a worthless old male grizzly with a record skull that trailed us up and had to be killed. Just what weight the largest bear reach up there on the Peninsula and on Kodiak I do not know. Some that have been weighed did not go much over 1000 to 1200 pounds, but there are all types up there, big heavy bear and smaller leaner ones. The one I killed was poor and had been in an awful fight. He was just as big as a big horse and would have weighed at least 1200 pounds. Doc Reising was an old veterinarian and had handled stock all his life. Jim Simpson, the outfitter, had also worked with stock a lifetime and I had skinned several hundred horses and critters. It required the combined strength of four of us to turn that old brute over, after he had stiffened, so he must have gone our esti-mated 1200 pounds. The skin measured 10 feet 4 inches across the paws unstretched, just laid out on the boat deck, and 9 feet 8 inches from nose to tail, so squared 10 feet. It would easily have stretched a foot at least and probably more each way. The skull when fresh and before shrinking measured 17 inches long by 10 wide with all meat pared off.

I have traveled hard gravel bars with a pack on my back, which with my rifle made my total weight of well over 200 pounds, and when I jumped up in the air and came down with all my weight on one of my Number 6 boots I could not even make a dent in that gravel. Yet there were the tracks of a big grizzly, much larger tracks than mine and sinking down into the gravel a full two inches, and they were fresh. The spread of his hind feet covered easily twice as much surface as my foot, or more, yet he had sunk in two inches in that hard gravel bar, so he must have had at least 400 pounds weight on each foot. I believe some of them, like the huge old male that O'Dale and I watched one evening at Iniskin Bay, would, when fat, weigh at least 1800 pounds. The front paws of my bear before skinning measured exactly 10 inches in width.

In southeast Alaska you have different country to hunt, much more timber and heavy brush as well, and visibility is much less. There seems to be more fog and the mountains are so much more densely covered with alders and timber that you seldom see a bear at any great distance except across some bay or up some stream. Arthur Kinnan and I made a trip for bear there in '39 with H. N. Busick of Baltimore. We used Art's fine boat the *Vermarco*, of 56-foot length and 16-foot beam. It was truly a de luxe trip with all comforts possible, as we lived and stayed on the boat. Jim Allen of Petersburg did the guiding and knew his business, while I went along to help with skinning and packing out the hides. Busick had killed a small grizzly, but had to empty his .30–06 with 225-grain Peters belted loads finally to stop her. He then decided to try my .333 O.K.H. with 300-grain Duplex loads on his next bear. We had anchored near a cannery on one of the islands and Jim, Busick and I worked our way up a salmon stream. The humpies and dog salmon were running very heavy and the stream was simply choked with them in places. A squaw stood near a pool at the mouth of the stream, throwing a line with weight attached into a pool. She had a couple of big grab hooks attached and each time she jerked on the line after the weight had carried it to the bottom, she would haul out one or two flopping salmon.

We worked our way up a trail along the side of the stream looking for bear sign. After about three miles we found fresh salmon heads along the bank and some big bear tracks. It was a veritable jungle. Huge trees towered up and shut out the sunlight and the underbrush cut visibility to about 10 yards in the timber, and rarely could we see 50 yards by looking across the stream. Jim took the lead and Busick the center while I acted as rear guard. We tested the faint air movement constantly by holding up a wet finger. Just as we were crossing a small glade in the timber, I saw a big black grizzly wade out into the river about 20 to not over 30 yards to my left. I stopped and whistled softly through my teeth. Busick heard me and turned around, his eyes two question marks as I slipped the safety and trained my .400 bore double rifle on the bear's shoulder. I whispered the one word, "Shoot." Jim stopped and turned to see if we were following him close and saw the action, and he also stopped. Nick Busick slowly raised my old .333 O.K.H. Enfield and when his sights steadied on the grizzly's shoulder squeezed the trigger. He made a perfect shot and the 300-grain Soft Point shattered the near shoulder, removed the aorta and finally stopped in the right lung.

The big brute went down instantly on his nose in the river. A rope of blood squirted out full three feet from his shoulder each time his heart beat for several seconds. Only his ears wiggled after he fell and he was so big and heavy the river simply flowed around him. The entrance hole was a full inch in diameter. Busick was taking no chances and still remembered how his sow would go down, then bounce to her feet again, so he threw the bolt and socked the old boar again in the front of the shoulder, the bullet ranging into and breaking the spine. It was not needed, but did not hurt his huge old hide any. The fall season had only been open a couple of weeks and his pelt was very short, with little fur along the top of the spine. One front claw and toe had been bitten off in a fight or trap. He squared nine feet and was a jet-black grizzly, not even a trace of white hair showing on him any place.

Alaskan bear hunts should be planned long in advance. If you take on a hunt from a shore camp, then hire a guide who well knows his country, either southeast Alaska, Kodiak or the Peninsula. You will have more hardship on a shore camp, but the right guide will take you back far enough to obtain a really good specimen of the big bear. You can expect hard work and plenty of it, but if you do secure a real big bear with good pelt, you have a trophy well worth the cost and the work. By such trips you can get back beyond the usual range of boat hunters and have a better chance for an outstanding trophy, but it will be a rugged trip.

If you decide on a boat trip and to hunt from the boat, then you can have every convenience and by moving from bay to bay have a reasonably good chance of a fine bear. My old partner, Arthur H. Kinnan, still operates up there, as do many other competent Alaskan outfitters, and good guides for the more northern hunting can be secured at Seward and Anchorage. It's a vast country and there are still plenty of places to go where you will find plenty of good hunting.

VIII

White-tailed Deer

ALTHOUGH there are many subspecies of both mule deer and white-tailed deer on this continent, deer occurring from Mexico north to Alaska may be divided into four general species. These are the small Sitkan deer of Alaska, *Odocoileus hemionus sitkensis* (Merriam), which occurs from the region of Juneau, Alaska, south to the mouth of the Stikine River in British Columbia. The Columbian blacktail, *Odocoileus hemionus columbianus* (Richardson), inhabits the heavily timbered coastal ranges from central British Columbia south into central California. Then there is the big mule deer with its many closely related subspecies, *Odocoileus hemionus*, which inhabits the western part of this continent, west of the Divide from southeastern Alaska south to Lower California and Tiburon Island in the Gulf of California and east of the Continental Divide, from Alberta to northern Mexico. Formerly this big deer extended east as far as Manitoba, Minnesota and the Dakotas, but is probably extinct over much of that range today. The whitetail and its many related species, *Odocoileus virginianus virginianus* (Zimmerman), inhabits the whole eastern part of the United States and southern Canada. It also extends west along the Canadian border and through Minnesota, Montana, Idaho, Washington, Oregon and California, as well as Colorado, Wyoming and some other adjoining states. Whitetail, in their various species and variations, also inhabit the Southern states, from the East Coast west to the Pacific, and to the Ozarks of Missouri and Oklahoma. It is by far the most widely spread species of American deer. Subspecies also range south through Mexico and Central America and into South America. A great deal of space would be needed even to classify the various whitetail as well as mule deer subspecies.

One subspecies of the whitetail is worth mentioning separately, and that is the little fantail. Formerly it occurred in Montana over the Continental Divide from the head of the Blackfoot River, and north of Helena, and also on the North Fork of the Blackfoot northeast of Ovando, Montana. I do not know whether any still exist there or not, but they were quite plentiful prior to 1919–1920. This tiny deer may or may not be related to *Odocoileus couesi* (Coues & Yarrow), but it is similar in size. I have seen tracks that resembled fantail tracks on the Lochsa, and have been told there were still some of these tiny deer there, but have never been able to verify it.

This is the smallest deer on the continent to my knowledge, and the tiny fantails that used to inhabit the Blackfoot country in Montana when I was a young lad may be an entirely different subspecies of the whitetail. Certain it is they were a whitetail and about the prettiest, sauciest little beast imaginable. Old bucks with five to seven points on each antler and their toes worn round with age would dress out about 60 to 80 pounds, and the does would dress about half that weight. Their tracks, in size, were but little larger than whitetail fawn tracks, a month or two after birth.

All descriptions I have read of the Coues deer indicate that they are similar, yet all pictures I have seen of the Coues show a much larger deer, with much larger and wider, as well as longer, antlers. These little deer were well known in that locality around 1917 to 1919. It may be they are still there, or the hard winter of 1919–1920 may have killed them off. Have often wished I had then taken the time to get a good specimen for my collection.

The Coues or regular fantail is similar in many respects, having a large tail for its size and being the smallest of the recorded whitetail. It is also a brush deer, yet is known only in New Mexico, Arizona and south into Chihuahua and Sonora. If I ever get back to that country in Montana, I will see if a specimen head or skull, or any of the tiny beasts, still exist, that can be sent in to the museum for classification, to determine if they are similar to the Coues deer or are a separate species.

The Alaskan Sitka deer is a larger animal than the Columbian blacktail and differs also in coloration. Though I have never hunted them, I have seen them many times when hunting bear in southeast Alaska and also examined many that were hung up by hunters. They are a very reddish colored deer, almost cinnamon. The tail is the same color as the back for two thirds of its length, only the tip being black. They are small deer and in some ways greatly resemble the whitetail. The heads resemble whitetail heads with long brow points and the main beam curving sharply forward, with heavy short points. They are more numerous on the islands of southeast Alaska than on much of the mainland and are more of a coastal island deer than a mainland animal. Large bucks will probably dress out about 125 pounds. Hard winters and wolves almost exterminate these small coast deer every so often. Hunting them is very similar to whitetail hunting, which we shall cover in more detail. The old sourdoughs up in Alaska call them by rubbing a blade of grass between the palms of their hands and thus emitting a sort of bleating sound, not very loud. They can be called in this manner for some distance. The southern extent of their range no doubt causes some interbreeding with the Columbian blacktail.

From central British Columbia and Queen Charlotte Islands south into central California occurs the true Columbian blacktail. It is a smaller deer than the Sitka deer and has a long bushy tail entirely black on the top or back of tail and entirely white underneath. This is also a brush and timber deer and is found in this thickest, most impregnable jungle imaginable. It is much darker in color than the Sitka. The winter coat is a dark brownish gray, with darker hair along the top of the spine. The face and brisket run very dark brown, with some black, the outer sides of the legs being more of a tan. The inside of legs and belly are white, as well as the underside of the tail. The horns of this deer are small and to my notion do not make much of a trophy, seldom having brow points, and the usual head is simply a main beam on each side, ending in a couple of points. There are of course many variations, as with all deer, but in the main the Columbian blacktail is a meat, not a trophy, animal. The ears are shorter, but almost as wide in proportion to the size of the deer as the big mule deer's and are larger than the whitetail's. Its range extends eastward through the Sierra Nevada and the Cascades and I have heard some sportsmen tell of seeing them almost as far east as Missoula, Montana, but have seen no single specimen of the species that far east myself. It is also said to intergrade with the mule deer in parts of California, but I have been unable to prove this and have never seen any specimen in either Idaho or Montana that indicated it was mixed with Columbia blacktail. The blacktail carries his big fluffy tail high, just as the whitetail, the Sitka deer and the tiny fantail when jumped, but the mule deer carries his down when running. Hunting the blacktail is so similar to whitetail hunting that it will be covered in the part of this chapter on whitetails, as will the Sitka deer and the tiny fantail.

The whitetail is the largest by far of all the timber deer. Like the Sitka deer and the blacktail, it inhabits the timbered sections of this country. The whitetail much prefers the timbered and brushy river bottoms and swamps and any heavily forested area, even close to civilization, but almost never is seen in the high open country that is preferred by the big mule deer. The whitetail is a skulker, preferring to sneak about in the dense

timber, the year round. Different type localities of these deer vary somewhat in color, but in general they are a beautiful reddish tan or brown,
have small ears in proportion to those of mule deer and very long, beautiful tails, with the sides and bottom snow white, and the extreme top the
same reddish brown as the back. In northern United States, east of the
Mississippi, they often run nearly as large as mule deer and many specimens have been weighed, hog dressed, that went 350 pounds and some
over that weight. Probably the average of large full-grown bucks would
run nearer 200 pounds hog dressed than over that figure. As with other
game, considerable time is required to grow a really big buck deer.

When jumped, whitetail often whistle at the hunter and throw the long
tail up in the air to its full extent each time they blow or whistle; they
also wave it when they run and carry it high at all times when startled.
There are of course exceptions to all rules and I once shot one that was
carrying his tail low when hit, but immediately elevated it as he ran past
us until he fell from the heart shot.

The whitetail inhabits much the same range as the mule deer over the
West, with these variations. While the big mule deer runs the high mountains and the ridges, the whitetail will be found, as a rule, lower in the
heavier timber and densely forested river bottoms. I have, however, seen
whitetails at high elevations, and one fall when we were camped on Little
Clear Water, a branch of the Selway, I loaned my .405 Winchester
to Swan Odegard for the day, as I was laid up with a foot injury from
sheep hunting. Late that evening I decided to hobble up the hill a short
distance and see if I could hear the pack string. We were camped about
two miles down from the Divide, between the Salmon and Selway Rivers.
The snow was over a foot deep and wet and heavy. On coming to the edge
of a little park, I stopped, as usual, to look it all over before moving out
into sight. Instantly I saw an old whitetail doe, followed by three fawns,
come out on the other side of the park. They crossed the park and went
on into the timber, heading down to their winter range on the Selway.
These deer may well have come over the Divide from the Salmon drainage. Soon Swan appeared, sneaking along right on their track, with the
old .405 shoved ahead, ready for a shot. I could tell by the actions of the
doe, though she never saw me, that she was being followed, so waited,
thinking that a whitetail buck would make his appearance. As Swan approached, I whistled and he soon located me. Instantly I saw the muzzle
of my .405 was caked full of snow and frozen hard and Swan knew nothing of it. It was a very lucky thing, both for him and for my rifle, that

The author, Dr. Reising and guide Ed Lovedahl with record Alaskan grizzly bear killed by author at 12 feet with .35 Whelen 275 grain. Author's largest bear; skin 10 feet 4 inches across the shoulders by 9 feet 8 inches from tail tip to tip of nose

Courtesy A. E. Ellinger

Mary Ellinger with her Alaskan brown bear killed with .375 Hoffman Magnum

Courtesy Don S. Hopkins

Record Alaskan brown bear squaring 10½ feet killed by D. S. Hopkins on Kodiak Island, 1941, with a .333 O.K.H. and 300 grain

Whitetails

he did not get a shot, as the barrel would surely have been blown off as far back as that snow and ice sealed the bore.

Whitetail are much harder to see in the timber than mule deer. The rump is completely reddish brown except for the sides of the tail, and whitetail have not that big white patch so peculiar to elk, mule deer and sheep that so often discloses their presence. This tail is also amply long to cover all the hind underparts of the deer, when he is not alarmed, and it is surprising how well that reddish-brown coat will blend with practically any timber foliage.

Hunting a whitetail calls for the very utmost care in still-hunting. He will almost always be found in dense timber, or brush, the same as elk that have been hard hunted, and for my money elk and whitetails that have been hard hunted are about the toughest still-hunting proposition we have, with the exception of black bear and cougar. To be successful, you must study your game — know where that particular buck usually feeds and when and where he prefers to bed; the direction of the prevailing air currents — then try to circumvent him. He will give you your money's worth at any and all times. Where whitetail are plentiful, the best method I have found to hunt them is to get out at daylight and again in the late evening after sundown and carefully skirt the edges of the little parks and wet meadows in the timber, spending a good part of your time seated, with your back to a tree and where you can watch. They will come out to feed and give you an excellent shot, and more will be taken this way than will be the case when the average city hunter attempts to match his wits and senses with the whitetail. They have excellent eyesight and their nose and ears are second to none of the deer tribe, unless it be elk. Many times I have run onto whitetail when carefully still-hunting for elk and on elk tracks, as I circled trying to cut in on them. Sometimes those whitetails have bounced out of their beds and whistled, and each time they whistled thrown that beautiful flag up and down, then departed with a tail wave of good-by. At other times I have caught them in their beds watching me, and have seen them slowly, almost imperceptibly, pull their heads even lower until their nose lay right on the ground in an effort to avoid detection, and they lay perfectly still until I had gone on past their beds. Sometimes they then rose slowly to their feet and skulked silently away, while at other times they stayed hidden in their bed until I was out of sight. I did not want them, being after larger game, and even in deer I preferred a big, fat, prime mule buck for my meat.

If the ground has a frozen crust, or crusted snow, or the wind is wrong for the particular section you wish to hunt, then you might just as well stay in camp as try for whitetail. You have an even better chance in camp for that matter, as you may see one traveling by. It is imperative that you hunt when the deer are feeding, for even though they feed very quietly, they do make some noise, but once they are bedded in the timber, I doubt seriously if a man is ever able to slip up on very many of them, without their first hearing his approach. I have never caught one asleep in his bed, but have seen many other animals asleep in their beds. If they think you will go on by them they may lie quietly, with head pulled down low on the ground, and simply wait until you go by, but if you once look directly toward them, they will be out of their beds and going in a flash and will wave you a good-by with that long tail. Their habit of whistling and jerking their tail upright and waving it gives away many a whitetail that would otherwise slip out unnoticed by the hunter.

The summer of 1920, I handled a pack string for the U.S. General Land Office Survey, first packing out of Ovando over into the South Fork of the Flathead and later packing from the Gordon ranch on Swan River, around Holland Lake, over the Divide and down to the Big Salmon Lake on the South Fork. I had ample opportunity to study whitetails a great deal that summer and fall. The Swan River was alive with them and there were a great many also in the South Fork. Early in the morning while hunting my horses, they would be plentiful around the little wet meadows and lakes, but during the day they would usually bed in some thicket adjacent to their feed grounds; then again in the late evening and on moonlight nights they would be out. One day I had missed my horses and as a last resort decided to look in a big fly shed on the Gordon ranch. When I poked my head around the narrow opening, some ten head of whitetails began whistling and flashing out past me, through the narrow opening. I pulled off my old Stetson and slapped one big buck across the rump as he flashed past. Instantly he lashed out at me with both heels, grazing my shirt under my outstretched arm. Needless to say I gave the rest of the band plenty of room to get out of that fly shed.

One fall I had camped on the Montour River north of Ovanda, intending to hunt elk, but first wanting to kill a good whitetail. I had located a good one and spent several days industriously trailing him around in about ten acres of thick timber, never getting more than a glimpse of his white flag as he waved me good-by. Finally, I decided to heck with him, I would pack up and go on into the hills after elk and kill a big mule buck for my deer.

With this thought in mind, I rose at daybreak and, taking a halter and my old Springfield, went out for my horses, intending to lead them in and saddle them before cooking breakfast. For some reason, they had fed farther away from camp than usual during the night, so I was working slowly upwind to a big park where I thought they might stop. As I approached, there stood my particular whitetail buck feeding in the park. One glance at his head with one deformed horn and I knew him for the same buck I had hunted so hard for several days. He did not see me and was about 60 yards away. The wind was in my favor so I slowly raised the old Springfield and slipped him a 220-grain Soft Nose in the right flank, ranging forward and out the chest, in front of the off shoulder, right through the heart. He simply jumped into a hard run as I worked the bolt, and flashed into the timber with his tail clamped hard down. I picked an opening and waited, and as his nose showed through it I fired again, holding well in front of his nose and lower, as he ran quartering away from me, as if the devil was after him. After the shot I saw no more of him, so circled and could not find his tracks leading away in the soft snow. I went back to where I had seen him when I shot and there he had hit the ground in a ball and rolled under some fir boughs.

My second shot had caught him about two inches from the first bullet hole and come out behind the off, or left, shoulder. He was a fat, beautiful specimen with one crooked deformed horn that I had marked when I first jumped him, several days before. The first slug had removed the top of the heart and the second was not needed, but I did not know it at the time.

More people hunt whitetails each year than any other deer, just as more people hunt deer as a group than any other species of our big game. The whitetail is a very intelligent beast and quite willing to match wits with you at any time. He will not line out across the country and leave, as will an elk or a moose, but if he can find good cover will simply circle around within a few miles or a few hundred yards and play hide-and-seek with you all day. Many times I have trailed them all day and never left one mountainside. They would simply circle and double back on their tracks, then jump off, usually over some high windfall or clump of brush, or down over a low cliff, in an effort to throw me off their trail. Even though I never stayed on the trail itself, but always circled to windward, they knew I was after them. They have a superlatively developed sixth sense in addition to all their other faculties. Several times I have trailed hunting cougar and seen where these wily deer had even outwitted the super-stalker of them all. Usually, if a whitetail is jumped in thick timber and starts circling, it is best to trail him only far enough to give him the idea you are after him, then backtrack until you locate some open place in the timber that will allow vision for some distance. Sit down on a stump or log where you have good cover, and in the course of an hour or even less your whitetail is apt to be along. You will have to watch with all senses fully alert or he will slip up on you and be in plain sight before you see him.

Having spent all day, many times, trailing them around in circles in dense fir timber, as well as stands of cedar, I have often noted this tendency to circle and finally found I could take advantage of it. When two hunters are working together, they can do even better, as they can travel on until a fair open space of reasonably good visibility in the timber occurs, then one hunter can drop out to windward of the trail and post himself where he will be out of sight, usually with his back to a tree, or stump, and wait. The other hunter can continue to trail the whitetail, until he dogs him around. This is, however, a job for experienced careful hunters, who know what they are shooting at before they shoot, and I would not care to so hunt whitetails with anyone I did not know well — his ability in the hills as well as his temperament. Any excitable fool may plug you for a deer, though the deer will be in sight first, as a rule, with this procedure. A whitetail buck can slip up on you unnoticed, unless you are a careful observer and have good game eyes that constantly sweep the surrounding terrain. A casual glance now and then will not do, as deer blend well with their surroundings.

Wary old whitetail bucks will practically always bed where they have excellent cover and in a place that usually allows them several exits in different directions, if hunters disturb them. Once they find such a bed ground to their liking and advantage they hate to give it up and will often come back and bed in, or near, the same place, day after day. I have known of old whitetails to be hunted for days in one small section of timber and doubt if they ever left it, or traveled more than a mile or two from it, at any time. Simply dogging them around produced no results for the hunter, as they were easily able to keep just out of sight. In other sections of the country they will line out and go a mile or two away when jumped. They usually have trails over which they like to travel and one should know where these crossings are.

If you get out at daylight and know of a crossing between bed and feed grounds, then nothing could be better than to slip quietly to windward of this trail and watch. The deer will be headed back for the bed ground shortly after daylight. I have even known old hunters to jump a wary old whitetail buck, take after him as fast as they could, trail him for a short distance, then quietly slip back and locate a good hideout in sight of his bed, and from this vantage point kill that buck within two hours. Sometimes whitetail will travel nearly all day before coming back to their bed ground, especially some of the big eastern whitetails, and if noisy conditions of snow, or frosted ground, tell them you are following them.

One can usually slip along old wood roads and do far better than by going through the noisy brush, and if you move carefully along such old roads in early morning and late evening, you will very often see more deer than if you hunted the timber religiously all day. They love old deserted orchards and are very fond of fruit, also old berry patches and slashings, and in parts of the East, as well as Utah, New Mexico and Arizona, they feed a great deal on acorns along the oak-covered ridges. In all big game hunting, one of the first and most important things to learn is what your game is feeding on and when it does this feeding, then the battle is half over. Remember the whitetail can smell you easily, many times as far as you can see him in the timber, so it is utterly useless ever to hunt downwind. Once you locate his feed grounds you have an excellent chance to surprise him while feeding, and deer are never as alert when feeding as when bedded. For some reason they seem much more wary and hard to approach during a storm, or hard wind, than when the weather is still and quiet. There are then so many forest noises and the deer are so busy evaluating them, on the chance of some of them being the approach of an enemy, that they are very nervous, wary and hard to approach. In still quiet weather they can hear and usually recognize any sound in the forest, but not so during a windstorm. When you consider the wonderful sense of sight, smell and hearing of the whitetail, combined with his red coat that blends perfectly with frost-struck leaves of maple, aspen and about all bushes, it's no wonder they are hard to see and obtain. Often I have found whitetails bedded in a frost-colored clump of brush, where the red of the leaves blended perfectly with their reddish coats. I have surprised mule deer asleep, also most other game species, but what whitetail I have surprised in their beds had already seen or heard me and were watching my every move.

If a strong cold wind is blowing, they will usually bed in the lee of some ridge. They particularly like to bed against some fallen log, or among the tangled roots of an uprooted tree. Their beds are nearly always well selected, with regard to background and cover, both to hide them from enemies and also to afford cover, while sneaking out from their beds. Deer that have not been hunted much are more prone to bounce out of their beds and flash their white flags than those that have been hard hunted. The latter will very often slip out of their beds without a sound and sneak off until they feel they are safe, before raising their flag, whistling and departing.

During the rut, which usually occurs during November in the northern range but may be much later in the south, the bucks are more easily hunted. At this time they travel around a lot, in search of the does, and are more apt to be caught out in early morning, or late evening along some meadow, lake or slashing, or old wood road. They will hide and thrive in close proximity to civilization. All they ask is plenty of food and cover and it doesn't matter if a train goes by daily or more often, or if a highway is close by, they will do all right so long as they have food and plenty of cover for protection.

If you are trailing whitetail on snow, and the deer start circling and stop feeding, then you can be sure they are searching for a suitable bed ground and usually it will be to windward of the back trail. Whitetail have regular trails, to and from their bed and feed grounds, and travel regular routes, far more than deer of other species. They also yard up in deep snow in the winter and beat out regular trails.

Though they may at times do unpredictable things, especially during the rut, as a general rule they are very wise and hard to outwit to obtain a chance for a successful shot — more so than any other of the deer on this continent. During the rut, old bucks may travel for miles in search of does, but at other times their range is usually very small and seldom encompasses more than a few miles of heavy timber land.

In eastern Canada a great many are taken annually by paddling silently along the streams and lakes in very early morning or late evening. Formerly they were taken by jacking as well, which is certainly a very unsporting way to kill any animal of the deer tribe. In sections where the timberlands are almost crisscrossed by winding streams and lakes, the canoe or light boat offers one of the best methods of hunting whitetail, as you can then move along almost silently and in late evening, or early morning, have an excellent chance of a good shot. Regardless of how long you hunt whitetail and how much you think you know of them, you will find individual bucks which will fool you, and which will not act according to Hoyle. They are individuals, very intelligent, and reason just as Homo sapiens, often to better advantage. In still-hunting whitetail, one should move only a few steps, then spend considerable time looking over every possible likely cover before moving again. It is slow tedious work, but you must remember that if the buck is bedded, he has every chance of hearing your approach if you make the slightest sound, and then lying quietly until you come in sight or he has made up his mind as to your identity. You must learn to discern a horn, or even an ear, or the white-edged tail, and especially the nose and eyes and alert ears, even when they are partly obscured by limbs, leaves or brush.

When the deer sees and hears you, he may sneak quietly away without a sound, or he may bounce out of his bed with flag waving and depart. Quite often deer will stop, if they have not been hunted, and whistle at you, and at each whistle the flag will be flipped up and down. Very often you can spot them by this white flag when otherwise you would never see them. At such times it is usually very hard to see them in their entirety, but quite often you may see the head or the rump and tail, enough in order to know how they are turned and where to hold, to place a slug in the vitals. Don't expect the pretty picture-book shots at them, for they will be few and far between, except around lakes and streams, meadows or old wood roads or clearings. In the timber you must learn to recognize any part of them and where to hold for a killing hit.

The bucks are invariably the most wary. They will investigate every clearing or road before crossing, usually while standing out of sight behind some screen of brush or trees. Often I have seen them standing in dense fir timber, with head thrust down near the ground so they could look under the low hanging bows of small fir trees and spot you or your legs, while a man standing erect would see nothing of them. This is just another reason why it is well to sit down while waiting for them, if such timber is prevalent. Bedded deer are usually hidden completely, except for the nose and eyes and sometimes the whole head, but often limbs will obscure all but the nose and eyes. They are very clever about selecting such a bed ground, and while an old mule deer will bed by the root of a big yellow pine, with rump clearly visible on one side and the head and neck on the other, you will very, very seldom find a whitetail bedded in any such conspicuous manner. It you do see one, freeze absolutely motionless, and when you raise your rifle take several minutes if necessary to bring it to your shoulder, as any quick movement on your part will stampede the deer out of his bed. If you see one and your head is not turned fully toward him, then do not look directly toward him at all, until the rifle is up, and then move your head very slowly if it is necessary to do so. The least movement, or the quick flash of your eyes, will tell him all he wants to know, and deer can tell the instant you see them, as a rule, unless you so camouflage your actions. Remember that sixth sense, they have it developed to a very high degree, like the coyote and cougar.

Usually during the rut you will see the does and fawns long before you sight the buck. The former will often walk out across openings, but not the bucks — they will hang back in a fringe of cover and watch the proceedings to see that nothing startles the does, before showing themselves. Like the Alaskan Sitka deer and the blacktail, whitetails can be called by experienced hunters who can imitate their bleat or use a blade of grass between the palms of their hands to make the call. I have never mastered the art, so cannot properly describe its use. Eastern hunters also bleat to stop jumped whitetail.

In the deep South where the deer country is largely swamps and very dense, hounds are used, and this is about the only sure way of obtaining whitetail in those sections. That prince of sportsmen, Archibald Rutledge, has written many fine accounts of such whitetail hunting. Drives are organized and the hunters stationed on stands at regular deer trails, while the Negroes and the hounds proceed to drive certain swamps. Shotguns are used altogether, and while this may not sound sporting to the uninitiated, fewer deer escape wounded than most people suppose, and I doubt if a fraction of the deer are ever wounded and lost when good hounds are used that are lost in regular whitetail hunting in the North, where a great many animals are wounded each year with rifles and lost. When good hounds are used, a wounded deer has relatively little chance of ever escaping, for once he leaves a blood trail, the hounds will follow him indefinitely, until he is finally brought to bay. I would not think such a deer, that had been run until he was hot, would be fit to eat, but I do seriously doubt if many ever escape wounded. Owing to the very nature of the dense semitropical jungle and the close proximity of the stands, shotguns with buckshot are invariably used as a safety factor. When heavy bore shotguns are used and a good buck load fitted to that certain choke, they are very effective, but anyone so hunting whitetail should carefully pattern his particular gun until he has found, or loaded, a buckshot load that will give good patterns and a certain killing range of 50 yards. I have tested thousands of shotguns with buckshot. In fact I tested 5000 in one lot at Ogden arsenal for Uncle Sam during the war and it was surprising how few threw a pattern that would have been effective, even at 40 yards. Some few guns, however, threw killing patterns to 60 yards, with all shot in a very small circle. I have an Ithaca Magnum ten bore with which Major Charles Askins, Sr., obtained 100 per cent patterns with a 20 buck load in a 24-inch circle at 40 yards, but when I tried a later loading with 15 buck to the charge, they would not stay on a 40-inch square of paper at 40 yards and would have been worthless as a deer load. So it is imperative that you select a load, or load one yourself, that fits the choke.

I believe it is also well to remove the top wad and pour melted tallow over the buckshot and allow to harden, then replace the wad. Another good system is to remove the shot and cut into each, then insert a string cord or light copper wire and space the shot along this string or wire and close the cut over it tightly. This will limit the spread of your load and you can then be reasonably sure of making a killing hit at 50 yards. If such precautions are used with double guns and those repeating guns which have a choke device can be regulated to give good patterns, then very few deer will escape, when driven by hounds, if the shots are taken within effective range.

In the North many hunters organize into large parties and conduct huge drives. Part of the party is stationed on runways, while the rest proceeds to drive a certain basin or swamp. I do not think much of this way of hunting whitetail, for while it does give some of the party a chance to kill an animal that they do not possess enough woods skill ever to outwit in fair still-hunting, it certainly is not a very sporting thing to do. I saw nine men line up here, two years ago, about a quarter mile apart and drive this rugged mountain terrain. They shot up everything they jumped, both bear and deer, and eventually killed their limit and then some, but game will not long last in any section if so hunted, and personally I would like to see such hunting abolished, except possibly in some swamp areas of the East where it is about the only feasible method. Many hunters are also killed by this method of hunting each fall, and it has also been the direct cause of rifles being prohibited by law for use on deer in some states.

The buck law helps somewhat in preventing hunters being shot for deer, but aside from this one mighty good thing, the safety factor, we do not believe in buck laws. In most states where the buck law has long been in effect the bucks deteriorate, and degenerate, until a good head is a very rare thing. Better by far to hunt both does and bucks as well as fawns, let them kill a deer, any kind they want, and quit. Wherever the buck law is in effect they will shoot does and leave them anyway. If bucks alone are killed, then there are often not enough bucks for the number of does and they are badly run down by the end of the season so that many does will go through a year without fawns while many others will have weak fawns. Then to top it off many of those bucks will die in March and April. Soon the vicious circle catches up with the deer herd and we have a surplus of dry does and not enough bucks left. We have seen it tried and do not believe the buck law is the answer. You need all those fine bucks so they will fight for supremacy and only the strongest, finest of them all will propagate the species, and when man kills out a great many bucks, leaving a surplus of does, he destroys the balance of nature and soon he will have no bucks whatever, with worth-while heads. It is much better to hunt deer; then whenever they show much of a decrease it is best to close the season, or shorten it, rather than set up the buck law.

A proper balance between winter range and the number of deer must be maintained, or excessive winter loss will occur. While in the West the coyotes and eagles, as well as cougar, kill a lot of deer annually, the East does not have the predators and the deer must be kept within numerical bounds by hunting. For this reason we believe the East would have better deer, with bucks having larger heads, and the deer on the average would run to larger size, if the buck law was abolished. I know I am treading on controversial ground in these statements, but having seen what the buck law has done in both Montana and Oregon, I am willing to take my hat off to the Idaho game officials who have as yet maintained an open season on both sexes of deer, elk and goat. The argument that less hunters will be shot for deer is not very conclusive, when you find does shot and left behind. Even in this country I have found where men, not sportsmen or hunters, but rather human jackals, had killed and dressed does as well as elk, then gone on hunting and killed other deer or elk and never come back to their first kills, leaving them to lie and rot. Such men are not entitled to be called hunters and really should be prosecuted to the full extent of the law; then some added punishment for good measure, such as flogging, should be administered. I have no use for any man, regardless of his station in life, who will wantonly kill big game and leave it, or who will kill one animal, then when he finds a finer specimen kill it also and throw the first away. I have seen many do this, but when I was guiding them they took out all meat of the first animal they shot.

It's surprising what the excitement of game killing does to otherwise normal persons, some of whom lose all self-respect and decency and revert to the primitive. I notice there seem to be just as many people shot for deer in states with a buck law as in states allowing the killing of both sexes, and any man who will shoot at a flash in the brush, or the sound of something, should be hung by his sling strap to the first tree available. He has no place in the hills and the world would be far better off without him.

The whitetail is a browser and eats far more browse than do mule deer. Almost anything in the browse line is acceptable, and in the winter they will even eat fir and cedar needles. Young cedar seems to be quite welcome at all times. In any acorn country, they eat great quantities of acorns and will be found along these scrub oak ridges. This feeding on acorns imparts a peculiar flavor to the meat. Some hunters prefer it, but we prefer the flavor of a big Idaho mule deer to that of any acorn-fed deer.

Whitetail hunting is about 95 per cent timber hunting and usually close range shooting. At times you will get long shots, across valleys, rivers, lakes or meadows, but in the main, more shots will be obtained at close than at long range. My friend Byron E. Cottrell of Pennsylvania often gets extremely long range shooting in his section of that state and employs long range rifles for the purpose. His hunting of whitetail is then more like mule deer hunting. My own experience has shown only close range shooting and for this reason I prefer a fairly large caliber, with long heavy bullets, for all my whitetail hunting. Further I prefer a fine double-barreled hammerless ejector, or a lever action, to a bolt action for such close range timber shooting. Both types of rifles have faster safeties and are quicker to get into action than the bolt gun. Further they are faster for running shooting. With the double rifle you have two shots at your instant disposal and with the lever action you have very fast repeat shots as needed. Right now I have three rifles here that suit me perfectly for timber whitetail hunting. One is a Lancaster double rifle for the .375 Nitro Express load, throwing a 300-grain bullet at about 2300 feet. Another is a little 7-pound double-barrel hammerless ejector for the .35 Winchester Model '95 cartridge and the third is a fine custom stocked Model '86 Winchester featherweight .45-70, with 22-inch nickel steel barrel, custom stock and single set trigger. I prefer any of these three rifles with their comparatively low velocity and large caliber heavy bullets to any and all high velocity rifles, for such shooting. They will all three wade through a lot of brush, leave a good blood trail, and are all excellent, certain killers. With the 405-grain Soft Point load in the .45-70, it is very hard to find a better close range timber gun and this rifle is within reach of all, while the fine doubles are very expensive, though the finest tools made for timber hunting. High velocity, while necessary for open country shooting and long range work, is a farce and a delusion in the timber and only results in blowing up your bullets on every twig or limb they strike. You want a heavy, preferably large caliber, slug for the brush. Other calibers I particularly like in the timber for whitetail are the .38-55-255, the .35 Remington 200 grain, the .33 Winchester 200 grain, .348-250, .30-40 and .06 in 220 grain and the 8 mm. with 236 grain. Smaller calibers like the 6.5 mm. and the 7 mm. with 160- and 175-grain bullets are also excellent if planted right, but they do not leave as good a blood trail as the larger calibers, and when you are hunting whitetails without snow on the ground, you desperately need a good blood trail.

High velocity small bore bullets either blow up on brush, before reaching the deer, or go into the deer and blow up, leaving no blood trail, and if the animal is not dropped in its tracks it very often is lost wounded. For the small Columbian blacktail and the Sitka deer of Alaska, which are both hunted in the same dense timber as the common whitetail, the same large caliber low velocity loads are advisable, but not necessary. These deer are much smaller and the .38–55 and .30–30–170 loads are excellent for them. Short rifles are much handier in the brush than longer arms and the double rifle gives one a very short weapon, for relative barrel length, shorter than any of the repeaters. This is also true of the good Farquharson and Winchester single shot rifles. Both are excellent in suitable calibers, but you must place that one shot, or not shoot. The little Remington 141 Model in .35 caliber and the Savage Model '99 in .303 and .300 caliber are both excellent and very fast for running shooting.

In Eastern states, where the use of the rifle is prohibited, we would prefer the rifle slug load to buckshot and would mount a Weaver IX shotgun scope on the 12-bore shotgun for such hunting.

IX

Mule Deer

THE mule deer are the largest and finest of all American deer. While they vary considerably in size and coloration in different localities, the finest and largest mule bucks no doubt are found in Colorado, Wyoming, Idaho, Montana and Alberta. In good virgin mule deer sections of these states, where the deer have unlimited low elevation winter range, they attain great size. Right here on the Salmon River probably occur some of the largest specimens of the species and I killed one old chap that weighed dressed, without feet or entrails or any innards, an even 400 pounds, cut in two sections. One killed by Pug Buster was even larger and heavier. In Montana I saw one killed by Judd and hung up and weighed on the Helena Meat Market scales that went 360 pounds dressed, but that was very large for that section. Here a 300-pound mule buck is not un-common, and many will go 350 or over. However, for every such huge old buck, you will find plenty of smaller ones. On the Middle Fork of the Salmon where the deer are too thick and not enough winter range, they are usually much smaller and more degenerated. While out with the Zane Grey party in 1931, I counted 1000 mule deer, from daylight in the morning when I went after the pack string, until two o'clock in the after-noon, when I stopped counting at Loon Creek. We were camped on White's Creek that morning and I started counting deer while hunting and gathering in the horses. They were everywhere and almost as thick as desert jack rabbits used to be. I saw several pairs of bucks fighting that morning, but in the 1000 deer I did not see a single exceptional head, or a single buck that would have dressed over 250 pounds. They are too thick in that section, and many years of scarce winter forage have caused them to degenerate and become smaller, just as in the Kaibab forest of Utah.

Here on the North Fork of the Salmon and down the main Salmon River, as well as the Selway River, the mule deer have ample winter range in normal years and can drop down to low elevations in the sagebrush. The result is some exceptionally large deer and some of the finest heads as well.

The mineral content of the water, however, has something to do with horn growth, and Colorado seems to have a corner on producing the greatest horn growth of all the states. I have seen a few very heavy record heads in this country and plenty of them are brought in each fall that would go well up in the records for the species, but the fine heads are usually killed by someone who does not appreciate them, with the result that he chops off the skull plate and nails it on the barn.

Except during the hunting season we have mule deer here on the ranch the year round. The does come down to have their fawns in the brush and feed in my hay meadow each summer, in fact they stay right here in the creek bottom until about two weeks before hunting season, when they seem to know it is time to pull out for the hills. Small spikes and two-pointers also summer at low elevations, but the old big bucks climb back along the Divide, just as high as they can find good feed. They like to summer up there where the wind will keep the flies away and where they have fine open and partly timbered country in which to grow their huge horns. The rut usually occurs here from the first to the tenth of November and extends through that month. Some years it may start as early as the twenty-fifth of October. For mule deer, as for whitetail, a few good hard early freezes and plenty of frosty nights will usher in the rutting moon. Each spring the bucks migrate upward to the highest slopes and in the fall they work down, during late October and November, toward their winter range. We usually have from twenty-five to fifty head in sight of the house every day during the winter, but from the fifth of October to the tenth of November they will usually be conspicuous by their absence. Now that I am writing this book, I usually get up at five o'clock in the morning and do most of my writing before breakfast, and nearly every morning I see mule does in the hay meadow, or licking salt by the garage. Having lived most of my life among the mule deer, I have had unlimited opportunities to study them at first hand.

In the spring and summer they are far more of a grazing than a browsing animal. While they will eat some browse at all times, they also eat a lot of bunch grass and curly buffalo grass as well as many other grasses. The old does also like the clover in the hay meadow. Right now they have their fawns in the brush, but are still keeping them more or less hidden, but by next month, August, they will appear in the meadow with the fawns. The fawns are usually born in May, and by hunting season will weigh from 40 to 60 pounds, buck fawns sometimes more. They are spotted at birth like the whitetail and elk, but soon lose the spots, so that by late August the spots are gone, then in September they start to turn blue gray. In color the mule deer is a beautiful glossy gray, shading to black on the brisket and white under the belly. The front of the neck also shades darker and has a white patch directly below the chin. The face is well marked with a dark brown or almost black patch in the forehead and white on the nose and lighter gray on the sides of the cheeks. The tip of the nose has a black strip and also one around the nostril. On each side of the under jaw well back toward the corner of the mouth is another small black spot. The chin is white. The eyes are outlined with a white or light gray border above the eye. As they grow old, the bucks become ever more gray, even to the brown patch in the forehead. The front of the huge ears is light gray with little hair inside the ears on old specimens. The back of the long mule ears is also gray. A darker shade of gray usually runs down the back of the neck and spine on old specimens. The white rump patch is fairly large, but not so large as on mountain sheep, while the tail is usually six to seven inches long and white for its upper length, with a black tip. It is round in shape, with very short hair except for the black tip. Mule deer have a habit of wiggling the tail a great deal, much like domestic sheep, as they feed. When they are jumped, the tail is usually carried clamped down, but when hit by a bullet they often raise and ring their tail in a circle just like a body-shot coyote.

When jumped, mule deer bound high in the air and come down with legs stiff and braced, then bounce again, not unlike big rubber balls. This peculiar bouncing gait is typical of scared mule deer and can be heard for a considerable distance. When hunting them in the timber you will jump many that have seen, heard or winded you, that you have not seen, but you can hear them thud quite plainly as they hit the ground. Old bucks will often clear small young trees and logs a good six feet tall as they run. Oftentimes they will see you in the timber and if they think you have not seen them, or are going to walk by them, they will pull their heads down low on the ground and remain absolutely still while you pass, so long as you do not look their way, just as an old whitetail buck will do. I have caught many of them in their beds in this way, when still-hunting in the timber, and I would size them up out of the corner of my eye, never looking directly towards them. If they were big enough to suit me, I would slowly raise the rifle to my shoulder and turn ever so slowly toward them for the shot. Usually when they saw I had spotted them they would be out of their beds in a bound and going in their high bouncing jumps that carry them a full twenty to thirty feet at a bound, depending on the slope of the mountain. Many times I have watched them slowly stand up out of their beds while they watched me, using one to two minutes at times, they rose so slowly, almost imperceptibly, from their beds, until they had gained a standing position. Then when I watched them from the corner of my eye without turning toward them, they would either stand motionless watching me, or turn and sneak quietly away to the cover of the first tree they could find, then start their high bouncing gait. A mule buck is the most adept at taking advantage of cover of any deer I have hunted, when only scattered pine trees are available. He will get behind one and run until near the top of it, then bounce over behind another tree and stay behind it until at the top, if going up a slope. A wise old buck can keep one tree between himself and the hunter until he is out of range if on level or nearly level ground, and even on steep slopes you won't see him for more than one jump at a time in the open, if there are trees behind which he can screen his getaway. They like to bed on a shoulder of a ridge, where one jump will carry them over the crest out of sight in any desired direction, usually behind some fallen log, in some clump of brush or by the base of a big yellow pine.

Many times I have found them bedded in a little clump of red buck brush a half mile from any timber and right out in the open, where they can see a hunter's approach for a half mile in any direction. When the cougar are working on them, they are prone to feed and bed in the open. If hard hunted, they will usually take to the steep, fir-covered north slopes, where the young trees grow so thick that visibility is cut to 50 yards or less, and will both feed and bed in such thickets. Then they depend on their long ears for protection and will practically always hear your approach, and the first you will know of their presence will be the sound of their high, hard, buck jumps, as they leave. If good thick cover is available, you will seldom see them. When the country is broken by steep hillsides and narrow creeks, or gulches, they will often cross the creek and then give you a good standing shot at 300 to 500 yards across a canyon. Mule deer, like whitetail, are very intelligent, and if they have been hunted they will use that intelligence to best advantage.

In the summer, the old bucks are solitary, or else live in groups of two or three. Then, when the first heavy snowfall blankets the higher mountains, they will work down to the bottom edge of the snow line. Often they will go down lower and feed during the night, then climb back up in the lower edge of the snow to bed for the day. Usually by the first of November they begin to band up and then the old bucks will start hunting for the bands of does and taking up with them. As the rut starts, the necks of the old bucks begin to swell, until by the time the rut is in full swing they are enormous in size and give the animal a topheavy appear-

Author with mule deer killed in 1945 with single shot from prone position at 300 yards with .285 O.K.H. 180-grain duplex load. 16 points

Mrs. Keith with big mule deer she killed with .333 O.K.H. 300-grain load

Author's best but not largest mule deer head, killed with single shot in chest from .405 Winchester at 60 yards. Head has 24 points and spread of 30 inches

Head of 18-point mule deer killed by author with .285 O.K.H. 180-grain duplex load, at 100 yards

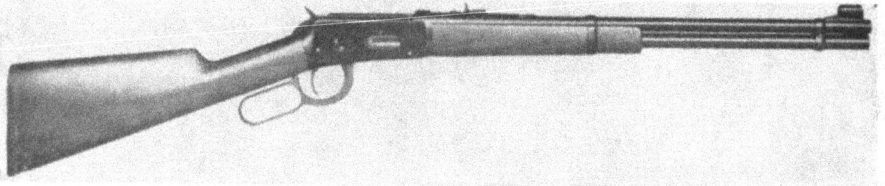

Winchester Model '94

Winchester Model 70

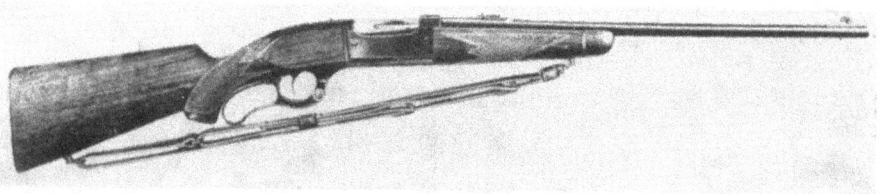

Savage Model '99

Remington Model 181

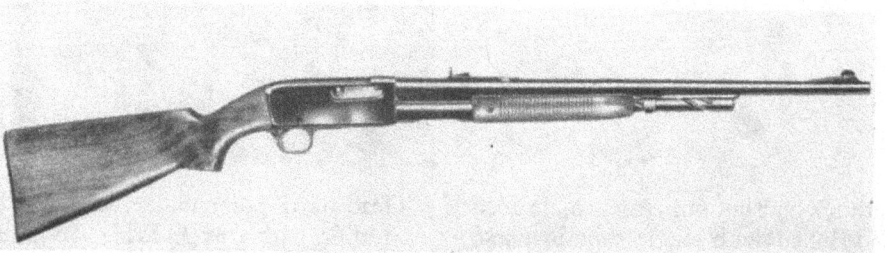

Remington Model 141

ance. The head in full rut is usually carried low and they will smell along the trail of a band of does and yearlings, exactly like a hound dog on the trail. When traveling down country to winter range, an old doe will usually be in the lead and with every sense alert, and the big buck will tag along behind, or with some doe he has singled out. Let another big buck approach, however, and his head will come up and he usually goes to meet him. They fight like the devil at such times, and I have watched them horn and push each other around for a half hour at a time, until both bucks were all in, if evenly matched. Sooner or later one buck will throw the other off his feet, then will give him a good goring with those sharp points until he leaves. I have killed many with deep festered wounds from such fights, others with blood still running from a fresh battle.

As with other species of big game, regardless of how tough a fight is in progress between the bucks, the does go unconcernedly about their feeding, seemingly paying no attention whatever to the fight, and regardless of which buck is the winner they accept him, just as though he had been with them all summer. Sometimes, as with the whitetail, their horns become locked and both animals die. I killed an old chap that had been hung up with another buck, and whose horns clearly showed where the other buck's horns had been locked for some time. He was thin and so strong we could not eat him at all.

By the first of October, the bucks are right at the peak of condition, sleek and fat as seals and with their horns well cleaned of velvet; then also they are at the finest stage as meat animals. They will often have two inches or more of fat on top of their rumps and are then the finest of all venison, at least to my taste. While having a stronger flavor than a fat elk, there is a peculiar tang to a fat mule buck that I like and which no other meat has. Mrs. Keith likes fat two-year-old bucks, but I prefer old-timers when fat, as they have a much better flavor than the young bucks, which are as veal compared to prime beef. When really fat and in their prime, bucks eight to ten years old are just as tender as anyone could wish, but rarely you will kill an old-timer that is tough and he will usually be a very old deer. If deer have been chased by hunters, or have been in a fight, then they may be both tough and strong, but usually at the start of the season they are about the finest venison imaginable.

I remember my first really big mule buck, killed in Montana when I was still a small lad. I had left the ranch early that morning on a fresh fall of snow, some three inches deep. Deer were not plentiful there then, but there were always enough for meat. I carried my fine old Creedmoor Sharps, caliber .44-105-520, with my own home-grown loads. Dan Floweree's father had brought that rifle to Helena by ox team, from Fort Benton. It saw service against both Indians and buffalo in those days, but is still in perfect condition. About a mile in back of the ranch I picked up the tracks of a buck and a doe feeding around the side of the mountain in heavy fir timber. They would browse on all small brush and mountain maple and the old buck would horn the brush. It was early in November and the rut was well started. After trailing them a mile or two and ever higher on the mountain, I could tell they knew I was after them, although I had neither seen nor jumped them. Nevertheless the tracks plainly told me they were watching their back track and knew I was following them. I would circle to windward for 200 yards or so, keeping a careful watch on all sides and then cut back upwind until I saw the trail, then circle again downwind from it. Several times I saw where they had backtracked, then jumped off over a high windfall in an effort to throw me off their tracks.

By noon, I had trailed them out on the more level top of the mountain some six miles from the ranch but still had not seen a hair of either the doe or the huge old buck. Then they split up and I of course worked on along the buck track. Clearly he was a wise old buck, as he doubled repeatedly and jumped down the mountain over the tops of brush clumps trying to elude me. Still I had never seen him, and by three in the afternoon I knew I would have to get a shot soon or I would be long after dark getting home. On coming over a low ridge onto a flat covered with big fir trees, I noticed the trail was double again and the old boy had come back, stepping exactly in each track until he reached a big windfall to my left. I had moved very slowly and carefully all day long, never moving ahead until I was certain that he was not in sight. Now when I again saw he had doubled on the trail I stood perfectly still behind a small clump of brush and looked over every inch of the scenery. Finally around to my left and 100 yards away, I saw him for the first time. The tip of his nose projected below a low hanging, heavy fir limb and the white rump patch showed to the right of the big tree trunk. Softly cocking the old side-hammer Creedmoor Sharps and setting the set trigger, I eased the rifle to my shoulder, knowing full well he was watching my every move and would be gone in an instant if I made a single quick move. When the long 34-inch barrel came up and the stock finally settled to my shoulder, taking a couple of minutes for the operation, I carefully swung the pin head through the center of the long vernier peep until it rested on the forward edge of the white patch of the rump and as close to the tree bole as I dared hold. Then, with a silent apology to mother, for punching a big hole through that fat rump roast, I touched the set trigger. Instantly all sight of the buck's rump and nose disappeared in a huge billowing cloud of powder smoke. The vernier peep sight smacked me a sharp rap on the eyebrow and the rifle barrel rose high in recoil. Then I saw the buck, down in the hindquarters and dragging himself swiftly over the shoulder of the ridge with his front feet. Reloading the big Sharps, I slipped over to the tree, then picked up his trail, where he had dragged himself down the mountain. I had him headed toward home, so followed after him as fast as I could, as I wanted to put him out of misery.

Reaching the bottom of the first draw, I saw him, so shot him through the neck with my .45 S.A. Colt sixgun. He was the largest buck I had seen at that time and I was a tickled youngster. I dressed him out and taking the heart and liver, spitted on a maple fork, headed down for the ranch, after tying my handkerchief on one of the big heavy horns to keep the coyotes away. He had a very pretty 26-inch spread head, with five and seven points, and weighed frozen, a month after killing, exactly 300 pounds. The back fat was fully three inches thick on top of his rump. One ear was split out from a previous fight. His neck was swelled out almost to the ends of his ears, but after hanging frozen for a month, he was as fine venison as I have ever enjoyed and I have been eating elk and deer each winter since I wore knee pants and long stockings. The heavy Sharps slug had torn a one-inch hole through the rump, then peeled a tree beyond and howled away.

Mule deer band together and herd together during the winter, but as soon as the new grass starts, where the snow has melted on the steep south slopes, they break up into little bands and scatter to the four winds. The big bucks work ever higher as the snow recedes under the influence of the ever-warming sun, while the does feed around the edges of the bottoms and later take to the brushy creek bottoms to have and rear their fawns. In the spring, when the old bucks have shed their big horns, you can still tell them from the does, almost as far as you can see them, by the angle of the ears to the head. The old bucks have carried their ears horizontally underneath those big horns so long that they still so carry them after the horns are shed. Also they are heavier bodied and the face has more white on it than the does'. Old buck mule deer, like elk of both sexes, carry the ears more at right angles to the head than does, which perk them up and forward, at a high angle.

Mule deer that have seldom if ever seen man are very curious, and I have often had them walk right up to me with nose outstretched as they attempted to get my scent. At other times, they have walked forward with ears outstretched and my scent in their nostrils, usually in summer

[157]

or early fall, before, or at the start of, the hunting season. Yearling bucks are particularly curious. Many days I have spent on the Salmon and Selway Rivers when I could easily have loaded a hay wagon with deer by using only a heavy sixgun, they were so tame.

The number of points on a mule deer is a very poor indication as to his age. As a yearling, he may and generally does have just a spike about six to eight inches long on a side, but sometimes there will be a forked horn on each side, and I killed one with a peculiar palmated set of short horns, with three flat points on one side and four on the other, and from his size and teeth judged him to be only a yearling buck. As a rule, however, they will have spikes the first year and two points the second, then the third year will have three-point heads. Some will have brow points, but most do not. At four years old they generally add the full four points, to a side, but may, or may not, have the brow point. Some old bucks never develop the brow points while others have several. My best head has twenty-four points all told on both sides and I saw one shed antler that was enormous and as large as a man's forearm above the burr. It carried full twenty-one points on the one horn, over an inch long. Such heavy palmated heads, with many points and the usual frog points projecting on the outside, make the most beautiful heads of all, to my way of thinking. A really fine one is a prize and makes a very impressive mount.

Mule deer heads deteriorate with age just as elk, moose and whitetail. Real old bucks often have a single long shoot from a main beam on one side with no points at all. At other times they will revert to a two-pointer with no brow points. At still others they may have a lot of points, but rather short, scrubby horns. Two years ago I killed such a head, a very old buck whose face was very gray, and while he had eighteen points all told, both points and main beams were short and scrubby.

One fall Mrs. Keith and I had driven to the end of the road on the Selway and hired a packer to take us out a full day's pack and drop our camp, then come back for us in a couple of weeks, or whenever I came out after him. Wanting some fat buck chops to eat, I soon located through the glasses a huge, old, rangy, Roman-nosed buck, feeding along a hillside about a mile away. I watched him feed around on the north slope soon after daylight and rightly surmised he would bed in the chaparral there. As he looked like a very big heavy buck and was in favorable country, I decided he would do for the little lady. We had breakfast, washed the dishes and started the long climb. I carried my old Enfield that C. M. Oneil had remodeled and rebarreled to .333 O.K.H. loaded with 300-grain Duplex loads containing 60 grains of 4350 Dupont to push the long, heavy, soft nosed slug. The rifle weighs eleven pounds, so I decided to carry it until we located the buck. Soon we were on top of the ridge and circled around and picked up his huge tracks in the soft sandy hillside. He was a big bounder all right, from the tracks, and very heavy. We climbed on up 100 yards above his course, then started around on the north slope. It was cut with many small gullies and these were partly covered with buck brush and the green chaparral. After cutting the heads of two of these deep dry washes, I spotted the old boy bedded below us. Mrs. Keith edged out in sight of him by sliding her feet ahead down the steep slope until she was over the comb, far enough to bring the rifle to bear on him and yet clear the brush in front of us. Just as she started the trigger squeeze, he got up and moved down the slope out of sight and started feeding again. This time only his horn tips showed, over the intervening brush. We had to work around to the left for some distance before we could again see him. Lorraine had a very insecure position and was digging her heels into the steep slope to keep from sliding down the mountain, but she soon brought the sights to bear and then I saw her slim finger tightening on the trigger. As the big rifle spoke, I noticed the barrel rise high in its characteristic slow recoil and it pushed her shoulders up and out of the sight of the corner of my eye. The sodden heavy plunk of the heavy slug told me all I needed to know. The buck jumped, then made a few steps across the draw, where he stood humped up until he filled with blood and rolled down the mountain, shot through the back of the lungs. We trailed him down the slope until we found where he had lodged against a big boulder, and turning him around I took some photos of her and the buck.

Another season, and across the Selway River, Mrs. Keith killed another very big buck that I later weighed at 300 and a few pounds over, but he was not as large as the first one she killed on the Selway, with the .333 O.K.H. This buck was, however, even older and his head was a freak. On one side he had a normal, but lightweight four points, and on the other just one long beam going upward and then curling inward. She won the prize for the best freak head that fall and a new automatic fly reel. That head was typical of real old bucks long past their prime, but his meat was tender and fat as a seal.

We have two general types of mule deer in this country and whether they belong to the same or different subspecies I do not know. One is a short chunky deer with short back, short legs and a pretty head with a fairly straight slope to the face and bridge of the nose. He will seldom weigh over 250 pounds, even in a very old buck, and although he often carries a very fine head it seldom goes to extreme spread. The other type of mule buck is a big, long-legged, very long-bodied and long-necked deer, always having a long Roman nose as well. He is the type that often carries an enormous head and I have seen them with over 40-inch spread.

The smaller, chunky deer are much the prettiest individuals, but those long rangy chaps are the ones that pack the venison, as well as the huge and heavy heads at times. Not all big deer have large heads, and the largest mule buck I ever killed, that weighed 400 on good accurate scales cut in two halves, had only a small 24-inch spread head, which I gave to Ben Comfort when he was out here. Incidentally, on that later trip, I obtained a good long range shot for Ben at one of the largest and finest mule deer heads I have ever seen, but he had his sights set about 100 yards too low for the damp muggy day.

Hunting mule deer is one thing and hunting old mule bucks something else entirely. In good mule deer country you will have no trouble seeing plenty of does and young bucks, but the old residenters you will have to hunt. I particularly like to work along a slope, either up or down, depending on the location of camp, which is regularly used by these old stagers — keeping down about 200 or 300 yards from the top and just above the heads of the springs, then watching every patch of aspen and other brush, as well as the shoulders of the little ridges between the springs. There these wise old chaps will usually hide out, in the early season. If you get heavy and early fall rains, you can look for them just over the ridge on the north slope, in the dense fir timber, where they will feed on mushrooms, of which they are very fond. They will then bed in these dense fir thickets on the north slope, just down from the top 100 yards or so. They are then very hard to get a shot at, as their long ears will practically always warn them of your approach and you will only hear them bounce away down the mountain. Get out among them at the first break of dawn and you will nearly always see some of them feeding or sneaking off to their bed ground.

Many times I have walked onto big mule bucks that had heard, but neither seen nor winded, me, and they would get up out of their beds and jump straight up in the air several times, coming down in the same place, as they attempted to get sight of me. They had not located my direction and would thus spring high in the air in order to see over the brush. This peculiarity of the mule deer often leads to their downfall. If you jump one and are well up the mountain, he will usually go downhill and quartering away, taking advantage of every tree he can get behind, to shield his escape. It is best to try and time your shots so that you catch them at the height of their jump, as they are then well up over any low brush and seem to hang and float in the air for a fraction of a second. Then is the exact instant to hang a bullet on them.

The fall I was out with the Zane Grey party, we had camped in lower Cottonwood meadow and needed a prime fat buck for meat. As the boys wanted to hunt alone and said they needed no guide, we let them do so, but when they said there was no game in the country we took exception to their statements. I offered to wager the entire proceeds of the trip against an equal amount of cash that I could hang up elk, deer and goat alone, in two days from that camp. They would not take me up and the upshot was that I was delegated to obtain a big buck for meat. Working down the left side of the creek on a flat tableland, I came out overlooking a huge basin that fell away toward the goat cliffs, farther down the steep creek. Below me and on both sides was as beautiful and ideal mule deer country as I have ever seen. Tracks led everywhere and by trailing Bob Carney's tracks from the day before, I found he had worked along with the wind at his back and jumped seven big bucks and a cougar and seen none of them.

I sat for a time overlooking the huge basin and sizing up the most likely places for an old buck to bed. The sun was high by this time, but I was in no hurry, well knowing there were at least twenty-five bucks in that basin some two miles wide by three miles in length. Finally I picked out a little spring below me and to the left about a quarter mile, that had a flat grassy basin some 60 yards in extent, while directly across the spring was about a quarter acre of heavy dense timber with many fallen logs. I felt sure a big buck would be bedded there, as trails went into and out of the spring from both sides, so I slipped down under cover of a line of trees to the spring. The gentle breeze was in my face and I smoked my pipe to keep track of the wind drift. Soon I was at the spring and carefully scrutinizing the timber about 125 yards away, across the gulch. Sure enough, a huge old mule buck was bedded just in front of a fallen log and he saw me the same time I saw him. He started to get to his feet and I honestly believe that deer put in three full minutes slowly rising from his bed to a standing position. He made no quick move and neither did I. As he was slowly unraveling his legs and gradually rising higher out of his bed, I was just as slowly turning the safety on the G & H Springfield and raising my rifle. He gained his full height just as the rifle butt came to my shoulder and the cross hairs centered on the base of his neck. A steady squeeze and the rifle barked, and he dropped back in his bed, dead as a mackerel from the 150-grain Remington Bronze Point shattering his neck. I dressed him out and carried heart and liver to camp that night, spitted on a willow fork. Next day we took the strongest, heaviest pack horse we had and finally succeeded in loading him. As we had no way to weigh him, we could only estimate his weight, but I have since weighed mule bucks at 350 to 360 that were not as large or heavy as that old boy. He had a nice heavy 31- or 32-inch spread head, with five and seven points, and was fat as a seal. The 150-grain bullet completely disintegrated when it struck the spine at the base of the neck and never went any farther. Three of us lifted long and hard to load him on the horse, which was all in and well lathered when we arrived back at camp.

Another time, a partner and I were camped on the west side of Horse Creek and had kicked the pack string around in a little basin, so they had to come to camp for water, as we were camped on the spring. Saddling my horse, I took the old Model '95 Winchester caliber .405 and decided to ride up the trail about three miles to the snow, then dismount and hunt around on that north slope of the Salmon, in some of the finest mule deer country we have. I forked my horse and climbed on up into the edge of the snow, soon locating a nice band of mule deer with three big bucks and several smaller ones, besides many does and fawns. On the way up I had also ridden onto a band of does and fawns that stood quietly beside the trail, while I rode past, not over 30 yards away. This big band, however, had several on lookout and they were feeding and bedded along a steep slope, with some fallen logs and heavy sagebrush. My only possible approach, as the .405 is a short ranged rifle, was to leave my horse and work around them in the heavy timber until I was a quarter mile above the band, and then work down through the heavy three-foot-high sagebrush to a fallen tree about 100 yards above them. This old fallen log lay right out on the rim of a small ledge and I knew would make ideal cover for the stalk. About an hour was required for the circle, but when I removed my hat and peeked through a sagebrush, there was the band about 125 yards below me. I sized up the three bucks, finally picking an old long-bodied, Roman-nosed chap with a good head that I later gave to Al Ellinger, bedded broadside, directly below me and in a clump of sage. His whole back and head were clearly visible. Poking the old .405 over the log, I held well down on the near shoulder and squeezed. At the shot, every deer froze into instant immobility. Those chewing their cuds stopped and the feeding deer also stopped in the exact position they were in when the rifle cracked. Well knowing I must have gone over the buck, and that the wind which was sweeping up the slope would deaden any sound, I carefully pulled back out of sight and reloaded the chamber as silently as possible, then shoved the rifle back over the log. This time I held down in the dirt under that big buck's shoulder and fired again. He sort of started and I heard the smack of the 300-grain slug. Then he slowly laid his head out in front of him to the full extent of his neck. That was the only move he made, as he did not even so much as kick.

The rest of the band were now in fast jumping motion, as they buck-jumped around the mountain to my left. I heard Brownie snort as they flashed past his postion in the timber. The bullet had struck on top of the shoulders almost in the center of the spine and broken it, then ranged downward and back as he was slightly quartering, and had stopped in that big grass and browse filled paunch. I finally found it, perfectly ex-panded, by emptying out the paunch. He was a fine big 300-pound buck, so I dressed him and, taking heart and liver, left him to cool with my old red handkerchief tied to one horn to keep the coyotes away. Next day I removed head and cape and skinned him back halfway. Then by manty-ing up the front end and folding the skin back over the end of the loin where I had cut him in half, I managed to load him on a Decker pack saddle and get him to camp.

Last fall after handling a hunting party from California, Oscar Bohan-non and I decided to get our own meat for the winter. We spent nearly a week hunting from the ranch and though there had been plenty of game there at the start of the season, while we were away hunting elk we saw only does and fawns that we did not want and many hunters. Each day we would spot several hunters, always seeing them first, when we would duck out of sight behind some tree and work over the ridge, hoping they did not see us and start shooting at us, as so many green hunters are prone to do. Finally we had enough of dodging hunters, so packed up and pulled to the head of the North Fork, back in where the hunters could not drive their cars.

That night we had a foot of fresh snow, so next morn, as soon as it was daylight, I started scanning the hillside across from camp. The range was very deceiving just as it had proved the evening before, when a buck I had thought was 200 yards away proved, on pacing the range, a full 300 yards. That is the usual effect at high altitudes. Soon I saw a nice buck well up on the other slope, so giving Oscar the .285 O.K.H. Mauser I told him to hold just at the top of the back behind the shoulders. At the shot, nothing happened, and I told him to hold just over the back the next shot. Again nothing happened and the buck started walking on around the sidehill. Then I asked him to hold about a foot over the top of the withers and just behind the shoulder, so that if the shot hit low it would not break a leg. Again the rifle barked and this time the buck jumped into a run for a distance, then stopped and bit at a foreleg. This gave us our clew and we knew the range must be greatly in excess of any 400 to 500 yards. There was a brush-filled creek bottom between us and the mountain some 200 yards or more across and the deer was high on the other slope. He toon turned directly up the mountain and started walking up a ridge. When he stopped, I told Oscar to hold the cross wires right over the top of the horns, and if we were going low, it should drop into him some place, as his whole body was lined up under the vertical cross hair. He did so and the rifle raised in recoil, then settled back down, then the buck flinched and turned around the mountain, walking slowly, as we heard the dull plunk of the slug striking home. The buck only walked about 50 yards and all humped up, with head held low, before lying down behind a clump of maple brush. We reloaded the rifle, went back to camp, cooked and ate breakfast. Then I walked down the trail with the .285 O.K.H. where I could cover the buck's position, while Oscar climbed the mountain with the double rifle. He had a hard time crossing the creek in the deep snow and required over a half hour to climb up to that buck, which was dead in its bed. After I had walked down the trail and had a chance to size up the range, I knew it must have been over 600 yards. Oscar dragged the deer down the gulch to where I had killed the evening before and we dressed and hung him in another tree. That slug had struck low in the right flank and ranged into the lungs and blown up, even at that distance. It is the highest velocity long range rifle I have ever used and with the flattest trajectory. A .300 Magnum would not have expanded at that range. Again we found the liver well demolished and only about half of it left, so Oscar remarked, "Guess we will have to eat heart and go for elk tomorrow," which we did.

Oscar's buck proved a very fat young animal, with a small head, and on the same trip I killed an old chap with seven and eight points. We had our mule deer and good ones as well, nor did we sight any hunters on the trip until we were back a few miles from the road, on the return trip. We killed our elk, then made two trips out to the ranch and back to bring out the camp and all meat.

When mule deer range dense timber, or have been hard hunted and driven into the timber, then all I have written on still-hunting and on such hunting of moose, elk and whitetails applies equally to them. Mule deer are very canny animals in the brush. They will also pack off a lot of lead at times, if it is improperly placed, or from too small a rifle. For timber shooting of mule deer, I like the same rifles as for whitetails, but prefer nothing smaller than .30 caliber or less than 200-grain bullets for my own use. For most average mule deer hunting, which will entail many long range shots, as well as some at close range, the modern scope sight long range high velocity rifle is the best. I used the .300 Magnum for years and the .285 O.K.H. is even better for the job.

You will sight many mule deer across deep canyons, where a stalk is impossible or the deer are moving and you won't have the time to make your stalk; then it is imperative that you have a flat shooting long range rifle for the job. The .270 Winchester is about the best of the small cartridges for this work and the .300 Magnum is even better. The old .256 Newton also worked well, as did the .30–06 with 150- to 180-grain bullet out to about 300 to 350 yards, but not over that, as .30–06 velocities are insufficient to expand the bullets reliably beyond that range. Regardless of where, or how, you hunt the mule deer, he is a grand game animal, both for meat and as a trophy, and after a lifetime of hunting him I have only respect and admiration for the species, the largest and finest deer on this continent. Their chief enemies are, in the order named, cougar, man, wolves, coyotes, eagles and bobcats. With Eastern whitetail man is the main enemy, while in the West it is problematical whether the big cats do not kill about as many or more deer than man. Coyotes kill plenty.

X

Caribou

THE caribou are our most northerly ranging deer species. Formerly caribou ranged from Washington, Idaho and Montana in the West and Minnesota to Maine in the East, far north into the Arctic Circle. They still range the North with Alberta and British Columbia as their extreme southern range. There may still be an odd specimen in Minnesota and Maine as well as the Yak Valley in extreme northwest Montana, but on the whole caribou must now be considered Canadian and Alaskan game on this continent. Their range circles the globe at or near the Arctic Circle, there being caribou in Siberia and also on Greenland and in Norway, though they are called reindeer in Norway and differ from other caribou species. Most of the arctic islands contain caribou.

Many different subspecies occur, even on this continent, the largest and finest being the big Osborn that extends from the Yukon south, probably to the Peace River. Its range merges into that of the mountain caribou. The mountain caribou of Alberta and southern British Columbia is, however, a darker animal than the true Osborn, and with more palmation of the top formation of the antlers than the true Osborn.

Just where the range of the Osborn in its southern extremity ends and the range of the mountain caribou starts I have never been able to determine. Have seen caribou called Osborn when killed ten days' trek south of the Peace River, and have also seen them classed as Osborn when killed as far as twenty days' travel north of the Peace. There can, however, be no doubt as to the caribou on the Cassiar being true Osborn in species. The Osborn usually carry the finest heads, though some mountain caribou also carry exceptional heads, but seldom as long as those killed farther north. At times the Barren Ground caribou of the far North will have just as long antlers as the big mountain or Osborn caribou. In size, however, the mountain groups are much the largest of the various species. Big bulls will weigh 800 to 900 pounds when fat. In comparison many of the largest Barren Ground species will probably weigh only 350 to 400 pounds.

The woodland caribou of Newfoundland, New Brunswick and formerly Maine have shorter antlers as a rule with much more palmation than the western and more northern species. The Woodland caribou is also a heavier animal as a rule than the various Barren Ground species; it is also a much darker-colored animal. Wherever found, caribou are most interesting animals. The cows have horns as well as the bulls, but in proportion they are very small and usually with few points, and compare with bull caribou antlers about as doe antelope horns would with those of a buck. However, they at times have considerable palmation to their short stubby horns. The more southern species are the darkest while the more northern Barren Ground species are the lightest in coloration. As a general rule the body is brown with white hair intermixed, often giving them a gray cast, while the neck is light gray on young bulls and cows and almost pure white on old bulls. The white neck on the old bulls often extends back across the shoulder and onto the ribs in the form of a lazy V, with the apex back about the middle of the animal. You can tell an old bull as far as you can see him with glasses, on account of the extent of the white patch that covers the whole neck and extends back in a V shape across the shoulders. The belly is usually white, top of tail brown and underneath always white. The face is usually a dark mahogany brown, shading to gray or white on the cheeks. The back of the ears is brown and the front or face usually gray or white. The legs are usually very dark brown to almost jet black. Just above the hoofs and around the top of the dewclaws is a ring of white. The mane of the bulls is long and heavy and white. The shank of the legs from the knee and hock down to the foot is slender, but the feet are huge. They have well-rounded, well-cupped widespread hoofs of very large size for the animal, being even larger than moose or elk that weigh much more. The dewclaws come down to the ground and also help support the animal, and his tracks always show both hoofs and dewclaws. These enormous feet enable the beasts to traverse almost any boggy country that would instantly bog any other species of the deer tribes, and also enable them to traverse hard crusted snow in winter without injury to their legs, when such crust would soon cut deer, elk, or moose legs raw. The big feet make such a large hole in the crust that they can pull them out without scraping their shins.

They are excellent swimmers and seem to like the water and will often be found around high alpine lakes. They do not hesitate to swim even large lakes or streams and seemingly have great endurance in the water.

The nose is blunt on the end, more like a domestic cow's than any of our other deer, and is completely covered with hair. The body coat in late fall and winter is very heavy, and having in addition to the long outer hair the usual hollow hair of most deer, it is so dense you can hardly part it. It is almost waterproof, it is so thick and dense. This extremely thick pelage protects them from cold and also waterproofs their coats to a great extent. The blunt muzzle is also covered with short hair that protects it from cold. The eyes are prominent and dark brown in color.

Caribou are very curious, and while they can spot you for a considerable distance if you move, they do not seem to have very keen eyesight. The horns differ from any of our other deer species. Usually just over the nose extends one and very rarely two brow points or shovels. Starting from the main branch in the form of a nearly round prong, this brow antler palmates, often to huge proportions and with many small points along its frontal edge. Occasionally a rare animal will be found with double shovels that come almost together and whose small prongs or points interlap. Farther up the main beam extend the bay prongs; these also run upward and forward and usually end in palmation with two or more points, some being quite heavy with many points on their front edge which often cup back and upward. Still farther up the main beam is a small upward curved prong on the back of the beam, usually occurring just about where the beam starts its upward and forward curve. There is nearly always one of these small upcurving prongs on the back of each horn. Thence the main beams curve upward and often forward as well, ending either in a series of branches or in wide and heavy palmation with small points along the top edge. We have seen many different types, and in fact saw one caribou killed by George Bates south of the Peace River in 1927 that had a typical elk head. The horns did not resemble a caribou's at all but looked for all the world like those of a small elk head.

Bulls in their prime will carry the finest heads, as is true of all the many deer species. When they get very old, the horns will often be just long main beams with a club effect at the top and without the usual brow and bay tines, and the small back points may be only small nubbins. We have seen many such heads. When you spot an old white-necked bull with the white extending well back behind the shoulders, you may well know it is a mature animal, but you will have to examine the head at closer range to determine if it is a good head or an old degenerated one with few or almost no points. A really fine caribou head is one of the prettiest trophies obtainable on this continent, but such heads are very rare. You will see hundreds of heads as a rule for every really fine one you find. Their striking, contrasting coloring combines with the peculiar shaped and palmated antlers to make a most attractive head.

Caribou are plump, round-bodied animals and in the late fall, before the rut, the bulls often carry an enormous amount of fat on their backs. Sometimes the layer of back fat will be from three to four inches thick. When really fat, they are fine meat, but a young, or poor caribou is to my notion inferior to either a fat elk or mule buck and far inferior to a fat mountain ram.

They have excellent noses and can wind you a long way. When they see you, the usual thing is for them to circle in order to get your wind. When startled or suspicious, caribou carry the head high and the tail is tipped up at a saucy angle of 30 to 45 degrees. When they are jumped the tail is thrown straight up and often waved as well. Old and very fat bulls seem unable to tip their tail up quite as high as younger ones or cows; this may be due to the heavy layer of back fat which extends well onto the root of the tail. The tail is shorter than a whitetail buck's in proportion, but much longer than an elk's. When jumped, caribou will make a few plunging jumps, then settle into their peculiar pacing or trotting gait which they seem able to keep up indefinitely, at least until they are completely out of sight in open caribou barrens. The gait always appeared more like that of a pacing horse to me than a true trot, and it seemed they threw the two feet forward on one side and then the two on the other at the same time. Either it is a fact, or an optical illusion with me alone, as all authorities claim they trot, but I have watched them many times for hours and this was my impression. When traveling, their feet make a great noise and whether it is the foot and ankle bones that rattle or the dewclaws against the hoofs I do not know, but I do know you can hear the rattling of their feet for a long distance.

In traveling, the hind feet are lifted very high, which must be a habit formed from centuries of muskeg and snow travel. When undisturbed and traveling, either at a walk or their peculiar swinging pace or trot, the head is held outstretched and on a line with the tail and the tail is also carried horizontal, but when suspicious or they see you, the head and tail both come up instantly. Many times I have run onto suspicious caribou who had seen me but could not determine what sort of creature I was, and they would extend their muzzles toward me and sniff, trying to get a trace of my scent, then would circle into the wind until they did get it, whereupon they would usually rise up on their hind feet and with the nose thrown high in the air emit a loud snort or whistle and make a few bounding jumps, then settle into that steady swinging gait, either a trot or pace, so peculiar to caribou and keep it up until out of sight. Many times I have seen them stand up on their hind feet to look at me when I was in plain sight, and when they snorted or whistled they nearly always threw their nose high in the air. Cows did this little stunt more often than bulls. When they line out and start traveling, the usual thing is for some wise old cow to take the lead, and during the rut the bull will tag along behind herding his harem together. They travel in single file a good deal but not as much as elk. Seemingly they have no set trails except during the migration of the northern herds, and all the mountain caribou I have hunted seemed just as apt to go one way as another, even straight up and over a high mountain when they could just as easily have gone through a low saddle. They are an animal without rhyme or reason at times and do the most unpredictable things of any beast I have hunted. I have seen old bulls past their prime stand for hours with their heads very low and almost against some small tree or bush, their only movements being an occasional shake of the head or stamp with a forefoot or a kick with a hind foot to fight off flies; they seemed utterly dejected and really looked as if they had lost their last friend. Why they will thus stand in one position for hours is beyond me.

At other times I have found stray bulls in dense fir timber before the rut and they would grunt at me. It is a peculiar noise, hard to describe and different from that of any other game I have hunted. Not so loud and hoarse as that of a moose but still a sort of coughing grunt, with an explosive nasal quality to the tone.

Caribou are as unpredictable as the direction of a March wind. They may be in one place in numbers one day and thirty miles away the next and probably still going. You never know which way they will go, or what they will do. Flies, mosquitoes and other winged pests deal them a lot of misery in the summer and they then like to live up on the high open plateaus and wind-swept ridges, where the breeze offers some protection against the pests. Caribou feed largely on lichens and moss, and you can instantly spot a caribou range by the feed present. At times they also eat wild pea vines, cranberries and crowberry and other small browse. While their summer diet is largely green grass and lichens, in the winter they add some browse, where it is available, to their caribou moss and dead grass diet. No hoofed animal is better able to paw away the snow from its feed than the caribou. Those huge feet are most excellent snow shovels. On the Pacific slope of their most southern ranges they also eat large quantities of the hanging tamarack moss, green in summer and black or brown in the winter. Caribou will subsist well where most any other game

Caribou

Courtesy Fred LeLacheur, Alaska

Caribou migration in Alaska

Courtesy J. Omar Cole

Very fine caribou killed by J. Omar Cole in British Columbia, 1932, with
.30–06, 180 grain. Length of beam 42 inches, spread 38 inches,
total of 35 points

A pair of caribou heads killed by A. E. Ellinger in British Columbia, 1939

would starve and they seem never to yard up, but prowl the wind-swept barrens and ridges in search of food. Some hunters believe that the brow antlers are used to break the crusted snow, but facts do not substantiate this theory as most of the big bulls shed their antlers early in the winter, long before the snow is crusted hard. They paw away the crusted snow in search of food, though young bulls and cows often carry their horns until nearly the end of the winter before shedding.

Caribou are not difficult to stalk if you can find cover leading to within range to windward of them, since they are not nearly as alert as sheep, antelope or many other species of herbivorous game. However, caribou seem to have no definite habits and I have seen them either traveling or feeding at all times of the day and traveling in the night as well by moonlight. You may locate an old white-necked bull and start your stalk, only to find him long since gone when you arrive in range of his former position. They may lie around or feed in some meadow or along some lake shore for hours, and suddenly throw up their head and tail and depart like all possessed, and for no apparent reason you will ever be able to determine. They are nervous, high-strung animals and seem to be eternally on the move. A caribou range may be covered with caribou one day; the next day they are gone. They may be back the next day, the next week or the next year, or never. Their continuous search for lichens may have had something to do with their habits over the centuries, as this caribou moss is scattered and obtaining it naturally leads the animals over a large area. In the summer months they are more apt to stay put than later, during the rut or hunting season. They delight in snowbanks during the hot summer days and spend much time around them and the resultant small lakes, especially during the fly season.

Enemies are chiefly man and the great arctic wolves that follow their migrations south in the winter. A grizzly occasionally catches a caribou, as both grizzly and caribou delight in the same range, and wherever you find good caribou range with plenty of lichens you will usually also find grizzly diggings, as the big bear dig out an enormous amount of roots for food. We have seen acres of ground literally torn up where the bear had fed. On one trip to British Columbia I found in a light early snow where a grizzly had stalked a cow and calf caribou. They had bedded some 30 to 40 yards from a thin fringe of alpine balsam shin-tangle and the great bear had used this for cover in his stalk, then in a rush he had carried himself in reach of the cow before she ever got really started to run and her rump bones and one hip bone were simply shattered where he had hit her with a paw. The cow was almost entirely eaten except the bones, but the calf still remained near the carcass when I found it. The light snow made reading the affair as simple as your morning newspaper.

Caribou are the vagabonds of the wild and no doubt travel more and see more country during their lives than any other horned animal on this continent. At the start of the rut, the bulls begin to gather up their harems and many fights ensue. I have seen them sparring, but never witnessed a real finish fight. One bull I killed in 1927 bore mute evidence of an awful fight. His entire body was full of holes and these were filled with pus. His meat was worthless and smelled very strong, as well as being poor. He had no back fat at all. Some holes were punched into his ribs clear to the lungs while others left his entrails showing, yet in spite of them he would have lived and was clearly boss of the little band I found him with. I believe the bay and brow antlers are their chief weapons in a fight, and this is borne out by the numerous scars and cuts along the scalp, over face and neck as well as shoulders.

Though bulls, cows and calves remain together in the winter after the rut, the old bulls usually go off by themselves in the spring, or in small groups, and summer alone. Then in the fall they will band together for the rut in September or early October on the southern end of their range. In Newfoundland they migrate to the southern part of the island, and in the extreme North the Barren Ground caribou band together, often as early as August, and start their southward migration. S. A. Camp and Jack Grigsby, two friends who have watched this migration in Alaska and killed their winter's meat from it, say it is a most impressive sight, with a continuous mass of caribou traveling along as far as the eye can reach. Camp said he had often picked a fat animal and shot it with his .32 Special Model '94 Winchester carbine, only to find the bullet had gone through the one shot at and also killed another on the other side.

While before and during the rut caribou wander in any direction, during the migration, which may or may not be local in character, they usually travel well-defined routes over which they have passed from time immemorial, unless hunted too hard at some section, when they may change the route to one side or the other. The southern herds of the Barren Ground caribou usually migrate south in the fall or early winter to the first of the scattered timber, while more northern herds often actually migrate to the north in search of better feed. Farther south, the Osborn and mountain caribou migrations are more local affairs and they seldom band into such huge congregations as do the Barren Ground caribou and the Newfoundland species to a lesser extent. Camp told me it was nothing to see thousands in sight at one time. Someday I would like to watch that migration and pick a couple of heads from it, and the Lord willing, so help me Hannah, I intend doing it before I get too old, if the wolves leave any.

Calves are usually born in late May and early June and there is usually only one, but twins are not uncommon. The time of the rut and the appearance of the calves naturally vary some in the different latitudes over which the caribou range extends. The Barren Ground species again migrates to the north about the latter part of March to their summer feeding grounds, while some bands east of the Rockies may migrate south in the spring on the more northern ranges. While small bands of caribou often travel in single file, with an old cow in the lead, when the migration comes in earnest there is simply a sea of antlers as a steady stream of animals file along. I watched elk in the fall of 1917 pass a single opening in the timber near the Yellowstone Park in a steady single file for three solid hours, so a caribou migration in the North must be a sight for any big game hunter to long remember.

The bulls usually clean their horns of velvet in August and I killed one bull some 200 miles north of Fort St. John whose antlers were clean and hard in August. Caribou and mountain sheep may often be found at the same elevation and in the same country, at least in those sections of British Columbia I have hunted.

Hunting caribou is different from hunting most any other species except possibly moose, in some sections of the North. The best procedure is to establish a lookout that will enable you to comb miles of their range with the glasses, with a good spotting scope to help you determine what an animal is when you do pick one up. When a good or promising looking bull is found, one should go after him then and there, for he will seldom be around the next day, unless it is very early in the season. After the rut starts they are constantly on the move and I have watched the bulls herding their little harem along, moving them constantly. During the rut the bulls make considerable noise grunting and stamping. Caribou hunting is a stalking proposition in the main, and while you will often run onto caribou while hunting other game, as a rule when you locate a good bull you will have to stalk him. Make sure you have the wind right as he has a very good nose. You may stalk into good range and again the bull may suddenly take fright, as you think, and run off, when he has neither seen, heard nor winded you. He is also apt to turn around and come back just as fast as he left.

If caribou do see you, the best thing to do is to remain motionless, preferably flat on the ground. They may stamp and snort for a time but unless hard hunted are apt either to come closer for a look-see, or else circle to get your wind. In either case their actions may bring them in good range. Nothing can ever be gained by following one as a caribou can easily outdistance any man, either on bare ground or in deep snow, with the hunter on webs, and once he knows you are after him he may leave the country entirely. If you have a good lookout from some high point and watch from it during the day, you have an even better chance than when traveling, unless you are in such broken country that you cannot cover much ground from any vantage point, when it is well to scout the high flat-top mountains and open ridges and particularly the heads of the streams and their little mountain basins which caribou love above all other terrain. Don't hesitate to go up high; they are often well above timber line in the North. Even south of the Peace River on the head of the Wapiti, I have seen caribou crossing the sheep pastures.

Powerful long range rifles are the best for caribou hunting for trophies and preferably scope sighted, as you may have to take long shots at some particular animal you want. In commercial rifles and loads the .300 Magnum Model 70 Winchester is my choice, and in custom rifles and loads the .285 O.K.H. with 180-grain Duplex load is the king of all rifles and loads for the purpose. It's one thing to kill meat from migrating caribou in the far North and quite another to hunt and kill a fine head earlier in the season, or farther south in the range of the Osborn and mountain caribou. One should always avoid breaking a leg of a caribou, as that spells his doom. Even though he may get away from the hunter, he is doomed, and the wolves will pull his innards out sooner or later, while he is still alive. Caribou shooting is usually in the open and they make most excellent targets, so one should place his shot right on them. I once saw George Bates put three 220-grain Western Boattails into a running bull's chest before he went down. All three bullets expanded perfectly and went through to the skin on the other side, as the bull fled past him broadside at around 200 yards. He was using a Webley & Scott .300 Magnum.

One time we were just starting to make camp on a short three-days side trip from the main camp. I was starting a fire under a gnarled old spruce tree when I glanced out across the muskeg meadow. There stood an enormous bull caribou. The white strip ran well back beyond his shoulders. His head looked enormous, wide heavy brow points, heavy palmated bays, long beams and a tremendous top formation. As far as I knew, I was the only man in the party then wanting a caribou, so asking Harry Snyder to put the glasses on him and post me, I slipped the sling of my old heavy barrel .300 Magnum Hoffman on my arm and bedded down prone for the shot. It was a good 400 yards and my rifle was sighted for 300. Harry took one look at the bull through his glasses and said "Shoot. He is a fine one." Just as my front sight top rested steadily near the top of the rear edge of the withers and I started the trigger squeeze, another member of the party who had already killed caribou and had said he was through with them said, "Wait, I want him." As I was helping with the guiding and cooking and preparing trophies on that trip, I turned the safety over on the old Magnum Mauser and went back to my fire. Taking an Indian with him, this lad attempted to circle in some timber and get closer to that bull, and never saw him again after leaving us. The bull simply snorted a couple of times and stamped the ground, then cocking up his little tail at a saucy angle he started off at his swinging gait that soon took him over a ridge out of sight. He was by far the finest caribou head I have ever seen in the hills.

Several years later my friend J. Omar Cole went back into that section of British Columbia on a sheep hunt, and while he did not find any sheep at all where we found them, he did kill a very fine caribou near that camp.

This experience well illustrates the necessity for taking a good caribou when you have the chance. It also illustrates what the presence of game sometimes does to a man. I could have killed that bull from camp with certainty and both Harry Snyder and I knew it. Harry gave me one long steady look as I turned back to my work. No words were necessary as we well understood each other.

Many times you will see a caribou bull's horns over the sky line of some ridge, before you see the bull. At other times he may be bedded with only his horns showing above the ridge, or above the tall grass of some wet meadow. Examine any suspicious looking object, especially if it looks like horns. Often caribou will bed with their head outstretched in front of them, but even then those big antlers usually project up into plain sight and there is no mistaking the big palmated top formation of a set of caribou horns. If you can locate a good lookout where you can cover a lot of terrain, you can spot a good bull for miles when the sun strikes his beautiful white neck and mane, as it simply flashes in the sun like a mirror.

Except in the southern extremity of the caribou range, there is seldom any use in going after a bull with a gray neck, or with the white of the neck extending back only to the point of the shoulder. These will nearly always be young bulls with small heads. But when you see an old chap with that telltale slash of white extending clear back across his shoulder and over the ribs, then you may know you have located a bull old enough to carry a head of trophy proportions. Examination, however, may prove him too old to grow good horns.

The last hunt I had in British Columbia in '37, Westley Brown and I located an old white-neck bull some three miles away. As it was late in the day and we were working out the tracks of a feeding small band of caribou, just in hopes of catching up with them, we decided to let the old bull go. We were after fat caribou meat at the time and wanted a young bull. There were two young bulls in the band when we came in sight of them and a careful stalk put us in long range, but when they jumped they came closer and I killed the larger. He carried twenty-two points but a very small, widely palmated head with very short beams, and had a lot of fat meat, which was what we wanted just then. Next day, Doc and Dick Brown went back for the old bull and strange to say he was still in that distant meadow. They finally got him down, only to find that his head, while fairly heavy and with long beams, had almost no points at all. An old residenter, too old to grow good antlers, he carried a typical head for a real old bull, long past his prime. Old caribou heads, like old elk heads, often run up in long heavy beams, but instead of many points have only a big deformation at the top. They had simply filled him full of Peters 225-grain .30–06 before he finally went down.

In 1927, we were camped on a branch of Fish Creek south of the head of the Wapiti River and all of us left camp hunting for the day, leaving Mac Farlane in camp to wrangle the pots and bake bread. Mac had no use for a caribou and did not want one at all, but the rest of us were looking for a really good head. Bates and I hunted hard all day and though we heard caribou grunt at us from the timber, we never did get to see them. Then when we returned to camp that evening, Mac took us across the creek and showed us the tracks. About the middle of the day, along had come a nice band of six or seven cows, driven by a remarkably fine bull. He had stopped, just across the creek from the camp and within 50 yards, and snorted and pawed the ground. Mac said he carried very wide and high double shovels with many points, big wide-spreading bays and long beams with a forest of points in the top formation. He tried to count the points and said he was convinced that bull carried thirty-five to forty, but sad to say, we never saw a hair of him again. Typical luck with caribou.

We saw a lot of caribou on that trip all told, but remarkably few really good heads. Perhaps the most interesting experience I ever had with caribou occurred on our way out to the C.N.R. We had crossed Fish Creek and were heading back toward Mount Ida and the Three Sisters and had camped in a wide valley. While packing up the next morn I was still eating a mountain sheep and biscuit sandwich when I happened to glance across the valley and spotted four grizzlies. We had a grizzly hunt in short order but that is another story. Anyway, after skinning out a fine black sow grizzly Bates had killed, Harry Snyder, who knew I wanted a good caribou, told me to take my horse and the rest of the day and see what I could do, as we would cross the Divide out of caribou country the next day. I lost no time in taking his advice and started north, heading for several high mountain basins with little lakes in their heads.

I saw several bands of caribou but nothing worth a second glance until I topped out, overlooking a big basin surrounded by high mountains. Near a little lake was a band of caribou with one old white-necked bull and an old cow off to one side of the main band. Two small bulls appeared with the cows and calves of the main bunch but the old bull was alone with a big cow some 50 yards to their right.

I tied up my nag in some fir timber and sat down to figure out an approach. The day was nearly done, and I knew I would have to connect then or not at all. By dropping back over the ridge I made a wide circle that put me within half a mile of the band, but there was no further cover except grass in that huge wet meadow. I watched them until all heads were down feeding, or turned the other way, and then crawled through water as fast as I could, keeping my rifle up out of the wet muskeg. In this way I soon halved the distance, then stopped for a rest, and laying my rifle across a hummock to keep it dry I studied the old bull through the glasses. He had lain down and only the tops of his horns showed, but the top formation looked good, with wide fairly, heavy palms and five and six points respectively. I decided that if he had any sort of bays and even one good shovel I would take him, so I watched until all heads were down and again started crawling forward. I was thoroughly soaked by this time and the water increased in depth to six inches in places. However I was bound to close the range as I wanted a caribou head badly. Soon the old bull got up and surveyed the scenery in all directions. I lay still as a mouse when he looked my way.

When he dropped his head again to feed, the cow turned my way and again I had to wait until she started feeding. The others of the band were now bedded down chewing their cuds, so I had no trouble from them. Finally I made it into good range and found a small hummock on which to rest my elbows. Then with tight sling and a strong wind blowing in my face, I turned the safety over on the Hoffman .300 Magnum Mauser and waited for the bull to turn around. I had estimated the range at 200 yards and decided to try a heart shot. When he swung around square

[177]

broadside, I held about four inches below the knuckle on the shoulder to allow for the rifle's being sighted for 300 yards and fired. The 172-grain Government Boattail which I had filed and drilled was backed by 60 grains of Dupont 15½ powder and I plainly heard the bullet strike him. He turned away from me, then reared up on his hind feet and held that pose for several seconds, while I threw in another round and debated whether to take him in the back.

Finally he pitched over sideways and started kicking with the top hind foot. The old cow ran over to him and nosed and smelled of him. Soon the rest of the band came over at a trot and the oldest of the two young bulls circled the old boy and proceeded to rake him with his horns and strike him with a forefoot. I knew he was down for the count, so I picked up my empty case and pocketed it, then rose erect for the first time in nearly a half mile and started pacing the distance to the bull. I had covered about half the distance when that old cow saw me and immediately she came for me at a fast trot, the rest of the band following her. The wind was still almost a gale in my face, so they could not smell me and I wondered what they would do. At 20 yards or less they formed a semicircle around me with heads and noses extended, the while they twisted their noses one way or the other in an attempt to get my scent upwind. I have never seen a prettier sight and simply stood there and watched them as I had no camera. The young bull had plainly taken up with the old cow and seemed glad I had bumped off his much larger rival.

Finally the old cow circled to the right and went almost around me before she caught my scent; then she stood on her hind feet and, throwing her muzzle high in the air, snorted and took off in her peculiar swinging rolling gait as fast as she could trot or pace, whichever it is. The young bull paced right along by her side, then while both he and the cow were in full flight and the rest of the band following, the bull mated with her and neither slackened pace in the slightest during the process. It was a beautiful sight and I have long wished I had had a good movie camera to record this phase of wildlife. That evening, when I told Snyder and the rest of the party of my experience, I am sure they thought I was crazy, but facts are often stranger than fiction.

The 172-grain doctored M-1 bullet had struck the knuckle joint as I intended, breaking it, penetrated square through the center of the heart, then the ribs and shoulder muscles on the off side, and lay just under the skin in the flat of the off shoulder. Wound channel was about 1½ to 2 inches in diameter and perfect execution. The slug was well expanded and furled back over half its length, showing ideal performance. The bull had one fair shovel and two good uniform bays, but with only two points on each. All told he carried twenty-one points and was the best head we obtained on the trip, so I was well satisfied. I skinned him complete and when I had finished and made skin and head into a pack to take back to the horse, I looked up and saw that old cow and her band still going as if the devil was after them and probably three miles away. They were on top of a high ridge, and through the glasses I could still see her throw her nose in the air and snort. Evidently I must have smelled very bad to her.

Pacing the distance from the bull to my muddy wallow where I had shot from proved the range just 220 yards. For all the concern those caribou showed after I killed the big bull, I might just as well have walked up to them and killed him. But maybe the old chap would have had far different ideas. At any rate I seriously doubt if that old cow or any of the rest of the band, with the possible exception of the old bull, had ever before seen or scented a man.

That head still hangs in my house as I write this and is still in perfect condition. Hunting caribou is like prospecting for gold—they are where you find them. A really fine head is, however, one of the most impressive and beautiful of all North American big game trophies.

X I

Elk

ALTHOUGH the American wapiti is closely related to several European and Asiatic species, it is the largest and finest of all the deer tribe with round antlers, on the entire earth. Wapiti were called elk by the early settlers, just as they misnamed the bison "buffalo." This name "elk" was no doubt brought from Europe where the moose is called elk. To Americans, the name will always be elk, just as our bison will be called buffalo.

Formerly the elk ranged most of the United States and the southern part of Canada, and was then more of a plains than a mountain animal, frequenting the cottonwood-bordered streams in the foothills and plains far more than the rugged steep mountains it ranges today. Time and the hunter's rifle have driven the remnants of the once great herds into the steepest, roughest mountains we have, with the exception of parts of Canada, mainly Alberta and some of B.C. and around Yellowstone Park. In New Mexico and also in Oregon, elk are found in less rugged country, but they have been replanted there after once being killed off completely.

Under favorable conditions, and where the animal has a fine high alpine summer range and can drift down to low elevations where the snow is light in the winter, they attain very large size. Elk live a long time if not killed off and often reach twenty years and occasionally live to be thirty-five years or over, as is well proved by one bull tagged and liberated in Montana, near Missoula, in 1909, and finally killed in 1944. They add weight and bulk as well, when they get older, as long as food is plentiful, until senility overtakes them. While Yellowstone Park elk dress out, for average, five- and six-point bulls, around 450 to 500 pounds with the entrails removed and feet removed, but skin and head left on; these are small elk, and sadly degenerated from what they once were in Montana and Wyoming. The Depot Agent at Gardiner, Montana, in 1917 had, he said, shipped out around 500, which he claimed averaged 450 to 500 pounds so dressed, for mature five- and six-point bulls.

Elk in the South Fork of the Flathead, the Clearwater drainage of Idaho, comprising the Lochsa, Selway and Clearwater Rivers and the Salmon River drainage, often greatly exceed these figures. Formerly the Wyoming elk were much larger also, when they had unlimited range, and seem to run to the widest spread of all elk, owing to the nature of the open parklike country they inhabit. Burt Ennis weighed one bull they raised from a calf in Jackson Hole, and when he was a fine prime bull they ran him on the scales in August, when he was at the peak of condition, and he weighed 1630 pounds. This is an exceptional weight, but I have killed three bulls fully as large — one in the South Fork of the Flathead in 1919 and another in the Lochsa in 1931 and another old boy here on the Salmon. I have also seen a few more of these huge old gentlemen. They were all huge-framed animals with heavy bones, and the youngest of the extra-large ones I believe would have been around fifteen years old. One bull I killed in the Flathead was weighed one month after killing. He was skinned out completely the day after I killed him and a month later the clear meat weighed 627 pounds frozen, and it had shrunk and dried out a great deal, from the extreme dry cold of Montana. No hide, head, feet or innards were weighed; just the forequarters and the neck alone weighed 71 pounds, cut off in front of the shoulders. That bull did not carry an ounce of fat, as he was killed the eighteenth of October, after the rut was over, and hence was at the lowest ebb in vitality. He would easily have carried over 200 pounds of fat the latter part of August.

Frank Waterman claims to have once rendered over 200 pounds of tallow from one huge old bull, when it was hog fat. The meat of that elk must have shrunk a good 100 pounds before I weighed it, as it loaded three horses when killed. If it had been weighed when killed and killed in late August, that bull would no doubt have dressed with just entrails and feet removed a full 1000 pounds, and would have weighed 1400 or over on foot. The complete hide and head would weigh over 100 pounds green. Last fall we obtained another such fine old bull for Mr. E. E. Wilkinson, but it definitely was not as large a framed animal as some I have killed; it loaded three horses and we packed the huge skull and horns out on our backs. Such elk are rare and they are also wise and have plenty between those huge horns besides bone, so the average hunter seldom runs onto them. For this reason a false impression of old mature bulls is often given as to size and weight. Of course these fine old residenters are far larger than the average run of bull elk, but they do occur where feed is plentiful the year round, just as some old mule deer will dress 400 pounds or over and some exceptional whitetail bucks almost as large. Today elk have been driven into the steepest, roughest and heaviest timbered regions left, here in Idaho and also in much of Montana I have hunted, so that they are far more of a timber animal than an open country or plains animal, as they were formerly.

The largest cow elk I have weighed dressed 600 pounds with feet, entrails and head removed, but the skin left on. She was much larger than average big cows, also much larger than many five- and six-point bulls I have seen over the years.

An elk is truly a grand animal, the finest of all the deer tribe, both as to fine meat and as to general symmetry and beauty. Take a big fat and mature bull from ten to fifteen years of age when he is ready for the rut, around the last days of August or the first of September, and if he also carries a big head, then you have the most beautiful species of deer it is possible to find on this green earth. The rut occurs as a rule around the first of September and extends through September some years, while in others it will start the last of August and be about over by the last of September. Some seasons it will not start until about the tenth of September and rarely as late as the fifteenth, and will then extend into October. At the start of the rut, the bulls carry an enormous amount of fat when on good range, but by the end of the rut the big herd bulls will be as poor as snakes and with slim flanks. After the rut the old bulls usually go off alone, on the north slopes, in the thickest alder patches they can find and then start to recuperate and put on more flesh before winter hits them. They are often in much better condition in December than they are in October. Further, the meat is stronger during the rut. In most sections the season is in October, and this is all wrong. If those grand animals could be killed in September or even late August, when they are in the peak of condition, they would average 200 pounds heavier and be much finer meat. However at that time the weather is hot and the flies are very bad and a kill made on a south sidehill simply must be quartered and moved into the shade to cool within an hour or two, or it will spoil and be flyblown.

I believe the best eating bull I ever killed was in the early season and killed the sixteenth of September. He was a young five-point bull, and though the rut was in full swing and had been for two weeks, the older bulls had whipped him out away from the cows, so that he had spent his time in the cool of the timber and mud wallows and was fat as a seal. I have also seen very old bulls, around twenty years or older, killed during October that were still hog fat, as they were so old that cows no longer interested them and while the younger bulls were fighting and losing weight, these old gentlemen were peacefully going about the business of adding more tallow for the long winter they knew was coming. Such really big bulls will run from 60 to 65 inches at the withers and around 112 to 118 inches in length nose to tip of stubby tail. They fight like the devil during the rut and many have broken shoulders or broken ribs, that somehow later heal up. Have killed them with many bones clearly showing where they had been broken and had knitted together again. Likewise I have found many of these old fellows with bullets incised in scar tissue in various places and small holes clear through the lungs, as shown by the strips of scar tissue where the bullet went through. One old chap I killed in 1931 had a 220-grain Soft Point .30 caliber slug and two .30–30 slugs incised in his muscles. He had been around awhile and was at least twenty-five or thirty years old when I killed him.

The calves are born in May as a rule, though I have seen some as early as late April, after a mild winter and when the rut had started abnormally early. Usually one calf is born, but twins are also very common and rarely three may be born, though I have never seen three calves with one cow, but have seen twins so many times as to think nothing of it. The babies are born with spotted coats like a deer, but soon change.

In fighting, the bulls will bugle back and forth for a time, gradually working closer as they bugle, grunt and horn the small trees; they simply strip all the branches from many and will hook their powerful horns under many spruce and fir tree roots when of small size and tear them out of the ground completely. At the start of the rut each bull usually has a favorite wallow, in mud or damp ground, and usually in heavy spruce bottoms. He will bugle and horn up all the small trees in this neighborhood. Then as the rut approaches the fights will start. Usually they will make a run at each other using the horns, but this soon stops and they stand up on their hind feet, each bull with his nose raised to his full height, and then they box with those wicked forefeet, striking tremendous blows, until one or the other is knocked over backwards, when the winning bull will drop to all fours and use his horns with telling effect as the other departs. Each bull will endeavor to gather up a small band of cows, and failing in this will attempt to whip some other bull away from his harem and take it over.

In all the wild, I know of no sound as beautiful as the full-drawn bugle of a mature bull elk. Old elk hunters can tell much about the size and age of the animal from the bugle. Young bulls have a higher pitched, shriller bugle and we call them squealers, as they really do squeal at times. Older bulls have the deep and beautiful melodious notes, while extremely old ones are much hoarser and sometimes their bugle is more the bray of a jackass than the beautiful bugle of an elk. Charley Oneil and I heard one old fellow that was so old only made a long hoarse call, more like an old jack burro than an elk, and he would of course add plenty of heavy deep grunts to the end of it. He preferred to stay down in a very heavily timbered basin, where we would have had to swamp for three days to get horses to him, so we left him alone.

The bugle usually starts with a low, coarse and very deep tone, then after a second or two is raised to a higher pitched key, and then after an interval is raised to an even higher key, ending in a shrill scream or squeal, after which hoarse grunts are emitted. At a distance you hear only the beautiful bugle notes. Late in the season, after the rut, when the bulls were calling the cows and leaving for the winter range, I have heard the bugle start high and then come down the scale to a coarser note. Cows will often bark at you in the timber and it is a very hard sound to describe, usually not unlike a small dog down a rain barrel.

During the rut, the elk usually frequent the high alpine basins which carry heavy spruce, pine or fir timber and you can get up on the rim above and listen to the most beautiful music in all the hills. One bull will bugle, then another will answer him from across the basin, and these beautiful notes will be tossed back and forth, as more join in the fighting. It is a very hard sound to locate exactly, even when comparatively close, and no animal is any more adept at hiding himself in the timber than an elk. While formerly elk were easily located and seen in the beautiful open mountain parks and are still so found in country where they have been little hunted, or where they have been transplanted and protected for years, they are an entirely different animal where they have been hunted steadily.

When jumped, they go off with thundering crashes through the brush and fallen logs, but I have seen them sneak out as quietly as a wise old whitetail buck, with never a sound. The bulls can tip their horns back along their sides until they can get through an unbelievably small hole, without disturbing snow on the tree branches. I have seen old cows spot me in the timber and show only one eye and ear around a tree bole, then, after they had made up their mind as to what I was, they would slowly, almost imperceptibly, pull their head back out of sight and then disappear as silently as a ghost, and examination often proved there were several in the band, when I had seen only half of one cow's head. Hunting has taught them to skulk away as silently as a whitetail, when necessary. At other times I have followed along behind a feeding band of elk all day long, continually circling in the dense cedar timber trying to cut them off, and never even got a glimpse of an animal, though I could hear them quite plainly, many times during the day. They can go through a jungle of fallen logs and brush that a man can only crawl through, and do it with ease. Further, when jumped they can clear even very high windfalls, or creeks, at a single bound. They are just as active as a big mule buck, but do not make the high bouncing jumps of mule deer. Rather they make each jump carry them a maximum distance from danger. Elk will climb around in the goat cliffs and I have found them bedded on small flat places, among the goat cliffs, so long as there was some timber for cover. They seemingly pay no attention to height at all and last fall we found where a whole band had bedded for days, among some knife-blade ridges where there was hardly room for beds and the slope fell away under them for 500 feet sheer. I have also seen their tracks where they had negotiated cliffs that the uninitiated would think only a goat or sheep could traverse.

Though big animals, elk are very active. They are also beautifully built and proportioned. In coloration, elk differ from all our other game. The face and neck are a mahogany brown, shading into almost black, long mane hair, while the sides of the neck tend to shade into a lighter brown and on old specimens it will be much lighter, almost a brownish gray, also on top of the neck. The feet and legs are also a dark mahogany brown, splendidly proportioned. The hoofs are shaped more like the hoofs of a cow, or a buffalo, than a deer and are cupped considerably, with blunt curving toes on old bulls and sharper on cows and young bulls. Dewclaws are well developed, but not to any such extent as on the caribou. Elk can negotiate swamps and muskeg better than many other deer species. The body is a buckskin color, shading to almost white in old specimens, and much darker, almost a grayish brown, on younger animals and barren cows. Calves, yearlings and two-year-olds are much darker with the back and sides a grayish brown. The rump patch is large and yellow, almost orange, on many specimens and the short, but very large and heavy tail is the same color. When fat the rump is as round as a huge butterball and has much the same color, though more orange. The tail is often tipped up above horizontal when the animal is frightened or even mildly alarmed, but is not elevated to the extent of caribous' and whitetails' and is so short and stubby as to be almost unnoticeable. The neck is long and on bulls very heavy as well. The mane starts just back of the jaws and extends down well toward the front of the chest. The brisket is usually a deep mahogany brown on cows and almost black on some bulls, while the belly of cows is white or whitish and nearly or quite black down the central line on bulls. A deep tear duct lies below and toward the nose, from the eye. The brown hair on the face, particularly around the horn bases, tends to curl on big bulls. Elk usually shed their huge horns in late February or early March, while young animals may carry them later. Usually the deer and moose are shed long before the elk.

Wounded elk, when mad, will fight a buzzsaw and give it any odds and we have had several turn on us. Even an old cow with a broken back gritted and ground her teeth together, the while she pawed herself toward me with fire in her eye, only to receive another slug in the brain. They are dead game animals and can take an enormous amount of punishment, in fighting as well as when shot, and they are also very good rustlers and will survive hard winters that will kill most other game, except moose.

In the summer they are grazing animals but also browse a lot, and in winter they will eat anything that has food value. They browse all willows and aspens and snow brush and will even eat the bark and limbs of small conifers when pressed. Last winter they cleaned out about all the grass in the river bottom above my orchard, and also most of the small brush had the limbs cropped. Up Sheep Creek, which flows into the lower end of my little ranch, they had eaten the smaller limbs from a great deal of the brush of various kinds, as well as pawing out all the wild timothy and other grasses they could reach under big trees. Out in the open the snow crusted too hard and deep, so they finished the winter on such browse.

These elk winter here on the North Fork of the Salmon drainage, but each summer three bands of sheep drive most of them out of Idaho and over into the Bitterroot drainage of Montana and the Big Hole basin, tributary to the Missouri, also in Montana. There they summer and stay until the next winter, when the deep snow drives them back into Idaho. If these three bands of sheep were excluded from the forest in this section, these elk would stay here the year round and benefit a great many sportsmen, as compared with the benefits derived by three sheep owners.

Elk are migratory only in the sense that they migrate up to the highest alpine meadows for the summer and down into the sagebrush flats for the winter. They do make long treks in some cases. Formerly the elk of Yellowstone Park had abundant winter range in Idaho, Montana and Wyoming, but as ranchers fenced in and turned their winter range into ranches for livestock, the elk winter range was sharply curtailed, until now only a fraction of it exists. Even with winter feeding of the herds by the Fish and Wildlife Service, formerly the Biological Survey, the herds do not do as well as in the early days, when they had ample range, and for this reason the park herds have deteriorated in size and are not now the big fine elk they were in the eighties. Many of the finest heads were also

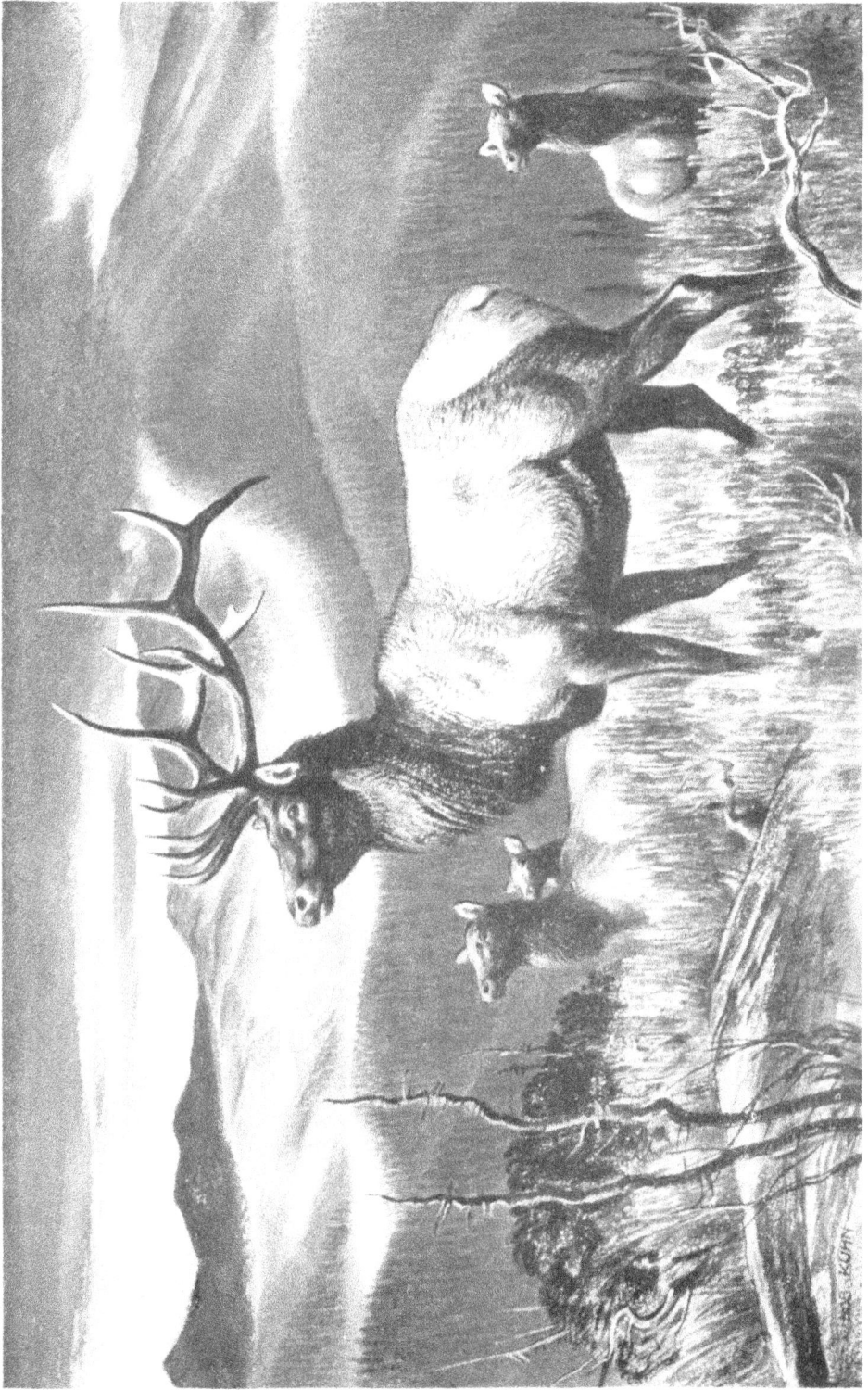

Elk

The author with record bull elk killed in 1919 with a .30–06, 220 grain, broadside in neck, which dropped him. He was finished with a .38–40 S. A. Colt after he nearly killed the author. Photographed by Captain W. R. Strong about two hours before he himself was killed accidentally for an elk

Victor J. Azbe with an Alberta six-point elk killed by him with a .30–06

taken at a much earlier date. Horns of those park elk usually run long and slender, while those of huge old bulls in this section are much more massive, seldom quite as long as the park elk, but usually much heavier and with much longer tines, both brow and sword as well as tip points. I have one set taken here on the North Fork that go seventh place in present records, but neglected to send in the measurements in time for the last book. Another head killed by Mr. E. E. Wilkinson last fall under my guidance would run very high as to weight of antlers, according to the new measurement charts by James L. Clark. I believe his measurement charts are much better than the earlier ones which took the total length of main beam as the main measurement in classifying the heads.

Yearling bulls usually have one long horn on each side, about 14 to 18 inches or two feet in length and the second year they usually carry two points but sometimes three to the antler. At four years they very often carry five points to the side, but good heads that are of trophy proportions are not reached before seven years as a rule and the finest and heaviest are nearly always taken from elk ten to fifteen years of age. After that they again deteriorate and very old bulls sometimes have only one long shoot with a club effect at the top and very few of the normal points or tines on the antlers. The usual head has just six points on a side, but quite often an extra point appears at the web between the high sword point and the extreme tip fork and this forms the royal or seven-point head. Some have more and I have seen them with ten points to a side and killed several with seven-point heads, also one with seven and eight points, and I have also seen heads with a great many points on each side and considerable palmation of the top formation. W. L. Dickey, while on a trip with me one fall in the Selway, killed a six-point bull that had a very rare horn formation of the right antler. About a foot from the base a heavy arm grew out at right angles to the main beam and fully as large as the beam itself, and ended in a huge knob as large as a man's fist. That bull had used it for a headrest when sleeping, as the outer side plainly showed.

Widespread heads usually occur where the elk range high open country in the summer, and those ranging heavily timbered alpine basins usually carry antlers of greater weight, but narrower spread. I have one head of a very old bull I killed on the Lochsa that has a 53½-inch spread and seven and eight points, but only a 49-inch length, as he was too old to grow the extreme long antlers he must have turned out in earlier years. The horns are, however, very heavy and massive. My best head has more typical horns with six even points to a side and the main beam measures 62½ inches for one horn and 60¾ for the other, with the greatest width between the two tip points of any elk I have ever seen. His spread was around 50 inches. A big elk head simply demands a shoulder mount, else the nose must be tipped down in a very unnatural position to mount it at all, and one needs a room ten to twelve feet high to display such a head properly. I have one in the Elks' Temple at Nampa, Idaho, and another fine one in the Haveman Hardware store at Salmon, Idaho. An ordinary dwelling house is just too small to display a big elk head.

The ears are large, but not as large in proportion as those of mule deer, and elk have a very acute sense of hearing — in fact I believe their ears are the full equal of any other of our hoofed big game, if not better. Their eyes are also excellent, fully the equal of deer eyes and I believe even better, as I have seen elk spot me, or the camp or pack string, many times at a distance where deer would have paid no attention to us. I believe they are, however, inferior to either sheep or antelope in the matter of eyesight. Their sense of smell is second to none among our hoofed game and probably is superior to that of any other species of such game. An elk can wind you easily at half a mile if there is any wind drift to bring him your scent.

When traveling, an old cow nearly always leads the band and the bull will be found bringing up the rear, herding the cows along and watching to see that none deserts his harem during the rut. I once watched a steady stream of elk pass single file on the drainage of the West Gallatin in Montana for several hours, and even at that distance, as they were over in the preserve, you could make out the old bulls by seeing them dip their heads, then the animal in front of them would break into a run for a few jumps. The horns were not visible at that distance.

In the South Fork of the Flathead I have seen old bulls round up an entire band of elk when we moved into the basin with a pack string, take them up on top of the Divide and herd them along for ten or fifteen miles before dropping down into another basin, and always some wise old cow took the lead while the bull drove the stragglers. They are very intelligent animals, much more so on the whole than most deer I have hunted.

During the spring and early summer, the old bulls go off by themselves and herd alone, high up on the wind-swept ridges and little alpine basins, where they can grow and cure their antlers. The cows will have their calves down in the heavy timber and then about the last of August the bulls will start their intensive bugling and start to gather up their harem and fight off any rival. When hard hunted, they will feed all night on moonlight nights and bed in the dense alder thickets, usually on the north slope in the daytime, where it is still-hunting with a vengeance. In the mountains, snow does not bother elk to the extent it does deer, and while mule deer will be found bedded or feeding just about the lower edge of the snow line in the fall, the elk will stay up high until the snow is much deeper unless they have an unmolested winter range far from civilization. Elk do not like civilization at all. They are far more wary than deer and prefer the solitude of the forests and high mountains in the interior, where they seldom get the man scent. On the West Gallatin, I have seen them wallowing through snow up to their bellies rather than come down into the sagebrush where they knew the hunters were waiting. However, on the Lochsa where they have plenty of winter range at low elevations and sagebrush and cedar thickets, I have seen them migrating down to their winter range in October. The fact that domestic sheep are run on the Divide all summer and the range eaten and trampled into the earth drives the elk off their summer range much earlier than would be the case if said sheep were excluded from our National Forests where big game is prevalent. This in turn forces them down on their winter range long before they should migrate, with the result that the winter range is soon eaten out and many starve during the winter. Then the game commission will hold early season hunts in an endeavor to limit the numbers of the herds, but nothing is ever done to correct the basic cause and remove the damn domestic woolies from their summer range. To any student of our wildlife here it is a sorry picture, and one wonders which is worth the most to the sportsmen of this great country, a few bands of domestic sheep or the great herds of elk and deer. The sportsmen are not organized, while the wool growers definitely are and maintain a powerful lobby in Washington. Most of the forest rangers, even though they would rather see the game than the sheep in this game country, have a job to hold down, must keep mum and part their hair in the middle, or lose their jobs. We need domestic sheep, but there is plenty of range for them on the desert and in non-game country, without ruining our best game sections by grazing them in the high forests during the summer. Further, we believe that the elk and deer such forests would support are worth far more, to a greater number of people, than a few bands of domestic sheep. An old bull elk standing on some shoulder of a ridge the while he issues his challenge to all and sundry is a far prettier picture to me than all the domestic sheep on our combined National Forests, and I would like to see said woolies removed forever from such sections as have good bands of elk and mule deer and wild sheep. Big game and domestic sheep can never be maintained on the same range. We need sheep—but not on big game ranges.

[189]

In and around the park, the bull elk usually run in groups and stay in close proximity to the cows and calves and young bulls, gradually working down on their winter range as the winter drives them in their search for food. Real old bulls usually range alone most of the time. They have been whipped out of the herds during the rut and lead solitary lives, though they will usually bugle their challenge during the season. When the rut is at its height, you can hear bulls bugling all night long, also grunting and fighting. I have had them answer my bugle many times while I was lying in my bed in the tent.

During the rut is the easiest time to hunt elk in this heavily timbered country; the elk stay in the timber during the day, coming out in the open parks only during the early morning and during the nights to feed. For that reason one has little chance of getting a fine head except during the rut, when they can be called. Elk will at times answer a bugle long after the rut is over, and while they seldom come to you then, they can be teased into answering and thus allowing you to locate their position, when you can sneak in and get a shot; at other times they will be wary and will circle enough to get your scent and depart.

Considerable time must be spent with the elk during the rut really to master calling them, and one should never bugle too often, or they will get wise. Likewise a false note is usually enough to send them on their way. I have, however, at times seen elk that would answer most any kind of a whistle and have often had them bugle at the bells of the pack string. When you get a good bull to answer in the dense forest and endeavor to call him up, it is something to be remembered, as he comes back with his beautiful long-drawn challenge and ends with deep, hoarse, guttural grunts. I always like to take my stand in some dense clump of timber that will permit observation on all sides and preferably above the elk that has answered, as I then have a much better chance of avoiding giving him my scent. If your bugling is right and you end the call with good hoarse grunts and then trample limbs and brush and rake a tree bole with a limb, you can usually get a bull fighting mad in short order, when he will come with his hair standing on end down his spine and his eyes glowing. They are grand game and one of the most thrilling to hunt of any.

I have made bugles of many different materials. Wild parsnip tubes make a very soft realistic bugle but its notes will not carry far and are very fragile. All metal tubes I have tried had a peculiar metallic sound that is not natural and I never used one, though I have had elk answer when I blew into an empty cartridge case. By far the best bugle, and what I have used for over fifteen years, is made from sections of common bamboo fishing pole. You take a long bit and bore out the middle node, leaving a tube some 16 to 18 inches long and ½ to ⅝ or even ¾ inch inside diameter. The larger the tube the more chest expansion and wind you will need. The larger tubes more nearly imitate the call of an old bull and the young squealer bulls will seldom answer them, and if they do they will not come, as they are afraid of a fight with a big bull. The larger inside diameter bugle is very good to use when you are after a big head. However, the old bulls will also get very mad at any young upstart challenging them and they will come to give him his lesson. I had one bugle that I used for some ten years that had a large tube and was 18 inches long. It required all the wind I could get in my lungs at one time, to produce the full, long-drawn, changing-note call. I gave it to Dee Vissing but doubt if he ever had wind enough to do it justice.

You fit a soft wood plug in one end and notch, forming a common kid's whistle, and leave the other end closed, with a node in the bamboo, or open as you choose. If left open you can hold a hand over that end and modulate and change the pitch of the call, while if left closed you can use it with one hand, but cannot get quite so wide a range in change of notes. I usually start with a low call by blowing slowly and softly into the bugle, then raise the pitch by blowing harder and holding each note as long as possible, finally increasing the tone to a higher key and ending with a shrill scream, with all the power of my lungs. Then I grab a breath and grunt if the bull is close enough to hear his grunts. The call will carry clearly for two miles or more in the still mountain basins and the cliffs will throw back an echo at times and further amplify it. It is best to tape the bamboo full length with black machinist's tape, to prevent splitting and checking. Also cement in the wooden whistle plug with spar or other waterproof varnish. A call doesn't sound quite right until the whistle is wet, when it produces a more natural tone, but don't expect to call elk the first time you try it, as you simply must spend many days with them and learn their various fighting talk and how to mimic it.

After the rut, elk will occasionally bugle on certain days, often before or during the early stages of a storm. Then is the best time to get an answer. You can bugle at intervals where elk are hid in the timber after the rut and they will make no answer, but if you can hear one bugle and answer him, you have every chance of getting an answer, and though they won't come then except on rare occasions, they will answer enough to let you locate them.

I usually carry a bugle in late elk hunting for this reason. At other times you may jump a band of elk in the timber that have not winded you and you can then sometimes stop them by a short bugle. The bull may not answer, but he will usually circle back for a look at you or to get your scent and this habit can be taken advantage of. Our elk hunting here, and in fact in most elk ranges west of the Continental Divide, is timber still-hunting. The game usually stays in the timber and there you must look for it. Just as well stay in camp as try to hunt elk with the breeze or wind behind you. You will have to bring into play everything you know of still-hunting to be successful, and when you do spot one you may have small chance of sizing up his head, unless it is during the rut and you are calling him.

Perhaps the hardest thing of all to learn is to see them. To the old guide this presents no problems, and he will see any part of a game animal visible, but sportsmen who are out from the cities and do not have good game eyes often look for minutes in vain, when the animal is in plain sight. Elk are big animals and not half as hard to see in the timber as deer, yet I have had to line my rifle sights on them many times before the sportsmen saw them. You must know what to look for, as well as where to look. It may be the turn of an ear around a tree, or a patch of that buckskin body, or a patch of the orange-yellow rump that is visible, and you must learn to pick it out through openings in the trees and know if possible what part of the beast it is. There is no earthly use in shooting such game in the rear end with a small rifle, unless you hit the spine, as elk will travel all day with 220-grain .30–06 slugs driven in from the rear unless the skeletal structure is broken down. Often elk will be bedded and you will see something that simply does not look natural. Investigate anything of that sort. A good pair of light binoculars will help, though they take the use of your hands, which may be needed to work the rifle at a split second's notice. You will be surprised how little timber it takes to completely hide a big bull elk and how he will take advantage of its cover if he has the least suspicion of your presence.

If you run onto a band of cows during the rut, then keep quiet and look for the old herd bull at the rear end of the bunch. Often a bunch of cows will cross an open patch in the timber while the old bull, if he has been hunted, may carefully skirt the edge, keeping himself concealed. You must know what the game looks like and then familiarize yourself with what each portion of him looks like, so you can instantly recognize any part that comes to view. Never shoot until you know exactly what you are shooting at. In 1919 I lost my best friend and hunting partner when hunting elk in the timber of Babcock Creek in the South Fork of the Flathead, simply because another man saw only a patch of Bill

Strong's buckskin shirt the size of his hand and promptly put a 150-grain umbrella point in it, for he was on a fresh elk track and thought he saw one. That slug missed me by inches, and many times since then I have raised my rifle and slipped the safety and waited for minutes for an animal to move and disclose its nature. Many of them have thus gotten away but some did not, and if I cannot see enough of the game to know absolutely where I am shooting it, I do not want the shot at all.

If you are after a trophy bull, you simply must see what kind of head he carries before shooting, and if you are out for meat, you also want to know what you are shooting. Old elk hunters in the late season will nearly always pick a big dark cow because she is apt to be either a young animal or a barren cow, and in any case she will usually be a dry cow with plenty of fat on her rump. I have seen very old cows whose bones were as brittle as glass when we quartered them up that were very fat and also fine meat, because they were dry. These old ladies were usually a pale yellow color. A small spike bull or a calf will be very tender, but not nearly so well flavored as an older, mature animal. However, after the rut the big bulls are skin poor, except those old chaps who, on account of age, have stagged off by themselves. They are sometimes fat, but often poor teeth or earlier injuries keep them poor the year round.

Remember that elk are prone to bed in the flat timbered bottoms and usually well screened by brush, or on the little flat shoulders of ridges, where they will usually bed by the side of a tree bole, log or stump.

I remember once when Chink Clark and I were working the north slope on Brushy Creek. The timber and brush were so dense and high we could only see about 30 yards and would climb up on logs and old stumps in order to see a bit more of the forest. I climbed or vaulted up on a huge fallen log, only to have a good fat bull jump from the other side of it. He was out of sight before I could turn the safety on the .400 Whelen, but by climbing higher on the stump of that log I could see his horns above the alders and placed a 350-grain slug into his paunch from the rear. He turned quartering away and moving slow so I knew he was hit and sick. I put two more into him, then waited; he soon stopped and we could hear him trampling brush, so I sneaked in and busted him in the center of the neck where it joined the skull. One slug had gone in under the tail and one in each flank, and all had stopped in that big water and grass filled paunch, which will weigh full 300 pounds in a mature elk. Recoil of the big rifle pushed me back off my perch to the ground each shot, and I had to climb back on the log and thence to the top of the stump for the next shot. I would not have attempted such a shot with any .30 caliber rifle as I well knew only a heavy slug would stop that elk when I could see nothing but the horns and had to hold down in the brush where I knew his body was located.

At times you may see only the horns of a bull around a tree bole or over a fallen log. At other times only the rump patch of a bedded elk may show around the bole of a big tree. You must be able to recognize game as soon as it is in sight. Old woodsmen who have hunted a lifetime have trained their eyes until they are constantly searching out every nook and cranny of the forest floor for the least suspicious sign. In time their sub-conscious takes over and they may go quietly along, slipping from tree to tree and stopping often, to listen and smell the wind. The instant any part of an animal is visible their eyes will see it, and the subconscious takes care of this almost without their knowledge. I have been accused of hav-ing the best eyes that my sportsmen had ever been out with, but know it is merely a matter of training. If you spend enough time at any one task you should in time learn something of it, and that has been the case with my eyes. Indians have good eyes at times, but no better than those of whites, and I have seen and recognized goats three miles away which the Indians swore were snowdrifts. You can improve your game eyes by going into the timber at every opportunity and studying bird life and any small animals you come in contact with. When you can spot a squirrel's eye and ear easily over a tree limb, you will also be able to see big game, but remember you are after an animal with very good eyesight and in the matter of hearing and sense of smell he has you licked before you start, so govern your travels accordingly.

Elk usually have regular trails worn deep in the ground in any alpine basin they inhabit, and you can travel best and with least noise by follow-ing one of these trails, if the wind is favorable. The trails will usually lead from their bed to feeding ground and will pass through the low saddles in surrounding ridges. Elk use the same ridges in their migration down to winter quarters year after year unless heavily hunted, when they will change their route. They are much more wary than deer and if you kill one in a certain basin today, you will have to go farther for the next. They can soon smell a kill and will move.

If you miss one, there is little use in continuing after it unless the going is good and you have snow, for elk will usually travel a long, long way before stopping again. Once scared, they line out and usually leave that section of the country, so it is imperative that you make your first shot good and all that is needed. When you see elk in the timber, they will usually be watching you, unless you have made a noiseless approach, and while they will crash off through the timber with all the stealth and silence of a runaway locomotive when jumped, they can also sneak away as silently as an old whitetail buck.

Many times I have seen them poke one eye and ear around a big tree bole and take one careful look, then slowly pull that side of their head back out of sight, taking several seconds for the procedure, then sneak away. Elk reason, just as do most all wild animals and, for that matter, some humans as well. They well know any quick movement on their part will be detected by the hunter, but many hunters do not reason as well and when they see elk in the timber, instead of slowly and quietly raising their rifle until it bears on said elk, they jerk the gun up, and probably also jump to one side to see more of the animal, and the net result is they see only a flash of very fast moving elk across various small openings in the timber.

Elk feed on moonlight nights and early mornings, then again late in the evening, and if hunted much they will shack up in some dense timber where the fallen logs and brush make a quiet approach almost impossible. They also have the uncanny habit of doubling and circling back before bedding, so that they can get the wind drift from their back trail, yet when merely traveling along they, as do many other game animals, like to travel into the wind so they can smell any enemy in front of them. The old bull will nearly always be behind and usually out of sight as well, and he will circle and pick up the wind from the back trail if he has any suspicions of anyone being after him. For this reason you simply must stay off the trail if you want to get a shot. If a band of elk feed slowly over some ridge and down into a timbered basin, you can be sure they will in time work out through some low saddle on the other side, and if they are traveling down country they will usually traverse the long slope of some ridge, usually where there is plenty of timber for cover.

They like old burns, with the scrub maple and laurel thickets, and often bed in these, just above a big old maple brush that the frost has turned all colors. Then their coat blends well with their surroundings and you will have to look close to see them. Elk dig out comfortable beds just above tree roots, fallen logs or stumps as a rule, and nearly always select a spot that well conceals them, yet allows them every advantage and a good view of their back trail. One has only to trail a few wounded elk to learn that he is after an animal with more than average intelligence. Even a badly wounded elk can usually cover more ground than you can in a day, so it is imperative that you stay clear of its trail and circle if you want the animal to bed and give you a shot.

[195]

During the migration down to winter quarters, many elk are killed by a hunter's selecting some vantage point along their route and simply sitting tight and watching, especially early in the morning and in late evening. When the brush and ground are dry, or when you have crusted snow, there is very little use in trying to still-hunt elk that are bedded in the timber, as they will invariably hear you and depart long before you get in sight of them. Elk hunting in this country, and for that matter in most of the elk ranges west of the Continental Divide, is usually tough hunting, but east of the Divide in the more open, rolling and parklike country of Montana and Wyoming, as well as Colorado and New Mexico, it is de luxe. There you can ride out until you cut the tracks of a band of elk and ride along to windward of their trail until you spot them, then with the glasses determine if a shootable bull is with the band and figure out the best approach. If you want to see plenty of elk and have easy hunting, and sometimes see some fine heads as well, it is very hard to beat Montana and Wyoming and parts of Alberta. In many ways the Alberta hunting is the nicest of all, as that is far more virgin country and the elk there run larger than the park elk. This country is so steep and heavily timbered that elk hunting is hard hunting and you must know all the rules of the game to insure success, and except during the rut you have relatively little chance of ever selecting a head. You may run onto one of the old residenters that will carry a far heavier head than most any of them now found in, or around, the park, but you may also see only small bulls. In the early season we formerly had here, from the fifteenth of September to the first of October, it was de luxe hunting also for an experienced elk hunter, as you could call them out with ease and look over any number of bulls.

Charley Oneil and I had such a hunt in September of 1936 in the Lochsa. We had Erikson pack us down the river, then forded it and crossed over to the south side and climbed well up on the slope of the main ridge, where we made camp at a little spring. An old burn surrounded our camp, and we had an early fall of wet snow that cooled the elk off a bit and stopped their bugling as we set up the camp. But the next morning they were bugling as we started up the ridge. We climbed to the top of the ridge and traversed it back for some three miles, walking right into a big old cow moose in the timber. Then I had an answer to my bugle far below us and across a small creek. It sounded coarse enough for a good mature bull, to me, so down the right side of the creek we went in an old elk trail. I would bugle and he would answer about every fifteen minutes, just enough to keep his location in mind.

In this way we worked down the creek to the first flat or basin, when the bull started up on the other side of the creek to meet us, getting his dander up. The timber was so thick it was hard to see over 50 yards except directly across the creek. Huge old spruce trees were mixed with tamarack and fir and snow brush six feet high, so I whispered to Oneil that we would take an elk trail that worked up toward the top of the ridge to our right and climb higher so he would not be as apt to get our scent, and from there we could see farther across the creek. We had no more than picked our position some 60 yards up the slope from the creek when the bull bugled hoarsely and grunted, then came up the other side at a run. He jumped the creek above our position with his hair all standing on end and plainly mad as a wet hen. One huge 30-foot bound carried him high over the creek and its fallen crisscrossed logs and he stopped at the trail, where we had come down. Then with neck outstretched he lowered his head and sniffed the trail. One sniff and he got our scent, just as a good hound dog would do. Instantly the hair dropped on his back and he was back across the creek, in an even wilder and higher bound. I bugled again, sharp and loud, and ended the call with several shrill sharp fighting notes, and this stopped him. He stood perfectly still and answered me right back. He was a beautiful bull with an average six-point head, and with his hair again standing straight up on his back and neck made a beautiful sight. I whispered to Oneil to follow me and silently worked down the trail some ten feet until I could find a good opening through which he could shoot. The bull was then about 60 to 80 yards from us and standing broadside. However, Charley did not follow me and was having a hard time trying to find an opening through which to shoot. Finally he fired, but I could not tell that he hit. The bull pranced back and along the bar then turned and presented the other side. Then I saw a dark plotch as large as my hand on the right flank. I could not tell whether it was mud or blood, but it looked like blood from the bullet exit. Though we did not know it then, Oneil had him, as his 250-grain .35 Whelen Soft Point slug had struck just back of the left shoulder and emerged high on the right flank, penetrating through the lungs. I kept up continuous fighting talk on the bugle as Charley shot twice more, but from his position so many limbs intervened that I doubt if either slug ever reached the elk.

Just then I saw a huge old black cow come along and sneak past the bull. She was a wonderful piece of meat but we both had bull licenses that year. The bull made no attempt to leave after receiving that heavy slug, but he neither flinched nor showed in any way that he was hit, except for that dark patch on his right flank. I whispered for Charley to bust him again, but he answered that his Lyman .48 was loose on the receiver and asked if I could see him. I answered in the affirmative and he asked me to give him another. I wanted Charley to come on down to me and finish the job so kept answering the bull on the bugle. Then, like many other wounded bulls I have seen, he turned and came out toward us, on the shoulder of the ravine over the creek, a short distance below where Charley had hit him, and again turned that right side to us. For 50 yards below him the creek was a jumble of crisscrossed fallen logs where we would have the devil's own time dressing him out or later getting horses. Well knowing we would have to pack him out of that log jam in quarters and up such a steep slope to the horses, I was very anxious for Charley to drop him where he stood. Finally Oneil again ordered me to bust him if I could see him, so, holding just back of the right shoulder, I gave him a 300-grain .375 Nitro Express load from my little double-barreled Lancaster rifle. He was mad as the devil, wounded, and had no intention of doing anything but squaring accounts with us, so he turned and came toward us right to the very brink of the ravine, bugling as he came, but his bugles had a strangling sound. Knowing my rifle, I had no intention of shooting again. He stood there facing us with legs widespread and blood running out of his mouth, until he tried to bugle again, then fell on his nose.

Oneil's first shot had done the business and mine was not needed, but without it he would have tried to cross over to us again and would no doubt have piled up in that log-choked creek bottom. We opened and dressed him, then skinned him out completely, Charley peeling the carcass while I removed the head and cape. We decided to call it a day and arrived back in camp very tired and hungry. That night the wind came up and we heard weird ghostly music all night, but could not locate the source of it. Sometimes it sounded like distant human singing, at other times like organ music. Finally Oneil thought it was a distant band of wolves howling until I told him there were only very few scattered wolves in the country. Next day we located the cause. Those old standing snags were all burned out inside and many had various-shaped holes burned where pitch limbs had been consumed. Through these various orifices in the hollow snags the early morning breeze played a tune, weird and hard to locate.

That day we had a hearty breakfast and taking a sandwich for lunch climbed up the ridge back of camp. After we crossed a low saddle we found a beautiful spruce basin lying below us to the left, and knowing it would be a good place for elk I stopped and bugled. Instantly a bull came back with his beautiful long-drawn melodious answer. I waited about ten minutes and answered him, and again he came back. We spent a half hour there talking to him on the bugle, but from the shrill end to his call I decided he was a young bull that the big ones had driven away from the cows and probably would be fat as a seal. He would answer, but did not want any fight and would not come to us, so I told Oneil to sit tight and I would go down into the basin after him. I slipped quietly along from one scrub fir tree to another, taking advantage of all the cover I could find, until I gained the cover of a good-sized clump of trees and with plenty of shin-tangle to cover my descent on to the bottom. Then I sat down and gave him the meanest fighting talk on the bugle I could muster, and he answered. I waited a long time and tried again, and again he answered, but plainly he was not going to come to me, so I started my stalk again, as I now had him located in a big boggy spring among some huge spruce trees. When I was about 150 yards from that little flat spring bottom I located him, bedded in a muddy wallow. He was a fine five-point bull, as fat and round as a seal, and as meat was what I wanted, not horns, I decided to take him. He was turned almost square broadside and I bugled at him again, as I was in excellent cover where he could not see me and I wanted him to get up. He answered but would not even get up out of the mud, so thinking that mud hole would be one hell of a place to dress him, I sat down and, resting my elbows on my knees, placed the tip of the gold front sight square over the platinum line in the open English rear sight and about halfway up on his ribs close in behind the shoulder, for a high lung shot, and squeezed off the left barrel. When the little .375 recoiled, I heard the sodden plunk of the 300-grain slug striking home. He bounced out of his bed into a hard run, for all the world as if he had been bedded on coil springs, and was out of sight in the spruce trees in two jumps.

Oneil called down the mountain and asked if I had got him. Knowing my rifle, I told him to come down as we would have a job to do, and I sat there silently thanking that bull for leaving his mud wallow. We had a smoke, then picked up his trail, but he only went about 15 yards from where I had last seen him and there we found him on his back, with his legs all sticking up in the air and horns driven deep into the soft muddy ground. He had evidently died running and turned a somersault that was never quite completed. We had a nice grassy place to dress and skin him out and plenty of huge trees on which to hang him. After skinning out and quartering, we found my slug had gone through the tops of both lungs and severed the big artery under the spine, then lodged under the skin at the back edge of the off, or right shoulder, perfectly expanded. I had made cases for the rifle out of .405 Winchester cases, by swaging them down to form and cutting off some of the end of the case, then filing the rims thinner so they would fit the shallow rim cuts in the British chambers. The load was 48 grains of Dupont 3031 powder and Remington 8½ primers with Western 300-grain Soft Point .375 Magnum bullets. Mrs. Keith claimed that was the finest elk meat I ever brought home. Since he was a young bull, the old bulls had whipped him away from the cows, so that all he did was lead the life of Riley and pile more fat on his back.

One of the most interesting elk stalks I have had occurred last fall while guiding Gene Wilkinson. We had climbed up to a high Divide, noting fresh elk tracks going both ways through the pass, and topped out in a beautiful 8500-foot mountain meadow. Scrub piñon pines and balsam decorated the edge of the valley, while very heavy and dense stands of beautiful large spruce interspersed with grassy wet meadows covered the valley floor. It was about a mile in length by a half mile wide. We slipped over the summit and sat down for a rest and to look and listen. No game was in sight, but soon we heard an old bull bugle, a little over a quarter mile below us and on the left side of the basin. This was great good luck, as we had not heard one for several days.

Filling my lungs to the utmost, I gave him the very best and longest answer I could muster and he came right back. We waited five minutes and then I called again. Again he answered, the tone telling me instantly it was an old heavy bull. Again I waited five minutes before calling and again he came back. We played with him for twenty minutes or more but he would not come. Then three more bugles answered my next call at widely spaced parts of the valley. They were all four in heavy timber and invisible. I continued to tease the old boy and told Gene we would go after him as he would not come. We slipped down on the left side of the valley and started skirting the wet springs and heavy timber. Each time I bugled all four bulls would come back at me and one, directly across the valley from the big bull, decided to come across and investigate.

Soon we were in the heavy timber where visibility was very short. We sat down and I bugled again. The hoarse tone of the old bull answered, but was definitely getting farther away. However the other three answered and the one across the valley started coming for us and bugling quite often. Clearly he was getting mad. While we were working through the next stand of timber to another open strip of meadow caused by a mountain spring, the wind shifted slightly, and our hopes as well. I was smoking to keep an eye on the wind drift and holding to the high left side of the valley as the wind seemed to be coming mainly from the right front at two o'clock. Soon we jumped a bunch of cows and they went out of their beds and circled around to the right and headed for the Divide in great style. They made plenty of noise and I saw the tops of three heads and ears flash past an opening not 30 yards away. The bulls of course heard their crashing exit, so I immediately bugled and gave them plenty of fighting talk to distract their attention.

This was too much for the bull directly across the valley and as we again slipped forward, for the old bull was plainly leaving, this younger bull came with a rush. Soon he was in the timber to our right and not over 100 yards away. His bugling seemed to make the old chap leave even faster. Telling Gene the old boy was the one we wanted, I held the bugle down low over a puddle of water and bugled again. This made the call sound more distant and the old bull stopped his retreat and answered right back. However the young bull also answered as well and now was only 50 yards away, in the timber to our right. I told Gene we would have to rustle as the old boy was still a quarter mile ahead, so we set out on a fast jog, when an opening made this possible, and I refrained from calling again until we had covered a good 300 yards. Then we stopped and I bugled. The bull behind us had still not crossed our track and came back with his long-drawn, ever-changing tone, ending in some hoarse grunts. He was plainly telling us what he would do if we had not run away. The old boy did not answer, so we slipped ahead across an open park and into another heavy stand of spruce, then I called again with bugle held almost in the mud, giving a low soft call. The old bull answered that with a heavy, full-drawn challenge, not 100 yards away. I motioned for Gene to go on ahead and kill him while I sat still and bugled softly, as I could hold him by so doing, but if I went ahead and bugled loud, he would travel again. Clearly he was an old chap that had had all the fighting he wanted, and he was climbing higher on the left sidehill into the scattered piñon pines. He wanted to get up above us so he could see the bull that was after him, and he was clearly leaving the basin.

Gene would not go on ahead, as he was afraid he would jump the old chap without seeing him, for by then he placed a lot of faith in my eyes. So, taking the bit in my teeth so to speak, I whispered for him to come on and set out on a run for the last heavy fringe of timber, as I knew the bull was beyond it and up the sidehill to our left. I stopped once and bugled very softly and he came back with a ringing challenge. That gave me his final direction and when we reached the farther edge of the timber, I told

Gene to get ready and stepped out. There was only a small clump of piñon pines above us on the left and the old bull had to be in them. Soon I saw his rump and high-held, heavy antlers, as he walked along the steep slope about 60 yards away, and pointed him out to Gene. His head was concealed by limbs and he had not seen us. Gene's first 250-grain .35 Whelen Soft Point missed him, the second caught him high in the right ham, breaking the leg. His next shot threw up white rock dust beyond the bull and must have missed cleanly, probably deflected by some of the numerous heavy limbs. One look at that huge head and I knew it was a record and one of the two finest heads I had ever seen in the hills. Gene ran forward, too close to my notion, and the old bull then did a grand thing. He made no effort to get away after receiving the crippling hit, but turned slowly around on three legs and headed back for Gene. He still had not seen him, and I ran out to the right, where I could see on both sides of that clump of pines and be in a position to help if necessary. Gene shot again, but again rock dust rose from the steep slope beyond the bull. The old boy had raised his head very high and was grinding his teeth, with the hair down the neck and back all standing on end. I knew he would go for Gene the instant he saw him, so yelled at him to plant some lead where it would do some good. Gene nicked the hair on the front of the neck as the bull swung around, then clipped him twice more through the edge of the neck, through trachea and windpipe, but without hitting the spine.

As the bull was above Gene and not 20 yards away, I well knew he would be on Gene in two jumps, if he did not stop him. His magazine had jammed and he was pulling single cartridges out of his pocket and feeding them into the rifle, one at a time, and shooting. It was beginning to look as if I would have to take a hand, so I slipped the safety on the .375 double rifle and threw the gun up, determined to give him both barrels in the left shoulder when he did see and go for Gene. The bull was still walking back when Gene caught an open place in the limbs, and just as that grand old elk saw him for the first time, Gene hit him solid in the front of the neck. He reared to his full height on his hind legs, then like a huge tree falling he came slowly over backwards and drove those huge heavy horns deep into the earth, then turned over in one somersault after another down the steep slope. When he reached a little flat below, he made his final somersault, then straightened out and pawed himself along a short distance with his front feet. I asked Gene not to shoot again, but to watch him. However, he shot again anyway, but where that slug went we never knew as it did not hit the bull. He soon died and we started the big job of skinning out and dressing him. He

Courtesy L. A. Cole

Bull elk with nice head that had been shot in chest with .333 O.K.H., down but not yet dead

E. E. Wilkinson with a very exceptional bull elk killed under guidance of author in 1945 with .35 Whelen and 250-grain Soft Point backed by 56 grains 4064 Dupont at 60 yards. Not the longest beam but it has exceptionally long points and is very heavy throughout, combined with perfect symmetry and evenness on each side

Courtesy J. Omar Cole

A band of bighorn sheep showing typical Alberta sheep country

was a huge old bull with a grand head, six very even, very heavy and extra-long points to a side, with enormous beams and swords points, the last two rear points turning out at widely divergent angles. In length the beams went around 55 inches and the spread was 47 inches, but the prongs were the heaviest and longest I had ever seen, with the exception of one head I have. The beams were so large that the state metal tag would not go around and close on any point of the main beam below any fork, so I had to wire the tag in place. Gene was delighted, in fact I have never seen such a happy hunter in my life. He hugged me and waltzed around like a ten-year-old kid. For over twenty years he had planned on someday taking an elk hunt with me and he considered a fine elk head the best trophy ob-tainable on this continent. I have killed a couple of heavier bulls, but have seen but one with a finer head. This elk loaded three horses and we packed the huge skull and antlers out on our backs, changing off on the heavy load as Gene would not think of letting us put them on a horse.

Gene's first 250-grain slug had broken the right hind leg, high up, and part of the bullet had gone on into the paunch. His last shot before the bull went down, that had struck solid in the front of the neck, had blown up and the core separated from the jacket. A small fragment of the core had gone on into the spinal cord between the joints, but that 250-grain bullet intended for only 2200 feet velocity had blown up and never broke the spine of the neck at all. A tiny sliver of lead had pene-trated the spinal cord and caused death. This shows what sometimes hap-pens when a bullet designed for low velocity is used at much higher velocity at close range. The other bull Gene hit about the same way and lost must have also stopped that 250-grain slug, without breaking his neck, though it floored the bull temporarily.

Later last fall, Oscar Bohannon and I packed back on the Divide for our own meat hunt. Hard winter weather hit early and we were wading in two feet of snow, which, combined with having to pack in baled hay and oats for the horses, made it a rough trip. We had hung up our big fat mule bucks and hunted out the head of several creeks before we located elk. We had come over a high ridge and stopped for a smoke out of the wind and the cold driving snow. Elk tracks and beds plainly told that we were at last near a big band of elk. Oscar carried my Westley Richards double-barrel ejector for the .400 Jeffery cartridge while I carried a .285 O.K.H. Mauser with 180-grain Duplex loads, in case we had to make a kill across a deep and wide canyon.

Working slowly down that wind-swept ridge and trying hard to keep from freezing, at around 8000 feet, we came on the band bedded right on top, in the deep snow. A spike bull was turned broadside at about 125 yards and Oscar picked him for his winter's meat. Oscar is a small man, but game as a goldfish, and though he is forced to wear glasses he is a good hunter. The driving snow was continually coating the lenses of his glasses. As he raised the big rifle for the offhand shot, I wondered if he would clear another low snow comb between him and the bull, as it looked to me as if he would hit the top of it. However, before I could whisper to him about it, he fired. The heavy 400-grain Soft Point clipped the snow comb and deflected just enough to miss the elk, by passing in front of his chest on the top of the snow. He was out of his bed in an instant and running for Montana, which was only 50 yards away. Instantly a small army of elk bounced out of their beds and went streaming toward and past us, on each side. Oscar shot again at the running bull, but by this time his glasses were fogged and he went just over his back. I picked a big dry cow, almost black in color on the snow, that was running directly toward me, and putting the cross hairs of the Lyman Alaskan scope in the center of her chest I touched the set trigger and told Oscar my job was done. The cow made one jump out of sight behind some trees when the slug hit her. The elk flashed past on both sides, running as if the devil was after them, in the hard driving snowstorm. Oscar bent over, opened the big rifle and saw the empty cases fly clear on the ejectors, then dropped two more long hulls in the barrels and closed the rifle, wiped his glasses and turned as another cow came through an opening in some timber, down the mountain to our right. He bored her through the lungs. She flinched at the impact of the heavy slug, took one jump down the mountain, then piled up and slid into some scrub fir trees. We backtracked along the trail of the elk, soon finding my big fat cow where she had slid down the mountain until the snow packed deep below her and stopped her descent. My bullet removed the aorta and lodged in fragments in the left ribs, the elk quartering toward us.

Elk hunting in this country is, nine times out of ten, the hardest kind of work one can get into, and often in the worst weather at high elevations. In sharp contrast, elk hunting east of the Divide is almost a picnic. I have hunted elk almost every fall since I was a small boy in knee pants, and this cow made my thirtieth elk killed for our own use, not counting a lot of cripples I have helped trail up and have finished off for others, with either rifle or sixgun. Since then I have killed one more bull.

Elk today are in no danger of extinction, but would be much more plentiful if more winter range was allotted to them and domestic sheep excluded from all their summer ranges in the forests. Then they would not travel down to winter quarters so early and many more would survive the long hard winters. Their range is today not extensive, except around the park, the South Fork of the Flathead in Montana and the Salmon and Clearwater drainages in Idaho. Some elk occur very far north and Edgar Dopp told me of finding a band of elk beyond the Musqua River and nearly halfway to the Liard River, in north British Columbia. The Indians also showed me a low range lying to the east of our course on a trip from Hudson's Hope to the head of the Wapiti River on the south side of the Peace River, where they assured me elk were plentiful. Continuous hunting, long hard winters and a steadily declining winter range make the finding of a record elk head ever more of a problem than it was in the old days, when they were so plentiful and had such a vast range all over the West. They are a grand meat animal as well as a trophy; a fat prime elk is just about as fine meat as one can find and second only to a fat mountain sheep. It is dark colored, but milder in flavor even than beef and usually very tender on prime fat animals. The elk get skin-poor each winter and all the meat on their frames is put on in a few short months, hence even old bulls, when fat, are fine meat. However, they should be killed before the rut when wanted for meat, rather than after, when they are run-down and the meat is strong.

The principal enemy of elk is man, with cougar next on the list, though coyotes and wolves will often pull down a stray in the winter when the snow is deep or in the spring when they are in a weakened condition. The big cats can, however, kill any young elk and may at times take a full-grown cow, but I have seen no evidence of their attempting to kill a big bull. A grizzly will occasionally stalk and kill an elk, any elk he finds, but the big bear are far too scarce to get many these days. Lack of winter range and consequent starvation kills more elk annually than all hunters added together and the answer to that problem is more winter range. It is up to the sportsmen of this country to decide whether they prefer domestic sheep on the forest or more game animals.

XII

Mountain and Plains Stalking

MOUNTAIN hunting may be either timber still-hunting or stalking, depending almost entirely on whether the mountains are densely wooded, or badly broken up in cliffs and gullies, or are open or partly timbered. If the mountains are densely timbered, then all we have written in the chapter on still-hunting applies. If they are open, or sparsely timbered, then stalking is usually necessary to get within rifle shot of the game. Many sections of the mountains present both types of hunting. Some mountain game, like elk, moose, deer and bear, usually adhere to the timbered section of the range, while game like sheep, goat, caribou and antelope will usually use the open, or partly open sections. Spring Alaskan bear hunting, as well as most spring bear hunting, is a stalking proposition. To be a really competent big game hunter one must be adept at both still-hunting and stalking.

In mountain hunting, like still-hunting, the prevailing wind direction must always be considered. Keeping the wind in your favor should be a prime desideratum. In some sections the wind is steady and blows in one direction most of the time, while in others it is always very uncertain. This is particularly true at high altitudes, in steep mountain basins and valleys. Ofttimes the wind changes so often and so radically in such localities that one has to simply trust to luck and a kind providence and keep going. Many times we have had it change just as often as we changed course. One thing of advantage to the hunter, however, is the fact that such erratic mountain winds seldom blow long in any one direction, and while they may be at your back where you then are, a hundred or two hundred yards in advance you may find them blowing in another direction entirely. Wherever they are steady, work into the wind at all times.

While stalking does not bring on the instant surprises of big game hunting, so typical when game is finally sighted in still-hunting the timber, nevertheless it provides a great many surprises and disappointments as well, and to my notion is the most interesting hunting of all. You often sight your game a mile or more away, then it is up to you to figure out an approach — considering wind, light and terrain in so doing. The problems are never the same, always varied, and will tax the skill of the best hunter to the utmost, at times. Many times after a long and careful stalk you will find the game has simply disappeared. It may have only fed over another ridge, or it may have obtained your scent from some freak air current. This often happens, even when you put in most of the day making a safe approach. A thorough knowledge of the game and its feeding and bedding hours is absolutely essential to success. No use starting a long roundabout stalk that will consume hours to bedded game, if you know it may get up and feed away in the interim. Likewise a stalk of traveling or feeding game that involves any great distance is always uncertain. Again, when all conditions are ideal, such as time of day and when the game is bedded and should normally stay put, it will pull out for no reason under the sun that the hunter can discern.

Sometimes such actions of the game, or a freak air current, may in turn bring the game to you. We have seen this happen. Several years ago Mrs. G. G. Nesbitt of Shreveport and I were hunting the north slope of the Salmon River for mule bucks, when we spotted a big bear nearly three miles away, feeding on the top of a ridge. He was cropping some green grass on the north slope, for all the world like an old cow. Careful examination for some time, until he showed on the sky line and we saw the hump on his shoulders, proved him a grizzly.

Even though we had but little over two hours good shooting light left for the day, we started across the heads of three shallow canyons to come out on the ridge just above a saddle below which the bear was feeding. In starting to cross the first gulch I heard something rattling a bunch of dried weeds in the draw below us, so stopped dead still and motioned for Mrs. Nesbitt to do likewise. Soon a nice small black bear appeared in a run, then stopped, and I whispered for her to take him and hold right behind the right shoulder as he quartered away from us. She planted the 130-grain Remington .270 Winchester slug just right and he snapped at the entrance and took off again around the slope into some timber. She missed him with two more shots, before he was out of sight. We waited and soon heard his death call. The wind was strong from the grizzly to us and he never heard the shots at all, so we hurried across until I located the black, dead as a mackerel about 200 yards from where he had been hit, with a heart shot that came out center of chest. We left the black draped over a big boulder and continued our pell-mell rush across rough, steep country. Finally I took Mrs. Nesbitt's hand and the rifle and fairly dragged her along. Crossing the last deep creek, we worked around the sidehill to come out above the saddle. The grizzly was still there and now only a quarter mile away and the wind was still in our faces.

We soon worked down to the upper side of the saddle, then for no reason that we could discern the bear started toward us, merely working up the ridge. I dug in my pack for the old Colt S.A. .45, for if he continued he would come around a small cliff and be within very short range when he came in sight, probably 20 yards. We were ensconced behind the trunk of a big pine, holding our breath and waiting. Just when everything looked made to order, the bear stopped and started twisting his nose this way and that and I whispered for Mrs. Nesbitt to shoot, but she could not see him from her position, owing to a leaning fir tree. Before she could move up the hillside, he caught our scent and turned and ran as if the devil was after him, back on the sidehill where he had been feeding. He stopped with his front feet on a big log at 200 yards, broadside, and again I whispered for her to shoot. The long run and the excitement were too much for the little lady and she missed him clean. He did not move at the shot, but stood still, listening, then when she worked the rifle bolt he got our direction and was gone in two jumps. A tricky mountain air current had sucked up from the opposite sidehill through that low saddle and given us away. It was dark long before we got back to the black bear kill and I literally towed Mrs. Nesbitt along by the rope on my pack. The black was located and dressed out by feel alone and we arrived in camp long after dark and just as the moon came up. Luckily we had a good government trail a quarter mile past the black bear kill or we would have had to find a big dry windfall, build a fire and stay for the night. Such is luck. We made the only approach possible, yet failed on account of a shifting air current. However, the old saying "a bird in the hand is worth two in the bush" proved true and we at least had a nice black.

Many times in steep mountain hunting, where the timber is quite heavy, one will see more game across canyons than by attempting still-hunting with a contrary wind, or when the ground and underbrush are too dry, or else are heaved up into brittle frost. At such times we prefer, where possible, to work along one sidehill and look into the timber on the other side and the small parks and bed grounds. If game can be located in this way, one can often work into range. Even long range is preferable to attempting still-hunting under unfavorable conditions. When the mountains are sparsely wooded, with big timber, you can search out every cranny of the hillside across the gulch from you; also up above 5000 feet, where the timber is often straight lodgepole pine, one can see game quite well from across a canyon, but a hunter on the same slope as the game finds his vision limited to 100 yards or less.

Game like elk and deer, and often bear as well, when jumped on a steep mountain hillside will often turn downhill and across the creek, or gulch, and come out on the other sidehill. Even though the timber on your side of the gulch is entirely too thick for a sight or shot at the game, you may be able to see it clearly when it crosses the canyon or gulch. Pile enough timber on an even slope and you cannot see through it, but put the same timber across a steep gulch from you and you can often look right down into it without difficulty.

When hunting fairly open mountain terrain, the same rule applies, and you will always be able to see more game, bedded or feeding, across a canyon than on the sidehill you are traversing. This for the reason that the small ridges and uneven slopes on your side limit your vision to a few yards, or a few hundred at most, while the opposite steep slope is spread out before you in its entirety, like a giant relief map, and you can look into every cranny of its surface.

Game of herbivorous type usually likes to feed in old burns, chaparral, or mountain maple thickets. You cannot see far in these on the hillside you are traversing, but across from you it is easy to spot the game. For this reason it is best to work through the heavier timbered sidehill, or the one with the poorest feed, while you watch the better slope across from you for the game. Such mountain hunting often calls for long range rifles and long range shooting, but will pay more dividends than busting brush under adverse conditions of mountain hunting.

Personally, I like to work along just under a ridge top, either up or down the ridge, keeping down low enough so I will not be silhouetted on the sky line, yet close enough to the top so I can slip over occasionally for a look-see on the other side, if it is also good country. In this way you can see game across from you with ease, and in addition have some chance of seeing it on your own slope as well. Then, if you do locate game across from you, you can easily swing upstream or down, as the wind dictates, and cross over, or if it is a small gulch, you may well be in range and can shoot across.

When game is located, it is well to note some landmarks where you stand, such as big or dead trees, cliffs or fallen logs, then do the same across where the game is bedded or feeding. When you circle upstream and cross over, the country is going to look different, and you may well need those landmarks to make a correct approach and know when you are getting close to the game. It is always best to circle above the game. The air movements are usually upward, especially if the sun hits and warms the slope, and game looks for trouble from below or on a level more than from above. If the country is covered with dense brush or alders some six to ten feet high, you may have difficulty in orienting yourself, once across the canyon; you can then look back to where you stood when the game was located, and if you have picked landmarks you will have a fair idea of your location. In open country, such as high alpine sheep country above timber line, or when hunting antelope in high open mountains, no such problems will be presented, but one cannot be too careful in a densely timbered country.

When you make a climb to the top of a ridge, it is always best to stop in the lee of the ridge and rest for a few minutes until your heartbeat is normal and you are steady, before working on to the top. Then approach the top where some timber or brush will screen you, and if you should see game just over the top, as so often happens, you will be steady and in shape for a good accurate shot.

In all mountain hunting, you should search out every possible game cover as soon as it comes in sight and determine if anything is in sight before you show yourself. Hunting high alpine game is best done with binoculars unless you have thoroughly trained game eyes. The experienced hunter knows what to look for and where to look for it and game will be instantly discernible to him that would be absolutely invisible to untrained eyes.

Many black spots seen at long range will be revealed as black stumps, while other stumps may turn out to be bear. Sometimes objects will be seen that simply do not look right or as if they were a normal part of the terrain. Examine them closely with the glass and many times they will turn out to be game. The old hunter spots such objects instantly, but the novice will usually see nothing out of the ordinary. This is the reason that good guides draw good money and are worth it to city sportsmen.

Many times you will carefully examine all the mountains, draws and slopes within your field of vision and see nothing. Then when you cross a small wash or draw, or come around the shoulder of a ledge, you will run right onto game and be caught flat-footed and out in the open. If it is not game you want, or if it is out of range but has seen you, the best thing to do is freeze still and remain so. Game instantly spots any movement, but if you remain perfectly still it is often unable to make you out or to determine whether you are dangerous or not. Many times I have been thus caught out flat-footed when the game was what I wanted. I have simply eased down into a sitting position and frozen there. At times the game became curious and started circling to get a better look, finally coming into good range. At other times it was does, or ewe sheep, or some other species I did not want at all, but to stampede them with fright would also have scared the game I was after, so there was nothing to do but remain fixed.

Another time, the late Julius Maelzer and I were hunting antelope and spotted a fine record buck across a wide and deep basin. The rut was clearly on and this old boy was chasing a doe. Between us and the big buck were about thirty head of antelope with many smaller bucks. We would have had to circle for miles to come around behind them and would then have been even farther away. We simply had to somehow work down across that big basin and up the other bank into some small cliffs and scrub mahogany, without frightening the band near us, in order to get within 500 yards of the old boy we wanted. I took the lead, bent over at the hips, and Julius hooked one hand in my belt and bent his body forward until his head rested on my back. We moseyed around that sidehill, bent very low, for over an hour, stopping for me to lower my head almost to the ground as though the two of us were simply a cow critter picking out scattered bunch grass. The whole band of antelope spotted us in short order, but we had the wind in our favor and they could not make out just what we were. Had either of us straightened up for an instant and revealed our true nature, they would have barked at us and been on their way. However, we held our pose, though it was painful back-breaking work, until we were down in the draw out of their sight, then had a good rest. Those antelope had stamped their feet and looked at us and some had come part way toward us, but we then remained perfectly still; finally they had lost interest in us and gone on about their feeding.

We worked up a deep brush gully, into the screening shelter of the cliffs and to a vantage point where we could see the big buck. He had also spotted our descent into the bottom of the creek, but had been unable to make us out and was watching for our reappearance.

We underestimated the range, and my first shot merely clipped a little short hair from the back side of one foreleg and kicked up a spurt of dust low and on beyond him. He turned and ran in a circle back to our left and getting closer. However, a very strong wind was whipping across the sparse short sage, or shad scale, and we could see no trace of him, yet my next shots, held for 500 yards, hit clear off to the right of the buck and beyond him. Thinking my scope must have been knocked out of adjustment, I picked out a small white rock some 200 yards down the gulch below us and where I knew there could be no wind and held on it with the 8 power Lyman target scope adjusted for 300 yards. I told Julius to watch and spot my shot, and if the scope was right the bullet from the .280 Dubiel Magnum should strike 4 inches directly over the center of the rock. It did print exactly there, so we knew it was wind that was kicking my shots out so far to the right. I had fired five shots at the buck and then one down the gully at a rock and the old buck was still swinging around to the left. He had stopped for each shot, then had run again. Just as I reloaded, after shooting at the rock, he stopped again, this time closer to us, at what I then estimated at 450 yards and so set the target scope. This time I held the cross wires a full two feet in front of his chest as he stood broadside, and after the rifle recoiled we heard that slug strike home and he went down to stay. Julius paced the distance at 450 yards and we found that instead of hitting him through the chest by holding so far ahead to the left of him, I had hit him through the kidneys, and fragments of the 150-grain W.T.C. Company bullet had broken his back. He proved a beautiful, even, 15-inch head with good prongs and was well worth all our long hot stalk. I can think of no other procedure by which we could have obtained this buck. When we stepped out from the screening cliffs the wind was so strong we had to lean into it to travel at all; no wonder my slugs, fired from a steady prone position, had drifted so far to the right.

Another time, Dr. Wilson L. DuComb and I were hunting sheep on the Salmon River. We had carefully searched the basin in front of us and spotted some mule deer and a ewe sheep. The wind was wrong, and the deer almost instantly got our scent and left in high bouncing jumps. The sheep stamped her feet and looked all around but we were looking through a scrub mahogany and she did not see us; finally she also got our scent and beat it for the high cliffs to our right. We waited a long time, hoping she would go on over the ridge and out of sight, then we sneaked on, hoping to cross that big basin and work up under the shadow of some cliffs opposite. However, we were out of luck, for as soon as we came out of a small draw and turned the corner of a ledge, there we were, in plain sight of a bunch of ewes. We wanted rams, not ewes, but knew if we scared them, they in turn would stampede any rams clean out of that section. We sat under a tree and watched them and they watched us for an hour or more. As the morning was wearing along we had to do something, so I suggested to Doc that we play cow as Maelzer and I had on the antelope. It worked, but took us most of the day to slowly work our way across that basin and up into a high crevasse of the cliffs, out of sight of that watchful harem.

Just before we reached the cliff a nice ram came out on the sky line behind the band of ewes, looking back upriver, toward camp and where we knew our comrades were also hunting sheep. I asked Doc how that one would do and he said fine. However, I saw little likelihood of my ever being able to get him in range of that ram, with a bunch of watchful ewes ensconced between us and him. We worked on up to the base of the cliff and then a huge old bonehead came out on the sky line above the smaller ram and also looked back. The smaller ram soon worked up to him. When I pointed him out to Doc and asked how he would suit, he said, "You can have the small one, but that huge head will suit me fine." The rams worked on around into the labyrinth of huge cliffs, overhanging the upper part of the basin and far above us. We worked upward until we climbed out on a shoulder, just barely below the top of the cliff we were on. From this vantage point I knew my .300 Magnum with scope sight could command all the open bunch-grass terrain above us to the top of the ridge, yet there was no possible hope for us to go higher without frightening the ewes and possibly also those watchful old boneheads above, so we elected to stay put and let the rams make the next move.

Soon, another smaller bunch of ewes came over the ridge where the smaller ram had originally topped out and in a hard run. They ran right into the other bunch, which had been bedded there watching our crazy antics all day long. Instantly the whole band was on its feet and streaming by under us and on over another ridge to our right, toward some towering sheer cliffs that overhung the river itself. Doc asked, "Now what shall we do?" and I answered, "Sit tight. Those rams are sure to see the ewes run by and all the dust they are raising and they may do anything, even come down and follow the ewes." The latter had hardly faded from sight and the dust still hung in the hot afternoon air when an apparition with huge horns suddenly bounced onto a ledge directly in front of us, and not 50 yards distant. My .348 Winchester which Doc was carrying stood in a niche in the cliff in front of us, and picking it up I cocked it, shoved it into Doc's waiting hands and hissed, "Shoot." He answered, "Hell, it's the little one." Again I hissed "Shoot," and this time Doc leveled the rifle and busted the huge old ram in the base of the neck, with 200-grain Soft Point. He dropped and rolled out of sight almost instantly. Then I grabbed my .300 Magnum, slipped the sling on my arm and asked Doc to watch for the small ram, as I knew he must be in the cliffs under us someplace. Then we saw him just topping the ridge to our right and 300 yards away and following the trail of the ewes. I could only assume a hasty and poor sitting position and hit him too far back with the 180-grain Open Point Boattail, but he went down and over the ridge out of sight. Doc was very anxious about his ram and insisted we hunt him up next. We spent over a half hour combing the foot of the cliffs before I found the gutter, or crevasse, he had rolled down and trailed him far below into the center of a dense clump of brush some six feet high. He was, of course, dead as a mackerel and a beautiful specimen, with 38½-inch curls and badly broomed tips and the widest spread of bighorn I have ever seen, going a full 26½ inches and still the widest *Ovis canadensis* in the present book of records. Just before finding Doc's ram, I looked around and saw my ram slowly climbing the farthest ridge from us, all humped up and fully 500 yards away. I located a big flat-top boulder, and with sling adjusted, stood behind it and rested my elbows thereon and held the top of the reticule up over the top of his horns as he climbed almost directly away from me. After the shot we heard the slug strike home; he turned down that ridge in a furious run and soon turned again, over into the cliffs out of sight.

We dressed Doc's ram, then worked over to the ridge and picked up the track of my twice-hit hard-head. He was easily trailed out to the comb of the ridge, then his tracks were mixed with those of all that band of ewes and when Doc asked how he could help me, I told him to sit tight and not make any tracks at all until I unraveled these. Finally, I trailed him to the edge of a cliff, finding a bloody smear on the rim. Looking far below I finally located him draped around a boulder nearly down to the river. We had our rams and only another strenuous day of backpacking before they were in camp, but we could never have obtained them any other way. Anyone can take advantage of definite cover and approach bedded or feeding game, but it is when the stalk must be made out in the open, with practically no cover, that all the hunter's skill is required.

This often happens in hunting sheep, antelope, caribou and sometimes moose and deer or elk as well. The clothing must be of a neutral shade that will blend well with the surrounding terrain, and the hat should be a sand-colored Stetson, preferably, or on darker ground the army hat is ideal. The brim should be kept down well over the eyes and the head kept as low as possible.

Crawl flat, do not try to travel on hands and knees as you are then easily spotted, and move forward only when the game has its head down feeding. If it is bedded and watching, you have a much poorer chance of ever getting in range unobserved. When at all possible, have the wind in your face and the sun at your back. Keep your face down, as nothing reflects light more, or is more easily seen, than the white of one's face. The hips must also be carried very low and one should wriggle forward, rather than attempting a true crawl. Avoid all dry weeds that will rattle and take advantage of every small sagebrush or clump of bunch grass. If possible to work in from behind the game, so much the better; they are not then as apt to spot you. Such stalks over smooth ground with little or no cover often consume hours, but they can be made. Do not overplay your hand. Crawl as close as possible, but if the game is still out of range, it is often best to lie quietly for a time and see if by chance the game will not feed your way. If it does spot you, lie perfectly still and you have a very good chance of the game's coming to investigate. The rifle must be carried forward with one hand, and be doubly careful to keep it low, as it will reflect light. Likewise any flashy cartridge belt or other object that will reflect light should be avoided at all cost. Never make any forward movement when the game is looking your way, even though it has not spotted you, but wait until it is looking in another direction or has started feeding again.

Prickly pear, cactus, rattlesnakes and scorpions, as well as anthills, are some of the things that can make such a stalk very interesting. Avoid them at all costs. In Mexico when the cholla burs have blown off the cactus and drifted into every depression, such a method of approach is absolutely impossible.

In stalking moose and caribou, when they are feeding or bedded around some alpine lake, one often has to crawl through water, and this also is far from pleasant but must at times be done. When the terrain over which you must make a stalk is sparsely covered with small clumps of brush, either sage, arctic birch or other growth, it is well to cut a bush and hold it in advance of you with one hand. Then when you stop you have some screen, and if the game looks your way he may not become curious of that small bush, but the Lord help you if you move it. There are many tricks to the trade, and after one does enough stalking he learns to know just about when the game will raise its head to look and when it will resume feeding. In time one becomes about half wolf himself, and the greater his knowledge of the game's habits, the better his chances of ultimate success, although an experienced stalker does these things without thinking and the semiconscious mind takes care of many of his actions, leaving the rest of his brain free for range estimation, judging the head, watching the wind, and so on. Smoking is inadvisable in any stalk on open ground as smoke is easily seen by the game. As with most other lines of human endeavor, getting a good instructor is the best way to learn about any game, and while much can be learned from books, it is hard to describe clearly all the important little details of approach which are best learned by actual hunting experience. We learn by our mistakes and this writer pleads guilty to making a great many mistakes, but the more experience you have under your belt, the better will be your chances of success. Many times you will have a stalk all but made when a shift in the wind will ruin everything. At other times, some beast may spot you and take alarm, or another animal may come along that you did not expect at all and spoil your stalk. These are just some of the unexpected things that can and do happen, to spoil the best laid plans.

The very word "stalking" brings to my memory some of the most pleasant hours of big game hunting I have ever enjoyed, also some of the most arduous. Where deer or antelope are hunted in open country, such as much of the West, and the game is used to seeing range horses around, one can then use a horse to advantage. You can often ride to within a half mile of a bunch of antelope without their paying you any attention; then if you have a small four-foot stick to tie to the bridle reins or hackamore, near bit or noseband, you can keep on the offside of your horse and slowly work him closer to the game by leading him via that push-pole method. Once a horse becomes used to being so led, he will soon catch on to what is wanted. Never approach the game directly, but always at an angle and with the wind in your favor, then tack back and allow the horse to feed a considerable part of the time. In this way, you can work a horse up fairly close to elk, mule deer or antelope when the game is used to seeing loose horses on the range. Once in good range you have only to let the horse graze, with reins down, if he is a well-broken cow horse, and sit or lie down for a sitting or prone shot, usually from the tail end of your horse, so the concussion will not be so hard on his ears. It is usually best to get down behind the horse and then crawl past him, so he will not be affected by the muzzle blast. Never make any quick movements, or jerk, or turn the horse quickly. Any hasty action on the part of either you or your horse will instantly attract the game's attention.

In many sections of the West, from Mexico north well into Alberta, one can use a saddle horse for hunting. When such open, or partly open, terrain, that is not too steep for the horse, is hunted, then there is no nicer way of covering a lot of country than from a good saddle animal. The horse, if used much for the purpose, soon learns what is wanted and seems to enjoy it as well. I have owned several good hunting horses and they became very adept at spotting game, often at considerable range. More often, however, they would get the scent of hidden game in the timber that we had not seen at all. Watch your horse's ears and nose. If he pricks up those ears and looks in some direction with eyes and ears alert and sniffs the breeze, you can bet he has either seen or scented game. You can see much more and better from a saddle horse than when on foot, for you are up higher, and the horse takes care of placing his feet and leaves you nothing to do but search for game. If the wind is favorable, your horse may well scent bedded game, for a quarter mile, that is totally invisible to you, and when he does it pays to locate his direction and search that section until you find what has alarmed him. He will always look in the direction the scent is coming from. Most horses do not like bear, and while they will become accustomed to some extent to black bear, the scent of a grizzly always terrifies them. They can tell the difference instantly, by scent alone, and ofttimes when the bear is out of sight of either horse or rider.

When you sight a bedded or feeding animal from your horse, notice if the game sees you, which it usually will if in range. It is best to pretend you do not see the game at all and observe it from the corner of your eye, while the horse continues to walk along. Usually by going on a little distance, then quietly slipping down from the horse and shooting as soon as your sights bear right, you can obtain the game. If you jump off your horse, probably also scaring him by your quick movements, the game will take fright and you will have only running shots offered. I have often ridden on as though I did not see a bedded animal at all, until I was even farther away and located a nice place to shoot from, in either a sitting or prone position, then slipped quietly to the ground with rifle all ready to go and before the game had made up its mind as to my intent, I had the sights laid right and shot.

At times you can also use your horse to attract the game's attention, while you make a successful stalk. I have employed this method many times. When you locate the game and it is watching you and the horse, simply ride along as though you did not see the game and go slow until you locate some draw, wash or ridge, behind or in the cover of which you can make a stalk. Then, as soon as the horse dips out of sight, slip off and work the horse on up in sight of the game, again keeping on the off side. Let the horse graze while you duck back and make your stalk. Game will often stand watching the horse and probably wondering what has become of his load for some time, while you approach in rifle range.

When you approach a ridge on horseback, do as you would on foot and work the horse up slowly, a step at a time, while you scan every foot of country carefully before moving your horse and your head higher, so your vision will command more country. Or you may slip off the horse just below the summit and work up on foot, which is the better procedure if you expect game over the ridge.

Two men can often make a stalk successfully where one would have a difficult time. Sometimes game may be sighted where approach to shooting range is very difficult. At such times, if one hunter works around, but clear of the wind and far enough away from the game so it will see him, yet not close enough to frighten it in any way, and remain in sight to attract its attention, the other hunter can circle around out of sight and then by crawling, only when the game is watching his partner, get in effective range. Many game animals are curious, and this fact should be used to advantage whenever possible. If one man moves into sight of the game, but off at extreme long range, and crawls around a bit on all fours, he will soon attract its attention. At such times it is much easier for the other hunter to make his approach. The Indians worked many such shenanigans on game and often with success. Game animals will often feed quietly along, raising their heads every now and then to watch some suspicious object, but if it makes no attempt to get closer to them, they will often not become alarmed.

When hunting moose in high mountain valleys it is best to get up on some point or ridge where you can overlook as much good moose country as possible and watch until you spot what looks like a good bull, then plan your stalk. If he is bedded, he will usually be hard to locate when you approach him, so make careful observation of any dead or otherwise outstanding trees, cliffs or small lakes near his bed, so you will know when you are near. If the sun is behind you, you will often see the flash of his palms in the sunlight to great distances. With all stalking game, it's best to be out at daylight when they are feeding, but as stated before, bear may be seen more often in the evening than early morning when it is cold.

Another method I have seen used to bring distant alpine game in range, when others failed, is to shoot beyond them at cliffs or dusty ground. To my notion, this is just about as sporting as jack-lighting deer at night and I have never used it. If game has not been hunted and does not know what the sharp ping of a rifle bullet going over means, it may often be driven back toward the hunter by such shooting at rocks or dry ground, or water, beyond. If it has been shot at before, the chances are it will only dust out of that particular neck of the woods. When it is not wise to the meaning of the bullets' passage, however, this throws it into a panic, and instead of running on it often runs back from the spurt of the bullets as they strike.

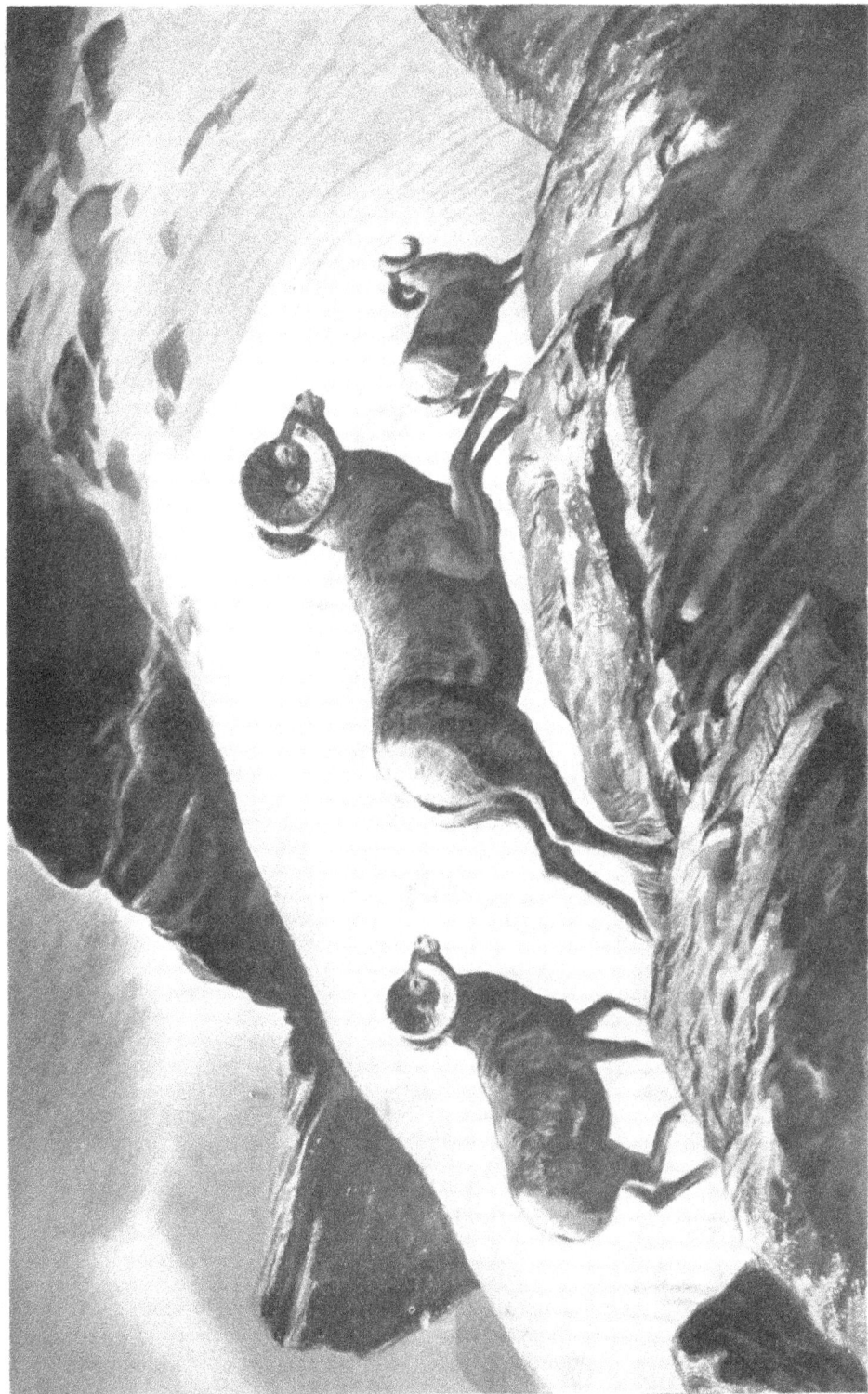

Bighorn sheep

Courtesy Helen R. Peterson

Helen Peterson with Billy Fan, the Indian guide, and her two Cassiar Stone rams

Westley Brown and the author with two Stone sheep killed by author, one at 400 yards and the other at over 500 yards in one shot each. The head at the right is in the records and shows amount of neck skin necessary for shoulder mounts

Many times in ordinary stalking you will shoot at a distant animal and overshoot, and when the bullet strikes rocks or dirt in the background the beast will run back your way. The sound of a bullet going past seems right in one's ear and it is very hard to locate the source of the sound; if the rifle is distant enough, the dull boom of the rifle itself is barely heard. Yet that sharp ping, apparently right by your head, is very real and the dust or white smoke rising from a rock in the background is enough to drive most animals back toward you. If they have seen or heard or winded you, then such things rarely occur, but when they do not know your location, or really what the sound is, they may come your way and usually will if they see the bullet strike beyond them.

In all stalking, watch the wind carefully. In much mountain terrain above timber line, or on open flat antelope country as well as caribou barrens, there may be very little to indicate the wind. When no trees or brush are available, a close study of dry grass, or weeds, or sagebrush through the spotting scope will usually tell you which way the wind is blowing. It may be blowing in an entirely different direction where you are than where the game is feeding or bedded. When no vegetation is present, look for mirage or heat waves. Focus the spotting scope, then back it off slightly just enough to throw it slightly out of focus, and if any mirage is running at all, you will be able to pick it up. This is just an old trick familiar to all long-range match riflemen, but is at times useful in the game fields as well. When a cold wind is blowing, at high altitudes, such game as sheep, antelope and deer will usually feed over on the windward side of the slope, and drop down just enough so the wind blows over them. It is well to remember this when scouting for distant game.

At times, one will think he has a stalk all made, when he suddenly learns how insignificant are the plans of man. Two California sportsmen I had out one fall in the Selway were after a band of sheep. We had trailed those rams down out of the deep snow and into scattered high basins and cliffs. Their tracks clearly indicated they were feeding and circling and would soon bed in the sun under some ledge. We had the wind in our faces and when the tracks worked through a small grassy basin and we could see where they had fed in the soft wet snow, we thought we had them.

I sneaked out to a ledge behind some scrub mahogany, fully expecting to see those old hardheads peacefully chewing their cuds on some ledge below, but instead saw their trails, each animal running like mad across the next basin. I knew we had disturbed no rocks, nor had we made any noise, and I was at a loss to know what had spooked them. Circling below the cliffs we soon found the answer. A hunting cougar had stalked them ahead of us, made a dash and a jump at one and missed, as the trail clearly showed. We then knew we were out of luck on that bunch of rams. We had made a good approach and if the big cat had made a kill, I believe we would have killed him anyway. His trail showed on after the rams, but he soon slowed to a walk, as they usually do when they miss a run at game. All our hard work was for nothing and we had to camp out that night and spend most of the next day getting back to camp. Such is sheep hunting. Cougar prefer sheep to any other meat, just as most all old mountain hunters do.

Whenever you shoot at game at long range, if you miss, watch closely for the strike of the bullet. Note in particular which way the dust, or smoke off rocks, drifts. If it drifts swiftly to one side and the hit appears to be to that side of the animal, then you can just bet you need considerable windage, so hold over for your next shot into the wind, if possible as much as the strike of the bullet is off from your first shot. If your shot apparently goes high, then you know it had too much elevation, or you may be shooting through an updraft, which often occurs in the mountains, particularly if you are shooting toward a cliff where the sun reflects. If the shot goes low, then it is probably farther than you figured and you need more elevation. Sometimes it may also be caused by a downdraft of air. So watch for the bullets' strike and make corrections.

Many stalks will be ruined by forces beyond your control. In Canada or Alaska, an old whistler may turn loose his long shrill whistle just when you are getting close to the game and put it on the alert. We have had this happen. At other times magpies, squirrels, jays and such will circle and scold you and give your position away. When this happens the game usually becomes not only on the alert, but also curious as to what has disturbed these birds or animals, and may come closer to investigate, often into good range. In Alaska we even had an old sore-headed grizzly, of record proportions, trail us up and stalk us while we were peacefully stalking a black bear, and we never knew the old brute had taken our trail until I saw him at 20 yards, coming right upwind of us and already on the prod. Though I killed the grizzly, we never did know what became of the black we were stalking.

At other times when crawling on game I have had golden eagles circle me slowly, and the game has thus spotted my location. In Mexico buzzards will sometimes do the same thing. Big game of most all species notice any such thing and get wise to your position in short order, though they may not know what you are. Once they become curious, you can look for them to either circle closer to you, or else circle into the wind to get your scent. Antelope, mule deer, caribou and bear are particularly curious, elk and sheep much less so. They will be curious, but not to the extent of coming to you, and are much more apt to circle for the wind, or farther away.

Raven in this country will circle a band of elk for hours. They are wise old birds and many successive hunting seasons have taught them that all they have to do is locate and circle a band of elk long enough and some hunter will come along and lower the boom on one. Then they know the offal is for them and they feed to repletion. They will also eat up the game as well, unless it is hung from spikes in trees, or well brushed. Golden eagles will also make hash out of any big game they find dead, so one must always brush it, or hang it, if these birds are prevalent. The same applies to Mexican buzzards.

The most interesting and productive sheep stalk I have ever been on occurred near the Musqua River and west of the present Alcan Highway in 1937. Edgar Dopp and I had hunted together for several days and seen only ewes and lambs, plenty of them, but no rams. Doc and Westley Brown had hunted in the opposite direction from camp with equal lack of success, seeing only ewes and lambs. We well knew from the amount of old sign and the many heads of old rams killed by wolves around the licks that we were close to the ram bands, but we had not located them. Finally Edgar, Westley and I scouted ahead of camp a few miles and back toward the head of the creek for a new camp site that would put us in reach of a high, but very open range farther west.

We located a fine site in a grove of timber with plenty of horse feed and water. Then on the way home we did actually run onto a bunch of four small rams, just crossing into the range we had so carefully hunted. They were all small in stature and with small heads, but Edgar declared he had eaten all the ham and bacon he could stand for a solid month, so we took one small ram at 475 yards with one shot from the scope sighted .300 Magnum on Edgar's license.

Then, bright and early, Allan Robinson started us off on a real sheep hunt with one of his incomparable hearty breakfasts. We traveled upstream for some three miles, turning up a branch to the left and south that brought us out on high rolling plateaus that looked good for caribou but not for sheep. The huge mountain range lay ahead some three miles more and naked of trees, but with the deep draws covered with short, stiff and stubborn arctic birch, willow and other scrubby shrubs and shin-tangle. We split up, Doc, Dick and Edgar taking the main canyon to our right, while Westley and I worked on toward that high open slide-rock range to the left. Westley and I traveled on foot while the rest of the party took horses in case we made a kill.

Westley and I worked up a long draw toward the main open range until we were about a mile distant, when I spotted an uneven row of white rocks in the distance, just under the slide-rock. I remarked that they looked like sheep, so we stopped and set up the little Mossberg 20 X scope we carried and sure enough they were rams. We dropped back into that shallow draw and proceeded another half mile before it played out, leaving us no further cover for an advance. We worked up behind the last shin-tangle and again set up the scope. There were two big old heads in the band. One was a beautiful white-necked Fannin, with wide sweeping horns with perfect points. His right horn swung lower than the left and with less curl, owing to its lower swing, while the right curled up and out above the nose. He was a beautiful specimen, even though one horn was of a wider and lower curl, and I decided to take him if we ever did get in range. The other big ram was one of those heavy base, short, wide curl types. His bases appeared very heavy but not very widespread, but each horn was a wide curl and badly broomed. We knew he would not carry much length of horn, but he was an old bunger for basal measurement. I decided to pass him up for time being, however. We lay there in the sun waiting for the sheep to move. Some fed along and some stopped and bedded. We saw the old Fannin dig roots with that low-swinging right horn, then eat them, and later saw him throw dirt up over his withers with that horn, much as a bull will throw dirt over his back with a fore-foot in fly time. Flies were no doubt bothering them as it was in August. Even though we had already sustained a six-inch wet snow, the weather had again turned fairly warm.

We watched those rams for several hours, as they contentedly fed around into the very head of the draw. Then they bedded for a time and finally the old boy with the heavy bases and short horns fed on around to the right side of the draw and down to within 200 yards of us. He was in easy range and I could have hit him in the heart easily, but wanted that finer old Fannin ram.

Then another ram, with one good horn and one that appeared to have been sawed off square about six inches from his skull, fed around above us. There was very little air movement, but we were afraid of it, knowing it should drift uphill to the sheep. We could not move as there was no cover whatever. As soon as the old short-horn boy with heavy bases fed far enough around to be out of direct sight of us, and the one with the broken horn also fed on around to a shoulder to our right, we managed to gain some yards up the slope, by keeping very low, until we came to a small ledge and some more sparse shin-tangle, beyond which was no cover at all— just the blue slide-rock and scattered small boulders. We lay there for some time, watching the rest of the band hidden out in huge boulders across the draw and above us, at some 600 yards. Finally they got up, stretched and started working across the gulch above us. One small ram worked down until almost in range, but that wise old Fannin held to higher ground. Just when it looked as though he would head down on the right side of the draw, over the tracks of the old heavy-base ram, he either saw some trace of us or else got a stray whiff, as he jumped into a hard run, followed by all the other young rams, and cut across the ridge to our right, high above us at 450 yards. I eased up into a sitting position and followed him through the scope, but was leery of attempting a shot when he was running like the wind, at such range.

Finally we decided to let them go and work on up to the right, into the saddle, and then attempt to work up that ridge in the broken cliffs until we were above them, then again attempt a stalk. Just as the Fannin and his bunch disappeared over the ridge into the cliffs, we heard distant and scattered rifle shots from the head of the canyon to our right where the other boys were hunting. It may have been some of the first of those shots that scared the old Fannin. We never knew, but as soon as all the sheep were out of sight, we sneaked higher up the ridge toward the saddle, only to be stopped cold by that one horn ram that had fed along behind the old heavy-base chap. He was fooling along the edge of some cliffs, and we watched him for some time. He would walk out to the very edge of a cliff that sloped downward at forty-five degrees, then broke off sharp and, apparently oblivious to height or danger, would stretch his head out over the edge of said cliff and nibble moss from the rock crevasses. Finally, he fed on around into the cliffs out of sight and we were able to straighten up for the first time in hours.

We worked up into the saddle. To our left extended a huge and high mountain, all slide-rock and smooth on the left, but breaking off into a series of cliffs and sharp precipices on the right almost down to the valley floor, when the cliffs ended in a shale slide below which was the ever-present thin shin-tangle.

We had just worked over the extreme top of the saddle to see if any rams were in sight on that broken north slope, when a huge old ram bounced into view and up on the top of a ledge where he stood silhouetted on the sky line at 400 yards. Instantly we dropped prone and I crawled to a slight hummock that would raise my elbows. The sling was adjusted tight on my left arm and the .300 Magnum Model .70 Winchester loaded with 180-grain Open Point Boattail factory loads and sighted for 300 yards point-blank. One look through the Hensoldt 2¾ power scope disclosed a huge right horn of wide spread and curving up and out, well above the bridge of his nose. He was standing quartering away from us and had not seen us. Clearly he had been scared by rolling rocks from the band running around above his hiding place in the cliffs, or else the broken horn and the old heavy-base ram had disturbed his snooze and he had come up to investigate. The rifle shots may have disturbed him. He was an old solitary ram, with a much larger head than the fine Fannin, and I waited just long enough for him to swing his head, showing he also had a good left horn.

Then, holding my breath, I ran the top of the post reticule level with his back and into the shadow behind his right shoulder for the 400-yard shot and squeezed. Following the report of the rifle, we saw him drop, then roll off the cliff as the plunk of the slug striking home came to us. He bounced sheer for fifty feet in the air, then disappeared over still another and lower cliff. Westley slapped me on the back and remarked, "There is one for the records."

This sudden and unexpected turn of events changed our plans, and I asked Westley to work up and around through the cliffs to where that old boy had stood and see if he could locate him, while I went on over the saddle and down the other side, following along the edge of the slide-rock and shin-tangle and watched back up and to my left for the old ram. I thought I had hit him right, but wanted to take no possible chance on losing that fine old head.

I was soon down in the shin-tangle underneath the slide-rock but could see no trace of the big ram, while Westley worked around to where he had stood and waved his arms and pointed down a narrow chute in the cliffs.

Just then the old Fannin and his younger companions came out on a ledge much farther up the canyon and even higher than Westley. His light-colored body, white neck, and rump showed clearly in the afternoon sun. He was so far away I had little hopes of being able to shoot him, but worked up to a small mound in the terrain, sat up the Mossberg scope on its tripod and looked him over. I sized up the distance from me to the foot of the cliffs, then that awful expanse of blue-black and gray cliff, extending far upward to the little ledge on which the Fannin and his band stood. They had heard my shot and were looking back. His head was held high, as only a scared old ram can hold his head, and with the right horn swinging back over his withers, as he stood broadside on to me. I finally decided he must be close to, or around, 600 yards and decided to try him. I had a fairly steady prone position with my elbows up on the little hummock and the sling adjusted tight. Holding my breath I eased the top of the post up on the withers, then upward until the top of the post was over the withers and just above the tops of the wide-spreading horn bases on the right, and squeezed. The rifle recoiled, then settled back. I jerked my head over to the spotting scope. It was just like the old days, when I fired on a .30 caliber rifle team at Camp Perry. I saw the old boy drop from the impact of the slug, then saw one hind foot raise up and kick the empty air, then heard the dull plunk of the bullet. The ram kicked once more, then lay still.

Westley heard me shoot and also heard the strike of the bullet. When I located him far above in the cliffs, he was waving his arms and signaling to me, so I waved him upward and on around toward where the Fannin lay, while I again assumed a prone position and watched the edge of that old ram so far above, just in case he did get up again.

Westley carried a .22 L.R. Colt Woodsman, and when he worked on around and higher, so he could see the rams, he decided to kill himself a ram with the little pistol. While I had been watching, first one and then another of the younger rams would walk up to the old Fannin leader and paw him, clearly trying to get him to get up and lead them away. They had probably never seen man and wondered what it was all about and could not understand what was wrong with their leader. We never saw anything more of the other two rams and supposed they had worked on through that maze of cliffs. Those young rams had lost their leader and did not know what to do. They stood on that ledge until Westley walked up to within 20 yards, selected the largest, and began slipping those tiny 40-grain lead slugs into him high behind the shoulder. Finally, when his gun was about empty, he landed one on the spine and the ram dropped and rolled all the way down over cliffs and ledges to the slide-rock below. I worked up the canyon just below him, then climbed up and watched while Westley came down. He finished off his ram and told me the Fannin was a beauty and he had dragged him back from the edge of the cliff.

We then went back to my spotting scope, and tried to estimate the distance from it up to the Fannin. Westley said 700 yards, so we decided to leave the scope right there until Doc and Edgar came back and had a look. In the meantime we resumed search for the old bonehead I had first knocked off the cliff. Westley was sure the Fannin was much the best head, but I thought differently. Westley climbed back to the ledge on which he had stood without locating him and I worked up from the bottom. Finally, when I had wondered if dead sheep ever turned into an angel and flew away, I saw him hanging by his huge horns, feet down, far up a narrow, sheer gutter in the cliff above me. He had dropped down this narrow chimney, until the spread of his huge old horns had caught and there he hung, twenty feet above the next ledge and ten feet down from the top of the chimney. Westley was soon down at my shout and finally managed to attach a rope to his horns. He was wedged tight, and I climbed up the chimney under him by holding to its sides, then lifted for all I was worth while Westley pulled from above. Finally I managed to work the tip of one horn loose and he swung clear over me. Westley Brown is in all probability one of the strongest men north of the Peace River, and he hoisted that ram up to his ledge hand over hand. Wes was just twenty-six years old and all muscle and weighed around 225 pounds.

My steel tape showed a base of each horn of 14½ inches and a length of the right horn of 39½ and left 38 inches — both badly broomed and some six inches gone from the longest horn and more from the left. He was a record and is now recorded in the last book of records for Stone sheep. We dressed him and I removed cape and head and carried that down that treacherous slope, while Westley worked the carcass down to the shin-tangle for packing. We took some photos of this big *stonei*, then climbed to the Fannin and did the same and dressed him out. I packed head and cape while Wes lugged the meat off the mountain. We soon located Doc, Dick and Edgar; they had their rams and some beautiful heads as well. Loading their meat and heads, we came down to my rams and they also estimated the distance from my spotting scope to the ledge where we dressed the Fannin at 700 yards. I still think it was around 600, not more, and afterwards wrote it up as being over 500 yards, but on publication was promptly called anything but a truthful man.

The Fannin ram was the most beautiful sheep I have ever dressed, but his head was much smaller than the big *stonei* ram. Bases went 13½ inches and the right horn had a 36-inch curl, while the sharper curved left horn went to 37-inch curl. I was well satisfied with both heads, as I had one good specimen of both Stone and Fannin rams. Westley, however, proceeded to kid me about packing a long, heavy, scope sighted rifle and spotting scope and killing rams so far away we had to hunt for them and they almost spoiled before we found them, while he packed only a little .22 caliber pistol and killed just as good eating meat at 20 yards. We packed up meat and heads and set out for camp.

Next day we put in skinning out heads and salting capes, while Edgar and Westley cut the meat in strips and jerked it from the extra quarters. That evening Allan Robinson treated us to the finest meal I have ever eaten. He took a whole side of sheep ribs, loin and all, after removing the shoulder. Then he cut the ribs at short intervals, leaving the meat hanging intact, and rolled the fat juicy ribs around the loin and a green pole. Next the pole was hoisted to the crotch of two poles, one at each end of a long bed of coals. One end of the pole he had not trimmed, leaving the limbs intact, so that he could turn the pole and tie it. He had slowly roasted that prime sheep meat all day long. Soon he spread a clean canvas manty on the ground, laid out that huge sheep roast and cut it into sections, one for each of us. Then with fresh-baked raisin bannock, canned butter, pickles, hot tea, mashed spuds and rich brown gravy he had made from the drippings from the huge roast, it was a feed for a king. If I live to be one hundred and hunt sheep many more times, I will still never forget that wonderful dinner, nor the others that followed on the long trail out to the Peace River, until the last of our fresh sheep meat was consumed. Until you have eaten mountain sheep ribs and loin from a prime fat ram so cooked, you really have no possible conception of this, the world's finest meat.

My Stone ram was hit quartering, the slug striking low behind shoulder, going through lungs and breaking the spine, but did not blow up badly. Most of it lay under the skin on the front of the neck. The Fannin ram showed even less expansion, hardly any in fact. The bullet entered the right side of the lungs low down and ranged upward, severing the big artery just under the spine and also the spine itself, and making only about a .50 caliber exit hole, even after shattering the spine, clearly showing the range was too great for expansion. Lucky I was to hit him so.

XIII

Stalking Rifles

WHEN we turn to stalking rifles and proper loads, we have an entirely different problem from that presented by short to medium range timber shooting. For stalking we need long range and flat trajectory and plenty of remaining energy out where the game is actually struck. Muzzle velocity means nothing if the bullet does not retain high velocity out to extreme ranges. While the blunt Round Nose and the Flat Point projectile are by far the best for close range timber shooting, they are entirely out of place in a long range rifle. The blunt bullet form piles up head resistance and sheds velocity as an old Mallard drake's feathers do rain water. What is needed in all calibers for long range is the spitzer or Sharp Point bullet with plenty of length and sectional density. High muzzle velocity is not nearly as important as high remaining velocity out at 300 yards. For this reason we need not consider any short, lightweight bullets. They are, one and all, wind sensitive and one and all have a very high rate of velocity loss per 100 yards. Further, those short, lightweight bullets are effective only on light, thin-shelled game, and when turned on our heavier game do not have that hydraulic shock effect and seldom penetrate deep enough to make more than a bad surface wound. Select medium weight spitzer bullets of the best possible form and sectional density and at high velocity if possible. Any time velocity is over 3000 to 3200 feet at most, you are better off with more bullet weight, rather than added velocity. Our .270 Winchester and .300 Magnum with 130- and 180-grain loads are simply devastating in their effect on our lighter game, when planted in the lungs or heart area, but turn them on a big bear, elk or moose and we would need a cartridge just about exactly duplicating the .50 caliber Government machine gun load with a 700-grain slug at around 3000 feet to give the same high velocity shock effect. Mere man cannot handle a rifle for such a load and pack it all day in rough country, hence we must depend on much lighter cartridges with long, fairly heavy bullets that will penetrate to the vitals with good expansion on our larger species.

Flat Base bullets are probably just as good to about 400 yards range; beyond that distance the Boattail no doubt gives slightly higher remaining velocity and flatter trajectory if started out in life at the same muzzle velocity as the Flat Base. Bullets must be made with thin jackets near the point and the best and most reliable types we have seen at long range were the plain Soft Point spitzers, or the small cavity, or Hollow Points, such as the W.T.C. Company and the excellent Western and Winchester Open Point. The Silver-tip spitzer shape is in reality a Soft Point. The Remington and Peters Core-Lokt line are some of our best designed bullets for timber or average ranges but the Blunt Nose is not suited to flattest trajectory over long ranges. If Remington and Peters would only point up their medium weight bullets in this line, such as the 130-grain .270, the 180-grain .30–06 and .300 Magnum and similar loads, then these Core-Lokt bullets would be ideal.

First let us take up the stalking rifles and loads suitable for our lighter game at long range, deer and antelope to caribou. The .256 Newton with 129-grain, or preferably 140-grain bullets is about the smallest stalking load that will give good average results on the lighter game. We have used this cartridge a lot in former years and found it flatter in its trajectory over long ranges than the .30–06 and an excellent killer when placed in the chest cavity of the smaller big game to 300 yards and occasionally to 350 yards. It is at its best with the 140-grain bullet hand loaded with 4350 Dupont powder. A. E. Ellinger has had very good success with it on all the lighter game and has even taken elk with it with carefully placed shots in the open. It is liable to be discontinued.

The 139-grain 7 mm. load, while it starts out in life at 2900 feet, loses velocity too fast for its bullet construction to be effective over 300 yards and we have seen it fail miserably several times at about that range. Up to 250 yards it usually works well on the lighter game when placed right.

The .265 O.K.H. designed by C. M. Oneil, Don Hopkins and the writer is a very effective small bore cartridge when hand loaded with Duplex loads. It drives its 160-grain Soft Point bullet to 2600 feet with standard loads from the revamped 7 mm. case and to a full 3000 feet with our best Duplex loads. It's a real killer on all the smaller big game and much superior to the lighter bullet .270 Winchester loads. It is also one of the most accurate rifle cartridges I have ever fired. However, it is a custom loading proposition and the rifles must also be custom made by Oneil. From my own experience with this little cartridge, I would place it on top of the list of all loads up to and including the 270 bore. It's a wonderful cartridge for the young lad or the lady who needs a light, short rifle, and yet wants actual killing power. Its long 160-grain 6.5 mm. bullets will expand to very long ranges — at its best for long range, of course, with Duplex loads and their higher velocity.

The .270 Winchester is probably the finest small caliber commercial load made today. It is flatter in its trajectory and usually more accurate than the .30–06 180-grain or 150-grain with its 130-grain load over long ranges. It is a fine killer of our lighter big game to 350 yards and sometimes to 400 if the bullet is placed in the chest cavity. We have seen it used on most game and while it failed miserably on elk and large game, it did a very nice job most of the time on the lighter game. The 130-grain load is the best for most long range work, but the 150-grain might prove even better if the bullet were pointed up and the twist increased enough to stabilize the longer bullet at long range. The .270 is obtainable in both Remington and Winchester factory rifles, as well as many fine custom rifles. The hunter can get about any weight or length desired. Barrels should be 24 inches long or longer for highest velocity.

Next we have the .30–40–180, the .303 British 174-grain and the 8 mm. with 154-grain bullets. All about on a par when used as stalking rifles and good on our smaller big game to about 300 yards. At times bullet expansion will not be too good, even at this range, but with proper thin jacketed bullets these loads will usually do good work out to about 300 yards. Properly loaded the 8 mm. is best.

In the .30–06, we have both the 150- and 180-grain loads for long range work. Both are very accurate and reliable on our smaller big game, when used with a bullet that will surely expand. The load is at its best under our observation with the 172-grain W.T.C. Company .30–40 thin jacket bullet and around 50 grains Dupont 3031 powder. This is the cartridge that with several makes of patent trick points has lost more big game wounded, under our guidance, than any other load. Many of the failures, in fact most of them, were due to bullets that failed to expand, or that blew out shallow surface wounds only. When used with the new Remington and Peters Core-Lokt and the Winchester and Western Open Point, or Silver-tip, results are usually very reliable. The cartridge has never given us the percentage of clean kills so many claim for it and we believe this is due to the fact that it attains really high velocity only with the 150-grain bullet, then sheds that velocity at a high rate due to low sectional density. With proper bullets of 150- to 180-grain weight that will expand reliably, it is a fine cartridge on all our lighter game out to 300 yards, but we have never found any factory load that showed much expansion on light game beyond the 300 yard range and many did not expand at all. The .318 180-grain Westley Richards about duplicates the .30–06–180. In eastern Canada and the United States, where the principal big game is moose, whitetail deer, black bear and woodland caribou, and the actual shooting ranges seldom exceed 150 yards except when shooting across ravines or lakes, the .30–06 with long exposed 220-grain Soft Point ammunition is adequate for all but moose. If those long 220-grain bullets are properly placed on moose they will take all Eastern game nicely. True, moose may not drop at the shot, unless brain or spine is hit, or the heart, when it is filled with blood, but pound for pound of animal tissue, the moose is the easiest big game animal to kill of any, in my humble opinion. Moose may not drop at the shot, but they give up and quit easily and will soon stop and bed down, or wait to see if the hunter is after them, affording another shot. A broken leg will usually stop them in a short distance, while an elk, mule deer, sheep, goat or antelope would travel for miles with the same hit.

Many readers may wonder why I consistently condemn the .30–06. It is simply because it has failed more often than any other load under my observation and on many species of game. Throughout this book many instances will be quoted, but a few more here may not be amiss.

One fall in the Selway I watched Mrs. Keith shoot a big mule buck at 150 yards up a steep slope above us. She used my .30–06 Springfield match rifle, with 180-grain Silver-tip ammunition. The buck stood broadside to us and her first shot struck the front of the right shoulder as he was slightly quartering, tore away one whole top corner of the heart and lodged in the left shoulder. All the energy in the load was expended in the buck. He jumped and ran down the mountain toward us for some distance, then stopped and turned around broadside again, presenting the same side to her. After two minutes by my watch he had not gone down, so she shot him again, this time low behind the shoulders, through both lungs. The slug hit a small maple sapling and expanded before it hit the buck and went completely through his chest and lungs. Again he ran down the mountain toward us and stopped. One front leg was broken at the shoulder, from the first hit. Buz Corbet of Salmon was with us and witnessed the shooting. After two minutes more, he was still on his feet, so I asked her to bust him again, this time high behind the shoulders, as he was again standing broadside. She placed that shot just right behind the right shoulder and it went on through the buck. After over five minutes all told, by my watch, he reared up and fell backwards dead. All three bullets apparently did all that could be expected of them.

On the same trip Mrs. Keith and I ran onto a fine big black bear feeding on elk offal fifty yards from the trail in dense timber. She was afraid of not hitting him right so asked me to shoot the bear. From a steady sitting position with left arm resting over a big log, I waited until the bear advanced the right foreleg, while he held the elk paunch down so he could tear away a bite with his teeth. Then aiming halfway up the side of his body and close in behind that advanced right shoulder, I gave him one of those Winchester 180-grain .30–06 Silver-tips. I aimed to break the off shoulder and did just that. He reared up at the shot and fell backwards over a log, but was up in an instant and running toward us with the left or off front leg flopping up level with the top of his back, showing clearly that the shoulder was broken. The timber was so thick I could not get in another shot and he would fall, then when I had held the rifle on the spot where he had disappeared in the jumble of fallen logs, until my arms ached and I had to lower the rifle, he would jump and run again, and again fall out of sight before I could get in a shot. He turned to the right and piled up in a log jam several feet above the ground, but all I could see was one ear and one hind foot, so I waited. Then he jumped up again and ran quartering away from us. I picked him up and shot again, but a small dead spruce came in line just as I shot. He went down, and again he was up and out of sight before I could even throw the bolt. Examination proved that shot went through the spruce and was headed right for the bear, but whether it hit him or not I'll never know. I trailed him as far as Mink Creek that night before dark and also spent the next three days in the rain without ever finding another track, though I worked both banks of Mink Creek down nearly a half mile to the Selway. A big peeled log lay on the other side of the bear when I hit him first, clearly showing that 180-grain slug stayed in him, as it did not mark the log. These two incidents happened exactly as described, on this one trip. I have seen the same thing happen so many times over the years that I long ago lost all faith in the cartridge, and never will use it again myself if anything else is available.

Frank Waterman, my neighbor, once shot a 300-pound black bear at 250 yards across a small canyon, as the bear walked along broadside. Ammunition, 180-grain Western Open Point Boattail .30–06. Frank aimed at the front of the shoulder, so as to land just behind the shoulder with the bear walking along. At the shot the bear turned and ran straight up the mountain for 75 yards, then turned to the right again and went a good 50 yards before crossing another opening in the scattered timber, when

Frank again shot and hit him. This time the bear rolled down the mountain about 75 yards. Then he regained his feet and stood up on his hind feet, the while he pulled up all the berry bushes he could reach with his front paws. Knowing he had placed his shots, Frank waited and finally the bear slumped down, then slid into a hole below in some slide-rock. On skinning him out Frank found the first 180-grain Open Point had gone in behind the right shoulder and literally blown the heart into shreds, but did not even mark the rib cage on the off side. The second shot caught him further to the rear, through the lungs and just under the spine, and went on through the bear. That little black lived long enough to have crossed the canyon to Frank at least, as he claims he must have been alive for at least four or five minutes. These three instances show three failures to kill even small 300-pound animals on the spot when the shots were placed exactly right.

One fall in the Lochsa, two of the party used .30–06 rifles with 180-grain U.S.C. Company patented spitzer point bullets, a modification of the old Ross copper tube. That bullet would not expand reliably on anything. Seven elk were shot through with it broadside all told, on that trip. Three of them were hit through the spinal column and killed, the other four all got away wounded and some we trailed a long way before losing the tracks. There were no blood trails. I also watched Bob Carney plug a mule buck in the seat of the pants, under the tail, at about 60 or 80 yards. The bullet came out his chest as near as we could tell from the blood on beds when he did stop. He simply humped up, kicked at his belly and departed, and we trailed him three miles before losing his trail in slide-rock. His few beds showed a little blood at each end and where he stood there was some hair from his chest thrown out by the bullet exit. That was 180-grain U.S.C. Company .30–06 load again.

I could fill this book with similar .30–06 experiences, but why go on. In conclusion, on this caliber, I must say that many other hunters report only clean kills and mostly one-shot kills at that with the cartridge over long periods of time, but such has never been my experience. I have never seen any man kill very many head of game with the cartridge without having some failures, even when the load was planted right, so consider it adequate only for our smaller game, or Eastern game, when hit right, and not to exceed 300 or 350 yards. I do not consider it adequate for elk, grizzly or brownies under average hunting conditions as we find them today, from here to Alaska, along the Rocky Mountain chain. Whether Western game, used to climbing steep mountains all its life, is more tenacious of life than Eastern game, living in less rugged country, I do not pretend to know, never having hunted the Eastern country. If the cartridge has done well for you, stick to it, but if it fails you as it has me so many times, then get something more adequate.

The .30–06 about concludes the list of long and medium range rifles suitable only for our lighter game up to caribou. Next we have the more powerful long range loads, ideal from every single standpoint for all our lighter big game, and in the hands of expert riflemen who will carefully place their shots or not shoot; capable of taking all our larger species. We believe heavier calibers than the next six loads listed should be used for all game heavier than caribou.

First we have the .275 H & H Magnum, which with 175- or 180-grain bullet is a most excellent long range load and good for our lighter game, with proper bullets, out to about 500 yards. It has never been used in this country except in British or custom built rifles, but Western did load the ammunition for a number of years. It is an excellent cartridge from every standpoint.

The .276 Dubiel is the same caliber but with a longer shoulder on the same cartridge case. Several of our friends have taken all species with this cartridge loaded with 175- to 190-grain bullets. At its best with 180 bullet and 4350 Dupont powder in all probability. It is extremely accurate and flat to extreme ranges and will expand well to 500 yards with proper bullets. Both the .275 H & H and .276 Dubiel are much more effective long range rifles than anything smaller, including the .270 and .30–06. They use bullets of great length and sectional density, with a very minimum velocity loss, hence retain high velocity out where the game is actually struck. At close range on heavy game, penetration may not be all that is needed, but when used in their proper sphere of usefulness, on our lighter game, they are most wonderful super-accurate long range loads.

The .280 Dubiel Magnum is an even larger case, really over bore capacity, but with 180-grain bullet is a mighty fine long range cartridge. With Boattail 180-grain handmade bullets it badly beats even the .300 Magnum H & H 180 grain for trajectory and remaining energy and velocity out at extreme ranges. I have used this cartridge a great deal on about all the smaller big game and to crazy long ranges. It always expanded reliably to 500 yards and sometimes even beyond that range. Have taken three record antelope with it, as well as having used it for years as a coyote rifle. It will do all the .275 H & H and .276 Dubiel will do, but really is little, if any, their superior, when the two latter cartridges are hand loaded with 4350 Dupont and 180-grain bullets. All three are most excellent long range cartridges. Harry Snyder used my hand loads in killing a museum group of our Canadian wood bison and they worked mighty well, even when he had to stop two charging bulls at close range with the 180-grain bullets placed in the center of top of neck, as the head was carried low in the charge. This performance speaks mighty well for their penetration with 180-grain W.T.C. Company bullets. Several mule deer that I bumped off at 450 to 500 yards with the 180-grain .280 Dubiel load all showed excellent expansion. The cartridge, like the .275 and .276, is a killer on our lighter game and carries the velocity out to long range; then combines a long heavy missile with great sectional density for wind bucking and penetration. All three are big Magnum cases and some of our firms should long ago have built a good rifle for one of these loads. They one and all lie closer to the wind and retain their velocity better than the same 180-grain weight of bullet in the .300 Magnum. Harry Snyder also used my 180-grain .280 Dubiel loads in African plains shooting with excellent results.

To my notion, the long sloping shoulder .280 Dubiel case holds a bit more powder than is needed, and if I were to have a rifle made up today, I believe the .275 or the .276 case would be the best bet. You would then have a much wider choice of 7 mm. bullets as well as the .276 bullets made by W.T.C. Company to our design for the .285 O.K.H. For standard loads in 7 mm. caliber, the .275 or .276 Dubiel is a mighty fine load and the .285 O.K.H. with standard loads will develop just about the same velocities, as the three cases hold about the same charge. The .280 Dubiel, however, is .2885 inches in groove diameter and uses only the fine W.T.C. Company bullets. Again, all of these loads are custom or hand loads and rifles must be custom made.

In a commercially made rifle and load for extreme long range work, the finest we have today is the .300 Magnum Model 70 Winchester with 180-grain Open Point B.T. loads. It's a whale of a good combination and when scope sighted with a 4 X scope and zeroed to 300 yards will give better average long range results on all our lighter game, antelope to sheep and caribou, than anything smaller in commercial production today (August 1948). We started using the .300 Magnum back in 1926 and have used the cartridge more or less for long range game shooting since that date. It has taken some of my finest game heads. When you want a commercial rifle and cartridge for extreme long range, that will give better results on the light game than anything else commercially made, then the Model 70 Winchester in .300 Magnum is your best bet. Fit it with the new Weaver K 4 scope in any good reliable low mount and sight the 180 grain for 300 yards point-blank. Hold about 4 inches low at 150 to 175 yards, dead on at 300, and about 5 inches high at 400 and over the back for 500 yards and you will get results.

The finest of all the long range cartridges for our lighter game to extreme long range is the .285 O.K.H. with 180-grain Duplex load. Designed by Oneil, Hopkins and myself, it has a load that badly beats anything extant, including the .280 German Halger. It has now taken, in our various hands and by J. Omar Cole, about all species of American game except arctic game. Practically everything else, including record Alaskan brownies, have been killed with the load. Velocity is very high, probably around 3200 feet. Velocity of the 180-grain .280 Dubiel load was chronographed by Colonel Whelen at the Springfield Arsenal at 2925 feet. Later I had my first .285 O.K.H. cut with a groove diameter of .2885 by Neidner and the rifle made up by Oneil. The regular .280 Dubiel W.T.C. Company 180-grain bullet that the .280 Dubiel load would drive almost completely through a mule buck at 300 yards, with the expanded slug staying under the skin on the off end, was simply blown to fragments at the same range by our .285 O.K.H. Duplex loads. Bucks hit in exactly the same place, with no bones struck, showed complete disintegration of the same bullet in the lung cavity. This could only be due to much higher velocity, as the bullets were from the same lot. The .285 O.K.H. also proved it would expand its bullets reliably much further than any other rifle cartridge we have ever used. I still do not know how far it will expand those modern W.T.C. Company tough jacket .276M 180-grain slugs. Last fall we hit one big buck in the flank at a good 600 yards and that bullet went on into the lungs and expanded into fragments. An eagle I killed at an estimated 700 yards also showed excellent expansion.

The first bullets W.T.C. Company brought out for us and marked .276 on the boxes were made with a hard brittle jacket considerably thinned at the point, and these blew to atoms on game at usual ranges; then the company brought out their .276M for us with a softer tougher jacket and probably thicker at the point as well. This bullet has worked perfectly on all game shot. It blows up badly, yet always gives deep penetration and is deadly on anything if carefully placed in the chest cavity. I had it fail me on elk that was hit with a raking shot, ranging forward through paunch and then through the right lung, but with a doctored and revamped Government M-1 bullet. We do not consider it a rifle or load for our heavier game, but there can be no shadow of doubt that it is the one most effective load ever devised for all our lighter game to extreme long range. I can guarantee it will expand reliably to a full 600 yards and I know of nothing else on this green earth in a sporting rifle that will do that. It's superbly accurate and lies close to the wind, as well as being much flatter over sporting ranges than even the great .300 Magnum 180 grain.

As a test I sighted in the .285 O.K.H. with 180-grain Duplex load at 400 yards and also sighted in a Model 70 Winchester .300 Magnum with the same 26-inch barrel length and same Stith mounted scope for the same range with factory 180-grain Open Point Boattail loads. When both rifles centered ten shot groups at 400 yards, I turned them on the 200-yard target without even getting up from the bench rest. Both rifles were fired with padded fore-end rest and no sling. The .285 O.K.H. 180-grain Duplex load printed just 5 inches high at 200 yards, for a ten shot group, and the .300 Magnum factory 180-grain load centered its ten shot group just 7½ inches high. In other words the .285 O.K.H. load was a third flatter over 400 yards range.

When turned on hard ⅝-inch steel plate at 20 yards the above 180-grain .300 Magnum load penetrated three fourths of the way through and badly bulged the back of the plate. Several shots were fired and always with the same result. Then the .285 O.K.H. 180-grain Duplex load was tested and blew a cork out of the plate at each shot. The plate was then moved back to 50 yards and it still blew out clean corks with complete easy penetration at each shot. Steel penetration is considered a very good criterion of velocity, so there can be no shadow of doubt as to the extreme velocity of the .285 O.K.H. load when one considers the bullet expansion tests on several head of game at the same range in comparison with the 280 Dubiel with same bullets, and then the trajectory and steel penetration tests in comparison with the .300 Magnum at 3060 feet velocity.

I first wrote up the results of our Duplex loadings in this cartridge in the *American Rifleman*, but finding that we were soon to be engaged in a war never did give out any further details, beyond the published reports on our patented claims. Duplex loading is simple enough and Oneil, while visiting me in 1936, was told my idea — namely the fact that I considered we were igniting the charge at the wrong end of the case, and that if we could only get the ignition carried forward so it would start the bullet by igniting and firing the front end of the powder charge, then the gas that pushed the bullet on its way would hold the remainder of the charge in the heel of the case until completely consumed. I had been experimenting with a .30 Newton case necked to .25 caliber that Oneil and Con V. Schmitt had made up, and that rifle heated up very badly in ten shots and its accuracy life was very short, around 200 rounds.

Oneil went home and soon designed a method of fitting flash tubes in the case to carry the primer flash to the forward half of the charge. I then wrote Hopkins about our experiments and he joined us in the work. We soon found we had something we did not want to have fall into enemy hands until the war was over, so Oneil obtained patents in the U.S. and Canada and applied for one in Britain and we kept mum on the development. Later while working in Ordnance at Ogden Arsenal I was ordered back to Frankford Arsenal, where I put in a month Duplex loading caliber .50 and gave them several loads averaging about 150 feet higher velocity than standard, with normal pressures, and my best Duplex load went on an average a full 202 feet higher in velocity than the standard Government .50 caliber load. Now that the war is over I have asked General Hatcher for permission to tell the tale and he has granted it.

The whole principle of Duplex loading is to compress the powder charge in the case with no air space. The case must be the right capacity for the bore, bullet weight and powder rate of burning used. Further it must have the right constriction at the shoulder for best results. Next the chamber must be tight over the body of the case to prevent undue case expansion that would in turn allow the fire to burn back around the bulk of the charge. Then with a tube in the case, and the primer flash carried forward to the front half of the charge, the forward portion of the charge is ignited and a relatively small portion of the total charge is used to start the bullet. After the bullet is in motion you can burn a hell of a powder charge behind it with normal pressures.

That is what we do and the rear end of the barrel remains cool during a long string and the muzzle back about to the tip of the forestock gets hot first. The powder charge, except for the front portion, is not funneled up the bore, but is held in the case until consumed. The proper place to burn a powder charge is in the combustion chamber itself, not funneled up the bore, in hopes it will be long enough to allow complete combustion of the charge. The pressure time curve is greatly extended, and the muzzle flash largely eliminated. This in turn leads to an accelerated bullet with velocity increasing as the bullet moves up the bore and the gas from the burning powder constantly increases in volume behind it. Like all good things it is simple, but when the right balance of components is secured it produces results not obtainable in any other manner. To Mr. C. M. Oneil is due the credit for this development. So much for this digression, as my mail has shown all riflemen are intensely interested in the development. The .285 O.K.H. case is made from .30–06 brass, and holds about the same load as the .275 H & H and .276 Dubiel with their larger but much thicker cases. With standard loads the cartridge develops around 2800 feet velocity with 180-grain bullet. Though our original Duplex loads were with just one powder, Dupont 4350, and that was used in the above .285 O.K.H. tests, Oneil later found we could further increase velocity by using a faster powder in the heel of the case, and even that three different rates of burning of powder would further increase velocities. I used some of those combinations for my highest velocity .50 caliber loads. The powder was not mixed at all. The fast powder was poured in the heel of the case, the medium rate powder next and lastly the slower burning powder. The case was kept straight up and handled carefully until the bullet was seated and the powder compressed tight so none of it could possibly move.

Such loads shoot the same uphill or downhill, as the charge is tightly compressed and does not move. Duplex cases are more difficult to make and loading takes more time, but results were what we were after and we obtained them. I do not know if the development will ever be commercially produced or not, but do know it gives results not obtainable by any other method of loading and firing a rifle cartridge today. It should work equally well in artillery and that is where I hoped to use it in Ordnance, but was put on caliber .50. It will produce normal velocities with very low pressures, or very high velocities with normal pressures. The flash tube is brass of smaller inside diameter than the original cartridge flash hole and screwed into the head of the case. Though this is the first time I have written the facts for publication, I may now let it out via the magazines since the War Department has allowed us to do so. It was held confidential during the war and until recently.

The .30 and .35 Newton have both been discontinued by the Western Cartridge Company. Now with no further supply of cartridge cases and with all rifles since the failure of the Newton Company being custom jobs, there is little need to discuss these two excellent loads. Both were brought out about twenty-five years ahead of their time and by a rifleman and ballistician who thought about that many years ahead of his time. The .30 Newton will do anything the .300 Magnum will, and in addition will handle light bullets to even higher velocity. The .35 Newton is an excellent long range load for our larger species and I have seen uniformly excellent results from it at all times and on a good many different species of game. They were mighty good loads but are due to fall by the wayside.

This brings us to the heavy caliber long range rifles, ideal for long range work on our heaviest American game and very useful against most of the game of Africa and India as well. The following calibers are not as flat in their trajectory as some of the more notable small bores, but throw much heavier projectiles, suitable for certain deep penetration on our larger fauna.

I have already discussed the .333 Jeffery and .333 O.K.H. Both are fine long range rifles with 250-grain spitzer bullets and will expand their bullets to much longer range as a rule than will the .30–06. This may be due to a thinner bullet jacket or more lead exposure. I have used the .333 O.K.H. to 300 yards on elk with the 300-grain Jeffery Soft Point bullet, and to a full 500 yards on mule deer, and obtained excellent expansion and wound channels at all ranges. Over 200 yards this 250-grain bullet driven at 2635 feet from the .333 O.K.H. seemed to beat the .35 Whelen, .35 Newton and even the .375 Magnum 270 grain for trajectory curve. This must be due to its greater sectional density and sharper point. It has a comparatively low velocity loss per hundred yards as compared with other larger bores, throwing shorter, more blunt form, projectiles. The Jeffery .333's 250 grain, however, is loaded to only 2400 or 2500 feet, and while a good long range load is not to be compared with our loading with the same weight bullet. But that Jeffery .333 case can be hand loaded with our American powders to give a full 2700 feet with 250-grain bullet with ease, under normal working pressures, and is then a mighty fine long range rifle for our larger game.

We have already discussed the lack of a proper bullet for both the .35 Whelen and .350 G & H Magnum, since Western discontinued the .35 Newton bullet of 250 grains. We understand Fred N. Barnes of Durango, Colorado, now makes excellent .35 caliber bullets in 250 and 300 grain, and these should put the two excellent .35 calibers back in their proper place. Both are exceptionally accurate and really fine cartridges for all of our heavier game. The .35 Whelen will work nicely through standard actions, but the .350 G & H is best served with the big Magnum Mauser action. That cartridge with a proper bullet of 300 grains for close range, and a 250 grain for long range, should do about the same work on anything as the .375 Magnum, and in addition should lie a bit closer to the wind and have a slightly flatter trajectory owing to its smaller caliber. I have used the .35 Whelen a great deal on most species, including black and Alaskan grizzly as well as lesser game, and have a very high regard for it when loaded with proper bullets. The .350 G & H Magnum I have never used; several friends who have used them report fine accuracy but improper expansion of the former 275-grain W.T.C. Company bullet. I found the same difficulty when this bullet was used in the .35 Whelen and had to drill out much larger and deeper cavities in the points to insure certain expansion on all but big bear. Even then it put three 275-grain slugs through a 1200-pound grizzly's shoulders at just 12 feet range, and two of them went on through and out of the bear, while the third lodged under the skin on the breast, which was the offside from where I shot him between the shoulders in the back, after my first slug had spun him around. Like the .333 O.K.H., these rifles and loads are custom jobs, but are good ones when used with proper bullets.

Next we have the .375 Magnum, now made by custom makers and also by Winchester in their Model 70. It is today the best American commercially made big load for long range on our largest game. At times no rifle will seem too large for our larger species as they differ so much in temperament and physical stamina. Last fall Jack Grigsby, hunting out of Anchorage, Alaska, ran onto a huge bull moose late in the evening. He jumped the moose, which trotted away at about 125 yards. Jack used the Model 70 Winchester .375 Magnum. His first shot caught the moose in the flank, ranging forward into the kidney area, where it stopped. He could not tell whether he had hit or missed as the huge bull never faltered in his stride, though he did turn almost directly away from Jack at the shot. His next slug caught said moose in the north end when he was headed south, right under the tail. Then the moose stopped and turned around and faced Jack. He shot him again in the top of the chest, ranging into the spine, but the bull did not drop, merely stood around awhile, then walked away and lay down. Jack threw the bolt for another round and found his magazine empty, and a frantic search of all his pockets failed to turn up another cartridge. He had left them all in the car. So Jack picked up a big dry limb and approached to throwing distance and heaved that at the bull. It struck his antlers and brought him to his feet instantly and headed for Jack, who left in high gear for the road and his car, some three miles away. He came back next morning early and found the bull dead a short distance from where he left him the night before. He did not state what weight bullet he used but it sounds to me like either the 235- or the 270-grain load, probably the former.

I have used the 300 grain to 360 yards on game with excellent expansion, but several friends report inadequate expansion of the 270-grain .375 slug at longer ranges. Walter Peterson, in particular, had difficulty with expansion of the 270-grain load on a real big Alaskan brownie in 1937, indicative of the need for greater lead exposure at the point of the bullet. We have not lately tested on game any of the 270 grain of recent manufacture, and this one fault may well have been corrected. It is one of our most accurate rifles and cartridges and with the 270 grain just about duplicates Springfield 180-grain trajectories. On large animals, one who knows his rifle should have little difficulty in hitting standing game to 400 yards from a prone or sitting position.

My own Model 70 .375 Magnum has two lateral cross wires in the Lyman Alaskan scope. The lower wire is zeroed for 400 yards with the 300-grain bullet and the upper wire for 200 yards with the same bullet. Then by actual test we found the upper wire would shoot to 300 yards with the 270 grain and the lower wire to about 500 yards with the 270 grain. Thus with the two loads and bullet weights we are all fixed for about any long range heavy game shooting in this country. This rifle placed for me, prone with sling and scope, 16 consecutive shots in just 1 9/16 inches at 200 yards, center to center of widest holes, with factory Winchester 300-grain loads, and that is about as fine accuracy as I have seen from any rifle to date. No rest, but a tarp spread over the snow, temperature about 30 degrees and overcast with no wind. Two shots were fired at a time and the rifle allowed to cool, then two more were fired and this procedure continued for the 16 shot string. When the big rifle was fired continuously, in usual slow fire cadence, the groups enlarged to 2½ to 3½ inches, due to heat waves over the barrel.

This brings us down to the king of all long range medium bore rifles for long range work on our largest American game. This is the .334 O.K.H., also designed by Hopkins, Oneil and myself. However, some twelve or fourteen years ago I had John Dubiel interested in just such a cartridge and he went so far as to make up the chambering reamers but he became sidetracked on some smaller calibers, including his earlier .276 and .280 Dubiel rifles, and he died without ever making up the rifle.

This cartridge is made from either the .300 or .375 Magnum case with an abrupt shoulder and in standard loads, handles 73 grains of Dupont 4350, with either 250 or 275 grain spitzers and 67 grains of the same powder with the 300-grain Soft Point Round Nose bullet. Velocity is too high for short ranges and I would prefer a .333 O.K.H. for all work up to 200 yards; beyond that range, however, the big rifle takes the cake over anything I have ever used. Velocity with the 250 grain is 2850 to 2900 feet, standard loads, and with the 275-grain spitzer around 2750 feet. With the long 300-grain slug velocity is around 2600 feet. Owing to its comparatively small bore for such bullet weights and their great sectional density, they far outrange any other big caliber for trajectory we know of.

I have had but one failure with the cartridge and that was due entirely to a 250-grain Barnes, extremely heavy jacket bullet that was closed too much at the tip and went through an elk's lungs at close range, then a small tree and then some 18 inches of frozen ground before it howled away. That elk was trailed until a snowstorm blew out the tracks, late in the afternoon and was about dead at that time, and we found but little left next day after the coyotes had worked on it all night. Aside from that one animal, all the rest of my shots have been clean one-shot kills from the big rifle, and one was at a mule deer at 600 yards, made on a bet and before a good many witnesses. To show what the terrific velocity does to the bullets at close range, I shot a big mule buck broadside in the lungs at 50 yards, or less, with the 275-grain load. He made about three short jumps and went down, but examination proved his lungs were demolished and the bullet completely disintegrated in the lungs, no part of it even marking the rib cage on the other side. I have killed two goats, one at 450 and one at 500 yards, one mule buck at 50 or less, one at 600, one at 450 yards and one, the last, at 300 yards, also one six-point bull elk at 200 yards and the above mentioned elk at close range. With the exception of that one failure the rest were clean one-shot kills. The shot at 600 yards was also made with one of those heavy jacket Barnes bullets and did not expand at all. It went through about the center of both lungs and the deer ran about 80 yards before dropping.

With all modern long range rifles, for either large or our smaller big game, we believe the hunting scope to be the best possible sight and to date have seen nothing superior for the purpose to the new Weaver K-4 scope, with cross hair reticule. No doubt other four power hunting scopes will be brought out ere long and may, or may not, beat this excellent Weaver, but so far we have seen nothing from any country that beats it for our own use.

In conclusion let me say that for the average tyro who is not, or will not become, an expert rifleman, there is no earthly use in buying and using such a long range rifle. Better by far for him to take only such shots as he can be sure of making. But for the trained expert rifleman hunter, there is a lot of pleasure in owning and using such a long range rifle. Until a man or woman can stay pretty well inside our standard military bull's-eyes at 600 yards, he or she has little business shooting at fine game animals at long ranges.

XIV

Mountain Sheep

HAVE you ever seen a mature bighorn ram silhouetted on the sky line of his rugged domain? If so, then you know that no word picture can ever quite do him justice. Ranging at or above timber line, no other animal so typifies, or is so symbolic of, the rugged grandeur of the lofty snow-covered peaks, beautiful glacier-fed lakes and alpine meadows of the Rocky Mountain chain. Some of the wildest, roughest and most beautiful country that God ever made. All big game hunters and most sportsmen and nature lovers consider the bighorn the prize trophy obtainable in America.

Sheep hunters and alpine climbers have much in common. Both love the beautiful high country and both must be physically fit to really enjoy the sport. A sound heart and lungs are an absolute necessity for the grueling climbs at high altitudes, often from 600 to 10,000 feet elevation.

Sheep hunters must often be gone from their base camp and its comforts for several days at a time, with only a back pack of food and the barest living necessities, and must often lie out around an open fire in freezing temperatures — although sheep may sometimes be taken with comparative ease and I have seen sportsmen ride to within a short distance of these grand animals and have a short climb to make to secure them. I have also seen sportsmen kill them from the boat on our Salmon River trips.

However, these are the exceptions to the rule and the sportsman who desires the head of a big ram for his home or office should count on plenty of hard work and hardship before his ultimate success. Truly this is a game for the young or the strong, and absolutely tops in American big game hunting. Sportsmen have journeyed from all parts of the world to hunt the various species of American wild sheep, and each fall hundreds of sportsmen make long trips back into the wilds of this continent by all manner of transportation — from pack horse outfits to boats and airplanes, and even by back-packing in parts of the North — for the express purpose of securing a big ram. Many thousands of other sportsmen and sportswomen plan and save for the time when they can also make such a hunt.

Formerly mountain sheep were very plentiful almost the length of the Rocky Mountain chain, from lower Sonora north far into the arctic in Alaska. Today, they remain much the same in the northern part of British Columbia, Yukon territory and Alaska. Mexico also has a goodly number left in Sonora and Lower California, in spite of a great deal of hunting. The picture in the United States, however, is not so promising. Of the once great bands of wild sheep that roamed most of our mountain chain, only scattered bands now remain, extending from Arizona and California north to the Canadian line.

The inroads of civilization have no doubt accounted for some of this great decrease, but by far the greatest single cause of the disappearance of the wild sheep from many sections was the introduction and grazing of domestic sheep on the range of their wild cousins. Mountain sheep are very susceptible to all domestic sheep diseases and such diseases are usually fatal to wild sheep, just as white man's diseases were to the Indians and Eskimos of the far North, who died by hundreds from them. Such diseases as scab alone killed most of the mountain sheep in the United States. At one time the Snake River canyon below Weiser, Idaho, contained a great many of the species, but domestic sheep scab killed virtually all of them in a few short years and many old-timers told me of finding whole bands dead in a very small acreage. The late Dave Lewis related how in 1931, while I was guiding the Zane Grey party on the middle fork of the Salmon, he had found over 200 dead bighorn sheep in the small basin at the head of a stream flowing into Big Creek, all dead from a domestic sheep disease. He carried out several of the heads for making stirrups and cinch hooks. Salmon City, Idaho, was once right in the center of a veritable mountain sheep paradise with many bands of wild sheep in every direction, but today the hunter will find only old bleached skulls and some wrinkled and shriveled horns in almost any small mountain stream he wishes to search in any direction from the town, but except for a small band ranging between the Lemhi and Pahsimeroi valleys and a small band ranging in the Bighorn Crags and another on the north side of the Salmon below the little mining hamlet of Shoup, bighorn are now completely gone from Lemhi County.

California, Arizona, Nevada, New Mexico, Colorado, Wyoming, Montana and Idaho still have mountain sheep in worth-while numbers, but they are decreasing rather than increasing in spite of the closed seasons. Miners and prospectors kill some for meat and some big heads are killed and smuggled out despite the law. Predators like coyotes and mountain lions and also wolves, in the North, take a heavy toll, but in this section at least the greatest cause of decrease in wild sheep population is domestic sheep and the golden eagle. This great bird preys a great deal on young mountain sheep during the nesting season and often kills every single lamb from some bands that is born in a season. The fall of 1937 I saw thirty-one head of ewes and not one single lamb in one band of bighorn, but golden eagles and their nests were very plentiful. When sheep were plentiful the eagle was here, as today, but in those times we did not have the U.S. Biological Survey carrying on poisoning campaigns against the rodents and thus driving more of the great birds down into the sheep range, where small game is very scarce indeed due to the very nature of the Salmon River canyon. Nearly every time man tries to improve nature by destroying some species, he in turn destroys the balance of nature so that other worth-while species suffer as a consequence. If steps are not taken in a very short time to control the golden eagle, then our mountain sheep in Idaho at least will soon be a thing of the past. The present price of gold has brought an influx of miners into our mountain regions, who must of necessity live chiefly on meat, and once they taste mountain sheep they will not hunt deer, for no other meat is quite so palatable and delicious as mountain mutton. Such meat hunting back in a country that is without a single game warden does not help the future of our bighorn. However, in all fairness I wish to state that most of the old-timers living down the river will go hungry before they will shoot a sheep for food, and use venison as their mainstay. With the influx of men new to the hills, mostly from the cities and totally lacking the inherent love of nature that is such a great part of the old mountain men, the situation is vastly changed and these new men lose no opportunity to kill and eat sheep and also to snipe a head or two and cache them in the caves of the cliffs, against a possible opportunity to sell them or sneak them out for sale in some other section of the country.

Such is the true status of the last stand of the grand old bighorn in the U.S. today.

The hunting and killing each fall of old mature rams with worth-while heads does not in any way decrease the propagation of wild sheep. This may seem strange to people unfamiliar with our wild sheep. By the time an old ram reaches such an age that his head is worth taking as a trophy, usually not less than ten years of age, then he is about all through as a breeder. Hunting of old rams each fall I honestly believe is beneficial to the species and helps to keep them on the alert and better able to take care of themselves, without in any way decreasing the breeding stock so necessary for perpetuation of the species. The killing of a ewe mountain sheep should carry a mandatory fine of not less than $1000 in all parts of our mountain sheep ranges.

If the golden eagle is controlled and domestic sheep taken from the mountains adjacent to all known bands of wild sheep, and a heavy bounty is placed on the cougar, together with rigid and adequate protection of the breeding stock, then mountain sheep can and will come back, but if the present state of affairs is allowed to continue, we in the United States will soon see the end of our finest big game animal.

In the North, especially north of the Peace River, in British Columbia on through the Yukon and Alaska, the wolf is the worst curse of the wild sheep and he alone is responsible for the greatest kill each year. In the Musqua and Prophet River sections, tributary to the Liard, I noticed that nearly all the sheep licks were covered with wolf tracks, and several kills were also found. Wolves are helpless against the agility of mountain sheep when in their rocky cliffs, and whenever attacked wild sheep run for the nearest cliffs where they can bounce around out of the way of any wolf. However when a hard and deep snowstorm hits that country as it does some seasons, then the sheep are sometimes driven down into the timbered valleys for food, and become easy prey for the great gray wolves of the North. Wolves have increased to an alarming extent in these regions as well as the Yukon and Alaska despite the bounty on them, and unless some means is soon introduced to thin their ranks, they will become as great a menace to the sheep of the North as is the golden eagle in the Salmon River drainage of Idaho.

In 1935 that section of northern British Columbia was covered with a four-foot blanket of wet snow in one great storm and many hunting parties were caught and temporarily snowed in. This storm completely covered the higher sheep ranges to such a depth that it was impossible for the game little beasts to dig out their natural food and they were forced down into the timbered valleys, where they could browse on the arctic willow and birch. That the wolves took a heavy toll was clearly shown by the mute evidence of many fang-marked skulls and scattered bones I saw when on a trip through that section in 1937. Canada has a ten-dollar bounty on wolves and a two-dollar bounty on coyotes, and Alaska has a twenty-dollar bounty on wolves and coyotes, but even so they are on the increase and something will have to be done. I would venture to say that for every sheep killed by man in northern British Columbia, north of the Peace River, at least ten are killed each year by wolves. Never have I encountered wolf tracks so thick as in that section in 1937.

Mountain sheep of North America may be divided roughly into four distinct species. Each of the four has several variations or subspecies, but the following species are sufficient to cover the main type variations. Climatic conditions under which each species lives are responsible for their chief difference in size, appearance and horn formation as well as coloration. In the South, we have the desert sheep, *Ovis nelsoni*, Mearns, Merriam, Elliot, and so forth, ranging in northern Mexico, Arizona, New Mexico and Southern California. Probably more of this species inhabits the peninsula of Lower California and the state of Sonora, Mexico, than elsewhere. Many subspecies of the Nelson sheep extend north to the southern boundary of Nevada, and at one time at least were found as far east as Texas.

From southern Nevada north to the Peace River we have the true range of *Ovis canadensis canadensis* and its many related subspecies, including *Ovis montanis*. At one time most of our Western states held many bands of this species but today they are extinct in several of these states. From all I could learn while on a trip down the Peace River in 1927, the range of *Ovis canadensis* does not extend as far north as the Peace River, but ends about 100 miles south of it. The next species is *Ovis dalli stonei*, beginning at latitude 56° on the north bank of the Peace. I saw tracks of several rams of this species within five miles of the Peace River at the Neparlepas Rapids a short distance below Finlay Forks in 1927. The range of *Ovis stonei* and its closely related subspecie, *Ovis stonei fannini*, extends north into Yukon territory. Just north of the Peace River occurs the true Stone sheep, while further north, around 57 to 58 degrees north latitude, the sheep are very much mixed in coloration between the true *stonei* and *fannini*, and still further north grade mostly to the *fannini*. North of the range of *Ovis stonei* and *fannini* occurs the true *Ovis dalli*, and his range extends far into the arctic of Yukon territory and Alaska.

The Nelson or desert sheep is lighter colored than *Ovis canadensis*, smaller in body but carrying almost as large horns. His hair is very short, giving this species a still smaller appearance. They appeared to me to be on an average slightly larger than the Stone sheep but not so large or heavy bodied as the *canadensis* species. I found one dead ram in Sonora whose bones were badly scattered and the horn shells had come off the bases of the skull. The thin horn shells at the base were badly shrunk and wrinkled, yet even then measured straight around 16⅛ inches in circumference, proving beyond a doubt they would have gone to a full 17-inch base in life, which is about as large a base growth of horn as the *canadensis* species ever carries, at least as large as any I have seen, although I have heard of 18-inch base heads. This old Nelson ram had a curl of over 36 inches and was broomed back to the second year ring, proving that those desert sheep often carry very large heads. Fresh killed heads that will measure 18 inches around the base usually shrink to 17 inches or less in a few weeks' time. One peculiarity I have noticed on all the desert sheep heads I have examined was the almost total lack of the deep year rings so common to all the more northern bighorn. With these desert sheep the year rings are so faint as to be almost indistinguishable and no one could tell the exact age of a ram by them. Living in an always summer land, with no winter to speak of and seldom any snow, they never become so poor and emaciated as the northern species.

With all species of northern bighorn the rams put on the greatest horn growth just before the rut in the fall when they are in the peak of condition. Then during the rut they become very much run-down, and this is followed by the winter, which further reduces their horn growth until it is practically stopped. In the spring as new grass starts, the horn growth starts again, increasing as the ram puts on fat until the peak is again reached in the fall. This stoppage of horn growth during the winter leaves definite deep year rings around the horns and is an exact measure of their age. With the Mexican desert species, this was much less prominent than with the northern species, owing to the fact those Mexican and desert rams stay fat most of the year and probably attain the lowest ebb of vitality just after the rut. This produces what faint year rings they do show.

With the Stone sheep, I have noticed by far the deepest and most prominent year rings. This is also true of the Dall sheep to an equal extent. The horns of these northern species show a decided bulge on the tip side of the year rings, showing clearly their great growth just before the rut and the winter and their slow increase in the spring. It also shows that the ram made his greatest horn growth during the fat fall months and attained practically no growth during the lean winter months. When spring comes the horn growth starts again, but is very slow during early spring and the horns are thus much smaller in diameter than when they were at their peak of growth the fall before; hence the deep grooves or year rings are left by the winters that clearly tell the age of the ram, when of the northern species from *canadensis* to *Ovis dalli*.

Rams grow very little horn the first year, merely a short spike, which by the time they are a full year of age in the spring may project up above the top of their heads two to four inches, seldom more than that, and by the time they are two years old the horns will show one year ring and be from 6 inches to 8 or 10 inches long. I have seen a five-year-old ram with a 14-inch base and a curl of 25 inches. On the other hand I have seen several nine-year-old rams that had from a 13⅝ to 14¾-inch base and a curl of from 27 to 36 inches, showing clearly the difference in individual horn growth. Have also seen five-year-old rams with a base of only 10 to 12 inches and horn length of but 19 inches.

As rams grow older the horn growth, while larger as a rule at the base for the first five years, is very much shorter each succeeding year, and in real old heads from fifteen to twenty years of age the growth often is not more than ¼ to ½ inch each year. Some heads show much greater growth per year than others. Some rams are very much larger than others of the same species, with correspondingly larger base of horns. Young rams up to three or four years of age often herd with the ewes and lambs. The old rams do not want them in their band and fight them off, so that they must stay with the ewes until they are three to four years of age, when they gradually start living apart from the ewes and, as they get older, take up with other rams. Mature rams and ewes run or herd together only during the rutting season and during the winter months when they band together for additional protection against predators, but even this general rule has its exceptions. Practically all very old rams ten or more years of age become old bachelors and live apart from the younger rams and ewes and lambs. They are fat, lazy old gentlemen and though their great horns may show places where huge chunks have been broken out from fighting, attesting plainly to the fact that in their younger years they also had their lighter moments, they now live either a solitary life alone, or else in company with one or more other old hardheads. In Mexico the rams seem to range apart from the ewes and young stock at all times except during the rutting season. However their range may crisscross that of a band of ewes and at times they will be seen close together, and if either band takes fright at sight of a common enemy, they may all jump and run off together. With all the northern sheep, when spring comes, the rams band together and move off to themselves, often five to ten miles from the range of the ewes and lambs, while at other times both rams and ewes may be on the same mountain. They thus live apart during the summer until the rutting urge brings them together again. At such times the ewes seemingly try to lead the rams as merry a chase as possible and both rams and ewes are constantly on the move a good part of the time. That is when most of the fighting of the rams occurs. Before the rut they fight like gentlemen.

They will back off, square away and, seemingly at a common impulse, almost as if someone had yelled "Go," they will run together with all possible speed, each striking the other on the huge heavy bosses of the horns. They often strike together so hard that both are thrown backwards off their feet. It seems utterly impossible that any animal could take such a beating and still live. After coming together they make no effort to go for each other while one is down and neither tries to take any advantage of the other, but they are gentleman fighters in the full sense of the word. Each will go back to his former station and wait until the other is apparently ready and then they run full tilt together again, each with his nose turned down to catch the blow of the other's horns square on his own. This makes a dull thumping sound that can often be heard a mile away at high altitudes as they fight.

When one is licked or has enough, he gets up and walks away and the other allows him to do so and that is all there is to it. My friend C. O. Maxwell has spent a lifetime with *Ovis canadensis* and told me of watching a pair of old Wyoming rams fight for over a half hour one day. They were fighting on a narrow shelf of cliff some six feet wide and extending parallel around the side of the mountain, one end of the ledge being considerably higher than the other. Maxwell said they would square off and come together, then each would quietly change places with the other so that each in turn had his own chance from the uphill position and could run downhill at his adversary. They continued coming together and each changing places with the other until finally one was knocked down and lay there for a time, when he got slowly up, turned around and walked away, the winner making no effort to carry the fight further. Many human beings could have learned a character lesson from that fight.

After the rut is in full swing, the gentlemanly manner of fighting is over. From then on it is a fight to the finish and best man take all the ewes.

At such times a whole band of rams, who have associated with each other throughout the summer, may fight to a finish, and the strongest or luckiest of them all will come out the winner and take the ewes. They are then anything but gentlemen in their fighting and when two are sparring and coming together, a third or fourth ram may come in from the side. Just as they near each other they spring into the air and usually hit head on while both are in the air. At such times a ram coming in from the side often puts one of the contestants out of the battle, and this also accounts for many badly broken horns. As one or another of the band becomes tired out, or knocked out from the pounding, he may lie down and rest, or walk slowly away, leaving the larger, more powerful rams to finish the struggle. This is Nature's own way of providing the strongest and largest rams for propagation of the species. As the ram's age increases he tends ever more to become an old bachelor, and after he is thoroughly licked a few times may leave the fighting and ewes entirely to the younger rams. He is then, usually, a trophy fit for a king.

The horns of *Ovis canadensis* are usually larger in basic measurement than any other species, the largest heads probably coming from the states of Colorado, Wyoming, Idaho, Montana, Alberta and British Columbia. I have seen larger base heads on an average from Montana, Alberta and British Columbia. Further north the *stonei* rams carry smaller base heads than do the true bighorn species of *Ovis canadensis* and related species, a base of 15 inches being large for the true *stonei* ram. The Fannin rams usually run to even lighter basic measurement and a 15-inch head is exceptionally large, and though I have learned of 16-inch bases in both stone and Dall sheep, they are very very rare and most hunters will not see one such in a lifetime. I have seen Fannin rams go 15-inch base and Stone rams go 15¼ but not larger.

The horns of both the Fannin and Dall rams usually are lighter in color than most desert *canadensis* and Stone sheep, being almost a light straw color at times, while the other species usually run darker. However with all old rams the tops of the horn will be badly weather-beaten and cracked and some will be a faded weathered gray in color. With all the Nelson, *canadensis* and Stone sheep, brooming is very common, and while an old ram of these species may rarely be found with perfect tips to his great horns, the usual thing is for the horns to be broomed back six to twelve inches from their regular length or rather the length they would have attained had they not so broomed. There are two types of horn, the narrow close curl type, with very narrow spread, and the extreme wide-spreading type, with the points coming out well away from the head. Of the two types the extremely wide curl sheep seem to be badly broomed more often than those with close curls. However neither type seems to have a monopoly on this brooming and many of the closest-curl heads I have seen were also the worst broomed. Many theories have been offered as to why the rams thus rubbed off or broke off their horn tips; some say it is because the horns come up over the eyes and shut off their view and they rub them away on stones in order to see. I do not believe this has anything to do with it. I have a photo of one head killed by a friend with the closest, most compact curl I have ever seen, the horn on one side coming up within three quarters of an inch of the eyeball, both horns badly broomed, but both broomed up above where the brooming would have allowed the ram more latitude of eyesight. He could see only straight ahead.

I think this brooming is more often caused by digging roots from the ground when food is dry and scarce and from fighting than from any desire to rub away the horns that are obscuring part of their field of vision.

I have many times watched rams dig in the earth with first one horn and then the other and then eat roots they had dug out, some old rams seemingly doing all the digging with one horn, so that that horn was worn back much shorter than the other. In 1937 I watched a big Fannin ram throw dirt and dust up in the air and over his back with his horns for all the world the way a mad bull will paw dirt and dust up over his back when getting ready for a fight with another of his kind.

In fighting, two rams come together so hard that if the points project up over the top of the nose, as is the case with most really fine old heads, those points will be broken back and cracked and battered until they in time are worn away. Most old rams have a heavy callus on the bridge of the nose from fighting. The rams carry their heads with noses turned down and back in the end of their charge so that any projecting tips of the horns may be hit by those of their adversary. That the horns of young rams are often badly sprung out of symmetrical alignment with their mates from fighting I am sure, for I have killed two such heads myself that have one horn setting much lower on the skull than the other, and these horns in turn make a wider, lower curl than their mates. The skulls of younger rams are not so hard or solid as later in life, and a hard blow that strikes on the boss of one horn more than the other I believe is the basic cause of so many heads having one horn carried at such a different angle from its mate.

Have also noticed that in such a head the horn that swings the lowest in its circle is usually broomed the most, which throws further light on the theory that much of this brooming is caused by digging roots and fighting, as this lower swung horn is of course much easier used as a grub hoe than its higher, more sharply curved mate.

The skulls of mountain rams are peculiarly well adapted to the terrific battering they receive in fighting. The top front of the skull is double, having a layer of bone, then a cavity or empty space, then another layer of bone around the brain pan proper. This is no doubt the reason why they can take such a terrible beating on those big horns without seemingly even getting a headache. Just in back of the horns on the top of the skull a heavy layer of cartilage starts and extends back over the joint between the base of the skull and the upper vertebrae of the neck, thus cushioning and protecting this joint. This cartilage is a full two inches thick in old rams.

The coloration of *Ovis canadenis* varies from a light sandy brown to very dark blue, almost black. Very old rams usually run much darker in color; however, this is not always true and some bands of bighorn I know of are all light, sandy-colored animals. I also know of one band of sheep in the Salmon River canyon that are all very dark blue, both ewes and old rams. This band are very large, heavy-bodied and long-legged animals, while the band in the Middle Fork section are smaller, shorter rams and also more chunkily built. I think food and the character of the country they inhabit have much to do with their size and coloration.

The Stone rams are the darkest of all, the body and neck often being a bluish black, and this color conforms also with the coloration of the rock slides and cliffs of the mountains they inhabit. The face of the true Stone sheep at the southern extremity of their range is usually more of a brown color than their body. Further north between the Prophet and Musqua Rivers all the old rams I saw had white faces and about half of them were Fannin rams. The bodies of the true Fannins were a light gray, some that I saw on the south side of the Musqua River almost white. The further south we went the darker became the average of these sheep and the greater percentage of them Stone sheep. The horns of the Fannini were also lighter in color than were those of most of the true Stone sheep.

The desert, *canadensis* and *stonei* and *fannini* sheep all have a large white patch covering most of the rump and extending further around on the sides of the hips than is the case with mule deer, elk and antelope. This white patch is also much whiter than in the other species, except antelope. With all three of these bighorn species there is a dark line, almost black, in Merriam and *canadensis* and quite black in Stone and Fannin, extending down from the top of the hips to the tail, directly over the spine. The tail itself is very short and jet black in Stone and Fannin and nearly black in *canadensis* and Nelson sheep. The backs of the legs and belly of all three species grade from very light gray to white, more white appearing on the two northern species than on the two more southern species. The bodies of the true Fannin rams are a light gray, some appearing almost white at a distance, while the bodies of the Stone sheep are the darkest of all American sheep, being almost black in many sections of their range.

The Dall sheep of the North are almost pure white and have the longest hair of any species. Occasionally a few black hairs will show up on them, however. All the other species have a white or light gray nose. Also albino bighorn occur on the Salmon River.

Mountain sheep that have been subjected to hunting for any length of time become the wariest and keenest sighted of all our big game animals. Their eyesight is simply uncanny, and I have many times seen sheep locate me when I was a mile away and stand watching me. I have also seen them locate my camp when three miles away. I could spot them as they appeared on the sky line and when crossing old snowdrifts, and when the spotting scope was focused on these tiny specks they proved mountain sheep that were clearly watching us and on the alert. Many claim that a ram has eyes that magnify distant objects as much as eight times and are the equal of eight-power binoculars. Of this I am not sure, as I have found no way of proving it, but I do know that they can see eight times better than many sportsmen can with the aid of 8-power binoculars. I have cut into the eye of dead rams and found a hard transparent lens, quite thick at the center and tapering to a thin edge on all sides. How much this lens magnifies I do not know. Sometime I am going to try and dry one and, if it will retain its transparency, attempt to determine the amount of magnification, if any can be detected by such procedure.

Mountain sheep have good ears, but they are not nearly so likely to take fright from a rolling stone as other big game animals. They spend their lives in and around cliffs and rough country and are used to hearing stones roll that are loosened by frost or by feeding sheep. A big band of sheep on the run certainly can roll a lot of stones and make plenty of noise. In hunting them the main thing is to keep out of sight. They have a very good sense of smell, but not nearly so acute as that of deer, moose and elk, or coyotes, wolves or bear.

Many times I have watched deer and sheep feeding together and then have had the wind change and carry my scent to the feeding game; in every instance the deer were the first to throw up their heads, point their long slim noses in my direction and then with a snort be on their way in their peculiar bouncing gait. The sheep would of course become instantly on the alert at the first startled move of the mule deer, but it seemed to take them considerable time to get enough of my scent to throw them into a panic and jump the band. However, if I had so much as shown an eyebrow around the edge of my protective clump of brush they would have spotted me and taken alarm long before the mule deer would have seen me.

So much for their sense of smell. Mountain sheep are the most agile jumpers of all our big game in the cliffs. I do not believe they can negotiate some of the places I have seen old mountain goats traverse with their slow majestic indifference to space, but on the other hand have many times seen them make jumps across deep crevasses and straight up to higher ledges that would have been impossible for the slower moving, sedate old mountain goat.

The feet of mountain sheep are slightly cupped on the bottom of the hooves, and the rear half of the hoof under the outer hard layer is composed of a mass very similar to soft rubber that will cushion the foot on hard long jumps and yet sticks or adheres to the sides of the rock like a crepe rubber shoe sole. Mountain goats have even more of this rubbery pad in the heel of their hoofs. No animal has a greater sense of balance or poise on steep cliffs than the mountain sheep and mountain goat.

With the exception of the lava beds of the Mexican Pinacate range and similar Mexican lowlands, and the canyon of the Salmon River in Idaho, I have found mountain sheep to inhabit the higher mountain ranges almost exclusively, usually at or above timber line. Timber line varies in elevation a great deal, extending up to 10,000 feet in parts of the U.S., while in Northern B.C. timber line often occurs at 4000 to 6000 feet. Sheep like the little mountain, grassy basins, just under the high peaks of such mountain ranges, adjacent to perpetual snowdrifts, where tender grass and fresh spring water from the melting snow or springs furnishes them their ideal food. They also like the long grassy slopes of the mountains adjacent to the higher and more rocky peaks, but no rule of thumb applies to all sheep ranges. In the winter they usually subsist on the cured grass on the high wind-swept ridges where the wind blows this feed free of snow. They are in the main grazing animals, but when pinched will eat all manner of rock moss, ferns and light browse among the cliffs, and along the Salmon River they winter mainly on the small bitter leaves of mountain or scrub mahogany, especially when deep snow covers their range. If driven off their natural high ridges by a soft deep snow they will browse just as a deer or elk or moose, but not from preference. When food is scarce or dry at high altitudes they very often dig out roots with their horns or hoofs and eat them. The ewes also have horns, but much smaller and shorter than the rams, seldom being more than long spikes projecting back and up from the head in the form of a scythe. I have never seen ewes use their horns for digging but did see one ewe cut into a cactus with her horns in Mexico.

In Sonora, the sheep live for months without a drop of water, and though they may have some deep well that they water from part of the year, they are in the main able to get along indefinitely without visible water. However the cactus in its various forms in that section furnishes ample moisture for them. They will break into the bisnaga with horns or hoofs and eat the watery pulp. They also girdle the giant Saguara cactus, as well as other species of desert cactus, and thus obtain some food and moisture. In the spring I saw ewes on the higher mountains eating various weeds while what rams I saw were down in the lava beds between the mountain ranges, living chiefly on weeds. Most of those desert growths seemed to me to have a much greater moisture content than plants of more temperate northern sheep ranges, and thus nature provides for the sheep in this arid hot climate. I have never experienced so dry or hot a place as the sheep ranges along the Gulf of California. The mountains there contain a great many caves and underground passages and at some times of the year the mountain sheep use these caves a great deal, probably to get out of the extreme heat during the hottest part of the day and to be up higher where the breeze will strike them and keep off the flies, even though that breeze blowing in from the Gulf is as hot as the air from an open oven. We also found it advantageous when in that country to shade up in some sheep cave during the hottest part of the day and thus conserve our precious water supply, without which a man will not last many hours in that arid heat.

Sheep that have been hunted at all habitually feed early in the morning and for a short time after sunrise, then usually bed on some warm sunny slope or ledge of a cliff or in the slide-rock below a cliff in the northern ranges and in the south usually in some cave in the shade. They again take to the feed ground in the late afternoon or early evening and feed until dark. Also, if hard hunted, they will feed a great deal by the light of a moon when moonlight is available and bed in the cliffs in the daytime. The harder they are hunted the more will they bed on the small ledges in the cliffs, where they can remain almost invisible to the average human eye and yet have a wide view of all the surrounding country for enemies. In such positions they can bound around the corner of a ledge and be out of sight of their enemies in a few short jumps.

One can often tell by observing the feeding and bedding habits of a band of sheep whether they have been hunted or not, and how wary they are. Sheep that have been hunted very much almost always post a lookout while feeding and also while the band is asleep. Whether this is done merely through instinct or at some sign from a boss of the band I have never been able to tell, but have many times observed one member of a band relieve another that had been on lookout while that animal also had its turn feeding or sleeping in the sun. I have seen an old dark-colored ewe stand still as a statue for over an hour at a time, only her head moving as she slowly scrutinized the surrounding mountains for sign of an enemy while the rest of her band fed. She had chosen a niche in a cliff above her companions where her dark body seemed to blend perfectly with the dark-colored cliffs and was almost invisible to the human eye. At other times I have seen rams doing similar sentinel duty.

At the first sign of danger, the sentinel will often stamp a front foot and sometimes snort. This always brings every member of the band on the alert and the first jump to safety taken by any one of the band is followed simultaneously by all members of the band. They seemingly all start at a given impulse. When surprised they will stand still for a second or two, sometimes longer, evidently deciding their best course of escape; after that there is no hesitation and they bounce away like the wind, regardless of how rough the going.

I have often seen some one ram or ewe in a bunch run to catch up with the others when feeding, or make a few short jumps, either playing or just enjoying life, without the rest of the band paying the slightest attention, but let a single animal make a jump or stamp when it has sighted an enemy and instantly the whole band is on the move. They seemingly have some means of instantly telegraphing a warning to all, but how it is done I have never been able to tell, except that when close to them I have often heard the sentinel snort, then their white rumps would go bouncing over the cliffs or around some ledge. If one heads out in a given direction on the run you can bet your last dollar the rest of the band will either travel over the same ground or very closely parallel the course of the first. They seem always to have a leader.

Twice in my lifetime of hunting I have seen the leader killed from a band of rams that had never been hunted, and the rest stood around in confusion seemingly not knowing where to go or what to do, but these are rare exceptions to the rule.

In bedding down for the day, sheep as a rule dig out a small bed in the slide-rock or earth, usually where they have a good wide outlook on the surrounding country, except in cases where hard-hunted old rams will take to a maze of cliffs and hide in the narrow ledges, often with only an eye and a horn showing over near-by boulders. Where mountain lions or cougar are working on a band they will usually bed in the open, and I have often noticed this same action with mule deer as well.

Some mountain sheep live to be quite old, though in all probability few reach 25 years of age. J. Omar Cole killed one old ram in Alberta with 24-year rings. The oldest head I have personally taken shows 18-year rings and a couple more 15-year rings. The two Stone rams had very bad teeth, the nippers practically gone and the jaw teeth in very bad shape, some knocked out and gone and the others grown so long on one side that chewing must have been very difficult for the beast. No doubt predators account for many before they ever reach such ripe old age.

Sheep ranges can be clearly located for miles with good glasses or a spotting scope in many sections of the country, such as Alberta and British Columbia. Wherever mountain sheep range or have ranged for any length of time they will leave their little telltale trails across the slides. These can be seen for miles. Search the slides just blow the cliffs and between patches of high mountain grass and those trails will show up if it is a sheep range. Sheep follow each other and the leader in moving from one high pasture to another and to high alpine springs to water, and in time the trails are gouged out of the small shale and slide-rock. I have even seen sheep trails worn deep into basic granite down the Salmon River and across the cinder slides in Mexico. In rough broken country they will not show up so plainly as farther north, but in Canada most sheep ranges will show that fine web of trails across all the high shale slides.

Once you locate a sheep range the next thing to do is to see if it is at present inhabited. The trails across the slides remain for many years in sections where the sheep have been long gone, so one must verify his find. If you locate ewes and lambs you can bet the rams are somewhere on an adjacent range or part of the same range, probably not over ten or fifteen miles away and at times less.

Do not try to camp on sheep, but place your camp where it will be well hidden and screened by trees or cliffs, preferably at least three miles from the sheep range. The camp should be located if possible well up on the last water, and where one can have an easy grade to the top. Expect hard climbs and harder work, for few sheep are taken otherwise. The pack string should also be grazed completely out of sight of the sheep range. Every possible precaution should be taken to keep the sheep unaware of your presence. Some sheep that have never been hunted may become only mildly curious, but any old rams who have been hunted will quickly quit that section if they locate you or your camp.

It's always best to get out at daybreak and be well up the mountain before the sun hits the range. If possible work up with the sun at your back and where you have a ridge to screen your movements from any grazing sheep. They can be seen at very long ranges when the sun hits them, having so much white on their rumps. When you approach the top of a ridge, try and locate some brush, if any, or trees, for a screen through which to search the slopes or basins on the other side, and if none are present select some broken bit of cliff and by all means get down on your belly and ease up with as little as possible showing. Remember sheep can and will spot you a full three miles away, if you walk over a ridge in sight. When they are busy feeding in early morning, they are not nearly as apt to see you, but once bedded for the day they see everything that moves within their range of vision. Even when feeding, they may have a sentinel posted.

If possible to do so, I always like to get up high, across from or above a band of sheep, while studying the heads or figuring out an approach to them.

If you have already located the range of a band, or are only desirous of searching out a basin, it is best to get up there before sunrise if possible. Then, when the sheep start feeding and the sun comes up, you have every advantage. If the sun is behind your back they will show up instantly when feeding, even over a mile away, by those flashing white rumps. You may see innumerable white rocks in your search for rams, but once you see a bunch of rocks that are strung out in line or appear to have about the same elevation, better put the glasses on them as they may turn out to be rams.

Once a band is located, you must plan your approach, always remembering it is better to get above them if at all possible. At times you can make a circle and come around the head of a basin and then work down on them. At other times you may have to go back over the ridge out of sight, then travel for miles to head a deep canyon and come around above the feed or bed ground. At other times you may have to chance crossing a gulch or basin and working up toward them, but such procedure is usually doomed to failure before you start, if the sheep have been hunted. At times, however, you may locate a strip of scrub timber or shin-tangle that will screen your approach, or a deep cleft or gulch or wash up which you can work out of sight of the band and then come at them on a level or from above. You have little chance of ever working up from directly below them.

Once you locate rams, it is also well to try and locate their feed as well as bed grounds before making a move, and I have often spent a day or so studying a band of sheep and their daily travels before ever attempting a stalk. They will usually feed for a couple of hours after sunup, then bed until about three or four in the afternoon, when they again start to feed. They may also travel a mile or so to water, usually holding about the same elevation and traveling around the slope to some hidden spring under a cliff, or in a deep gulch, or at the foot of a glacier. At times they may use hard-crusted snowdrifts entirely for their water supply. In Mexico, they may even do without water for months on end.

Bedded sheep are always harder to approach in rifle range than feeding sheep, so govern your actions accordingly. At times you may locate a band and work as close as you can and simply have to lie and wait for the sheep to make the next move. When you are unable to get closer without scaring them, this is the best procedure, especially if you are on the trail where they will feed, or move, after coming off the bed ground. They search everything below and to the side of them, but unless you are silhouetted on the sky line or roll a rock to attract their attention, they seldom seem to look for trouble from above and for this reason the best approach is from above them.

At times they may bed in timber, or in very broken cliffs. My advice is then to leave them alone and wait until they come out to feed, as it is very difficult to get a good shot in such timber or rocks, and you will have little opportunity to pick a head once you jump them. Better, by far, to wait until they come out for their evening feed if you have the time. One should always carry a pack sack and a couple of days' iron rations of some kind, either jerky or other light but wholesome food that will see you through, and by all means include a good windbreaker that will do to lie out in overnight. The Bauer down jacket has proved admirable for this purpose and is light yet warm.

Many artists depict rams in bottomless canyons or on narrow ledges of cliffs, when in reality they are seldom found in such places and then only when traveling through or when scared and have taken to such places to hide. What they like is long, high, grassy slopes and open alpine basins, with cliffs and rougher country adjacent. They often feed down quite low in back sections where they are not molested, but if hunted they hang close to cliffs, timber or other good cover for protection. An old sheep hunter can just look over a range of mountains and tell you if it looks good to him or not. Oftentimes the mountains may be quite heavy timber up to timber line, but if the tops have those long grassy slopes or grassy benches and shoulders and little high glacial valleys, then it is good territory for sheep.

In making a stalk, remember the wind usually sucks up the draws and up the south slopes. The sheep will usually be found just over the top out of the wind and probably within 200 yards of the top, when said top is an open grassy slope. After you have picked out a shootable head, if others are with him, make sure your stalk won't bring you to some outlying member of the band who will jump up and scare the others before you get in sight of the ram you want. This can happen. If the band is located too late in the evening, as is often the case, better to leave them and start before daylight the next day than to attempt a stalk too late. At times you will run into traveling rams right on the trail, or where least expected, but this is unusual and as a general rule you will have to work long and hard for every one you get.

In most sheep country the season is over before the rut starts. During the rut rams are much easier hunted as they will soon find the ewes, and the hunter has only to locate a big bunch of ewes at the start of the rut to be sure of seeing rams sooner or later. He may get some good heads in this way, but usually the very fine old records will not be with the ewes at all, but off alone, or with some other solitary bachelor.

In the sheep country of Montana, Idaho and Wyoming, the sheep rut usually starts about the first to the fifteenth of November, but the season varies and we have seen them traveling as early as October 20, and at other times have seen bands of ewes and lambs as late as November 15 unattended by rams. Some years winter may have started before the rut occurs. We have never had the opportunity of observing the sheep rut in either the desert species of Mexico or the northern species of Dall and the subspecies of Fannin and *stonei*, but have watched the bighorn a good many times.

Mountain sheep are all stocky, sturdily built animals and the old rams in particular have massive quarters and necks for their size. A big mature bighorn ram will easily go 350 pounds, while the Mexican sheep I have seen, probably Merriam, would not weigh over 225 to 230 and the larger Stone sheep I have seen would run around 225 to 250 pounds in my opinion, but I have never had an opportunity to weigh them. The ears of the *canadenis* and desert sheep are usually longer and larger than the northern species. As before stated color varies greatly but of one thing you can be sure—sheep, wherever found, will have a color of coat that will blend in well with the country they inhabit. The things that give them away are that big white patch on the rump with its little black line down to the black tail and the white strips extending down the backs of the legs. When the sun hits them these are plainly visible at longer distances than the sheep themselves, if turned facing you. No game animal holds its head up so erect as a mountain ram and this also helps to give them away, even when bedded.

In all sheep hunting it is well to see where the ram will roll to when shot, before shooting. They have the habit of falling or rolling into the most inaccessible places, or over a cliff where they are badly battered by the fall. When possible, it is well to wait until they cross such a place so that when shot they will stay put. Most times, one has enough to do to get in a killing shot, without regard to where the animal may fall or roll to, but when possible and time permits it is well to keep this in mind. It may save hours of dangerous work getting the old boy off a ledge far below. Always pack 30 or 40 feet of light but strong rope, sufficient to lower the weight of a man; it may and often does prove very useful. Sheep horns are seldom damaged by a bad fall but the cape may well be ruined; we had one ram tear his whole nose off.

One of the easiest successful sheep hunts I was ever on occurred in 1927 in British Columbia. Jim Ross and his Indians, Pete, Joe and Sam Calleau, had already done the hard work; they had located three good shootable rams some three miles from our camp. Carrol Paul, George Bates and Harry Snyder had each taken one good ram and had one to go to fill our licenses. We took pack and saddle horses and simply rode to within sight of the mountain over whose crest they had seen the rams the day before. There we stopped and combed it all with the glasses to be sure the sheep were still on the other side, then forked our cayuses and rode up to within a quarter mile of the top. Leaving the horses, we climbed the rest of the way, then one man wormed his way to the top and, with hat removed and holding his head as close to the ground as possible, inched his way up and over until he located the three rams, down the ridge to our left some 400 yards and about 150 yards down from the top and out of the wind. We dropped down a little on our side of the mountain and made a circle to come out directly above the three bedded rams. Carrol Paul was selected to take the choice, while Harry Snyder, who had already killed a 42-inch record bighorn, agreed to take the smallest ram and George Bates would take the next best from the first shot. Paul inched his way out in plain sight of the rams and in a sitting position, and as they jumped up out of their beds and stood for an instant he busted his ram through the back edge of the shoulders with his 20-inch Mannlicher type G & H Springfield and Remington 220-grain express. It simply dropped and rolled. The other two sheep took off to the right in a hard run but swung around and stopped at 200 yards for another look back. Instantly Harry Snyder, who is a very fine and deadly game shot, took his smaller ram through the lungs with his .300 Magnum and my 172-grain W.T.C. Company bullet hand loads. It went down at the shot and the third and heavier ram again ran and at 275 yards hauled up and swung around facing us, and Bates planted a 220-grain Western Soft Point B.T. in its chest from his Webley & Scott .300 Magnum and the job was done. We simply had a job of skinning out heads and dressing meat and packing it all over the ridge to the pack horses. All three were fat nice rams, with good shootable heads. Those sheep had never before seen a human in all probability, hence acted so strange for wild sheep.

Sheep migrations are mostly local. They will feed to the highest mountain tops in summer if suitable range is thereon, and back down to lower levels in winter, but remain up on the high wind-swept ridges where the snow blows off and the grass may be obtained even in the dead of winter. A heavy wet snow with no wind is the worst curse of the sheep, as it covers everything and makes food very difficult to obtain. If they are forced off their lofty ridges and cliffs, they become an easy prey to coyotes and wolves as well as cougar.

In most mountain sheep hunting you can well expect long range shooting to be the rule. At times you may hunt a broken, partly timbered country, where shots will be obtained at close range, and if so they may often be quick running shots. For such work a fast lever action is mighty nice, but the bulk of sheep hunting will offer more long range difficult shots and the modern bolt action, scope sighted, high velocity rifle is the best tool for the purpose.

The first ram I ever saw killed passed Father and me at a trot at about 30 yards, during the rut. We were hunting mule deer and I spotted this old chap coming for a half mile, but when Father saw it was a ram instead of a mule buck he asked me to give him the shot, which I gladly did. We simply sat in the snow among old blackened fire-killed snags and let that ram come. He apparently never saw us at all and Dad busted him through the heart at 30 yards as he trotted past. The little 117-grain .25-35 had no visible effect at all and he went on for 80 yards before stopping, turning around and shaking his big head at us three times. Then he stiffened out and slowly turned over down the mountain like a wooden sheep.

Of six mature rams I have personally taken, the closest shots were at 300 yards, two different rams being first hit at 300 yards and later finished at longer ranges. Have seen many killed at much closer ranges, but in many sheep ranges the fact remains that you will get more long difficult shots than close easy ones.

One trip by boat down the Salmon River, when I handled a party from Holland, Michigan, composed of Eddie Landwehr, Herman Prins, Larry Kolb and Dr. Chet Sulkers, well illustrates what sheep hunting was like on the Salmon before they closed the season.

Captain Harry Guleke and I ran the big scow, and Bob Hagel helped me with the guiding. Max Oiler flipped the flapjacks and fried the steaks. We had fair luck on game other than sheep, but after scouting several sheep ranges with no luck at all moved on down the Salmon to my old sheep camp. Here luck changed for the better. Bob was guiding Larry Kolb and spotted a huge old solitary ram in the cliffs at about 150 yards range. He must have been a dandy, as Bob said his horns came well up above the nose, with a very heavy and wide turn, yet the points were broomed off until they were almost as wide as his hand at the tips. When Bob whispered to Larry to take him, Larry did not see the ram and started kidding Bob about having located one. Then when he did see the ram, he planted a Remington 180-grain Bronze Point .30-06 too far back, about the middle of the ram as he stood broadside, and that sheep got away in the cliffs. In spite of continued search next day they never saw him again and lost his trail completely in the cliffs. That 180-grain Bronze Point is notorious for penetrating almost through a beast before it expands and a great deal of game has been lost with it under my observation.

Larry never obtained another shot on the trip. Dr. Sulkers obtained a fine 36-inch heavy and massive head with well-broomed points and Eddie obtained a young ram under peculiar circumstances, of which more later.

One of the toughest days I have ever put in was the day I obtained my ram. Dr. Sulkers and I had worked down the river from the boat, angling up an old sheep trail to the top of the ridge and then heading into a huge basin, where I had obtained sheep for other hunters and later got Dr. Du-Comb a ram that is still the widest head in the present book of records. Finding no sheep in that basin, we worked on across it and over the top of the next high ridge, where we could comb the heads of numerous steep rocky canyons, leading down to the main Salmon River.

We finally decided to drop down from the ridge and circle through the head of the next big basin as we had seen no sheep, only a few tracks showing on the ground we had covered. While working around a steep mountain, sparsely covered with big yellow pines and bunch grass, we stopped and sat down for another good search of the basin and particularly of a huge cliff formation lying between the two forks of the small creek, far below us. Doc was using the glasses, while I depended on my eyes to spot anything that did not look like part of the scenery. Finally I picked up a small spot on the top of a cliff overhanging the forks of the creek that did not look like part of the cliff to me, so I set up the little Mossberg 20 X scope I then carried and focused it on the spot. Instantly a big black bighorn came to life in the field of view. While no record, he was a nice shootable head, and I well knew he would be the best chance I would be offered on that trip so decided to take him.

I was carrying a .348 Winchester, while Doc had his .30-36 Remington Express with a 22-inch barrel and Zeiss Zielkein scope. We were well equipped for either short range running shooting or long range work. Swapping the .348 for Doc's scope sighted .06, I started the long stalk. Nearly a half mile of steep open sidehill with but very few tree boles had to be negotiated to put me within 300 yards. To make matters worse, the ground was very dry, hot and dusty and the least dirt disturbed would immediately rise in the air. Then the slope was thickly studded with dried sunflowers which made an awful racket at the slightest touch and the surrounding cliffs of that big basin would echo any slightest sound.

[265]

I managed to get a tree bole between the ram and my approach for the first 100 yards, then had to lie down on my belly and crawl down the steep slope. This was the only way I could catch and stop rolling rocks, and dig a small hole in the ground to hold them, and yet keep as flat with the ground as possible. I tried going down feet first, but dislodged too many rocks— also found I had to raise my knees up above the bunch grass and sunflowers —so had to quit that and crawl headfirst. Did you ever try crawling head-first down a hot south mountain slope, at a snail's pace, under such conditions? Very soon I was soaked with perspiration, but finally managed to get behind the top of another yellow pine and straighten up for a change.

When I arrived down at the base of that tree, the old ram was still bedded and the spotting scope showed him chewing his cud, so I rested awhile and started down headfirst again, keeping my body perfectly flat and pulling myself along with my hands. After an hour and a half I reached the bottom of a slight draw leading into the main gulch below the ram, and could then travel on hands and knees. In spite of my best efforts, I managed to touch one of those cursed dry sunflowers when nearing the top of the next ridge, and the ram was up on his feet instantly, swinging his big head around looking for the source of the noise. I froze perfectly still for several minutes, until he turned his head to look the other way, then quickly worked onto the top and moved to one side of a clump of dry bunch grass, so the rifle muzzle had an unobstructed view of him at 300 yards, across the canyon, before he again swung his head back in my direction. I believe he saw the top of my head then, as he continued staring at me and I saw one forefoot stamp, just as I settled in the sling for a good prone shot. Knowing Doc had sighted the rifle for 200 yards with the 180-grain Remington Bronze Point ammunition, I knew it should drop about 9 inches at 300 yards, so held the top of the post almost level with the top of his withers and squeezed. At the shot, he jumped into a high bouncing run, then I heard the slug land on him. Working the bolt I followed him through the scope, waiting to see if he would stop or continue to run. He stopped and swung around broadside at about 350 yards. This time I held about the same except to run the top of the post reticule just over the top of the withers for the added range and shot again. This time he dropped at the shot and as he rolled down the steep slick black granite rock, I heard the slug hit. Could clearly see his white belly flash in the sun as he turned over, then he simply disappeared. He had been bedded on a flat-top cliff and had run along the slope of that black rock, where it did not seem possible for a fly to hide. I lay there in the sling with ready rifle, while Doc came down to me on the double. Still no sign of the ram. He neither got up and left, nor rolled over

Dr. Wilson DuComb and author with widest spread of bighorn in present book of records, killed by DuComb in one shot with the author's .348 Winchester, 200-grain Soft Point load

Sheep and grizzly skulls; animals killed by J. Omar Cole with .285 O.K.H. 180 grain and by J. H. Shirk with a .30–06

J. Omar Cole with a fine record Alberta bighorn head in 1930. Bases 16¼ x 41½ inches and 16⅜ x 42

Author's best sheep head, a *stonei* killed at 400 yards from a prone position with .300 Magnum Model 70, 180-grain Open Point B.T. Record head with 14½-inch bases, spread of 26½ inches and longest curl of 39½

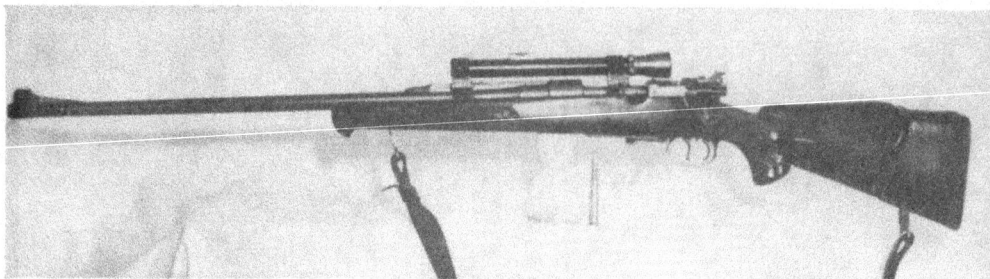

Author's .285 O.K.H. Mauser with Lyman Alaskan scope in Pachmayr mounts, Pachmayr special sights; rifle by Oneil and stock to author's design by Frost

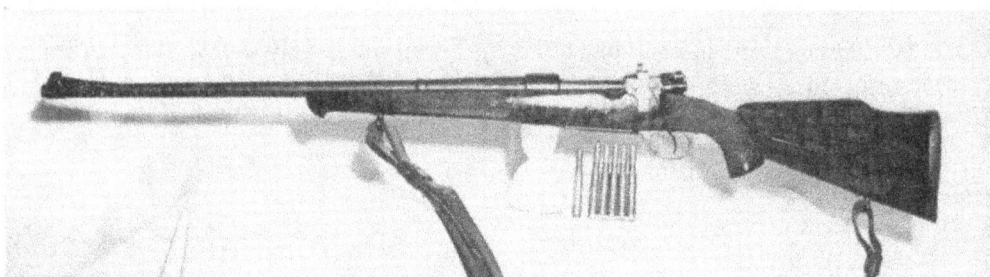

Mrs. Keith's .333 O.K.H. Mauser by Oneil with stock by Frost to author's design

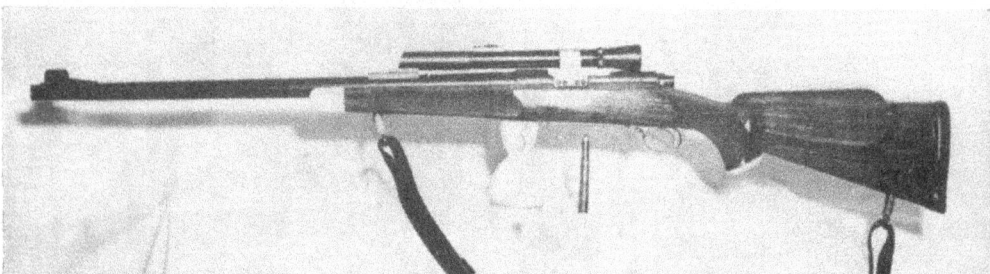

Author's .375 Magnum Model 70 Winchester, stock to his design by Frost. Lyman Alaskan scope with Stith mounts

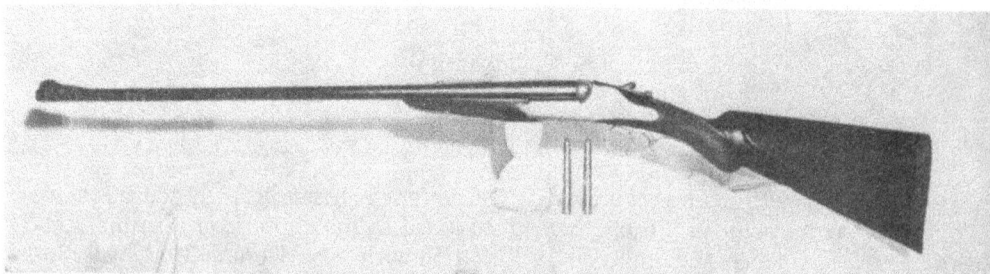

Photos courtesy Keith Barrette

Author's .375 Nitro Express double rifle by Lancaster, automatic ejectors and self-opening action, side locks and side clips

the rim into the canyon where I would have seen him instantly. I asked Doc to work his way up the gulch and down into that box canyon and across and try to find a crevasse up which he could gain the top, while I continued to watch all avenues of escape in case the ram should get up. Doc made it down into the bottom of the box canyon, but had an awful time finding a way up the other cliff. Finally he found a crevasse with some scrub mahogany growing in it and finally made the top. He soon walked over to where the ram had stood when my second slug went through him and marked the rock on the off side; found some blood where he rolled but no trace of the ram. I could not understand it and Doc looked in every direction with no success. I yelled across at him to trail the blood back toward me the way he had rolled. Then Doc let out a yell that was welcome to my ears. He said the ram had rolled into a hole in the cliff that extended down for nearly 100 feet and came out on another ledge below, and that the sheep was hanging in the top of a big scrub mahogany growing in that hole.

I had a hard time getting to the bottom of the canyon and an even harder time negotiating the opposite cliff but finally made it up on top of that flat rock mesa. There sat Doc looking down into a huge hole some ten feet across. Approaching the edge, I could see the old boy hanging by his horns in the fork of the mahogany some six to eight feet down from the surface. How a tree, even a mahogany, ever managed to grow in a crevasse of that old blow hole is beyond me, but there it was and some 75 feet of sheer drop below it to the next ledge. Taking a hank of rope from the pack I snubbed it to a rock and had Doc lower me down into the top of the mahogany. Then taking a hitch on the ram's head, Doc pulled while I stood in the crotch of the tree and lifted upward with all my strength. Though he would have weighed a full 300 pounds, we finally got him up clear of the treetop, but could not get him higher. I then climbed up the other end of the rope to the surface and between us we heaved the old boy out on top and dressed him. He proved to be an eleven-year-old ram.

Those 180-grain .30–06 slugs had landed just right for elevation but a full 18 inches to the left of where I had held them. Doc had sighted the rifle with bench rest without the sling, and my use of the sling strap under heavy tension caused the rifle to shoot the full 18 inches to the left at that range. The first slug had entered about the center of the body through the liver and had expanded almost none at all, making only a small exit hole, and the second had landed about three or four inches higher and broken the back and also made a very small exit hole, clearly showing why

Larry had lost his ram and why we had had so much trouble with wounded game the entire trip. The head went 14½-inch bases and 34-inch curl, small but a very nice head at that, and I was well satisfied.

After skinning out the head for a good shoulder mount and taking a pattern from the meat on a piece of canvas, I made it up into a pack and told Doc we should go back the way we had come; I was afraid to try any other course as all those creeks turned into box canyons with many sheer drops below us to the river.

Doc took one look down at the canyon we had crossed and the long steep slope on the other side and insisted we should work on to the right and down into the creek and go down it to the river. This course did not look good to me as I had been ledged up and spent too many nights tied to a mahogany on just such cliffs as I visioned below us. However, Doc insisted, so against my better judgment I agreed to try it. We made it along nicely for a quarter mile, then the canyon walls became sheer on each side and we came to a fifty-foot sheer drop. However an old dead pine had long ago rolled into the canyon and now leaned up the face of the cliff with many broken limbs projecting out for hand and toeholds, so we climbed down the length of that tree bole to the next flat in the bottom of the creek.

After another quarter mile, we came to another very narrow box canyon, but the slope was not over 45 degrees. It was all slick black rock, with the creek covering the whole surface of the bottom, but the walls were so narrow that by holding onto the sides with hands and knees we slowly worked our way down that steep watery descent with the creek building up behind us and fairly soaking us with ice-cold water. Then said Doc, "We now have easy sailing." A half mile farther down the chasm we came to another sheer drop, this one of sixty to eighty feet at least, as I now remember. It was sheer with the water pouring over on huge boulders below. Knowing it was utterly impossible ever to get back up that slick chute behind us, we were clearly up against it.

On our right was a narrow crevasse extending from the bottom of the cliff up the sheer walls and above us but out a good twelve feet to our right. If we could only reach those scrub mahogany bushes growing in that crevasse we could climb down them to the bottom of the cliff. We spent some time looking vainly for some toehold or way of getting over that crevasse. Finally I spotted a tiny projection on the smooth slope to our right, about the size of the end of my thumb and a half inch high. Doc held my feet while I spread out and tested it, finding it solid. So he removed his shoes and I gripped that small pimple on the face of the rock with my hand, telling him to step on my hand and jump for it. Doc was game and with a flying jump he hit my hand and bounced on into the mahoganies, which he grabbed and stopped. Then I tossed over the rifles one at a time and he removed and fastened the sling straps together, and tied the rifles to a mahogany bush with a shoe lace. I next swung him the heavy sheep-head pack, that was still tightly roped up, and he caught and anchored it to another mahogany, the while balancing on the roots of another that grew out over a sheer drop to the bottom.

Having no one to hold a hand on that small pimple for me, I knew Doc would have to unrope the sheep head, unless our belts and the sling straps would reach across. However they reached nicely and I made one fast to my right wrist, had Doc take a good turn on a mahogany and jumped as far as possible, when Doc swung me over that chasm into the thin line of mahoganies in the crevasse. Never have scrub mahoganies looked so good to me, either before or since. Many times before that I had cursed them, while trying to bring a heavy pack board, loaded with sheep or goat trophies, up a narrow crevasse, only to be hooked by those stiff limbs, just when I was reaching for another hand hold. This time, however, they looked like heaven to me and we were soon down to the bottom with both rifles and sheep head.

The next half mile down was easy going, then we came to another box canyon that looked even worse from above, but careful search located an easy way down on the left side and we were soon in the bottom of the gulch below the cliffs. Then we jumped a bunch of mule deer and as both Doc and I wanted a fat venison, we sat down and each rolled one over. Laying aside the sheep head pack which was eating into my shoulders and back by this time, we dressed them out, brushed them to keep off flies and magpies next day and worked on down to the river with the sheep head.

We traveled upstream for over a mile along the north side of the river, finally coming to a cliff extending down into the water, but by probing ahead of us with poles found we could wade around it. After a couple such experiences, we came to a cliff that hung far out over a deep pool, so knew our progress up the river was definitely at an end. The sun was down and it was fast growing dark as we started up a narrow and very steep crevasse, hoping we could gain the top of the ridge and work back, far enough to cross that next box canyon and then continue on up the river to the boat and camp. I had visions of a good hot meal after a drink of whisky and an air mattress bed, but told Doc I did not think we could possibly make it. We were completely all in when we reached the top and in total darkness. I never remember a blacker night. Finding we could not go on up the ridge because of more cliffs, Doc thought we might work down the cliff to our right and thence up the other side, but I told him it was hopeless and dropped a rock over. We listened for some time before we heard it strike far below and Doc gave up. We went back down that slide and back to the river where I remembered seeing some dead mahogany. By that time it was very cold and a strong wind blowing upstream. Camp was easily two miles above us and a bottomless canyon we had headed in the morning between us and camp. We built a good fire on that narrow strip of sand and also built up a rock wall to turn the wind. Doc suggested we skin out the sheep head and take the tongue and cheeks for roasting meat, but I thought of a better plan and picked up the .348 and fired into the river three times. Soon we heard an answering shot from camp. Next the boys in camp attempted to work down on the north side of the river to us in spite of Captain Guleke's telling them it was impossible and he should run the boat down as there were no rapids in that stretch. However they tried it and eventually arrived on the opposite rim of that canyon with the gas lantern and had to retrace their steps back to camp. The Captain then had them load camp in the boat and drifted down to us, with a gas lantern in each front corner of the boat.

He heaved out the gangplank, then held up a jug of whiskey and invited us aboard. After each of us had a long pull on the jug, Max yelled, "Come and get it." As it was then after midnight, no word could have sounded better and we consumed huge quantities of hot chili and venison steaks, while Captain ran the boat across the river to a big sand bar where we made camp. That completed the toughest one-day sheep hunt I have ever had. Doc remarked, "Never again will I tell the guide which way to go to camp."

X V

Mountain Goats

ACCORDING to scientists our mountain goat is not a goat at all but belongs to the antelope family. Be that as it may, he is to us a mountain goat and will so remain. Just as we know the bison as buffalo so the term "mountain goat" will stick. Goats inhabit the roughest, rockiest, most Godforsaken sections of the whole Rocky Mountain chain, from far north in Alaska, south as far as the Snake River Valley. I have never heard of one being killed south of the Snake River on the west side of the Divide; likewise have never heard of goats inhabiting the Continental Divide east of this locality which embraces the Lemhi and Pahsimeroi Valleys — the former being just over the Divide from the headwaters of the Missouri in Montana, south here of the Sawtooth Range, while the north drainage of the Snake River seems to be as far south as their range extends. Whether they extend south of the Columbia River in Washington I do not know but have never heard of it, if they do. North of here in Montana, their range extends east as far as the headwaters of the North Fork of the Blackfoot and the head of the South Fork of the Flathead. I killed my first billy on the head of the South Fork of the Flathead in 1917 with an old .45 Single Action Colt. Their range extends north far into Alaska, at least to the Copper River, and maybe beyond. Goats differ in size very materially in different localities and the Montana goats are the smallest I have personally seen.

The animal is peculiarly well adapted to the awful terrain it inhabits. It is a thin, slab-sided animal with very high boss ribs, extending high over the spine at the shoulders, and is generally shaped more like our buffalo or bison than any other animal. Very fine old billies may reach a total length from nose to tail of 70 inches, and many fine old specimens will weigh a full 450 pounds on foot with some going even to 500 pounds. In some localities, however, the largest animals will be much smaller and mature billies will not weigh over 250 or 300 pounds on foot.

The horns are small but dagger sharp and curve upward and backward and also diverge at their tips. The tips are sharp as needles and blue black or jet black depending on the season. Just behind the base of the horn is a big ugly blue-black oil gland. It is also a musk gland and most active during the rut, which usually occurs, at least in this section, in late November. The face or skull is long and thin, the tip of nose wide, heavy and deep. The whole body is covered with one of the finest grades of wool imaginable, protected with very long, shaggy and coarse guard hair. Many specimens have a few black or brown guard hairs, especially along the mane. The mane extends up high above the neck, six to eight inches on large specimens, and then almost ends just behind the shoulders, but starts again over the top of the rump and out to the root of the tail. This gives the animal a sway-back appearance when seen from the side. Heavy wool and coarse guard hairs extend well down the legs to the knee and hock joints and hang even lower, making him look as if he were wearing chaps. The color in general is almost snow white, with a creamy yellow stain on old billies and also dirt stain on the buttocks. They sit down on their buttocks much as a dog or cougar, and I have observed them in this position for hours at a time, often with their front feet braced on the extreme edge of some ledge between their hind legs which extended off into space.

Goats are perfectly at home on any cliff and none is too steep or too high for them. Usually they inhabit the broken cliffs of the north slopes as high as the mountains rise above sea level, but in some sections they may be found low down, and along the Salmon River below, Shoup, Idaho, I have seen them right down along the river as well as back along the Divide at the highest possible elevation. Elevation makes no difference in their young lives — what they want and will find is cliffs, and if those cliffs are down at 2500 feet along the river, they will inhabit them just the same as some on the very heads of side streams at 8000 to 10,000 feet.

The pelts are at their best in January, long after the season is closed, or when any self-respecting hunter would be out after them, and usually during hunting season in this section, in October, the pelts are short. For best rugs they should be hunted here in December or January, but by that time the mountains are heavily covered with deep snow and anyone who wishes to hunt white goats in the cliffs at that time of year can have my full share of the sport. Farther north, in Canada and Alaska, the pelts are very much better during hunting season and exceptionally long pelts may be obtained in October or late September. Even there they would be much longer if killed later in the winter. Both nannies and billies carry horns, the billies having the larger basal measurement but the nannies having equal length, and in fact the record is a nanny. Length runs to about a maximum of 13 inches. Goats differ as much in facial appearance as do human beings and vary just as much in weight of individuals as do humans. Bob Hagel killed one on the Salmon River that had by several inches the longest skull I have ever seen. It was a horse-faced old billy with an unbelievably long ugly nose. His head was so long that Bob thought he carried short horns until he had killed him and measured them.

The meat is very fine grain or texture and requires longer cooking than any other game I can think of, unless it be a tough old bull buffalo or grizzly bear. The flavor is sweeter than deer, and fat young billies, or dry fat nannies, are most excellent meat; not as tender as sheep and antelope but very finely flavored, and I personally like fat young nanny or billy goat just about as well as anything short of sheep. When young, say up to three years old, it is firm but tender, and when fat makes most excellent chops. Old billies are, however, tough and during the rut strong as well. The first one I killed was used to feed a Government Survey crew, and Russian Charley, our cook, had an awful time with it.

Goats may fight at times, but I have never seen them do so, and have seen billies running with the nannies and kids during the rut. During the summer months the old billies usually live alone, or in company with one or two other old males, but younger billies may be found with the nannies at all times. I have also seen old billies consorting with a nanny and kids all summer long. Where goats are scarce, whole families are apt to range together, but where they are more numerous the old billies with fine trophy heads will usually be found off by themselves. Though I have never seen them fight, I have seen nannies prod an old billy out of his bed during the rut, evidently forcing the lazy old gentleman to get up and take notice of them.

Their enemies are mainly eagles, cougar and man. Man is the worst enemy but eagles take an awful toll of young kids. We have even observed a pair of eagles trying to knock a four-year-old billy off his perch high on a cliff along the Salmon. One bird would make a pass at him and rake white hair from his withers with his claws, the while the billy would swap ends and hook upward viciously with his little black horns. I never saw the goat hit the birds but did see birds pull hair from the goat's withers with their long meat hooks. Though we have found ewe mountain sheep and also full-grown mule deer does killed by eagles alone, I have never seen where they had killed a full-grown goat. They will break the back of a doe deer or sheep or antelope, and one eagle killed an old doe just back of my barn last winter.

Goat hunting is probably the most dangerous big game hunting we have on this continent. The goats themselves are not dangerous and I have never seen one show fight even when wounded, but the country they inhabit makes their pursuit the most dangerous of all, as one must often negotiate narrow ledges, shale slides and ice-covered crevasses and slopes, where a single slip would precipitate one into eternity. I know many years of goat hunting have given me a wholesome respect for the species and I have been in more tight places and come nearer getting killed hunting goats than any other game.

Goats do not bother anyone at any time, nor do they ever get down where they will damage crops. They spend their entire lives, both winter and summer, up in the cliffs, picking a living among the rocks where the wind has blown away the snow. They live chiefly on various rock mosses, weeds and some grass, and browse as well in the winter, the small scrub mahogany being one of their chief foods here when deep snow covers their range. As long as a goat can find a toe hold for two of his feet, he is perfectly at home, regardless of the fact that there may be a thousand feet of space below him. The hoofs are peculiarly shaped, almost square or oblong, with the toes almost as blunt and square as the heels. Ofttimes it's hard to tell at a glance which way a goat track is headed in the snow. The ball of the foot is well cushioned with a substance very like crepe rubber and will adhere to any rock slope regardless of how steep. All told, they are a beautiful beast and with any sort of protection will maintain their numbers. They should be hunted only for trophies and only the best old specimens taken, leaving the young to propagate the species.

They are slow stolid beasts, nothing seems to excite them, and I have seen an old billy walk sedately along a narrow ledge the while he received killing hit after hit from the most modern rifles. They are tough phlegmatic beasts, absolutely impervious to shock, and react less to the impact of a rifle bullet than any other animal I know of. As a rule goats like secluded spots, the rougher the better, and the farther from civilization the better. On the other hand I know of one goat family within three miles of this typewriter, and others some ten miles away. Unless some friend wants a specimen rather badly and would appreciate it when he did get it, their secret will remain with me, as I would much rather know they were still enjoying their rugged wild country than being taken by someone who would not appreciate them. Down the Salmon we have a good many goats, also along the Bitterroot Range. North in British Columbia and Alaska there are large herds in many sections, often numbering a hundred or more.

The kids are usually born in early June and twins are about as common as singles. I have never seen triplets, though they may rarely occur. The old nannies have an awful time protecting them from the eagles, at least in this section, and usually have the kids in dense fir timber atop the cliffs where the big birds cannot reach them. Contrary to popular opinion, goats like the timber and often spend months in dense fir timber above the cliffs or adjacent to them, bedding and sleeping in the timber and working out on the cliffs for feed in the late afternoons. They water at the little high springs, in and under the cliffs, and may go for days without water. They also eat snow for water a great deal, from the hard-packed drifts. I have also seen them dig out depressions in the soft shale under perpetual snowdrifts and drink from the melting snow water.

As a rule they live their lives out in one section, but if nannies are scarce old billies may trek to another mountain range during or before the rut. Once I watched an old billy in August come down off one mountain range and cross the valley, swim the South Fork of the Flathead and climb the mountain on the other side. He was all alone and evidently going places. His gate was the usual shambling trot, breaking into a short gallop at times as he hopped from boulder to boulder. He swam high, with head and top of withers completely out of the water, and was a lot more graceful looking in the water than on land.

Goats often remain in a section of rugged cliffs and fir timber unknown to hunters for years, even though said hunters may hunt other game in that section for years on end. Unless they take the time to climb the cliffs and look for beds and tracks as well as droppings and shed wool, they may pass by goats and never know they are there. When hunted much, goats will bed out of sight in fir timber on top of the ledges, but when not molested they like to work the open cliffs, and usually bed on the top of some spire where only an eagle can reach them. Where goats have long ranged there will be well-worn trails leading down the steep ridges to the feed grounds. Usually they travel down in the afternoon and feed until night, then climb back to their lofty perches for the night and following morning. At times I have seen them feeding in the morning, but more often only late in the afternoon and evening. Nannies and kids seem to feed regularly, but old billies, under my observation, do not. I remember one old chap I watched for three days. We were camped and hunting sheep just over the Divide to the south from the head of the Wapiti River in British Columbia. Our camp lay in a beautiful high alpine basin, good caribou and grizzly country, and the mountains rose up in long slide-rock slopes around the camp. This old yellow-colored billy was bedded in the slide-rock high above camp. As I was busy preparing trophies and skinning out sheep heads, I had ample opportunity to watch him for three days. Two or three times a day he would get up, turn around and bed down again on the other side. He was there at daylight each morn and he was still there as the last rays of daylight left the valley each evening, for three straight days. If he fed or watered, he must have done so during the night, as he never left that bed in the daytime.

On the same Canadian trip in 1927, George Bates and I had made a short circle looking for caribou and were several hours behind the pack string. Bates had his saddle horse, while I walked, as we were short of pack animals and I had given up my saddle horse as soon as we reached game country, some ten days south from Hudson's Hope. I could cover more country on foot than a horse could in that country during a day. As we were climbing toward the Divide, between the Wapiti and a branch of Fish Creek, and following the tracks of the outfit, we spotted a pair of billies working along under a huge cliff to our left. They were traversing slide-rock and looked to be about 400 yards away. The rear goat was an old yellowed billy that looked exceptionally good to me. Bates had already secured his goat, so I decided to take him. I asked Bates the range, as he was studying the goats through his glasses. He said, "At least 500 yards," so bedding down to the side of the trail I held the tip of the front sight over the top of the goat's withers. The rifle, a .300 medium heavy 26-inch barrel Magnum Mauser by Hoffman, was sighted for 300 yards. Using a hand load of 60 grains of Dupont 15½ powder, Frankford Arsenal No. 70 primer, and the Government 172-grain Service Boattail bullet, I filed and drilled at the point.

My shot threw up a cloud of rock dust just over the goat's withers, so I knew the range was less than 500 yards or it would have dropped into him. Next, I held on the withers, near the top, and shot again from a comfortable prone position with sling. This time I obtained results. The goat dropped and another cloud of white rock dust rose behind him on the slide. He slowly regained his front feet, but his hindquarters refused his bidding. After struggling for a few seconds, he toppled over sideways and rolled end over end for over 200 yards down the slide toward us, ending up in a patch of shin-tangle. He was dead when we reached him and examination and pacing of the range put it around 400 yards. The bullet had expanded well and went through the shoulders just below the spine. Exit hole was about 2 inches in diameter. He was a beautiful specimen and would have weighed fully 450 pounds. Bates took some photos for me and then rode on over the top of the Divide, searching for caribou on the top, some three miles distant. The remaining billy worked on around under the cliff, apparently in no hurry, and often stopped to look down at me and the old billy, seemingly not understanding why his partner had quit him so suddenly. The old goat was so heavy I had all I could do to roll him over during the skinning out operation. Finally, when I had his complete pelt, with head and feet attached, made up into a pack, I looked up to see what had become of the smaller billy. There he sat, over halfway up that seemingly vertical cliff on a narrow ledge. He was facing me, and as near as the glasses showed had about an eight-inch ledge to sit on. His front feet were braced between the crotch of the hind legs and the hind legs and feet projected out into space. He was sitting on his rear end, just like a dog, and how he ever got up there is beyond me. I have often wished I had taken time to watch him while skinning the old billy, just to see how he ever negotiated that vertical cliff. My goat hide and head made a pack fully 100 pounds in weight and the skin on the buttocks, where he had evidently done a lot of sitting down, was over an inch in thickness. I have skinned out many goats since that day, but have never seen a specimen with thicker skin on the buttocks. His roll down the slope had broken off over a half inch of each horn and they still measured $9\frac{5}{8}$ inches with heavy bases, so he was about as good a billy as a man has any right to expect and would have gone well over 10 inches before he rolled, and in the records. I later filed the horns to a point before mounting them.

Goats have very good eyesight, not the equal of sheep, but plenty good enough to spot you long before you get in range. Their ears are very small and pointed, and being used to living where rocks roll a lot, they usually do not pay as much attention to small sounds as do other game. Their hearing, while not as acute as that of deer, bear, moose and elk, is nevertheless much better than that of human beings. Goats' legs, from the knee and hock joints down to the hoof, are very short. Their gait appears awkward in the extreme, yet they are anything but awkward. When disturbed, they usually go around a ledge or else climb upward, unless they are on top, when they will break over into the cliffs. Unless you are very close they will simply walk and occasionally trot a little, also jump from boulder to boulder, apparently in no great hurry, yet their gait is deceiving and they will soon put a lot of distance between you and them and do it with ease. Never try to make a stalk uphill in sight of goats, or you will invariably find on reaching their location that they have moved on upward and are just as far or a trifle further away than when you first started the stalk.

In the spring, when the snow starts to slide and when melting frost loosens rocks, the goats are used to hearing these slides and rocks rolling down the mountain. The slides also take their toll of goats, as we have many times found their skeletons and skulls in the bottom of the canyon below cliffs where snowslides had occurred. They may also slip on the ice and fall, but I for one cannot imagine any such happening, so believe that slides or rolling boulders account for most of their bones found in the canyon bottoms.

Some may be killed fighting — of this I do not know, never having seen goats fight or tracks indicating anything beyond a mild, playful scrimmage. I have watched the billies and occasionally nannies as well hook the mountain mahogany with their horns before the rut and also watched them rub their horns on various brush, polishing them up and no doubt oiling them from that pair of big stinking glands behind the horns. Those glands seem most active in November and no doubt leave plenty of their musky odor on the brush for other goats to smell when they come along. This may well be one means of leaving signposts for other goats to know their location, just as about all animals do in one way or another. Of one thing you can be sure — if old billies did fight, it would be a mighty short fight and one or the other would very soon be dead and rolling down the slope. Have skinned out a great many of them and never found them scarred up as I have so many other animals. Old bull elk, mule deer, rams and moose very often have broken and healed bones and heavy and thick scar tissue in various places from old wounds, as well as deep scar tissue running through their muscles where a horn has penetrated, but the only trace of old wounds I have found in goats has been old bullet wounds, or a few old healed scratches on their backs that must have been caused when they were young, by eagles.

Lions no doubt kill a few of them, but I seriously doubt if the big cat has much relish for a tussle with an old billy. Harry Snyder told me the party that went through the British Columbia wilderness from Hudson's Hope south to the C.N.R. before we did in 1927 found a grizzly and an old billy goat lying below a ledge on a cliff. The bear still had one of the goat's horns driven upward through his heart, and the goat's body from the shoulder to the rear was simply pounded into a pulp. I did not see this and can only report it as I heard it.

One time, while scouting for goats on Cottonwood Creek, a tributary of the Salmon River, I worked around a narrow ledge, across the face of a cliff. I wanted to get past that cliff without having to climb a chimney clear to the top, so decided to try the ledge as it appeared good footing and the rocks were polished from goats using it. There were also some tracks showing in shale and hair on the brush. Rounding a corner of the cliff, I met a huge old yellow-colored billy at a few feet. I jerked my six-gun out of the holster, expecting trouble. The billy was just as surprised as I was and for two or three minutes stood his ground looking at me, then he bunched his feet and somehow started to turn around. The ledge was hardly wide enough, so he backed up a bit to a wider place, turned and beat it around the ledge on a shambling awkward run. I did not want him myself and could have killed him easily with a brain shot when I first saw him, but he would have rolled a quarter mile and probably busted his horns in so doing. He made no effort to fight, but did stand his ground a few minutes.

Another time Art Kirkpatrick and I had located goats a few days previously and climbed a steep ledge and then a very steep knife-blade ridge up to where they had been. We each wanted a goat for a head and rug. I wanted a fine old nanny particularly, while Art wanted a good rug and not too large. Rounding a small ledge and looking over, as we traveled on an old goat trail, we saw the band across the canyon from us some 400 yards away. They spotted us instantly and got up out of their beds. I told Art to slip over on the trail and find a good prone position and I would do the same behind him; then he agreed to take the lead goat and as the one in the tail end of the procession looked particularly good to me, I told him I would take that one. Art was using my old remodeled Enfield for the .333 O.K.H. with 250-grain spitzer at 2635 feet velocity, while I carried my scope sighted .334 O.K.H. with 275-grain bullet, at about 2750 feet velocity. Art shot, but from a sitting position, and landed just behind his goat. They were then walking swiftly upward and to the left and across the deep canyon. He evidently landed just behind the goat as he had set the sight for 400 yards. I had been following my goat through the scope and with the 300 yard cross hair held just forward and level with the top of the long hair on the withers. At his shot, I simply touched the set trigger on the big rifle. While the barrel was raised in recoil, I heard my slug strike home at about 450 yards, and my goat dropped and rolled about 50 yards and caught on some rocks and lay still. Sliding another round into the chamber of the big rifle, I set the trigger again and watched Art. He hit his goat, but too far back and not a center hit. Then I saw him crease it across the front of the face, as examination later proved. This turned it from him, but the goat soon turned back to the left again to go over a low ridge. It had now dropped to the tail end of the procession. Then Art shot again as it hopped along and we saw dust rise under its tail. He had not led it enough. Then he asked me to help him before it got over the ridge out of sight. Just as it was skylined on the ridge and walking to the left, I held the 300 yard cross wire up over the withers and about over the head to allow for lead and again touched the set trigger. We saw the goat drop and roll out of sight and then heard the plunk of the heavy slug. Range a good 500 yards.

Nearly an hour was required to negotiate that steep and treacherous slope, down to the canyon and thence up a narrow chimney to the flat on which the goats had been. Mine proved a fine old nanny with horns over 9 inches in length, just what I wanted. Art's goat was nowhere in sight, though we found the crevasse down which it had rolled. Horse Creek Connors, who was with us, decided to help me skin out the nanny while Art climbed down that chute after his goat. The nanny was fat as a seal and knowing she would be fine meat we took not only the complete skin and head but also every scrap of the meat and loaded it all on our pack boards. Then we worked down into the canyon.

The bottom was a jumble of slide-rock, huge stuff from three to ten and twenty feet in diameter and slick with moss. It was most treacherous going, but we put plenty of faith in the seat of our pants and slowly slid and worked our way from boulder to boulder down that steep chasm. When we finally reached the bottom of the crevasse into which Art's goat had rolled, there stood Art and there also stood the goat by his side. It was a small three-year-old, just what he wanted for a rug, but very much alive. Art is a big fellow over six feet and he was petting the goat. My bullet had gone through the base of the neck just over the spine and had not opened a very large hole at a range of 500 yards. The goat had a bad crease across the front of the skull just above the eyes and a flesh wound through a ham. Art said he had found the goat on a ledge and simply driven it on down to the bottom and waited for us. He petted the goat and it made no effort whatever to fight in any way. I took a series of pictures, then as we had no possible way of getting a wounded goat out of that awful canyon and did not want to leave anything wounded, Art killed him and skinned him out. We took all meat and both skins complete and surely earned our goats before we reached the main river.

When darkness overtook us we cached both skins and meat and finally managed to negotiate all that steep river slope around cliffs in the dark and reached camp. My goat was hit squarely through both shoulders and spine at 450 yards and the bullet opened about a two-inch exit hole, killing instantly.

Another time Herman Prins and I were out for a goat. He wanted a medium-size specimen for complete mounting and we finally located a fine young billy across the canyon from us. As per usual, the canyon was all goat cliffs and huge rock thrown in every possible and conceivable shape and position. We managed to work up on our side until above the goat and out of sight, then crossed the raging stream on a pole and started the long and treacherous climb to get up as high as or higher than the goat. He had been bedded on the top of a granite spire and we had located another higher ledge some 100 yards above him that looked favorable for a good stalk. After many narrow squeaks, when we managed to stay on that cliff only by the grace of God and sheer luck, we worked out to the edge of the higher ledge and looked over. Sure enough there was our goat. Herm carried his old Springfield and I a new .348 Model 71 Winchester loaded with 150-grain factory ammunition. Wanting to know how it would work on goats, Herm took the .348 and carefully planted three slugs in that goat's chest, not even staggering him, and we later found they stayed under the skin on the off side. The goat got up and down from his perch to a ledge and started to walk around it out of sight. Herm yelled for me to stop him with the Springfield and I planted a 180-grain Remington Bronze Point on top of his rump as he walked out of sight. It dropped him but he was up and out of sight even as I reloaded and I only had the rear half of him in sight to shoot at. Herm then took the Springfield and worked down to the right and out on another vantage point where he could see the billy. He carefully planted the remaining five 180-grain Remington Bronze Points in the goat at less than 100 yards and finally got it down. Then, we worked down to the goat, but it was not dead, and that game little billy got up and started to jump over the ledge, where he would have fallen sheer for a quarter mile. Herm grabbed his hind legs and braced his feet on a scrub mahogany bole and managed to hold him on the cliff ledge while I knifed him to the heart. Those 180-grain Bronze Points had penetrated almost through before expanding at all, hence had very little shock and their exit holes were only about a half inch in diameter. We roped him to the mahogany and carefully skinned him out entirely, for a whole mount, then took leg bones and cleaned them. I would very much have liked to have the meat in camp, as he was only about a four- or five-year-old, but there was no chance of our getting anything but his skin off that cliff. That goat made no attempt whatever to show fight, even when Herm grabbed him by the hind legs, and if he had not done so the goat would have done the usual—jumped off into space and broken himself on the jumble of huge boulders far below.

These experiences are typical of goat hunting. You can expect the hardest and most dangerous kind of work in getting your goat and even then you may wind up with no pelt or head, and the billy getting your goat. Another time, while guiding the Zane Grey party in 1931, we were camped on lower Cottonwood meadows. Zane Grey's son-in-law, Bob Carney, and a lad named Jack Frost each wanted a goat. Bob killed his goat on the top rim of the lower Cottonwood canyon without difficulty, but in so doing, and not waiting until Jack also had one located, he spooked all the goats down into that God-awful maze of cliffs and slides. My partner and I had to take Jack the next day and go back to get his goat. Jerry worked down through the cliffs, as he is almost as good in cliffs as the goats themselves, while Jack and I worked the left rim of the canyon. In places it fell away sheer for hundreds of feet, at others slides and crevasses ran down through the cliffs. We worked down to the lower end of the big basin without seeing anything. Both the Cottonwood and another stream from Black Lake came together in the basin. It is one of the most awful messes of cliffs and slide-rock I have ever seen on this continent. The basin was probably two miles across and the cliffs on our side dropped down for well over 1000 feet before the shale slides started. Then the bottom was a huge expanse of jumbled boulders, each as large as a small house, with the creek in sight in places and at others running merrily along over 100 feet down under the boulders. In the center of that huge expanse of rock below us was a small patch of timber, mostly dead and dry, and the creek ran on the surface there through the patch of timber, probably an acre or two in extent.

Late in the afternoon we had seen or heard nothing of Jerry below us in the cliffs, but did locate a nice billy out on a small ledge and some 500 yards away. He had seen us and was ready to leave. We also located a great many goats far across the canyon from us but a couple of miles away, bedded and feeding among the spires on that side. Assuming a good prone position, we put two .30–06 150-grain Remington Bronze Points through that billy's shoulders at 500 yards by holding the cross hair of the Noske scope up over the top of his withers. He flinched slightly at each shot and then walked slowly around a ledge out of sight.

Many deep and sheer cliffs and crevasses extended between us and where the billy had stood, so we decided to work down a narrow chute,

Mountain goat

Courtesy J. Omar Cole

J. Omar Cole with a fine mountain goat killed by him at 300 yards with a heart shot

Courtesy George Bates

Author with a good specimen of British Columbia mountain goat killed in 1927 at 400 yards, prone position, with a .300 Hoffman Magnum rifle, M–1 Boattail filed and drilled and 60 grains 15½ Dupont powder

Snapshot of a live mountain goat taken by the author through a small opening in the rocks on a cliff a quarter of a mile above the Salmon River

or chimney, to a ledge far below and then work around it and try to locate the goat from below. We had not worked down 30 yards before a small ledge under my feet peeled off, and away I went head over heels down that chimney. I still retained my rifle in the left hand, and as I turned another somersault under the low-hanging boughs of an old gnarled and wind-twisted fir tree I grabbed a stout limb with my right hand. The shock nearly tore my shoulder out of joint, as I turned on over and hung in mid-air by one hand. Jack worked down to me and helped me regain my feet. That right shoulder hurt like fury. As soon as I recovered and looked on down the quarter mile I would have fallen sheer to the rocks below, I thanked God for that fir tree.

We worked around that ledge and into a crevasse below where we had last seen the goat. The ledges and spires here were covered with scrub mahogany, offering good hand holds. The goat had left plenty of blood, Jack said, as he climbed up to the ledge where he had stood when hit. Jack elected to climb on around that narrow shelf while I watched from below. He gave me strict orders to shoot the goat if I saw him and finish the job. Finally he scared him out of another chimney and again he ran around out of Jack's sight. Jack could not negotiate the deep chimney the goat had jumped across, so worked back down to me. I could see the goat's head and neck as he looked over at me. We were standing in a narrow chimney in soft shale, but the walls were only about four or five feet apart and the goat directly above us. I told Jack if we busted him he would come down that chimney on us, and we would have to time his bouncing and either run up under him or dodge lower down and try to run up when he bounced in the air again. Jack agreed and asked me to finish the job, so I broke his neck offhand. He dropped off the ledge, then bounced twenty feet in the air, then hit again and bounced higher. It looked to me as if he would land right on us, so I yelled for Jack to climb for all he was worth, which we did. The goat came down with a thump right where we had stood, and if we had not climbed higher when we did, he would have surely smashed us to a pulp. He bounced several more times down that awful chimney, then rolled out into the fine slide-rock at the top of the long rock slide leading to the canyon floor far below. The fine soft shale made excellent footing when once we got down out of that treacherous chimney and we literally ran the rest of the way down to the goat in the gathering darkness.

The two 150-grain Bronze Points through the shoulders had not ex-panded at all, but the one in the center of the neck had blown up in great shape. We skinned that goat out entirely for a rug and in record time.

Then I cut under the shoulder blades and threw the forelegs forward out of the way and removed both loins complete, as I well knew we would not see camp that night. Rolling the loins in the skin, we made up a pack and headed down for that patch of timber, just as a small fire lighted up under a big boulder far below us. We knew where Jerry was then and that he had selected the best hotel possible for the night.

The slide grew ever coarser as we progressed downward. While we were able to run down for a time, the rock soon changed to big stuff and darkness closed in. It was one of the blackest, completely cloudy nights I have seen. Soon the boulders were the size of cookstoves and we had to climb laboriously over each one; then they increased to the size of small houses. It was slow, ticklish work. We made it down to within a quarter mile of the campfire, then got out on a huge boulder the size of a house and could find no way off it in any direction. We had jumped down on it and could not go back up, so there we sat and yelled for Jerry. He yelled back that he had got stuck on that same rock, but had found a way off of it before dark and would be up with the flashlight after us. He was as good as his word and in a half hour made it up to us with the flashlight and we were soon off that piece of rock and on down to camp.

His first question was "Did you bring any meat?" I told him we had billy-goat loins for supper and breakfast and that satisfied him as we each carried salt. He had selected one of the finest hotels I have ever seen in the hills. A huge flat-topped rock extended out from the creek for twenty yards, a regular ledge some fifteen feet high and sloping back underneath, affording a perfect windbreak from the cold wind now blowing down the Cottonwood canyon. Under this ledge which shed the now falling rain was a fine springy mat of that sticky rock moss, several inches deep and as springy as a fine set of bedsprings. Six feet in front of this long strip of moss was a jungle of dead logs and brush which he had set afire. It made a roaring fire and burned all night and was still burning next day, but being surrounded by nearly a mile of rock in all directions, and being about all dead timber, it did no harm. We lay there in perfect comfort, roasting slices of the tough, fresh-killed goat meat, on sticks. I had brought plenty of fat for basting the meat and we had a grand night, eating all the meat we wanted and sleeping well until daybreak. The meat, while too fresh to be tender, was very well flavored and Jack and I enjoyed it very much, but Jerry insisted he could still taste it a week later.

Next morning we climbed right up that canyon, over one rock the size of a house and then another. We would crawl to the top on hands and knees, then slide down the far side, putting plenty of stress on the seat of our pants. We turned up Black Canyon, thinking it would be better going as we could not get back up the sheer wall we had worked down the night before. You can go down where you never can hope to get back up again. Soon the seats of our pants were completely worn out and we each badly needed a breechclout.

Black Canyon proved even worse and at times we were walking on dead logs thrown down by snowslides, that were fully fifty feet above the jumble of jagged boulders below. At times we could only hear the creek hundreds of feet under us in that huge slide, and at other times it would briefly come out on top for a few yards. Arriving at Black Lake late in the afternoon, we negotiated the steep climb onto the timbered slope above that hell hole of a goat canyon and were glad to be back where solid ground again afforded decent footing. We made it to camp late that night and I'll bet Jack Frost will never forget how he obtained his goat. Over twenty years of such guiding has now convinced me at least that there are other and easier ways of making a living, including punching this hunt and peck machine.

Big game hunting is usually mostly hard work, but of all species of game on this continent, my vote goes to old *Oreamnos americanus*, for usually producing the most dangerous and tiring hunting of all.

In all goat hunting the best procedure is to climb a slope across from the goat cliffs and first locate your goats across the canyon. Then plan your stalk; also select ways of getting in range of the goats. If they are up on top of the rim, then you have only an easy circle to make to come in range. If they are bedded down on spires below the top of the rim, you may have to wait for them to work up, or down to feed, or select a ledge you can work around. Never shoot a goat until you are sure you can get to him; no use in killing and wasting a fine trophy. If you cannot see an easy way to get to him, don't shoot. Also never shoot unless you are reasonably sure you can drop him where he is, without his falling over a ledge. Remember also that badly wounded goats, when cornered, will invariably walk or crawl to a ledge and throw themselves over. I have seen them thus commit hara-kiri many times. It is the usual thing and can be expected. If you have a hard-hit goat in such a place, either shoot him again or leave him alone and let him lie down and quietly die, for if you crowd him, he will jump over the ledge and be a battered, broken-horned wreck when you do find him far below, unfit for either food or trophy. It's far better to leave them alive than to waste them. If you locate goats on a cliff face, then when you circle above them are unable to see them, you can usually bring them up in sight by rolling a big boulder down a crevasse. Select some vantage point that will give you as good a view as possible, then roll a boulder over and the goats will soon be up to investigate, if they have not been hunted.

You can usually locate them easily across a canyon, but when you get in a maze of cliffs, it is hard to locate them at times. For this reason it is best always to locate them across a canyon in advance of the stalk. Never try to work up under goats as they will invariably spot you and leave. Goats are beautiful animals, with their snowy white coats and long chin whiskers, which, combined with the heavy and long hair on the legs, the high arch of hair on their withers and rumps, make them a trophy worthy of the best hunter. While the horns are not large or imposing, the coat of the goat is. They make most beautiful rugs. When a rug is desired, the head and feet should be left on the skin, and when only a head is wanted, the rest of the pelt and feet should be saved; then if some other member of the party also obtains a goat for a head, the two body skins can be joined where the capes were removed, tanned, lined and made into a beautiful and unique rug. We have sent a good many to Jonas Brothers for sportsmen, for such rug making.

If you kill a young billy, save all the meat if possible, and if a nanny is wanted for a trophy, then select a dry one with no kids in attendance, and save the meat. Hang it up in sacks to age for a week and it will be found to be firm, but delicious. I do not believe in killing a nanny with kids — the youngsters need their mother for that first year, to teach them the ropes; so be careful and select a dry nanny if you want a specimen for your collection. Further, I do not believe in killing either sheep or goats for meat alone. They are too fine and rare a trophy to be taken solely for food except under dire circumstances. The sportsman should make it a point to select a fine billy for a trophy or one of each sex, then take care of them and leave the rest of the goat tribe for posterity.

Goats do not have the springy effortless grace of a bighorn in the cliffs and we have watched sheep bound around cliffs where a goat would walk sedately and slowly, but the goat will go places where no self-respecting ram would think of going; he will even sleep and live right there for months on end. They do no possible damage to anyone or any crop, yet are one of the grandest sights in their native habitat of all our big game animals. I hope many successive generations of sportsmen will be able thus to see them and on occasion take a fine specimen as a trophy. Goats are not on the increase here, and they breed slowly. We have often found nannies and yearlings together, so do not believe they have kids each year, as so often happens with both deer and antelope. Properly protected and hunted only within limits and on a special license, they will remain with us for centuries. License fees should be high on goats in all countries where hunted, just as on sheep. This will automatically eliminate the meat hunting lad who wishes to kill one merely to be able to say he has killed a goat. If you do not appreciate such a fine animal as a trophy and think enough of him to accord him the expense of proper mounting, then he should be left in his wild state. We believe license fees should be high enough to prohibit hunting them as meat animals. Idaho has taken a step in the right direction in putting a ten-dollar special license on goats and we really believe it should be even higher. Given reasonable protection they will increase, but the golden eagle, their worst enemy, should carry a ten-dollar bounty on his yellow head in all states and Canada, regardless of what some Eastern sob sisters think of that grand old bird, the worst predator of our lighter big game we have today. Coyotes will kill off the diseased and old and feeble animals, but the eagle takes the cream of the crop, the young kids.

When hunting goats, always carry a pack sack or pack board, on which to carry out your trophy and meat. The pack board is much the better of the two. Also pack some light but warm jacket, as you may have to lie out around a fire at any time. We have found the Bauer down jacket excellent for the purpose. Always carry about fifty feet of strong but light rope, like sash cord; you will need it. One should also always carry plenty of salt and matches as well as either jerky, cheese or some other light but nutritious food that will keep him from getting too hungry for a couple of days. When you start after a goat you never know when you will get back to base camp, at least in this country, and it's well to go prepared. I have even had to rope myself on a ledge to a scrub mahogany and spend the night in such an uncomfortable place and nearly freeze to death without a fire, so it is well in goat hunting to select a good hotel under some ledge, about three or four o'clock in the afternoon, where plenty of fallen limbs or other firewood is available. While you may often get a very close shot at goats, you will also have to take them at extreme long range at times, and for our money the best commercial made rifle and load for the purpose is a scope sighted .300 Magnum, with 180-grain bullet, and the next best is the .270 Winchester with 130-grain bullet.

Some years ago, some of our eminent authorities got off on the wrong foot by recommending thick jacket heavy bullets for goats, as they claimed the goat's hair was hard to penetrate. In my experience just the opposite is true and you need a flat shooting rifle with high velocity and a thin jacket bullet, that will surely expand out at long range and that will blow up as much as possible inside your goat, not on the scenery on the other side. They are easily penetrated but all too many commercial bullets go through before sufficient expansion occurs. I watched Dr. Chet Sulkers shoot through a nanny from stem to stern, then, as she turned, he shot through her again broadside, through both lungs. This was with a .30–06–180 Remington Bronze Point, and at 100 yards. That goat got out of sight and ran nearly three miles before Doc again obtained some long range shooting across a canyon and finally broke her back. She never even flinched from the hits, and the first one traveled the length of her body. Even my old .45 S.A. Colt with 250-grain slugs and black powder loads penetrates about the length of a big billy, sometimes going clear through, and I have used it on several crippled goats as well as killing my first billy with the old gun. A heavy sixgun load, however, usually penetrates deeper than an expanding, high velocity rifle bullet and this is as it should be. Don't underestimate mountain goats, they will give you your full share of thrills any day.

If you want to stalk to very close range of goats, have a white parka made from an old sheet, with hood to cover your face, and large eye holes and also sleeves. Let it come down to just below the knees. Then if you will temporarily discard your hat, keep the wind in your favor and work in from above or from the side, and keep bent over, you can approach very close to goats at times. I once exposed a whole roll of film, sixteen exposures, at just 12-feet range at a young bill, taking the photos through a hole in scrub mahogany.

Good footgear is of utmost importance. My favorite for goat hunting is loggers with ten to twelve inch top that fits tight and snug around the ankle. If you are absolutely sure of being on dry rock, such as in early hunting here in Idaho, then rubber soles are good, but if it rains or any snow is encountered, rubber soles are almost suicidal. The best bet for all-around work in goat and sheep country is good loggers coming up well above the ankles and lacing tight enough to support them. They should be large enough for a pair of light pure wool socks and also a pair of heavy wool socks. The heels should be slightly undershot and about 1¼ to 1½ inches high to hold you when running down shale slopes. The soles and heels should be well covered with good logger's drive calks, not those worthless screw-in kind that tear out on the first rock and must be constantly replaced. In addition to the calks you need a couple of rows of hobnails all around both soles and heels near the edge, or better still a complete edging of Swiss hobs, that not only cover the bottom edge of the sole but also come up on the sides a quarter inch. Such footgear when kept well oiled and pliable is the safest and most comfortable of all for high mountain work.

XVI

Antelope

THE American antelope is one of our strangest game animals, differing in several ways from any other animal on this continent. The horns are hollow at the base and the skull runs up in pronounced bony prongs, over which the horns grow, yet the horns are shed each year, or at least with all the younger bucks. The horns do not shed as do the Cervidae, nor are they maintained for the life of the animal, as with the Bovidae groups. What really takes place is that after the rut, or during early winter, a new horn starts to grow inside the base of the old one and between it and the bony base proper. As growth progresses, the old horn is raised ever higher, which accounts for some of the long tales we read of antelope with horns over 20 inches long. (The record is 20⅝ inches, killed in 1899.) At such times an antelope might have a very long combined measurement, but it would be the length of both the old horn and the new inner horn. When growth has progressed far enough, the outer shell becomes loosened and the animal usually hooks it off on the sagebrush. A great many shed horns will also be found along barbed-wire fences adjacent to antelope ranges, showing they pull them off on the wire as well. The horns are a hairy growth becoming hard and slick as they age. The beast has solid bony horn bases, yet actually sheds his horns. Another peculiarity of antelope is that they have no dewclaws whatever, merely a bump, well rounded, where these occur on all other herbivorous game, except the Javalina, which has but one on each hind foot and thus also differs from other game.

Another peculiarity of antelope is the fact they can erect the entire white rump patch when alarmed, or frightened, or flashing a signal to other adjacent antelope. This is a peculiar action; the white or creamy-white rump patch is large and when erected makes an antelope look for all the world as if someone had tied a big white pillow to his rump. In fact when one is running directly away from you, little of the animal can be seen, except head and neck and those flying nimble legs above and below that huge white rump. Halfway up the body, on each side of the barrel, is white or creamy white, and this extends from the hip and hind leg forward onto the rear part and knuckle of the shoulder. The brisket is also white and with white strips extending up from the brisket on each side and tapering to a point just in front of the shoulder. Above this on the neck are two white bars across the frontal section of the neck or throat. Sides of the face, lower part of the upper lips and the lower jaw are also white. A white strip runs back under the middle of the chin and is fringed on each side with their beautiful reddish tan. Around the eyes is usually quite dark or black and the long eyelashes are black. Just to the rear of the jaw and below a line from eye to ear is a black patch, which is also one of their numerous oil and scent glands. The back of the neck has a stiff coarse mane of brown or black, and with some white hairs also at times. A narrow, dark cinnamon line runs from top of the rump down to the tail, which is usually the same color on top and white underneath. It is short and inconspicuous and when the flag or rump hair is erected does not show. The belly and inside of the legs are a creamy white, shading to tan, and the outside of the legs the usual tan. The rest of the body is also a varying shade of tan to cinnamon, young bucks in their prime being much darker and more reddish, or cinnamon, in color, while old bucks grow quite gray and have much more white hair on their faces. The top of the nose is usually a dark mahogany brown. Ears are small, pointed and edged with black. The black neck mane also extends well up to the back of the head.

The horns grow right above the eyes, in fact the eyes are almost set in the base of the horn. They are large for the size of the beast, but not prominent as in sheep, deer or any other herbivorous game. On the contrary, they have a sunken appearance and are a dark color with little light or pupil showing, just a dark, sad expression. The horns tip forward and are well separated from the ears by several inches of the skull proper. The does also have horns, after about the second year, but they are merely slim pencil-size gray spikes usually two to four inches long.

The legs are very small in diameter below the knee and trim as those of a ballet dancer. When feeding slowly along over a sage flat at a distance, they look for all the world like a huge beetle bug, especially the old bucks. The hoofs are shaped about halfway between sheep and deer, and are rather short with wide heels like sheep, the toes cupping somewhat.

They are the most deceiving of all American game, when it comes to estimating their range. One time they may appear to be 100 yards or so away, then, when they change position as they feed, they may appear to be twice that far. As they change position, the sun strikes the numerous white patches, giving them an entirely different appearance. At times under hot sunlight or mirage they appear to be white.

Formerly, during the buffalo days, they numbered into the millions and the plains antelope annually migrated northward to some extent in the spring and southward to the Black Hills in the winter; but antelope were then spread from far into Canada down into Old Mexico. Today they are again on the increase, but in the past thirty years were almost wiped out. Old-timers considered them the best summer meat of all and they were hunted almost to the point of extermination. Under sound game management, they have staged a remarkable comeback, in many sections. We have plenty antelope here in Idaho and are now trapping and shipping to other sections where they have long been extinct. The late Julius Maelzer, an old friend of mine, told me that thirty years ago it was a very rare occurrence to see an antelope in the Pahsimeroi Valley; now there are probably 5000 there.

The rut occurs early in September, but varies somewhat from year to year. At this time, the bucks rub their horns on their oil and scent glands, then rub them on the sagebrush, until they fairly shine. They also rub the horns on those oil glands, then over their body, until their coat is covered with a fine oil. At such times the horns may be almost jet black. At other times of the year, the horns will be more of a blue black or blue gray. They are small, big bucks usually running from about 90 to 125 pounds, but a rare exceptional animal may well go to 140 or 150 dressed. I have seen just one such antelope and he stood a full 6 inches higher at the withers than other bucks that had horns over 16 inches in length in the band. His head with uneven twisted horns still goes seventh place in the world's records, with a length of $17\frac{1}{2}$ inches for both horns and a spread of $17\frac{1}{2}$. I have recently made an oil painting of the old boy, just as he looked in 1936 before I killed him.

Antelope are curious animals at times; they are also very intelligent little beasts, and when hunted a bit will give the sportsman all the work he wants to get in range — if he gets out and hunts them like a man, either from a saddle horse or on foot. Running them with cars has long been against the law, but here at least it is never enforced and I even saw one state game warden, with his party, chasing a band of antelope and promiscuously shooting both bucks and does, but when we reported the fact, nothing was done about it. Properly hunted, on foot or with a horse, antelope hunting is next thing to sheep hunting for real sport, but when hunters run them down in cars and then jump out and shoot them, there can be no sport about it and the meat is likewise not fit to eat after becoming heated. Antelope that range the sage flats and eat shad scale and alfalfa around the ranches are seldom good meat. Usually they are as strong as a sage jack rabbit killed in February, but antelope killed up on the high mesas and high ridges at 7000 to 10,000 feet, where they live on the fine buffalo and bunch grass, are almost as fine eating as sheep — a little drier meat, but wonderfully well flavored. If you go after antelope like a man, you will find some of the finest sport, and one of the finest stalking animals, on this continent. But if you shoot them from an auto, little sport, or knowledge of the beast, will be obtained.

Antelope have wonderful eyes but never the equal of mountain sheep. They can see you for miles, but do not seem to be able to tell exactly what you are, as a mountain sheep will do. They seldom take alarm at extreme distances as will mountain sheep. Further, if horses or cattle graze in the same range, antelope will often be found associating and feeding with them, seemingly enjoying their companionship. Thus a saddle horse can usually be ridden fairly close to antelope without exciting them. When alarmed, an antelope will usually raise its head very erect and stare at you. The entire rump patch will stand on end, giving the little beast a most curious appearance, then he will probably stamp a foot and bark at you, before taking off. Sometimes they will continue to stand and stamp and bark for several seconds before jumping, usually into a stiff-legged long stride trot, with head very erect, then breaking quickly into a run. When really scared, they run flat with the ground with head well extended in front of them, the same as a race horse, and do not really get wound up and into high gear until they have run a mile or so and have their mouths open and their tongue hanging out. Then they can really fly. As long as their heads are held high they are not really running. Buster and Vern Coiner and I once wanted to see how long were the horns carried by a particularly large buck that ran with a band of about a hundred animals on a sage flat on the Pahsimeroi. It was long before the season and we had no intention of harming the animals, but we wanted to see the length of that old boy's horns at close range. In the Chevrolet we chased them for a good six miles over more or less broken ground, then after negotiating a bad wash we thought we had them, and in second gear we were doing over 30 miles an hour and fast closing. Then they simply let out another notch and ran right around and across our front as though we were standing still. I still do not know how fast they can actually run. The old buck was a very large and fat animal and ran well to the rear of the band.

The tops of his horns rose straight up, so I knew he would not go over 14 or 15 inches and lost interest in him for the coming season.

The bark of an antelope buck is a peculiar sound, like nothing else I know of. It's a sort of nasal snort, but sounds very much like the cawing of a crow, only more of an explosive nasal twang, in some ways resembling the bark of a small dog. It can be heard for a considerable distance, and while of the same nasal type as the whistle of a buck deer, has more tone to it and more resembles the crow. Buck antelope are beautiful, dainty little beasts, proud as peacocks, and seem to take the same pride in carefully oiling their hair and polishing their horns on sagebushes before the rut starts. No doubt they are our fastest game animal.

Antelope were formerly plains animals, staying out on the open flats, but today, in many sections, they have turned into mountain animals and now range where mountain sheep did in former years, before scabies killed them off. I have even jumped several antelope that were bedded in dense timber. At other times during our season here I have sat on a high open ridge and watched the dust trails all over the valley floor, as hunters stirred up and shot at band after band. Many of those antelope headed straight for the mountains and showed no hesitation in climbing up through a half mile of dense fir timber to reach the open mesalike tops of the mountains and ridges. I have even seen old solitary bucks bedded in the slide-rock, right under the highest cliffs, where one would never expect anything but sheep or goats. This shows what civilization and the ultimate change in environment have done to the antelope's habits. The elk used also to be a plains animal, but is now a mountain animal. Antelope are supposed never to jump washes or fences. I have seen them jump narrow washes many times and last winter when the Idaho Game Department rounded up several bands with an airplane for shipment to other sections of the state, some few antelope actually jumped an eight-foot canvas fence set up to corral them. I believe that changes in habitat brought about by the ever-encroaching inroads of civilization have driven them to be more of a mountain than a plains animal, at least in this section.

The rut starts early in September and the fawns are born in May or early June, nearly always two in number. I have never seen triplets as I have with both whitetail and mule deer, but they may occur. The old doe usually selects her fawning ground with care and quite often another doe will take up her claim a short distance away, in sight of the first doe. If many antelope are present, this fawning ground may be quite extensive. I believe it is done for mutual protection, by one doe warning the next of the approach of any enemies. Coyotes and golden eagles are their worst enemies. In late winter, coyotes may occasionally run antelope into deep crusted snow and eat them alive, as the sage wolves can travel easily on top of the crust. At fawning time a single coyote has little chance of obtaining a fawn as the does are very watchful and will attack a coyote without hesitation, usually striking at him with the forefeet if they can make him run. If he starts to run they will chase him and administer a sound drubbing with those forefeet, usually chasing him for a quarter mile from their fawns. Then some other doe may take up the task if any be present. When two coyotes work together they have more luck, and one may attract the doe's attention and endeavor to lure her away from the fawns while its mate makes a kill. Doe antelope are very canny, however, and will usually spot both coyotes and stick closer to the fawns' bed ground. The little fellows, all legs and innocence, are usually hidden in the sage, and except for the soaring old golden eagle are hard to find. But that great bird does get a lot of them. The golden eagle is also perfectly capable of breaking the back of mature antelope and often does so when rabbits are scarce and hunting particularly hard.

Antelope are stalking game and as such second only to mountain sheep. The best bucks are nearly always solitary individuals, before the rut. During the winter they band up for mutual protection against their enemies, but when spring comes the old bucks go off by themselves, and usually there is little use in looking for a record buck among a band before the rut. Nearly always, only small, or young bucks, with horns not over 14 inches, will be found with the does, while the wise old boys are off alone. They will feed and bed alone, usually where they can see everything that moves within a quarter mile of their bed or feed ground. Like sheep and goats they also seldom look for trouble from above, and one should stalk from above where possible. Delmer Coiner, a friend and I once located a big band of antelope on a steep slope of a long ridge, running back to the Divide. We made a circle of some three or four miles, then worked down the top of that ridge above the band of antelope. There were some bucks in the band, and several that looked to have fair heads. When we were almost over the band, a couple of hunters started walking directly toward the antelope from a neighboring flat. Of course, the antelope instantly spotted them and started working up the ridge just under the comb where we sat, ensconced in a jumble of boulders. Those hunters both emptied their rifles at the band, which was far out of range, then waved their hands and shouted at us. The antelope were watching those two hunters and filed past us at a trot not 50 yards away, directly below us. I readied my rifle and sat there watching them; not seeing anything with exceptional horns, I turned the safety back on the .285 O.K.H. Mauser and enjoyed the scene. The antelope all streamed past us and on up the ridge, gradually working out into a basin on a level with us about 200 yards; then they spotted us and started running in earnest, the while those dizzy hunters far below continued to wave and yell, not understanding why we did not shoot.

An old prong buck bedded out in the open, as they usually do, will give you your money's worth any time you attempt to stalk him, and if you do succeed, you will know you have earned him fairly. They have very good noses and can wind you a quarter mile very easily. Likewise they have most excellent ears and as before stated their eyes are second only to those of mountain sheep. Many times you will attempt to stalk on a wary old buck, either bedded or feeding, and some doe or other buck you had not seen will spot you, take alarm and flash a warning with that white rump patch; instantly your buck will be on his feet and watching in every direction. Like coyotes, they seem to have a very well-developed sixth sense, and several times I have stalked them, knowing full well I had never shown an inch of myself or hat, yet they jumped to their feet when I was either in range or just out of range and barked and stamped their dainty feet, plainly aware of my presence, but not knowing where I was at, as they would turn and look in first one direction and then another and ofttimes beat it, usually away from me as well.

During the early stage of the rut is the best time to hunt them. Then the fine old bucks are on the move, searching for a harem, or else with a band of does and intent on fighting off any young upstarts who wish to challenge their position. If a band of does is located, you can be sure bucks will be along before the rut is over. Usually, however, there will be younger bucks with a band and the old record heads will stay off alone, until the rut is well started. As a general rule, it is well to put the telescope on a band of does to determine if a worth-while buck may be with them, but most of your time should be spent searching out the little pockets and ridges as high as the grass extends, for they will often be found, at least in this country, up to 8000 or 10,000 feet elevation. The fine old bucks nearly always like to summer at the highest elevations, where good open ridges or flat-top mesas are available. They are a grazing animal and only browse occasionally on shad-scale and other small sage when grass is very scarce. What they can do to an alfalfa field is a caution, but that is seldom the place to look for a good one. They feed early in the morning and again in the late afternoon, usually spending the heat of the day bedded where they can watch in all directions. In this country they will usually come in to a spring and water once each day, either after feeding hours in the morning or before feeding hours in the evening. Desert antelope of Mexico, however, may go for days and weeks without water, obtaining sufficient moisture from the desert growths.

Mother Nature has well camouflaged the antelope. Although it is one of our most flashy colored animals, like a pinto horse or a Stone or Fannin ram, those changes in color tend to break up the outline of the beast when off at any considerable range. Often it is very difficult to show antelope to novice hunters, even though they are in plain sight and out in the open. The various white patches, while conspicuous, also help the beast to blend with his surroundings. If the sun is bright and any mirage running, they often appear to be pure white at a distance. Estimating the range of a band of antelope is a tricky business. They usually range at high elevations except in Canada and down south in Mexico, where the clear air of high altitudes often causes one to underestimate the range.

When after a head, you should make every effort to stalk to certain killing range, then drop the buck with one clean shot, if at all possible. Likewise use a high velocity rifle, that will expand its slugs to extreme range. If you do not make a clean kill and the animal jumps and runs a distance before falling, it may pile up in a bunch of rocks or sage and scrape most of the hair from a shoulder in falling. When an antelope is wounded, the hair falls out or scrapes off, easier than that of any game animal I know of. It is just like a well-stuck turkey, whose feathers are seemingly loose when it is dying. Head and cape should be removed where killed if you want a nice cape, otherwise the very brittle hollow hair is easily broken or damaged.

W. L. Dickey, Delmer Coiner and I were out for antelope in the Pahsimeroi Valley in 1935. I soon located a very nice old buck in some broken ridges where an easy stalk was made, but he sensed our approach and jumped and ran to 300 yards across a steep gulch. There he stopped, barked and stamped his foot at us, as Dickey settled in the sling and trained the 8-power Lyman Target scope on the old boy. Just as he started to take off Dickey's bullet caught him high behind the shoulders, breaking his spine and cutting that last bark short. He proved a beautiful 15-inch head with wide heavy bases and very wide paddles or prongs. The head appeared short, but was not, as the tips made an exceptional long curve back and down and had white tips.

We loaded Dickey's trophy after removing head and cape and started back for the ranch, then next day, turned our horses to higher country. Just after noon we had topped out on a big mesa, or sage flat, high on the ridge, when I spotted another that looked good at a distance. A man named Jess had asked to go along and was with us. In view of his later actions I will not give his last name. Leaving Delmer and Jess with the horses for the buck to watch, I slipped behind a huge black, flat-topped boulder that lay about two thirds the way to the bedded buck and started my stalk. Arriving at the boulder, I set up the old Mossberg spotting scope and took a look at him through the sage. He was a beauty, and I estimated him at well over 16 inches. His horns swept up and out, then the tips curved inward in a perfect lyre shape. Remembering that Delmer had often stated he would surely like to kill a lyre-shaped buck with record horns, I slipped behind the rock and signaled for Delmer to make the stalk also. The buck was still bedded, apparently watching Jess and the horses. Delmer made it successfully, though he had to squeeze down and wiggle as flat as paint over a portion of the ground. I told him it was just the head he wanted and he crawled up on the flat-top rock. The old buck jumped to his feet to stamp and bark at us, but Delmer caught him just over the heart with a .257 Remington Roberts 100-grain — my rifle, and the same one Dickey had used earlier. The 100-grain Remington Open Point staggered the old boy and he started to back up a ways, then whirled and ran another 100 yards to our left and stopped again. Instantly Delmer caught him again, this time too far back, but it put him down. We had to kill him with a knife, then, to avoid further damage to the fine trophy which went 16⅛ inches both horns as I now remember. Dressing the buck and removing head and cape, which we carried on with us, we rode around into another high basin some two miles distant and soon spotted a band out on a flat near a small lake. We had already looked over at least 500 antelope including many big bucks that day, but only Dickey's and Delmer's heads appeared to be in the record class, so we passed up all others.

Soon we located another band in the big basin and one buck appeared to have a fair head. Jess immediately said he would take that one and asked to borrow my rifle. He was carrying an iron sighted Model 54 Winchester .270, so I gladly loaned him my .280 Dubiel Magnum Mauser with heavy barrel and 8 X Lyman Targetspot scope. Delmer and I had a ringside seat as he started his stalk. He made it in fine style for some distance, then an old doe spotted him and the buck also took alarm when still 500 yards distant, then the whole band left on a run. While waiting for Jess to return, I had been searching an even higher mesa, to the north and some two miles away. Finally, I made out what appeared to be the largest buck antelope I had yet seen, bedded right out on top, where he could watch in every possible direction. His horns looked heavy through the 20 X spotting scope even at that distance, so I decided to go after him as soon as Jess returned with my rifle.

Delmer said he would stay with the horses. Jess asked if he could go with me for the fun. I answered, "Sure, as long as you keep to the rear and out of sight." So we started. One long gully looked as if it would offer cover for the first mile and a half; after that we would have to trust to luck, as the scope did not show much cover — merely a slight falling off in elevation of the ground and some very short sparse sagebrush, beyond the head of that gully. It was steep climbing and at 10,000 feet elevation we had to stop often to get our breath, but finally made it to the top rim of the gully. The old buck was still there, about a half mile away, and another look through the scope convinced me he was the largest buck antelope I had ever seen and carried a head that should go well in the top of the records.

To our delight, there was another swale that extended well around toward the buck. From our position, flattened in the sage on the rim of the gulch, I could not see its extent, but it headed around to the windward side of the old boy, and as long as he stayed in his bed it looked as if it might well allow us to approach in good rifle range. After another hot arduous crawl for over a quarter mile, we knew we were in range of my big rifle, but could find no place high enough to shoot from, so had to continue our crawl to a small knoll about 200 yards farther. After removing my hat and slowly raising my head in the sage, I saw the old boy bedded not 200 yards distant and looking our way, too close. There was also high ground between us, so I knew I would simply have to adjust the sling on my arm for a prone shot and crawl up in sight, then take him as quickly as possible, whether running or standing.

Just then young Martiny came over the other side of the mesa behind the big buck at a swinging lope. He did not know we were there at all. The old buck was on his feet instantly and running quartering toward us, even though Martiny was a half mile away. He was hunting horses and would never have ruined our stalk if he had known we were in the vicinity. I rose to a sitting position, turned the safety, picked up the running antelope at about 30 yards from me as he passed and started to squeeze the trigger, with the cross hairs on the front part of the shoulders. Jess yelled "Don't shoot." I asked why, and he answered, "He don't look so good." Then I said, "He is plenty good enough for me," and again started to bust him. By then the huge buck was 100 yards away and going fast. Then Jess yelled, "I'll match you to see who gets him." At this crack I saw red, and turning the safety on the big rifle told him to take him. The buck stopped on the rim of the next ridge, at 200 yards broadside on, and Jess shot, missing him completely. Then he proceeded to miss him running with the remaining five cartridges in his .270 magazine. After which he simply fell off the moun-

Antelope

The author with record antelope, having horns 16¾ inches long, killed with .280 Dubiel Magnum and 150-grain bullet at 202 yards

The author with his best antelope, also a record animal, length of both horns 17½ inches and spread of 17½. The largest antelope the author has ever seen and killed in one shot, prone position, at 360 yards. He used a .280 Dubiel Magnum and 150-grain bullet

tain, grabbed his horse from Delmer and rode back up on the mesa. He spent the rest of the day chasing and shooting at that big antelope with no success at all. Delmer and I were thoroughly disgusted with him and his rotten show, so we headed back for the ranch some ten miles away and arrived long after dark. When Jess arrived he informed all and sundry that that huge buck with the crooked left horn was his meat and no one was to shoot at him. Though all the rest of us were thoroughly disgusted with him, we decided to hunt one more day from that ranch before moving, in case I did not connect with a good one.

Next day we drove a pickup high up an old wood road and climbed the back of the escarpment on foot to the same high mesa. On poking my nose over, I spotted another big record head bedded a half mile distant. Examination through the glasses proved him a fine buck, but with more symmetrical horns than the huge old boy I had so successfully stalked the day before. Jess took one look and immediately informed us it was the same buck. I remonstrated, and told him I was positive this was a different buck, but told him if he was so greedy to come with me and we would drop back out of sight, make a half-mile circle under the rim of the escarpment to our right, and come up again with a big dead and fallen log between us and the bedded antelope. Then from that position we could have another look with the scope and if I was right I would take the stalk, and if Jess was right he could have my rifle for the job. He looked again and decided I was right, so declined to go with me. So we left Delmer sitting in plain sight of the buck, while I dropped back out of sight and made the long circle through the jumble of cliffs and rock.

Finally, I made it around to a position with that fallen log between me and the buck, then inched over the rim and started wiggling forward like a snake to that fallen tree. It lay with its extended roots toward the bedded buck and the top toward me. The rest of the mesa was as bare as a dance floor, so I knew I would have to keep out of sight. Finally I made the distance to the tree trunk and stopped for a rest. No brush or small limbs were in evidence to screen me. However, one huge tree root had a six-inch hole near the bole of the tree, so I rose to a stooped standing position and sidled along the trunk of the tree out of sight, to this hole in the roots. Peeking through, I saw the old boy up on his feet, barking and stamping a forefoot, but looking in first one direction, then another, clearly showing he sensed danger, but did not know where it was. I had a strained uncomfortable off-hand position, with rifle poked through the hole, but settled the cross wires of the 8 power Lyman scope in the white patch just behind his shoulder and squeezed the trigger. The rifle was sighted at 4000 feet elevation and for

300 yards. Granted a four or five inch rise at 200 yards, it still struck far too high, merely scraping the top of his back with the 150-grain W.T.C. Company bullet. It put him down and I saw hair fly, but he was up on his forefeet instantly, as I walked forward, so I shot him again in the lungs, this time holding lower and at closer range. The first shot was at 202 yards.

That first slug had merely blown all skin and muscles clear of the vertebrae, just behind the shoulders, but had not touched the spine. Its extreme high velocity had put him down from shock alone. The second slug blew up in the lungs at close range and stayed in the antelope. By this time Jess had gone on over the top of the mesa and after the big buck, which he again saw but did not land. My buck proved a beauty, both horns going 16⅜ inches and well up in the records. He was a very large antelope and Delmer and I estimated his dressed weight at around 135 pounds. We removed head and cape, then tied the feet for back packing and took off down that steep slope for the pickup, leaving Jess to chase the huge old buck with the crooked left horn. While stopping for a rest, I kicked at a bone lying in the trail and was amazed to dig up a perfectly good and huge old bull buffalo skull, clearly showing buffalo had once grazed that 10,000-foot mesa in the distant past.

Later that fall, when I was in town, I was informed Jess had left word that he finally killed the big antelope, some five miles from the mesa. I have never seen any man demonstrate a more total lack of sportsmanship in my life.

Next year C. M. Oneil came out from Minnesota for a hunt with me. We were also experimenting with the .250 Magnum rifle and developing that cartridge at the time. We hired young Martiny to pack our light camp over the top of the Divide to an old abandoned mine cabin, near a spring in the timber, while we made the long pull upward from 7000 feet on foot and hunted all the way in to camp. For some reason we saw only three bucks in that long climb and some ten miles of travel through the high basins. The year before, that country had been full of antelope, with big bands in every deep gulch containing water, but this year they were conspicuous by their absence. Just before dusk, we circled the south side of the mesa as it was starting to rain and snow. The wind was cold, and we were wet with perspiration from our long, all-day climb upward. We had seen two bucks but neither worth going after, then in the timber on the south side of the mesa I located several antelope. Though Charley wanted to go on and find camp before dark, I stopped and set up the spotting scope for a look at the distant antelope. Imagine my surprise and delight when the first antelope to come into focus proved the same old huge crooked-horned buck that

Jess had chased so long the year before and later claimed to have killed. There could be no doubt of its being the same buck. His left horn was twisted and the prong or paddle projected straight out to the left, while the tip curved in and forward at the top. He was feeding with only three does in sight and I then told Charley I was going to kill that old gentleman, or go home without an antelope, even if it required the entire ten days of the season. Too late to go after him then, in the driving rain and wet snow, so we climbed on over the pass and found our camp where Martiny had left it.

We moved into the pack-rat infested cabin, whose roof had a huge hole in the center, cooked and ate supper and rolled out our beds. We had little sleep, however, on account of the rats. Next day we worked back into the pass and set up our spotting scopes and started searching the mesa. Soon we located a big band of antelope. Careful scrutiny proved them all does but one huge old buck. He was my old friend of the year before and had gathered up over twenty does for his harem. Soon, three more big bucks came over the sky line and attempted to join the band, but the old crooked-horned buck went for them with a vengeance. He was so old his knees were beginning to buckle at the joint and he looked like an old buck-kneed ram. He was still plenty fast on his feet and soon whipped out the younger bucks. Two of them looked to carry well over 16-inch horns, but the old boy stood a good six inches higher at the withers, and whenever he reached one of the smaller bucks, we could see the hair fly from the tips of those crooked horns. He was wicked with them. The other bucks stayed well out of range of the band after he gave each of them a good drubbing, but they would not leave the vicinity. Clearly the old buck had gathered up all the does on the mesa and was not in any mood to share them with his rivals.

We watched this beautiful scene for a couple of hours. Occasionally one of the smaller bucks would make a quick dash for the herd of does and the old boy would be after him in a flash and those long horns would again send the hair flying. The younger bucks were no match for him and would not make a standing fight, so that he usually raked their rump or sides as they were in full retreat.

Finally they fed around above a point of timber about a quarter mile to the left and west of where I had stalked him with Jess, the year before. Charley and I arranged signals, so he could signal to me which way the band fed, and I started my long mile and a half stalk. Oneil signaled they were feeding to the left, so I worked into a point of timber that ran up on the right of a steep gulch, toward the top of the mesa. When I had reached the extreme tip I found I was within 400 yards, just nice range for a prone shot for the big rifle. The old buck was turned rump to me, horning at a small scrub piñon pine tree. Not wanting to plaster him in the rear end, I waited for him to turn to a more favorable position. I had an excellent prone position, with tight gun sling, and had about settled down from my hard climb.

Then, just as it looked as if my dreams were finally coming true, the wind changed, the band winded me, an old doe barked first, then the buck, and with their white rumps all flashing, with hair standing on end, they ran back up the slope and circled to the right. I slipped back over the ridge and ran up that steep slope for all I was worth, in an effort to catch them at the head of the draw. They soon flashed around the head of that basin and again stopped at 500 yards. Setting the scope up from 400 to 500 yards, I bedded down for a shot. Finally the old buck exposed his chest, and just as I started squeezing the trigger the band again took off in a hard run, around to the right, but not getting much farther away. Again I dropped back out of sight, crossed the draw and worked up under cover of some larger sage on the other side. Soon the band again came in sight at 500 yards and stopped. The does started feeding, but the old buck was looking my way. I believe he had caught a glimpse of me. From a good prone position, I watched for an opening. His back and head were clearly visible over the does but for some time they gave me no opening. Finally, they fed clear of him, leaving me a clear shot, and I instantly brought the cross wires to bear on the center of the white patch just behind the shoulder and started the trigger squeeze. When only an ounce or so remained on the trigger pull, a doe jumped forward, just behind the buck. Knowing at such long range the slug would go through both animals, I refrained from shooting. I am sure the old buck saw me then, for he left that band of does on a hard run and went back to the left, out on the extreme top of the mesa, where he could see everything in all directions for a full half mile. The younger bucks instantly joined the band of does. I lay out of sight in the sage while Charley climbed up to me.

There was no possible chance of getting onto the old buck again that day from all indications, so we watched the band feed on around the mountain top to the east, and after they had been gone for a half hour, Oneil and I slipped along after them. We decided we might as well try to get in range and allow Charley to kill the next finest head, if possible, and try for the big boy again the next day. I was determined to kill him or none. We worked clear around the east slope of the mesa, seeing only tracks of the feeding band and old beds in the slide-rock, much like mountain sheep beds. Nearing the north shoulder of the mesa about a half mile from where I had killed my buck the year before, we located the band in a big grassy swale some half mile across. We picked up a shallow draw and crawled up it to the head, where it ended in some sparse but tall sagebrush. The band then looked to be fully 500 yards away and Oneil did not want to chance a shot at such a range with the .250 Oneil Magnum he carried, nor would he consent to using my .280 Dubiel. The best buck was a beauty, with very symmetrical even head, which was what Charley wanted. The left side of his neck, however, was marked differently than any antelope I had ever seen before. Instead of the usual two white bars it carried a mass of tan spots in a solid white background, a pinto.

The sun had come out hot, and with no further cover available and the band still out of range, we decided to simply lie there and await developments. My old buck was still on his high ground about a mile to the west and there he remained most of the day, watching in all directions and making no attempt to bed down. The day wore along slowly for several hours and Oneil went to sleep. Lying on his back he snored prodigiously. We had the wind in our favor, but about four o'clock in the afternoon, I believe, an old doe must have heard his snoring, for she started working our way, stopping to look directly at our position in the sage, then advancing again. Clearly, she was excited and had seen the top of us, or heard Charley's snores, so I woke him up and bade him get ready as the bucks were also liable to take alarm from the advancing doe and come our way. Sure enough, all three bucks jumped up from their beds and started watching the doe as she advanced. Soon she started barking, clearly giving the alarm. Then the bucks came across the swale in a run and joined her. Charley asked me the range and I told him it looked like 300 yards as near as I could tell, lying as flat to the ground as humanly possible. The bucks also raised their white rump patches and started looking our way and barking occasionally, but they had not seen us. The doe was clearly the worst alarmed and started running to the right. They stopped just across a small wash and I told Oneil to shoot at the buck farthest to the left and be quick about it, as they were going to take off. I held my breath and waited for his shot until I almost had heart failure. Then, just as the leaders started to move, the .250 Oneil Magnum barked and Charley's pinto buck went down in a heap. The rest of the band ran on around the slope and over a shoulder out of sight, while we remained hidden until the last animal had disappeared and for some time afterwards — to make sure no buck or doe turned back higher up the ridge for a look-see and spotted us. After a half hour, none appeared, so we straightened up for the first time in several hours. Imagine our surprise on pacing the distance to find it only around 150 yards. Had we been able to rise up and study the intervening ground, we could have made a better estimate. Oneil's rifle was sighted for 200 yards as I remember and the bullet took his buck in the top of the white patch, directly behind the shoulder, and blew up in the lungs; one fragment had also severed the spine, putting him down and out instantly. He was a beauty with 16⅛-inch horns and Oneil was delighted.

We dressed him out, after removing the beautiful head and cape, and flagged him with our handkerchiefs to keep coyotes away until the morning, when we would come back for the rest of him. We worked up over the top of the mesa through a low saddle as the sun went down, entirely satisfied with our wonderful day's hunt. We had dropped down the other side of the top and out on the mesa for a quarter mile, when, looking to the west, where the old buck had spent the day, I saw him on the sky line at 500 yards. Instantly I dropped to prone position and turned the safety. Having no time to change the scope for 500 yards, and knowing it was zeroed for 300 down at 4000 feet, I raised the cross hairs up just level with the tops of his wide-spreading horns and started squeezing the trigger. I knew that slug should drop into his chest someplace, as he faced directly toward us. However, again I was not in time, as he whirled and ran before I could shoot and I silently cursed that single trigger and its military pull. If it had been a double set trigger, that buck would have been mine, right then. He was only in sight one jump, but that one jump showed him headed back around toward the basin where Charley had killed his buck, so I jumped up and ran that steep quarter mile back to the top of the saddle as fast as I could leg it. Charley followed but could not keep up with me. Just over the top, I flopped prone in a little flat and waited. I well knew that old buck would stick to the high ground, and unless he had already crossed ahead of me would soon be along in search of his harem. He was much too wise to drop down below the ridge tops, and no doubt he had heard Charley's single rifle shot. Soon his huge horns appeared over the sky line to my left and about on a level with me. He was heading on around the slope to where Oneil had killed his buck, working lower on the ridge. I waited, with the rifle trained on those horns, then his head appeared and he stopped for a look all around. Dusk was fast approaching and I lay well screened in the shadow of some sparse sage, so he never saw me. He continued to work down that ridge, with more of his body coming into view each time he stopped for a look. Soon the whole of his body came in sight and by this time I had taken up all slack on the trigger and put considerable pressure on the main pull, when he stopped again. As the cross wires settled steadily in the white patch behind the right shoulder, I finished the trigger pull. The big rifle recoiled, and I had a momentary glimpse of the buck making a long twisting jump downhill out of sight, as I jumped to a standing position and threw out the fired case. Then, just as I thought I had missed, for no reason I could understand, I heard the bullet strike home. The range had looked to be only 200 yards, but again I had little time or chance to size up the intervening ground, and when I rose up could see two more low ridges lying between me and the one on which the buck had stood. Charley soon came over the saddle; said he had stopped and held his breath and waited at my shot, hoping to hear the slug strike, but when he did not hear it had concluded I had missed; then the plunk of that slug had come to him clearly, even over the top of the ridge, as he had been higher than the antelope. He had pulled off his hat and yelled in sheer joy. I told him where I had held, so we started pacing the distance, knowing the buck should have received a fatal hit. Soon we saw the top of one huge horn projecting up above the sparse sage and made the distance at just 360 long steps of a yard or over downhill. One of us paced it at 360 and the other at 362, so we decided to call it 360 yards as both had long checked our pacing by a yardstick and knew we were about right. The 150-grain slug had struck low behind the right shoulder, penetrating the lower tip of the heart, and gone on through the body. He had made only a few jumps and piled up. Luckily, no hair was rubbed from his lower shoulder and we marveled at the size of him and his huge head. Oneil and I each took some pictures and due to the high elevation they came out swell, even in late evening dusk. We removed his grand old head and dressed him out as darkness fell, then worked over the summit and down to Oneil's head, after flagging the carcass with one pair of my socks. I knew no coyote would ever come near that carcass after all the sweating I had done that day. If he had been at lower elevation I would have missed him clean, as the rifle shot high.

After cleaning and curing the skull, it measured 17½-inch length for both horns with a spread of 17½. For a time it held fourth place in the world's records for the species and still goes seventh place in the last book of records. The head hangs over my desk as I write these lines and an oil painting I did this winter of the old buck with a doe, in typical natural setting, hangs from an adjoining wall, fitting tributes to the finest antelope I have ever seen, or ever expect to see. I have killed record antelope since that day in 1936, but never expect to kill a finer one, or a smarter old buck who will afford so much genuine pleasure in the taking. He was a grand specimen, well worth all my efforts over two seasons and one of the finest trophies I have ever taken. These experiences will give the novice an idea of what can be expected when you go after antelope on your own two hind legs, in a sportsmanlike manner. They are one of our finest game animals, even though of small size, and I hope they are maintained in fair numbers for many generations of sportsmen to hunt, until eternity.

XVII

Tracking and Managing Wounded Game

Tracking

EXCEPT for men who live in the hills and spend much of their life trailing either game, horses or cow brutes, and the natives who *must* be able to trail their game, tracking is fast becoming a lost art in this country. The skilled old hunter, trapper or cowman is usually a very good tracker, but the average city-raised individual can follow only a fresh track in the snow. Many years' experience are required to become an expert tracker. Our old Indian scouts were usually very adept at the art. Likewise many Indians are wonderful trackers.

As in most other accomplishments, one must use his head as well as his eyes, if he would become really expert. Some folks believe the native Indian is a better tracker than an equally well-trained white man, but in my experience this has not proved true, when whites were equally well trained in the art. In fact I have, myself, found trails after the Indians had quit and curled up under a spruce tree and have seen the same thing happen many times, with other whites and Indians.

To the expert, a misplaced stone or dead limb, scuffed leaves or a broken twig, all tell their tale. Such men usually started trailing the milk cows when quite young, or trailing up their saddle horse, or working out the tracks of small game when trapping, and as the years go by they quite naturally become ever more expert in reading sign. A real hunter must of necessity be an expert tracker, for tracking is part and parcel of all big game hunting. Until you can instantly pick up game tracks, even though very indistinct and over difficult ground, you are not a good hunter. Regardless of how cool and deadly a game shot you may be, you must still be able to trail the game, or else you need a competent guide who can and will do so, when necessary.

No hunter likes to wound and lose game, even temporarily, but the best hunters and rifle shots who ever lived have wounded and lost big game. Those who haven't have done all their big game killing from a swivel chair. In spite of every precaution, you will sooner or later have a hang-fire that will throw you off, or the game will jump just as you shoot and you will inflict a fatal but slow-killing wound and may well lose the game. I have had this happen many times, both in my own game killing and also when guiding sportsmen. Van Stull and I were slowly working our way up an Oregon hillside with pack and saddle horses, intending to make the top of the ridge and traverse it for some miles. Nearing the top we jumped a nice fat two-point mule buck. Needing meat badly, I simply fell off my horse as the buck ran past me at 30 yards. Pulling the Springfield from the scabbard, I held for his heart when he stopped on the ridge top at 100 yards. He was standing, quartering away from me, and I intended slipping the 172-grain W.T.C. Company bullet in behind the left foreleg and out front of chest, so as not to injure any meat. Just as the rifle cracked, that buck jumped, and instead of hitting his heart I cut off the right hind leg above the hock joint and saw it swing and the foot fly up above his back, during that last jump in sight. Though both of us had long been expert trackers, that buck went over the ridge and down on the steep Snake River slope that was covered with scattered timber and large slide-rock. He left no trail on those big boulders and though we spent the rest of that day, all the next and part of third day we never found him, only a few drops of blood leading down on the river side. He left no marks on the big hard slide-rock and no moss was present to peel and scrape. Neither did our circling ahead and into every likely cover for several miles produce that young buck.

Usually game will cross some patch of soft ground, or will disturb grass or break some brush or knock moss from logs or rocks, sufficient to allow a good tracker to follow them, or at least get the general direction of flight or traverse, but when you get into the big dry slide-rock with neither moss nor patches of soft ground, or hillsides covered with dense and thickly grown bear grass, then you are out of luck unless you have a blood trail, or the patch of rock or bear grass is small in extent. Then you can usually circle and pick up the trail on more likely ground. A bird dog does not circle and quarter the ground for nothing, neither does a good Walker foxhound, and the hunter can well emulate them. Usually if you circle long enough and in ever-widening circles you will be able to pick up the trail, but in some instances we have seen the best men in the game stopped cold, when the terrain was such as described and continuous in every direction.

Big heavy animals are always more easily trailed than smaller big game such as deer, sheep and goats. The larger animals have so much more weight that they will roll or move rocks on which the lighter animals would skip along without leaving a trace. Heavier game also cuts down into grass to a much greater extent. Goats in particular are very hard to trail at times, especially when they stay on solid cliffs where a mere man has an awful time traveling at all. Running game is always easily trailed, in comparison with slowly walking game. When running their hoofs or claws will turn up more sod, or roll more rocks, or break more limbs, or disturb more grass or leaves.

Many times we have lost the trail of animals in big spruce bottoms where a solid carpet of dead needles lay six inches deep on the forest floor. A walking deer will often leave no trace on such ground because the needles will spring back in place after his passage. Likewise a bear or cat can walk slowly across such a spring carpet without leaving many traces. If they run across such ground, it is a different matter and they are then easily tracked.

Only last fall I lost two wounded animals when guiding Gene and Virginia Wilkinson. I had teased an elk bull with the bugle until he finally came for us, stopping at sight of us at about 100 yards on a steep mountain slope. He was standing perfectly still facing us at Gene's shot from the .35 Whelen with 250-grain Winchester Soft Point bullet at around 2700 feet. Gene hit him square in the front of the neck. He dropped, then started kicking with his hind feet and I asked Gene to bust him again, but he replied he had hit him in the chest and did not want to shoot again. Again I asked him to bust him, as I was sure it was not a chest shot and that he would regain his feet. The bull finally got his hind legs under him and kicked himself down the mountain for 30 yards, rooting his nose in the ground before he regained his feet. Then in a flash he was around a tree bole and gone and Gene's second shot struck the tree.

An elk shot in the chest would in most cases have staggered and whirled and run for a distance, or dropped cold if the heart was hit when full of blood. This bull acted like a neck shot to me and trailing him soon proved that was the case. A six-inch hank of the long mane hair was found clotted with blood, proving the slug struck the center of the neck as he faced us. That 250-grain bullet intended for 2200 feet and driven 500 feet faster had simply blown up on reaching the spine of the neck. We proved this to be the case later on a still finer bull. The mountainside was crisscrossed with both old and fresh elk tracks, of both bulls and cows, and even after Gene's two shots I obtained an answer on the bugle from another bull. Tracking was very difficult, owing to the dry nature of the ground and the many tracks going in every direction, some walking and feeding and some running. Our bull made only a few jumps to take him out of sight, then slowed to a walk, picking his trail through every patch of bear grass and slide-rock he could find. After the first 50 yards, only a minute drop of blood showed occasionally. We trailed that old chappie from just after daylight in the morning until one o'clock in the afternoon with neither breakfast nor lunch. Tracking was far too difficult to let Gene try it so I had him hold the last track I had seen with a drop of blood until I found another. Finally, out on the open ridge where the ground was flinty hard and mostly all rock, and other elk had crossed during the night, we lost the trail completely, but knowing elk I figured this one would head past a spring and through a low saddle, so we circled ahead and sure enough picked up his trail again and followed it over the Divide and onto the north slope in dense second growth timber where about all the ground was covered with bear grass. He had practically stopped bleeding and I well knew was then miles ahead, so we had to give him up.

If that slug cut his trachea or windpipe, he died, if not he may have recovered, and such I hope is the case. Later on the trip, Virginia had her Krag loaded with Western 220-grain Soft Point Boattail bullets intended only for heavy game and shot a nice buck behind the shoulders broadside. We could plainly see the dust fly on the other side as he stood on the steep sidehill, and also saw hair fly as well. He was about 125 yards away across a deep gulch. He staggered a couple seconds, then whirled and ran around and over the shoulder of the mountain. That buck died but we never found him. The elk I had trailed over two miles and I trailed this mule buck about the same distance. He was in a bad way and fell over a cliff and fell down several times in jumping windfall. He bled only a very occasional drop, showing clearly that bullet did not expand much, if any, on his thin rib cage and lungs. Finally, after falling over another cliff, he negotiated a huge patch of very large slide-rock, each boulder being two to three feet in diameter, and on these he left only an occasional drop of blood while a few short sheared hairs fell out of his coat, but we managed to take him across that slide and into a big spruce bottom. We trailed him to the creek, but after crossing never could tell his tracks from others and finally lost him completely after putting in most of the day. His bleeding had by then completely stopped and we were out of luck. Later, when packing out the camp, our horses scented him up the hillside in a dense thicket and within 100 yards of where we had searched for him. Of course he was then spoiled to high heaven.

Early morning dew, or frost, aids materially in both picking up tracks and in determining their age. Likewise as the sun dries the dew or frost from the tracks, the dirt will crumble around the edges of said tracks, again giving the experienced tracker considerable assistance in determining their age. The more knowledge you have of the game hunted, the better will be your chances of following it over difficult ground, when wounded. Unless an animal is wounded, never stay on its trail, but always keep well to windward, if you would ultimately get a shot.

In general, tracking over fresh snow or after a hard rain and on soft ground is very very easy, and anyone can then follow a trail with little or no difficulty. At times you may wound an animal during a hard snowstorm. We have seen this happen many times, and if the storm is severe enough little time can be given the animal — one must take the tracks immediately. The best one can then do is to stay clear of the tracks and well to windward and circle in hopes of obtaining a finishing shot.

Again, game may be wounded late in the evening. This is very often the case, and as daylight fades little can be done about the matter. If you have a good blood trail, the game may not go far and can be followed by the aid of a flashlight, but as a rule, wounded game lost in gathering darkness will be spoiled when found next day and only the head or trophy will be saved. Just another reason why we should make every effort to hit game right the first shot. Also another good reason for being out in the game country at the first break of dawn, when you have the whole day before you.

Game, except for bear, always feeds and travels more in early morning and late evening than at any other time of the day, also many animals travel and feed at night, particularly on moonlight nights, and bear and cats are both nocturnal. Generally speaking, black bear will be more often found feeding in late evening than in early morning. They are lazy animals and, like city folks, often stay up late at night and sleep late in the morning.

Though game often feeds and travels upwind, so as to get the scent of any enemy in advance of them, it practically always circles enough to also pick up the scent of anything trailing it. Animals, as a general rule, expect trouble in the form of a hunter or predator following their back trail, which is just another reason why we must stay clear of that back trail, except to cut it occasionally, to be sure of its course. Once an animal has scented you and knows you are on its trail, it's virtually impossible ever to get to see it in timber country, if you stay on the tracks. On the other hand if you merely cut the trail occasionally, then circle well to windward and keep the wind in your favor, you have every chance of ultimately getting ahead of the feeding game or seeing it to one side of your general course. Watch always to each side as much as to the front and even behind you as well, as you never can tell just which way circling feeding game will ultimately decide to go.

During the rut, it is well to follow a band of circling does or cows as they feed along, likewise staying clear of their trail as much as possible, for at such times the wary old males you are after are also hunting the females and will trail them for miles until they come up with the band. We have watched bull elk and caribou as well as moose trailing the cows, and also buck deer and rams as well, so even though you are circling well to windward of the trail of the band, keep a sharp lookout on all sides and behind you, as a buck, or bull, may be doing the same thing and come in from behind.

Elk, moose, caribou and deer use their nose a great deal in trailing a band of females, and we have watched them quarter the ground over which a band of cows or does had fed, for all the world like a hound dog. At other times they would sniff the brush through which the band had passed, picking the scent from the twigs and brush. The nose of many big game animals will tell them instantly far more than mere man can learn of a trail by several minutes' close scrutiny. They know instantly which way the band is feeding, just as a dog can instantly tell which way game has traveled.

There is little use in trailing a traveling buck or bull when he is alone during the rut, as he will cover far more ground in a day than the human hunter and most likely keep to windward of his back trail to catch the scent of any man following him. The more he has been hunted the more religious he will be in occasionally circling and picking up the scent of his back trail. Further, he travels day and night until he finds a harem of his very own or whips some other rival away from the band. Better by far to locate a band of females or a section of country over which they feed daily and watch from some vantage point, or watch their back trail, rather than attempt to run down a lone buck or bull who is traveling. If two or more bulls or bucks are together, then you have a much better chance as they will stop and feed and bed, but the lone males, when traveling, hardly stop for food and eat a little as they travel.

All horned animals are much easier hunted during the rut than at any other time, once you know their ways and where to look for them. Only by being able to read sign correctly can anyone correctly size up a new game country. In all sections of the West that I have hunted, from Mexico to Alaska, you will find game pockets and other sections lying adjacent that from every practical standpoint are just as suitable for the game, yet for some unknown reason will not be inhabited by the game at all. Why this is, no one seems to know. The feed may be ideal and even better than in another valley a few miles distant, yet several species may regularly use the poor valley while none at all use the good one. Of course stray animals like a traveling grizzly or wolf, or a traveling ram or bull, may cover a wide range in their fall search for the females of the species, but the fact remains they will not stop long in some sections that to the human eye appear ideal. Success, then, depends to no small extent on being able to correctly interpret the sign you cross. If you or your guide cannot find tracks of the game desired in a few days' scouting, it is a pretty safe bet none exist and it is better to move to another locality, even though only a few miles distant, as it may be a game pocket.

One can soon learn to tell the different animal tracks, but more time will usually be required to tell the bucks from the does, or bulls from cows. Also one must see enough tracks to learn the variation in size and those that spell a big male, as well as the average tracks that can often be either sex. A short distance will often reveal the sex of the animal even though the tracks are of a size which could be either male or female.

Moose tracks look more like a gigantic deer track than anything else and have long sharp points to the toes. The stride and width of the track as well as the length help in determining sex. Also one should watch all beds, wallows or other similar places for signs of sex. The bull will disturb snow from branches where a cow would slip quietly through without knocking it off. With elk, the tracks more closely resemble those of domestic cattle, the toes of older bulls usually being well rounded, while the young bulls and cows make similar tracks, but the bulls will always be much wider.

With deer tracks the large buck will always stand out instantly, while the smaller buck is much harder to tell from the does. Usually, in the hunting season, you will find where the buck or bull has rubbed his horns or urinated in his bed or at some rubbing tree. Also when in soft ground or snow the buck's dewclaws show more plainly than those of a doe. Also in deep snow the buck will drag his feet out of each track to a much greater extent than will does, and this fact is true of about all our big game of the horned species. A big heavy animal will always print deeper, and if very fat may spread the toes somewhat.

Caribou tracks look like nothing else on this earth except reindeer. They are very large and very rounded and spread widely. Further the caribou always shows his dewclaws as they bear on almost any ground. Years of traveling muskeg have made him that way, and the combination of wide flaring rounded hoofs of great size for his body and the supporting dewclaws enables him to cover marshy ground that would bog almost any other animal. Big bull tracks are quickly and easily distinguished from those of the cows on account of the size and spread of the print, as well as by the extreme blunt curve of the toes and the depth of the dewclaw prints.

With mountain sheep we have a different track entirely. The heel pad is more square on the back and forward the track is cupped much more than that of deer or moose. Elk, as well as caribou, show considerable cupping of the hoofs, while deer and moose have distinct pads almost the full length of the hoof. Sheep tracks will show considerably more raised centers than deer tracks and once you know sheep tracks they are instantly seen for what they are on most any ground. Old rams will almost always be much larger and wider than ewes and the points of the hoofs will be more uneven, and often one side will be longer than the other. Old rams will also have quite blunt toes. Their beds are always prominent on any ram range and you can nearly always determine the sex from them. Usually they will dig out a small depression for their bed, the size of which is an instant indication of the sex of the sheep.

Mountain goat tracks differ from all others and are much more nearly square, the front of the toes being almost as blunt and square as the heels of the hoofs. In snow it is often difficult to tell at a glance which way the beast is going, owing to these peculiarly shaped feet. When you do get a good print in snow or mud around some cliff spring it is unmistakable. The old billies have much larger feet than the nannies and are instantly seen for what they are. Like the sheep they have soft rubber cushions for heel pads and the whole hoof is nearly as wide as it is long.

Antelope have very small hoofs and their tracks resemble sheep more than deer. Old buck tracks are discernible from their width and length as well as their spread from one side to the other of the body. This spread of tracks is also an immediate indication of sex of all our hoofed game. Antelope have no dewclaws and their tracks in snow instantly show this, but many of our antelope range where little snow will be found during the hunting season. The antelope track is fairly short for its width on old bucks, more like sheep tracks, while the does, like ewe sheep, will have longer, slimmer tracks.

With bear one can instantly tell from a good impression whether the animal is a grizzly or one of the black species. The black's claws will strike very close to the toe pads while the grizzly's claws will strike much farther ahead, except during late fall when they may be worn down considerably from a season's digging. Even then in soft earth where he has dug for roots, or ants, or bugs, the grizzly's claw will lie flatter to the ground and will show more of its length, while the black's claw will show only the short curved points hitting the ground. Again size is a good indication of the type of bear and the grizzly has a more pointed heel than the black.

On hard ground the grizzly's claws will lie more closely together than those of a black but on soft ground either species will spread the toes and claws. With all species, unless the animal stops and turns, you will usually see the hind track overlapping the front one. With all the horned species of game, the older males will often show the hind track lagging slightly while younger animals will often overreach with the hind foot. Heavy old males will also show heavier heel prints while does and young cows travel more on their toes and this is quickly evident from the tracks.

Cat tracks are unmistakable, being nearly round. Cougar and bobcat tracks have much the same characteristics, except that the cougar tracks are so much larger. Lynx tracks on the other hand are different. The foot, being completely covered on the pads with fur, will show as a big round ball of cotton in the snow or mud, and while the weight on the foot and toe pads will make a deeper impression, showing the unmistakable cat outline, it will not show the clear pad impressions characteristic of the cougar and bobcat. Lynx tracks will also be much larger than bobcat's and often quite as large as a fair-sized lion's.

Coyote and wolf tracks are easily distinguished from dog tracks, due to their much greater length in proportion to width, and due also to the fact that the toes are carried closely together on all hard ground and the two longer toes project a considerable distance ahead of the next two. Fox tracks on the other hand, while usually furred over like lynx tracks, are more round and much more closely resemble a dog track in general contour.

With bear, a good indication of the size of the beast, and also whether it is a grizzly or a really big black, is the width of the trail. Really big bear have wide treads and leave considerable grass or snow between their left and right legs in traveling. The wider the trail the bigger the bear is a safe bet.

Managing Wounded Game

Whenever you shoot at a big game animal, watch its reactions to the shot very closely. Most game will react to the impact of a slug but some

Two old photos by the late Mr. Huffman taken in 1882 outside of Miles City, Montana, showing a killing of cows and spike buffalo and the skinning. Note the old Sharps buffalo rifles and the spacing of carcasses

Bull buffalo killed by author with his 16-pound .45–120–566 Sharps buffalo rifle

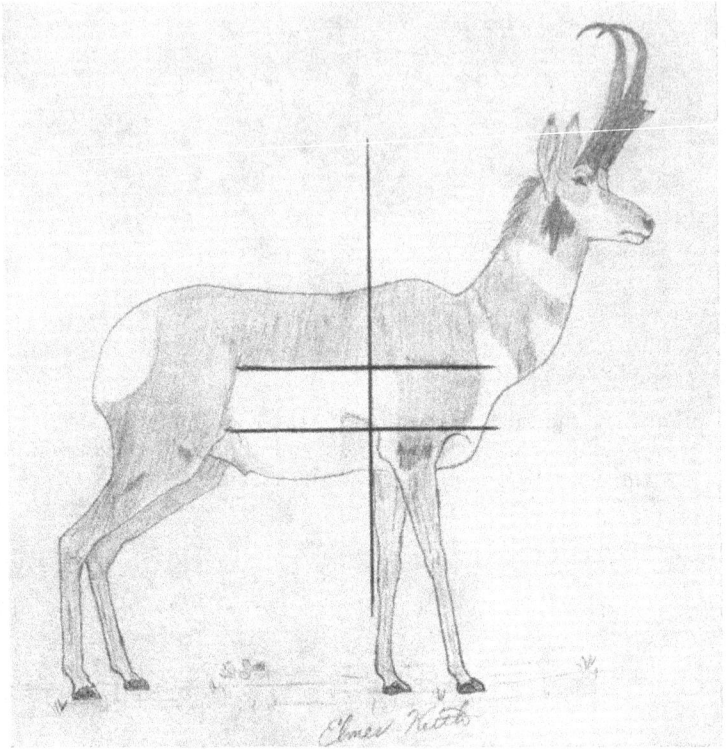

Aiming points for antelope
Top: high lung shot; *bottom:* heart shot

Aiming point for mule deer
Heart shot

game animals do not — namely mountain goat and elk and often moose, which will absorb vital hits with no apparent reaction whatever.

Bear and cats almost always react instantly to the impact of a slug, as do most deer, sheep, antelope and caribou. They may jump into a hard run, or they may merely flinch or hump up their backs. At any rate, observe them closely, whether they stand, go down, or jump into a run. If they run, that first jump often tells the tale. They may carry one ear lower than the other, or it may be a twisting crooked jump that plainly spells a hit. At other times they may simply start or flinch at the impact. Usually when they stand still and hump up the back, the bullet is placed too far to the rear, through paunch, guts or liver. Observe also, if they run, whether it is an intelligent course they are pursuing, or whether it is just blind flight and the animal crashes into trees and brush as it runs blindly from a fatal hit.

At all times, remain in your tracks. If the game goes down, well and good, but reload as quickly as possible and watch the creature. If it raises itself up on either front or hind feet, bust it again, striving for a heart or lung shot. If the game does not go down, then unless you are very sure from long experience of both your aim and the cartridge you are using, shoot again. Ninety per cent of the meat we have seen wasted was on the dead and soured frames of animals that were lost wounded, either through improperly placed bullets or through the use of inadequate cartridges. It's far better to mess up a few pounds of stew than to lose the whole animal, trophy and all.

If the animal goes down and stays down at the shot, watch it and remain in a position for an instant shot if necessary. Give it plenty of time to die, then approach slowly. Many animals will play possum until you are almost on them, then jump up and run, and in the case of big bear they don't always run away. Never lay your rifle down until you are certain the beast is dead. This can best be determined by examination of the eyes. So long as the eyes are clear and with expression in them, stay away from the beast and only approach after the eyes turn glassy. Make no attempt to dress the beast too soon, as muscle reaction may kick your knife into your person. Give them plenty of time, then while standing in back of the beast lean over and whack the hind shins with the back of your knife. If any life or muscle reaction is left they will kick.

If the beast jumps and runs at the shot, sit down and have a good long smoke. If it went off in a blind rush, crashing through brush and timber, you can listen and probably soon hear it fall. If it was hit too far back, then best to give the beast an hour to bed and stiffen, unless a heavy snowstorm, or rainfall, or coming darkness prevents.

Next go to the spot where the beast stood, and it is well always to locate the exact spot by some stump, rock, tree or other landmark, or you may have trouble finding it if at long range or across a canyon in dense brush. Mark the spot plainly in this way, then go to that exact spot and determine if possible where your bullet struck. Look for blood, also sheared hair, and for the impact of the bullet in the earth unless the beast was on level ground or sky line. In such cases look for its impact on any trees that may have stood behind the beast. Make every possible effort to locate the strike of the bullet if it missed or went through the animal, as much can be learned from it.

If you have broken a leg, the trail will clearly show it, as that leg will not print on the ground but will swing and scrape dirt or snow. If the animal was one of a band, be doubly careful as another member of the band may brush against it in flight, rub off some blood on itself and then it too will leave a blood trail, especially on snow. Often some animal of the band may be standing closer to you than the one shot at, and when they take off, this animal may run in the tracks of the wounded beast, further confusing the hunter. Note the color of the blood where the beast stood, if any is present. Dark brown blood spells gut or paunch hits while bright blood may be either legs or other body hits. Bright frothy blood always spells a lung hit.

Any wounded animal can always be depended on to watch its back track if it is still in its right mind and will very soon circle to see if any pursuer is still on the trail. It will invariably bed downwind of its trail so as to catch your scent, long before you get in sight. Take nothing for granted when trailing a wounded animal. If the ground is bare and no blood trail present, as so often happens when sharp pointed high velocity bullets are driven into a big beast, you may have to follow the trail more or less, but with reasonably good tracking on either ground or snow, stay clear of the trail — merely cut it enough to get its direction and circle well to windward, always watching for any likely bed ground. You can expect the beast to bed where it is well screened by trees or brush from its back trail and you simply must see it first if at all possible. If it is hard hit, and given an hour to stiffen, you will very often find the tracks are circling as the beast looks for a suitable hide-out; then is the time to be doubly cautious and try to locate it in its bed.

Observe closely all logs over which the beast jumps — these will show blood if any is present; also observe all limbs, boughs and brush through which it passes as the height of blood on these will tell much about the placement of the wound. If you are using a small bore high velocity rifle, don't think you have missed because no blood is present, for such loads usually go into the beast with a very tiny entrance hole, then blow up inside. The first jump of the animal usually moves the muscles sufficiently to seal the entrance hole, and then you have no blood trail but a fatally hit animal to trail up. That is one reason I personally prefer rifles throwing long, heavy, round or blunt nosed bullets for all timber shooting, driven at moderate velocities and with sufficient penetration always to go through the beast on broadside shots. Such loads leave a blood trail. Some folks labor under the delusion that big game lives and acts only on instinct, but the writer is certain in his own mind at least that all big game animals reason, and often to far better advantage than some humans we have seen hunting them. If the beast is hit, it knows well enough you will trail it up. It expects to be trailed, for predators have trailed it since it was born, and it will take every possible advantage of cover in its flight.

Many times we have seen old mature deer, elk and sheep that were hard hit use every possible means to cover their trail. Often they would take to a small stream, at other times head along some flinty hard rocky ridge where the tracks would not show. Many times we have seen them double back on their tracks, stepping exactly in each previous hoof print, then when a big windfall was reached or some dense clump of brush or second growth, they would leave the trail in one mighty bound and land far below the brush or log. Even fawn deer and calf elk will double on their trail and jump off to confuse their pursuer, and this is not instinct, but gray matter being put to use.

When trailing a wounded beast, look for and expect him, not directly in front on the trail, but off to one side in some cover, as that is where you will usually find him bedded. As a general rule, we do not like running shooting. It may be lots of fun to the hunter, but produces more gut-shot wounded game than any other form of game shooting. However, when a wounded beast is jumped a second time, get another slug into it if you can, even a leg hit, for you may well know it will travel a long distance if it is able before giving you another chance. In cases where wounded game is jumped, running shooting is justifiable and one should make every possible effort to connect, as long as the game is in sight, and so put the poor beast out of its misery. If animals are running quartering or broadside, don't forget to lead them and get your slug into the front half of the beast when at all possible. Remember, however, that another slug in the rear end is far better than no hit at all.

All wounded game is notoriously hard to kill, because the first bullet imparts about all the shock its nervous system can assimilate. After that first hit, you must strike the brain or spine or bleed the beast empty with heart or lung shots if you would put him down. Remember this, and strive to place that first shot vitally.

If the beast is fatally hit in the chest, its trail will always show this, as it will run blindly with no choice of direction and usually in the same course its nose was pointed when hit. At such times the beast pays no attention to small trees, logs or limbs but simply crashes straight through them, and will jump over a cliff just as quickly as it will go along level ground. Usually you have nothing to worry about when the trail indicates such a hit. Merely load up and smoke out your pipe, then take the trail and you will find the animal dead.

Such wounded animals will go in a hard run as long as life lasts and are then very easily trailed; you need not circle — simply follow the tracks. It is when the beast is gut-shot and able to think and reason that he will run a distance, then walk and use every trick in the trade to cover his tracks or mix them with those of other animals to confuse the tracker. Then you must watch the wind and stay clear of the trail as much as possible, always circling ahead and trying to catch sight of the beast in some open spot. Wounded game can, however, be depended on to take advantage of every vestige of cover at all times. As a general rule game hit too far back behind the belt will jump and kick at its belly the first jump, with one or both hind feet. If too sick to jump, from the shock of a heavy bullet, it will usually hump up and stand with head low and mouth open. When such is the case, better give it another and better placed slug as quickly as possible.

Over twenty years of big game guiding have taught me a lot on this subject and I will try to pass along all the information I can think of in this chapter. If you are not steady when you shoot, and even though you think you have missed, it's always best to trail the beast a half mile or a mile and make sure. A great many times sportsmen have told me they missed. In some cases I could clearly see the beast was hit, at others it showed no signs of being hit yet I found it dead in a half mile of trailing. As above stated, the jumps of broken-legged animals will be shorter if a hind leg and the trailing broken leg plow up ground or snow. The gut-shot animal will make short jumps and will soon slow to a walk if not molested. Remember always that the beast lives in the bottom half of its body and the spine is often nearer the center of the body at the shoulders than at the top of the back. Shoot into the bottom third or half of the body whenever possible. High shoulder shots over the spine may put a beast down temporarily but it may regain its feet. Neck shots that miss the spine are always very unreliable and many animals drop as if pole-axed, then are up and away and often get well in time.

Many hunters will tell you that a deer when hit will drop its tail on the impact of a rifle bullet. With whitetails, this is usually the case, but not always. The first whitetail I killed, when still a small boy in Montana, was running toward us down an old wood road. A cougar had jumped him and was still following him when I shot, as the tracks later showed. We saw the deer first and I sat down in the snow, swung the sights to bear on the chest and gave that particular whitetail a 220-grain .30–06 slug in the center of the chest, wrecking the heart and coming out behind the left shoulder. At the impact of the bullet, the tail, which had been carried down, was flashed up in the air and continued to wave over the deer's back as he ran past my father and me and finally piled up about 100 yards beyond us. Knowing both rifle and load and exactly where I had shot, I made no attempt to shoot again, but that whitetail continued to wave his flag until he dropped. Another time a partner and I were peacefully eating breakfast on Horse Creek, a tributary of the Salmon. Dense fog hovered over the mountains and its lower level reached down to within 100 yards of camp. I had just asked my partner for another cup of coffee, which he was pouring, when my eye caught sight of a big mule buck in the lower edge of the fog and not over 100 yards away up a steep slope. I asked my partner if the buck was good enough to suit him.

For answer, he carefully sat the coffeepot on the coals and reached behind him for his old .35 Model '95 Winchester, which reposed in easy reach against a big yellow pine bole. Swinging around into a comfortable sitting position, just as the buck turned his rump toward us, feeding, he shot him behind the right shoulder, ranging forward through the heart with that 250-grain Soft Point. At the shot that big buck started right up the steep slope at a fast trot, with his tail up and going round and round like a windmill. He continued right up the mountain into the fog with his tail wringing like mad for some 30 yards, then stopped and rolled over backwards and down, right into camp. This buck acted true to form from a heart shot by going in the direction he was headed when hit. Likewise my first whitetail ran right on past us after being hit and never lowered his tail. As a general rule, however, whitetails will raise and flourish their flag when jumped and will also, as a rule, clamp it down when hit, but such is not always the case.

Another fallacy is the age-old saying that a wounded animal will always

[319]

go downhill. While this is usually the case with animals hit too far back and also with three-legged animals, it does not always hold true and we have seen many badly wounded animals turn directly uphill. As before stated, the vitally chest-hit animal will usually go in the direction he is pointed when hit, but many three-legged elk, deer and sheep have, under my observation, gone uphill. Usually a three-legged animal will go either directly uphill or downhill and quite often quartering downhill. That broken leg as it swings bothers its stride when it attempts to go around a sidehill and for this reason it is more apt to turn downhill or else straight uphill.

The sound of the bullet striking also tells the experienced hunter a great deal about the location of the hit. Paunch hits usually produce a dull plunk, while lung hits produce a lighter sound, if the distance is great enough clearly to hear the strike of the bullet after the rifle's report. Leg or other bone hits such as skull hits usually produce a more brittle, sharp sound on impact. If the animal is off any considerable distance, I can usually tell a broken leg by the sound of the slug striking home. It's a sharp tick, like breaking a twig or limb, as compared to the dull sodden plunk of a body hit. Of course, when the range is so short that the rifle's report and the bullet striking home blend together, one will seldom hear the slug strike unless he is using a low velocity rifle like the old .45–70–405 load. At other times, and particularly at long range, if the wind is favorable or you are above the animal, the strike of the slug can often be heard quite plainly. When the game is above the hunter, it is much harder to hear the bullet hit, but often it can be heard.

Wounded game should always be approached with the utmost caution. You never know whether it will run, or decide to fight. I have had three bull elk turn on me and come with a vengeance, and have seen others turn on other hunters I was guiding. Have also seen several buck mule deer go for the hunter and to a finish.

Trailing up a wounded grizzly or Alaskan brown grizzly is always ticklish business. Grizzly will invariably circle and bed in some dense timber or alder thicket where they can get your wind before you see them, and then either sneak quietly away or in some cases lie for you until you are close enough for a charge to carry home. Such a job is always best handled by two men, one keeping a sharp lookout on all sides with rifle ready, while the other does the trailing. At best it is no fun, but occasionally must be done to secure that bear rug or to prevent the escape of a wounded bear.

One instance will suffice. We had crossed the Divide from the Siccanni

River over onto the Halfway River in British Columbia and I was riding along in the extreme rear of the pack string, with the scope sighted .300 Magnum cradled in my left arm. I was watching all the surrounding mountain slopes closely for possible game, a habit formed from so many years in the hills. Two big Stone sheep heads of my killing bobbed along on top of a couple of the packs and I was at peace with the world and thoroughly satisfied with the long two months' trip by pack string. Suddenly I spotted something a half mile away on a side slope that did not look right. Stopping my horse, I whistled to Westley Brown, who was just ahead of me in the trail. He also pulled up his horse, the while whistling to Allen the cook and Edgar Dopp, who were ahead of the string. Telling Westley that if we were in Alaska I would swear that was a grizzly, I raised my rifle and looked at the object through the 2¾ power Hensoldt scope. Sure enough, it was a nice grizzly, peacefully digging roots. I waved to the boys and slipped off my horse. Westley and Al held the pack string while Edgar and I started the long stalk up through a narrow strip of timber and brush that we hoped would put me in at least long range of the bear. Edgar also carried my .375 Magnum, also a Model 70 Winchester. My .300 Magnum was loaded with 180-grain Winchester Open Point Boattail ammunition. Finally we reached the comb of the ridge, only to find the bear was much higher than we were and over 500 yards away across the gulch. Just then he threw his head up, sniffed and started over the mountain. He must have winded the pack string, as we had the wind right as near as we could tell, but one can never be certain of the eddying currents of air in the mountains. At any rate I flopped into a prone position behind a log, and holding the top of the post reticule up over the grizzly's rump the full height of his body, squeezed one off. The rifle kicked up and settled back, then the bear went down and we heard the dull plunk of the slug. We knew it was a good solid hit. The bear, as usual with them, started rolling down the mountain and Ed said, "Hold your fire," which was darn good advice, but wanting to get as many of those tiny 180-grain slugs into him as possible, I held over him again the height of the body and shot. In my haste I had forgotten that he was rolling down the mountain and we saw the slug kick up dust over the rolling bear. Then the bear regained his feet, but was apparently dizzy from the first slug and started walking around the side of the mountain. Again I held over him the height of the body, but forgot that he was moving; and we saw that bullet kick up dust at perfect elevation but behind the moving bear. This shot turned him back up and over the mountain. As my position was very strained, I jumped up over the log and assumed a good sitting position. I was using the sling and had the rifle zeroed for 300 yards. Again I held the height of his body over him and fired. This time he went down again and later we heard the slug strike. We clearly saw all four of his feet extended up in the air, and throwing the bolt and reloading I held just over the level of those extended paws and fired my last round in the rifle. We heard this bullet strike plainly also and knew it was a good solid hit. Then, as I reloaded, the grizzly regained his feet and went on over the ridge out of sight.

Edgar and I climbed our ridge to the same level as the bear had been, then crossed the gulch and looked over the tracks. He was bleeding only a drop or so at a time though we knew he had received three good solid hits, but at such long range it was problematical if any of the three bullets had expanded at all. We trailed him up on top of the ridge, finding where he had dug under a log and lain down for a time, and there we found some blood and silver-tipped hair. After looking the sign over carefully and knowing he had a long distance to the next camp, Edgar decided to go on with the pack string as he did not think much of my chances of ever obtaining that grizzly.

Westley joined us and we asked Edgar to tie up our saddle horses and a couple of packs, with our beds and some grub. We would catch up with the outfit in a day or so, but we were definitely going to get the grizzly or exhaust all possibilities before giving up.

I exchanged the .300 Magnum with Edgar for my .375, as it looked much better to me for the job in hand. The ground on top of the ridge was covered with stiff springy lichen and moss as well as dense huckleberry brush, already turned red from the fall frosts. Over this carpet the bear left no tracks at all. Westley tied up his old saddle horse and we started trailing that bear, one of us with ready rifle while the other progressed foot by foot on hands and knees. When a drop of blood was found, no matter how tiny (and some were no larger than No. 6 birdshot), one man held that spot while the other crawled along until another was found. From years of trapping Westley was also an expert and we progressed over the top of the mountain and down the other side in about an hour and a half. We found several places where the grizzly had dug out the moist earth under spruce trees, where their low-hanging bows would completely conceal him. He had lain for a time in each of these damp earth beds. At each he left a little blood. Then with his wounds coated with soft damp earth the blood would stop dropping and we had only an occasional turned leaf or stone or broken twig, or an occasional shot-off hair that dropped to the ground, to guide us. It was slow ticklish work, as we could not see more than 10 yards and often not half that distance, in the dense covered north slope of the mountain. Even though it was very brushy, and there were plenty of evergreens, with boughs extending clear to the ground, the footing was good for a horse; and well knowing a horse could smell that bear much farther than we could see him, Westley went back for his horse, then rode a slow circle in front of our position. That wise old horse cocked his ears on down the mountain and sniffed but did not snort, so we tied him up again and proceeded with our slow trailing.

Getting tired of trailing, I had just straightened up and taken over the watching business, as Westley crawled in front of me. We had not traveled more than 200 yards beyond where the horse had looked down the mountain when Westley hissed, "I see him." The grizzly had dug out a pocket under another big tree root, and as I stepped to the side for a shot he rose out of his bed on his hind legs to his full height, and started to swing around toward us. He had heard, but not seen us. He never finished that swing around, as I broke both shoulders with a 270-grain slug and down he went in a heap. He groaned for several minutes before passing out, while we watched him with ready rifles. That proved the finest bear pelt I have ever obtained. Skinning him out while Westley boiled the kettle and made bannock revealed that two of the 180-grain .300 Magnum slugs had gone in the left ham and out the right flank without any trace of expansion at all. The third 180-grain had struck right under the tail and must have expanded in the water and root filled colon, as it lay in pieces under the skin of the right flank. The 270-grain .375 Magnum fired at only a few feet range broke both shoulders, cleaned the aorta off the top of the heart and lodged under the skin of the right shoulder, also in pieces but leaving a two-inch wound channel through his vitals. I doubt if one man in a hundred would ever have been able to trail up that bear, and neither would we, except for many years' experience. His pelt was a beauty, black ears, legs and feet, and the whole top of shoulders and back cream colored with silver-tipped guard hair, perfect in every detail and a real trophy for any hunter.

What little air movement there was was uphill, in our favor, after the bear went down the north slope, and we constantly smoked in order to check said movements, or we would probably never have seen him again.

A wounded grizzly should never be allowed to escape if it is possible to trail him up, as in all probability he will later become an old sorehead and may cause some innocent person trouble. A good percentage of unprovoked bear charges are by old bear who have previously been wounded by man. If you are faced with the charge of a wounded bear, which is rare, then you must be ready for instant action; further, you need a good powerful rifle that will put him down, preferably with one shot. If the bear comes around a sidehill at you, a shot to the shoulder on the lower side will nearly always put him down long enough to get in more killing hits. It is not a fatal shot but will nearly always roll him over and stop his course and give more time for the finish. It is often more effective at very close range than a shot into the chest, as a stopper.

Wounded bear should never be crowded. Give them plenty of time to make a bed and stiffen up. They will nearly always dig out under a log or tree root to rub their wounds in the cool damp earth unless snow covers the ground. While all herbivorous game, if left overnight without dressing out, will sour and spoil, a bear is usually more tenacious of life and may well be found still alive the next day, when trailed up. Likewise all hoofed game is much easier tracked under difficult conditions than the soft pads of bear or cats.

If you are using a saddle horse and hunting partly open terrain, it is well to watch his ears and actions when he catches strange scents. Horses can smell game a great distance, and much farther than you can see it in timber. Sometimes the horse's nose can thus be used to advantage when the track of a wounded animal is lost. He will usually let you know if he scents it.

Remember exactly where your front sight or scope reticule lies on the game, when the rifle recoils. Then, if you do have a cripple on your hands, check by the amount of blood, if any, how far it is thrown out from the body, which would indicate arterial or lung flow, or whether it merely runs down a leg of the beast. If the beast beds, check carefully where the blood is in the bed. In this way one can often determine exactly how the animal is hit and how best to manage its pursuit. If the beds and trail show a paunch-hit beast you may well have a long trail ahead unless it is given plenty of time to stiffen. If you have a good reliable camp dog within a few miles and plenty of daylight hours available and no snow, it is well to leave the beast for a time and get the dog before working out the trail. The beast may then be stiffened until it will not get up, and if it does the dog may be able to trail it where you would not.

Practice trailing at every possible opportunity, either game or livestock or your pet dog or cat, and see how far you can trail it. Such practice will sooner or later come in very handy in big game hunting. Learn the effect of frost on tracks and game beds and how the tracks look as their edges crumble from the sun, in either wet earth or snow. In time you can tell within a very few hours when the tracks were made. The age of the droppings can also be told by their moisture content. For old hillbillies like myself, reading sign is habitual; we do it without thinking. The ground to us is a newspaper and we constantly read it from day to day, as a city man reads his morning paper over the breakfast table. I never come home from town without a glance at the road telling me if I have had company in my absence, either by car, saddle horse or on foot, and very often I know who was at the ranch by the horse tracks or the tread of the car or the size and shape of the human tracks. As the years go by the person living in the hills learns all this as a matter of course, but the average city man will see little or nothing and the services of a good guide will usually pay him dividends. It is impossible for him to emulate the skill of a man raised in the wilds, but he can soon learn if he will only apply his senses. As I have many times stated, I like to do all my hunting before I shoot, and this should be the motto of every hunter.

If you hunt extensively, you will sooner or later shoot at an animal in late evening and wound it, and before anything can be done about the matter it will be dark. If it is a horned trophy animal, one can often find it next day and save the head, though the meat will be wasted. In some sections of game country birds and coyotes are scarce, but in most of the western Rocky Mountain chain they are plentiful. These undertakers of the wild will, as a rule, soon find any dead or wounded animal.

Many times while trailing wounded game, on either snow or soft ground, we have had coyotes cut in on the trail ahead of us, and when these little sage wolves take a track ahead of you, you can be sure the game will be pushed hard if it is bleeding badly. Several times as darkness closed in and we were forced to give up a trail for the night and camp, we have heard a coyote calling his family in the direction taken by the wounded beast. Then, by daylight, all that would be left of the poor beast would be a few scattered bones and hair and the paunch. Sometimes the head can be found if it is large and heavy, but I have had coyotes clean up both cow elk and doe deer in one night, leaving nothing but a few scraps of hide, some of the vertebrae around the shoulders and the paunch. The coyote won't help you in your search, but he will demolish your trophy overnight. With a bull elk or bighorn ram, you may find the horns intact, but usually the scalp of sheep will be ruined.

Magpies, ravens and golden eagles, however, may well help you find the wounded beast in time to save it. In the Southwest and Mexico the buzzards will soon locate any dead or wounded animal and their circling can be seen for miles. Over the years, the magpie has saved me many trophies, both when hunting on my own and when guiding. If the beast is hard hit and you lose the trail in open, or partly open, country, the magpies will usually find him in short order. Many times I have simply climbed to some good observation point where the country ahead, and into which the wounded game disappeared, could be watched. Usually in a short time, if the beast was close, a magpie will start his chatter and soon they will come from all directions. They have saved me many animals, and when hunting coyotes are the one best bet after tracking fails. The golden eagle and ravens will both circle and clearly indicate the presence of wounded or dead game and will both feed to repletion on a dead beast.

On the Salmon River magpies are very plentiful, and they have several times found wounded, or dead, elk, sheep and deer for me as well as a couple of bear. Watch their course and work slowly in toward the section they are heading for and you can soon locate the game. Whenever I lose an animal in the cliffs along the river, the best bet is to cross the stream and climb the other side and watch the magpies and an occasional eagle; if the birds are present in any numbers your patience will soon be rewarded.

While I was hunting in Sonora with the late Charley Ren, we lay down for a cat nap during the heat of the day under the doubtful shade of a paloverde tree, and very soon several buzzards were circling just over our heads on noiseless sinister wings, waiting to see if any signs of life remained. Some dried and well-cleaned human bones we found south of the Pinacates clearly indicated what became of a hunter who ran out of water in that section. I really believe, if we had lain perfectly still long enough, they would have alighted on us and started picking out our eyes.

Mother Nature's undertakers will help you find game in many cases if you will simply watch from some vantage point and clearly read their course. In the timber, when wounded game is on ahead of you, listen for the chatter of the pine squirrel. You can tell when he is merely singing of his good health, or scolding some animal that has intruded in what he considers his own domain. They are particularly vociferous when a bear, cat or coyote comes along. One can often clearly trace the passage of an animal through a basin of scattered timber by listening to the squirrels and magpies if both are present in goodly numbers. Usually, if game is present in large numbers, the undertakers will also be on hand and it behooves us to learn to use them to our advantage.

XVIII

The Bison

AS a game animal the bison, known in this country almost entirely as the buffalo, is gone. Canada still has a wild herd of the original wood bison, now mixed somewhat with plains buffalo, that were moved north from the Fort Wainwright herd. This herd still lives around Slave River and Slave Lake. It is the only wild herd left on this continent. The Yellowstone Park herd is still maintained, as well as various small herds all over the West. One is on the bison range between Kalispell and Missoula, Montana. Another small herd, now mixed somewhat with cattle, is called the House Rock herd of Arizona. Many other small private herds are maintained over the western part of this country, so that the animal is now in no danger of extinction.

The great Wainwright herd, numbering upwards of 27,000, was killed off at the orders of the Canadian government by Purchell. He carefully slaughtered them, a few at a time, as he and his helpers could properly handle both meat and skins. It was just a huge job of butchering, requiring several years for completion, and they were mostly corralled before killing. This was done to make room for the training of troops, so I have been told, but it is a pity the herd could not have been moved and retained alive. No doubt it was composed largely of descendants of the old Flathead herd that was sold to the Canadian government when I was still a small boy. The Crow Indians have a small herd on their reservation in Montana.

Formerly the bison ranged in untold numbers from the Great Slave Lake to the Rocky Mountains, at the northern extremity of its range, southward to latitude 25° in Old Mexico along the westward side. To the east it extended from Great Slave Lake southeast to the Great Lakes, and from there south to Georgia. Only small numbers occurred east of the Alleghenies. In the northern Rockies the section of the Liard River was about its northern extremity. In Montana, Idaho, Wyoming and Oregon,

[327]

it occurred far west of the Continental Divide. The main range, however, was the drainage of the Mississippi River Valley and its tributaries. Over this section, comprising most of the plains of the continent, the buffalo once ranged in countless millions and even as late as the early seventies herds still remained, numbering well into the millions. West of the Rockies it once extended as far as the Blue Mountains and the eastern extremities of the Sierra Nevada.

I have found old bleached skulls over much of Montana as a boy, and just over the north rim of a 10,000-foot mesa, between the Pahsimeroi Valley and the Willow Creek–Lost River drainage in Idaho, and as far north as the low hills north of Fort St. John, I have seen the ancient buffalo trails still worn deep into the soft hillsides. Along the Missouri River many old trails still show where the great herds came down to water and cross the river. At one time there were no doubt between 50 and 100 million bison on this continent. Today but a few scattering small bands exist, and the one wild herd in northern Canada, of all the vast herds that once roamed the plains.

North of the Peace River, at Fort St. John, old Indians claimed that very hard winters, with heavy snowfall, killed off those herds completely, but farther south and in the United States, white men decimated the buffalo herds for hides, tongues and meat. Mostly they were killed for the hides and tongues. The Indians killed only for meat and hides for their lodges and lived with the buffalo for centuries without decreasing their numbers. Even after the first Spaniards brought horses to this country and the Indians obtained horses, the buffalo were in no danger of decreasing as the Indians killed only what they needed for food and shelter and their total killings weren't a drop in the bucket for the vast herds then existing.

Buffalo do not tame worth a whoop and are never reliable, so the vast herds had to go, in order to settle up the plains territories of this country. It still seems a shame that more land could not have been set aside for them, to roam in their natural state. Further, I cannot condone the senseless slaughter of such a vast store of wildlife, simply for the hides and tongues. During the Indian wars the army, as well as the settlers, knew that once they killed off and exterminated the buffalo, they had the wild Indian whipped and deprived of his living and home, so no effort was made to spare the buffalo. Occasionally the Indians both decoyed and drove herds over cliffs and wasted far more animals than they could hope to use, but in the main they killed only what they needed and usually selected the animals. They rode fast horses, and as horsemen the world has never seen better than the plains Indians. With a handful of arrows and a short buffalo bow and themselves and their trained buffalo horses stripped naked, except for a thong half-hitched to the lower jaw of the horse, they had no trouble getting up alongside the running buffalo. Arrows were then driven into it from a few feet range, usually the high flank shot driving forward into the lungs and taken from the right side of the animal. One arrow so placed well forward in the flank or ribs and penetrating down and forward into the lungs, and that animal was done for, and in the course of a half mile to a mile at most would stop and soon go down from hemorrhage.

Later the whites hunted them in the same way with fast horses and all types of arms, from the old muzzle loading rifles to the Colt Dragoon, and many buffalo were killed by competent horsemen armed with nothing more than a pair of the huge old Colt Dragoon revolvers, which would drive their .45 caliber round ball completely through the lungs of the huge beasts at close range. Many early plainsmen and the boatmen taking supplies up the Missouri and returning with boatloads of furs killed all they could use with the old Plains type percussion rifles, the most famous of them being the .52 caliber Hawken, throwing a half-ounce ball with a very heavy powder charge. This rifle when used with 80 to 100 grains of black powder, driving the half-ounce ball through the buffalo's lungs, accounted for a great many buffs. It was absolutely certain when it placed the ball in either heart or lungs and deadly to at least 200 yards.

Later, when a market for the hides was obtained, a great army of ex-Civil War veterans and plainsmen turned to hide hunting as a livelihood. None of them ever got rich from the job, but they did make a living and some did even better. They were not slow in finding out that the Civil War rifles all lacked power, and this demand for ever more powerful rifles was the direct cause of the development of the great Sharps buffalo rifles of the late sixties, seventies and eighties. Probably the great bulk of the buffalo were killed during the seventies with these powerful, long range, single shot rifles. The early Sharps, made at Hartford, Connecticut, were usually in .50 caliber, the .50-95-473 being very popular. They usually had a silver fore end tip. They were not marked OLD RELIABLE in a rectangular box as were the later Bridgeport Sharps. Their use on the buffalo led to the fine Bridgeport Sharps being brought out. Many calibers were used from the .50-95-473 down to the .44-77-470 in the Hartford Sharps. Later the Old Reliable, often known as the Model 74, was brought out for even more modern cartridges, the prime favorites being the .40–90–370, the .45–100–550 and the .45–120–550, and a few of the Big Fifties with 3¼-inch case and handling up to 170 grains of black powder and up to a 700-grain bullet.

These rifles were superbly accurate when properly loaded and were peculiarly well adapted to the job in hand. They were paper patch bullet loads and the hunter had only to purchase a few kegs of powder and sufficient lead and caps and cartridge cases and one of these rifles to be well fixed for months of hunting. Probably more .50–95, .44–77 and .45–100 calibers were used than any other, the longer 3¼-inch cases not coming into general use until along toward the close of the buffalo hunting days. Of the later and finer cartridges, probably none attained such popularity as the .45–120–550 with 3¼-inch straight case, but the .40–90–370 in both bottleneck and straight 3¼-inch persuasion was almost as popular. As few men living today know much of the loading and management of these old rifles, a brief description should be of interest.

As a boy in Montana, and being then an invalid to some extent from third-degree burns that covered a full third of my body, I spent many months in the close companionship of old buffalo hunters. One of them, who taught me a great deal about using and loading the old Sharps, was Waldo P. Abbott. He had been raised in Kansas and his father was killed in the Civil War. His earliest recollections were of his older brothers, loading two four-horse wagons each year and going west into the buffalo range, where they would kill and jerk enough buffalo meat to last the family a full year. Later he had taught school, scouted during the Indian wars and hunted buffalo. His favorite rifle was the .40–90–370 Sharps straight Model 74. I also knew and hunted with several other old-time buffalo runners and they taught me about all there was to know of the loading and use of the Sharps.

The .45–120–550 has always intrigued me and after thirty years' use of that great buffalo cartridge I still have only respect and admiration for it. The bullets were cast about one part tin to sixteen of lead and I usually use one part tin to twenty of lead. The slug is 1½ inches long and is then patched with hard bond paper. The patches are cut diagonally and wet on the tongue, then rolled on so that the last lap will be on top in the direction the slug will spin. The cutting in of the deep lands tends to slit the double patches and they whirl off at the muzzle of the rifle as the slug rotates. The powder charge was 120 grains of best shiny black powder, F. G. Curtiss & Harvey English powder being the best, but early Laflin & Rand and Dupont was also used. The powder was poured through a long brass tube to settle it in the cartridge case and then a thick card was pressed down firmly on the powder. Next a wad of tallow, or bees-wax, about ⅛ inch thick was forced down the mouth of the case. Some hunters then placed a thin card wad over the lubricating disk and some did not. I long ago quit using this thin wad and pushed the patched bullet into the case friction tight, onto the lubricating wad.

The patches are rolled onto the bullet very tight, but wet and then allowed to dry. The tail of the patch is twisted into a curl and if hollow base bullets are used, the tail is pressed down into the cavity of the base; if flat base bullets are used it is curled up and allowed to dry, then snipped off short and square. Chambers of good Sharps rifles were very close and the fired case expanded none at all, so that when reloaded the next patched bullet fitted them friction tight. The old folded head Berdan cases used Berdan primers, and the later solid head cases used the old 2½ black pow-der modern primer. After firing, the cartridge cases were decapped, then washed in boiling water and thoroughly dried, then recapped, when they were ready for loading.

Hide hunters usually carried them in pouches made especially for them, or in wide soft cartridge belts that would protect the paper patch bullets as the lower ends of the loops were closed. Each morning the hunter would ride out until he located a band of buffalo, then would dismount and stalk them upwind, usually trying to get to within 200 to 300 yards. That was close enough for the more expert hunters and they all told me they preferred to shoot at around 200 yards rather than closer, as the noise of the gun was more apt to disturb the herd if too close. They would then lie down, or sit down, and spread out their cartridges and usually a small bottle of water and a cleaning rod, to swab the bore when it got too hot. Then using rest sticks, they would select an animal in the middle of the herd and carefully shoot him or her through, about the center of the diaphragm. The stricken animal would immediately get very sick, walk around and lie down, when others of the herd would rush up and sniff the blood and paw around the down animal. The hunter would then carefully pick the animals on the outside of the herd and drop them with neck shots, or more generally simply plug them through the lungs close in and high behind the shoulder, being careful not to shoot through a small animal and wound another on the other side. Lung-shot animals would usually flinch at the shot, then walk or stand around until their lungs filled with blood, when they went down from suffocation. Heart shots were usually avoided, because heart-shot animals usually jumped into a run in the direction they were pointed. At times an animal off to one side of the herd that was pointed into it would be purposely shot through the heart and would then jump and run into the herd. This was what the hide hunter called a stand and when one was obtained, through careful shooting and management, they were often able to kill all the animals they could skin with their entire crew, before they would spoil. I have heard of fifty to seventy animals being thus killed from one stand and sometimes even more, but few hunters had crew enough to skin even that many before they spoiled.

The buffalo seemed to pay little attention to the report of the rifle or the smack of the heavy slugs, and if animals were shot always on the outer edge of the herd, they would often mill around until the entire band was down. I have seen photos taken by Huffman of Miles City that clearly showed the terrible execution of the big Sharps, and still have two of them showing a killing of cows and spike bulls. Those animals were dropped one after another by the old .45–120–550 Sharps, and the cartridges show plainly in the belts of the hunters while the old rifle rests against a fallen buffalo, as they skin them out.

Abbott told me he killed his last buffalo in the late eighties with the .40–90–370 Sharps straight with a single lung shot, and that it was a mountain buffalo, a very old solitary bull. The .45–120–550 Sharps load developed close to 1500 feet velocity with best black powder, usually of English make, and was truly a most lethal cartridge. Even today it is a far better killer on our heavier game than any single modern cartridge made for sporting use in this country, even the .375 Magnum. It was finely accurate and deadly to a half mile on buffalo. The long heavy slug expanded into a huge mushroom on heavy animals on impact, and penetrated clear through on lung shots broadside on buffalo, to the skin on the off side. It tore large, even wound channels and a buff hit through the lungs had only a short time to live at the most.

I have watched Abbott and others of the old buffalo hunters shoot the big rifles at 200 yards. They usually kept their shots well inside a four-inch circle at that range and Abbott practically never missed a small white rock the size of a man's fist. As a class, this country has never produced a group of men who were as deadly game shots as the old buffalo hunters, either before the buffalo killing days or since then, and in my humble opinion we will never again see as good game shots as a class. We will never have the game to kill, in order to learn as they did. With them it was a business, and the cost of wagons, teams, skinners, cooks, grub, powder and lead had to be balanced against the skins brought in. They hunted for money, not sport. It was a cold-blooded business of killing the great beasts cleanly and with a single shot each, wherever possible.

Even today, I seriously doubt if we have a better rifle or cartridge than the 16 pound Model 74 Sharps in caliber .45–120–550, for killing buffalo cleanly with a single shot. I have used the cartridge enough on elk, mule deer, horses and other game to know that it is still the best killer ever produced on this continent for sporting use, with the exception of the Big Fifty Sharps with its 3¼-inch case and 170 grains of black powder and 700-grain soft paper patched slug. That rifle was not in such general usage, but was even more powerful and a quicker killer.

I have two Sharps buffalo rifles that were actually used on the buffalo during the hide hunting days. Both rifles have the old percussion set trigger action remodeled and fitted with heavy .45 caliber barrels. One is caliber .45–100–550 and was used by Hank Waters in the Dakotas, Montana and Wyoming. He killed a great many buffalo with this rifle and later sold it to J. D. O'Meara, from whom I bought it about 1918.

The other is a .45–120–550 Bridgeport Sharps side hammer and also with set triggers, in a 16-pound weight and used in the hide hunting days in North Dakota. I bought it of W. H. Lenneville. These two old rifles will still shoot; one is perfect inside, the other nearly so. The .45–100 won thirty-four turkeys for me one winter in Montana, shooting at 200 yards, against all manner of Springfield .30–06, Krags and all sporting modern rifles. In one match it took the last seven turkeys for me, including the shooting off of three ties. The target was a six-inch bull's-eye at a measured 200 yards, with two inner circles, the center being about the size of a dollar. Of ten shots I fired that afternoon, I did not go out of the center, which was numbered 15, and the next adjacent ring numbered 14. Factory loaded cartridges were also sold to hide hunters, as well as factory swaged and patched bullets, patches, caps and empty cases. Sharps and Winchester both furnished tools and molds. The .45–120 factory loaded cartridge sold for two bits each on the buff range.

Though some scattered buffalo remained in the mountains until about 1890, the great herds were decimated mainly in the seventies. Theodore Roosevelt speaks of killing buffalo, here along the Divide between Montana and Idaho, in the eighties. Once they were driven to the mountains, hard winters no doubt completely finished them. When Lewis and Clark came down the Lemhi River from the head of the Missouri, after crossing the Divide in 1804, there were no buffalo in the Lemhi Valley and they nearly starved, except for some salmon that were trapped by the Lemhi Indians and given to them, where Salmon City now stands. Yet the valley is full of old buffalo skulls and the ranchers still plow them up when breaking new ground, so these buffalo must have winterkilled many years before the Lewis & Clark Expedition, just as hard winters later killed off the herds on the north side of the Peace River around where Fort St. John now stands. Their trails were still clearly in evidence there in 1937. Much of that country north from Fort St. John would still make a better buffalo range than anything else and herds should be transplanted there again.

Buffalo were first exterminated east of the Mississippi. As early as 1800 they were on the decrease in the Eastern states and by 1820 practically all buffalo east of the Mississippi had been killed off. The great plains herds were killed off mainly in the seventies, but their slaughter continued almost through the eighties. Some wise old ranchers like Scotty Phillips caught a few calves and started the nucleus of many of the present small herds left in the United States. At one time American cowboys shipped two mature bulls they had ranch raised to Mexico, for fights with the Spanish bulls. They bet everything they owned on the outcome of the fight. Though the buffalo bull paid no attention to the first Spanish bull turned into the arena until the domestic bull took the initiative, he then proceeded to kill that bull and also two more that were turned in in record time, by simply charging them and goring them as he picked each up and flung him high over his back with a toss of the great shaggy head. The best in Spanish bulls were no match for the bison.

A general description of the typical plains buffalo will give anyone not familiar with the animals a very good idea of all species, both the two now living as well as the two extinct subspecies. The mature bulls would average around 1800 to 2500 pounds in weight and some have been weighed that went to 3000 pounds for very old fat animals. Cows usually average around 800 to 1500 pounds when mature but some no doubt went heavier than those figures, especially old barren cows. Both cows and bulls have horns, but the bulls have much larger skulls and heavier wider horns, as well as longer. The face is covered by long hair, except for the muzzle and around the eyes, and the hair on the top of the head practically obscures the tips of the horns and is often 10 inches to a foot in length. The neck and shoulders are covered with very long heavy hair under which is a fine softer wool. The lower jaw back of the mouth is covered with long hair forming a beard, often 10 inches in length and hanging down far below the nose of the animal. Cows average darker than bulls except across the shoulders. The young calves are a very light brown, but turn darker as they grow older. I have a robe from a two-year-old heifer, one of the last of the old wild herds in Montana, and it is a dark glossy brown where unworn. The horns curve outward and then up and inward and the wood bison heads show even more inward curve than the plains type.

The boss ribs are very long and high, extending far above the shoulders and spine at the withers. This was known as the hump and was a very popular roast, with both whites and Indians. The horns are black and very heavy on old mature bulls, often being worn or broken at the tips but usually quite sharp on the cows. The Indians used them for headdresses, as well as many useful implements. From just back of the withers and shoulders the hair is much shorter and without the long guard hair over the rear half of the body, if it could be called half, as the rear end of the buffalo is much smaller than the huge massive shoulders. He is shaped much like a mountain goat, only having still more massive front quarters and higher boss ribs in proportion. The tail is short, 20 to 30 inches long on mature specimens. The general body color is a dark brown, being almost black on the lower front legs on some specimens. This long hair hangs down to the knees and makes the beast look as if he was wearing chaps on the front legs. The head is carried very low and the fact that the hump is so high gives the head an even lower appearance. The animal lives in the lower third of its body and the spine at the shoulders is down fully halfway from the top of the withers, when the animal is viewed on foot. This is partly due to the extreme long guard hair on top of the wooly hump at the withers.

They are great game, the greatest cloven-hoofed beast of this continent and a magnificent beast comparable in size and beauty with anything in the bison or buffalo line on the globe. While heavier than the African Cape buffalo, they are probably lighter in weight than the gaur ox of Indo-China and India. A big mature bull stands around 6 feet at the withers, is some 9 feet or more long in a straight line and may be anything from 30 to nearly 36 inches in width at shoulders and paunch. They are clean bodied and not paunchy like domestic critters. A big mature bull will weigh from 2500 pounds upwards and the Records of American Big Game speak of 2900- and 3000-pound bulls as being recorded, but we have heard of two bulls in Oklahoma that weighed 3900 and one over 4000 pounds.

Although the rut is supposed to start in July, and no doubt does, we have seen it carried on several months in Montana and as late as December have seen tiny embryo buffalo, no larger than a silver half dollar, taken from fat heifers that were being slaughtered. They mature much faster than domestic cattle and a two-year-old bull buffalo may easily dress out around 750 pounds. Their eyesight is not keen and they seldom seem to notice a person on foot more than a quarter mile away and may not see him at that distance, but they have a wonderful nose and can smell an enemy a good mile at least. The ears are very small and it is doubtful if their hearing is very keen.

Good bull heads will run in spread from around 25 to 35⅜ inches and the length of horns will run from 15 inches to around 22 for the top records, while the bases will run on good heads from 13 to 16 inches in diameter. The horns on old bulls are invariably badly broomed at the tips, both from fighting and from digging wallows. Buffalo never bellow or bawl as some fiction writers would have us believe. They snort when scared, much like a buck deer, and also grunt when fighting and sometimes when wounded or scared, and during the rut at least they will occasionally roar almost like an African lion, but they never bawl, or bellow. Their grunts sound very similar to those of a hog.

A buffalo has almost no neck; seemingly the head hooks onto the front of the hump over the withers. This fact, combined with their enormous shoulders and quite 18 inches to two feet of dorsal ribs over the top of the shoulders proper, accounts for their enormous strength.

In former years when buffalo were plentiful, many died in bog holes, and almost all old springs and bog holes contain their bones and skulls. Many more were drowned when attempting to cross the various rivers on the ice and it gave way with them. They are excellent swimmers, but have no chance when the ice breaks through with them. Today the northern herd has its quota of wolves that take care of any old or crippled animals just as the buffalo wolves of the plains used to do.

When a buffalo gets mad, he usually curls up his tail at a saucy angle before charging, and at times will paw the ground with a forefoot just like a domestic bull. When attacked by wolves, the old bulls usually will stand in a circle and protect the calves, but buffalo do not come to a stand as do musk oxen, and when man scent is picked up they invariably stampede.

The buffalo is the only animal that faces directly into a blizzard, and instead of standing still for its duration, old-timers always stated they walked steadily forward right into the teeth of the storm. In this way they kept up circulation and their long shaggy shoulders protected them from the direct blast. Some think blizzards killed off many of the bison, but I believe it is far more likely that extremely long winters combined with very heavy deep and wet snowfalls, that later crusted hard, were the cause. Certain it is, such snowfalls killed off the Peace River herds and probably also accounted for the herds that once ranged the Lemhi

Valley above Salmon, Idaho. The chief enemy of the bison was man, though the great grizzly also killed many in old times, before he was exterminated on the buffalo range. Wolves hamstrung and killed stray calves and old broken-down bulls, but were no match at any time for healthy vigorous animals when grown. The grizzly did kill even prime bulls for meat, when he was able to stalk them. After hide hunting decimated the plains herds, the remnants were driven into the mountains, where hard winters with heavy snowfall no doubt finished the job.

The life span of the wild herds was probably not over twenty years, as by that time the old bulls would be whipped out and the wolves would kill them in deep crusted snow. Under more favorable conditions, or as the few small herds are run today, buffalo should reach the age of twenty-five years, if not killed off before that time. Many old-timers I knew spoke of seeing stray old bull buffalo around for several years after the herds were gone, and these old bulls had been driven out of the herds before the latter were killed off. Buffalo meat is coarse and dark, but very good when taken from a fat two-year-old heifer. The Indians preferred fat ribs, both side ribs and the high boss ribs over the withers, and roasted them before the fire.

We still have a great deal of country in the West and Southwest that is used only for grazing livestock that would support good-sized buffalo herds, and it is a moot question if such buffalo herds properly managed would not benefit far more people and to a much greater extent than the stockmen who annually graze them. The buffalo is a very hardy beast and will find ample subsistence where any kind of domestic critter will starve to death. Many sections of the United States and Canada that could support buffalo are now used for sheep grazing, or are not used at all, as is the case in much of Canada.

Buffalo in the wild state always bed with their heads facing any prevailing wind. They should always be approached upwind. Today, if one is lucky enough to get the nod to kill a surplus bull from a herd or to engage in a hunt such as was conducted down in Arizona to thin that herd, he should use the most powerful rifle he can procure and shoot for the lungs or heart. A clean lung shot with a heavy caliber, such as the .405 Winchester or .375 Magnum, will do the trick, and the old Sharps buffalo rifle will still prove an even better tool for such work. Of course, if the animals are driven into a corral and shot, any modern rifle will do the trick with a full patched long heavy bullet if placed in the brain pan. The brain is comparatively small in the huge head and shots will have to be placed. Hard Point bullets should be used for brain shots. I loaded the 180-grain .280 Dubiel Magnum ammunition with which Harry Snyder killed his museum groups from the wood bison herd, but Harry would have been much better off if he had employed some of the fine old Sharps rifles I sold him in former years. The .280 Dubiel killed a couple of charging bulls with frontal neck shots, when the head was lowered in the charge, but did not work so well for heart and lung shots on the huge beasts. One 17-pound .45-120-550 I sold him had already killed a great many buffalo and should have been used on that expedition.

I have killed but one buffalo, a huge and beautiful prime bull, probably ten to twelve years of age. Old buffalo hunters with whom I hunted and camped for months as a youngster always told me they shot for the heart or lungs, usually the latter, and then left that particular animal alone while they turned their old Sharps on some other member of the band. They claimed that a buffalo often lived for from three to ten minutes with a good heart or lung shot from the big .40 to .50 caliber Sharps. Only a spine or brain shot would put one down instantly. W. P. Abbott, Samuel Fletcher O'Connell and others I hunted with as a boy claimed they had killed them as far as 600 to 800 yards with the .40-90-370 and .45-120-550 Sharps but always preferred to work in close to around 200 yards or less if good cover offered. As long as they and the smoke of their big rifles did not attract the attention of the buffalo, they were in no danger. However, they claimed that when a wounded bull did locate them, he would sometimes come for them, in which case they would break a shoulder and stop him, then give him another in heart or lungs. None of these men ever spoke of shooting them in the head.

My bull was in a little open basin with some scattered timber at the lower and upper ends. Iver Henricksen was with me, while Mrs. Keith and our two children with Mrs. Henricksen followed behind to see the show. I used my 16-pound .45-120-566 Sharps side hammer buffalo gun that had already killed hundreds of the great beasts in North Dakota during the hide hunting days. I had cast the 566-grain slugs one part tin to sixteen parts lead and carefully paper patched them. The load was 120 grains of best shiny F.G. black powder, then a card wad $\frac{1}{16}$ inch thick, then $\frac{1}{8}$ inch of deer tallow and then the 566-grain slug seated friction tight about $\frac{1}{8}$ inch in the $3\frac{1}{4}$-inch U.M.C. case. Primers were modern $2\frac{1}{2}$ Peters make. Owing to our families being with us, I told Henrickson I would break a shoulder and under-pin the old bull if he ever turned a shoulder in line with the heart.

At about 120 yards the bull first saw us and turning around came for us, quartering slightly to my left, with tail erect. When his left shoulder was fully exposed and in line with the heart and lungs, I held the front bead on it through the long peep sight and touched the set trigger from a sitting position in the snow. We could plainly hear the heavy plunk of the big slug striking home, mingled with a hoarse grunt from the bull. He came for us very fast on three legs, in long twisting jumps, with his head held low and tail erect and wringing, then stopped. The left shoulder was broken and he seemed to require several minutes for the shock to wear off. Soon we could see he was recovering from the shock and Mrs. Keith, from behind me, urged me to "bust him again." It was apparent that for some reason that heavy slug had not gone on back into the heart and lungs, as he started shaking his head at me and showing the whites of his eyes. Knowing I would have to hit him again to prevent his coming, I ran out to the right as he turned towards me, but as soon as I had a good quartering shot at the heart back of the shoulder, I dropped to a sitting position and planted the next 566-grain slug just behind the shoulder and a little above the knuckle for a center heart shot. He had just started to come forward again, evidently seeing the family as well as Iver and me, when the second slug took him square through the heart. This stopped him, except for one long twisting jump, but after what seemed at least five minutes he was still on his feet, not bleeding at the nose or mouth, and I began to wonder just how long he would live with a center heart shot. Mrs. Keith again urged me to "put him down," so knowing that even a big Sharps slug would not damage either meat or robe, I again held just at the top of the shoulder knuckle with the bull turned squarely broadside, after again running to the right of him. At the impact of the second slug he had made another long twisting jump toward us and grunted when the slug hit him, and he did the same identical thing after the third shot. By now he was very apparently in trouble, but continued to stand on his feet and shake his head and occasionally wring his tail upright for several minutes more, probably three to five minutes, before he staggered and then fell heavily on the left side. Even then he continued to breathe and kick for another five minutes. I had never before seen any American game take such punishment and stay on its feet, when shot with one of the most powerful sporting cartridges ever made in America, only the Big Fifty (.50–170–700) being more powerful. This was also a Sharps buffalo cartridge.

He proved a magnificent beast in prime coat, the hair on top of his head being around 14 inches long. When skinning him out we found the second and third slugs under the skin on the off side. They had penetrated the ribs, heart and lungs and the ribs again, and lodged under the tough heavy hide. After quartering we could find no trace of the first slug coming through the rib cage into the heart and lung area, so knew it was still in that left shoulder which it broke. The skin on top of the head and neck and also over the frontal plate of the skull was fully 1½ inches thick and it was like trying to skin a board loose from the skull. All three recovered slugs showed some upsettage, the second one considerable, as it went through a rib on the near side. The one planted in the shoulder expanded back halfway and perfectly mushroomed. I would have bet anyone the Sharps would go right through the beast broadside, but surely learned a lesson. The clear meat of the four quarters weighed 1011 pounds, without heart, liver or tongue. Both slugs tore good-sized holes through the big heart, but he required a long time to die of hemorrhage. The chest cavity was filled with blood when opened. I could have put him down instantly with a spine or brain shot, but by the time the cape was removed it would have been too late ever to bleed the meat properly, while the heart shots did an excellent job in this respect. He was dead before the shock of the first heavy slug could have worn off so did not suffer, but he surely showed quite plainly that he was mad after that first shot. Had I given him the first shot in heart or lungs instead of breaking a shoulder, he would no doubt have charged in the direction he was headed, and as he was headed our way I decided to "three leg" him the first shot. Before this experience, I would never have believed that the heavy shoulder bone would completely stop a .45–120–566 Sharps slug at such short range, but it surely did so. I have seen them rake a big elk full length and often go on through the skin on exit, but an elk is much softer muscled than an old bull buffalo. The head should go around thirty-eighth place in the records. Spread 26¾ inches extreme, and tip to tip 21¼ inches. Bases both horns 14¾ inches and the right horn 16¾ inches in length and the left 16¼ and tips of both badly broomed off. This, my 127th head of big game, proved one of the most interesting animals I have ever killed and the largest. He should have weighed around 2200 to 2500 pounds on foot. The combination of head and cape was all two of us could drag and the robe was also a load for two men.

Killing this bull was a very interesting experience. The crash of the big Sharps cartridge, blending in with the plunk of the heavy slug and the hoarse deep grunt of the bull at each shot, was an experience I will never forget. We were all convinced that had I not broken a shoulder at the first shot, we would have sustained a nasty charge, and as it was, he made all tracks in our direction, but seemingly had his attention fixed on me alone and I had to run to the right and shoot quickly for the second and third shots to get them into the heart from the side, before he could again swing my way. The old Sharps packs an awful wallop, but I hesitate to think what the results would have been if I had used a light caliber modern rifle. Colonel Lykins and his son Guy from Salmon, Idaho, also witnessed this buffalo kill.

From the size and appearance of the .45 caliber bullet wounds through this buffalo, I believe there is no use in ever using Soft Point bullets on an animal of this size, and were one using a modern rifle I believe he would be better off with long, heavy, Round Nose full patched bullets. Light Soft Point high velocity bullets would no doubt give insufficient penetration and I believe one should use solids in modern rifles and place them correctly on beasts of such size and weight.

XIX

Arctic Game

Polar Bear

I HAVE never had an opportunity to hunt arctic game, which consists largely of seal, walrus and polar bear, with musk oxen in some isolated instances in the extreme far north; and for this reason must depend on what several good friends have told me of such hunting, who have spent a winter or two in the arctic.

The polar bear is no doubt the finest trophy of the North. From all I can learn, at times he attains the same great size as the Alaskan brownie, though is of course different in build. The head is long and narrower and the forehead is convex and more the shape of a black bear's than a grizzly's. The neck is longer and slimmer also, while the body is often more rangy than a grizzly's. The center of the back is the highest portion except for the head, not unlike a black bear, though the body is longer in proportion. The feet are huge and furred over the bottoms, the claws more curved than in the grizzly and very sharp. Teeth are large and long and also sharp, on all but very old bear. The winter coat is very long, heavy and shaggy, to protect him in extreme temperatures. The eyes are very small, as with grizzly, and appear dark. The tip of nose is also dark. His coat blends perfectly with the ice pans and floes he inhabits. The rut must occur in late June, from all I can learn, and possibly extends into July. As with black and grizzly bear, the cubs are born in the den, are born hairless and with closed eyes, and are about the size of a squirrel at birth. Usually one cub is born each time, but two are not uncommon and rarely three have been seen with one sow. The males attain the greatest size, as with other bear species. Polar bear skins usually run longer than their width, unlike the grizzly, and this is due to the long rangy body and the long neck. A perfect, well-furred and well-tanned polar bear skin is one of the most beautiful trophies imaginable. The tail is short as with other bears and well furred, but often a trifle longer than on grizzly in proportion to the size of the animal.

Polar bear are probably the best swimmers of all four-footed animals and are quite often encountered hundreds of miles from any land and with no pan ice in sight. They can, when necessary, swim and live for days in the open water. Under the skin is usually a very thick layer of fat, to protect them from the cold. They do not sink when shot, as a grizzly will, but often drift under pan ice in the ocean currents and are then lost to the hunter. Their eyesight is probably keener than that of any other bear, though inferior to many other game animals.

Their food is chiefly seals, which they stalk and kill on the ice pans. They will also stalk and kill walrus at times on the ice. A walrus is an awkward animal when on the ice and the white bear is more than a match for the young walrus and may at times take old ones as well. In the water, the walrus would have every advantage over the bear. While seal is their principal *pièce de résistance*, polar bear will kill a young, or iso-lated walrus when they can stalk him on the ice, as the walrus sleeps. They invariably hunt upwind. Walrus being seldom found far from the ice packs and also close enough to shore for them to dive and dig up their natural food, the bear usually have a good chance at sleeping walrus herds on large pans and ice packs. They also eat anything available, and will eat a dead whale or walrus once it drifts up on shore, as well as food caches stored by the natives when they can reach them. In summer, they at times feed some on fish, as they run up the streams to spawn. The polar bear is the only bear that will stalk a human being and kill him for food. When hungry they are very bold, during the arctic night. In summer, they usually have an abundance of food. Just when they hiber-nate, or for how long, or where they den up, I have never found anyone that knew. There must be months when food is entirely unavailable and they must hibernate as long as, or longer than, the more southern species, but I have as yet failed to find anyone with the answers to these ques-tions. Like other bears, I presume they may at times be out even in the dead of winter. Far northern posts and Eskimo camps record their ap-pearance late in the fall and often far inland from the ocean. They travel and range much farther than any other species of bear.

In the spring and summer, melting ice floes and the ocean currents carry them far to the south, as far as Newfoundland on the east coast and the Aleutians and the north side of the Alaskan peninsula on rare occasion on the Pacific side of the continent. No doubt they range completely around the Arctic Circle, wherever seals are available for food. In the main, they hunt upwind and can scent their quarry long before they can see it. In spite of their great weight and bulk, they can stalk as silently as a cat.

The Eskimos of the far North often hunt them with packs of dogs, and in the old days sometimes made the kill with a long spear while the bear was engaged with the dogs. Usually some of the dogs were killed in the melee. White hunters rarely have a chance to thus hunt them on the pack ice with dogs, unless in company of the Eskimos. A sportsman will have the best chance of obtaining a polar bear on a well-equipped ship, outfitted especially for an arctic cruise, as soon as the ice breaks sufficiently in the early summer to permit their nosing northward into the broken pack ice and floes. When such an expedition reaches bear country, usually pack ice adjacent to land, a lookout is usually stationed in the crow's-nest at all hours. In this way they are often sighted several miles from the ship. Another favorite method of obtaining the great white bear is to keep a small smudge pot on deck burning seal or walrus blubber and preferably with some bacon scraps for good measure, while the lookout keeps a sharp watch downwind. Bear will come for miles when they get the scent of the burning blubber. It can also be thrown on the fire, in the galley stove, with equal results, and when the hunter is on land and the wind blowing to sea and any pack ice is evident, such a smudge pot will attract the bear as far as they can get the scent, which may be several miles.

If a dead whale can be located, it is a sure bet, if any bear are in the neighborhood. Whale, seal or walrus blubber makes attractive scent when thrown in the fire, while gas or diesel oil fumes will scare them away. Usually they are found singly, except in cases of a sow with cubs or yearlings, but I once saw a very dim movie film brought back from the western arctic, showing the killing of three bear together. A hunter ran out ahead of the camera toward the three bear, knelt on one knee and with an old '95 Winchester started the show. At his first shot a big one went down and the other two started to run. His next shot brought another bear down, the smaller of the two left on foot and running away. At this, the third bear turned and charged, probably an old female. She was again promptly knocked flat, but was up and coming as soon as the rifleman could work the lever and reload that old Model '95. His next shot turned her in a somersault, but she floundered up on her forefeet, with mouth open at close range, when another shot put her down for keeps. Then as the rifleman reloaded, or started to reload, the first bear regained his feet and started toward the hunter, who closed the action, probably on a single round, and taking a long careful aim shot again.

This time the great bear, the largest of the three, slid to a stop and sagged in a heap. I could not tell the caliber of the rifle from the movie, but from the way the hunter's shoulder jerked and from the upchuck of the rifle's muzzle, it looked as if he must have been using a .35 W.C.F. or .405 W.C.F. Lighting of the picture was too dim to tell anything about the empty cartridge cases, or even to see them. That film was shown when I was a small boy, and was evidently taken on an ice pack, as some huge cakes were in evidence, tilted up on edge.

The Eskimo uses bear pelts for sleeping bags, socks, parkas and much of his winter clothing. The fat and meat are also used for both human consumption and dog food. The meat of young polar bear, properly cooked, is very good and similar to pork, from what those who have eaten it have told me, but old ones are often very strong and tough. The skins of young bear and many females are usually a beautiful white, while those of older bear, particularly old males killed late, are usually a yellowish cast, probably stained from seal fat. Just when they shed I do not know, but have seen a couple of pelts from Hudson Bay killed in the summer that had a very short crop of new hair and were both thin and very short, not over an inch in length, while all the pelts I have seen from the Pacific were even and long-furred, beautiful skins.

Some Eskimos take their rifle, sleeping bag and food and go out to a vantage point on the pack ice, where they can watch and see everything downwind and simply lie in wait and let the bear hunt them; then when he comes in range, they rise up and kill him. As the Eskimo lives on seal, walrus and white whale and fish, he no doubt smells fit for food, to the great bear. Many have been taken in this manner by hardy souls among the Eskimo.

Like the black bear, polar bear are more often taken on chance encounters than when actually hunting them, unless an Eskimo is out for them with his trained pack of sledge dogs, or a ship is keeping a constant lookout and burning blubber for a scent bait, in or adjacent to good bear country. Eskimos often hunt them with dogs during the early arctic night, when visibility is very low and they must be shot at close range and with only a hint of rifle sights available for the job.

When encountered in open water, or on small pans of ice from a ship, bear can usually be approached to very close range, when almost any high power rifle of good penetration will do the trick, as the bear is then at a great disadvantage, but when hunted on foot, or with dogs in the pack ice, the killing of a polar bear is something else, and in the summer shots may have to be taken at long range. For this reason, powerful long range rifles

[345]

are the best for the purpose and the .300 Magnum and .375 Magnum, as well as the heavier caliber lever actions, such as the .35 and .405 Winchester and .348 Winchester, are all good, but the first mentioned bolt action calibers will be the best for all long range work over 200 yards. The 220-grain bullet should be used in the .300 Magnum and either 270 or 300 grain in the .375 Magnum.

The great white bear is never to be trusted and no man traveling the arctic by dog sledge should ever be far from his rifle. Polar bears have been known to come right into the outer entrance of igloos and kill dogs and attack humans as well. A great many cases are recorded of their coming upwind and stalking the hunter. The best way of securing a good one and the easiest, as well as the most expensive, is on an arctic expedition by ship. Formerly, whalers brought back a great many skins, both to this country and to Denmark and Norway, but now that less whaling is being done, the great bear should increase. Certainly he has no immediate danger of extinction. His chief and almost only enemy is man, and aside from arctic expeditions and the few white explorers and trappers who have wintered and lived with the Eskimos, comparatively few whites have ever seen the white bear in his native habitat. Now that air travel has become so common, more hunters may in time be able to take a hand in hunting the bear, but even so, there are only a few short months of each year when air travel is possible, or reasonably safe, and fewer still when visibility would permit success to such a venture.

Walrus

Two species of walrus are recognized, the Pacific and the Atlantic. The Pacific walrus occurs from the Bering Sea northward into the Arctic Ocean; the Atlantic species from as far south as Labrador northward into the Arctic Sea. Both species are very large and differ materially from the true seals and sea lions. Old bulls may reach a total length of 12 feet and weigh a ton and a half. Cows are about three fourths this size.

The Pacific walrus is the finer of the two species and usually carries longer, heavier and more divergent tusks. Both species range far northward in summer and come south with the drifting ice in the fall. They must have some open water, as they feed on the bottom of the sea along the continental shelf and are not found in really deep water. In the summer they drift northward and in September and October again drift southward with the pack ice. Some sections that are eternally frozen over have no walrus for this reason.

The walrus in general is peculiarly well adapted to the ice pans along the Arctic Coast. Walrus furnish meat, fuel, leather and ivory for the Eskimos, who would have a tough existence were it not for the walrus herds. One friend of mine, now dead, who spent two winters in the Pacific arctic claimed that one has a craving for blubber up there and that he could eat a piece of seal, walrus, polar bear or white whale blubber and relish it just as much as he would a chocolate bar down in the States. The extreme cold and lack of sun, he claimed, brought on a craving for fats of all kind. Certain it is, they are a godsend to the natives.

Both cows and bulls have long ivory tusks, but the bull tusks are heavier and larger in diameter. The Eskimo hunts the walrus with his spear and rifle. When walrus are found on ice pans, the native sneaks up close and attempts to kill them with brain shots from his rifle, but once in the water, the walrus is first harpooned, the spear having a long line and float attached, and then, when it comes up, is dispatched with a head shot. The float keeps the animal from sinking.

Like seal, walrus will sink when shot in the water. We have shot seal and if you can take them through the brain just before they are ready to slip under water when the lungs are filled with air, they will float for a time, but if you shoot them when they first come up and the lungs are being emptied, they will sink, almost immediately. I have seen some shot when the lungs were but partly inflated and they sank to a certain depth, then floated there, and you could clearly see them down in the clear water. Walrus, however, are said to sink whenever killed in the water.

Walrus are most easily hunted from a good ship, outfitted especially for an arctic expedition, the same as polar bear, unless one wishes to spend a season with the Eskimos. They can then be located from the crow's-nest for great distances when the fog rises, and boats can be put over-side for the actual hunt. If they can be approached upwind, close range shots can often be obtained while they are asleep on the pack ice. Individuals with the best tusks and lying farthest in from the edge of the pan should be selected and preferably a side shot taken about 15 to 16 inches back from the end of the muzzle, so as to strike the brain and kill instantly. Long heavy bullets, with good penetration and at moderate velocity are best for the job. Body shots are seldom effective and will usually not prevent the mammal from flopping to the edge of the ice and throwing himself into the sea. One would probably need an elephant rifle or an old Sharps .45 caliber buffalo gun for effective body shots, and even then the walrus would often get into the water unless the spine was struck.

The rut occurs in the summer and the calves, one or two in number, are born in the spring. The cows take every precaution to guard their calves and a herd that is once disturbed and has taken to the water is very dangerous to anyone in small boats, if calves are present, as the cows will fight anyone and anything at that time, to protect their young. The principal enemies of walrus are man, the polar bear and killer whales. Man is no doubt their number one enemy, with the great white bear ranking second and the killer whale third. Man, both Eskimo and white, hunts the walrus on the ice packs and also from boats, while the bear attacks only on the ice pans, and usually takes a young walrus. Once in the water, if killer whales are present, they can make it tough for a herd and at times drive them out on the ice pans. As before stated, never having had an opportunity to go on an arctic expedition, I can only repeat what several friends have told me of walrus hunting. I believe they have given me the straight of things, however.

During the rut, the herds are very noisy and their bellowing can be heard for miles, when the wind is favorable. Unlike the polar bear, they are never found far from pan or pack ice, for they must feed on the bottom and have the ice pans on which to rest and sleep. Walrus are most easily hunted after a prolonged stretch of bad weather, when a clear warm day is obtainable. After such a stretch of weather, they will bask in the sun and sleep on the ice pans and can be approached at very close range upwind before they become disturbed. When the water is smooth, one will have a fairly good platform of his boat from which to shoot, but in rough water it is very uncertain and the animals will probably have to be harpooned and then shot. At such times and with the herd in the water, anything can happen, and many natives have been killed by walrus. Usually when a herd is attacked, the animals will hover around and fight rather than try to leave the vicinity. They may come up alongside or directly under small boats and thus endeavor to upset them and get the men out in the water. All who have hunted them agree that walrus hunting is very difficult during bad weather, and it is best to wait for a calm clear day, when they like to sun and sleep on the ice pans. They can then be approached quite easily and either killed on the ice or harpooned and then shot in the calm clear water. Walrus are said to be on the increase. Use long heavy bullets and shoot for the brain and only when the head is above the water or on the ice, as no rifle will penetrate much water with any part of its energy left to hit the walrus. An old bull walrus has a very heavy layer of blubber under his tough thick hide, to protect him from the cold, and this layer covers about all parts of the body except the skull. It necessitates considerable penetration from a rifle bullet and also further protects the great mammal in fights with other bulls. The walrus strikes downward with his tusks, and has ample power to drive them through, or into any living thing in the arctic. He is also a most cheerful boat wrecker when aroused.

Musk Oxen

Musk oxen are native only to the northern reaches of the North American Continent. During the glacial period musk oxen inhabited what is now New Mexico and even later lived in Alaska. Their fossil heads are still dug up in the placer mines at Fairbanks, as well as those of a buffalo appearing much like the African buffalo. The great mastodon tusks and skeletons are excavated as well.

During the Pleistocene epoch the musk ox was also a native of Europe, but has long been extinct on that continent. Musk oxen are divided into three subspecies, the Barren Ground, *Ovibos moschatus moschatus* (Zimmerman), *O. moschatus niphoecus* (Elliot) and *O. moschatus wardi* (Lydekker). The first two are native of this continent, the first, or Barren Ground, musk oxen living from about 60 degrees north latitude and from Hudson Bay west. It is now extinct over much of its former range. The second subspecies occurs from about Wagner Inlet west to Great Slave and Baker Lakes, but its exact range is probably still unknown and no doubt it gradually merges with the Barren Ground species. It is darker colored as a rule than the Barren Ground musk ox. The third subspecies listed is native of Greenland, Banks and Grant Land and is by far the most numerous of the three species today. Musk oxen have been planted in Alaska near Fairbanks in more recent times and are said to be doing well in their new home.

The musk ox is a shaggy, long-haired animal, with a very heavy and dense underfur or wool, somewhat resembling the pelage of the mountain goat but with much longer, heavier underfur and much longer and coarser outer hair. The pelage is so long and heavy that the exact shape of the animal cannot be seen until it is skinned. It is peculiarly well adapted to its bleak arctic range. Both bulls and cows have horns of the same general type, but the bosses of the bulls are much wider and cover much more of the forehead. They are also longer and heavier. The horns of both species curve sharply downward, then out and up at the tips, the broad bases practically covering the top of the skull on old bulls, much as the horns of an African buffalo. Hair and fur extend well down on the legs and feet. He is a sturdy, stocky animal, smaller than a domestic ox but heavily built.

Musk oxen live on moss, grass, lichens and what arctic willow they can find and paw down to, even in the worst weather, for food. They were formerly circumpolar in their range, and their skeletons have been found with those of the great hairy mammoth. Most scientists class the musk ox as belonging to the oxen as well as to the sheep species and claim they are about halfway between the two species in general characteristics. The underfur is really a wool and covers the complete body, but since there is less guard hair on the back and especially behind the shoulders, this whiter underfur or wool shows through to a greater extent. The outer hair is very long and heavy and the bulls have a heavy mane, making them appear much larger than they really are. The nostrils alone are not covered with hair or underfur.

The heavy undercoat of wool is shed each summer much as the mountain goat's. It loosens from the skin and gradually works out from the heavy guard hair in patches. At this time of year the animal appears ragged and patchy, as well as lighter in appearance than when he has again acquired a normal winter coat. This wool is often collected by the Eskimos and is said to be the finest wool on earth. Usually the wool is shed by late June and then the musk oxen is dressed only in the darker guard hair, but by winter he will have another heavy undercoat. Greenland musk ox have a white patch in the forehead of young bulls and cows, that later turns darker as they grow older. Life span is thought to average around 15 to 20 years, but may extend longer. The horns of bulls start growing downward at about two years old and are not fully grown, either as to length or the spread of the flat bases, until about seven years of age.

The rut occurs at the different latitudes from late August into September. Herd bulls gather up all the cows they can and fight off any stray bulls. Most bulls are whipped out of the herd at about four or five years of age and usually these outcasts band together while the stronger bulls take the cows. They fight much like mountain sheep, probably due to their inherent sheep ancestry. The cows, like most other game, pay no attention to a fight between the bulls. The calves are born from late April into very early June and bleat much like domestic sheep for a time. The cows have four teats like a domestic animal; they do not wean their calves but allow them to nurse until almost time for the next calf to be born. In summer and even during the rut, the bulls that have been whipped out of the herds band together, often three or four in a bunch, and live a solitary life, but in winter they all band together for mutual warmth and protection. When a blizzard strikes, they bunch closely together and turn their tails to the wind, with the big bulls on the outer fringe next the wind. The next larger bulls will then take up their position, leaving the cows farthest from the wind with the younger animals packed among the larger ones and the calves under the bellies of the cows. They can stand thus packed together for warmth for days on end, but as soon as the storm is over they are out cheerfully rustling for food. Their brain is very small in proportion to the skull and they certainly are not overly intelligent, but in turn are marvelously well adapted to their rigorous climate. Possibly an animal that must endure that climate should not have too much in the way of gray matter.

When attacked by either wolves or man, musk oxen form a circle, with the calves and younger animals in the center, and stand with lowered heads. While this works admirably with wolves, it is the worst thing they could do with man, for if you kill an animal or two, the rest will stay there as a rule and guard the carcasses until you cannot get to them, unless you kill them all. For this reason you should select animals from very small groups rather than try to kill from a big band in the winter. They are not game, in the true sense, and are even easier to kill than were our wild bison in the seventies, for they will make a stand when danger is present, while the buffalo, at least, knew enough to run when once he did recognize danger. All scientists and explorers who have killed musk oxen claim it is just about as sporting as killing cows in the barnyard. If specimens are to be taken for museum groups or game collections, then old solitary bulls should be selected, away from the herds, that will not in any way injure the propagation of the species, as they lead solitary lives in the main.

Musk oxen are said to be the finest meat in all the North and many claim it is even better than any other game on this continent. It would be a shame if such a species were to be exterminated. They have few enemies except man. Wolves may at times get an old one that is caught alone, or a stray calf, but this is rare, and while the polar bear may kill an occasional musk ox or even a Barren Ground grizzly, these occurrences will be few and far between and if the musk oxen are given protection, they should increase. When specimens are wanted, they should always be selected from solitary lone bulls and the cows or calves should never be killed. They are just as polygamous as domestic sheep and one bull can take care of a fair herd of cows, so only old bulls that have been run off the cow range should be taken. When properly protected and managed, the killing of a few of these old specimen bulls each year would do no harm to the future of the species.

They are a survivor from a far distant age and should be preserved as such, for posterity. However, I can see no reason why the lone bulls that lead solitary lives and have no part in the propagation of the species should not be taken as specimens by sportsmen who would really appreciate them, so long as their taking is properly managed and no other killing occurs.

Musk oxen are not difficult to approach or kill, but fairly powerful rifles should be used with long heavy bullets of good penetration and preferably lung shots taken, so that all meat could be saved and used. No doubt more musk oxen have been killed by natives and polar expeditions than by sportsmen, and at times they have thus saved human lives, when no other meat was available. They should be maintained wherever possible in the North, as they are among its most interesting animals.

X X

Cougar and Jaguar

Cougar

THE only large cats native to North America are the cougar and the jaguar of the Southwest. The cougar is known by various names, such as mountain lion, puma and panther. Here it is called the cougar, while in the East and South it is always called the panther. The scientific name is *Felis concolor*. Whatever name is given it, it is one and the same animal and mountain lion is probably as fitting a name for the species as any. It once ranged from Alberta and British Columbia in the north and Quebec in the east, south throughout the Southern states and Old Mexico, as well as about the whole of South America. Today it has been exterminated in most of the eastern Canadian provinces and the eastern United States with the exception of Florida. We still have plenty of the big cats in this section and they will be found plentiful anywhere that deer range in great numbers, unless continuous hunting with dogs has reduced their numbers. Scientists have divided the cougar into twenty-five subspecies that we shall not attempt to cover, but for all practical purposes it is one and the same animal, though differing in size due to the amount of deer and other game on which it feeds. Probably the largest specimens occur along the Rocky Mountain chain in British Columbia, Montana, Wyoming, Idaho and Colorada as well as Utah, which in turn is the home of the mule deer. It is the most adept still-hunter on God's green earth, and any time anyone thinks he is a really finished still-hunter, I would recommend that he start trailing cougars on foot and without dogs in an attempt to get a shot. A good many cats have been killed here on the North Fork of the Salmon the last seventeen years by hunters, but they were all chance encounters and not one of those hunters was trailing, or hunting for, cougar when sighted. More of still-hunting can be learned in a week of hunting cougar alone and without dogs than any other way I know of.

When I was a boy around Helena I used to spend every Saturday and Sunday I could get away trailing a big cougar that then inhabited Nelson Gulch. In the winter I always had tracking snow, but often it was crusted, or wet and poppy. At other times it was ideal. By actual record I spent, all told, over two months trailing that big cat over the years and never did I get even a glimpse of his tawny hide. He seemed to enjoy the game as much as I, and though I carried a good Sharps or Winchester, loaded, all the time, he never gave me an opportunity to bust a cap. It was a game of hide-and-seek and as soon as the great cat sensed I was circling on his trail, he would take to the dense fir thickets on the north slope and there he would stay, regardless of how many miles we circled in a day. I usually had only to trail him a mile or two to have the uneasy feeling that he was in turn trailing me, and such always proved the case. It got so in time that when this sixth sense warned me, I would turn around and work back carefully on my own tracks, always finding where I had jumped him, as he was trailing me up. This got to be a game with us and I believe that old tomcat enjoyed it. At least he never failed to circle and trail me, when I was after him. He was a big cougar and I believe would have gone 200 pounds or more. Deer were not plentiful there at that time, having been hunted out for many years by hunters from Helena, and the old cat ate about anything he could catch. I have found his deer kills, also porcupine, grouse, snowshoe rabbit and once a horse kill made by him. I was just a skinny kid at that time and knew little of the habits of the cougar, but was determined to find out all I could and always hoped to make a rug of his hide, but I never succeeded. It was simply uncanny the way he could sense he was being followed and he would always double around in thick timber, or under cliffs, where I could not see him, and then I would get that uneasy feeling that he was behind me and it never failed to prove true, when I backtracked. If I had had the sense at that time to lead him to more open country when he was following me, and then lie in wait to windward of some more open timber, I might have gotten a shot, but I left Montana without ever seeing the big cat.

One day I had been out primarily for snowshoe rabbits and carried a double Ithaca 16 bore and of course my old Single Action Colt sixgun as well. I had filled the back of the hunting coat with the big-footed white bunnies, until there were all I could lug. Those jumped and running I had killed with the shotgun and those I found sitting on some stump or log I had killed with the sixgun. I had all I could possibly carry and the blood was dropping out of the back of my coat into my trail, as I learned next day. Night caught me after I had supper with an old-timer who lived in the gulch and made a living by placer mining. I started up the old wood road from his cabin before the moon came up, intending to go on over the Divide and down Grizzly Gulch to Helena and home. While going up this wood road in the dark and on crusted snow, I had the warning I was being followed. I stopped and listened and quite often could hear the big cat, first on one side of me and then on the other side, or behind me. I stopped and waited for some fifteen minutes under a big fir tree, but never saw anything, then moved on up the gulch in the dark. I could see a short distance in the timber, but none too well, and it was a ticklish feeling to know I was being trailed and yet be unable to see well enough, in case the big cat did actually try for me. Finally the moon came up and it was a welcome sight, as I neared the head of Nelson Gulch.

After hearing the cat behind me, I again heard him breaking through the thin crusted snow to the right and slightly ahead, and on rounding a bend in the road with my eyes peeled, I saw a big square head project from the bole of a tree, just over a big limb and some six feet above the side of the road. Instantly I thought it was the cougar, so threw up the sixteen bore, now loaded with BB shot, and gave him both barrels in the face. Out fell an old horned owl, as I knew from hearing the clicking of his beak as he died, and at the same time I clearly heard the big cat run on the crusted snow. He had been standing behind that tree and slightly further up the slope and I never saw him. Next day I came back with my rifle and again spent the day trailing the old boy, after first determining that he had trailed me all the way from the cabin to where I had shot the owl.

One time a partner and I were trailing a cougar in very deep soft snow. We were on webs, but the country here is so steep that we made entirely too much noise to ever get a shot. We had two pot-lickers with us but they were about worthless as cougar dogs. They would chase the big cat until they were about 100 yards out of our sight in the timber, then sit down and wait for us and usually get on the tails of our webs and throw us headlong in the deep snow. That cat was never more than 200 yards ahead of us all day, but we could not get the mutts to show enough spunk to put him up a tree. With good dogs it would have been easy. We saw where he had made a deer stalk. He had slipped up on the deer, to about 35 yards, from behind the band and slightly above, then had made a run and a flying leap, but the deer had beat him to the jump. As soon as he missed the deer, he had sat down in the snow and meditated on a misspent life and then quit that bunch of deer and gone over a ridge to hunt another band. It was while going down the other slope that we jumped him. He never did circle and trail us as they have so often done with me, when I was alone without a dog. Probably he was aware of the dogs from the start and surely after they chased him through that fir thicket.

I have never heard a cougar scream, but several of my friends have and describe it as being similar to a woman's scream, when she is in mortal terror. I have, however, heard cougars call on numerous occasions, but never have I heard them utter anything resembling a scream. When living in Missoula in 1911 my father and brother were out for mule deer and heard a cougar calling, but it was not a scream at all but a coarse heavy cat yowl. Dad said it sounded much like a tomcat on the back fence only magnified many times and more of a roar. They finally saw the cougar sitting on a ledge, about 300 yards off, and attempted to get closer for a better shot, but he saw them and slipped away. While living at Winston, Montana, on a cow ranch, I heard a big one call for some time one moonlight night, as I was milking the cows. He was up on a dense fir-covered slope, about 400 yards above the cow barn, and called for some time. It was a bloodcurdling cat yowl, long drawn, coarse and heavy, almost a roar at the finish of each call. There was six inches of fresh wet snow on the ground at the time and next day I climbed the mountain with my rifle and circled it very carefully. The only tracks on that entire mountainside were of snowshoe rabbits and pine squirrels and one huge cougar track that walked out onto a ledge overlooking the ranch. He had sat there for some time, as the snow was melted down and frozen where he had sat. I know nothing else could have made that noise. It was an unearthly noise, very loud and long, but instantly gave you the impression it could be nothing else but a cougar. That old cougar always crossed that fir-covered sidehill in his periodic rounds. We saw his tracks many times and he would work on down through the foothills to Beaver Creek, then follow down it on the ice, and he always crossed the road by going under the bridge on the ice.

There is no set period for the rut and it may occur any month in the year, as I have heard these calls at rare intervals over thirty years and during practically every month I have been in the hills. The kittens are born any month and friends have found them in cougar dens about all months of the year. Usually the litter runs from two to three, but occasionally four, or even five, have been found. The kittens are spotted with scattered black spots over most of the body.

While running a martin and lynx line back of Williams Lake and out along the Divide to Taylor Mountain the winter of 1929 and '30 I jumped five cougar in one bunch, an old female and four kittens. I had a mighty good cow dog with me and was on webs. We jumped the band of cats about the head of Iron Creek, in dense, but small, lodgepole timber, at around 8000 to 8500 feet elevation. Bobby, my dog, took after the old female and the trail clearly showed where he had pulled hair out of her tail several times, but she had turned and jumped at him, then run again and the dog after her. I could hear them fighting and the spitting of the cat several times, but never did get sight of any of them and they would not tree. While following the dog after the old cougar, one of the young ones had sat behind a fir tree until I had passed, then run in the opposite direction, and I did not know he had been there until I retraced my steps and found his trail cutting out and into my web tracks. Next trip over the line I took a saddle horse as far up the mountain as the snow permitted, before donning my webs. Saw nothing of the cats on the trip along that high trap line, but soon after getting back to my horse I jumped the five again. I had borrowed another dog of a neighbor, my good cow dog having been poisoned in the meantime by a Biological Survey coyote pill. This dog would only run the cats for 100 yards and come back to me, and as the horse was scared to death at the scent of them, I had to give it up. The next year one of the Kiel boys who spent the winter there ran onto the five in the open and killed three outright and wounded another before they got out of sight — that is, the two that did get away.

An adult cougar will average fully one deer a week the entire year and may often kill more than that average. I usually find several kills around the ranch here each year. Some are coyote and eagle deer kills during the late winter, but others are cougar and in the summertime. While they tend to keep the deer herds down and will congregate where the deer are thickest, I believe the cougar should be kept down in numbers a great deal more than is done at present. Those deer might as well be left for human consumption, and better to allow two deer per man than to use them for cat feed. Further, if the bounty were raised from $50 to $100 and kept at that level, men could afford to bring in dogs and hunt them out. I do not believe in completely exterminating the great cat, but do believe we could do nicely with far less of them than we have at present and have far more deer to eat each year. The only successful way to hunt cougar is with well-trained cougar dogs. They will put him up in a tree or corner him on some ledge with little difficulty, when he can be approached and shot. Care should be used either to make a brain shot if one has a small rifle or a six-gun, or else to use a powerful rifle and attempt to break both spine and shoulders the first shot, so he won't be able to kill the dogs when he falls out of the tree. Cougar are powerful animals and will kill any dog once they get a hold on him. They usually grab a dog with the teeth and

[357]

front paws, then bring up the long hind legs and kick his entrails out with the hind claws. Two cougar were killed in sight of my house last winter while I was down with pneumonia.

As before stated, I consider the cougar the greatest still-hunter on the face of the earth, unless the leopard has him beat. Cougar do not jump off ledges and limbs onto game, as most artists portray them, but simply stalk their game — often a deer — upwind and from behind always, then when close enough they make a short rush and spring on the deer's withers. They sink their teeth in the neck and then bring up those terrible hind feet and kick the deer's guts out as he runs, unless the long fangs have reached and shattered the vertebrae. They usually kill the largest, finest animals in a band and if they can find mountain sheep, they will not eat deer, as they prefer sheep meat to venison. I have found and analyzed many kills. Many have occurred in good tracking snow, so that the whole tale was as plain and understandable as your morning newspaper, more so in fact than some newsprint I have tried to read, after the printer's devil had mixed his lines. After eating their fill, usually under some tree or ledge, they drag the carcass to where they can cover it with dead limbs and pine needles and may return later for another feed if deer are scarce, but if plentiful they are more apt to kill a fresh one for the next meal. I have seen cougar tracks walking down a trail in fresh snow, and noted where the cat had stopped and crouched, then jumped 15 to 20 feet to one side of the trail. There were a few feathers where he landed, clearly showing the great cat had heard or smelled a grouse under the fresh snow.

Many have been captured and raised from kittens, but you must remember they are still cats and not to be trusted. Frank Allison raised one from a kitten until he was a big 200-pound cat. He was tame and they never suspected trouble from him; then one day when he went to feed him, the big cat jumped Frank, got him down and was feeling for his throat and neck spine with his long fangs when the hired man's .30–30 ended his days.

When hungry, a cougar is never to be trusted and I have known of four authentic cases where humans have been killed and two of them eaten by cougar. One was a 21-year-old man schoolteacher in Colorado, another a small boy in Washington. The third was a schoolmarm in Washington and the fourth a boy in Oregon. Usually cougar are the most cowardly of all beasts and if they had half the spunk and guts of a bobcat, they would be a menace to human life. Likewise if they were as game as the little weasel, we would have to exterminate them.

There is little danger in hunting cougar with dogs except for the possibility of getting a bad fall. True, you should not stand directly under one when you shoot him out of the tree, nor barge in on a cornered cougar, as he will then maul you in short order. Usually he will jump out of a tree and take off again, if you try to approach too close for the shot, and it is better to shoot as soon as you are in effective range, but making sure of a clean kill if possible so that cat won't come down among the dogs, still able to do them damage. If the dogs are tied up, as is sometimes the case when the cat shows no signs of jumping, then you can shoot him out with impunity. The Rood boys who live on Panther Creek kill a good many every winter and they have repeatedly stated that any good dog with a little gumption will tree most any cougar, unless he is up in lodgepole pine, which for some reason they do not like to climb very well. But they also state that if you trap a cougar and let him fight a trap all night, he is then a very different animal and has about the same sweet disposition as a sow grizzly with a sick cub.

In 1934 some neighbors and I had killed three big mule bucks high on the shoulder of Eagle Mountain, on the north side of Sheep Creek, a tributary of the North Fork that empties into the latter stream on my ranch. One buck had died promptly and another had been wounded and circled until he received the *coup de grâce* near the first animal, but the third had led us a long chase down onto the brakes of Sheep Creek before I finished him with a 180-grain .280 Dubiel slug through the lungs. We had dressed out the upper two kills and I had selected a big fat buck as my own meat. We had trailed up the wounded buck and finished him, then slid him down into Sheep Creek and loaded him on a horse. Next day, two of us went back for the other two bucks, intending to ride up there and pack our saddle horses and walk back. We loaded one buck, the upper one, on Buck's horse and then dropped down to the trail where I had left my big buck. Imagine our surprise to find all the hams and the entire saddle eaten away and a big pile of hair all tramped down, where the cougar had licked it off the carcass before starting his meal. He had then sat on that mat of deer hair while he ate about all the best of that big buck.

I decided there was nothing left worth packing out, except the head, and decided to forgo taking even that much. We lit out for the ranch, Buck leading his loaded horse, while I fogged it through and rustled a pair of traps, one a Newhouse No. 4 wolf trap and the other a Newhouse No. 14 with offset jaws and teeth. Those were the heaviest traps I had on hand at the time, so taking them and some wire, I made old Brownie haul me back up that long steep trail to the kill. There I wired the rings of both traps together, then wired them to a piece of light dry aspen about three inches in diameter and about three feet long. I buried the toggle and chains in the snow and the two traps in that mat of deer hair, setting each carefully and covering just enough with deer hair to cover the traps and the teeth on the No. 14. Twice before I have had cougar step directly on the pans of No. 4 Newhouse traps, but always when they had frozen down and would not trip, so I bedded these traps in deer hair and knew they would not freeze, unless we had a big thaw.

Next day I rode back up there, taking an old three-legged stock dog with me. When I approached the set, the deer had not been touched, but the bed of deer hair was disturbed and the traps and toggle gone. A huge cougar track led into the set through the foot-deep soft snow, but I looked for some time and finally circled before I found where he had left, landing far down the mountain and over a big clump of brush, when the teeth of that No. 14 had clamped on two toes of his big right forefoot. I tied up Brownie by dropping his reins in the trail, and with my old Model '95 Winchester caliber .35 W.C.F., my camera and S.A. Colt .44 Special sixgun took the track. The old dog hobbled along in front of me, sniffing in each track. The cat had crossed the gulch, then attempted to work his way up the steep opposite slope in dense stands of scrub fir and quaking aspen. He had bitten off scores of the little aspens when his toggle and the extra trap had hung up on them, and all told I believe he had wallowed down nearly an acre of the snow during the night. Then, finding he hung up at every attempt to get over the ridge and into the huge cliffs into which that side of Eagle Mountain falls away, he had gone straight down the steep gulch. I trailed him down a good half mile, when I saw him for the first time, about 150 to 200 yards below me. He was turned diagonally away from me and tugging slightly at the trap. The toggle and extra trap were wrapped around the tops of a big Salalle or snow brush. This was my first good look at a wild cougar. The nose is carried low and pointed down as though the animal were looking at the ground, when in reality the eyes look straight out from the face. After watching him for a few minutes, I purposely stepped on a dry limb above the snow and broke it. Instantly he turned my way and saw us. He then sat up, just like a big house cat, and made no further move to get away, but sat facing and watching our approach. His head seemed about three feet above the ground as he sat there. The old dog had not seen him and continued his slow working out of the tracks, shoving his nose down into each track in turn. I walked down to within 35 yards of the cat and saw two toes were firmly clamped in that toothed trap, and knowing cats from many years of bobcat and lynx trapping I thought that would hold him nicely, so I leaned the rifle against a tree bole and drew the sixgun. Old Prince continued on toward the cat and still did not look up and see him, so I yelled at him. He then jerked his head up and seeing the big cat watching him and only ten feet away, the old dog started backing up. When he came to me I spread my feet wide and he backed up between them, then turned and sneaked up the hill and lay down behind a fir tree.

When I tried to sick him on the big cat, he merely wagged his tail, which projected around the other side of the tree bole. I walked on down to within six feet of the big cougar and adjusted the camera. Then I stamped my foot, the while holding a cocked sixgun on him with my right hand. He lunged out toward me, the full extent of the chain, opened his huge mouth, hissed, then yowled at me, heavy and coarse. When I looked down into the finder of the camera, he closed his big mouth like a trap and I repeated this several times, the while he got madder each time. However, I was afraid to take my eyes off his and when I looked down into the finder he would close his mouth. I have never seen any animal that could open its mouth so wide; he simply dropped the lower jaw down on his neck, exposing the long yellow fangs. Then, when I started to snap a picture, he turned and went back into the brush and lay there broadside, snarling and hissing at me. I took one picture of him in that position, then worked around below him, as his right paw was stretched its full length toward the snow brush by the trap. From this position, I thought I could take one step closer and have a picture that was all cat, with only a fringe of the white snow around for a frame. He was looking directly away from me, seemingly oblivious to my presence, and I know he could not see me make that move, but the tip of his tail switched back and forth. I decided to take that one step forward, and as I raised my right foot the tail switched faster, the while I held camera in the left hand and cocked sixgun in my right. Things happened too fast for the eye to record. I never finished that step and was conscious only of the big cat being in the air and headed for my face, as I shot from the hip by merely tipping up the muzzle of the gun and jumped as far as I could to my left and down the slope. At the shot, his big head fell down on his chest and he flashed over my right shoulder and landed plop on his big belly, up the mountain beyond where I had stood. I landed down the mountain in the longest standing broad jump I ever made and with the old single action again cocked and on his shoulders. However, no second shot was needed. His tail was still held vertical and it slowly came down to the snow, just like the tail on a woodchuck when it dies. The head and neck seemed alive and he reached out and bit off every small quaking asp he could reach, but his whole body was paralyzed. The left paw was extended up the mountain, still reaching for me, and the right paw still back along his side dragging the two heavy traps and the light toggle, but he could not move his feet and the tail soon straightened out. I grabbed him by the tail and pulled him down the mountain into the opening and took one more photo as he gasped his last.

Old Prince still remained behind his fir tree until I called him out, but he was very reluctant to come close, even after the cat was dead and would not touch him. He proved a very large old male. The tips of his ears had been either chewed or frozen off to mere stubs, and the tip of his tail was likewise gone. One fang had broken off about halfway, and on skinning him out, after getting him home, I found his skull had been badly fractured clear across the top, over the zygomatic arches and back over the brain, and had healed, but the whole skull was a bloodshot reddish color.

I climbed back up the gulch and rode Brownie down to him. The wise old horse had packed out many a deer and some bear and goat, but he refused to go near that big cat until I walked up and put my foot on him and kicked him, telling the horse he was dead. Finally Brownie edged up with his reins trailing to one side and pawed the cat with a forefoot, just as he used to do with deer before he would let me load them, then he was satisfied and took no further interest in the cat. I led him to a wash about two feet deep and then dragged the cougar to him, but found I could not lift the beast as Brownie stood 17½ hands at the withers. Even when I had him in the wash I still could make no headway trying to lift that big cat into the saddle. Finally, I lugged a couple of dead quaking aspens up and leaned them against the horse, one in front and one just behind the cantle board of my old bronc saddle. Then by getting the big cat across them I found I could slide and roll him up and finally managed to flop the hindquarters over the saddle. I lost no time half hitching the hind legs to the cinch ring, while Brownie stood still as a mouse. It was then the work of seconds until I had the paws likewise lashed to the cinch ring and the cat loaded. I also tied tail and head with the cantle strings. I removed the head and cape from my buck remains and led the horse back out to the trail and the ten miles back to the ranch. Though I reset the traps and ran them every day for a week, no further cougar tracks showed near them and I finally pulled them up.

On laying the cougar out on the ranch house floor, I measured him before skinning, and found he measured exactly 7 feet 6 inches from tip of nose to tip of tail. Where they get these 9- and 10-foot cougars we read about in the sporting magazines and funny papers is beyond me. After skinning him, I quartered him up and weighed the four quarters, the innards and the skin with head and feet attached, and the whole works weighed exactly 200 pounds. Of course I lost the weight of the blood. There was nothing whatever in the stomach except the soles from a porcupine's feet and a few quills, so he must have had an awful fast turnover to dispose of all the huge bate of deer meat he had eaten the day before, or else I caught a different cat from the one that had eaten my deer. He still goes third place in the last book of records for the species.

The 250-grain .44 Special Keith Lyman bullet, backed by nine grains of Dupont shotgun, a light grouse load, had entered the center of the chest, taken off the aorta and lodged against the spine between the shoulders. It did all right, but I would have been safer with one of my heavy charges of Hercules 2400 behind that slug. He lived only two or three minutes after the slug had hit him. Even when I was watching him carefully, with every sense on the alert, he moved so fast in turning and tearing the traps loose from that snow brush that my memory only records a picture of him flashing toward me with that left paw outstretched and his big mouth open. The sixgun sounded and felt like a .22 in recoil. My respect for *Felis concolor* increased in no small degree after that experience.

At times cougar will kill every young colt they can find and sometimes attack full-grown horses. It used to be very hard to raise a colt in the Jim Ball basin, northeast of Helena, on account of cougar depredations. Cougar have a wide range, and though when deer are plentiful they will stick close to one small locality, if deer become scarce they will travel a considerable distance at times.

Cougar hunting nearly always entails the hardest kind of climbing and endurance, except in a country where you can ride a horse, and a good pack of dogs is an absolute necessity if results are desired. Once a cat is treed, you should not crowd him too close. It is much better to shoot from some distance, for if you try to get too close, he will often jump out and continue to lead you a merry chase. It's grand sport. If you follow the dogs on foot, by all means take a light pack with plenty of food for a few days and also a heavy coat or light sleeping bag for a bed. You will need both before the chase is over. Several friends of mine have eaten cougar meat at the end of such a chase, and claim it is not bad.

Jaguar

Never having hunted the jaguar, I must depend on what friends have told me of this animal. The late Charley Ren hunted jaguar quite a bit farther south in Mexico with dogs and the late Zane Grey told me of shooting several of them while on a trip by boat down a Mexican river with a Winchester .351 Self Loader. Though he hit them hard, all cats hit with the .351 escaped wounded. He wished for his old '95 Winchester on that trip, after losing several fine specimens of the jaguar that they encountered along the tropical riverbank.

Felis onca is much the largest of the American cats, and formerly its range extended as far north as central Texas, New Mexico and California, but at present it probably does not occur except very rarely north of southeastern Arizona and the adjacent Rio Grande River Valley. It extends southward far into Argentine. Much of the jungle region of Mexico, Central and South America is excellent jaguar range. The jaguar is a beautifully and gaudily marked animal, resembling the African and Asiatic leopard, but being larger, heavier and much stronger as well. In Mexico and South America, he is usually known as the tiger. In the Southern United States jaguar are usually found only on, or adjacent to, the range of the peccary or javalina, as he is very fond of these wild pigs. Jaguar will kill and eat deer, cattle, hogs, sheep or horses and most other wild game when hungry, but do not seem to concentrate on deer to the extent that cougar do. The beast is large and powerful enough to kill all species that inhabit its range. Its call is more like the roar of an African lion than the call of the cougar. The rut varies all around the calendar with no set season, much as with the cougar, and the young are born some 100 days after mating and are from two to four in number.

In many sections of Mexico and South America, the great spotted cat preys largely on domestic cattle and is hunted extensively for that reason. My friend C. W. Thurlow Craig, formerly ranch foreman for the International Products Corporation of the Paraguayan Chaco, killed a great many jaguar with a sixgun when cornered or treed by dogs. However, an American, Bob Eaton, who later took over that job when Craig left, killed even more with a .357 S & W Magnum sixgun of long barrel. A Britisher named Henry Gorman has the record for that section of South America at least, as he killed in one year forty full-grown tiger or jaguar with an old Colt New Service in caliber .44-40. They hunted them entirely with dogs and worked into the brush, when the dogs brought them to a stand. Owing to the spotted camouflage, they all claim it is often difficult to see a jaguar even at a few yards' range as his coloring blends so perfectly with the jungle.

In Brazil, the jaguar is particularly hard on domestic cattle and with the largest weighing well over 300 pounds, it's no wonder the ranchers are continually at war with the big cats and usually employ or keep good packs of tiger dogs on hand to deal with them. Like the cougar, the jaguar is seldom seen, except when chased and treed or stopped by dogs. Likewise it seldom attacks man. It is large and powerful enough to deal with a man, but like the cougar seldom tackles man unless cornered. When cornered or treed by dogs it will attack a man on sight, ignoring the dogs in many cases. Some jaguar hunters employ not only a well-trained pack of dogs and a good heavy-caliber sixgun but also carry a long-handled spear, and when a cat jumps them they drop the butt to the ground and let the big cat impale himself on the spear point.

When goaded to fury by the dogs, a cat will roar and jump for a man with little additional provocation. The American and Mexican species are usually smaller than their South American cousins, and while still plentiful in many of the tropical regions of Mexico, are now very scarce along the border of the United States.

XXI

Placing the Bullet on Big Game

IN all big game shooting, proper placing of that first bullet in a vital area is of utmost importance. The hunter simply must have a fair knowledge of the anatomy of the game hunted, in order to be certain of so placing his shot. If the first slug be carefully and correctly placed on the animal, and an adequate caliber is used, the results will be clean one-shot kills, with a very minimum of suffering for the animal, or none at all. This is only clean sportsmanship and should be the aim of all true sportsmen. Wherever possible to do so, the shot should be placed ahead of the diaphragm.

Big game usually drops at the shot and stays down only from spine or brain hits. Occasionally the heart may be exploded when it is filled with blood, resulting in an instant kill, but the usual thing for a heart-shot animal is for it to jump into a hard run and go anywhere from 50 yards to a quarter mile and live long enough to get well out of sight or, in the case of a big grizzly, to reach the hunter.

If the first shot is correctly placed, the animal either goes down at once or in a short time and stays down, but if the shot is improperly placed it may live for hours or days and travel a long way. The first bullet that strikes an animal administers all the shock his nervous system will stand, and after that first hit succeeding bullets seem to have little or no effect, unless brain or spine is hit. If that first shot lands in a vital area or strikes a nerve center the job is done, but if it fails to do so, one may often literally shoot the animal to pieces before getting it down.

Life is something we know all too little about and much will ever remain unknown. Animals differ just as much as do human beings, both in appearance and also in stamina and temperament. A shot that will put one animal down for keeps may have little effect on another animal even though it hits exactly the same spot or area. Once an animal is frightened or enraged, it is much harder to kill than if hit when it does not even suspect the presence of man. An animal shot in its bed as it peacefully chews its cud will often never regain its feet and dies quickly. The same beast, once jumped and scared, may carry on for a considerable distance with exactly the same placing of the shot. Likewise an animal hit when feeding may be caught off balance when the slug strikes and go down instantly, whereas if it were hit with legs in a different position, it well might not go down at all, but simply jump and run. The killing of a few head of any species does not give one any concrete idea as to how hard or how easy they are to kill. Whenever you think you have solved the mystery and can always kill cleanly with one shot, then along will come an animal that defies all rules and simply will not die from the same hit, at least not at once. I have seen many animals go down and stay down from a heart shot, and have seen a great many more simply jump into a hard run and carry on for several hundred yards unless a heavy cartridge was used on them. Even a brain shot is not always instantly fatal as many would believe; I have seen animals with part of the brain destroyed live for hours, and the same is true of man. After you see enough game killed yourself and also answer thousands of letters annually from other hunt-ers, and compare their notes on the different game, you finally arrive at a much more accurate conclusion than you ever would from your own hunting alone. What one animal does with a certain hit is, however, no criterion as to how the next beast will act, similarly hit.

Some shots such as brain or spine shots we know will always drop a beast, if an adequate rifle is used. Others we know will be fatal in a short time, such as lung and heart shots, but just how soon they will be fatal on different beasts we will never know, as the beasts vary too much in vitality. Some hits we know will injure or impair locomotion and thus offer more time for a killing hit. All these things must be considered, plus the fact that game very seldom offers the exact same placement of the shot. Nine times out of ten we will get a different presentation of the ani-mal than we expect, and we must be able to instantly recognize the vital area of the beast and know how to direct our slug to reach it, regardless of how it may be turned when hit.

If the heart of an animal be filled with blood at the time of the bullet's impact, it often sends a hydraulic shock effect over the entire nervous system and ruptures the blood vessels in the brain, causing instant demise, but if the heart is pumped empty when the projectile strikes, it is then just a muscle and death occurs as the result of hemorrhage alone. Many men of small experience will tell you exactly what an animal will do when hit in the heart, but you can be sure they then need more experience. In all game shooting one should, wherever possible, shoot with both eyes open and have a definite sight picture on the beast when the rifle recoils. This will give the hunter a very definite idea of where his bullet should have landed. Never shoot at an animal as a whole—always pick the spot on him you wish to hit; even in fast running shooting try to get your slug ahead of the belt and into that vital forward area of chest and shoulders.

Yes, we have read many briefs from those chaps who always hit the head or neck, running or standing, at all ranges, to and beyond 300 yards, but to date and after a lifetime of game experience we have yet to see the man who could always place his shots exactly right under average hunting conditions, unless all running and difficult shots were passed up.

It is well also to consider the type of rifle load you are using, and its average penetration and effect on different size game. We know that very high velocity rifles like the .270-130, .275 H & H, .276 and .280 Dubiel, .30 Newton and .300 Magnum, .30-06-150, .285 O.K.H. 180 grain and 334 O.K.H. 250 grain drive their missiles at extremely high velocity and tend to disintegrate on impact at close range, with maximum destruction of tissue but minimum penetration. We know that these general types of high velocity loads will kill a beast in a minimum of time if placed in the heart or lung area, and so placed that they will surely get inside the boiler room before blowing up. We also know these loads will seldom if ever get forward into the chest cavity, if fired into the flank or rump of the beast. Especially is this true on our heavier game, like elk, moose and big bear. On the other hand we know that rifles like the .35 and .405 Winchester, 6.5 mm. 160 grain, 7 mm. 175 grain, 8 mm. 236 grain, .30-06-220, .45-70-405, .333 Jeffery 300 grain, .333 O.K.H. and .334 O.K.H. 300 grain will practically always drive their long, heavy, moderate velocity bullets through to the vitals from rear raking hits on our smaller game, and even on our larger game they will often do so if the paunch is missed. If that big, fluid and food filled paunch is hit on large herbivores, it usually stops all slugs except those of very moderate velocity with plenty of sectional density. We know these slow heavy bullets will not kill as quickly from heart or lung shots as the high velocity types, yet we also know they are much more reliable when they must of necessity be driven into the rear of the animal, as is so often the case in fast running shooting.

Many sportsmen say it is not sporting to shoot a beast in its bed, but we believe it far more sportsmanlike to thus kill a beast cleanly than to jump him and cripple him in running shooting, often breaking a leg and allowing the poor beast to hobble along for miles on the stub. Running shooting is lots of fun, but produces more crippled and poorly hit game than any other phase of big game shooting. We prefer standing or bedded shots and clean one-shot kills to the so-called sport of running shooting. Consider the type of rifle load you are using and also your own ability in your selection of an aiming point. It's safer to select a large aiming point that will insure a clean kill in a few minutes than chance a very small aiming point that must be centered exactly to kill, with the possibility of a wounded animal escaping if the shot is not placed right.

Let us first take up the least desirable shots, those most often presented to the tyro hunter. These are rear and raking shots, usually on departing animals that have been jumped. Let us consider these shots first on herbivorous animals. If the beast is going directly away from you, the best bet is to aim at the center of the rump bone just over the root of the tail, for a certain hit. If you strike this thin shell of bone the animal will go down instantly and is then anchored, as both hind legs will be utterly useless and it can only drag itself with its front feet. Little or no meat will be damaged and there is but slim chance of injuring the cape if it is a trophy animal. If your shot should go high it will still strike the spine or withers or the back of the neck and will usually put the beast down. If it strikes the withers only it may or may not range into the spine and kill the beast, but it will usually put him down. If it strikes the back of the neck and centers the spine the beast is of course killed instantly, but if it misses the spine he will regain his feet and depart. There is also a great chance that it will emerge through the front of the neck, leaving a huge gaping hole in the scalp on our lighter game, but no damage at all on such beasts as elk and moose. If the shot should go low, then you are in for trouble unless the pelvic bone is shattered. In any case a low shot in the rump will ruin a lot of meat and probably range into the intestines or paunch, or both, and badly taint the meat through the lymph vessels, unless the beast is killed and dressed immediately. Avoid all low shots in this area as you would a pestilence. To my notion, unless it is a fine trophy head, you are better off to miss cleanly with a high shot than to hit an animal in the seat of the pants and badly mess him up.

Nearly every fall we pass up such shots rather than dress out gut-shot game. If the game is running hard or bouncing up and down, as is so typical of mule deer, then the task of placing the bullet is even more difficult. On running game we believe in shooting when the beast is at the height of its jump. Merely a matter of timing, and if you will watch a few run you will see that they sort of hang in the air for a fraction of a second at the height of their jump. Then is your best chance and if you have the sights on them and following their every jump, it's comparatively easy to shoot as they near the top of their bound. They are then up in the air and more clear of intervening limbs, shrubs and brush than when they hit the ground and present a better target. Strive always to hit that top of rump just above the root of the tail or the back of the head or neck if the animal is shot for meat only. The rump shot will not be instantly fatal, but it will anchor the beast and allow plenty of time for a clean killing lung or head shot. One should always carry both Hard and Soft Point loads for his rifle when procurable as the Hard Points are very nice to slip into the rifle for such finishing shots, where a minimum of mutilation is desired.

Next let us look at the quartering, going-away shot. The top of the rump is then harder to hit and if the beast is running only slightly quartering, the lungs are well covered by the hips and flanks. The back of the neck is also much more difficult to hit due to the lead factor. If the right flank is presented, then a long heavy bullet in proportion to its caliber will usually drive forward into the liver, diaphragm and lungs. The paunch lies on the left side in all herbivorous game, remember, and a slug driven forward through the right flank will usually range well forward into liver and lungs, very often without touching either entrails or paunch.

If the cartridge is large enough for the game hunted, it is a very reliable shot and one preferred by my friend John Burger for African buffalo. He uses a .333 Jeffery with 300-grain Solids or Hard Points, as we call them, for this shot and with excellent results. I have used it many times on elk, deer and goats and it is a killer. Game so hit usually continues to run for some distance, but is dead as a mackerel when trailed up. It also does not damage a pound of meat. In making this shot one should figure on aiming for the lungs as the ultimate destination of his bullet and the shot should be placed high rather than low, just under the spine in the right flank. If it goes higher it will usually range into and break the spine, and if lower will usually hit the intestines and badly wound and mess up the animal. Low shots in this area are to be avoided at all costs.

When the left flank of the beast is presented, in quartering running shots, it's another proposition. The paunch lies against the left flank and will stop practically all our modern high velocity expanding bullets. A hard point or solid .405-grain .45–70 will penetrate through the paunch and into the lungs, but it will also let the paunch contents out into the abdominal cavity, and if the beast is not killed quickly will result in tainted meat. We do not like our meat so flavored, hence do not like this shot at all. Many times we have seen elk and some moose so hit, even with our most powerful modern rifles like the .375 Magnum 300 grain and the .405 Winchester 300 grain, as well as the .400 Whelen 350 grain, and that big water and grass filled paunch stopped all bullets. The beast would go down but get up immediately and travel for miles from the smaller loads, and often some distance from the three heavy calibers above listed. Usually, however, such calibers sickened the beast until it stopped under 100 yards, but with .30–06 and similar cartridges it was able to travel all day or get completely away.

When the beast is going away at a more quartering angle, either to left or right, then one has a fine opportunity for making a raking chest shot, either through lungs or heart, or both. This is a fine placement of the bullet and it should be driven in behind the shoulder, so it will drive through heart and lungs and emerge in the front of chest. No meat will be damaged at all if the bullet is placed right and only a pound of ribs on the near side will be punctured before the bullet reaches the lung cavity. It is an excellent shot at such running game from either side but the aim should usually be just to the rear of the shoulder, depending of course on the angle the game is going and the distance and speed as well.

This is an excellent shot for our larger game when they must be killed with small caliber high velocity cartridges or with any load for that matter. The thin rib cage does not offer enough resistance to stop even a .270–130 and of course the heavy calibers will always penetrate this area nicely. Aim to strike the heart and lungs and remember they lie in the lower third of the body. Such placement of the shot will not damage any meat except the heart. If you like baked heart, aim a trifle higher to penetrate lungs and the aorta. These shots are equally good at standing, bedded or running game, but with standing or bedded game one can aim directly at the spot he wishes to hit, rather than having to lead that spot as in running shooting. Such shots, with the bullet entering and traversing a lung and then ranging forward through the heart, or the aorta above the heart, are very deadly and the game either drops at the shot or jumps into a hard run and continues to run until it bleeds out and drops. The bullet can thus be kept clear of the shoulders and relatively little meat is damaged. On opening the beast you will find that the blood will all have drained into the chest cavity. We like such shots on all herbivorous meat animals. They are very reliable stew producers.

When an animal is turned broadside, you have an even nicer shot offered. We prefer to place the bullet high in the lung cavity and just behind the shoulders, but under the spine. There is a big artery that carries all the blood back from the heart and lungs to the after portions of the animal;

this lies just under the spine and is usually noticed when severing the liver and diaphragm in dressing an animal. If a slug is so placed it drives through the top of both lungs, causing them soon to hemorrhage to such extent as to fill the lungs completely and suffocate the animal. Game so hit with an adequate rifle never goes very far. If it is a big slow heavy bullet, it expands and tears a good wound channel through both lungs and out the other side, leaving an excellent blood trail, and if it is a high velocity rifle with a long heavy bullet it will usually demolish the top of the lungs and sever this big artery, causing death in a very short distance. However we have seen 150-grain .30–06 and 130-grain .270 cartridges go into elk on such shots and blow out a small crater in the near lung about the size of an egg, and the elk took five or six such shots and traveled a long distance. In the case of one bull elk we watched a ranger plant six shots behind the shoulder with 129-grain .256 Newton before he emptied his gun. The shots could have been covered with the crown of your hat but that bull went about a quarter mile. His off lung was not even damaged. Another time I planted five 150-grain Remington Bronze Point .30–06 close in behind the shoulder on a small bull that stood broadside at 300 yards, all in a space some eight inches in diameter. That bull took them all and merely flinched. Then my partner ground an old Winchester Model '94 .25–35 carbine empty and hit him twice back in the paunch. He merely humped up a little and turned around facing us. My next shot was a 6-degree 1923 National Match load and the Full Patch spitzer entered the base of neck and penetrated the length of the spine, coming out on top of the rump and killing him instantly. Examination disclosed that my five 150-grain had merely gone into that near right lung about two inches and blown up, ruining that lung but still leaving the other in good condition.

A .30–30-170 in the same place would have been more effective as it would have cut through both lungs with one shot. This shows the fallacy of trying to use short light bullets at high velocity on heavy game of any sort.

A low lung shot placed with the animal broadside is deadly, but very slow to kill in proportion to the high lung shot, since it simply bleeds the animal out and if a small rifle is used he may travel a mile or more. If enough lung tissue is destroyed, such as is usual from a .35 W.C.F. or .405 W.C.F. on elk or moose, the beast seldom goes very far and always leaves an excellent blood trail. The fact remains, however, that the high lung shot kills much quicker through the filling of the lungs with blood and the resultant suffocation of the animal. Further, you are very apt to sever that big artery with a bullet fragment even though the slug passes below it, and this also leads to very quick death. If the shot should go a bit high, it will strike the spine and kill the beast almost instantly, if it has sufficient penetration. If still higher and over the spine, it will knock the beast down but won't always keep him down, unless the spine is injured. For all herbivorous meat animals this high broadside lung shot is my favorite, but I believe in using powerful heavy bullets that will surely drive through both lungs and out the other side. The animal either humps up and stands around until he drops from suffocation, or jumps into a run and travels until he drops. In either case I have an excellent blood trail and can be absolutely certain of finding a dead animal at the end of it. No shot is more certain, though it is not as quick in results as a heart or spine hit. When opened, the animal is always perfectly bled out and the blood will be found in a huge clot filling the chest cavity. I know of no better way to kill a beast for meat and also stick and properly bleed him at the same time. If it is a trophy animal, then the scalp or cape is never injured in the least, neither are the shoulders, and my meat and trophy are in perfect condition.

If one desires to hit the heart from such broadside shots, then aim at the rear edge of the shoulder knuckle or just behind it. If using a light bullet high velocity rifle like the .270–130, the .30–06–150 or the .256 Newton 129-grain, then you should always shoot just to the rear of the shoulder knuckle. We have seen elk shoulder bones blow up and stop all these loads cold and they never got into the chest cavity at all. If long heavy bullets are used at moderate velocities, they will break the shoulder and drive on into the heart or through it, but short, light, extremely high velocity missiles will not do so on elk, moose or big bear. The heavy shoulder bones cause them to disintegrate. We have seen four bull elk lost completely with the shoulder thus broken when such heart shots were taken with the .270–130 load. Others similarly hit were trailed up and later finished, but those four got away on three legs.

If you are using a 220-grain bullet in the .30 calibers or a 150-grain in the .270, it will usually break the shoulder and go on into the heart. We have sometimes taken such shots on a bet just to show they would hit the heart, but do not like such broadside heart shots, as one or both shoulders are usually damaged and the heart blown up and ruined as well, and baked or boiled heart is a choice titbit with us. If you are using a powerful rifle with long heavy bullets, this is a very certain shot and will not only break one shoulder but also destroy the heart and cause the beast to go down in a short distance. Not wanting the shoulders shattered even this low, or the heart blown up, we prefer the high lung shot to all other broadside shots at meat animals. We like to bleed out our meat animals quickly but at the same time stay clear of all four quarters with the bullet channel.

Neck shots we are off of for good and ten days. In 1919 I shot an old bull elk in the neck at about 60 to 70 yards with .30–06–220 load. He stood facing me but with head turned to the left as he looked down the mountain. That 220-grain slug missed the spine but put him down as if stone dead. When we approached and looked him over he was apparently dead but his head was under the snow so I could not see his eye. While standing directly in front of him, I prodded him on top of the withers with the muzzle of the rifle. He came up on his feet with the suddenness of a dynamite explosion, catching me on his brow points and hurling me off down the mountain. I lost the rifle in the sail down the hill and landed on a log just under the snow, temporarily paralyzing my left arm. Only a good single action Colt sixgun saved the day, but since then I have refrained from ever attempting a broadside neck shot at any game. That 220-grain slug lodged under the skin on the off side of his huge old neck, missing the spine by less than an inch. Game so hit will go down as if killed but will later regain its feet and get away unless hit again. I have known several hunters who were injured by deer and elk when they thus approached game and stood their rifle up against a tree to dress out the animal. If I had planted that 220-grain .30–06 in the lower part of that bull's chest as he faced me, with the long slug ranging back through his heart, he would in all probability have simply whirled and run off around the mountain, leaving a good blood trail, and would have been dead and well bled out when I trailed him up. Instead, I had a fight on my hands and narrowly escaped with my life.

Years ago we saw several old cow horses that had been captured from bands of wild horses by the simple expedient of shooting them through the top of the neck with Hard Points. The scars on their necks bore mute evidence as to how they were captured and no doubt many more were killed by spine hits in an attempt thus to crease them.

There is a lot of meat in a bull elk's neck or that of a big bull moose and the spine is hard to find at any great range. For this reason many neck shots only penetrate the muscles and miss the spine and the animal soon recovers. If the shot is low it is very apt to sever the jugular veins and bleed the animal to death, but if placed over the spine results in only temporarily stunning the beast. Anyone can have my full share of neck shots. They are too uncertain to suit me. If the animal is broadside and close to you and you want to make a neck shot, then the best place to aim is right where the skull joins the neck — you then have a fair target for close range and a bullet so placed will kill instantly.

When an animal faces the hunter, you have an excellent opportunity for either a frontal neck shot or a chest shot. My preference is the chest shot. It's a larger target and you are certain of results. If the beast is slightly quartering, the bullet should be aimed to take off the aorta, just over the heart, and cut the ribs behind the shoulder. If it is facing you squarely, you can shoot through top of heart and back through lungs into paunch if the rifle has that much penetration, or you can aim higher and break the spine at the base of the neck. The latter shot will kill instantly, but messes up the front quarters when the spine is hit. The chest shot, into the heart, will damage little or no meat and will bleed the animal out perfectly. For some reason unknown to me, an animal shot from behind nearly always drops at the shot, while one shot from in front into the chest nearly always whirls and runs, often with no sign of being hit. Just why this is the case we would not even hazard a guess, but it is a fact that has stood out over the years. Even small mule bucks shot in the chest, when the heart was almost totally destroyed, have jumped and run for 50 to 200 yards, as though unhit, before dying on their feet. The shot from the rear seems to produce a great shock effect, while the one from the front of the chest seems only to produce fatal hemorrhage.

When the frontal shot is aimed at the base of the neck, the hunter has a maximum-sized target. A high shot will still break the neck, if centered and an adequate load is used, while a low one will drop into the chest cavity. A shot to either side of center will break or damage a shoulder and an extremely high shot would hit the head. For these reasons this center shot to the base of the neck is a good one to employ for a long range shot at an animal facing the hunter.

Broadside shoulder shots, aimed to also strike the spine, are very deadly and will put an animal down instantly when properly placed, but are also very injurious to the front quarters of meat animals and for this reason we prefer the heart or lung shots to hitting the spine in the shoulder region. A shot through the tops of the withers or shoulders, over the spine, will usually drop an animal and sometimes keep him down. This is a shot often made by tyro hunters. You must remember that many game animals have high boss ribs over the spine at the shoulder, particularly the buffalo, mountain goat and elk as well as moose. Even a mature bighorn ram measures just nine inches from the top of the hair on the withers down to the center of the spine. The animal lives in the lower third of his body at the shoulders, so shots should be placed in that lower third for heart and lungs and not over halfway up for a spine hit.

This leaves us the head shot on meat animals. It should never be employed on a trophy animal as the skull will be shattered, even with a small rifle, and blown to bits with a heavy cartridge. It is, however, a nice shot for close range, standing meat animals. One should remember to keep his point of impact at or above the level of the eyes. If a frontal shot is presented, and the head is level with the hunter, an imaginary line from the base of one horn across the other eye, to cross and intersect a similar imaginary line from the opposite horn and eye, will give you the location for a center brain shot. This is the age-old system used in shooting beef cattle, also hogs, except that with the latter the line is taken from one ear across to the opposite eye, then another from the opposite ear across to the other eye, and if the head is at the proper level this intersection of the two lines will give you the proper location. If the head be held high the aim should be lower and if held low, the aim should be higher. When a side shot is presented, a bullet driven in at the very base of the ear, or between the eye and the base of the ear, will reach the brain. Avoid all low shots from the side, as we have found several animals dead and soured that had run a long way with the lower jaw shattered and had either bled out or starved to death. The head shot should never be employed except at close range, where you can be certain of exactly placing the slug.

A further note on broadside shots at such meat animals at long range. Broken-legged animals will usually go a long way and it is best always to avoid breaking a leg. For this reason when I take a shot at long range at a standing broadside animal, I aim to hit either the chest and lung cavity behind the shoulder or to miss completely. It's far better to drop below the chest with a clean miss than to aim for the shoulder and then have a drop from the point of aim simply break a leg below the chest cavity and lead to a long chase.

The back of the head of meat animals presents a very good target, as a low shot will break the neck while a high one will miss cleanly. Game so hit will die instantly but will not be as well bled out when dressed as if shot through the heart or lungs.

Next we have bear and cats. With both bear and cats, it is imperative that you break them down whenever possible. For this reason different aiming points are necessary than on herbivorous hoofed game. Wounded bear or lion leave a much poorer trail to follow than a running hoofed animal. Further, they are harder to stop on the spot and one should always strive to break down the spine or a shoulder, thus destroying the powers of locomotion.

When the rump or rear end of a bear or cat is presented, no shot is more certain than one driven into the rump bone above the root of the tail. This will instantly put the hindquarters out of commission and leave you a very mad animal, but one that can travel only by pulling himself along with the forepaws, allowing ample time for a killing hit to be administered. A grizzly or cougar so hit presents a spectacle you will not soon forget. We have seen big bear so broken down bawl and pound the ground with one paw, then pull themselves forward toward you in a desperate effort to close with you. They always then present ample opportunities for a killing hit. When a bear or cat is turned quartering away from you, it is well to strive to break the spine between the shoulders. Remember a grizzly also has a high hump over the withers and the shot should be aimed only about halfway up from the bottom of the chest. A raking shot into the loin, just in front of the hip to the spine, is also good but presents a smaller vital target than one driven in behind the shoulder. If the bear or cat be turned nearly broadside, but still quartering somewhat, then it is best to drive your slug through the lungs, with the ultimate intention of breaking the spine and off shoulder. You simply must be able to visualize where the spine and off shoulder lie regardless of the angle at which the animal is turned. Wherever possible, one should strive to break one or both shoulders and try to hit the spine at the same time. If the beast is quartering toward you, aim in front of the near shoulder, to hit either the aorta or the spine and thence range into that off shoulder. You simply must break a big bear down to stop him quickly. If the animal is square broadside, then a shot through both shoulders at a level with the spine is very deadly and will practically always anchor the beast if an adequate cartridge is used.

When the animal faces the hunter, a bear will very often rise up on his hind feet, presenting a chest shot. It should be directed into the center of the chest at the level with the shoulders and aimed to hit the spine, regardless of whether the beast faces you squarely or is turned slightly. Aim to break the spine, and if you can drive the slug through heart and lungs before hitting the spine so much the better. Many black bear have a small white spot in the breast that makes an excellent target when they are facing you on their hind feet. If the bullet misses the spine and heart, it may only put the beast down temporarily, but if it is planted right it will kill him almost instantly.

Jack Grigsby was back-packing on a hunt in Alaska, and was heavily loaded with bedding and food on his pack board. In addition he had an old 8 mm. Hanel Mannlicher carbine slipped in a canvas boot on the back of his pack board. Coming down a bear trail to a salmon stream, he surprised a huge old boar or male brownie at close range. The bear rose to his full ten feet of height in the stream, as Jack reached over his shoulder and hauled the little short Mannlicher out of its canvas boot. He had purposely cut the stock off shorter than normal, to reduce weight, and had to shoot with his nose almost against the safety. He turned the safety and aimed in the center of the huge old brownie's chest and gave him a 236-grain long exposed Soft Point bullet. Though directed right it never penetrated the spine but did utterly ruin the aorta. At the shot, the big bear shuddered, then stood on his hind feet swaying from side to side for several minutes as Jack debated shooting again. Then he simply settled down in a heap, dead.

If a bear is down on all four feet and facing quartering toward you, it is well to aim for the spine, at the base of the neck, so that your bullet will range on into the opposite shoulder. This is a very deadly and certain shot on big bear if placed right. Usually it is safer to try to penetrate heart or spine and hit the off shoulder rather than to hit the near shoulder first, as it may blow up and stop your bullet before it ever gets into the chest cavity. When a grizzly is coming your way, however, a shot to the shoulder on the downhill side of the bear will practically always roll him over and give you time for another hit. It will stop or turn a big bear quicker than a center chest shot as a rule. In a charge the head is carried low enough to almost cover the base of neck and upper chest and usually the skull is wanted undamaged. Bear move fast and a frontal head shot on a fast moving bear is very apt to strike the teeth or the top of the skull, when it may deflect upward. If the beast is still, and the head held low, a shot between the eyes with a powerful rifle will range back into the brain. If the head be carried level with the hunter, the bullet should be aimed into the orifice of the nose. A bullet entering here will drive back through the thin nasal membranes of the skull proper over the brain and penetrate it easily. A sixgun bullet or even a .22 L.R. High Speed solid bullet will usually penetrate to the brain on a big bear when thus directed, as there is relatively little to penetrate but nasal membrane and the brain itself has a thin bone covering at the back of the nasal passages. If the beast is up on his hind feet, a much safer shot is to the center of the chest if he faces you, and if standing on his hind feet but facing away from you, then shoot to break the spine between the shoulders.

The brain of a bear or cat lies in the extreme rear end of the skull and

Aiming point for bighorn sheep
Heart shot

Aiming points for mountain goat
Top: spine and shoulder shot; *right:* high lung shot; *bottom:* heart shot

Aiming point for elk
Heart shot

Aiming points for mad grizzly
Top: brain shot; *bottom:* heart shot

Aiming points for bear
Left: brain shot; *right:* top shoulder and spine shot; *bottom:* heart shot

unless the head is low, so the bullet will penetrate the heavy frontal bone squarely, or the head is held high enough for the bullet to go back through the nasal passages to the brain, it may and often does deflect the slug. When a side shot is presented and you wish to hit the brain, as when using too light a rifle for such work, aim at the very base of the ear. A slug striking here will drive into the center of the brain without difficulty. Walrus and sea lion, as well as seal, also have the brain pan in the extreme rear end of the skull. The sea lion and seal brain is easily reached from a shot in the end of the nose when facing the hunter, but the walrus presents a smaller target as the heavy tusks root up on each side of the nasal passage, and on walrus it is much safer to wait until the head is turned sideways and shoot into the rear portion of the skull, a trifle below a level of the eye.

Walrus shot in the water will sink; so will a grizzly bear for that matter. One friend of mine shot three grizzlies one spring while running the Peace River and all sank and were lost. They were shot with a .300 Savage rifle while swimming the river. Edgar Dopp also lost one into which he emptied a 9 mm. Luger, when it barged into his pack string. The bear, a nice grizzly, rolled into the river and never came up. A bear's skull is comparatively thin on each side, though protected somewhat by very heavy jaw muscles, but almost any modern rifle will penetrate to the brain from the side. On a frontal shot, the slug must go back in the nasal passage to be sure of reaching the brain, and the frontal skull bone being quite heavy, as are the teeth, a shot placed at random from the front may well disintegrate on skull or teeth without ever reaching the extreme rear end where the brain lies. Usually the skull is desired as a trophy and for measurements, so whenever possible it is best to kill bear with body shots.

Cougar are usually hunted with dogs and shot out of trees. Usually a clean kill is wanted, so they will not fall out with enough life left to kill a valuable dog. A .22 L.R. solid bullet high speed driven into the bottom of the skull from almost directly underneath the cat will drive up through the thin throat muscles and into the brain. A heavier rifle is always advisable or a heavy sixgun. This shot is deadly when it can be obtained. When a side head shot is wanted, the bullet should be driven in at the very base of the ear. If the skull is wanted undamaged, then it is best to break spine and shoulders at the same time if possible. Don't aim too high and go in over the spine. Most shots will be from below the cat and you must visualize the exact location of the spinal column from any angle. In all big game shooting the hunter should study the anatomy of any beast hunted until he knows the exact location of spine or heart and lungs as well as brain, regardless of how the animal may be turned. Then he must shoot for that vital area and not just at the surface. In a way it's much like playing billiards and the expert billiard shot knows almost instinctively exactly where his cue ball must contact the other ball. Likewise the hunter should know his game well enough so he can tell at a glance exactly where to direct his slug so it will range into that vital area. With all bear and cats, you must always strive to kill instantly or else break the beast down with the first shot. Once a cat or bear is wounded, he will present only a very fast moving target and one very difficult to hit right. It is always poor policy to shoot at a rolling bear. Both bear and cats react to a bullet's impact quicker than any other beast, and the usual thing with bear is for them to drop and roll if the hit is well placed. It's best to wait until they stop rolling and regain their feet before shooting again so you can have some idea of where you are hitting them. Cats go into a frenzy of movement when hit and are then virtually impossible to hit right.

It is always safer to shoot bear from above than from below, because they will invariably drop and roll when the slug strikes them. If it does not strike a leg or spine, they may only swing their head and bite at the bullet entrance, but if hit in spine or near a nerve center they usually drop and roll. They are very hard to hit right when rolling. In all bear shooting take nothing for granted, and remember it's far safer to drive another slug into the spine-shoulder area and be sure. If they do regain their feet, they may do so very fast and then present only a fast moving target that is hard to hit right. Another bullet hole will not hurt the pelt and may save you a fine trophy. With expanding bullets, I know of no single modern American cartridge that will shoot through the shoulders of a big grizzly or brownie, and a big polar bear presents the same resistance.

In all bear shooting, the placing of that first slug just right is of vital importance and I have watched old bear hunters take half an hour in carefully approaching a bear and even then wait until he turned and presented the exact shot they desired before shooting. They well know that first shot is the best one they will get and they also know the importance of placing it exactly right, or waiting until they can do so. No game is dangerous until it arrives at close quarters. While an unwounded bear will often rise to his hind feet when he sees or suspects your presence, I have never seen a wounded one rise on his hind feet after a charge is started. Bear come for you with just one purpose, and that is to get in reach of you and come fast and on all fours. If you have them out in the open, a cool head can easily stop them with a good rifle, but if in dense alders where your movements are limited, it is sometimes a different proposition. Shots to the chest will kill them in time, but unless a very heavy rifle is used may not stop them in time to save your own pelt. A shot breaking a shoulder will stop or turn them and a brain shot through the end of the nose will of course kill instantly, but is very hard to make on a fast moving bear.

It's much safer to take a little more time when same is available and make that first shot good, then you usually have the job finished. Trailing up a wounded grizzly or brownie in dense alders is always ticklish business, and best avoided by killing or completely disabling him with your first shot; so take every possible precaution to make that first shot on bear a killer.

XXII

Skinning and Curing Big Game Trophies

PROPER skinning and care of trophies after they are killed is absolutely necessary if one would ultimately wind up with perfect mounts or rugs. When sportsmen hunt with competent guides, this phase of big game hunting is usually well taken care of by the guide. However we have seen many guides who did not know how to properly skin, or prepare a cape or skin after skinning, to insure its reaching the taxidermist in perfect condition.

For every hunter who hunts with a competent guide, there will be at least ten hunting on their own. For this reason all persons interested in the taking of big game for later use as trophies should understand the rudiments of skinning and curing of capes and skins, so they will reach the taxidermist in perfect order. Only thus can they hope to do the work themselves, or to be able to check on the work of their guides. We have seen literally hundreds of fine trophies ruined, by improper skinning, by throat cutting, or by failure to properly cure the scalp or pelt after skinning. The long-suffering taxidermist is in the end the goat and is blamed if the trophy does not look up to par, when in reality the fault is often with the hunter or guide who prepared the trophy.

First let us take up proper skinning, either of horned beasts for head and shoulder mounts, or of bear or cats for rugs. Forget the sticking or throat-cutting operation. Game hit with a high power rifle seldom bleeds at all, or if it does then only in very small quantities when the throat is cut. This for the reason that the shock of a heavy rifle bullet paralyzes the heart action, so that blood is no longer pumped through the arteries, and coagulates in the blood vessels and around the perimeter of the bullet wound. The thing to do is to open the beast as soon as possible after killing and the blood will be found largely in the chest cavity around the lungs and heart.

For animals of the size of deer, sheep and goats, which are usually

[382]

wanted for meat as well as trophies when having suitable heads, one need only open the beast full length from tail to breastbone and remove all innards and heart and lungs and drain out in cool weather. After the blood is all removed, one should wipe the inside of the carcass dry with leaves, boughs or a cloth, so that the meat will seal and dry as soon as possible. Many simply coat all the meat exposed with blood and allow it to dry, and this is a mighty good method though it leaves the tallow coated with blood and does not produce as nice appearing a job.

When heavy animals like elk or moose are shot for meat, they must be opened further or they will often sour even in cold weather. There is a lot of weight and thickness to an old bull elk's neck and the same is true of a moose, and the cape must be removed and also the trachea and wind-pipe and air allowed to circulate around this portion or it will not prop-erly cool in time to prevent souring. When deer are killed in very warm weather, also all elk and moose, they should be completely skinned im-mediately, so they will cool out. If flies are prevalent the meat should be well peppered with black pepper and covered with cheesecloth, either wrapped or sacked so the flies cannot actually blow the meat. In the case of heavy game it should be hung from trees by either ropes or spikes until thoroughly cooled before packing out.

Meat can be kept perfectly for a couple of weeks even in very warm weather if hung up very high at night and all covering removed, then taken down and wrapped and put in a cool shady place during the day.

The secret is to get the meat dry on the outside, so that a crust is formed, sealing the meat against the air. If hams are to be kept for a great length of time and the weather is comparatively warm in the day, then the best procedure is to sew them up in common flour sacks or similar cloth and immerse in a boiling brine that will float a spud or an egg for about one to two minutes, then hang in the shade, or on the north side of the cabin. Deer and elk hams so prepared will keep from hunting season until spring. The boiling brine sears the outside and a rind soon forms that is impervious to flies or weather with its cloth coating, and the meat inside will be found fresh and properly hung months after killing.

When hoofed game is taken for trophies, one usually desires a head mount. For a real head mount the brisket and points of shoulders should always appear on the finished mount if it is to look really well. First turn the beast on his back, then pull the forelegs back along the body. With game of deer to sheep size cut square across the breastbone between the forelegs, leaving at least six inches of the brisket and breast skin on the neck

[383]

or scalp end, or if you are in doubt, just take the skin off behind the shoulder. Uusually one can cut across the legs well down below the shoulder, leaving this upper leg skin on the cape, then run the cut up on each side to the top of vertebrae, skinning from a point well back of the point of the shoulder and leaving all the front of the shoulder skin on the cape. Next turn the beast on his belly and make a cut from a point on top of the shoulders, up the back of the neck, forward to a point about between the ears. Next cut from the end of this incision to each horn, making the cuts in the form of a V from the main cut up the back of the neck.

This leaves a flap of skin extending back from between the horns in the form of a V. That is all the splitting needed to properly skin out any horned game head. Next peel the skin back around the horns and sever the ears close to the skull, being careful to leave all skin and hair on the cape with none left around the base of the horns. Care should be exercised in skinning around the eyes, to leave the inner eyelids on the scalp, and care should also be used in digging out the tear ducts just forward of the eyes, leaving this skin unbroken and all on the cape. Next cut into the mouth well back from the lips, leaving all the inner lips intact on the cape. The same must be done with the nostrils, as the taxidermist needs both the inside of the lips and the inside of the nostrils for three fourths of an inch back from the orifice of mouth or nostrils.

When the cape is completely removed, you will find the beast is skinned from the rear part of the shoulders and about half of the breastbone forward to its nipper teeth. If front leg mount is desired the skin should be cut around the beast in back of the shoulders, and a small cut run down the inside rear part of each front leg to remove the bone and meat and the leg should be unjointed at the hoof. Aside from the cut around the beast at the back of the shoulder, the only splitting is along the back of the front legs extending into the cut across the lower breastbone, and the splitting up the back of the neck to a point between the ears and then out to each horn base with a separate cut.

Next turn the skin inside out and carefully remove all flesh and fat. Start skinning the back of the ears, turning them wrong side out, but separate the skin from the cartilage *only on the back* of the ears, letting it adhere to the cartilage on the inside of the ear. This separation of back ear skin and cartilage must extend from the extreme edges of the outer ear and to the extreme tip of the ear as well, and great care must be used or the skin will be broken or cut through. In the case of mountain goats with their extremely sharp pointed ears, one should separate this back ear skin clear to the extreme tip. With elk and mule deer, the ears are very large, and this ear skinning represents considerable work, but it must be done or the skin will spoil and the hair slip before the scalp reaches the taxidermist. When the ear is turned completely wrong side out, sever the ear base from the scalp, leaving only a small orifice.

Next take the eyes. There is a thin inner membrane and this should be very carefully split from the outer covering or eyelids, working slowly and carefully with a razor-sharp penknife until the inside lid is skinned back to the extreme edge of the outer eye covering. With practice one soon learns to tell by the feel of the skin when he has reached the extreme edge and no undue thickness remains. Next do the same with the lips and nostrils, carefully skinning back the inner membrane and leaving it intact with the outer skin, until the inner lips are split free of the outer lip yet no hole is cut through at any place. The taxidermist sews these inner lips together in making a closed-mouth mount or glues them up inside the mouth when making a bugling elk mount or one of deer or sheep with mouth open. All surplus fleshy tissue must be removed around the lips and eyes, yet retaining the entire inner lining on the scalp.

When the skinning and splitting is completed spread the scalp in the shade and rub in all the fine table salt you possibly can, in every portion of flesh-exposed skin, being careful to put plenty around base of ears, nostrils and mouth as well as eyes, then coat it with salt an eighth inch deep if possible and keep in the shade. This salt will form a brine. Fold the head skin back over on the flesh side of the neck skin and roll up. Keep in the shade for thirty-six hours until the brine has penetrated every possible portion of the skin, then spread in the shade and allow to dry slowly. Scalps thus prepared will keep almost indefinitely and hide bugs will not bother them, but hair moths will cut the hair the next spring, so get them in the taxidermist's hands as soon as possible after curing.

Next take the skull. Cut off every possible bit of meat and dig out the eyes, skin off the inner mouth covering and remove and clean the jawbones. Next saw off the small round skull joint until a small hole appears to the brain cavity and remove the brains with a brain spoon or common teaspoon. If you want a lifelike mount, the complete skull should be preserved. Salt and pepper the skull inside and out heavily and tie the lower jaw in place. Only with the natural skull complete can a competent taxidermist make up a manikin that will exactly duplicate the original skull. Animals' skulls differ just as much as do those of Homo sapiens and their faces vary just as much, so if you want the mount to appear as the animal originally did, cure the complete skull.

Most taxidermists have manikins in three sizes and many outfitters simply saw off the skull plate to eliminate as much weight as possible. When this is done the skull plate should always include the eye sockets, but if you want the taxidermist to model the manikin to exactly conform to the original skull, then he must have the original skull to follow. After curing, capes should be sacked in burlap bags that will allow free circulation of air until they reach the hands of the taxidermist. Be sure and wash out all bloodstains as they impregnate all hollow hair like that of deer and sheep and are very hard to remove once dried. With white sheep and goat pelts or scalps it is virtually impossible to remove all bloodstains after they have dried into the hair, so wash them clean as soon after killing and skinning as possible.

With bear and cat skins, split from the rectum forward to the throat with beast lying on its back, then split from throat forward to *only* one corner of the mouth. Next split from the belly side of the rectum out each hind leg, being careful to keep the cut on the inside of the leg to the foot pads. Also split from about the center of the breast out to the pad on the inside of each foreleg. Skin around the pads, leaving them on the carcass until you reach the toe pads. Do not split the toe pads but turn the skin wrong side out until the claw itself can be unjointed. The head skin should receive the same treatment as to eyes, ears, lips and nostrils that I have outlined for horned beasts. Next remove all fat; this can best be done when skinning the beast by using a sharp knife and leaving the fat where it belongs, on the carcass. After skinning carefully pare away all remaining fat, turn ears and split around lips and nostrils and eyes, then salt very heavily and roll up to form a brine. Examine the pelt daily and turn it over so that the brine formed from the fine table salt impregnates every single pore of the entire skin. Be sure and pour the toes full of salt and do not be stingy with it.

We have saved one fine grizzly skin with only three pounds of salt available, by first carefully removing all fat and flesh and then thoroughly rubbing the salt into every pore of the skin, and it arrived at Jonas Brothers in perfect condition over a month after killing. It is always better to have plenty of salt and use a surplus, as it preserves the skin and makes tanning easier.

The tail of bear and cats should always be split from the rectum to tip of tail and on the underside, and this also cleaned of fat and well salted. Skins thus prepared will keep for weeks and arrive at the taxidermist's shop in perfect shape. Proper preparation of big game heads and skins and scalps is work, but if the beast is worth hunting in the first place, then it should be accorded proper care after killing. One has only to visit any big taxidermy shop like Jonas Brothers and examine the scalps and pelts shipped them for mounting to know why taxidermists grow old early, as they will see many bloody, dirty scalps and pelts, often with the throat cut and too short for even a good neck mount; but with full instructions for a full shoulder mount. No taxidermist can do a perfect job on a poor or improperly skinned specimen, and all hunters should consider it a disgrace to ship such specimens for mounting. In taxidermy as in other things, you get just about what you pay for and we advise the best. There are hundreds of really competent small taxidermists throughout the country, but unless you are familiar with their work and know it is good, then our best advice is to ship to competent taxidermists like Jonas Brothers with a national reputation and be sure of the best. Formerly the James L. Clark studios also produced work above reproach but Mr. Clark closed his business when he took up work with the Museum of Natural History at New York. So, unless you know a really good small taxidermist, we would advise shipping to Jonas Brothers at Seattle, Denver or New York and be sure of the best work available.

Before going on a big game hunt, it is well to visit your taxidermist and obtain complete skinning charts and instructions so you do not have to leave it all to memory.

Now a further word on keeping meat. Remove all bloodshot meat and especially shattered bones from the carcass as soon as possible after killing. Shattered bones sour and spoil first and bloodshot meat next. Meat that is bloodshot need not be thrown away. Remove it, wash it and separate the muscles, and the blood clots will be found to lie between the muscles and tissues rather than in them. These blood clots can be removed, after which that meat will make excellent stews or mulligans for immediate consumption. Use up the thin rib portions of the carcass first as the heavy hams will keep longest. Meat is usually at its best after it has hung and aged several days.

Improperly handled and dressed game animals as well as improperly prepared big game specimens are the badge of a tenderfoot. If you would endear yourself to your guide and get the most from his services, then by all means learn to prepare, or at least help in the preparation of, your trophies and leave him more time to scout and perform his multitudinous duties. You will also find your taxidermist will accord your trophies earlier and better mounting if they reach him in perfect shape.

Big bearskins can be best shaved clean with a currier's knife, but it takes a lot of experience even to learn to properly sharpen and curl the edge of these heavy two-handled knives and the layman will never master them unless he has worked in a taxidermy or tanning shop. One familiar with their use can, however, thin and clean a heavy elk or moose cape or big bearskin to perfection. A large smooth fleshing beam is necessary and the skin must be cleaned of burrs or mud so there will be no bump underneath to cause the knife to cut through the pelt.

For most hunters the big heavy currier's knife is out, for obvious reasons, so they must learn to skin the beast clean and then to pare away any remaining flesh or fat. For skinning heavy game, we prefer a properly shaped sheath knife. Ofttimes the hands are numb with cold and a jack-knife, however large, is awkward to open and does not afford as secure a grip once opened as a good well-shaped sheath knife. There are many excellent shapes on the market. The blade should not be too long, about five inches maximum. Those extremely long blades are useful to cut steaks or to stick pigs but are awkward in the extreme for skinning. The ideal would be two knives, a small straight-blade ripper for all splitting and a wide heavy blade with considerable curve to the point for peeling. When one knife must do both jobs it should have a straight clip to the back of the point to enable the skinner to run it along smoothly and evenly under the skin for splitting, and still maintain a wide curved point for peeling. It should always be razor sharp, but not too thin, as a too thin knife will chip easily.

Many times the hunter will be caught out with only his sheath knife, and it should be heavy and strong enough to permit removing a forefoot and shank which can then be used as a club to pound the knife right back through the brisket. The pelvis can usually be separated easily enough, if you follow the white seam, but if you miss it, the knife will have to be pounded through with a forefoot used as a club, on the back of the blade. Some hunters carry a long heavy knife that is very awkward for skinning, but by having the back of the blade filed into saw teeth, they do have a good efficient bone saw incorporated in the knife. We prefer a good stout five-inch blade with plenty of width and strength and thickness that can be pounded through the brisket and pelvis where necessary. A much better tool is a small belt ax. They add weight, but when of very light, strong construction like the little Marbles axes are well worth their weight. You can easily split both brisket and pelvis and in addition you can also split the vertebrae when quartering elk or moose, and also have an excellent tool for blazing out a trail from your kill. Never leave a kill in heavy dense timber without landmarks, without blazing out a trail that you can find and easily follow back. It should also be blazed high enough so that a heavy snowfall will not cover it. Remember that the timber, hills and, in fact the whole terrain, will look differently after a heavy snowfall.

Always orient yourself and the location of your kill by cliffs, dead trees, mountains, streams or other prominent landmarks that you can see as far as possible and then blaze a trail to them, so you can always find your game when you come back. We have known of many animals being lost and never found, due to the fact that the hunter, in his excitement over making a kill, had neglected to mark the spot or to blaze out from it, if in heavy timber.

For such blazing a small belt ax is the best tool but a good heavy sheath knife can be used nicely if you do not have an ax. In addition to blazing trees, cut into and break over the tops of small stuff; this will always show, even after a heavy blanket of wet snow.

Each fall a great deal of game, especially deer, is dragged out from the spot where killed. If the snow is deep enough to cover logs, rocks and so on this can be done to advantage, but we personally do not like our meat dragged over dry ground at any time. Far better to cut it up and pack it out. We have even seen four men thus drag out elk and often over rough terrain. When their camp was reached the hair was all rubbed off, the skin scored through and dirt ground into both meat and skin and the meat badly bruised as well.

When a heavy buck has to be packed out by hand and is too heavy for one man, then the best procedure is to skin him halfway back. If the head is to be saved, one can remove the cape, then skin back to the middle of the beast and cut him in two sections, but leaving two ribs on the hindquarters and simply unjointing the spine. The skin can be rolled over the end of the loins on the hindquarters and they are then ready to lash on a pack board. The front half and the cape should be mantied up in good clean canvas and then lashed on the other pack board. It is well to cover the horns, or turn them down and flag well with red handkerchiefs, so some nitwit will not shoot you for a deer, if the hunting is in heavily hunted sections. A heavy buck can thus be packed out much easier than if swung on a pole between two men. I know of no more awkward load than a deer slung on a pole between two men, and even though his front legs be hooked up over the horns and allowed to stiffen and then lashed to the pole so he will not swing, it is still an ungainly, ill-balanced load and the steps of one man on rough terrain will never match those of his partner. Better by far to halve the buck and make two loads of it that can be handled easily and surely.

With mountain sheep and goats, the cape must be removed at once, and the same procedure is best when packing out sheep or young or fat goats wanted for meat. I have often taken the head and cape and neck of a ram down in one trip, then made two more trips for the rest of the meat, when alone. Two men hunting together can usually take a whole ram down off the mountain if they will bone out all the heavy bones and leave them behind. Meat so boned out will not keep as long and may have to be jerked, but it is one way to get all the good meat off the mountain and is far better than simply taking the hams and saddle and leaving the front quarters for the coyotes, as so many do. For boning meat you need a thin slim blade. Some jackknives will do but are usually too small in the handle and too short, as well as having the blade set at the wrong angle from the handle. The old Swedish pocket knife with birch handle and a blade that folded into its own bolster and was locked inside the handle for carrying, and also locked out in position for use, is one of the best little boning knives we have used.

In boning out an animal, first skin him out completely, then start on the shoulders, remove them and bone them, shaving the bone with the knife. Next bone the neck meat, then the ribs, and unjoint them from the hams and saddle. This can be packed down in one piece or, if necessary to bone further, unjoint the hams at the hip joints and bone the rest of the saddle and spine. We like to always take that saddle and rump and hams home, as nothing makes a finer roast than a fat rump of ram, mule deer or other game. However, by boning the neck, ribs, shoulders and front half of spine you can eliminate an awful lot of weight, so that two good men can then take out head, cape, and all meat of a big ram if they take their time and have good pack boards. There is nothing the equal of a good pack board for heavy packing. A rucksack will do, but makes an uncomfortable load and heats the back as well as always prodding it. A good pack board is best and when a hunter is hunting with a good guide, the guide can carry the two pack boards, leaving the hunter free to use his rifle; then when an animal is secured, he has the pack boards to bring out all usable portions of the carcass.

The cape or scalp should always be removed where killed, to prevent damage to the brittle hair; then if a clean six-foot square of light canvas is carried, half the meat can be wrapped in that and the remainder in the body skin and all kept clean and usable.

When heavy game like elk and moose is to be packed out, the meat should be left hanging until dry on the outside, or else frozen. All animal heat should be out of the meat before packing, then each quarter should be carefully wrapped in a canvas manty and cargoed up. In cold weather the moose and elk can simply be quartered with an ax and hung until stiff and cold and the skin left on each quarter, unless the skin is desired for leather. This system works well in cold weather and keeps the meat in its original skin wrapping and clean. It is well to also manty up these quarters to protect the flesh side from dirt. At times, elk will be killed on steep slopes that are frozen, when it is impossible to get horses within reach of them. Then it is best to attempt to slide them down to where horses can hold their feet for packing out. It is hard work at best, but with the aid of long ropes elk can be let safely down very steep slopes by dallying the rope on first one tree and then another. If snow is deep, they can simply be slid down. Moose are often killed from canoes and are then handy for loading and boating out to camp, but the good Lord help the lad who makes a kill where he can neither boat nor pack with horses, for he is then in for the hardest, most backbreaking work imaginable. It is then best to bone everything, to cut down weight. Having thus packed out more elk than I like to remember, I much prefer to hunt and kill my game where horses can be brought direct to the kill.

When a kill is to be left out overnight, or for several days, it should always be heavily brushed if left on the ground to prevent birds from eating it. Magpies and ravens, as well as eagles, will very soon make a mess of a fine animal. Scalp and head should always be removed and taken to camp, as it may be hopelessly ruined overnight. Coyotes will very seldom touch a carcass the first night, and if you flag it with a sock or handkerchief they will never touch it, but birds will work on it in spite of a flag. If it is a heavy animal and is quartered up, you should carry a few heavy spikes and hang the four quarters up in trees as high as you can lift them. This will prevent birds from working on them if they are brushed a bit, but nothing will stop a prowling bear, who will pull them down and eat the best portions in a single night. A hungry cougar will also ruin a fresh-killed animal. Marten and weasel will also work on a carcass, and there is no way of preventing their doing so unless it be near camp where they can be trapped or shot.

Once the meat is packed to camp and hung up, it will keep indefinitely in freezing weather, but in wet rainy weather it should always be under some sort of roof, even a batch of spruce or fir bows nailed up above the meat. Wet weather is the worst possible thing for meat, but if you can once get it dry and keep the rain or wet snow off it, it will keep. In warm weather, you should throw a rope up over a limb as high as possible and swing it in the air each night, free of all covering, then pull it down and wrap in canvas and lay in some cool shady place during the day. Meat can thus be kept for two weeks in the mountains, even in warm early fall weather. In many sections of the hot arid Southwest, meat will have to be used up or jerked, as the hot dry air will very soon jerk it anyway and we have seen hams that had dried out completely in a very few days even when hung in the shade.

Once the meat of an animal has been boned from the skeletal structure, it will have to be used up or jerked if the weather is warm, but in freezing weather it can be frozen and kept indefinitely. Meat keeps best hung in large sections or quarters, and when cut up, as in boning out it will soon dry and too much surface is exposed to the air to keep long unless jerked or frozen. When meat is to be put away in lockers in the freezer, it may well be cut into steaks and roasts if for reasonably quick consumption, but if thus stored in small packages over long periods of time it tends to dry out and will then have to be soaked overnight in water, or it will resemble a piece of leather. When it is to be stored in the freezer over long periods of time, we prefer to cut it up into large chunks of ten or fifteen pounds each, then wrap in wax paper and put in the quick freeze, before storage, where it will keep for much longer periods without drying out, except on the surface.

Many expeditions into distant game countries have suffered for lack of grub before the trip was ended, when they had wasted enough good meat to have enabled them to live in style the entire trip, if they had only taken time to save and preserve the meat they killed as they went along. I remember one trip when we ran out of flour and all essentials except meat and lived well enough on straight meat and tea for the last three weeks of the trip, but had we not taken the precaution of jerking and saving meat we would have gone hungry before that trip was over.

Kill only such game as you want for meat and trophy, then take time to properly preserve what you do kill and many head of game will be left in the hills for posterity. You will have a better trip by so doing and feel that you have not wasted game.

XXIII

Pack Outfits and Tentage

Pack Outfits

USUALLY the outfitter takes care of both packing and tentage on about all mountain pack trips. Some sportsmen, however, wish to own and run their own pack outfits. Having packed four years for the government when a small kid, besides having had my own pack outfit while guiding and outfitting up to this last war, I will give the benefit of my thirty years' experience for what it may be worth.

Mules are by far the best pack animals, are more sure-footed than horses, less excitable, better rustlers and, last but not least, will pack just about double the load a horse will and stay fat. Further, mules are much easier handled, and easier wrangled. All you need with a mule string is an old gray mare along to pack the bell. You can slip out at daylight, catch your old bell mare and bareback her to camp. When you get there the donks will be there also, ready to receive their Deckers and halters. I always like to pack a few oats, and give each animal a small feed each morning after saddling it. This is not only good for the animals, but they very soon learn to look forward to it and are always on hand ready to go.

One should saddle his donks and give them their light feed, then cook breakfast and pack the camp while the donks and saddle animals are taking their morning siesta. A well-trained pack string will follow the bell horse or mare to camp, accept their halters and saddles and small feed of oats, then each will drop a hip and go sound asleep while the packer cooks and eats his breakfast and packs camp. Next wake up each donk in turn and cinch him up. The saddle animal should be saddled and each donk added to the string as soon as packed. As soon as the entire outfit is packed it should move out. Make your pull as early as possible in the morning and preferably get it over with in eight hours or less. As soon as a camp site is located, unpack the animals first thing, unsaddle and pile your saddles, turn the bell loose and kick them out on good feed. Horses or mules must chew every bite they eat, and not having a second stomach and a cud to chew like cows, must spend a lot more time getting their daily supply of food. So it is imperative that you get out early and make your day's trip as soon as possible, then get the pack string on good feed and water at the earliest moment if you would keep them in good condition. Fifteen miles per day is plenty for a heavily loaded pack string, though most out-fitters make twenty or more, but it will soon kill off the string.

Horses should never be loaded over 150 pounds each, while good tough cayuse mules raised in the mountains can pack 250 to 300 if they weigh 1000 pounds or more. If you are traveling good government trails without a lot of windfall and mud holes, you can make better time by tailing up the entire string. A loop of quarter-inch rope should be tied in the rear hoop of the Decker pack saddle, then the halter shank hitched to this loop. Give them enough slack to travel freely, but not enough to feed. They must have sufficient slack to make sharp turns in the trail and to allow them to jump some windfalls or mud holes, also some leeway when they bust open that inevitable rotten log full of yellow jackets.

If the trail is poor and dangerous, and animals liable to roll or slide off the trail, or the trail is liable to peel off with them, then you must turn them all loose, as there's no use losing a whole pack string because one animal comes to grief. If they have to swim any streams they should also be turned loose and their halter shanks tied up so they cannot feed while en route. A pack string will always make better time and arrive in better condition if tailed up, but you need good trails for such procedure and if the trail is bad or dangerous, or full of muskeg swamps, then each animal must be free to pick his own way and to flounder out of such places alone.

The ancient sawbuck saddle is now obsolete. It always placed the load too high on an animal, giving it a tendency to rock and cause sore backs. Get the Decker pack saddle complete as sold by the George Lawrence Company of Portland, Oregon, the Hamley Saddle Company of Pendelton, Oregon, or Max Oiler of Salmon, Idaho. This outfit has a heavy leather rein-forced canvas boot that should be filled with dry bear grass or curled hair from some old automobile junk yard. The famous diamond hitch is also obsolete for packing over good trails; all you need for good trails is the heavy half-inch swing rope on the Decker saddle. If much up and down going is in progress you can run the swing rope down through the cinch ring and take a final pull on it. Breast collars should be taken up and breech-ings let out when you start a long climb; when you start down a long slope,

Courtesy J. O. Cole

Nice Alberta sheep country

Author and part of pack string on spring bear hunt ten miles from his ranch on the Salmon River

The author's son Teddy heading the pack string which is carrying the author's 1946 elk killed with a .400 Watson double rifle

Courtesy Union Pacific Railroad

A big game hunter's camp on the Middle Fork of the Salmon River

let out the breast collars and tighten the breechings. Such an outfit will move more freight and keep the stock in better condition than any sawbuck type of saddle.

All packs should be just two heavy side packs, no top packs. Each side pack should exactly balance its mate and they should be swung exactly the same height so they balance perfectly on the animal. As soon as the string walks a short distance you can see if any single pack is riding heavy on one side, and if so, stop right then and raise it so they balance, after which you may well travel all day with no further trouble. With the old sawbuck saddle and the diamond hitch you pack up, and when the diamond is pulled tight neither you nor the devil can tell whether the load is perfectly balanced or not, and you will travel all day, or until the animals have loosened their cinches, before you can see if one pack is riding heavy on a side or not. In really bad country, where many yellow jacket nests are on hand and where plenty of logs must be jumped, the diamond hitch will bind the pack to the animal better than the swing rope alone, but it is always hard on the animal, and if he gets down in a mud hole with only his nose and eyes and pack sticking out, then it is very difficult to remove said diamond hitch without the necessary sheath knife. For this reason we prefer the Decker saddle and heavy swing rope and let the old diamond hitch, which used to be the badge of a packer, hang in the shed at the home camp. It is now a relic, nothing more, of the good old days that were and will never be back.

For blankets, I like one good heavy pure wool blanket that will fold to about three thicknesses, or better by far a double Navajo blanket next the animal's back and then a heavy thick pad of deer hair or curled hair. The deer hair pads are cooler and preferable. Padding should be sufficient for the animal and some razor-backed individuals require more than others. Likewise the Decker pack saddles should be fitted to each individual animal, by bending the hoops together at the bars or spreading them until they contact the animal's back evenly and surely. The tips of the bars, particularly at the front end, should be curled up somewhat so they will rock, rather than dig into the withers. Some rock is advisable on the tips of the bars at the back but not much. This will prevent kidney sores in real rough country. Each outfit, complete, should be individually fitted to one animal and his name painted on the saddle, blankets and manties. You need about two to three heavy canvas manties for each animal. Only two for the usual side pack, but very often you may want to roll up lunches, or coats or some small items, and pile them between the hoops for a very light top pack. These canvas manties are best of waterproof material, of ten to twelve or not over fourteen ounces and should be about seven feet square. Cargo ropes should be three eighths inch rope and the entire side pack should be carefully mantied up in this waterproof canvas and then cargoed hard and tight, so it will remain waterproof and tight the entire day. Then if an animal rolls, or is bogged down, your equipment is protected. I very much dislike top packs of any sort, though lunches and extra jumpers, and so on, can be put on the top of the first animal behind the saddle horse. Alforjas and similar sacks for pack saddles are out with us. You seldom get them perfectly balanced and they are slow and unhandy. Forget them, or that they ever existed, and you will be ahead. At the start of the day's pack, cinch every donk as tight as you can, as he will soon shrink on the trail and a loose cinch is the cause of more sore backs than any other single item. Water your string at each creek if they want it — it tightens the cinches. A steady three-mile gait is best and make your move and get the packs off as quickly as possible.

When packing, it is well to tail up the string and hang the lead donk on the saddlehorn. Then spread each mule's load on each side of the trail. Lead them up between their respective loads and lose no time throwing on the packs. The sooner you get them all loaded and move out, the better for the outfit. Absence of the diamond hitch makes such procedure easy, and one man to each side of the string can pack an animal easily and surely in two to three minutes per animal. The first day will always be the worst. The animals are green and their backs soft and the loads will seldom be in perfect balance that first day, so make it short and sweet. Each successive day you can travel a bit farther until your string is gradually hardened in and the packs and loads are perfectly balanced.

If you have an old well-broken pack string, no worry is encountered about their leaving you if the saddle animals are hobbled up, or are used to camp life so that they need no hobbling. However, if you have a mixed string, gathered up from different ranches, you are in for trouble. The first few nights they will split into their separate respective bunches and each should have a bell, or you may spend most of the next day hunting horses. Just another reason why we prefer a string of donks. Then all you need is to run them together with a bell mare between hunting trips and you have no worry about finding your string in the morning. The packer should be out after the string at the break of day, and if it is a well-trained string, he will usually be back in camp by the time the cook yells "Climb a wagon wheel." The party should be taught to pack and lay out their personal belongings in two even-weight packs for each animal so the packer can quickly cargo them up into side packs, and they should endeavor to keep their personals in such shape that they will make up into two even-weight packs for each day's move.

When camp is made and the animals unpacked, the donks should be unsaddled as soon as possible. Each pack saddle should be laid out on poles and its blankets spread evenly on top after the ropes are half hitched up to the hoops. The next mule in the string should have his outfit stacked on top, and so on to the end of the string and in rotation, just as the animals travel in the string. The riding saddle should be stacked on top of the heap and all covered with a waterproof tarp. All cargo rope should be gathered, coiled and piled on top as well, and the halters should also be placed handy in a corner of the wrangler's tent or on top of the saddles and also under tarp. There is no worse curse to the packer than a lot of wet ropes. They are hard to pull, won't render and also slack up as soon as the sun hits them, so every effort should be made to keep them dry.

After over thirty years of packing I have had a sneaking longing to someday change my name temporarily, hire some unknown outfitter for a pack trip and then deck myself out in choke-bored pants, high shiny tan boots and all the usual dude equipment, then play the tenderfoot in style. I would even insist on having the outfitter tail me up on my saddle horse. However, I am afraid if I ever got rich and could afford such a trip, I would soon give myself away, for it's impossible for an old hand to watch a rider for more than a few yards, or while he mounts a horse, and not know whether he is an old hand or not. It would be lots of fun for a day but would be a very hard role for an old hand to play.

There is no nicer way of taking to the tall and uncut than with a well-trained pack string and a crew who know their business. You get up at daylight and pack your duffel, then wash in cold water to bring the sleep from your eyes and eat a good hearty breakfast. Then swing onto a good live saddle horse for the move. At the end of the day make camp, have a hearty meal and listen to the horse bell as the string goes about its nightly feeding. If the weather is nice and frost only at night, no tents need be set up, and all you need is a tarp to keep the frost off your bedding. It's a healthy vigorous life and the finest I know of in the hunting season. Once you make such a trip, you will want another one and so it will go until you are old and gray headed.

When a green string of pack and saddle animals are used for the first time after a summer's rest, it is always best to wash off their backs the first few nights, after they have been unsaddled, with cold water into which you should pour a handful of table salt and a little alum. This will remove all caked sweat and dirt and also greatly aid in toughening their backs. Watch out for any soreness, and be sure there are no wrinkles in the blankets. Occasionally pine or fir cones may get under a saddle bar, or twigs, and cause a sore spot, but if care is exercised you should be able to make long trips with no sore-backed donks or saddle horses. Make every member of the party sit up straight and ride his horse, and if he gets tired let him get off and lead the animal but do not permit him to ride on one side with his weight on one stirrup. Nothing will sore a horse's back quicker. A load should always be in balance on a saddle or pack animal, and if you carry a rifle on one side, hang the rope on the other, or extra coat or whatever you have, to balance the load.

If a sore back does develop, then it is best to take an old extra curled hair pad or deer hair pad, cut out a hole where the sore spot is, sew up the edges and place the blanket or pad on the animal carefully so that it will pad and take the weight around the sore with no weight on it. Powder it each night with boric acid. A small bottle of turpentine in the outfit is good for the usual bad scratches or snag cuts on the animal's legs and will keep flies away, and contrary to most medical opinion will heal up an open cut in very short order. When flies are bad, a mixture of bacon grease and a little turpentine added and rubbed on the breast and under the jaws and around the junction of the forelegs will help keep the flies away. Many times in some sections flies will be so bad, particularly the big horseflies, that smoke sheds must be made for the animals. These can be thrown up in a hurry from small leaning fir or spruce trees; then build a good rotten wood smudge. I have seen old pack horses stand for hours in the dense smoke of a fly smudge. You will find flies particularly bad in the North in July, when you must go in on many long trips, back to the Stone sheep country. Treat your animals well and look out for them and your kindness will be fully repaid on every trip. By this, I do not mean for you to get soft with a recalcitrant donk. With one of these you must make strong medicine and a damn good club is the thing, but apply it to the rear end of the donk, never on the head as I have seen many Indians do. You must have a mule's respect, but he must also know you for his boss. Any sign of softness or fear is instantly known by the animal, and he will take advantage of it. Horses and mules are individuals the same as humans, some good, some bad, and you must be the master. When an animal tries to do the right thing, treat him accordingly, but be firm with an ornery mule even though it necessitates working him over with a shillelagh.

Be sure and pack sufficient salt for the string, in addition to all that is needed for curing skins and capes. When you make a more or less permanent hunting camp, then is the time to put out the salt near camp, so the animals will stick around and on good feed. Do not salt them in camp or they will drive the cook crazy; salt them in some clump of timber close by. Many old pack animals used to camp will simply wreck your camp if everyone is absent from it during the day. They get used to eating stray hotcakes and many know all about the cache of oats and will sneak in during the night, grab the tarp with their teeth and pull it off, then grab a sack of oats by one corner and swing it around their heads until it bursts open. Then a good time is had by all the string, while the wrangler cusses and chases them away in his shirt tail. It is best to either hoist oats high in a tree, if one is available, or else store them in the tent, or use them for a pillow. Wise old pack animals are sometimes almost as bad as a bear at camp wrecking, so if any such are present in the string, adequate precautions should be taken.

Treat your animals firmly but kindly. I have no use for anyone who will abuse his animals. Further, when such a man does abuse his string at any and all times and treats them meanly, they will take advantage of him at the first opportunity. What you want is a gentle, thoroughly trained pack outfit, that are not afraid of you but know you for a friend; then when you get in a jackpot they will be patient and help you out of it. Never try to force an animal to swim a stream he is afraid of and give him plenty of time if he is afraid of a bridge or bit of bad trail. I have known wise old pack animals to demonstrate far more gray matter than the man who owned them. Likewise pay strict attention to the ears of your saddle horse and the donks, they will very often wind or sight game that is invisible to you. One should always carry a good sheath knife and have either a heavy sixgun or a rifle instantly available when on a pack trip. You never know when some animal may roll off the trail and you will need the knife to free him to save his life, or when you may have to shoot a crippled animal or may meet a bear that has other ideas besides getting off the trail. Treat your animals with due respect and kindness and you will be more than repaid on every trip you make. Animals soon learn to come to you for protection, and several times I have had the string overrun the camp during the night, as they tried to get as close to me as possible when a grizzly scared them. They usually pay little attention to a black bear, but a grizzly will scare them to death. I have seen a whole string go wampus for several days, just because we had a grizzly hide and skull carefully wrapped in canvas in one of the packs, yet they could smell it through all the canvas. Even though we had packed a black bear for days in plain sight on top of one of the packs and they paid no attention to it, as soon as we packed up with the grizzly skin in one pack the whole outfit tried to buck off the packs and all animals fought the one who carried the skin, until it was forced to travel in the rear of the string. Horses and mules are both very intelligent, and in the timber they can smell a bear much farther than you can hope to see it. Packing and the various hitches are something that simply must be learned under the watchful eye of an experienced packer, so I am not going to write anything further on the subject. There is absolutely no substitute for experience and it is is one thing that cannot be learned from books. If you want to learn, get a packer to teach you the art.

Tentage

For summer pack trips or early fall, less tentage is needed than for late season hunting in deep snow. Where one needs only a light camp and the party is small, I like the lean-to tent with a fly. It's adequate and very comfortable for all early fall trips. Dr. H. A. W. Brown, formerly Indian Agent at Fort St. John, and now living at Parksville, British Columbia, made the best one I have ever seen, of about ten-ounce waterproof duck. This particular lean-to was long enough to adequately take four beds laid with the foot of each toward the open front. It must have been about eight or ten feet from front to back and ten to twelve feet in length. A single lodgepole served as a ridgepole and it was handy and quick to set up. The back of the tent had about a three-foot wall, and a fly extended out in front for another eight feet. This could be dropped down to completely enclose the front of the tent in bad weather. A mosquito netting fly was also incorporated and we usually turned this down in front to keep out all mosquitoes and black flies when we went to bed. Such a tent is just about ideal for a light camp on early fall trips.

With a good log fire in front of it, it is plenty warm and very cheerful as well. Such lean-to tents can be had in any desired size from a small one, suitable for one or two people, up to a large one suitable for four. By making kindling the evening before and whittling shavings, one man can slip out of his bed and start the fire and soon the lean-to is cozy and warm. You can cook over the fire as with any open fire and still have the fly for a roof in rainy weather. For a light tent for early camping I know of nothing nicer.

Another excellent tent for summer, or early fall, camping is the regulation Umbrella tent. I have one, size of about 9 x 11 feet, of waterproof material that is excellent. The door opens to the top and can be extended for a fly. When this is done, one can have a fire in front of the tent for cooking and heat before going to bed. It is a thoroughly waterproof tent and adequate for two people and three could sleep in it on a pinch. These Umbrella tents necessitate packing the poles and the folding steel top frame, but the pole unjoints in the middle and will go nicely in a couple of long side packs. For early fall trips, I suggest the lean-to or the Umbrella type of tentage; where no camp stoves are packed, the cooking is done over an open fire. Of the two, the lean-to is the more comfortable, as it exposes the whole front to the warmth of the fire and is nice to lounge around in on a rainy day and also better to cook from on a wet day than the Umbrella with its small narrow flap. The Umbrella type is a sleeping tent, pure and simple, and good for little else, but the big lean-to is a comfortable camp home in all but bad weather.

When the trip is to be late, when zero temperatures may be encountered, or subzero, and deep snow is in order, or continuous heavy rains such as are usual in the Lochsa, there is no substitute for a good big tent in which you can have a stove or fire. Of the two the big wall A tent is the heavier to pack as you must also pack a good camp stove; this in turn necessitates packing a Swede saw to cut the wood the right length. The other type is the Indian tepee or lodge. When plenty of lodgepole pine is available at all camps, I know of no more comfortable tent than the big Indian lodge or tepee. It should be large, 18 to 20 feet, and a 20-foot diameter lodge will do nicely for four people. It should have a good deep ground cloth that ties to the inside of the lodgepoles some six feet up from the bottom, then drapes down and under the beds on the ground for another foot or two. This type of tent will stand more heavy snow and more continuous rains than anything else I know of, and in really bad weather is the most comfortable tent I have used. It must be made right, pitched right, and the smoke flap adjusted right, to be comfortable, but when this is accomplished it will be the most ideal of all camp homes for really cold or bad weather. The fire need not be large, only a small fire being necessary in the center of the floor space to provide adequate warmth and light, as well as no stove to pack. Where lodgepole pines are available for the poles it is my choice of all big tents. The Indian lived in it for centuries and the white man has not yet improved on it. Small inadequate tepees with low ceilings and no room inside are a nuisance. It should be large enough so you can stand up in it, away from the steep walls and the fire as well. The air sucks up between the ground cloth and the tepee proper and creates a good draft, so that when the smoke flap is properly adjusted it is free of smoke at all times. In warm weather the ground cloth can be rolled up on one or more sides to allow plenty of air and in really cold weather it can be anchored down by beds, wood and camp impedimenta until it is tight and snug. A Swede saw and a good double-bitted ax will furnish all the wood necessary. It need not be cut to any certain length, but can be cut in four-foot poles very nicely, and when burned in two in the middle the ends can be fed into the fire. I still remember one time when a two-foot fall of wet snow during the night in the South Fork of the Flathead country brought our 12 x 14 foot wall tent down on top of us and the entire camp and bedding were soon wet. We had a miserable time of it until an old Flathead Indian who was camped near by with his squaw came over and invited us into his lodge for the night. In sharp contrast to our inhospitable wall tent, his big 20-foot lodge was perfectly dry and warm and the snow did not stick or collect on its very steep sides. We had plenty of food, including sugar and coffee, while the Indians were down to straight meat, so we spent the rest of the trip in the comfort of his lodge and his squaw proved not only a clean, but very capable cook. That trip happened many years ago, but taught me the difference between the Indian and white man's tents. The native has camped much longer than the white man and his home is much more comfortable in really bad weather, when no stove is packed.

The next best compromise is the big wall tent, and for four people it should be at least 12 x 14 feet and better even larger. Such tents require a large space to set up and two long ridgepoles if untreated and a fly is needed, or one long ridgepole if it is a waterproof tent. It should also have a four-foot wall to insure adequate headroom. Then you need a good camp stove on which to cook as well as to heat the tent. If the tent is of untreated canvas or duck, you should have a full-length fly, otherwise rain will beat right through it and any time you touch the roof or ceiling it will start leaking at that point. But with a good fly stretched over an extra ridgepole it will be warm, dry and comfortable, but, with stove included, much heavier to pack than the Indian tepee. For one or two people, a much smaller version is indicated, but you still must have the camp stove, either the common ordinary sheepherder's sheet-iron stove or one made from a ten-gallon oil drum, which is even better when properly made. In pitching the wall tent, it is well to use a couple of poles on each side at the right distance and elevation from the ground so that all guy ropes can be stretched evenly and uniformly from the bottom sides and corners of the roof. The stovepipe should be the telescope type that folds into one joint and the top should also be capped by a screen funnel to prevent sparks from balsam or other resinous wood from setting the tent afire during the night. Personally I despise a small cramped wall tent with low wall, which necessitates stooping over all the time. The wall should be four feet high on all such tents, even an eight by ten, to insure headroom.

In the far North and many other sections as well, it is virtually impossible to find lodgepole pine and the Indian tepee is out for this reason. In such countries the wall or lean-to tent is the only answer. When the weather is continuously bad with continued rain, you need a good warm camp where you can cook and eat and also dry clothing in comfort. You can then rig light rope slings just under the ridgepole of the tent, on which to hang wet clothing, rifles and other things such as your binoculars, which you wish to keep dry. The same can be done on the inside of the Indian tepee, but if lodgepoles are not available the wall tent is the answer.

Another good tent, but one that is harder to pitch correctly, is the 16-foot square army Sibley tent. It has good headroom and a high steep roof that sheds water or snow very well, and can be set up with one long pole in the center. It is a mighty good rag house, but one that requires a lot of stakes to set up properly. Ample room is provided in the army squad tent for four people, including a place to eat and store the food and camp impedimenta. With the army Sibley or the common wall tent you must also pack a gas lantern, candles or coil oil lantern for lighting, while with the tepee the fire furnishes ample lighting.

For use in desert country where snakes, scorpions and centipedes are prevalent and where the nights only are cold, I prefer the Umbrella type tent with floor and the door to come up at the bottom at least a foot, and with a flap that can be buttoned up even higher at night against snakes and insects. Most Umbrella tents are closed up a foot at the door and for use in such desert sections an additional flap can be sewed on at the bottom of the door opening, that will usually prevent snakes from moving in with you. Rattlers particularly like to crawl into blankets or your discarded clothes for warmth during the cold desert nights, and I once found a small one camped in my riding boot when I started to pull it on one morning in Montana. I was punching cows at the time and when the boss rolled me out of my buffalo robe at 3 A.M. I put on my hat, next I pulled on my pants, then picked up a boot, and as it felt heavy even with the heavy bronc spur attached, I set it down and picked up the other boot, and shaking it found I had stored some hard cash and extra sixgun shells in it for the night, so pocketed them and pulled the boot on, then when I picked up the other boot it still felt heavy so I shook it and was rewarded by hearing the angry buzz of a rattler. He had crawled into my boot during the night as it lay under my clothes at the head of my bed. I yelled at the cook that

I had a buzzer in my boot and he asked me to bring him over and shake him out in the fire, which I did, while the cook herded him back in with a long-handled frying pan until he was well cooked. That experience has lived in my memory and I now never pull on a boot without shaking or looking into it first. An Umbrella tent closed against such pests is a fine thing in such country.

In 1931, when I had the Zane Grey party out, we camped for two weeks at Williams Lake, fishing and waiting for the big game season to open, and most of the party were equipped with such tents, which was a good thing, as rattlers were plentiful and we killed several in camp during the two weeks' stay. Such tents should be equipped with mosquito netting over windows and also a drop over the door for warm weather in many sections of this country and for summer or early fall camping in Canada and Alaska, where the mosquitoes are often terrible. Even a lean-to should have a front flap of mosquito netting that can be dropped down to enclose the sleeping portion of the tent for the night, after the fire has died down and the pests swarm about.

When a permanent camp is to be made the tents should be pitched in a clump of thick spruce or fir timber whenever possible, so that if you do get a hard blow and snowstorm, you will have protection. I have seen hard snowstorms as early as late July and early August and as late as late June at high altitudes, even in this country, and a tent pitched out in the open is usually blown away during the night, or at least brought down around your ears. Neither is a pleasant experience, so it is well to select your camp site with care and put the tents where they will be well protected from the wind by cliffs or thick clumps of trees. When in game country, the camp should also be well concealed in the timber. Sheep, goats and caribou as well as bear will spot it out in the open and you never know when a really worth-while head of game may stroll right into camp if your tents are at least partly hidden, but placed so that you can watch the best adjacent game country during daylight hours. Such places can usually be found with little difficulty and adjacent to good water, at least in most mountain camps. I for one dislike a camp pitched out in the open where the first hard wind will blow it away, or pitched in a hole in dense timber where you cannot see any of the game country adjacent. Sometimes in heavy dense forest it is necessary, however. Then one should look out for standing dead timber that the first wind may bring down across the wigwam during the night. Any such leaning or slightly rooted dead trees should be felled at once or the tent pitched where they cannot reach it if they blow over.

When a permanent site is reached, or one where you will stop for a week, you should first put up a good camp before starting your hunt and a half day so spent usually pays dividends in the long run. If you start right out hunting and make a kill, then you have an awful mess on your hands when you return to camp and try to pitch it in the dark, to say nothing of caring for your meat and trophy, so it should be the rule to make camp first. Many times on the trail you will encounter a good moose, or caribou, or grizzly and kill him, when it is necessary to make at least a temporary camp on the spot for the night, or until the game can be taken care of.

One side of your double-bitted ax should be ground thin and stoned keen for chopping, while the other should have a very short, thick but sharp edge for chopping bones in splitting a moose, caribou or elk, so it will not chip when splitting the hard bones of an old animal. A little forethought in the selection of the camp equipment and of the camp ground pays dividends. Cooking equipment should be of the nesting type so that it will go into a minimum of space on the pack animal and it should be packed into a box or boxes that will also serve as cupboards in a permanent camp. Water pails should be collapsible canvas. Aluminum is nice for the cooking kit and also for plates, but for heaven's sake don't get aluminum cups as they will still burn your lips long after your coffee is stone cold. For desert country, take along some canvas water bags that will keep your water cool through evaporation even in hot weather.

Camp gear is endless in variety, but the wise hunter will take only just what he really needs and cut weight and bulk to the very minimum. One should have enough to be comfortable but it is a good rule to avoid anything not absolutely necessary. Go light but right. Take along plenty of heavy canvas bags for the various food items and also some large ones for meat, while a few common burlap bags are best for head skins and bearskins, as they allow more circulation of air. Take plenty of salt both for the pack string and for curing skins. An extra tarp or light small tent is advisable for short spike camps out from the main camp when a big party is in the hills, otherwise they will not be needed. I never did like oiled silk tents as they become hard and brittle in cold weather, even rainy weather, and are then easily torn by a hard wind, and a hole can be punched in them even by a swinging tree bough. Better by far to get waterproof duck of eight-ounce weight. In a cloudburst country, avoid camping in the mouth of some deep gulch where you may get washed away, just as you would avoid camping below an unprotected snowslide in the spring on a bear hunt where an avalanche might bury you and your camp from any cause. Take along a couple of mouse traps and also a couple of No. 1 Newhouse traps. You will invariably find white-bellied timber mice at any old camp ground and they will raise merry hell with your groceries in a night or two. At any permanent camp they will move in on you in a short time and the mouse traps are a necessity. Also you may camp near some cliff and have the pack rats lug off all your small belongings and the two No. 1 steel traps are the answer. At other times a marten or weasel may come in to camp and help himself to any meat you have hanging up or laid out for an early meal. These traps will add his skin to your collection in short order. It's well always to include a small roll of light flexible stove wire. It comes in very handy for many camp uses. A few big spikes for hanging quartered animals and a few small nails for the cook to use in fashioning a table and cupboards are also advisable.

XXIV

Equipment

AS I have said, the cardinal rule in outfitting for a big game hunt is to take only what you actually need. The tyro almost always takes more than is needed and usually many unnecessary articles as well. These load horses that are needed to pack meat and trophies as well as food. Rifles have already been discussed. As to ammunition, it is better to use 60 rounds in practice before the trip and to get acquainted with your rifle and its trajectory and have 40 rounds left for the hunt, than to start out with 100 rounds and not be in good form with your rifle. If you really know your rifle, then a box of 20 cartridges is usually more than you will need for an entire trip. The worst thing you can do, and the thing that will endear you to your guide the least, is to wait until you are in the game fields to sight up and practice with your rifle. This should be done well in advance of the trip, and unless you are an expert rifleman you should practice weekly at least for months before a trip after big game. Forty rounds of ammunition should be ample for even a long trip into Canada or Alaska if you know your rifle and shoot only when you can be sure, or reasonably so, of making a killing hit.

Next let us look at binoculars. In much lowland timber hunting, a light pair of wide field, low power glasses are of very great advantage at times. For such low elevation timber hunting the 6 x 30 Bausch & Lomb are excellent, also the lightweight 6 x Zeiss if you can get them, or the Hensoldt. You will usually need them at close range to determine the size of a head, or how an animal is turned, and a light glass of about six power is usually all that is needed for such hunting and gives very good definition in the low muggy atmosphere.

For higher elevations, as in most all Western or Alaskan hunting, I would not recommend anything below 7 power, and the best 7 x glass I know of to date is the new coated lens Bausch & Lomb 7 x 35. The 8 x 30 is very good but the 7 x 35 is a better night, or late evening glass, as it gathers more light. For sheep, goat and caribou work and bear at long range, the 9 x 35 Bausch & Lomb is excellent and my own choice of all makes and powers of binoculars. I have tested them alongside Zeiss, Hensoldt and many other makes for high alpine hunting and the 9 x 35 B & L suits my eyes best of any tried. Ten power or stronger binoculars are usually very heavy, like the big 7 x 50 marine glasses — usually altogether too heavy to carry in stiff mountain climbing. The 7 x 35 and 9 x 35 are as heavy as I want to carry and weigh in the old construction 26 ounces, but can probably now be obtained in lighter weight. Get the coated lenses by all means, as they give a much better color rendition than uncoated lenses and also a brighter image. This better color rendition alone is well worth any extra cost, as it better enables you to pick an animal out in his neutral colored surroundings. The 8 x 30 glasses of B & L, Hensoldt and Zeiss are also excellent mountain glasses and usually a trifle smaller and lighter than the 7 x 35 and 9 x 35, but the added light gathering power of these special B & L glasses is well worth the extra weight. For boat use along the Alaskan coast, or the East Coast, where you do not have to lug them, the big 7 x 50 glasses are excellent also, for late evening or night use.

Likewise the little Miracle 8 x 24 Daylux glass is a wonderful glass for the man who wants something very light and that will fit in one shirt pocket. It is really surprising what you can do with this little glass, especially in the high clear air of high altitudes. It is excellent for sheep hunting where you want a very minimum of weight and bulk. Down at sea level, the 6 x 30 B & L would be the better instrument, but up at high elevation this little Miracle glass has given excellent results in our hands and should for others.

Regardless of what glass you choose to fit your particular hunting, get it with individual focusing of the eyepieces, as this construction is much stronger and much more dust and moisture proof than the dual focusing with central adjustment for both ocular lenses.

In addition to a good pair of binoculars, a really good spotting scope with light portable and adjustable tripod, to be carried by the guide, will prove of inestimable value, and once used by the guide he will not kick at packing it, as it will save him many weary miles every few days of the hunt. It should be of 20 power, and one of the finest I have seen and used is the new Argus super grade, with coated lenses. The Bausch & Lomb of similar power is also excellent and you cannot go wrong on either glass. Even the little 20 x B & L draw tube and the Mossburg 20 x draw tube are good, and if nothing better is available are well worth taking along. Where you can afford it, we would advise the Argus or B & L prismatic spotting scope. It should be set up in camp and the surrounding mountains covered with it when anything suspicious is seen through the glasses or with the naked eye. Many times you will locate game at long range and be unable to tell with binoculars whether it is what you want in the way of a trophy or not. That is when the spotting scope pays dividends, for you can set it up and tell at a glance whether you are looking at rams or ewes, and the size of the heads as well. Roll them in your bed when traveling.

Next the camp bed. Nothing is more important than a comfortable bed. Forget this old stunt of taking along a couple of blankets and a tarp. That is O.K. for the old seasoned hillbilly or the cowpuncher who would not sleep in a good bed if he had one. I well remember the days, after a summer in the hills, punching cows or packing for the government, when I would come home and be totally unable to sleep on a soft bed with good mattress, and finally in desperation would roll up in some blankets or quilts and sleep on the hard floor. Those days are now gone for me, and though I have slept comfortably in the slide-rock by digging out a trench to keep from rolling down the mountain and wrapping myself in an old buffalo robe, I now need a good comfortable bed and a good night's sleep, to be able to keep up the hard strenuous climbs, day after day.

The foundation of any bed is the mattress. You can make a very comfortable one if you have the time and the spruce or fir boughs, but very often you will have neither the time nor the boughs. A good bough bed takes an hour to prepare, even when boughs are plentiful, and soon mats down. The best mattress is a rubber air mattress. Get the best and I would suggest the full length, though some folks get along very well with the three-quarter length. Get one that is wide enough to permit you to turn over with ease, as one rolls around a good bit during the night after a hard day and a heavy meat meal at the end of it. Get one that you can blow up with your breath, as those with pumps have a habit of getting separated from their pumps. Also take along a small BOTTLE of rubber cement and some cold patches. You may throw your bed where a porcupine has died and get a quill or two through it in the night, or a man may step on it with corked boots, or some other mishap occur, so take along a small bottle of rubber cement and some patches. Cement in tubes has a bad fault in that it will dry out and be worthless; further, it is easily busted and the contents spilled in your bedding or other container.

Next comes the bed itself. Blankets and fur robes are all heavy and bulky and the best and lightest bed of all is the Woods or other make such as the Bauer eiderdown robes. Get the heavy arctic weight for the Northwest and the lighter weight for the Southwest. I prefer the big 90 x 90 size, then you can turn over with ease and if a stranger drops into camp without a bed for the night, you can double up. I have seen two 200-pound men sleep comfortably in one 90 x 90 Woods arctic robe by sleeping head to foot and with both ends left open. Get the "lift the dot" rather than the zipper fastening, as those damn zippers have the habit of going haywire when you need them most. Further, with the "lift the dot" you can open the robe along the side at any point, if the weather is unduly warm. When a man and his wife are out together, nothing is nicer than a big double air mattress, made especially for a double bed, and a pair of 90 x 90 robes of eiderdown with "lift the dot" fasteners. Take a very light but small feather pillow. You will need it more when sleeping on the ground than at home. Also fold a pair or two of cotton pajamas and pack in your bed. Next get a good waterproof heavy duck, or canvas shell for the complete robe and air mattress. In camp, it is best to spread a pack manty on the ground, then your mattress on top of it, and then lay your shell and robe complete on top of that. This keeps the robe and the shell from drawing moisture. Avoid any of these oil silk coverings, as the body gives off a lot of moisture through the pores of the skin during sleep after a hard day, and you want something that will allow this to escape and dissipate, while an oiled silk covering will simply hold the moisture in your bedding. Hang the robe in the sun every few days if possible, to thoroughly dry out any moisture, and be sure to get a shell that is amply large for you when you are in the robe. Most of them are so narrow you cannot turn over in bed. Next take one light blanket, cotton or light wool, and use inside the robe to keep your robe clean. You can wash this blanket occasionally or at least at the end of the trip. Such a bed will cost as much as a fine rifle but is well worth it, and will do for a great many years. When moving camp, roll it up, then manty up with a heavy pack manty and cargo it so that stray limbs will not snag your bed or canvas shell.

Next your toothbrush, comb, soap and towels, and take a can of dental powder instead of toothpaste. It will look much better mixed with your belongings than paste, if the container is busted under a diamond hitch. Take your shaving outfit and a cake of shaving soap, rather than shaving cream which comes either in a heavy jar or else in a fragile tube that is easily broken in the pack. Take a good spool of heavy linen thread, some extra buttons and some heavy needles; a good buckskin needle is advisable as well. You should have a spare front sight, a few small files and a good pair of pliers. A small coil of copper wire will often come handy, also a few spare parts for your rifle if of the Springfield type, such as ejectors, an extra extractor and striker. Next take your cleaning tools. These should include a good jointed steel rod such as Marbles and Belding & Mull put out, some Hoppes No. 9 and a can of Fiendoil or a small can of Rig; plenty of cleaning patches and an old shammy well saturated in Rig, for wiping the outside of the rifle. This cleaning outfit should be packed in a strong container, either leather or a tin can that will not mash easily. Leather cases are preferable. Your ammunition should not all be put in one package, but place some in your bed as well as your war bag; then in case one horse rolls and the outfit is lost, you may still have some ammunition.

For knives, take a good jackknife with extra blades and preferably with a leather punch, and then get yourself a good sheath knife. For the money I know of nothing better than the ones advertised and sold by R. C. Ward & Sons, Missoula, Montana, or the excellent Marbles line, but be sure and have a good heavy leather sheath made, well riveted so it cannot punch through and injure you in a hard fall. The blade should be a combination ripper and peeler and heavy and wide, so it will stand pounding through pelvis and brisket with the foreleg of an animal used as a club, also for blazing out from a kill in dense timber. If you are going to hunt elk and moose, then a small belt ax like the Marbles is best, as well as the knife. Never get a blade length of more than 5½ inches for the sheath knife and 4½ to 5 inches is usually better. Take along a small Arkansas oilstone and one of the little ten cent carborundum stones.

A small flexible steel cable with snobble end and sharp point on the other end, and a can of patches that exactly fit the bore of your rifle, make the best field cleaner. These patches can be soaked with solvent or Fiendoil and carried in the pocket when hunting; then if you get snow in your rifle barrel, or rain water, or shoot it and have to lie out overnight, you can clean it properly. A light waterproof case of cloth is a good thing to carry along, as you can put it in the pack during the day and slip it on your rifle at night, if you have to lie out in the rain or snow. You should also have a good saddle scabbard for the rifle. The best and cheapest is the government cavalry boot, remodeled, so that the sights lie up when you are on the horse. Also the usual straps must be rearranged on it and the rear one extended farther to the rear of the scabbard and a slit cut through so the strap will stay in place. Take a small steel tape, notebook and pencils for recording measurements of game in the field.

Next you need a good rucksack, or a good light pack board, if you are to hunt sheep and goats and possibly have to lie out overnight as well as move heavy loads of game down to camp on your back. The pack board is much the best when any heavy load is to be packed, but a good packsack with comfortable shoulder straps is plenty for carrying a windbreaker, lunch or jerky, extra shells, camera and such.

You must have a good waterproof war bag to hold all your clothing and the above-mentioned items, something that is both strong and waterproof, as your whole outfit, with exception of your rifle, will go in this war bag and your bedroll.

If you are out for big game, it is best to forget all about killing small game of any kind, as even the popping of a .22 will often scare away a fine animal that might otherwise walk right into camp. When I am out for big game, I hunt that to the exclusion of everything else. The northern spruce grouse or fool hen can, however, be easily snared with a noose of copper wire tied to the end of a pole, and you can walk up on them and slip the noose over their heads and jerk it tight, if you work slowly and carefully.

If you are going to be in good trout fishing country it is well to take either a light rod, with short joints that can be rolled in the bed, or at least flies, leaders and a good line that can be wound up and put in the war bag. A few full power Hard Point or Full Patch bullet loads are always advisable for any big game rifle, as they are nice to finish down and wounded game and can be used to shoot a fox or other small pelt you want, without damaging the fur.

I do not care much for the idea of packing reduced loads, unless they are put up with bullets differing radically from the big game loads in appearance and are then kept religiously out of the rifle when hunting, because you will sooner or later shoot a big game animal with a light grouse load and lose him. When hunting, it is best to carry your cartridges in a small leather clip pocket on the belt, and a couple of such clip pockets, holding ten rounds altogether, with a loaded rifle are enough to lug. Cartridges will soon wear through the best of pants pockets and also rattle when walking or jumping logs. A good waterproof match safe is a necessity and a good reliable, but small, compass is advisable, if you are hunting without a guide, especially in flat timbered country. Marbles makes an excellent match safe. A good pocket lighter is also good for long trips, with extra flints, like the "Cache" lighter sold in Canada. Gas or kerosene for it should be carried in several small bottles rather than one. We used such lighters almost altogether on one two months' trip north from Fort St. John to the Musqua River and had the misfortune to have the bottle of gasoline spilled. We found that Fly-tox would work and used up our supply of that, then in an old abandoned trapper's cabin we found a bottle of Sloan's

Liniment and discovered it also would work in the lighters, but it surely imparted a strong taste to the first few puffs on our pipes.

If you smoke a pipe, take along a couple of extras and plenty of pipe cleaners, and usually it is a safe bet to figure on about twice your normal supply of tobacco. Evening campfires are hard on the tobacco supply and nothing is worse than to be out with a man who has suddenly decided to stop smoking while on a trip, so take plenty. It may come in handy, and on northern trips nothing is more acceptable for trade to the Indians than an extra sheath knife or two or good pipe tobacco. You may want to swap for some moccasins or a moose skin case for your rifle, and these items are always acceptable in addition to money and often far more so than currency.

It is well to take a small tin can with tight-fitting lid and fill it with matches carefully placed on end; then pour melted paraffin over them until they are covered, let it harden into a pack and wrap in oiled paper. The matches are then impervious to water and if you also carry half a tallow candle you can get a fire under almost all conditions.

A good first-aid kit for two or more people should be included in every outfit. One is enough in the camp, but it should be a good one and fairly complete. Likewise some good liquor should be included. I do not favor much drinking in a hunting camp, but a good hot one when you come in at the end of a hard day is beneficial and helps no end. Many times on our first long two months' trip in British Columbia we unpacked the camp in cold driving rain, when everyone was so wet, glum and numb with cold we could hardly unpack the animals. Then, the first thing I would do was get a kettle of water boiling and with sugar and a bottle of 132 proof rum make every man a good strong hot one with a lump of butter and some nutmeg added. It is surprising what it would do, and soon the horses were unpacked, unsaddled and hobbled, and the bells tinkling merrily as they fed; the tents would be up in a jiffy and wood cut and the evening meal well under way. The liquor should be under the control of one man who never drinks to excess and rationed as needed, or you may run short before the trip is over. Likewise one good drink is enough for an Indian on one day. Indians do not handle their liquor well. One good drink will bring a numb, half-frozen Indian to life and make a good man of him, but two will ruin him.

Clothing

To do good hunting one must be comfortable, and next to a good bed comfortable clothing is of utmost importance. You should have clothing that will enable you to be warm and comfortable in any kind of weather likely to be encountered on the trip. For the Southwest, lighter clothing should be used as the days will usually be very warm, though the nights are cold, and for the North and Northwest you should be well prepared for any emergency.

First let us take the underwear. I favor wool union suits amply large so they will not bind. Some folks can wear wool next their skin and some cannot, and those who cannot will do well to wear a light cotton union suit next their skin and a light pure virgin wool suit over it. In extreme warm weather, in early season, the cotton will be all that is needed, but when bad weather sets in the wool suit is a necessity. It should be large enough so it will not bind and I favor union suits over two-piece underwear, because they are less bulky around the waist and usually more comfortable. You should take two suits on short trips and three on long trips. Wool will absorb perspiration, but will not get cold and clammy afterwards, as cotton does, so wool is the safest to wear. Women going on long hunting trips into the North should be likewise equipped. They won't like the idea of them at first, but if they get caught in a blizzard they will accept them without undue comment. Pink panties and pale people have no place on a big game trip back into the wilds. Next come shirts. You should have three good pure wool shirts. The U.S. Army shirt is almost unbeatable, but if you cannot get them, then Pendleton, Bean, Woolrich, or other good virgin wool shirts are also excellent. They should be roomy and have two good large flap-covered pockets. Two will be ample for short trips, but on long trips, three shirts are preferable. If the weather is warm, a cotton shirt is advisable, and for the Southwest the wool will only be needed in the cool of evening or early morning, but in the North and Northwest, after the first of September, wool is usually very comfortable except in the heat of the day.

Next you need at least two pairs of good wool pants, cut roomy and of virgin wool, of very tight weave that will stand hard service. This can be varied by taking one pair of such heavy tight-weave pants and one of heavy cotton for warm weather and a pair of chrome-tanned light horsehide pants that will stand an unbelievable lot of hard service and yet will dry soft when soaked by a hard rain. Pants are something that come in for a lot of hard wear on a long trip and it is better to have three pairs than to be caught short and have to patch a single pair innumerable times on a trip. For all timber hunting they should be wool like the shirts, so they will not scrape on limbs and brush. Nothing is worse in the hills than a pair of canvas pants, or a pair of corduroys that scrape and creak at every step. Two pairs of good wool pants with a pair of good soft cotton will usually be adequate for even a long trip. I do not favor choke-bored army pants at all, as used by the army before the last war. They were entirely too tight in the knees and when wet simply hobbled a person, until he could neither climb nor mount a horse. L. L. Bean of Freeport, Maine, does, however, cut a roomy pattern of choke-bored pants for sportsmen that are excellent. They are very loose and roomy through the knees, as they should be, yet fit snug around the calf and allow socks to be pulled up over them. Such a roomy choke-bored pant is excellent and better than slacks. Never tolerate long baggy slacks, especially with cuffs at the bottom, as they will hook on every snag you come in contact with and sooner or later you will hook a dead limb that is pointed downhill, do a record pole vault and land right on your nose. I always take such trousers to a log and chop them off so they will come about on a level with the top of my boots. Then if you whip the seams with heavy linen thread, so they will not rip apart, they make excellent hunting pants if of good material. Whatever you take in this line, put them on and wear them on hikes before you go hunting so they will show up any defects long in advance of your trip.

Next let us look into footgear, the most important item in your clothing. You should be equipped for both snow and dry weather in the West and Northwest and only dry weather as a rule in the Southwest. For hard, day in and day out mountain work, nothing beats a good pair of Whites or other good logger's or packer's shoes. They should have a sole a half inch at least thick and be large enough to allow your wearing a pair of light pure wool socks and also, over them, a pair of heavy wool socks. Remember your feet will swell to beat the devil, if you are not used to such climbing, so the boots should be large enough to accommodate the one light and one heavy pair of socks at all times. The heels should be about 1¼ inches high and slightly undershot — that is, set ahead — so they will be comfortable in the saddle and throw the stirrup far enough forward under your instep so it will not rub and chafe your shin at the top. These higher than normal heels are also the best thing possible for holding you securely when going down steep scree or shale slopes, as they dig in and hold you,

[415]

while a big low and flat heel will merely act as a ski and send you off down the slope at every step. The soles should be covered with logger's drive calks, put in at the factory by men who know how to calk a logger, then around the edges should be two rows staggered close together of hobnails, or else the entire rim of the sole or edge should be covered thickly with Swiss edging hobs that not only coat the bottom edge of the sole, but also come up around the outer edge. Having put in many months of continuous mountain work over the roughest terrain on this continent, I have found nothing to quite equal these loggers made by the White Boot & Shoe Company of Spokane, Washington. They should be best quality and are practically waterproof. The tops should be at least 14 inches high and seldom higher than that, unless you are very long-legged, when they could be 16 inches high and no higher. The boots should be made to measure over the socks you will wear and will cost around $20 but will last you many seasons, and will give you more solid comfort than anything you ever wore in the hills. They should never be high enough to bind the calf of the leg, but should never be less than 14 inches, so they will properly fit and support the ankle and protect the shin from sharp rocks and fallen logs and limbs. You can cat around over ice, scree slopes, or walk logs all day long in these boots, with ease and comfort. Many other companies make equally excellent loggers, such as Kern, Bergman, Cutter and others. They will be heavy, but I have seen more sportsmen crippled up and confined to camp by using light thin-soled shoes than from any other cause.

Loggers are also indispensable for rock work in the snow and when icy, as when hunting sheep and goats or grizzly. Low shoes are out with me for any hunting use. When you run down a slide, they will fill up with rocks and your feet will be black with dirt each evening. Also they give no support to the ankle in the many twists and wrenches it will get daily, as well as offering no protection to the shinbone. Likewise any sort of leggings, or puttees, are out of the question. You absolutely must have such loggers made well in advance of a trip and get out daily if possible, or at least weekly, for months in advance and properly break them in by actual hiking. Once they are broken in and fitted to the foot, you have footgear that will stand up and give you safe, sure footing on almost any terrain. For dry rock work alone, rubber tap soles and heels on these loggers are excellent, but get the least skim of snow and you will break your neck if you are not lucky. If you cannot stand wool next your skin, take a few pairs of silk or cotton socks for wear next the skin and then use the wool socks over them. However, cotton soon wrinkles or rolls up, from perspiration, and will make your feet sore, so pure wool is the best sock you can wear in the hills at any time of the year.

Next, for the West and Northwest, you need a pair of Bean's leather-top rubbers. They should be same height as your loggers and about the same fit. He furnishes them with different width last and they should be amply large for the two pairs of socks, one of which must be very thick and heavy, and if they are even larger and permit a good felt or arch-support sheepskin inner sole, so much the better, as the insole will absorb perspiration and also insulate your foot against the cold of the rubber bottom, than which there is nothing colder on a cold day. These rubbers should have oil-tanned tops and you should take along an adequate supply of good shoe grease like Hubbard's or Bean's, or other good varieties. If you run out and kill a bear, try rubbing the raw bear fat on your boots. In addition to the loggers and the Bean's leather-top rubbers, you should have a good, comfortable but sturdy pair of camp slippers that will enable you to remove the loggers or rubbers when you reach camp, slip into a clean dry pair of wool socks and the camp slippers and be comfortable.

For the level Eastern hunting, many like Russell pack boots with moccasin soles. Never having hunted that country, I do not know how well I would like them, but do know they are not worth a whoop in steep mountains, when they are covered with snow and ice, or on fallen logs where the bark will peel off with you, often when you may be crossing some deep stream and ten feet above the water. For our country and all of Canada and Alaska I have seen, inland from the sea, the loggers have given best satisfaction, but they must be made to fit *your individual* foot and properly broken in long before the hunt.

In addition, you must toughen up your feet preparatory to a hard hunting trip, if you are used to walking only on city pavements. Hard hiking as often as possible, combined with soaking your feet in strong salt and alum water for a half hour of evenings, will soon toughen them. Nothing kills me off as quickly as walking a city pavement, so my hat is off to those who have to do so. However, in many years of guiding I have doctored enough feet to know what is best in the wilds. Thin, light-soled shoes, while very light, offer no protection to the feet and you are soon down with stone bruises or blisters. If you like light footgear, you can have your loggers made with lighter uppers, but don't dispense with the thick heavy sole and the calks for mountain work.

When it comes to socks, take plenty of them. A half dozen pairs each of both heavy and light are not too much for a long two to three months' trip, while for a short ten days' or two weeks' trip, three or four pairs of each will be ample. You should change them often and wash them, as nothing will put your feet out of commission quicker than dirty socks. We favor white, pure wool, next the skin.

In the Southwest you won't need the Bean rubbers and then you had better add in their place a pair of light but strong rubber-soled shoes, preferably with 12- to 14-inch tops. Don't forget the camp or house slippers, but they should be good chrome leather or leather with sheep-wool skin lining. They are very handy to slip on around camp and to rest the feet.

Next hankies. Take along a half dozen at least but get red ones, the regular old bandana. White handkerchiefs have been responsible for many men being shot for deer in whitetail country, so take red ones. For headgear, nothing beats a good wide-brimmed Stetson hat that will keep the rain, snow and pine needles from falling down your neck and also afford a good sun shade. The old army campaign hat will do, but I personally like a wider brim. It should be either belly beaver (sand) color or else the olive drab of the army. If you are apt to be out in blizzards, then a good warm cap with ear flaps, with fur lining, is good insurance, or you can do as I usually do and pack a silk scarf to bind over the ears in bad weather. A pair of comfortable, short buckskin gloves are usually all that is needed in dry weather, but when wet weather and snow come, several pairs of cotton gloves or rubberized cotton are advisable. Two or three pairs of these will suffice. If real cold weather is on the ticket, ten to twenty below zero, then heavy fleece-lined mittens are about the only thing that will keep the hands warm. Never try to shoot with a glove on your shooting hand — it will only get you into trouble, sooner or later.

Next you need a good windbreaker to pull over your shirt when you have made a climb to high altitudes, where the wind will soon chill you. A buckskin shirt is excellent, as is also the Bauer down jacket, and even the light army field jacket is very good. None of these have any appreciable weight. Where you are apt to have to lie out at night when hunting sheep and goats, the Bauer down jacket will be the warmest of the three. In addition to this light windbreaker jacket, you need one heavy warm jacket. I do not like Mackinaws, because they are too heavy and bulky. A good pure woolen stag shirt of heavy material with double shoulders is much better and allows more freedom of movement. If you are hunting in the North, in Canada or Alaska, where hunters are scarce, then by all means get neutral gray or olive drab colors, but if you are hunting in these United States, where the hills will be overrun with an army of hunters for the next few years, get a bright red for your outer jacket or shirt, as well as your hat. It looks like the devil, to both game and man, but is cheap life insurance. Only a pretty woman looks well in a red hat, but they are a great protection against some trigger-happy nitwit who may think he sees a deer.

You need some kind of waterproof outer garment — for use when you must travel in driving rain. A light oiled silk jacket or short slicker is the most comfortable but will snag badly in the brush. It is also less noisy than a heavy slicker. The Filson waterproof stag shirt is excellent and I prefer it where the rain is not too steady, but it also is noisy in the brush. However, you need some such garment for the long cold rides in the rain. If you are going on a long pack trip, chaps are a godsend in wet weather, or when the brush along the trail is covered with wet snow.

The ladies may not think much of the clothing I advocate for the mountains, but if they are ever out for several months in the wilds, they will soon come to the point where they will see its value. A good leather waist belt about completes the picture unless you are one of those chaps who sport a bay window, when a pair of heavy suspenders is indicated. The strong leather waist belt is useful even then, to support your sheath knife and cartridges. Such an outfit will keep you warm and comfortable in most any weather you are likely to encounter in the Northwest and will all go in a good big war bag.

If you are going to hunt the coast of Alaska for brown bear, you can dispense with the loggers, but will need good cleated-soled hip boots, knee or hip length slicker and a rain hat with a chin string attached. If you are going into the arctic you will have to have a good parka and native footwear as well, if you intend being there in cold weather. In addition, take along several pairs of long leather shoelaces; they come handy for many purposes. Such an outfit will enable you to enjoy the beautiful scenery of the wild and the game to the fullest.

Films should be packed in some sort of waterproof container, in case your outfit gets a dunking in some stream, and I have seen large-necked bottles used for the purpose for roll film. The camera should be packed with the glasses in the bedroll when being shipped or, better, carried on the person, and you should have it with you when hunting or on the trail, as you will have many opportunities for its use.

In the preceding pages I have endeavored to give the reader the benefit of my own experience, for whatever it may be worth, and if it helps sportsmen toward having a better trip, I feel the work was well worth while.

In conclusion, let me again admonish all hunters to kill only what game they want for specimens and trophies, or need for meat, as by so doing they will help preserve the many different and beautiful species for posterity. To all readers of this book I wish hearty good hunting.

Elmer Keith

NORTH FORK, IDAHO
July 24th, 1948

We hope you enjoyed this title
from Echo Point Books & Media

Before Closing this Book, Two Good Things to Know

Buy Direct & Save

Go to www.echopointbooks.com (click "Our Titles" at top or click "For Echo Point Publishing" in the middle) to see our complete list of titles. We publish books on a wide variety of topics—from spirituality to auto repair.

Buy direct and save 10% at www.echopointbooks.com

DISCOUNT CODE: EPBUYER

Make Literary History and Earn $100 Plus Other Goodies Simply for Your Book Recommendation!

At Echo Point Books & Media we specialize in republishing out-of-print books that are united by one essential ingredient: high quality. Do you know of any great books that are no longer actively published? If so, please let us know. If we end up publishing your recommendation, you'll be adding a wee bit to literary culture and a bunch to our publishing efforts.

Here is how we will thank you:

- A free copy of the new version of your beloved book that includes acknowledgement of your skill as a sharp book scout.
- A free copy of another Echo Point title you like from echopointbooks.com.
- And, oh yes, we'll also send you a check for $100.

Since we publish an eclectic list of titles, we're interested in a wide range of books. So please don't be shy if you have obscure tastes or like books with a practical focus. To get a sense of what kind of books we publish, visit us at www.echopointbooks.com.

If you have a book that you think will work for us,
send us an email at editorial@echopointbooks.com

www.ingramcontent.com/pod-product-compliance
Lightning Source LLC
Chambersburg PA
CBHW050448270326
41927CB00009B/1653